MW00986463

Knowledge of Meaning

Richard Larson and Gabriel Segal

Knowledge of Meaning

An Introduction to Semantic Theory

A Bradford Book
The MIT Press
Cambridge, Massachusetts
London, England

© 1995 by the Massachusetts Institute of Technology

All rights reserved. No part of this book may be reproduced in any form by any electronic or mechanical means (including photocopying, recording, and information storage and retrieval) without permission in writing from the publisher.

This book was set in Times Roman by Asco Trade Typesetting Ltd., Hong Kong, and was printed and bound in the United States of America.

Library of Congress Cataloging-in-Publication Data

Larson, Richard K.
  Knowledge of meaning : an introduction to semantic theory / Richard Larson and Gabriel Segal.
        p.   cm.
  "A Bradford book."
  Includes bibliographical references (p.   ) and index.
  ISBN 0-262-12193-X. — ISBN 0-262-62100-2 (pbk.)
  1. Semantics. 2. Semantics (Philosophy) 3. Generative grammar. I. Segal, Gabriel.
II. Title.
P325.L298   1995
401'.43—dc20   95-5324
                                                                      CIP

We dedicate this book to our parents:
Mary E. Larson and Orville K. Larson
Hanna and Paul Segal

Contents

Preface

This book is designed to present, motivate, and defend a particular approach to semantics for natural languages. It is an introductory work aimed primarily at undergraduate and graduate students of philosophy and linguistics. Yet if we have done our job properly, it should be accessible to readers with little or no background knowledge of the field.

Our approach has strong theoretical commitments. Although we have tried to be fair to alternative approaches, we do not intend our work to provide a general introduction to them. We do believe, however, that our approach provides a good framework within which to raise many of the important questions of semantics, from fundamental conceptual and methodological ones to detailed empirical and technical ones. Many of the questions raised within our framework are of general concern, and our discussion of them is intended for anyone interested in semantics, whether or not they share our specific views.

We have commitments at two levels. We have background, methodological commitments about the general nature of semantics for natural languages. We believe that semantics can and ought to be pursued as a science, specifically, as the empirical study of a particular human cognitive competence, the competence to understand the meanings of words and sentences. Our views about the nature of this science derive largely from Noam Chomsky's work in syntax and phonology. We have merely carried those ideas over to the field of semantics. We introduce these matters in chapter 1 and illustrate their application throughout the book as we deal with various particular kinds of natural-language structures.

We also have commitments concerning the formal structure of a semantic theory. Here we follow Donald Davidson's idea that a truth theory of the kind developed by Alfred Tarski can serve as the formal basis of a semantic theory.

This core idea is introduced in chapter 2 and, again, is applied and developed throughout the book.

By laying out and defending our approach in detail, we hope to make clear exactly what it involves, why it is plausible, and, inevitably, what its weaknesses are.

We believe that our formulation of the subject matter has intellectual attractions both for linguists and philosophers. Over the last two decades, formal linguistic semantics has stood largely alone. Connections to syntactic theory have rarely been pursued beyond the level of using trees motivated by current syntax as the objects of semantic interpretation. There is little notion of a common subject matter or a shared program. Likewise, connections to the philosophy of language have rarely been pursued beyond the narrow confines of possible-world semantics. In the linguistics literature it is rare to see discussions of the interesting work on the nature of meaning, of predication and quantification, of linguistic knowledge, and so on, that have enlivened the philosophy literature. Finally, connections with other domains of cognitive psychology have rarely been pursued within formal semantics, despite the very interesting work now being done in aphasia and children's acquisition of knowledge of meaning. The result is that a large amount of very interesting and relevant work, especially in philosophy, is largely unknown in the field. We have tried very hard to draw on this work and to show its vital links to linguistic semantics. We hope that linguists will find a good deal of new material here to stimulate their interests.

Similarly, philosophy of language has often been pursued without a great deal of attention to detailed empirical matters. We believe, however, that attempts to address even the most general philosophical questions about linguistic meaning benefit greatly from serious study of empirical linguistics. From this methodological standpoint we have taken up many of the central questions in philosophy of language, for example, questions about the relation of meaning to the world, of meaning to mind, and of mind to world. We believe that philosophers will find this scientific approach both challenging and invigorating.

Our formulation of the subject matter also has attractions for the teacher. The approach developed here offers a way into truth-conditional semantics that is substantially different from Montague grammar, which has been a dominant force in linguistic semantics over the last two decades. In our experience, the vast technical apparatus of Montague grammar, and the substantial effort that students must expend in mastering it, limits the time that can be spent on the fundamental conceptual questions of semantics or on specific empirical problems. Our approach offers a simpler formulation of truth-conditional semantics, one that preserves the general virtues of formal rigor and explicitness but one whose technical toolbox is lighter and a good deal easier to carry about. Although truth conditions continue to play their central role, gone are models, types, lambda abstraction, lambda reduction, characteristic functions, functions from functions to functions, higher-order intensional logic (IL), and a great deal more. Those trained in Montague grammar may be surprised to discover how many of the results of formal semantics can be retained without these devices. In teaching this material, instructors will find that they can spend much less time building technical skills and correspondingly more time on empirical and conceptual matters.

Acknowledgments

Writing this book has turned out to be a much-longer-term project than either of us anticipated, and we each have inevitably accumulated many debts of thanks along the way.

Richard Larson

Professionally I owe special thanks to three people: Noam Chomsky, James Higginbotham, and Peter Ludlow. Chomsky and Higginbotham were not only terrific colleagues at MIT; they were also largely responsible for shaping my views of linguistic theory. Their influence is present on every page, from technical details to metatheory, and I am profoundly grateful to them both. Peter Ludlow first introduced me to the modern Davidsonian program in semantics. We have argued over all aspects of this material and have cotaught it on numerous occasions. It has been a pleasure to have him as a friend and colleague.

Special thanks also to Barry Schein, Jason Stanley, and Kathrin Koslicki for many pleasant discussions and arguments about all the issues in this book, and many more besides.

Finally, my deepest personal thanks to my wife, Susan, and my daughter, Gwendolyn, for their love and support and for making clear what is most important in life.

Gabriel Segal

I have many people to thank. As with most of my work, my contributions to this book have been greatly helped by lengthy discussions with a group of philosophers that meets more or less assiduously every second Monday at 19 Gordon Square: Tim Crane, Keith Hossack, Mike Martin, Lucy O'Brien, David Papineau, Barry C. Smith, Scott Sturgeon, and Bernhard Weiss. I have presented various sections of the material at various meetings in King's College, London, and I am grateful to all my colleagues there for their constructive comments, support, and encouragement; in particular, to Tad Brennan, Chris Hughes, M. M. McCabe, Richard Sorabji, and Alan Thomas. Jim Hopkins kindly read some chapters and made helpful suggestions. So too did Mark Sainsbury, to whom many thanks are also due for numerous fruitful discussions.

I have also benefited greatly from discussions with many friends, in particular, Ned Block, George Boolos, Don Davidson, Alex George, Marcus Giaquinto, Peter Ludlow, Fraser McBride, Stephen Neale, Terry Parsons, Chris Peacocke, Peter Simons, Bob Stalnaker, Jason Stanley, Stephen Schiffer, and David Wiggins.

I owe special debts to two of my teachers when I was a graduate student at MIT: Noam Chomsky and Jim Higginbotham. Noam was an excellent teacher —kind and supportive. He remains a friend and constant source of inspiration. Jim also taught me well and has continued to be a good friend. Over the past nine years I have spent many hours discussing semantics with him and have learned a great deal as a result. It will be apparent to anyone who knows Jim's work that his influence on me has been broad and deep.

Richard Larson and Gabriel Segal

Many colleagues provided us with comments and suggestions. Our thanks to Martin Davies, Ernie Lepore, and Barry Schein for detailed discussion and criticism on every chapter of the manuscript and for helping us to make this a much better book than it otherwise would have been. Thanks also to Kent Bach, Noam Chomsky, Rob Cummins, Norbert Hornstein, Peter Ludlow, Robert May, Stephen Neale, Paul Pietroski, and Stephen Schiffer for comments, suggestions, and many bracing challenges.

We have also had considerable assistance from the folks at the MIT Press during the process of writing this book. Our thanks to Harry and Betty Stanton, who were with us at the beginning five years ago, and to Teri Mendelsohn, who gave us (many) timely pushes in the later stages and got us to the end. Thanks also to our copyeditor, Alan Thwaits, for many very helpful suggestions, for patience, and for a lot of hard work. Amy Pierce supervised the final stages of publication and we are grateful for her assistance. Finally, we thank Rudy Fara for help in reading proof and for philosophical discussion, Xuan Zhou for numerous corrections, and Aleen Marsh for aid in preparing the indexes.

The material in this book has been presented in classes at Kings College, MIT, and SUNY at Stony Brook, as well as at the 1992 Linguistic Society of America Summer Institute at UC Santa Cruz and the 1993 Girona International Summer School in Linguistics. The students who participated in those classes provided enthusiasm and fun, as well as many helpful comments on everything from terminology to problem sets. Our use of their names in the example sentences of this book is a sign of the warm affection and sincere gratitude that we feel for their help.

Knowledge of Meaning

1   The Nature of Semantic Theory

Semantics is the study of linguistic meaning. Ultimately, its goal is to provide theoretical descriptions and explanations of all of the phenomena of linguistic meaning. In this chapter we introduce the general subject matter of semantic theory and attempt to chart its place and responsibilities in the study of language. Our aim will be to answer certain broad but fundamental questions regarding the data of semantic theory, the object of semantic investigation, the nature of semantic principles and rules, and the task of semantics in relation to other, sister sciences.

1.1   The Pretheoretical Domain of Semantics

Like any scientist, the semantic theorist must begin with whatever data are pretheoretically available and seek a satisfying explanation of them; the semanticist must start by addressing the pretheoretical domain. We begin our explorations by examining the kinds of phenomena that initially present themselves as facts about meaning, and hence the kinds of things our semantic theory might plausibly be responsible for. Considering the data in a rough, intuitive way, we may distinguish three general subdomains. First, there are facts about linguistic expressions themselves, including various properties that they have and various relations holding among them.[1] Second, there are facts about the relationships between linguistic expressions and the world we live in, discuss, and sometimes argue about. And finally, there are facts about the relationships between linguistic expressions and the speakers who use them to formulate thoughts, communicate ideas, persuade, and act. Let us examine these domains briefly.

1.1.1 Semantic Properties and Relations

Among the semantic properties that we would ascribe to natural-language expressions, the most obvious are surely the **actual meanings** that those expressions have. The following, for example, are simple and immediate facts about the actual meanings of three sentences of English and French:

(1) a. The English sentence *Camels have humps* means that camels have humps.
   b. The French sentence *Les chameaux ont des bosses* means that camels have humps.
   c. The English sentence *Camels have humps* does not mean that reptiles have wings.

Clearly, facts of this kind represent primary data that we would want any semantic theory to account for. We want to understand what it means for a sentence or phrase to have the particular meaning or range of meanings that it does, and how it comes to have that meaning rather than some other.

   A second semantic property that we recognize immediately is **ambiguity**, the property of having more than one meaning. The sentences in (2) give sample facts of this kind:

(2) a. The English sentence *Pedro jumped from the top of the bank* has two meanings.
   b. The English sentence *Mad dogs and Englishmen go out in the noonday sun* has two meanings.
   c. The English sentence *John saw her duck* has two meanings.

The ambiguities arise from different sources in the three cases. Sentence (2a) is ambiguous according to whether we understand the word *bank* as referring to a financial institution or a fluvial embankment. Ambiguity here arises from one of the component words. By contrast, (2b) is ambiguous according to whether *mad* is taken to apply to both *dogs* and *Englishmen* or to *dogs* alone. Here ambiguity arises not in the words of the clause but rather in how we understand those words as combining. Finally, (2c) involves a combination of what occurs with (2a) and (2b). The pronoun *her* is ambiguous between a possessive form (as in *John saw her book*) and a simple object form (as in *John saw her*). The word *duck* is ambiguous between a noun and a verb. And the phrase *her duck* is ambiguous between a sentencelike phrase meaning she ducked and a nominal phrase meaning the duck that she owns. Again, an account of ambiguity and also of how ambiguity can arise would appear to be the province of semantic theory.

A third semantic property that we might wish to recognize is **anomaly**: the property having an aberrant meaning. Anomaly is illustrated by the famous sentence in (3), from Chomsky 1957, and by the lines of the children's rhyme in (4), drawn from Leech 1974:

(3) Colorless green ideas sleep furiously.

(4) I went to the pictures tomorrow,
     I took a front scat at thc back;
     I fell from the pit to the gallery,
     And broke a front bone in my back.
     A lady she gave me some chocolate,
     I ate it and gave it her back;
     I phoned for a taxi and walked it,
     And that's why I never came back.
     (Opie, *The Lore and Language of School Children*, p. 25)

In (3) and in each of the verses of (4), we can identify some form of oddness; the sentences are all nonsensical in some way. It seems reasonable to think that semantics should tell us about anomalies and their sources.

Along with semantic properties that hold of individual expressions, we also recognize various semantic relations that hold among them. These include, for example, **logicosemantic relations** such as contradiction, implication, and synonymy. Examples (5) through (7) illustrate:

(5) a. *John believes that the Earth is flat* contradicts *John doubts that the Earth is flat.*
     b. *John claims that the Earth is flat* contradicts *John denies that the Earth is flat.*
     c. *Some mice migrate* contradicts *No mice migrate.*

(6) a. *John is a human* implies *John is a mammal.*
     b. *Mary was laughing and dancing* implies *Mary was dancing.*
     c. *Mary usually takes the train* implies *Mary sometimes takes the train.*
     d. i. *This is a blue gun* implies *This is blue* and *This is a gun.*
         ii. *This is a small moon* implies *This is a moon* but not *This is small.*
         iii. *This is a toy gun* implies *This is a toy* and *This is not a gun.*

(7) a. *John sold a car to Mary* is synonymous with *Mary bought a car from John.*
   b. *Felicity is a female fox* is synonymous with *Felicity is a vixen.*
   c. *John saw Mary* is synonymous with *Mary was seen by John.*
   d. *Alice gave a present to Frank* is synonymous with *Alice gave Frank a present.*

The relations in (5) through (7) arise from different sources. Sometimes they issue from relations between particular pairs of words, such as *believe/doubt, claim/deny, usually/sometimes, buy/sell.* In other cases they come from from individual words, like *and.* In still other cases, the relations arise from pairs of sentence forms, such as active/passive, (7c), and an oblique dative versus a double object, (7d). The examples of (6d) make it clear that such data are in fact rather subtle: although each of the right-hand sentences involves an adjective-noun combination and all these combinations are superficially similar in form, the implicational relations are quite different in the three cases.

A second and slightly less familiar family of semantic relations is the group of **thematic relations** illustrated by the examples in (8) to (11), from Jackendoff 1983. Each of these triples displays a common pattern in meaning, a semantic parallelism. Thus the sentences in (8) all express the idea of an object undergoing a change of some kind. In (8a) it is a change of location, in (8b) a change of possession, and in (8c) a change of properties. The sentences in (9) express the common idea of an object traversing some path. The sentences in (10) all express the idea of an object extending over some path. And the sentences in (11) express the idea of an object being oriented along a path:[2]

(8) a. The train traveled from London to Paris.
   b. The inheritance passed from John to Mary.
   c. The substance changed from liquid to gas.

(9) a. John ran into the house.
   b. The mouse skittered toward the clock.
   c. The train rambled along the river.

(10) a. The highway extends from Denver to Indianapolis.
    b. The flagpole reaches (up) toward the sky.
    c. The sidewalk goes around the tree.

(11) a. The sign points to Philadelphia.
    b. The house faces away from the mountains.
    c. The cannons aim through the tunnel.

It is a fact about English that the sentences in these groups express the same (or significantly similar) thematic relations. A semantic theory should attempt to account for them.

1.1.2   The External Significance of Language

The second main area within the pretheoretical domain of semantics concerns the relation between language and the world, the "external significance of language," to use a phrase from Barwise and Perry 1983.[3] For example, it appears to be a fact about certain words that they make **reference** to specific objects, and a central part of learning these words lies in learning what object or objects they refer to. Thus a crucial aspect of the competent use of the name *Marilyn Monroe* lies in using it to refer to the same Hollywood actress that other people use it to refer to, (12a). Similarly, mastery of the French term *Les Etats Unis* crucially involves learning that it refers to the United States of America, (12b):

(12) a. *Marilyn Monroe* refers to Marilyn Monroe.
     b. *Les Etats Unis* refers to the United States of America.

Reference is not a relation like contradiction or implication, which holds between linguistic expressions; rather, it is a relation between expressions and extralinguistic objects, such as people and countries.

A similar class of semantic facts involving language and the world are facts about **truth** and **falsity**. Many of the sentences in any natural language have the property of being either true or false, and for any of these sentences, the property of being true or false depends crucially on meaning. More exactly, the property of being true or false depends on two things: what the sentence means, and how things are in the extralinguistic world. Thus *Camels have humps* is true because it means what it does and because camels do, in fact, have humps. If camels did not have humps, the sentence would be false. And if *Camels have humps* meant that fish are reptiles, again the sentence would be false.

The relationship between meaning and truth is a complex and intimate one, and we will examine it in detail in the next chapter. However, even at this preliminary stage we can see important connections. Observe that this relationship supports the two inference schemata shown in (13):

(13) a. S means that p b. S means that p
         S is true p
       ──────────   ──────────
         p S is true

Thus if *Camels have humps* means that camels have humps and *Camels have humps* is true, then camels have humps. And if *Camels have humps* means that camels have humps, and camels do indeed have humps, then the sentence *Camels have humps* is true.

That meaning and truth are related in the way shown in (13) underlies the obvious but enormously significant fact that a natural language is **informative**, both about the world and about its speakers. Suppose that Barry telephones us from southern California and utters the English sentence *The air in L.A. is absolutely foul*. Knowing what this sentence means and also knowing that Barry is a truthful person (i.e., a person who speaks true sentences), we learn something about atmospheric conditions in a place thousands of miles from our homes. We do this by employing scheme (13a) as in (14):

(14) *The air in L.A. is absolutely foul* means
      that the air in L.A. is absolutely foul.
      The air in L.A. is absolutely foul is true.
      ──────────────────────────────────────
      The air in L.A. is absolutely foul.

Similarly, suppose that we are trying to determine the truth of a statement whose meaning we know, but whose truth we have cause to doubt. We do this by investigating the world. If Florence tells us that choosy mothers chose Jiff peanut butter and we know what this sentence means, then we proceed by employing scheme (13b) as in (15):

(15) *Choosy mothers chose Jiff* means
      that choosy mothers chose Jiff.
      Choosy mothers chose Jiff.
      ──────────────────────────────
      Choosy mothers chose Jiff is true.

Upon discovering whether choosy mothers do indeed choose Jiff peanut butter, we are in a position to assess the truth of Florence's statement.

The observation that language has external significance—that we can learn things about the world through speech and that we can learn things about sentences (their truth or falsity) through the world—is, of course, a commonplace, one that we rely on constantly in our daily lives. What is important not to miss, however, is the central role that meaning plays in this: It is meaning that allows us to reason from from facts about language to facts about the world, and vice versa. It is meaning that is responsible for the essential informativeness of language. This is clearly a fact about meaning that we would want any semantic theory to capture and explain.

1.1.3 The Internal Significance of Language

Finally, the pretheoretical semantic data about natural language also include facts about the relations between language and its speakers. Meaning relates language not only outward to the world of smog and peanut butter but also inward to the mental lives of speakers. Meaning is connected not only with world-oriented notions like truth and reference but also with speaker-oriented notions like saying, believing, asking, ordering, doubting, etc. Again, the relationship between what sentences mean and the assertions, beliefs, questions, and commands that speakers express by using sentences is complex and subtle. However, in paradigm cases some connections are clear. For example, if a woman sincerely utters (16) under typical circumstances, then it is very likely that she is asserting that it is snowing, that she believes that it is snowing, and that she wishes to inform the audience that it is snowing:

(16) It is snowing.

Similarly, if a man utters the interrogative form (17), then under typical circumstances he would be asking whether it is snowing, indicating that he does not know whether it is snowing and that he wishes to know whether it is snowing:

(17) Is it snowing?

Of course, matters are often less straightforward. When someone is being sarcastic, that person may utter a sentence that means that p without themselves wishing to assert that p, without believing that p, or without wishing to inform the audience that p. Equally, someone might utter (17) knowing full well that it is snowing: the addressee might, for example, have promised to fix the central heating next time it snowed, and the utterance of (17) might serve as a timely, if somewhat oblique, reminder.

Once again, the observation that language has internal significance—that we can discover what people believe, want, demand, and might do on the basis of what they say—is a commonplace that we draw on implicitly every day of our lives. And once again, meaning plays a crucial role. In paradigm cases, the meaning of a sentence directly reflects the content of an internal, psychological state. A speaker utters a sentence meaning that p. By that act, the speaker asserts that p, indicates a belief that p, indicates a wish to inform the audience that p, and so on. In these cases the speaker says exactly what he or she means. And even in other cases there are evidently crucial connections between the meaning of the sentence uttered and the content that the speaker expresses. In the case of the speaker who uses (17) as a reminder of a promise, it is surely no accident that a sentence normally used to ask whether it is snowing is chosen to convey the meaning.

1.1.4   The Pretheoretical Domain as *Pre*theoretical

Our three subdomains present a fund of data and apparent data to which a nascent semantic theory should be addressed. But it is important to keep in mind that a mature semantic theory will not necessarily take these data as given and explain them under their pretheoretical guise. True, we must begin with a pretheoretical domain of facts. But like any scientist, we must bear in mind that what initially presents itself as relevant data may turn out not to be so further down the road. In the process of constructing a rigorous and explicit theory, we must be prepared for elements in the pretheoretical domain to be reanalyzed and redescribed in various ways.

For example, some data may end up being rejected altogether as merely apparent data, "facts" whose initial inclusion in the domain was based on false beliefs. The daily motion of the sun and planets is a case of this sort. At its inception, the pretheoretical domain of astronomy included the "fact" that heavenly bodies rise in the east, traverse the sky along the ecliptic, and set in the west. But, of course, this fact turned out to be merely an apparent one: the planets do not actually circle the Earth each day; rather, the Earth turns.

Other pretheoretical facts may end up being retained as genuine data but reassigned to some other discipline or collection of disciplines for explanation. The motion of the tides illustrates this case. The explanation for the regular ebbing and flooding of large water bodies was once thought to belong to geological theory: tidal motions were believed to be explained by the local properties of the earth.[4] Later, following the work of Kepler and Newton, it was recognized that tidal movement is not properly a geological phenomenon but rather an astronomical one: tides are not caused by the motion or inner workings of the Earth but rather by its gravitational interaction with extraterrestrial bodies. Tidal motion was retained as a genuine fact, but the responsibility for its explanation was transferred to planetary astronomy and gravitational physics.

Still other data may be kept as part of the domain in question but significantly redescribed in the process of being brought within a precise theory. Pretheoretical data about the weight and heat of bodies are examples of this kind. While pre-eighteenth-century physics routinely used these familiar, homey notions, modern physical theory significantly redescribes them. The phenomena of weight are reinterpreted in terms of abstruse concepts like gravitational fields and inertial mass. The phenomena of heat are likewise redescribed in terms of the motion of molecules and other elementary constituents of matter.

Thus although our three semantic domains provide a fund of initial data, we must allow that the developed theoretical domain of semantics may count and classify these data in very different terms than those we began with. The process of constructing a systematic and explicit semantic theory from the pretheoretical domain may well involve a considerable amount of rejection, reassignment, and redescription.

1.2   Semantic Theory as a Theory of Linguistic Knowledge

Semantic facts like those surveyed above are verified by the judgments of native speakers. As native speakers of English, we judge the presence of ambiguity and anomaly, of implication and contradiction, and of thematic parallelisms. We judge the reference of terms, and the truth and falsity of sentences. And we judge what people have asserted, queried, or denied on the basis of what they have said, asked, or written. In our view, these judgments do not merely confirm the data of semantics but actually constitute them in an important sense. Human languages are, after all, the products of human minds. Languages have, to a large extent, just those semantic properties that their speakers ascribe to them. It is because English speakers take the string of words *Camels have humps* to mean that camels have humps that those words have this meaning in English. If English speakers all took the sentence to mean that reptiles have wings, then this is what it would mean.

Our ability to make linguistic judgments clearly follows from our knowing the languages that we know. Monolingual speakers of French or Warlpiri are not able to assess the semantic relations between the English sentences in (8) through (11), they are not able to judge the truth or falsity of English sentences like *Camels have humps,* and they are not able to assess the beliefs and thoughts of English speakers on the basis of what they say. We are able to make the judgments that we make because we English speakers have come to know the language that we know. And those who lack this knowledge lack the corresponding abilities. Given this simple observation, one way to construe semantic theory—the theory that attempts to describe and explain semantic facts—is as a theory of knowledge of one special kind. We can see semantics as a theory of the knowledge that underlies our ability to make semantic judgments. Semantic theory addresses one part of our linguistic knowledge: *knowledge of meaning.*[5]

To view the subject matter of semantics as linguistic knowledge is to locate the place of semantic theory within the general enterprise initiated by Noam Chomsky (1965, 1975, 1986a), for whom linguistic theory is a theory of the real knowledge of speakers. This project contrasts with a variety of other commonly held views of the subject matter. For example, some have taken semantics to be a theory of the semantic relations holding between expressions (including inferential and thematic relations).[6] Many others have construed semantics as a theory of the relations holding between language and the world.[7] Still others have insisted that since languages are abstract objects, linguistics (including linguistic semantics) should be pursued as a branch of mathematics.[8] Our conception differs from all of these. On our view, semantics is part of a theory of speakers' knowledge. Facts about language-to-language and language-to-world relations may furnish important clues about the content of this knowledge—they may furnish data—but they are not the object of inquiry itself. The object of inquiry is knowledge of language.[9]

As Chomsky (1986a) has especially emphasized, once we focus on knowledge of language as the object of investigation, three natural questions present themselves:

1. What do we know?

2. How do we come to know it?

3. How is this knowledge used?

In our view, these questions should be approached from a **cognitivist perspective**, according to which knowledge of language is knowledge of a body of (largely unconscious) rules and principles that assign representations and meanings to the physical forms of signs (be they phonetic, visual, or tactile).[10] On this conception, an answer to question 1 would specify these rules and principles and show how they affect the required mapping from sign to structure and meaning. An answer to question 2 would specify how such rules and principles are acquired, including what knowledge the language learner has at the outset and how this interacts with experience to yield adult knowledge. An answer to question 3 would specify how the rules and principles known by speakers are deployed in speech and understanding, and how they interact with other systems of thought and with action. Let us examine these points more carefully.

1.2.1   Properties of Semantic Rules

If knowledge of meaning is knowledge of a body of rules and principles, what sorts of rules and principles would these be? A natural idea is that some of them would tell you about the meanings of individual words and morphemes and others would tell you how these meanings interact when their corresponding expressions are put together in a sentence. Consider the simple example in (18) from this point of view:

(18) Boris kissed Natasha.

Roughly speaking, understanding (18) would involve rules specifying what *Boris* and *Natasha* refer to and what relation is expressed by the verb *kissed*. It would also involve rules that identify the subject of the transitive verb as the agent of the relation (so that it's Boris who does the kissing) and the object of the verb as the patient (so that it's Natasha who is kissed). Semantic rules of this kind are said to be **compositional**. They give the semantic content of a sentence by specifying the semantic contributions of its parts and the semantic significance of putting those parts together according to a definite mode of syntactic combination.

The hypothesis that we know a set of compositional semantic rules and principles is a highly attractive one having a great deal of explanatory power. In particular, it accounts for three notable and closely related features of linguistic competence. First, it explains why *our understanding of sentences is sys-*

tematic—why there are definite, predictable patterns among the sentences we understand. For example, we would confidently predict that anyone who understands (18) will also understand (19), and vice versa:

(19) Natasha kissed Boris.

This is explained by compositionality. Once you know the rules yielding the meaning of (18), you already know enough to understand (19). The same rules allow for the interpretation of both sentences.

   Second, the hypothesis accounts for the obvious but important fact that *we can understand new sentences*, sentences that we have never come across before. This too is easily explained if we have a body of rules that allow us to infer the meanings of new sentences from prior knowledge of the meanings of their parts and from knowledge of the semantic significance of their combination.

   Third, the hypothesis accounts for the slightly less obvious but equally important fact that *we have the capacity to understand each of an indefinitely large number of sentences*. Consider, for example, the set of sentences in (20), from Platts 1979:

(20) a. The horse behind Pegasus is bald.
      b. The horse behind the horse behind Pegasus is bald.
      c. The horse behind the horse behind the horse behind Pegasus is bald.
      d. The horse behind the horse behind the horse behind the horse behind Pegasus is bald.
          $\vdots$

Clearly this list could be extended indefinitely. Yet in some obvious sense, we seem to be able to understand them all. Of course, our actual capacity to use or react to these sentences is limited in certain ways. When the sentences get too long, we cannot get our minds around them: we forget how they began, or we get distracted, or we simply lose track. Consequently, we cannot show our understanding in the usual ways. For example, we cannot explain what the sentences mean or use them in inferences. But it seems that these limitations reflect constraints on such things as memory and attention span and have little to do with specifically linguistic abilities. If we had unlimited attention spans, memories, and so on, we would presumably be able to understand all the sentences in the set.

Such collections of examples show that our linguistic competence is rich enough to yield an infinite number of distinct judgments. But since our brains are finite objects with finite storage capacity, it is clear that this competence must have a finite form. The compositionality hypothesis accounts for this in a straightforward way. If we know a finite vocabulary and a finite number of the right kinds of rules for deriving what sentences mean from what words mean, then we could generate infinitely many results. For example, suppose that the words and phrases in (20a) are grouped together in the way shown by the traditional tree diagram in (21):[11]

(21)

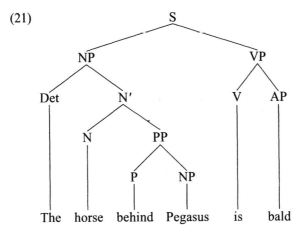

Suppose further that we could assign some kind of semantic contribution or value to each of the leaves of this tree (i.e., to each of the individual words), and suppose that we could give a way of combining these semantic values for each of the branches.[12] Thus, we would have a semantic value for *bald*, for *Pegasus*, for *behind*, etc. And we would also have a general way of combining the values of nominals (N′) and prepositional phrases (PP) in the configuration [$_{N'}$ N PP], a way of combining the values of verbs (V) and adjectives (AP) in the configuration [$_{VP}$ V AP], a way of combining the values of noun phrases (NP) and verb phrases (VP) to yield the meanings of sentences, and so on.

If we could give such semantic values and combination schemes, then we could directly account for our ability to assign meanings to the unbounded sequence of sentences in (20). Consider the tree underlying (20b), depicted in (22):

(22)

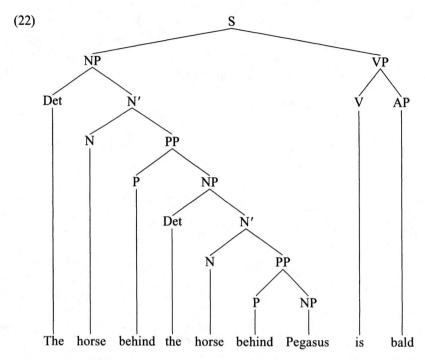

The   horse   behind   the   horse   behind   Pegasus   is   bald

This tree differs from (21) in having extra [$_{NP}$ Det N′] and [$_{N'}$ N PP] branches involving the lexical items *the*, *behind*, and *horse*. But all of these elements already occur in (21). That is, (22) involves recycling the configurations [$_{NP}$ Det N′] and [$_{N'}$ N PP]. It is clear how this recycling occurs. NP introduces an N′ node, which in turn can introduce a PP node, which in turn can introduce an NP again. Configurations of this kind are called **recursive**, and the rules that generate such configurations, rules that have the property that they can apply to their own output, are called **recursive rules**. Given the recursive nature of the configuration in (21), it follows that if we have the semantic resources for computing the meaning of (21), we will "automatically" have the resources for computing the meaning of (22). A compositional semantic theory specifying values and rules for combining them will deliver meanings for (20a), (20b), and indeed *all* the sentences in the list.

It is not difficult to figure out in rough intuitive terms the rules involved in the understanding (18) and (19). But the situation is much less clear with many other examples. Consider the pairs in (23) and (24), adapted from Chomsky 1986a:

(23) a. Boris ate an apple.
      b. Boris ate.

(24) a. Boris is too clever to catch Rocky.
      b. Boris is too clever to catch.

Sentence (23b) means that Boris ate something or other edible. Comparing (23a) and (23b), then, one might think that whenever a transitive verb appears without a direct object, the patient, or undergoer of the action, is taken to be arbitrary: some typical example of an appropriate patient for the verb. But the pair in (24) shows that this rule is much too simple. Sentence (24b) does not mean that Boris is too clever to catch something or other catchable. Rather, it means that Boris is too clever for anyone to catch him. Interestingly, the implicit subject of the verb *catch* is now taken to be arbitrary, and the direct object is understood as *Boris*.

These examples reveal two important further points about knowledge of language. The first is that some of the knowledge that goes into language understanding is unconscious or **tacit**. We are simply not aware of why we assign grammatical relations in (24) the way we do. Introspection does not reveal the rules that we are following, and indeed there is no obvious explanation of the features noted in (24). We can easily imagine a language in which (24b) meant that Boris is to clever to catch anyone. This would be a perfectly respectable meaning for the sentence to have. But (24b) does not have this meaning in English. Why not? The answer to this question turns out to be exceedingly intricate. What accounts for the meaning of (24b) lies deeply buried in our minds, does not emerge after a few moments of reflection, and indeed very probably cannot be accessed through any form of introspection.

A second point illustrated by (23) and (24) is that to understand a sentence, we are compelled to view it as more than a superficial string of words. In particular, we are led to attribute *structure* to sentences, or better, to take sentences as structured things. To understand (24a), you need to know that *Boris* is the subject of the verb *catch*. To understand (24b), you need to know that the subject of *catch* is not *Boris* but an implicit element meaning approximately the same as *one* or *anyone*, and that *Boris* is the object. Understanding a spoken or written string of words thus involves at least two components: there must be an assignment of structure, and there must be an assignment of meaning based on the meanings of the individual elements and the effect of combining them in that particular structure. The rules that account for the first component are syntactic rules, and those that account for the second are semantic rules.[13] We will discuss the relationship between syntax and semantics in more detail in chapter 3.

1.2.2 Acquisition of Semantic Rules

Knowledge of language is something acquired over a period of time. When born into a linguistic environment, a normal human infant will, after a few years, gain knowledge of the rules of language. This distinguishes human infants from rocks, chimpanzees, and indeed everything else. Human infants thus have some property P lacking in rocks, chimpanzees, etc., that enables them to learn language when placed in a suitable environment. P, together with the infant's experiences, account for its acquiring linguistic competence.

An answer to our second question about knowledge of meaning—how we come to know it—will explain how adult knowledge of semantic rules and principles is achieved and the nature of the property underlying this achievement. More precisely, it will specify what semantic knowledge is available to the child at the outset of the learning period, and how this knowledge interacts with experience to yield adult competence. This task is a formidable one, since, as in so many other domains of human learning, there is a considerable gap between what adults come to know and the evidence by which they come to know it.

Consider first an example from the domain of word meaning due to Susan Carey (1984). Imagine a child in the process of acquiring the meaning of the English noun *rabbit*.[14] The child's parent shows it a number of pink, velour, stuffed rabbits. Each time the parent picks up a rabbit, it says the word *rabbit*. What conjectures can the child make about the meaning of *rabbit*? One possibility, of course, is that *rabbit* means rabbits, the concept that adult speakers eventually acquire. But clearly there are other hypotheses fitting the data that the parent has provided; indeed, there are indefinitely many such hypotheses. For example, *rabbit* could mean toy rabbit, or pink velour, or pink, or rabbit or chicken, or rabbit or planet, or rabbit or prime number lying between 8642 and 8652, and so on. Some of these hypotheses might be tested and corrected against further data, but clearly for a great many possibilities (like the last), such checking would be difficult to do. Furthermore, there are some hypotheses that no such empirical tests will serve to distinguish. For example, suppose the child is attempting to decide whether the word *rabbit* means rabbit versus undetached rabbit part, that is, piece of a rabbit connected to a whole rabbit.[15] Since picking up a rabbit always entails grasping some un-disconnected piece of it (a paw, a tail, an ear, etc.), any evidence for the former hypothesis will also be evidence for the latter. No simple visual presentation will tell them apart.

In a similar vein, consider the child exposed to verbs like *chase*, *buy*, and *give* in a context where the parent is using hand puppets to act out various scenes while uttering sentences like *Big Bird is chasing Oscar*, or *Ernie is buying a block from Kermit*, or *Fozzy is giving a block to Bert*. In these circumstances the child might indeed conjecture that *chase* means to chase, *buy* means to buy, and *give* means to give. However, as Gleitman (1990) points out, for each of these predicates, there is another available alternative. Any situation in which *Big Bird is chasing Oscar* is true will also be one in which *Oscar is fleeing Big Bird* is true; any situation in which *Ernie is buying a block from Kermit* is true is also one in which *Kermit is selling a block to Ernie* is true; and any situation in which *Fozzy is giving a block to Bert* is true is one in which *Bert is getting a block from Fozzy* is true. *Chase*, *buy*, and *give* each have a symmetric counterpart describing a closely related situation involving similar roles for the participants. In view of this, it will also be plausible for the child to conjecture that *chase* means to flee, *buy* means to sell, and that *give* means to get. In and of themselves, the scenes presented by the parent will not tell these conjectures apart.[16]

Finally, consider a child in the process of fixing the meaning of nominal structures of the form $[_{NP}$ NP's N'$]$, as they occur in examples like *Rosa's book* or *Kyoko's picture of Max*. One possible conjecture is that $[_{NP}$ NP's N'$]$ refers to the object NP possesses having the property described by N' (thus, the object Rosa possesses that is a book, the object Kyoko possesses that is a picture of Max, etc.). This is roughly the interpretation rule that adults come to know. But an indefinite number of other hypotheses are also possible. Thus children might conjecture that $[_{NP}$ NP's N'$]$ means the object that is NP and is an N' (e.g., Rosa, who is a book), or they might take it to refer to the object that NP either possesses *or* likes, having the property described by N', etc. Again, some of these hypotheses will be eliminable through simple stimulus data, but not all them. For example, suppose the child takes $[_{NP}$ NP's N'$]$ to refer to the object NP possesses that has the property described by N' and is either a number or else not a number. Then there will be no simple situations in which the "correct" adult rule yields a true sentence and the alternative rule yields a false one. That is, *Rosa's book is red* will be true under the adult rule exactly when it is true under the alternative rule.

These examples illustrate the basic **induction problem** facing theories of semantic acquisition: the rules that children ultimately adopt regarding word
and phrase meaning are substantially underdetermined by the evidence that
the learning environment provides. Given this disparity between knowledge
and evidence, the conclusion seems inevitable that there are a priori principles
in play allowing children to make the right choices. That is, in acquiring the
meanings of words and sentences, it seems that children must be guided by
antecedently known constraints permitting them to select appropriate hypotheses in the face of minimal data.

At present, the principles children deploy in acquiring word and phrase
meanings are only beginning to be understood clearly. And indeed, different
kinds of principles and data appear to be involved for different parts of the
grammar. For example, in resolving whether a noun like *rabbit* refers to
rabbits or undetached rabbit parts, it appears that children deploy principles
involving knowledge of objects and their properties, and their familiarity with
the word that accompanies the object.[17] Thus if children are presented with an
unfamiliar object (a rabbit) under an unfamiliar term (*rabbit*), they will generally conjecture that the term applies maximally to the object as a whole (so
that *rabbit* refers to rabbits and not rabbit parts). On the other hand, if a
familiar object (a rabbit) composed of an unfamiliar substance (e.g., velour) is
presented under an unfamiliar term (*velour*), they will conjecture that the new
term refers to the substance of which the object is composed (*velour* refers
to velour material). And so on. Such reasoning evidently requires children to
have a substantial theory allowing them to isolate objects and their properties,
and a variety of experimenters have argued that such a theory is available
from a very early age.

In fixing the meanings of vocabulary items like verbs, more specifically linguistic data seem to be involved. A number of researchers have argued that
children are able to deduce substantial aspects of the meanings of predicates
from the syntactic structures in which they appear. Consider the case of *chase*,
buy, and *give* versus *flee*, *sell*, and *receive*. One prominent difference between
these predicates involves who is the agent in each. Although *Ernie is buying a
block from Kermit* and *Kermit is selling a block to Ernie* are true in the same
circumstances, we understand Ernie to be the agent in the former but Kermit
to be the agent in the latter. Suppose, then, that children deploy universal
linking rules specifying that in a structure of the relevant kind (that is, roughly,
NP_1 V NP_2 P NP_3), the subject noun phrase (NP_1) must always refer to the
individual playing the agent role. Then they will be able to distinguish *buy* and

sell correctly in terms of the environmental data and the syntactic forms that accompany their presentation. Hearing *Ernie is buying a block from Kermit*, observing the situation described, and knowing the linking rule just given, the child can reason that V denotes events of commercial exchange in which the recipient of the object exchanged is also the agent. That is, V denotes buyings. On the other hand, hearing *Kermit is selling a block to Ernie*, observing the situation described, and knowing the linking rule, the child can reason that V denotes events of commercial exchange in which the source of the object exchanged is also the agent. That is, V denotes sellings.

The picture that emerges from these results is a familiar one under the cognitive perspective. The child appears as as active agent who must deduce the rules of its language on the basis of available evidence. Given the underdetermination of hypotheses by data, such deductions evidently require the presence of substantial constraints limiting the space of possible conjectures. Without them, the language learner would be forever in search of data to rule out extravagant hypotheses. Since the principles in question apply to all human language learning, they will clearly constrain the possibilities of all learnable languages. Only languages whose rules conform to the principles will be humanly learnable. So, to pursue the above example of *rabbit*, it seems plausible to conclude that whatever principles intervene to fix the meaning of the English noun *rabbit* as rabbit, and not rabbit or prime number between 8642 and 8652, will also be the operating in French to fix the meaning of *lapin* as rabbit, and not rabbit or prime number between 8642 and 8652, and similarly for many other nouns and many other possible hypotheses. Such principles specify universal constraints on human language, and so are appropriately called **universal grammar** (UG). On the cognitivist view, property *P* is knowledge of UG, and a cognitivist answer to question 3 would specify UG and show how knowledge of particular languages results from the interaction of UG with experience.

As we commented above, it seems clear that the ability to learn languages must be a species-specific property of humans (Chomsky 1975, 1986a). No nonhuman animal or other earthly object learns language when placed in a typical human habitat. Moreover, children of all races and nationalities appear equally able to learn all languages: a child born of English parents but brought up by Japanese speakers will typically learn Japanese. To be sure, not every human can learn language. But those that cannot are atypical of the species in precisely that respect. So it is reasonable to conclude that it is part of our genetic endowment.[18]

1.2.3   Use of Semantic Rules

Knowing a language is not sufficient by itself to enable one to understand and to speak. Such knowledge must be applied to the problems of interpreting the sentences one hears and finding the right words and structures to express what one wants to say. An answer to our third question—how knowledge of meaning is used—would describe the mechanisms that access this knowledge and explain how they work. We will confine ourselves to some very brief remarks on the topic.

When we express ourselves in language, we move various parts of our bodies (our vocal chords, our tongue, our lips, our lungs, our hands) to produce the words we wish to produce. These motions result from the intention to produce just these words and no others. Very little is known about how such intentions are arrived at. Introspection is of little help. When we converse, it often appears as though we think our thoughts even as we speak them. If this appearance is correct in at least some cases, then in these cases the problem of explaining how we find the words to express ourselves (what Chomsky calls the "production problem") is a subproblem within the much larger general problem of how we arrive at the thoughts we have. If the appearance is not correct, then the alternative hypothesis is presumably that the thought is present in our minds in some form prior to its expression and some cognitive processes are responsible for selecting the best words of natural language to convey the thought.

It is clear that at least sometimes there is a gap between thought and its expression. To borrow an example from Higginbotham 1987, someone might be on the verge of using a particular sentence, realize that it is ambiguous, and so choose another one instead. In such a case, a small aspect of the subject's deploying knowledge of meaning is introspectively revealed: he or she knows the candidate sentence is ambiguous and reasons that it is unsuitable for communicating. But this casts little light on the larger process: what leads the subject to the initial idea of uttering the first sentence, and what leads to the choice of the next sentence? About such matters almost nothing is known.

The process of using knowledge of language in understanding perceived sentences is slightly less mysterious. We can distinguish at least three kinds of processes involved. First there is what is called **parsing**. When you hear a sentence of your own language, you need to identify the speech sounds for what they are, that is, you must identify its phonological form. You must identify the syntactic arrangement of its constituents. You must also identify the meanings of its words and how they compose. This much seems clear and is widely accepted. What is not clear and is much more controversial is how all this is carried out. It seems possible a priori that the process is serial: first you identify the phonology, then the syntax, then the semantics. But it is also quite possible that the task is staggered or occurs fully in parallel, so that, for example, you compute the semantics at the very same time you are computing the phonology. Research in this area is very active at present, and both the serial and parallel views are under intense scrutiny and debate.[19]

Parsing concerns the application of strictly linguistic knowledge only. Linguistic knowledge will provide only what we might call the **context-independent meaning of an utterance**. To fully understand an utterance of a sentence, more than this is often required. For example, if someone utters (25), your knowledge of the language will not tell you who *she* refers to on this occasion or which place is identified by *here*:

(25) She is here.

These are context-dependent features of utterance meaning. Your knowledge of language will tell you, very roughly, that the utterance means that some independently identified female is near the speaker. The second kind of process involved in language understanding, then, concerns identifying the relevant features of context and combining them with knowledge of language to arrive at a full interpretation of the utterance.[20]

The third kind of process is the application of knowledge of general conversational principles—**pragmatics**. Knowledge of language provides only the literal meanings of sentences. But there is often a gap between what is said with a sentence (fully interpreted in a context) and what a speaker using the sentence intends to convey. Pragmatics is required to bridge the gap. Consider how you would understand the following testimonial by Professor Williams about Dr. Stevens, who is a candidate for a philosophy position:[21]

(26) Mr. Stevens command of English is excellent, and his attendance at
      tutorials has been regular.

By writing (26), Williams conveys the message that Stevens is not very good as a philosopher. How so? Grice (1975) suggests that there is a general principle of "quantity" governing linguistic communication: make your communication as informative as required. Using this principle and one's general knowledge of the circumstances, one can infer the conveyed message: Williams is surely in a position to comment on Stevens's philosophical ability and knows that this is what she is supposed to be doing. Williams must therefore have some reason for not wishing to provide the required information explicitly. But since she has bothered to write, she must wish to get the information across in some other way. The natural conclusion is that she thinks that Stevens is no good at philosophy.

Semantic knowledge is thus used along with a variety of other kinds of knowledge in understanding language. It is used along with knowledge of phonology and syntax in the parsing processes that deliver the literal, context-independent meaning of a perceived sentence form. This knowledge is combined with knowledge of relevant features of context in further inferences to yield an interpretation of the sentence in the context. And it is combined also with knowledge of pragmatics in yet more inferential processes that provide conclusions about what people are saying.[22]

1.3   The Place and Responsibilities of Semantic Theory

Semantic theory as we have sketched it here is a component of the larger enterprise of cognitive linguistics. As such, it rests on two major empirical assumptions. Like cognitive linguistics as a whole, it assumes that linguistic competence consists of an unconscious body of knowledge, what Chomsky has termed the "language faculty." Furthermore, it assumes that the language faculty contains a specifically semantic module: a particular, isolable domain of linguistic knowledge beyond phonology, morphology, syntax, etc., that is concerned with meaning.

In our picture, the semantic module has contents of a very specific sort. The module contains specifications of meaning for the simplest expressions of the language and rules for deducing the meanings of complex expressions on the basis of the meanings of their parts and the structural configuration in which they occur. Moreover, the semantic module occupies a definite place both within the language faculty and within the larger cognitive system. In the language faculty, semantics is connected to syntax, yielding meanings for the structures that syntax provides. It is also connected to those modules mentioned under the heading "Use of Semantic Rules": the pragmatics module and the parser (figure 1.1).

In the larger cognitive domain, we will later see grounds for thinking that semantics is connected to a module containing knowledge of inferential principles (tacit logic), and to the modules containing our implicit theories of objects

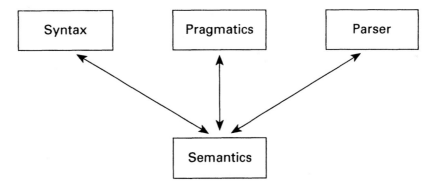

Figure 1.1   The place of semantics in the language faculty.

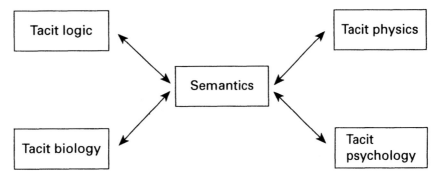

Figure 1.2   The place of semantics in the larger cognitive domain.

and forces (tacit physics), of creatures and their goals (tacit biology), and of people's cognitive states and their actions (tacit psychology) (figure 1.2).[23]

The task of semantic theory, then, is to specify precisely the contents of the semantics module. We must say what knowledge is contained in it, and we must show that this knowledge is sufficient to fulfill its purpose and explain semantic facts. If the enterprise fails, this will reflect back on one of the two assumptions on which the theory is built: Our efforts will fail because the whole enterprise of cognitive linguistics is mistaken. Or they will fail because there is no semantics module. It is worth reflecting on this latter point, since, however plausible it may seem, the assumption that there is a semantics module within the language faculty cannot be demonstrated a priori. It is conceivable that the genuinely modular areas of this faculty—the areas that contain a definite set of rules and principles with a well-defined role in cognition—do not include a semantics.[24] In such a case, syntactic knowledge would feed directly into a variety of different processors containing different kinds of knowledge and serving different tasks involved in speech, understanding, and (no doubt) other matters as well.[25]

There is no quick way of establishing the truth of either of our guiding assumptions. In both cases we must wait on the development of the best over-all theory. To establish the correctness of cognitivist linguistics as a whole, it is necessary to develop a relatively detailed and complete theory and to demonstrate, first, that it works—that if it were true, it would account for a very significant body of data—and, second, that it outperforms competitors (if there are any). To establish the existence of the semantics module, one must work within linguistics and show that the most successful linguistic theory overall is one that includes semantics as a part. It is to the latter task that this book is addressed. In the next chapter we articulate the general form of semantic theory, explaining exactly what kinds of rules and principles are involved in semantic knowledge and showing how a theory of this form could play the role assigned to it. In chapter 3 we specify in detail the relations between semantics and syntax. In the following chapters we deal with a variety of constructions in natural language and develop detailed and well-supported, specific theories of their semantic functioning. We conclude, in the final chapter, with a deeper and broader discussion of the conceptual issues and methodology underlying our approach.

2   Knowledge of Meaning and Theories of Truth

We have been pursuing semantics as a theory of the real but unconscious knowledge of speakers. We have argued that what is known by speakers is a set of rules and principles that are finite in number and compositional in form. These underlie our grasp of semantic facts, our capacity to make semantic judgments, and our ability to communicate with and understand others. Precisely what does this knowledge consist in? What kinds of rules and principles are known?

The idea we will adopt and develop in this book derives from the work of Donald Davidson, who proposes that the work of a semantic theory can be done by a particular sort of formal theory called a **truth theory**, or **T theory** for short.[1] A T theory for a particular language L is a deductive system that has the resources to prove something about the truth value of every sentence of L. More specifically, for each sentence of L it proves a theorem of the form in (T), where S is a name or description of the L sentence and p has the same truth value as the sentence referred to by S:

(T) S is true if and only if p.

The language from which S is drawn is typically referred to as the **object language**. It is the language that we are theorizing about. Here the object language is L. The language used to discuss the object language is typically referred to as the **metalanguage**. It is the language in which our theory is stated. Here the metalanguage is English. A T theory produces theorems that pair a sentence S of the object language L with a sentence p of the metalanguage. These two are paired together by the relation "is true if and only if" (henceforth abbreviated "is true iff").[2] Theorems of the form (T) are called **T sentences** or **T theorems**.[3]

2.1 T Theories

The easiest way to understand the workings of a T theory is to examine a concrete instance. So let us consider a sample T theory for a small sublanguage of English that we will call PC, since it includes some elements of the propositional calculus. PC contains an infinite number of sentences, although they are all of a highly restricted form. In particular, PC contains the three elementary sentences *Phil ponders*, *Jill knows Kate*, and *Chris agrees*. PC also contains all sentences that can be produced from the basic three either by joining them together with one of the sentence conjunctions *and* or *or*, or by prefixing them with the negation *it is not the case that*. For present purposes, we will assume that the elementary sentences are generated by the three rules in (1), and that the remainder are generated by the rules in (2). Rule (1a) may be read as saying that *Phil ponders* is a sentence (an S), and similarly for (1b, c). Rule (2a) may be read as stating that any two sentences (Ss) joined by the word *and* is also a sentence, and similarly for (2b, c):[4]

(1) a. S → *Phil ponders*
    b. S → *Chris agrees*
    c. S → *Jill knows Kate*

(2) a. S → S *and* S
    b. S → S *or* S
    c. S → *It is not the case that* S

Under these rules PC will contain all of the example sentences in (3) (among infinitely many others):

(3) a. [$_S$ Phil ponders]
    b. [$_S$ Chris agrees]
    c. [$_S$ Jill knows Kate]
    d. [$_S$ [$_S$ Phil ponders] or [$_S$ Chris agrees]]
    e. [$_S$ [$_S$ Jill knows *Kate*] and [$_S$ [$_S$ Phil ponders] or [$_S$ Phil ponders]]]
    f. [$_S$ It is not the case that [$_S$ Jill knows Kate]]
    g. [$_S$ It is not the case that [$_S$ [$_S$ Phil ponders] or [$_S$ Chris agrees]]]

The **labeled brackets** in (3) depict the derivational histories of complex sentences. For example, (3g) is formed by our first connecting *Phil ponders* and *Chris agrees*, using *or* to form a disjunction (as permitted by (2b)) and then attaching *it is not the case that* to form the negation of this disjunction (as permitted by (2c)). These derivations may be also depicted by means of familiar tree diagrams or **phrase markers**.[5] Thus (3d) can be associated with the tree in (4a). Likewise, (3f) can be represented with the tree in (4b):

(4) a.

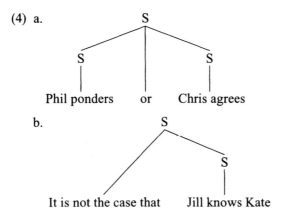

b.

The three elementary sentences *Phil ponders*, *Jill knows Kate*, and *Chris agrees* appearing as the leaves on these trees are treated as complex words in PC. That is, they are assigned no internal syntactic structure. Following standard terminology, we will refer to these elementary sentences as the **terminal nodes** in the tree. And we will refer to nodes with internal syntactic structure, for example, the built-up Ss in (3d–g), as **nonterminal nodes**.

A T theory for PC will allow us to derive a T theorem for each sentence of PC. The T theory we wish to explore consists of three basic parts. First, there are interpretation rules for the terminal nodes in the PC grammar. These assign a semantic contribution to the basic components of PC, as in (5):

(5) a. *Phil ponders* is true iff Phil ponders.
    b. *Chris agrees* is true iff Chris agrees.
    c. *Jill knows Kate* is true iff Jill knows Kate.

Second, there are interpretation rules for the nonterminal nodes. These allow us to derive T sentences for configurations with internal structure from the T sentences for their smaller component sentences. Thus for *any* sentences S, S_1, and S_2,[6]

(6) a. $[_S\ S_1\ and\ S_2]$ is true iff both S_1 is true and S_2 is true
    b. $[_S\ S_1\ or\ S_2]$ is true iff either S_1 is true or S_2 is true
    c. $[_S\ It\ is\ not\ the\ case\ that\ S]$ is true iff it is not the case that S is true
    d. $[_S\ \alpha]$ is true iff α is true (for any elementary sentence α)

Third and finally, there are **production rules**, which license inferences of certain specified kinds. These allow us to reason from the elementary and general semantic rules and to prove results using them. For PC we will adopt two production rules. The first is called substitution of equivalents, abbreviated (SE). This rule is defined as follows:

(SE) Substitution of equivalents

$$F(\alpha)$$
$$\alpha \text{ iff } \beta$$
$$\overline{}$$
$$F(\beta)$$

According to (SE), if we have proved a statement involving α (i.e., $F(\alpha)$) and have proved that α is equivalent to β, (i.e., α iff β), then we may conclude the result of substituting β for α in the statement (that is, we may conclude $F(\beta)$). The second rule is universal instantiation, or (UI):

(UI) Universal instantiation

$$\text{For any S, } F(S)$$
$$\overline{}$$
$$F(\alpha)$$

Universal instantiation will allow us to apply the general rules in (6) to particular instances.

The three elements specified above may be viewed as jointly specifying a deductive system. The interpretation rules in (5) and (6) function as semantic axioms from which we can prove a T sentence for each sentence of PC, using the production rules (SE) and (UI).

2.1.1   A Sample Derivation

We can illustrate how this system works with example (3d). Recall this string of words receives the structure in (4a), which we represent with labeled bracketing as in (7):

(7) [$_S$ [$_S$ Phil ponders] or [$_S$ Chris agrees]]

To derive the T sentence for this structure, we begin at the top (leftmost) S node and interpret it in terms of its subsentences. We do this by applying (UI) to the axiom in (6b):

(8) [$_S$ [$_S$ Phil ponders] or [$_S$ Chris agrees]] is true iff either
     [$_S$ Phil ponders] is true or [$_S$ Chris agrees] is true (by (6b), (UI))

The axiom in (6d) tells us how further to unpack each of the two disjuncts on the right-hand side of "iff" in (8):

(9) a. [$_S$ Phil ponders] is true iff *Phil ponders* is true (by (6d), (UI))
　　 b. [$_S$ Chris agrees] is true iff *Chris agrees* is true (by (6d), (UI))

The clauses in (5a) and (5c) then tell us how to spell out the T sentence for each of the two elementary sentences on the right-hand sides of the "iff" connectors in (9):

(10) a. *Phil ponders* is true iff Phil ponders. (by (5a))
　　　b. *Chris agrees* is true iff Chris agrees. (by (5b))

To complete the T sentence for (3d), we now use the production rule (SE), working our way back up the tree. Suppose that we let (9a) be $F(\alpha)$, "*Phil ponders* is true" be α, and "Phil ponders" be β. By (10a), we have "α iff β," so we can use (SE) to conclude "[$_S$ Phil ponders] is true iff Phil ponders":

(11) [$_S$ Phil ponders] is true iff *Phil ponders* is true　　(9a)
　　　Phil ponders is true iff Phil ponders　　　　　　　　(10a)
　　　───
　　　[$_S$ Phil ponders] is true iff Phil ponders
　　　(by (9a), (10a), (SE))

We now reapply the same strategy, this time letting (9b) be $F(\alpha)$, letting "*Chris agrees* is true" be α, and letting "Chris agrees" be β. By (10b), we have that "α iff β," so again, using (SE), we may conclude that (12b):

(12) a. [$_S$ Phil ponders] is true iff Phil ponders (by (9a), (10a), (SE))
　　　b. [$_S$ Chris agrees] is true iff Chris agrees (by (9b), (10b), (SE))

Next let (8) be $F(\alpha)$, let "[$_S$ Phil ponders] is true" be α, and let "Phil ponders" be β. By (12a), we have "α iff β," so we can use (SE) to conclude that (13):

(13) [$_S$ [$_S$ Phil ponders] or [$_S$ Chris agrees]] is true iff either
　　　Phil ponders or [$_S$ Chris agrees] is true (by (8), (12a), (SE))

Finally, let (13) be $F(\alpha)$, let "[$_S$ Chris agrees] is true" be α, and let "Chris agrees" be β. By (12b), we have "α iff β," so, using (SE), we conclude that (14):

(14) [$_S$ [$_S$ Phil ponders] or [$_S$ Chris agrees]] is true iff either
　　　Phil ponders or Chris agrees (by (13), (12b), (SE))

We have shown that the PC sentence *Phil ponders or Chris agrees* is true if and only if Phil ponders or Chris agrees. Intuitively, of course, this is a true outcome.

2.1.2   The Nontriviality of T Theorems

Results like that in (14) are achieved by means of a formally precise theory using explicit procedures. Nonetheless, they may appear entirely trivial at first sight. After all, how informative is it to learn that *Phil ponders or Chris agrees* is true if and only if Phil ponders or Chris agrees? In fact, such results are quite informative and the initial impression of triviality is really an illusion of sorts. It is important to locate the source of this illusion and to dispel it.

Like other scientific statements, T theorems state facts or hypotheses about certain phenomena, specifically, about linguistic phenomena. T theorems thus make statements *in* a language *about* a language: language is mentioned in the T theorem, and it is used to formulate the T theorem. Given any object-language, there will be a vast array of languages in which we can formulate T sentences for sentences of that object language. We can give the truth conditions of a sentence of English using a T sentence formulated in Chinese. We can also give the truth conditions of a sentence of English using a T sentence formulated in English. This is the case with the T theory for PC. The object language, PC, is a small fragment of English. And the metalanguage in which we give our axioms, production rules, and results is also English.

Now it is a simple fact about sentences and their truth conditions that any sentence of a language L can be used to state its own truth conditions in L. That is to say, T sentences of the following homophonic form are (almost) always true for any sentence S of English:[7]

(T*) *S* is true if and only if S.

It is partly this fact that gives results like (14) their air of triviality. The T sentence (14) mentions a sentence of English (*Phil ponders or Chris agrees*) and then goes on to use this very sentence to state its truth conditions. Part of what is obvious about T theorems like (14) is thus their truth. Nonetheless, it is important to see that despite the obvious truth of (14), this T sentence is far from trivial.

The general informativeness of truth theories can be seen most clearly when we consider examples where the object language and metalanguage diverge. For example, consider an alternative T theory for PC in which the metalanguage is German rather than English. Under this choice, (5) and (6) would be replaced by (5′) and (6′):

(5′) a. *Phil ponders* ist wahr genau dann wenn Phil nachdenkt.
   b. *Chris agrees* ist wahr genau dann wenn Chris zustimmt.
   c. *Jill knows Kate* ist wahr genau dann wenn Jill Kate kennt.

(6′) a. [$_S$ S_1 *and* S_2] ist wahr genau dann wenn S_1 wahr ist und S_2 wahr ist.
   b. [$_S$ S_1 *or* S_2] ist wahr genau dann wenn S_1 ist wahr oder S_2 wahr ist.
   c. [$_S$ *It is not the case that* S] ist wahr genau dann wenn S nicht wahr ist.
   d. [$_S$ α] ist wahr genau dann wenn S wahr ist (fur jeden Elementarsatz α)

These results are evidently neither uninformative nor trivial. For a monolingual speaker of German, (5′) and (6′) will provide information about an infinite set of English sentences. Using these rules, the German speaker will be able to determine the truth conditions for all of the sentences comprising PC. However, (5′) and (6′) do not say anything different from what is said by the original (5) and (6). Indeed, they say just the same thing! They attribute the same truth conditions to the same elementary sentences of PC, and they provide the same rules for dealing with complex sentences of PC. It's just that they say these things in German, and so make them available to monolingual German speakers.

Why, then, do homophonic T sentences appear trivial? The answer is not too hard to find. If someone is in a position to understand a T sentence, then, obviously, they must understand the metalanguage, the language in which the T sentence is formulated. Or, more precisely, they must understand as much of the metalanguage as is used in the T sentence. For example, to understand any T sentence of the form of (14), it is necessary to understand as much English as is used in its formulation:

(15) S is true iff Phil ponders.

Understanding this includes understanding the RHS, "Phil ponders." Now anyone who understands the sentence *Phil ponders* knows that it is true if and only if Phil ponders. Understanding *Phil ponders* requires this at the very least. Consequently, anyone who is in a position to understand any T sentence of the form of (15) already knows what is stated by (5a): *Phil ponders* is true if and only if Phil ponders. But, of course, (5a) just is a T sentence of the form of (15). So anyone who understands (5a) must already know that it is true.

In a sense, then, homophonic T sentences are uninformative: anyone who is in a position to understand them already knows enough to know that they

Table 2.1 Truth table for the material biconditional, "iff"

p	*q*	*p* iff *q*
t	t	t
t	f	f
f	t	f
f	f	t

are true. But it certainly does not follow from this that what is stated by such a T sentence is not highly substantive. It is highly substantive, as we can see by the nonhomophonic cases. The purportedly unsubstantive (5a) says no more and no less than the evidently substantive (5′a).[8]

Although T sentences are not trivial, at the same time we should emphasize that by themselves they carry less information than one might think. In a T sentence the "if and only if" that appears is just the ordinary **material biconditional**, defined in standard logic texts by the truth table in table 2.1. According to this table, a sentence made up of two sentences *p* and *q* joined by "iff" is true whenever *p* and *q* are either both true or both false (and false otherwise). Since the "is true" in a T sentence is just the usual predicate "true," any T sentence in which the sentence on the left of "iff" has the same truth value as the RHS will be true. For example, (16) is perfectly true.

(16) *Snow is white* is true iff pigs have curly tails.

The upshot is that although T sentences carry nontrivial semantic information relating the truth value of a sentence to a worldly condition, the information they carry is somewhat limited. As we will shortly see, the issue of exactly how much information a T sentence carries is a central one.

2.2 T Theories as Theories of Meaning

We began our investigations by characterizing semantics as the study of linguistic meaning, more precisely, as the study of knowledge of meaning. From this perspective, it may seem quite puzzling to be told that knowledge of meaning amounts to knowledge of a T theory. After all, a T theory like the one for PC proves statements about the truth of sentences, for example, those in (17). It proves nothing directly about the meanings of sentences; it does not give results like (18):

(17) a. *Phil ponders* is true iff Phil ponders.
    b. *Phil ponders or Chris agrees* is true iff either Phil ponders or Chris agrees.

(18) a. *Phil ponders* means that Phil ponders.
    b. *Phil ponders or Chris agrees* means that either Phil ponders or Chris agrees.

But then what is the relation between the two? How are we to understand the claim that knowledge of the one might be responsible for our grasp of the other?

As a step toward clarifying the connection, note first that although our T theory for PC doesn't derive explicit statements of meaning, its results are similar to the latter in an important respect. Observe that while the sentences in (17) differ from those in (18) in involving the relation "is true iff" instead of the relation "means that," the two sets of statements are alike in pairing exactly the same object language sentences and metalanguage sentences together. That is, the relation "is true iff" defined by our truth theory for PC (that is, by (5), (6), (SE), and (UI)) is similar to the relation "means that" insofar as it associates an object-language sentence with a metalanguage sentence that intuitively gives its meaning. We will call a T theory that yields the same pairing as that given by "means that" an **interpretive T theory**. And we will call the T sentences yielded by an interpretive T theory **interpretive T sentences**.

We propose that knowledge of this special kind of T theory, an interpretive T theory, is what underlies our grasp of semantic facts, our ability to understand our language in the way that we do. That is, we propose the following empirical hypothesis about knowledge of meaning:

The T hypothesis A speaker's knowledge of meaning for a language *L* is knowledge of a deductive system (i.e., a system of axioms and production rules) proving theorems of the form of (T) that are interpretive for sentences of *L*.

On this view, speakers who know the semantics of their language have internalized a system of rules like those in PC. The deliverances of this system, its (interpretive) T sentences, are what the speaker draws upon to encode and decode utterances, to make semantic judgments, and so on.

To explain the connection between interpretive T theories and semantic knowledge more fully and to show how the former could serve as a theory of meaning, it is useful to consider the T hypothesis in the light of two important questions that arise naturally in connection with it. First, under the T hypothesis, speakers are claimed to have internalized an interpretive T theory. But is it really possible to define such a T theory formally? Since "is true iff" and "means that" are different relations, is it possible to give a set of axioms and deductive principles for a natural language whose T theorems pair all and only those paired by "means that"? We call this the **extension question**.

Second, under the T hypothesis, knowledge of interpretive T theorems is claimed to provide the information that underwrites judgments about semantic facts. But would knowing an interpretive T theory be enough to tell you what the sentences of a language mean, to ground judgments about semantic properties and relations, and to account for the external and internal significance of language? Again, since "is true iff" and "means that" are two different relations that appear to talk about two very different things, truth versus meaning, a positive answer is by no means clear. We call this the **information question**.[9]

2.2.1   The Extension Question

There are two separate parts to the extension question. First, there is the question of whether we can give a T theory that's sufficiently productive, that is, one that proves an interpretive T theorem for every sentence of the object language. Second, there is the question of whether we can give a T theory that's not overproductive, that is, one that proves no uninterpretive results.

Both of these questions appear to be fundamentally empirical ones, to be answered by providing an interpretive T theory of the kind required. In subsequent chapters we will explore such theories for a wide variety of natural-language constructions, including such central ones as predicates, names, quantifiers, descriptions, anaphoric elements, modifiers, and embedded clauses. And there are other constructions not discussed here, such as comparatives, that have also been more or less satisfactorily dealt with. There remain, of course, elements of natural language that have so far resisted satisfactory T-theoretic treatment. Subjunctive conditionals are one well-known example. As we will see, however, the track record of T theories is a strong one— strong enough to warrant optimism about their power in principle to account for the full range of natural-language structures.

The second part of the extension question—whether it's possible to give a T theory that proves no uninterpretive results—is a bit more complex. As described earlier, a T theory consists of two basic parts: semantic axioms for interpreting lexical items and phrasal structures, and production rules for deducing results from the axioms. T theorems are the product of these components acting together, and including either the wrong axioms or the wrong production rules can yield uninterpretive results. For example, suppose that axiom (5c) (repeated below) were replaced with (19), or suppose that we simply added (19) to PC as it now stands:

(5c) *Jill knows Kate* is true iff Jill knows Kate.

(19) *Jill knows Kate* is true iff Jill knows Kate and 2 plus 2 equals 4.

Then we could obviously deduce uninterpretive T-theorems (including (19) itself). This is the case even though (19) is perfectly true, as are all the new T theorems that would result from its addition to the original theory.

A similar result holds with the production rules in the T theory for PC. This theory includes the highly restricted rule of substitution (SE) (repeated below). However, suppose that we replaced (SE) with the alternative rule (SE′).

(SE)   Substitution of equivalents

$$F(\alpha)$$
$$\alpha \text{ iff } \beta$$
$$\overline{F(\beta)}$$

(SE′) Substitution of equivalents, version 2

For any formula β such that α iff β,
$$F(\alpha)$$
$$\overline{F(\beta)}$$

The two differ as follows: under (SE), we are allowed to substitute a formula β only if we have *proved* that it is equivalent to α as part of the derivation whereas under (SE′), we are allowed to substitute *any* β that is materially equivalent to α.[10] Such a change will once again yield uninterpretive results. For example, it is a fact of logic that the equivalence in (20) holds.

(20) Jill knows Kate iff Jill knows Kate and 2 plus 2 equals 4.

Accordingly, from this fact and interpretive axiom (5c), (SE′) will allow us to prove an uninterpretive T theorem, as shown in (21):

(21) *Jill knows Kate* is true iff Jill knows Kate.   (5c)

Jill knows Kate is true
iff Jill knows Kate and 2 plus 2 equals 4.   (by (20), (21a), (SE'))

The original production rule (SE) blocks this result because it does not allow substitution of arbitrary equivalents but only βs that have been proven equivalent to α as part of the derivation. This feature essentially encapsulates the derivation, blocking the importation of extraneous results like (20). Hence uninterpretive consequences like (21) are not derivable.

The contrast between (SE) and (SE') illustrates a further important point. Readers familiar with logic will note that the alternative substitution rule (SE') is not a bizarre one in any sense but is just the rule for substitution of material equivalents standardly assumed in logic texts.[11] What we see, then, is that one of the standard inference rules of logic is not admissible in our semantic theory. This result is in fact quite general. If one were to add to our T theory for PC even the ordinary, truth-preserving rules of standard logical systems, one would easily be able to prove uninterpretive consequences, such as the T theorem in (22):[12]

(22) *Chris agrees and Jill knows Kate* is true iff it is not the case that either it is not the case that Chris agrees or it is not the case that Jill knows Kate.

That the inference rules of logic allow too wide a class of deductions for semantic theory is not an accidental fact but rather follows from the very different goals of logic and semantics, as conceived here. As Frege (1956 [1918]) succinctly put it, logic is the general theory of truth. The inference rules of logic are motivated by the conceptual or philosophical goal of characterizing the set of true inferences from a given set of axioms. By contrast, semantics is a theory of speaker knowledge. The production rules of semantics are motivated by the empirical goal of describing part of what speakers know about a language. On the assumption that what speakers know about meaning is an interpretive T theory, it is clear that semantic production rules cannot aim to yield T sentences that are merely true. Rather, they must yield T sentences that are both true and interpretive, since these are what underlie knowledge of meaning, according to the T hypothesis.[13]

Since most familiar logical systems are not adequate for the purposes of semantics, it is an interesting but, at present, largely unexplored question as to what rules or production procedures should be employed in their place. The semantic theory given for PC restricts the class of deductions from its (interpretive) lexical axioms to those derived by (UI) and (SE). As we will see in subsequent chapters, if the semantic axioms for the PC fragment are modified in even relatively simple ways, it becomes necessary to introduce additional production rules to prove the most basic interpretive results, and this immediately brings the risk of overgeneration. The production rules proposed in succeeding chapters do in fact produce only interpretive consequences. But there is no general theory at present of what formal procedures are best suited to the job of building interpretive T theories. This is an area of research that may ultimately draw on the resources of logic (proof theory) and psychology (reasoning and cognition).[14]

2.2.2   The Information Question

The T hypothesis not only assumes that it is possible to give an interpretive T theory for a language. It also asserts that knowledge of such a theory underlies judgments of actual meanings—that the information necessary for the latter is present in the former. This claim is strong and controversial. And, initially at least, it looks very dubious. The problem is that there just doesn't seem to be enough information in a T theory—even an interpretive one—to support judgments of meaning.

   To see why this is so, consider the hypothetical situation in which you know no French but have at hand a T theory for French written out in English. Suppose that this theory is interpretive but that you don't know it is. You are now faced with the problem of finding out what certain French sentences mean, for example, the sentence in (23):

(23) Les oiseaux ont des plumes.

You can use the T theory to derive T theorems, such as (24):

(24) *Les oiseaux ont des plumes* is true iff birds have feathers.

But do you now know what any French sentence means? Do you know what *Les oiseaux ont des plumes* means? No. For (24) neither says nor implies (25), nor does anything else in the T theory.

(25) *Les oiseaux ont des plumes* means that birds have feathers.

The point here is a simple one. Since there are many true T theories for French in English that are not interpretive, you have no way of knowing in advance whether the particular theory before you is interpretive or not. And since you don't know that the theory is interpretive, you can't move from (24) to (25). What goes here for explicit theories would seem to go for tacit ones as well. If you had tacit knowledge of an interpretive T theory for French, then you would not seem to know enough to know what French sentences mean.

It is tempting to think that this problem might be solved by specifying some new additional theory that, if known, would allow speakers to discover whether their T theory were interpretive or not. If you had a second, independent theory permitting you to deduce that the T theory yielding (24) was interpretive, then you could indeed pass from (24) to (25). On reflection, however, this does not seem to be a promising strategy. After all, a theory allowing you to deduce that (24) is interpretive would be one telling you that "birds have feathers" gives the meaning of *Les oiseaux ont des plumes.* But this is just the job we want our T theory to do! We wanted the T theory to correlate sentences with their meanings. Hence it looks like we could succeed in this strategy only at the price of putting our T theory out of a job.

T Theorems Treated as Interpretive

To motivate a more promising line on how a T theory might underlie judgments of meaning, let us recast the problem situation. In the previous little scenario, you had an interpretive T theory, but you didn't know that it was such. Because you didn't know this and couldn't deduce it, you didn't know you could use the theory to interpret French. Suppose, however, that because of your basic makeup you were compelled to take the T theory in your possession as interpretive, regardless of its actual status. Suppose, for example, that you are the kind of person who can't stand uncertainty, and to avoid it when dealing with Frenchmen, you simply decide to treat any T theory for French that comes into your hands as giving the meanings of French sentences. Whenever you are presented with a French sentence, you turn to your T theory, calculate a T sentence for it, and take whatever results on the RHS of the biconditional as giving its meaning.

Notice that in this circumstance, the knowledge gap noted earlier is still present: you still do not *know* that your T theory is an interpretive one, and the theory neither contains this information nor allows you to deduce it. Nonetheless, the T theory does underwrite judgments of meaning for you, since you use it to interpret and produce French sentences and you behave toward French speakers as if it rendered the meaning of their words. Given your constitution, you proceed as if the gap in question did not exist, as if you already knew your theory were interpretive. Notice furthermore that if the T

theory coming into your hands were in fact interpretive, then all your judgments and acts would be appropriate: you would correctly render the meanings of French sentences, you would form correct beliefs about what French
speakers were trying to say to you, you would plan actions correctly in accord
with these beliefs, and so on. Thus a T theory could serve as a theory of meaning for you, and do so successfully, if you were constituted to treat any T
theory as interpretive and if events conspired to bring an interpretive T theory
into your hands.

   We suggest this second scenario as our answer to the information question
—as a picture of how T theories might successfully serve as semantic theories
for human speakers despite containing no explicit information about the
meanings of expressions. Suppose that as a matter of biological endowment
(that is, of universal grammar), humans are designed to acquire T theories.
These theories are not written out in some natural language in a book but
rather are represented internally in the brain. In the course of learning a language, speakers fix axioms and production rules yielding T theorems as outputs. Suppose further that humans are designed to treat whatever T-theory
they acquire as interpretive. That is, whenever they are called upon to produce
or interpret their own sentences or the sentences of others, they draw on the
results of their internalized T theory and treat its theorems as interpretive:
they take the RHS to give the meaning of the natural-language sentence mentioned on the LHS. Finally, suppose that events conspire to give speakers an
interpretive T theory in the course of development. Then, although the T-
theory contains no explicit information about the meanings of words and sentences, it would still be responsible for the semantic abilities of speakers. They
would use it to make the judgments they do. The knowledge gap, though
present, would be irrelevant to understanding or action, since speakers would
proceed as if they already knew that their T theory were interpretive. Furthermore, since speakers would have learned an interpretive T theory as a matter
of fact, all interpretations, beliefs, and actions undertaken in accordance with
it would be appropriate ones. The use of the T theory as a theory of meaning
would be successful.

   The success of this proposal evidently turns on the correctness of its three
central assumptions:

- Humans are designed to acquire a T theory.
- Humans are designed to treat any T theory they acquire as interpretive.
- In the course of development humans learn a T theory that is interpretive
  in fact.

About the first assumption we will say nothing more except that it is an obvious one, given our general approach. People acquire knowledge of meaning, and since we are assuming that a T theory underlies this knowledge, obviously we must assume that people acquire a T theory. As usual, checking the truth of such an assumption will be a highly indirect matter, involving the success of the larger enterprise as a whole.

The second assumption—that the mind treats T theorems as if they were interpretive—is also hard to spell out further here, given our present understanding of cognition and the brain. One potential way of conceptualizing the assumption is in terms of the familiar idea of the mind as computer. We might imagine the brain as manipulating an internal T theory that takes sentences of a natural language as input and computes T sentences for them in some "brain language" or "language of thought." Suppose that the outputs of these computations are passed to the various mental processors or modules responsible for inference, belief formation, planning of action, and suppose that these modules process the information to infer, form beliefs, plan, etc. The processors that need information about the literal meanings of sentences receive T theorems as their inputs and then proceed under the assumption that the RHSs of these T theorems give the meanings of what's mentioned on the left. In this way, information derived from a theory of truth is treated as information about meaning by the very way the mind passes information around—by the mind's functional architecture, so to speak.[15]

Our third assumption, that speakers acquire an interpretive T theory in the course of development, requires a bit more comment and involves a number of interesting subtleties. First of all, it's clear that this third assumption interacts strongly with the other two. If we are designed to acquire a T theory and to treat any T theory we acquire as interpretive, then we had better acquire the right one. If we somehow came to possess a noninterpretive T theory of French, then by assumption, we would necessarily apply it to the words of French speakers, misunderstanding them, forming wrong views about their beliefs, acting inappropriately toward them, and so on. How is it, then, that we acquire an interpretive T theory, and what *ensures* that the T theory we acquire *is* interpretive?

We suggest that nothing guarantees that the T theories we acquire are interpretive for those around us. Rather, this is a contingent result. That people do quite generally acquire an interpretive T theory is, we suggest, the product of two factors: universal grammar and the very context in which natural language is acquired. In the first chapter we observed that there must be principles of universal grammar heavily constraining the hypotheses that natural-language learners make about the meanings of words and phrases. A child acquiring *rabbit*, for example, has available as hypotheses not only (26a) but also (26b), (26c), and an indefinite number of others:

(26) a. *Rabbit* refers to rabbits.
  b. *Rabbit* refers to undetached rabbit parts.
  c. *Rabbit* refers to rabbits, and either dogs are shaggy or dogs are not shaggy.

Similarly, a child acquiring the meaning of the structure $[_{NP}$ NP's N'$]$ has available (27a) but also (27b), (27c), and an indefinite number of other hypotheses:

(27) a. *Rosa's book* refers to the book that Rosa has.
  b. *Rosa's book* refers to the book that Rosa is.
  c. *Rosa's book* refers to the book that Rosa has, and 2 is an even prime number.

Incorporating (26b, c), (27b, c), or any other equally wrong axioms into the T theory will produce uninterpretive T theorems for sentences containing *rabbit* or the possessive structure *Rosa's book*. Since we assume that UG constraints on lexical and phrasal acquisition play a role in excluding these candidates, UG will serve to guide learners to an interpretive T theory.

A second important factor in acquiring interpretive T theories, we believe, is the very situation in which natural language is acquired. Languages are internalized in the context of communication—in the context of activities such as speaking and understanding. As T theory learners, we hypothesize and fix our rules while engaged in the practical tasks of trying to get our thoughts across to others and trying to grasp what others are trying to say to us. The primary data we use to fix semantic rules in the first place is thus speech produced in communicating with others. Semantic rules are, if you like, fundamentally hypotheses conjectured and tested so as to be interpretive of the speech of others, that is, so as to make sense of their meanings and to make our speech meaningful to them.

What is involved in testing such hypotheses? Briefly put, it seems that we try to see whether interpreting people's speech in the way we conjecture makes sense of their overall motions and interactions with the environment. That is, we try to see whether our interpretation of their speech makes their interactions appear *rational*. In the learning situations described above, for example, a child might plausibly decide between (26a) and (26c) on these grounds. If sentences containing *rabbit* are interpreted using (26a), then such sentences are simply about rabbits. If they are interpreted using (26c), however, then sentences containing *rabbit* are about rabbits and shaggy dogs. Presumably, a child or other learner would be able to determine by context whether shaggy dogs are under discussion or not, for example, by noting whether the person speaking held up a picture of a dog, made sounds like a dog, or in some other way introduced dogs into the subject matter. By examining the behavior of the speaker and making basic assumptions about the rationality of their actions, we can hypothesize about the meanings of their words. The principles of reasoning we are employing here are, of course, ones that apply not only to speech behavior but also to human action as a whole. We evaluate not only our hypotheses about the meaning of others' speech in this way but also our conjectures about their beliefs, motives, fears, etc. All are judged under the goal of trying to make maximal sense of their actions and behavior.

It is worth stressing, in conclusion, that our answer to the information question—our claims about how knowledge of T theorems might be capable of supporting judgments of meaning—is predicated on the assumption that there is a positive answer to the extension question. It remains a separate hypothesis that an interpretive T theory can actually be given for a full natural language. Our point here is that, on the assumption that such a T theory can be given, knowledge of this theory could account for judgments of actual meaning. In principle, then, judgments of actual meaning are within the scope of what T theories can explain.

2.3   The Theoretical Domain of Semantics

We began chapter 1 with an account of various phenomena constituting the pretheoretical domain of semantics. And we also noted certain important properties that semantic rules should have, such as compositionality. Let us return to these phenomena and see how the T hypothesis accommodates them.

2.3.1   Recasting the Pretheoretical Domain

In discussing the pretheoretical domain of semantics, we said that we have to be ready to adjust our view of the data in the course of articulating a formal theory. We have to be ready to see the data significantly redescribed, or even moved out of semantics and assigned to another discipline. The T hypothesis, under which semantic knowledge is knowledge of a T theory and semantics is the theory of internalized T theories, provides a good illustration of how a formal theory leads to such adjustments.

Redescription

Actual meanings provide an example of how data end up being redescribed. Recall that we began our survey with data like (28), simple facts about what sentences do and do not mean.

(28) a. The English sentence *Camels have humps* means that camels have humps.
   b. The French sentence *Les chameaux ont des bosses* means that camels have humps.
   c. The English sentence *Camels have humps* does not mean that reptiles have wings.

In chapter 1 we shifted our focus from what a sentence means to what it means for a speaker: the speaker's knowledge of meaning. And in the last section we argued for the empirical hypothesis that what it is for a sentence to have a certain meaning for a particular person is for that person's internalized T theory to prove a certain T theorem for the sentence. The correspondence we argued for could be expressed as follows:

Redescription of meaning   A sentence S means that p for an individual i iff it is provable in i's internal T theory that S is true iff p.

In view of this, we recast (28) in terms of the formal counterparts in (29):

(29) a. It is provable in some i's internalized T theory that *Camels have humps* is true iff camels have humps.
   b. It is provable in some i's internalized T theory that *Les chameaux ont des bosses* is true iff camels have humps.
   c. It is not provable in any i's internalized T theory that *Camels have humps* is true iff reptiles have wings.

Pretheoretical talk of actual sentence meanings is thus replaced by theoretical talk of theorems of internalized T theories. And talk of the meanings of subsentential expressions is replaced by talk of the semantic properties assigned to these expressions by internalized T theories. What we have, then, is redescription: the pretheoretical data, originally described in terms of the meanings of sentences, get redescribed in the terms of the truth-theoretic properties assigned to these sentences by individual speakers.[16]

Redescription has the effect of placing central data for semantic theory at some remove from direct observation. A semantic theory for an individual will produce statements about the contents of the individual's internalized T theory, including the T theorems. But an individual's internalized T theory, including both contents and theorems, are not directly observable either by that individual or by others. What is observable—explicit judgments of actual meaning, synonymy, etc.—is the result of the semantic module (which deduces T theorems) acting together with modules (like the pragmatics module) that involve nonlinguistic knowledge.

Redescription also carries with it the possibility of divergence between the pretheoretical concept (or concepts) of meaning and the theoretical concepts of internalized truth theories. And indeed, there appear to be cases in which explicit judgments of meaning depart from the results of the truth theory. For example, consider the two sentences in (30).

(30) a. Chris agrees and Jill knows Kate.
     b. Chris agrees but Jill knows Kate.

Grice (1975) argues convincingly that these two sentences should be paired with identical metalanguage sentences, as shown in (31).

(31) a. *Chris agrees and Jill knows Kate* is true iff Chris agrees and Jill knows Kate.
     b. *Chris agrees but Jill knows Kate* is true iff Chris agrees and Jill knows Kate.

Nonetheless, native speakers routinely judge (32) to be false.

(32) *Chris agrees but Jill knows Kate* means that Chris agrees and Jill knows Kate.

The meaning of *Chris agrees but Jill knows Kate* is understood to involve an element of contrast that is missing in *Chris agrees and Jill knows Kate*. Grice suggests that the judgment about (32) results from what he calls "conventional implicature." Someone saying "*p* but *q*" would, as a matter of convention, be committing himself to the view that there is some element of contrast between the truth of *p* and that of *q*. However, this person has not actually said that there is this contrast. On our view, one's knowledge of conventional implicature lies outside the semantics module proper, even if it is intuitively an aspect of meaning.[17]

Reassignment

A more radical fate than redescription is reassignment, in which facts initially ascribed to one domain turn out, in the light of theory, to belong to another. The treatment of ambiguity and anomaly in a T theory illustrate this result.

Ambiguity

We saw that strings of words in English can sometimes have multiple meanings, with this ambiguity arising in a number of ways. As it turns out, within a T-theoretic framework it is plausible to hold that ambiguity is not really a semantic property at all but rather a syntactic property. On this view, strings of words that are ambiguous in meaning are always also ambiguous in form, and the ambiguity in meaning simply follows from the ambiguity in form.

We can illustrate this idea with a string from PC: *It is not the case that Phil ponders or Chris agrees*. This string is ambiguous in form, being derivable in either of two ways: we can first prefix *it is not the case that* to *Phil ponders* and then conjoin the result with *Chris agrees* using *or*; alternatively, we can first conjoin *Phil ponders* and *Chris agrees*, and then prefix *it is not the case that*. We represent these two derivations with the labeled bracketings in (33):

(33) a. [$_S$ [$_S$ It is not the case that [$_S$ Phil ponders]] or [$_S$ Chris agrees]]
    b. [$_S$ It is not the case that [$_S$ [$_S$ Phil ponders] or [$_S$ Chris agrees]]]

The PC string is also ambiguous in interpretation, having the two meanings in (34):

(34) a. Either it is not the case that Phil ponders or else Chris agrees.
    b. It is not the case that either Phil ponders or Chris agrees.

According to (34a), the string asserts that something isn't true or something else is. According to (34b), it asserts that neither of two things is true. There is an obvious correlation here: the structure in (33a) matches the meaning in (34a), and the structure in (33b) matches the meaning in (34b). And indeed, the T theory for PC actually provides this result. If we apply it to (33a), we prove (35a), and if we apply it to (33b), we prove (35b):

(35) a. [s [s It is not the case that [s Phil ponders]] or [s Chris agrees]]
         is true iff either it is not the case that Phil ponders or Chris agrees.
     b. [s It is not the case that [s [s Phil ponders] or [s Chris agrees]]]
         is true iff it is not the case that either Phil ponders or Chris agrees.

Having two T sentences is thus a consequence in PC of having two structural representations. Ambiguity of meaning follows from ambiguity of form.

This general strategy of uniformly analyzing ambiguity as syntactic ambiguity can be applied to other examples from chapter 1. Thus the ambiguity of *Mad dogs and Englishmen go out in the noonday sun* can be ascribed to its having the two different structures in (36):

(36) a. [s [[Mad dogs] and Englishmen] go out in the noonday sun]
     b. [s [Mad [dogs and Englishmen]] go out in the noonday sun]

Under a suitable T theory, these inputs will yield appropriately different T theorems. Likewise, the ambiguity in *Pedro jumped from the bank* can be analyzed as syntactic, although the ambiguity here would be located in the basic parts of S and not in how they are combined together. Here we recognize two different words *bank*$_1$, meaning embankment and *bank*$_2$ meaning a commercial savings institution, but both pronounced [bæŋk]. The ambiguity in the sentence would thus be a matter of which word was involved. Again, under a suitable T theory, these two different inputs would yield appropriately different T theorems:

(37) a. *Pedro jumped from the bank*$_1$ is true iff Pedro jumped from the embankment.
     b. *Pedro jumped from the bank*$_2$ is true iff Pedro jumped from the commercial savings institution.

Ambiguity is thus a property to be reassigned to syntax. A single string of words receives distinct interpretations only by receiving distinct syntactic structures, which are assigned the distinct interpretations.[18]

Anomaly
Under the T hypothesis, the property of anomaly, or having an aberrant meaning, also plausibly falls outside the realm of semantics proper. Consider the examples in (38):

(38) a. John's toothbrush is trying to kill him.
     b. Max went to the pictures tomorrow.
     c. Colorless green ideas sleep furiously.

We noted in chapter 1 that such sentences are perfectly respectable from a syntactic point of view. Presumably, then, a truth theory will apply to them straightforwardly, yielding results like (39):

(39) a. *John's toothbrush is trying to kill him* is true iff John's toothbrush is trying to kill John.
   b. *Max went to the pictures tomorrow* is true iff Max went to the pictures tomorrow.
   c. *Colorless green ideas sleep furiously* is true iff colorless green ideas sleep furiously.

The latter appear to be legitimate T theorems, correlating (38a–c) with specific truth conditions. *John's toothbrush is trying to kill him* is true if and only if a certain dental hygiene instrument belonging to John is attempting to end his life. Similarly, *Colorless green ideas sleep furiously* is true if and only if colorless green ideas (whatever they are) sleep furiously (however that would be). And so on.

What is the source of oddness in (38a–c)? Briefly put, it seems to arise not from an absence of truth conditions for these examples but rather from the presence of truth conditions that we do not know how to evaluate. The truth conditions in (39) all seem to involve some kind of misapplication of concepts that make it difficult for us to see how or in what situations they could actually apply. For example, murderous intentions are only attributable to sentient beings that can plan and act. But in the world as it is constituted, dental instruments do not and, it seems, cannot fall into this category. Similarly, past conditions like those specified by *Max went to the pictures* seem incompatible with occurrence in the future (tomorrow). Since time is noncircular, what was cannot also be part of what will be, and so such a situation is ruled out. Finally, we do not know what it would be for an idea to be green or to sleep, or for something to sleep furiously. Somehow these concepts just don't fit together.

These points suggest that if there is a theory of aberrancy to be developed, then it lies outside semantics proper and within a more general theory of human concepts. The T theorems in (39a–c) require situations not merely that do not obtain but that cannot obtain, given our conceptual map of the world. The general theory of this map, which may lie entirely outside of linguistics, depending on the ultimate relation between language and thought, would presumably tell us which concepts are compatible for humans, and so what could constitute truth conditions framed in compatible concepts.

Mixed Cases

Along with semantic properties, we also considered certain logicosemantic relations, like synonymy, implication, and contradiction. At first sight, their fate might seem to be simple redescription, with a formal counterpart of each being reconstructible within a truth theory as illustrated in table 2.2. On this view, a subject would judge that two sentences α and β are synonymous just in case that subject's processor can prove a statement of the form "α is true if and only if β is true," and so on.

In fact, however, the situation is more complicated, even granting the correspondences in table 2.2. Given the highly constrained nature of the deductive rules in interpretive T theories, it is clear that we cannot in general expect that all, or even most, judgments of logicosemantic relations will be ratified by the T theory alone. One case where this is possible is (40):

(40) *It is not the case that Phil ponders* contradicts *Phil ponders.*

With only the semantic rule for negation in PC ((6c) from section 2.1), we can derive instances like (41) directly:

(6c) [$_s$ *It is not the case that* S] is true iff it is not the case that S is true

(41) *It is not the case that Phil ponders* is true iff it is not the case that *Phil ponders* is true.

This general reasoning might be taken to underlie our judgment that the negation of a sentence contradicts it.[19]

In many other cases, however, semantic resources alone will not be sufficient. For example, even the simple entailment (42) lies beyond the reach of the T-theory for PC:

(42) *Phil ponders and Chris agrees* implies *Phil ponders.*

Table 2.2   The redescription of some logicosemantic concepts

Judgment	T-theoretic counterpart
α is synonymous with β	α is true iff β is true
α implies β	α is true only if β is true
α contradicts β	α is true iff it is not the case that β is true

To underwrite this judgment in the way indicated by table 2.2, the T theory would have to prove (43):

(43) *Phil ponders and Chris agrees* is true only if *Phil ponders* is true.

But such a proof requires production rules that are not part of the theory. In view of this, the implication in (42) must be regarded not as a purely linguistic matter but as a logicolinguistic matter: one that results from the meanings of the sentences involved plus additional rules supplied by logic.

It is often a complex question as to when judgments of logicolinguistic relations arise from purely semantic sources and when they must be supplemented by extrasemantic information. Consider (44), for instance:

(44) *John believes the earth is flat* contradicts *John doubts the earth is flat.*

Even if we suppose that the relevant T theorems of the T theory are equivalent to (45), it is very unlikely that the theory could prove (46):

(45) a. *John believes the earth is flat* is true iff John believes the earth is flat.
      b. *John doubts the earth is flat* is true true iff John doubts the earth is flat.

(46) *John believes the earth is flat* is true iff it is not the case that *John doubts the earth is flat* is true.

There are simply no resources in the T theorey to establish the required relations between believing and doubting. In this case we have to look elsewhere for the missing resources. For example, it might be that humans have some nonlinguistic theory with the consequence that nobody can believe and doubt the same proposition. This might be a consequence of the basic psychology that all humans appear to know innately.[20] If nobody can believe and doubt the same proposition, then evidently the truth conditions of the two sentences *John believes the earth is flat* and *John doubts the earth is flat* cannot be met simultaneously. Consequently, given (46), (44) follows. Here what needs to be added to the T theory is not just pure logic but also a theory of the essential nature of belief and doubt.

On the other hand, it's possible that the information required to prove (44) could be present in the T theory after all. For example, suppose that the lexical entries for *believe* and *doubt* were very rich and specified the facts in (47):

(47) *Doubts* applies to a person x and a proposition y iff x does not believe y.

Then the T theory alone would indeed entail (46). At present we know of no evidence deciding whether the information in (47) is available to the language module itself or lies in some other part of the mind, although we strongly suspect that the latter is true.

Most cases of entailment appear to have the character of (44), where it is unclear whether the judgment at issue is given through purely semantic means. The crucial point at issue, of course, is the boundary between semantics and other theories, such as logic, psychology, and so on. The ultimate fate of logicosemantic relations is thus a mixed one under the T hypothesis. Pretheoretical logicosemantic relations can be largely reconstructed in terms of formal T-theoretic relations. However, the resources for proving that those relations hold appear to fall in many cases outside linguistics. Logicosemantic relations are thus subject to both redescription and reassignment within a semantics that is based on T theories.

2.3.2 The External Significance of Language

We noted that a crucial property of our knowledge of meaning is that it allows us to reason from language to the world and vice versa. If we know the meaning of a sentence and we are told that it is true, then we learn something about how things stand in the world. And if we know the meaning of a sentence and we find out the appropriate facts about the world, then we can learn whether the sentence is true or false. From this we saw that knowledge of meaning must be relational: it must relate language to the world.[21]

T sentences have this relational character, as we can see by considering the sample T sentence in (48), in which the object language is French and the metalanguage is English:

(48) *La neige est blanche* is true if and only if snow is white.

This T sentence, like all T sentences, goes from the mention of linguistic expressions to their use; it relates language to the nonlinguistic. This property of going from mention of language to use of language is sometimes referred to as the property of being **disquotational**, the idea being that one can remove the quotes around a mentioned expression.

Because they are disquotational, T sentences will support reasoning of the kind we attribute to semantic knowledge. That is, knowing T sentences will allow us to make inferences of the kind that arise from knowledge of meaning.

Thus, suppose that I know (48) and further that I know the French sentence *La neige est blanche* is true. Then I am in a position to conclude something about the world, namely, that snow is white:

(49)   *La neige est blanche* is true iff snow is white.
        La neige est blanche is true.
        _____
        Snow is white.

Similarly, suppose that I know (48) and that I also know that snow is in fact white. Then I am justified in concluding something about the French sentence *La neige est blanche*, namely, that it is true:

(50)   *La neige est blanche* is true iff snow is white.
        Snow is white.
        _____
        La neige est blanche is true.

Knowing (48), I can reason in either direction: from language to facts about the world or from the world to facts about language.

A Nondisquotational Theory

Although it is evidently crucial that statements of a semantic theory be disquotational, it is easy to imagine theories lacking this feature. Suppose that instead of delivering theorems of the form in (T), our theory yielded theorems of the form in ($T^\dagger$), where S is a sentence of language L_1 and S′ is a sentence of some other language L_2:

(T)   S is true if and only if *p*.

($T^\dagger$)   S is true if and only if S′ is true.

Observe that unlike (T), ($T^\dagger$) is not disquotational. It does not pass from mention of language to use of language. Rather, the LHS side of the biconditional mentions an expression from one language and the RHS goes on to mention an expression from yet another language. ($T^\dagger$) correlates sentences of L_1 with sentences of L_2, but it does not disquote them.

Because ($T^\dagger$) is not disquotational, knowledge of a $T^\dagger$ theory will not allow us to reason between language and the world in the way required of semantic knowledge. Suppose, for example, that we know the $T^\dagger$ sentence in (51):

(51)   *La neige est blanche* is true iff *Der Schnee ist weiß* is true.

Then knowing that *La neige est blanche* is true will not entitle us to conclude anything about the world; in particular, it will not allow us to conclude that snow is white, witness (52), where the crosshatch (#) means "is an unacceptable inference":

(52)   *La neige est blanche* is true iff *Der Schnee ist weiß* is true.
     La neige est blanche is true.

      # Snow is white.

At most we can conclude that *Der Schnee ist weiß* must also be true. Similarly, knowing (51) and knowing that snow is white will not allow us to conclude anything further, in particular, we cannot conclude anything about the truth or falsity of the French sentence *Le neige est blanche*, witness (53):

(53)   *La neige est blanche* is true iff *Der Schnee ist weiß* is true.
     Snow is white.

      # *La neige est blanche* is true.

In order for (51) to support deductions of the kind we need, we require further statements in which *La neige est blanche* or *Der Schnee ist weiß* appear and the relevant sentence is disquoted. That is, we need the equivalent of what is delivered by a T theory.

The contrast between T theories and $T^\dagger$ theories makes clear that semantic theory cannot be a matter of simply correlating the sentences of two languages, of translating from one language to another. Indeed, this should have been obvious from the start. For if you ask someone the meaning of the French sentence *La neige est blanche* and you get the answer "The French sentence *La neige est blanche* means the same as the German sentence *Der Schnee ist weiß*," then clearly this is only helpful to you if you already understand the German sentence. Without such understanding, you are forced to ask further for the meaning of *Der Schnee ist weiß*, and so on, until you finally obtain disquotational knowledge, and so break out of the circle of language.[22]

2.3.3   The Internal Significance of Language

We observed that the meaning of sentences is crucial to the communicative activities of speakers. We said that in paradigm cases the semantic content of the sentence uttered gives the content of the speech act performed. For example, someone might utter (54) and thereby assert that it is snowing:

(54) It is snowing.

We also noted that in nonparadigmatic cases there might not be such a correspondence of content between speech act and sentence. For example, Lord Peter Wimsey might utter (55), thereby commanding Bunter to shut the window:[23]

(55) It is cold in here.

And we said that even in nonparadigmatic cases, the literal meaning of the sentence would surely figure as part of the explanation of how the utterance comes to possess the inward significance that it does possess.

On the theory adopted here, the notion of the literal meaning of an expression is replaced by that of the semantic properties ascribed to the expression by an individual's internalized T theory. Thus when a speaker utters an indicative sentence and intends to speak literally, the meaning the speaker intends to convey will be the truth conditions his or her internalized T theory ascribes to the sentence. The story is similar for when a hearer hears a sentence. The hearer's semantic processors will compute a T theorem for the sentence, the RHS of which will give the literal meaning of the sentence. So, if a speaker *a* utters (54), speaking literally, and *a*'s internalized T theory has a T theorem equivalent to (54'), *a* will intend to communicate the thought that it is snowing:

(54') [$_s$ It is snowing] is true iff it is snowing.

If *b* hears this utterance and assumes correctly that *a* and *b* attach the same literal meaning to (54) and assumes further that *a* is speaking literally, *b* will correctly conclude that *a* has said that it is snowing. In this way *b* can discern the communicative intention behind *a*'s utterance.

When a speaker speaks nonliterally, the reasoning required to discern the communicative intention may be more complex. For example, when Bunter hears Wimsey's utterance of (55), his semantic processors will compute a T theorem for it, and this will serve as input to further processors, which will treat the theorem as interpretive. Thus Bunter will take the literal meaning of Wimsey's words to be that it is cold in here. Bunter may then reason somewhat as follows: "It is obvious to Wimsey that I know that it is cold here. So his utterance of (55) cannot have been intended to inform me that it is cold here. So he must have had some other communicative purpose in mind. Since it is one of my duties to maintain a comfortable temperature in this room, the fact that it is cold here entails that it is my duty to shut the window.

Consequently, Wimsey's utterance should be taken as a command to shut the window."

As we emphasized in discussing our approach to the information question, very little is known about the cognitive subsystems responsible for speech production and understanding. For this reason, it is pointless at this stage to attempt detailed speculations about how these subsystems make use of the T theorems that come from the semantic module. To motivate this approach, all we require is the simple point that T theorems would be suitable inputs for these subsystems, provided that these subsystems treat them as interpretive.

2.3.4   The Compositional Form of T Theories

When we considered the general properties of linguistic rules, we saw that the grammatical knowledge of speakers must account for the fact that our understanding of sentences is systematic, and allows us to understand both new sentences and infinite collections of sentences like (56):

(56) a. The horse behind Pegasus is bald.
     b. The horse behind the horse behind Pegasus is bald.
     c. The horse behind the horse behind the horse behind Pegasus is bald.
       ⋮

On the basis of these points we conjectured that our semantic knowledge consists of a finite set of rules and principles allowing us to derive the interpretations of sentences from smaller semantic contributions. That is, we suggested that semantic principles are compositional.

The T theory given for PC illustrates a finite, compositional semantics of the kind we need. It derives the truth conditions for the phrase markers of PC from seven axioms and two production rules. Furthermore, if it is the semantics underlying our knowledge of sentence conjunctions and negations for the fragment of English represented by PC, then this explains why our understanding of (57a) is systematically related to our understanding of (57b); it would explain why, if we understand (57a), we are also able to understand a new sentence like (58); and it would explain why we are able to understand each member of the collection of PC sentences indicated in (59), despite its infinite size:

(57) a. Jill knows Kate, or Phil ponders.
     b. Phil ponders, or Jill knows Kate.

(58) Jill knows Kate or Phil ponders, and Chris agrees, and Chris agrees.

(59) a. Jill knows Kate, or Phil ponders.
  b. Jill knows Kate or Phil ponders, and Jill knows Kate or Phil ponders
  c. Jill knows Kate or Phil ponders, and Jill knows Kate or Phil ponders, and Jill knows Kate or Phil ponders.
$$\vdots$$

Hence T theories, even our little illustrative theory for PC, are capable of meeting the crucial requirement of accounting for the systematic and open-ended character of semantic competence.

A Noncompositional T Theory

Again, although compositionality is clearly a desirable property for a semantic theory to possess, it is not difficult to imagine alternative theories lacking this feature. For example, consider the theory for PC in which its axioms and production rules are all replaced with the single rule (R):[24]

(R) For every sentence S, S is true if and only if S.

Under this one rule, we derive T sentences for every clause of PC without appeal to semantic rules for its component parts. T sentences are directly assigned without mediation of syntactic structure.

A semantic theory for PC employing (R) has some of the features of the compositional theory. Thus it assigns an interpretive T sentence to every sentence of PC, including infinite collections like that in (59). And it assigns a T sentence to any new sentences of PC that we might encounter, such as (58). At the same time, however, the theory with (R) also departs significantly from the compositional theory in assigning no systematic patterns of semantic relatedness among the sentences of PC. Because all clauses of PC receive their T sentences through one and the same rule (R), there are no distinctions of semantic derivation. Thus whereas our original theory groups the T-sentence derivations for (57a) and (57b) as involving the disjunction rule, and thus distinguishes them from the derivation for *Chris agrees*, the theory containing (R) derives T sentences all in the same way, and hence makes no derivational distinctions.

We will shortly discuss various kinds of evidence that might help us to chose between extensionally equivalent semantic theories like these two—ones that agree on the final T sentences they assign but differ in the derivational routes by which they assign them. As it turns out, however, there are independent grounds for excluding a grammar with a rule like (R). There is an important feature of this rule that immediately eliminates its interest under the view of semantic theory we have been pursuing.

To see the problem, simply imagine us trying to use rule (R) as a semantic rule for interpreting a language we ourselves do not speak. To what languages could (R) be applied? If we try to use (R) to interpret a German sentence like *Jill protestiert* or a French sentence like *Les chameaux ont des bosses*, we will obtain linguistically mixed outputs, as in (60):

(60) a. *Jill protestiert* is true iff Jill protestiert.
   b. *Les chameaux ont des bosses* is true iff les chameaux ont des bosses.

What appears to the right of the mentioned sentence in both cases is a blend of English and German or French. These are not well-formed sentences of English, or any other language for that matter; hence they are not well-formed T sentences either. Indeed, it's clear that the only object language to which (R) can be appropriately applied is one that is the same as (or at least contains) the metalanguage. That is, the only language to which (R) can be applied is English, the language in which it is formulated.

But reflect now on what this means. Our goal in semantic theorizing is to specify the tacit knowledge that underlies a speaker's grasp of meaning. Since this knowledge is supposed to explain speaker understanding, clearly it cannot be formulated so as to essentially presuppose this understanding. Otherwise, we would be assuming just what we are supposed to explain. But this is just what would be the case with a rule like (R). If we are using (R) to interpret another language, presumably we understand the language in which (R) is framed. But (R) can be used to interpret only the very language in which it is framed, and hence one we already understand. Hence use of (R) presupposes understanding of the only language to which it can be applied. Evidently such a rule cannot be part of a theory that seeks to explain knowledge of meaning.

2.4   The Reality of Semantic Knowledge

On the view developed above, semantic theory is a branch of individual psychology, and therefore a scientific theory. Correlatively, what semantic theory a person knows is a question for science, a matter of determinate empirical fact. This means that even if we discover a number of interpretive T theories, all successfully predicting the various kinds of speaker judgments discussed above, at most one of these can be the theory actually internalized by the speaker.

It is natural to look for various lines of evidence that might help us to decide which interpretive T theory a speaker really knows. One important source of evidence comes from neighboring theories of syntax, phonology, psychology, biology, etc. As it turns out, many T theories assigning the right truth conditions to surface forms can be ruled out by their failure to mesh properly with these other theories. We will see examples of this in later chapters. There are also various kinds of evidence that bear more directly on the structure of the various T theories that we may attribute. We can illustrate this with a language related to PC.[25]

Imagine a population of individuals speaking the sublanguage of PC whose sentences include the following: the three elementary strings *Phil ponders*, *Jill knows Kate*, and *Chris agrees*, the negations of the basic three, and all their binary conjunctions. We'll call this sublanguage PC⁻. As is easy to see, PC⁻ is finite, containing exactly the 24 sentences listed below:

(61) a. Phil ponders.
     b. Chris agrees.
     c. Jill knows Kate.
     d. It is not the case that Phil ponders.
     e. It is not the case that Chris agrees.
     f. It is not the case that Jill knows Kate.
     g. Phil ponders, and Phil ponders.
     h. Phil ponders, and Chris agrees.
     i. Phil ponders, and Jill knows Kate.
     j. Chris agrees, and Phil ponders.
     k. Chris agrees, and Chris agrees.
     l. Chris agrees, and Jill knows Kate.
     m. Jill knows Kate, and Phil ponders.
     n. Jill knows Kate, and Chris agrees.
     o. Jill knows Kate, and Jill knows Kate.
     p. Phil ponders, or Phil ponders.
     q. Phil ponders, or Chris agrees.
     r. Phil ponders, or Jill knows Kate.
     s. Chris agrees, or Phil ponders.
     t. Chris agrees, or Chris agrees.
     u. Chris agrees, or Jill knows Kate.

v.   Jill knows Kate, or Phil ponders.

w.   Jill knows Kate, or Chris agrees.

x.   Jill knows Kate, or Jill knows Kate.

Consider now two very different grammars that generate and interpret PC⁻. The first, G_1, is similar to the grammar of PC. It has a syntax containing seven rules: the three rules in (62a–c), stating that each of the elementary strings is a "clause" (Cl), and the four combination rules in (62d–g), stating that every clause is a sentence, that every negation of a clause is a sentence, and that every conjunction of clauses with *and* or *or* is a sentence:[26]

(62) a. Cl → *Phil ponders*

b. Cl → *Chris agrees*

c. Cl → *Jill knows Kate*

d. S → Cl

e. S → *It is not the case that* Cl

f. S → Cl *and* Cl

g. S → Cl *or* Cl

G_1 also has a T theory containing eight semantic axioms, together with the production rules (SE) and (UI) (not listed):

(63) a. *Phil ponders* is true iff Phil ponders.

b. *Chris agrees* is true iff Chris agrees.

c. *Jill knows Kate* is true iff Jill knows Kate.

d. [$_S$ Cl] is true iff Cl is true.

e. [$_S$ *It is not the case that* Cl] is true iff it is not the case that Cl is true.

f. [$_S$ Cl$_1$ *and* Cl$_2$] is true iff both Cl$_1$ is true and Cl$_2$ is true.

g. [$_S$ Cl$_1$ *or* Cl$_2$] is true iff either Cl$_1$ is true or Cl$_2$ is true.

h. [$_{Cl}$ α] is true iff α is true (for any elementary clause α).

The second grammar, G_2, is radically different. Its syntax contains 24 distinct phrase-structure rules, one for each sentence of PC⁻:

(64) a. S → *Phil ponders*

b. S → *Chris agrees*

c. S → *Jill knows Kate*

d. S → *It is not the case that Phil ponders*

e. S → *It is not the case that Chris agrees*

f. S → *It is not the case tht Jill knows Kate*

g. S → *Phil ponders and Phil ponders*

h. S → *Phil ponders and Chris agrees*
    ⋮
p. S → *Phil ponders or Phil ponders*
q. S → *Phil ponders or Chris agrees*
    ⋮

And its corresponding T theory includes 24 separate semantic axioms, one for each S generated by the syntactic rules:

(65) a. [$_S$ Phil ponders] is true iff Phil ponders.
          ⋮

      d. [$_S$ It is not the case that Phil ponders] is true iff it is not the case that Phil ponders.
          ⋮

      g. [$_S$ Phil ponders and Phil ponders] is true iff both Phil ponders and Phil ponders.
          ⋮

      p. [$_S$ Phil ponders or Phil ponders] is true iff either Phil ponders or Phil ponders.
          ⋮

G_1 and G_2 assign distinct syntactic representations to the strings of PC⁻. For example, G_1 assigns the labeled bracketing in (66a) to *Phil ponders and Chris agrees*, whereas G_2 assigns the one in (66b).

(66) a. [$_S$ [$_{Cl}$ Phil ponders] and [$_{Cl}$ Chris agrees]]
      b. [$_S$ Phil ponders and Chris agrees]

Furthermore, because of their syntactic differences, the two grammars assign T theorems following different derivational routes. Like PC, G_1 assigns its T theorems indirectly, through proofs that involve combinatory rules and substitutions. By contrast, G_2 assigns them directly: every T sentence it "proves" is an axiom of G_2. Nonetheless, despite these differences, G_1 and G_2 still associate the same strings of PC⁻ with the same truth conditions. Both yield the T theorems in (67), for example:

(67) a. [$_S$ Phil ponders] is true iff Phil ponders.
      b. [$_S$ It is not the case that Jill knows Kate] is true iff it is not the case that Jill knows Kate.
      c. [$_S$ Phil ponders and Chris agrees] is true iff both Phil ponders and Chris agrees.

    d. [$_s$ Jill knows Kate or Phil ponders] is true iff either Jill knows Kate or Phil ponders.

More generally, for each of the 24 sentences of the object language PC⁻, G_1 and G_2 assign T theorems that are identical (up to syntactic differences in the object-language sentences).

    The fact that G_1 and G_2 assign the same truth conditions means that one grammar will be interpretive for PC⁻ speakers if and only if the other is. And because of this, the two will support all of the same semantic judgments of actual meaning, and hence share central predictions. Nonetheless, semanticists adopting a realist view of their subject matter must take it to be a genuine empirical question as to which of G_1 or G_2 our PC⁻ speakers have internalized. Speakers must know (at most) one or the other, their equivalence notwithstanding. How could we answer the question? Would there be empirical evidence to decide the matter?

    Noam Chomsky and the philosopher Gareth Evans have observed that speakers who know different semantic theories will have knowledge that is differently structured.[27] This will in turn predict specific differences in speaker abilities. For example, consider a population that knows the T theory G_1 rather than G_2. Because the former divides the job of deriving T sentences among a number of axioms that interact together, its speakers' semantic knowledge will have a certain articulated structure: we can talk about their knowing a semantic rule of negation, a semantic rule of conjunction, and a semantic rule of disjunction. Furthermore, we can talk about their assigning a meaning to a certain complex sentence in virtue of knowing two or more interacting rules; it makes sense to see them as able to interpret (61d) in virtue of knowing (63a), (63d), and (63e). By contrast, under the semantic theory in G_2, speaker knowledge doesn't have this structure. G_2 doesn't "factor" the semantics of PC⁻ into separate axioms for negation, conjunction, and disjunction. Rather, its semantic rules for PC⁻ sentences are all completely independent. The semantic rule assigning the T sentence to *It is not the case that Jill knows Kate* is completely independent of that assigning the T sentence to *It is not the case that Chris agrees*, and so on. Accordingly, it makes no sense to talk of G_2 speakers' knowing "a rule for negation." Nor does it make any sense to talk of them as being able to interpret a negated sentence in virtue of knowing a number of rules. Rather, they know only separate rules for separate negated sentences. Similarly for conjunction and disjunction.

    As Chomsky and Evans observe, this difference in the way that knowledge is structured by the two theories entails different predictions about speaker behavior in situations involving **partial knowledge**. For example, consider the situation of language acquisition, where speakers are in the process of learning PC⁻. If they are acquiring PC⁻ under G_1, we expect a pattern of semantic acquisition as follows: the interpretations of the three basic sentences (61a–c) should be learned individually, since mastering each involves adding its own semantic rule. By contrast, the interpretations of sentences involving negation (61d–f), conjunction (61g–o), and disjunction (61p–x) should be learned as groups, since mastering the interpretations of each involves adding a single rule: (63e), (63f), (63g) respectively. Thus we would expect that a child who could interpret *Chris agrees, It is not the case that Chris agrees*, and *Jill knows Kate* would also be able to interpret *It is not the case that Jill knows Kate* and so on. G_2 predicts a very different pattern of acquisition for speakers acquiring PC⁻. In brief, we would expect the interpretations of all sentences of PC⁻ to be acquired following the pattern of the basic sentences (61a–c). Since each PC⁻ sentence is interpreted by means of its own special semantic rule, each must be learned separately and independently under G_2. There is no prediction that a child able to interpret two simple sentences and the negation of one should be able to interpret the negation of the other, because in G_2 there simply are no semantic relations among negated sentences, among conjoined sentences, or among disjoined sentences.

Chomsky and Evans note that similar kinds of evidence are potentially available from studies of language deficit—situations in which selective portions of linguistic competence are lost through trauma or pathology. Again, definite patterns are predicted according to the structure of the knowledge lost. Under grammar G_1, we would expect that interpretations of the three basic sentences (61a–c) could be lost separately, since each involves a separate rule. But we would expect the interpretations of sentences involving negation (61d–f), conjunction (61g–o), and disjunction (61p–x) to be lost as groups, since their interpretations involve one rule in each case. If an individual were able to interpret *Chris agrees* and *Jill knows Kate* but not *It is not the case that Chris agrees*, we would not expect this person to be able to interpret *It is not the case that Jill knows Kate*. By contrast, under grammar G_2, we would again predict the pattern to follow that of the basic sentences (61a–c). Since each sentence involves its own semantic rule, the ability to interpret each would be lost separately. Accordingly, we should allow for an aphasic who is able to interpret two simple sentences and the negation of one but not the negation of the other.

These reflections show how even with semantic theories that yield equivalent results, we might still find empirical grounds for choosing among them as the theory known by some group of speakers. Differently structured theories entail differently structured knowledge, which may in turn predict different patterns of acquisition, loss, and revision. Of course, this is not to suggest that patterns of acquisition and decay will always be able to adjudicate between rival semantic hypotheses. It might be possible to construct some ingenious model of the mental structure of speakers who have internalized G_1 under which they would exhibit just the patterns of acquisition and decay predicted for speakers who internalize G_2.[28] And indeed, if semantics is a branch of science like any other, we expect such a result. We expect that it will always be possible in principle to construct alternative semantic theories for any given set of data. Our point is simply to stress that "Which semantic theory do they know?" is a factual question to be answered on factual grounds, and that often we can discern the grounds that might yield a decision.

Theory and Exercises

The Theory PC (Propositional Calculus)

Axioms for Terminal Nodes

(1) a. *Phil ponders* is true iff Phil ponders.
   b. *Chris agrees* is true iff Chris agrees.
   c. *Jill knows Kate* is true iff Jill knows Kate.

Axioms for Nonterminal Nodes

(2) a. $[_s S_1$ and $S_2]$ is true iff both S_1 is true and S_2 is true.
   b. $[_s S_1$ or $S_2]$ is true iff either S_1 is true or S_2 is true.
   c. $[_s$ It is not the case that S] is true iff it is not the case that S is true.
   d. $[_s \alpha]$ is true iff α is true (for any elementary sentence α).

Production Rules

(UI) Universal Instantiation

   For any S, $F(S)$
   _____
   $F(\alpha)$

(SE) Substitution of Equivalents

$$F(\alpha)$$
$$\alpha \text{ iff } \beta$$
___
$$F(\beta)$$

Exercises

1. Give two different ways of inserting quotes into the following (due to R. Cartwright) so that it makes sense and contains no obvious falsehoods:

   According to W. V. Quine,
   Whose views on quotation are fine,
   Boston names Boston,
   And Boston names Boston,
   But 9 doesn't designate 9.

   If any of the following is either false or senseless as it stands, remedy matters (if possible) by supplying quotes. Look for "best" solutions, i.e., solutions that involve as few additional symbols as possible (these problems are taken from Cartwright 1987, 257):

   (1) Boston is north of Providence, but Providence is not south of Boston.

   (2) The last word of the best solution for (1) is Boston.

   (3) Moore's wife called Moore Moore.

   (4) It is not the case that Moore's wife called Moore Moore's surname.

   (5) The last word of (5) is obscene.

   (6) The last word of (5) is obscene.

2. Give full T sentence derivations for each of the following strings of PC, providing structures and indicating how each step in the derivation is justified by axioms or production rules:

   (1) It is not the case that Phil ponders and Chris agrees.

   (2) Phil ponders, and it is not the case that Chris agrees.

   What elements must be added to the theory PC in order to derive appropriate T sentences for the following:

(3) Chris ponders, and Jill knows Kate.

(4) Rolf promises a cookie to Chris, and Chris agrees.

(5) It is the case that Phil ponders.

3. The set of English connectives includes not only *and* and *or* (as found in PC), but also *if*, *only if*, and *if and only if* (abbr. *iff*). Extend PC to include these three particles; that is,

   ■ give syntactic structures introducing *if*, *only if*, and *iff* ;

   ■ extend the semantic apparatus of PC so that sentences containing these connectives are interpreted appropriately.

   Provide full derivations for the following examples:

   (1) Phil ponders only if Jill knows Kate.

   (2) Chris agrees if it is not the case that Phil ponders if and only if Chris agrees.

   As always, be sure to show how each step in the derivation is justified by the T theory.

4. In propositional logic, the particles *if*, *only if*, and *iff* are assigned the following truth tables:

If . . . then			Only if			Iff		
p	*q*	if *p*, then *q*	*p*	*q*	*p* only if *q*	*p*	*q*	*p* iff *q*
t	t	t	t	t	t	t	t	t
t	f	f	t	f	f	t	f	f
f	t	t	f	t	t	f	t	f
f	f	t	f	f	t	f	f	t

According to these tables, "if *p*, then *q*" and "*p* only if *q*" have the same truth conditions. Both express implication; the only difference is that in the former, the subordinating conjunction (*if*) attaches to the antecedent, whereas in the latter, the conjunction (*only if*) attaches to the consequent.

   This result predicts an equivalence between *if* and *only if* examples that is found in some cases. Consider (1) and (2) (from McCawley 1981a):

(1) a. If all men are mortal, then Aristotle is mortal.
    b. All men are mortal only if Aristotle is mortal.

(2) a. If a set has only finitely many subsets, then it is finite.
    b. A set has only finitely many subsets only if it is finite.

In many other cases, however, equivalence fails badly. Consider (3) to (8) (also from McCawley 1981a). In (3) to (5) the sentences with *if* are normal but the ones with *only if* are bizarre. In (6) to (8) the converse is true:

(3) a. If you're boiled in oil, you'll die.
    b. You'll be boiled in oil only if you die.

(4) a. If Mike straightens his tie once more, I'll kill him.
    b. Mike will straighten his tie once more only if I kill him.

(5) a. If we're having fish, we should order white wine.
    b. We're having fish only if we should order white wine.

(6) a. I'll leave only if you have somebody to take my place.
    b. If I leave, you'll have somebody to take my place.

(7) a. My pulse goes above 100 only if I do heavy exercise.
    b. If my pulse goes above 100, I do heavy exercise.

(8) a. You're in danger only if the police start tapping your phone.
    b. If you're in danger, the police start tapping your phone.

What's going on here? Why does the predicted equivalence fail, in your view?

Another equivalence predicted by propositional logic is between "*p* only if *q*" and "not *p* if not *q*." Does the expected paraphrase relation between the two forms actually hold up in English? If so, why? If not, why not?

5. The examples in (1) to (3) below are all odd and/or unacceptable as sentences of English. Sentence (1) is syntactically ill formed and semantically uninterpretable. Sentence (2) is syntactically well formed but semantically anomalous. What should we say about the nature of the oddness in (3)?

(1) Boris Olga to herself asked kiss.

(2) The number 2 asked a thought to baste itself.

(3) Olga asked Boris to kiss herself.

Consider the logicosemantic relations in (4) and (5). What is the status of these relations from the standpoint of semantic theory? Are they to be accounted for by semantic theory alone, by linguistic theory alone, or by linguistic theory in conjunction with other theories?

(4) *John is human* implies *John is a mammal.*

(5) *John saw Mary* implies *Mary was seen by John.*

3   Meaning and Structure

The unbounded and systematic nature of our semantic abilities argues strongly for a compositional account of semantic knowledge. Knowledge of meaning must specify the content of clauses and phrases in terms of the content of smaller parts and their modes of combination. This result implies a close relation between meaning and structure in semantic theorizing. To explain its particular body of facts, semantic theory must attribute a definite structure to linguistic forms. In this chapter we will examine various conceptual, technical, and methodological issues concerning semantic structure. And we will introduce some important hypotheses that will guide us in the construction of T theories later on.

3.1   Notions of Structure

A compositional semantic theory analyzes sentences and other expressions into constituent parts. More precisely, it seeks to isolate certain basic items and state their semantic content. It also seeks to determine the modes of combination for these basic forms and state the semantic significance of combining them in these ways. We will call the structure attributed to sentences and other expressions in the process of bringing them within an explicit semantic theory (such as a T theory) the **semantic structure** imposed by that theory.[1]

Semantics is not alone, of course, in attributing structure to linguistic forms; other sciences taking natural language as their object of study do so as well. Syntax, for example, is traditionally conceived of as the study of how sentences are structured from parts.[2] Syntacticians study the categories of these parts (parts of speech); their form, linear ordering, and grouping in various constructions; the principles by which these structures are generated and licensed; and how this structure bears on judgments of acceptability, ambiguity, and so on.[3] In the process of analyzing expressions within a syntactic theory, they are led to attribute a definite **syntactic structure**.[4]

Logic has also been concerned with sentence and discourse structure. Logic is traditionally conceived of as the study of the various inferential relations holding among sentences and sets of sentences. In attempting to account for these relations, logicians standardly isolate certain elements of sentence forms and take these as determining when we can validly draw an inference from some sentence or collection of sentences (the premises) to another sentence (the conclusion). Here too the process of analyzing expressions and their relations within a theory of inference leads them to postulate a definite **logical structure**.[5]

Since the goals of these three disciplines are different, there is no a priori expectation that the structure they ascribe to a given set of forms will be the same. It is fully conceivable that the three might diverge. Consider once more some familiar strings from PC:

(1) a. Phil ponders or Chris agrees.
    b. It is not the case that Jill knows Kate.

A semanticist is interested in the meanings of PC sentences and in how these meanings are derived. Under the general view of meaning adopted here, this involves giving an interpretive T theory for PC along the lines sketched earlier. Thus we isolate three sentences as basic forms (*Phil ponders, Jill knows Kate, Chris agrees*) and give their semantic contribution in terms of three elementary T sentences. Next we assume three modes of combination from more basic forms in PC (conjunction, disjunction, and negation) and give the semantic significance of these modes of combination in terms of T-sentence schemes

(2) a.

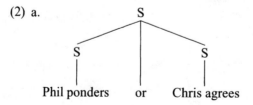

b.

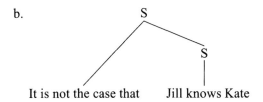

It is not the case that   Jill knows Kate

The trees in (2) show the semantic structure of (1a, b) according to the T theory.

A syntactician would be interested in a different set of questions about PC, and hence a potentially different set of facts.[6] Such questions might include, What are the possible sentences of PC (regardless of content), and what formal rules or principles determine these possibilities? Data relevant to these issues would include the fact that examples like (3a, b) are well-formed sentences of the language, whereas (4a–c) are not (as indicated by the asterisk), the fact that *and* and *or* pattern similarly in PC, occurring in the same position in clauses containing them and being mutually exclusive with respect to any position where either can appear, and the fact that *and* and *or* show a very different distribution from *it is not the case that.*

(3) a. Phil ponders or Chris agrees.
    b. It is not the case that Jill knows Kate.

(4) a. *Phil ponders or and Jill knows Kate.
    b. *Phil ponders Jill knows Kate and.
    c. *Chris agrees it is not the case that.

The syntactician might also note the intuitive judgment of native speakers that English conjunctions seem to group more closely with the following sentence than with the preceding one, a judgment supported by the difference in acceptability between discourses like (5a) and (5b):

(5) a. *A*: Phil ponders.
        B: Yes, and Jill knows Kate.
    b. *A*: Phil ponders.
        B: *Yes, Jill knows Kate and.

In explaining this different set of data, the syntactician might give rules and principles imposing different structures than would the semanticist, for example, those structures shown in (6).[7]

(6) a.

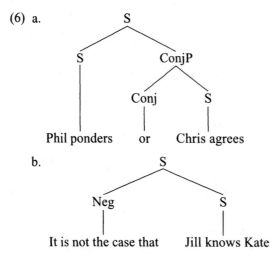

b.

The similar patterning of *and* and *or* versus *it is not the case that*, and the ill-formedness of (4a–c) are accounted for by assimilating *and* and *or* to a single category Conj, and by positioning this category between clauses; a separate category with a distinct position is given for negations, Neg. Finally, the close grouping of conjunctions with their following sentence is captured by placing the two in their own separate syntactic constituent, conjunction phrases (ConjP), which excludes the preceding clause.[8] The trees in (6) give the syntactic structure of the sentences in (1), according to this theory.

Finally, the logician would be interested in PC from yet a third angle, different from that of either syntax or semantics. Crucial questions for the logician would be, What sorts of inferences hold among PC sentences? What arguments are valid in the language? Relevant data from the logician's perspective would include the fact that the first member of each pair in (7) through (9) implies the second member of the pair, and the fact that arguments like (10a) are valid in PC (at least on one construal of the premises), whereas arguments like (10b) are not:

(7) a. Phil ponders, and Chris agrees.
     b. Phil ponders.

(8) a. It is not the case that it is not the case that Jill knows Kate.
     b. Jill knows Kate.

(9) a. It is not the case that Phil ponders or Chris agrees.
     b. It is not the case that Phil ponders, and it is not the case that Chris agrees.

(10) a. It is not the case that Phil ponders and Chris agrees.
Phil ponders.
————————————————————————————————————
It is not the case that Chris agrees.

  b. It is not the case that Phil ponders or Chris agrees.
Phil ponders.
————————————————————————————————————
It is not the case that Chris agrees.

To explain these facts, the logician might identify certain constituents as logical elements—here, the connectives *and, or,* and *it is not the case that*—and attribute a definite structure to their occurrence in PC sentences, for example, the structures shown in (11):[9]

(11) a. $[_s \, And \, S_1 \, S_2]$
  b. $[_s \, Or \, S_1 \, S_2]$
  c. $[_s \, It \, is \, not \, the \, case \, that \, S_1]$

The logical relations among the PC sentences would then be captured by general rules of inference making reference to this structure, for example, the rules in (12) through (15):

(12) $[_s \, And \, S_1 \, S_2] \rightarrow S_1$

(13) $[_{S_1} \, It \, is \, not \, the \, case \, that \, [_{S_2} \, it \, is \, not \, the \, case \, that \, S]] \rightarrow S$

(14) $[_s \, It \, is \, not \, the \, case \, that \, [_s \, or \, S_1 \, S_2]]$
  $\rightarrow [_s \, and \, [_s \, it \, is \, not \, the \, case \, that \, S_1] \, [_s \, it \, is \, not \, the \, case \, that \, S_2]]$

(15) $[_s \, It \, is \, not \, the \, case \, that \, [_s \, and \, S_1 \, S_2]]$
  S_1
————————————————————————————————————
  $[_s \, It \, is \, not \, the \, case \, that \, S_2]$

The articulation in (11c) would be the logical structure according to this theory. Here again this structure differs from that postulated by either semantics or syntax.

3.1.1 Semantic Structure and Syntactic Structure

This example shows how the different projects of the semanticist, the syntactician, and the logician might in principle lead them to attribute different structure to linguistic forms. Nonetheless, for a variety of reasons, it is attractive to think that structures might converge to some extent, particularly with syntax and semantics.

One reason is the systematic nature of our linguistic knowledge. On the view embraced here, syntax and semantics both attempt to characterize certain aspects of our knowledge of language. Syntax pursues knowledge of formal structural principles, and semantics pursues knowledge of meaning. Both partition this task in the same way: both attempt to discover the content of this knowledge, how it is acquired, and how it is deployed in speech and understanding. It is reasonable to think that our knowledge of language is unified to a certain extent, that it forms a **cognitive system** distinct from other cognitive systems. If this is correct, the parts of our linguistic knowledge should interact and interrelate in principled ways. One natural way of conceptualizing this arrangement is in terms of shared representations (or sets of representations) to which the various principles of our linguistic knowledge apply. That is, it is attractive to see our knowledge of language as organized into separate modules of rules and principles—a syntax module, a semantics module, a phonology module, etc. (each perhaps with its own division into submodules)—all applying to some common representations (or sets of representations) $\mathfrak{R}$:

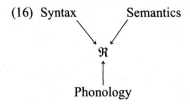

(16) Syntax   Semantics

$\mathfrak{R}$

Phonology

Such a picture is not, of course, a novel one and is indeed broadly assumed in modern linguistic theory. For example, various phonological properties of phrases and sentences including prosody, stress, and intonation contour are widely thought to arise through phonological rules applying to structures licensed independently by the syntax. That is, syntactic and phonological rules operate over a common set of forms. It is natural to think that semantics and syntax are related in the same way.

A second reason for expecting common or compatible structures is learnability. We saw earlier that the goal of providing an interpretive T theory for a language may allow a number of solutions: there may be a number of distinct, extensionally equivalent interpretive T theories, each assigning different semantic structures, that execute this task.[10] In view of this underdetermination of theory by data, it is clearly necessary that theory choice be constrained if learning language is to be possible. Without such constraints, the job of acquiring the semantic theory becomes insurmountable.

One simple way of constraining theory choice is to subject the hypotheses made by the language learner to a number of independent demands. Suppose that we require the semantic structure posited by a language learner to be compatible with that required independently by syntactic theory. That is, suppose we require semantics and syntax to yield overlapping forms. For a given sentence or other expression, the language learner would then be obliged to find a structure that both explains its syntactic properties and provides an articulation of constituents suitable for an interpretive T theory. It is plausible to think that this constraint would sharply limit the choice of available structures. In effect, the learner would be in the position of someone trying to find a single solution to a set of independent, simultaneous equations. The demand that all the equations be solved in one go restricts the class of solutions.

Shared representations would also strongly augment the information available to the language learner. If syntactic and semantic structure are closely similar at some level, a child will be able to gain syntactic information about a sentence from its semantics and semantic information from its syntax. For example, suppose that from formal, distributional data, a child determines that the sentence contains a major constituent division into a subject phrase and a predicate phrase. Then it would at the very same time be learning something about the semantic composition of the sentence, namely, that it is constructed from the semantic contents of a subject and a predicate. Likewise, if the child fixes the semantic constituents of some expression, it will at the same time be fixing the distribution of parts relevant for purely grammatical relations. Such a picture offers an attractive partial answer to the question of how children are able to acquire knowledge of language at the speed they do, in the face of incomplete and often "defective" data. If the resulting knowledge is interrelated in the way sketched, there will be a number of routes through which it can be acquired.

Finally, convergence between syntactic and semantic forms is suggested by the separate results of these enterprises themselves. The structures assigned by syntax and semantics to our PC examples in (1) are clearly different in absolute terms, with the syntactic structures being somewhat more articulated than the semantic ones. Nonetheless, the similarities between the two are far more striking than their differences. The syntactic and the semantic representations for conjunctions each isolate two subsentences (S_1 and S_2) and a connective (*and, or*) as distinct structural parts. Likewise, the syntactic and the semantic representations for negation each isolate a subsentence and a negation element (*it is not the case that*). The presence of these fundamental similarities itself suggests that the two should be brought together.

3.1.2   Semantic Structure and Logical Structure

At first sight it might seem that our reasons for thinking that syntactic and semantic structure converge should extend to logic as well: that logical relations among sentences should draw on the same forms. On reflection, however, it's not so clear that this is true, at least if logic is construed as the discipline that attempts to account for our knowledge of such relations among sentences as implication, contradiction, synonymy, and so on.

In the last chapter we considered how familiar logicosemantic relations between sentences might be captured by T-theoretic means. We suggested that relations like implication, contradiction, and synonymy correspond to (provable) T-theoretic statements shown in table 3.1. For example, our proposal was that when a speaker judges that two sentences α and β are synonymous, that speaker's implicit T theory yields a statement of the form "α is true if and only if β is true," and so on.

We further saw that the resources necessary to prove interpretative T-theoretic statements of the required kind very plausibly go beyond those provided by semantics alone. These additional resources take the form of additional inference rules of logic, allowing us to underwrite a semantic judgment like (17) on the basis of a deduction like that shown in (18):

(17) Phil ponders and Chris agrees implies Phil ponders.

(18) a. *Phil ponders and Chris agrees* is true iff Phil ponders and Chris agrees.
      b. *Phil ponders* is true iff Phil ponders. (by rules of the T theory)
      c. Phil ponders and Chris agrees only if Phil ponders. (by rules of the logic module)
      d. *Phil ponders and Chris agrees* is true only if Phil ponders. (by (18a) and (18c))
      e. *Phil ponders and Chris agrees* is true only if *Phil ponders* is true. (by (18b) and (18d))

Table 3.1 How logicosemantic relations between sentences correspond with interpretative T-theoretic relations between sentences

Logicosemantic judgment	Interpretative T-theoretic counterpart
α is synonymous with β	α is true iff β is true
α implies β	α is true only if β is true
α contradicts β	α is true iff it is not the case that β is true

Observe now that if this general view is correct, then logicosemantic relations between sentences of PC (and more generally of any language) are not accounted for by logical rules of inference defined over expressions of the object language. There is no rule of logic here allowing us to infer directly from *Phil ponders and Chris agrees* to *Phil ponders*. Rather, the inference is established indirectly through the T theory and the *metalanguage*. As in figure 3.1, the T theory relates a sentence of the object language to a sentence of the metalanguage; the rules of logic then relate that one metalanguage sentence to another; the T theory then relates the last back to a sentence of the object language. One way to picture this is to think of a subject's internalized T theory as proving the equivalent of (18a, b), where the object language is a natural language (here English) and the metalanguage is an internal "brain language" or "language of thought." The subject's logic module then licenses further deductions through various inference rules defined over statements of the brain language, that is, rules stated in terms of the structure of brain language expressions. The T theory then relates the results of brain-language inferences back to the natural language.

Whatever the strength of this particular computational picture, the upshot is that even if logic must ascribe structure to sentences in order to account for inferential relations, it is far from clear that accounting for the logical knowledge of speakers requires attributing logical structure to the *object* language. It is altogether possible that the rules and principles accounting for this knowledge are defined over expressions of the metalanguage. In such a case,

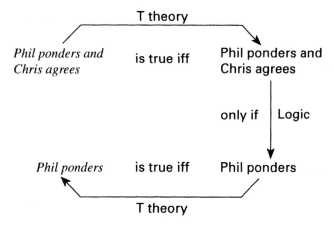

Figure 3.1 The derivation of a logicosemantic relation.

our logical rules would not concern themselves directly with the object language at all.

3.2   Constraints on Semantic Rules

The assumption of a compatible form for syntax and semantics is, of course, an empirical hypothesis and, as such, potentially false. Indeed, we have already noted how syntactic and semantic investigation might arrive at different structures for identical strings of PC. If the assumption of compatible forms is to be maintained, then divergences between syntactic and semantic structure would clearly have to be reconciled when they occurred.

At first sight this challenge might not seem to be a terribly difficult one. If we look at the syntactic forms in (6), for example, it looks simple enough to adjust the semantics for PC appropriately. Suppose that we replace our original axioms for conjunction, disjunction, and negation with the ones shown in (19) through (21), for instance:

(19) $[_S S_1 [_{ConjP} [_{Conj} and] S_2]]$ is true iff both S_1 is true and S_2 is true

(20) $[_S S_1 [_{ConjP} [_{Conj} or] S_2]]$ is true iff either S_1 is true or S_2 is true

(21) $[_S [_{Neg} It \ is \ not \ the \ case \ that] S]$ is true iff it is not the case that S is true

Then despite the new structures, we derive the same metalanguage sentence on the RHS of the biconditional as before. Where the earlier theory proved the interpretive T theorem in (22a), the revised theory proves the interpretive result in (22b), and so on.

(22) a. $[_S [_S Phil \ ponders] \ and \ [_S Chris \ agrees]]$ is true iff both Phil ponders and Chris agrees.
      b. $[_S [_S Phil \ ponders] [_{ConjP} [_{Conj} and] [_S Chris \ agrees]]]$ is true iff both Phil ponders and Chris agrees.

On reflection, however, things really aren't so simple. Note that the results in (22) are achieved only by introducing a new and undesirable feature in the rules in (19) to (21). In the original T theory there was a very close relation between interpretation and form. Specifically, constituents of the object-language expression appearing on the LHS of the biconditional corresponded directly to expressions of the metalanguage appearing on the RHS of the biconditional. Consider conjunction as show in (23):

(23)

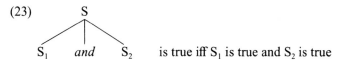

is true iff S_1 is true and S_2 is true

The rules in (21), however, abandon this close relation. The ConjP and Conj nodes on the LHS of the biconditional in (19) and (20), for example, have no counterpart on the RHS in (24):

(24)

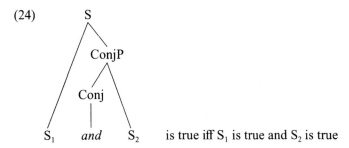

is true iff S_1 is true and S_2 is true

In effect, the semantic rules in (19) through (21) simply ignore the additional structure introduced in the syntactic representation. They interpret no more than what was interpreted by the original rules for PC.

The loss of a direct connection between meaning and form in (19) to (21) is not a small thing. In fact, it's easy to see that if we allow semantic rules to ignore form, we undermine one of our central grounds for taking syntax and semantics to converge in the first place. Recall that one reason for taking semantic and syntactic structure to coincide was that this would restrict the class of grammars available to the learner and increase the information that the learner received. But clearly if the relation between syntactic structure and semantic rules is permitted to be a loose one, these grounds are forfeit. If semantic rules may ignore structure, knowledge about the semantics will do little to help fix the syntactic theory, and vice versa.

These points make it clear that if the hypothesis of a common form for syntax and semantics is to have force, it must involve certain fairly strong **constraints on the formulation of semantic rules**. Such constraints must determine, for example, how much structure semantic rules can appeal to, whether they can ignore structure (as in (19) through (21)), and perhaps whether they can introduce structure of their own. Let us consider one constraint that is particularly attractive from this point of view.

3.2.1   Strong Compositionality

We observed in the last chapter that the T theory for PC is compositional in the general sense required of any semantic theory. That is, it derives the semantic content of complex sentences (the T sentences) from the semantic content of smaller constituent clauses. In fact, the semantic axioms for PC go beyond the requirement of simple compositionality and exhibit this property in a particularly strong and restricted way. These rules not only interpret a syntactic node $[_X Y_1 \ldots Y_n]$ in terms of its constituents; they interpret it in terms of its *immediate subconstituents* $Y_1, \ldots, Y_n$. They never look down any deeper in the tree. Furthermore, these rules interpret structure given by the syntax, and they interpret *only structure given by the syntax*. They never introduce structure of their own.

Thus consider (6a, b) from the last chapter (repeated here):

(6) a. $[_S S_1 \ and \ S_2]$ is true iff both S_1 is true and S_2 is true
     b. $[_S S_1 \ or \ S_2]$ is true iff either S_1 is true or S_2 is true

These rules state the truth conditions of conjoined Ss in terms of the truth conditions of S_1 and S_2, the immediate structural daughters of S. Furthermore, S_1 and S_2 are nodes produced by the syntactic component; the only object-language expressions appearing on the RHS of the biconditional also appear on the LHS. We might summarize this situation by saying that the semantic axioms for PC have the property of being *strictly local* in scope and *purely interpretive* in contribution.

Being strictly local and purely interpretive are not necessary properties that any compositional semantic rule must possess. Consider (25a, b), for instance:

(25) a. $[_S S_1 \ and \ [_{S'} S_2 \ or \ S_3]]$ is true iff both S_1 is true and either S_2 is true or S_3 is true
      b. $[_S S_1 \ and \ S_2]$ is true iff $[_S$ *it is not the case that* $[_S$ *it is not the case that* $S_1]$ *or* $[_S$ *it is not the case that* $S_2]]$ is true

These are compositional in form and yield true T sentences for the structures they analyze. Nonetheless, (25a) fails to be strictly local in that it gives the interpretation of the node S in terms of the interpretation of its daughter node S_1 and its granddaughter nodes S_2 and S_3. Likewise, (25b) fails to be purely interpretive in that it gives the interpretation of a conjunction in terms of a negated disjunction that it introduces.[11]

Although being strictly local and being purely interpretive are not necessary properties of semantic rules in a logical sense, they are nonetheless very appealing properties for semantic rules to have. Indeed, it is attractive to suppose that being strictly local and being purely interpretive are universal constraints governing the syntax-semantics interface. This idea might be stated in the form of a "strong compositionality" hypothesis:

Strong compositionality $\mathcal{R}$ is a possible semantic rule for a human natural language only if $\mathcal{R}$ is strictly local and purely interpretive.

The chief attraction of strong compositionality is that it makes the construction of a T theory for a language highly sensitive to the syntactic configurations over which the T theory is stated. As observed above, this is a very desirable result from the standpoint of language learnability, given the basic "induction problem" for grammars. A highly constrained relation between syntax and semantics limits the class of grammars that a learner must potentially conjecture. It also increases the deductive richness of the theory, allowing a child to gain syntactic information about the language from its semantics and semantic information from its syntax. We will show how strong compositionality enforces this interconnectedness by considering a simple alternative grammar for the language fragment PC.

The Alternative Theory PC′

The original grammar for PC included the syntactic rules in (26), which yield the structures in (27).

(26) a. S → S *and* S
      b. S → S *or* S
      c. S → *it is not the case that* S

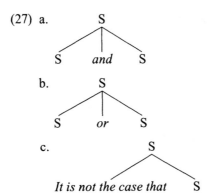

(27) a.

      b.

      c.

In the trees in (27) the conjunctions *and* and *or*, and the negation *it is not the case that* are not analyzed as independent words belonging each to a grammatical category of its own. Rather, they are analyzed more or less as "syntactic features" of the larger conjunction or negation structure in which they occur, and hang directly from S. This may be expressed by saying that (26a–c) treat the conjunctions and negation as **syncategorematic elements**. This syncategorematic treatment is directly reflected in the semantics for PC. Under the axioms in (26), *and, or,* and *it is not the case that* are not analyzed as independently meaningful expressions making some specific semantic contribution of their own. There are no separate axioms for *and, or,* and *it is not the case that.* These elements make a semantic contribution only through the larger structure in which they occur.

Consider now the alternative syntax, PC', discussed earlier. The rules in (26) are replaced by those in (28), which assign the new structures in (29):

(28) a. S → S ConjP
    b. ConjP → Conj S
    b. S → Neg S
    c. Conj → {*and, or*}
    d. Neg → {*it is not the case that*}

(29) a.

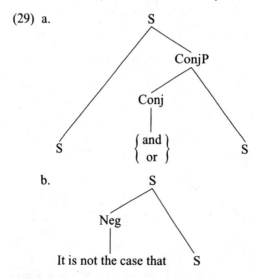

b.

Substitution of (28) for (26) produces no difference in **weak generative capacity**; that is, the resulting grammar generates exactly the same strings of English words. However, it does produce a change in **strong generative capacity**: the grammar in (28) follows a different derivational route to a given string of PC, assigning a different structure. More specifically, (28) treats *and, or,* and *it is not the case that* as **categorematic elements**: they are analyzed as independent formatives belonging to their own lexical category Conj or Neg.

The difference in syntactic analysis introduced by (28) need not entail any real difference in semantic analysis. Following earlier remarks, suppose that we allow the fit between syntactic and semantic rules to be a loose one and adopt the rules in (19) through (21) (repeated below):

(19) $[_S S_1 [_{ConjP} [_{Conj} and] S_2]]$ is true iff both S_1 is true and S_2 is true

(20) $[_S S_1 [_{ConjP} [_{Conj} or] S_2]]$ is true iff either S_1 is true or S_2 is true

(21) $[_S [_{Neg} It is not the case that] S]$ is true iff it is not the case that S is true

Then the semantics operates essentially as before, despite the categorematic status of the conjunctions and negation. *And, or,* and *it is not the case that* receive no individual semantic interpretations and contribute only as part of a wider structure. In effect, these semantic axioms simply ignore the structure introduced by the Conj and Neg nodes and look directly at the material they dominate. If, however, we adopt the tighter constraints on the syntax-semantics interface imposed by strong compositionality, then (19) through (21) are immediately excluded. We are permitted only semantic axioms that analyze a node and its immediate daughters.

On reflection, the job of providing strongly compositional axioms for structures like those in (29) is not a trivial one. Note, for example, that this will require an axiom analyzing the mother-daughter configurations $[_S S ConjP]$ and $[_{ConjP} Conj S]$. Since these represent the parts of a coordination structure common to *both* conjunctions and disjunctions, we cannot assign this structure the fixed semantic significance of either. Roughly, what we must find is some semantic contribution made by the constituent sentences, some *general* semantic contribution made by the conjunction phrase ConjP and the conjunction Conj, and some way of combining these contributions to get the interpretation of $[_S S [_{ConjP} Conj S]]$. That is, we need axioms like this:

(30) $[_S S ConjP]$ is true iff
   a. the semantic contribution of S is x,
   b. the semantic contribution of ConjP is y,
   c. x and y are put together as follows: ....

(31) The semantic contribution of [$_{ConjP}$ Conj S] is y iff
    a. the semantic contribution of Conj is z,
    b. the semantic contribution of S is w,
    c. z and w are put together as follows: . . . .

But what kinds of contributions can these be? We know that sentences are associated with truth conditions, but what is the semantic contribution of a conjunction phrase, what is the general semantic contribution of a conjunction, and how do we combine these with the contributions of sentences?

In a similar way, strong compositionality will require semantic axioms analyzing the mother-daughter configurations in (32).

(32) a. The semantic contribution of [$_{Conj}$ *and*] is ...
    b. The semantic contribution of [$_{Conj}$ *or*] is ...

Presumably, these analyses will state the particular semantic contributions made by *and* and *or* within the general type of contribution proper to conjunctions. But again, what kind of contributions are these? The sentences joined by conjunctions are true or false, but surely conjunctions themselves are neither true nor false. How do we fill in the ellipses in (32)? As it turns out, a very interesting answer can be given to this question. The principle of strong compositionality not only excludes some candidate semantic axioms, like those in (19) to (21) for the interpretation of (29a, b), but also motivates the introduction of a new and important feature in the axioms that replace them.

3.2.2 Introducing Semantic Values

Our discussion of T sentences has so far implicitly accepted the familiar intuition that truth and falsity are properties of sentences. We have spoken of sentences as being true or false, just as we might speak of them as being short or long, complicated or transparent. In his *Grundlagen der Arithematik*, the philosopher-logician Gottlob Frege (1953 [1884]) proposed an alternative view that was not only strikingly original but, initially, rather bizarre-sounding. Frege suggested that truth and falsity are in fact not properties applying to sentences; rather they are **objects** that sentences may have as their **semantic values**. Frege's idea was that there are two distinguished objects in the universe —call them the True (t) and the False (f)—and that a true sentence is one having t as its semantic value, whereas a false sentence is one having f as its value. For Frege, all true sentences have the same semantic value, t, and all false sentences have the same semantic value, f. Frege referred to t and f as **truth values**.

The semantic axioms we have developed to this point can all be recast straightforwardly along Fregean lines. All statements that speak of a sentence S as being true (or false) are simply replaced by ones that state that S has the semantic value t (or f). We will abbreviate this by writing "Val(t, S)" (or "Val(f, S)").[12] Under this revision, the general form of T sentences thus changes from (T) to (T$^+$):

(T)   S is true iff *p*
(T$^+$) Val(t, S) iff *p*

Correlatively, our T theories change so as to allow us to prove things of the form T$^+$. Our original axioms for PC are recast as in (33) and (34), where every occurrence of "α is true" is replaced with "Val(t, α)":

(33) a. Val(t, *Phil ponders*) iff Phil ponders
     b. Val(t, *Chris agrees*) iff Chris agrees
     c. Val(t, *Jill knows Kate*) iff Jill knows Kate

(34) a. Val(t, [$_s$ S$_1$ *and* S$_2$]) iff both Val(t, S$_1$) and Val(t, S$_2$)
     b. Val(t, [$_s$ S$_1$ *or* S$_2$]) iff either Val(t, S$_1$) or Val(t, S$_2$)
     c. Val(t, [$_s$ *It is not the case that* S]) iff it is not the case that Val(t, S)
     d. Val(t, [$_s$ α]) iff Val(t, α) (for any elementary sentence α)

These revised axioms allow us to prove T theorems for all the sentences of PC using the production rules (SE) and (UI), just as before.

New Axioms for PC

The Fregean semantics for PC might seem at first to be a simple variant of our original account: one that adopts a peculiar view of truth but is basically equivalent. In fact, however, the new analysis introduces a significant shift of view. Previously we conceived of the semantic contribution of a sentence in terms of its truth conditions. Under Frege's idea, we are led to see the semantic contribution of a sentence S in terms of a specific *object* that S takes as its value—a truth value, t or f. This object-oriented perspective can be directly generalized to other constituents. Other sentence elements can be viewed as contributing other kinds of objects as their semantic values.

Table 3.2   Semantic values of the conjunctions *and, or*

Lexical item	*and*	*or*
Semantic values	$\langle t, t \rangle$	$\langle t, f \rangle$, $\langle f, t \rangle$, $\langle t, t \rangle$

We can illustrate this point through our problem of how to get strongly compositional axioms for the structures in (29). Recall that we needed to interpret the shared structure in (29a), and that this required isolating some general semantic contribution made by conjunctions. We also needed to talk about the specific semantic contributions made by *and* and *or* within this general type. Under our earlier semantic account, we didn't know how to do these things. By contrast, under the Fregean analysis, a natural approach offers itself. Think of it this way: syntactically, conjunctions are expressions that join pairs of sentences together. Furthermore, we're now assuming that the semantic value of a sentence is a truth value. Suppose, then, that we think of conjunctions as semantically joining truth values together. The semantic value of a conjunction would then be a pair of truth values:

(35)

Truth value   Pair of truth values   Truth value   Semantic values

This idea allows a natural answer to the question about the contributions of *and* and *or*. If conjunctions in general contribute pairs of truth values, then we can take *and* and *or* to provide certain specific pairs of this kind. In particular, since a conjoined sentence with *and* is true just in case both of its conjuncts are true, we can let the value of *and* be $\langle t, t \rangle$, the pair containing two t's. And since conjoined sentences with *or* are true whenever one of their conjuncts is true, we can let the value of *or* be any one of $\langle t, f \rangle$, $\langle f, t \rangle$ or $\langle t, t \rangle$, the pairs containing at least one t (table 3.2).

These general points are made concrete in the axioms in (36) and (37), which interpret the coordinate structures in (29a) in a strongly compositional way, looking only at immediate mother-daughter node configurations:

(36) a. Val(t, *Phil ponders*) iff Phil ponders
       b. Val(t, *Chris agrees*) iff Chris agrees

    c. Val(t, *Jill knows Kate*) iff Jill knows Kate
    d. Val($\langle z, z' \rangle$, *and*) iff $z = $ t and $z' = $ t
    e. Val($\langle z, z' \rangle$, *or*) iff $z = $ t or $z' = $ t

(37) a. Val(t, [$_\text{S}$ S ConjP]) iff for some z, Val(z, S) and Val(z, ConjP)
      b. Val(z, [$_\text{ConjP}$ Conj S]) iff for some z', Val($\langle z, z' \rangle$, Conj) and Val(z', S)
      c. Val(t, [$_\text{S}$ α]) iff Val(t, α) (for any elementary sentence α)
      d. Val($\langle z, z' \rangle$, [$_\text{Conj}$ α]) iff Val($\langle z, z' \rangle$, α) (for any conjunction α)

In (36) are the semantic axioms for the basic expressions of the grammar. The first three are the familiar axioms for the basic sentences of PC. The last two are new axioms for the conjunctions *and* and *or*, which are now treated as independent lexical items. In (37) are the semantic axioms for the phrasal configurations of the grammar. According to (37a), a sentence consisting of an S and a ConjP is true if and only if there is some (truth value) z that is the value of both. The axiom for ConjP, is similar: this phrase has the value z just in case there is some (truth-value) z' such that the pair $\langle z, z' \rangle$ is the value of the conjunction and z' is the value of S. Axiom (37c) states that the semantic value of an S node dominating an elementary sentence is to be passed down to that elementary sentence. Axiom (37d) states that the semantic value of a Conj node dominating a lexical conjunction is to be passed down to that conjunction.

New Production Rules for PC

As it turns out, the new axioms in (36) and (37) are not quite enough to interpret the structures in (29). In addition, we must include three new production rules, one each for the conjunction (CJ), disjunction (DJ), and negation (Neg) structures:

(CJ) Conjunction

$$\frac{\phi \text{ iff for some } x, y, \text{Val}(x, S_1) \text{ and Val}(y, S_2), \text{ and } x = \text{t and } y = \text{t}}{\phi \text{ iff both Val}(t, S_1) \text{ and Val}(t, S_2)}$$

(DJ) Disjunction

$$\frac{\phi \text{ iff for some } x, y, \text{Val}(x, S_1) \text{ and Val}(y, S_2), \text{ and } x = \text{t or } y = \text{t}}{\phi \text{ iff either Val(t, } S_1) \text{ or Val(t, } S_2)}$$

(Neg) Negation

> ϕ iff for some z, it is not the case that $z = t$, and Val(z, S)
> ───
> ϕ iff it is not the case that Val(t, S)

(CJ), (DJ), and (Neg) are similar to the earlier rule (SE) but involve statements of identity in place of statements of material equivalence.

A Sample Derivation

To see that these axioms and rules do yield the desired T^+ sentences for PC under the syntax in (28) and (29), let us return to the example *Phil ponders or Chris agrees*, with the labeled bracketing in (38):

(38) [$_S$ [$_S$ Phil ponders] [$_{ConjP}$ [$_{Conj}$ or] [$_S$ Chris agrees]]]

As always, we begin at the top (leftmost) S node:

(39) Val(t, [$_S$ [$_S$ Phil ponders] [$_{ConjP}$ [$_{Conj}$ or] [$_S$ Chris agrees]]) iff for some z,
      Val(z, [$_S$ Phil ponders]) and Val(z, [$_{ConjP}$ [$_{Conj}$ or] [$_S$ Chris agrees]])
      (by (37a), (UI))

We continue by applying the rule for ConjP (40):

(40) Val(z, [$_{ConjP}$ [$_{Conj}$ or] [$_S$ Chris agrees]]) iff for some z', Val($\langle z, z' \rangle$, [$_{Conj}$ or])
      and Val(z', [$_S$ Chris agrees]) (by (37b), (UI))

The contribution of the disjunction is spelled out in (41) to (43):

(41) Val($\langle z, z' \rangle$, [$_{Conj}$ or]) iff Val($\langle z, z' \rangle$, *or*) (by (37d), (UI))

(42) Val($\langle z, z' \rangle$, *or*) iff $z = t$ or $z' = t$ (by (36e) (UI))

(43) Val($\langle z, z' \rangle$, [$_{Conj}$ or]) iff $z = t$ or $z' = t$ (by (41), (42), (SE))

Using (40) and (43), we derive (44a) by (SE); using (44a) and (39), we derive (44b) by (SE):

(44) a. Val(z, [$_{ConjP}$ [$_{Conj}$ or] [$_S$ Chris agrees]]) iff for some z', $z = t$ or $z' = t$
          and Val(z', [$_S$ Chris agrees])
      b. Val(t, [$_S$ [$_S$ Phil ponders] [$_{ConjP}$ [$_{Conj}$ or] [$_S$ Chris agrees]]) iff for some z,
          z', Val(z, [$_S$ Phil ponders]), and $z = t$ or $z' = t$, and
          Val(z', [$_S$ Chris agrees])

This sets us up to apply the new inference rule (DJ) as in (45):

(45) Val(t, [$_S$ [$_S$ Phil ponders] [$_{ConjP}$ [$_{Conj}$ or] [$_S$ Chris agrees]]) iff
either Val(t, [$_S$ Phil ponders]) or Val(t, [$_S$ Chris agrees]) (by (44b), (DJ))

With all truth-value variables now replaced by t's, the semantic contributions of two disjuncts can be elaborated using (37c):

(46) a. Val(t, [$_S$ Phil ponders]) iff Val(t, *Phil ponders*) (by (37c), (UI))
b. Val(t, [$_S$ Chris agrees]) iff Val(t, *Chris agrees*) (by (37c), (UI))

The elementary clauses in (36a) and (36b) tell us how to spell out the T sentences for each basic clause, and so by (46), (36), and (SE), we can conclude (47) and (48):

(36) a. Val(t, *Phil ponders*) iff Phil ponders
b. Val(t, *Chris agrees*) iff Chris agrees

(47) Val(t, [$_S$ Phil ponders]) iff Phil ponders (by (46a), (36a), (SE))

(48) Val(t, [$_S$ Chris agrees]) iff Chris agrees (by (46b), (36b), (SE))

Combining the results in (45), (47), and (48) and using (SE), we can now conclude the final T sentence (49):

(49) Val(t, [$_S$ [$_S$ Phil ponders] [$_{ConjP}$ [$_{Conj}$ or] [$_S$ Chris agrees]]) iff
either Phil ponders or Chris agrees (by (45), (47), (48), (SE))

This is, of course, the desired outcome.

These results illustrate a number of important points. First, we see that it is indeed possible to interpret the alternative syntax for PC in a way that respects strong compositionality. The new semantic rules assign appropriate T sentences, and do so in a way that is strictly local and introduces no new syntactic structure. Fregean semantic values thus provide a concrete answer to the question of how to give a strongly compositional semantic analysis for PC under the syntax in (29).

Second, we see that although the new axioms produce appropriate T theorems, they do so by means of derivations that are more complex than those given under the original T theory, or under the noncompositional T theory in (19) to (21). This is in fact generally the case in linguistic theorizing, where the choice between elaborating the account of specific constructions versus elaborating the content of general principles (such as strong compositionality) arises routinely. Although the choice in such matters is ultimately an empirical issue, it has often proved useful as a research strategy to prefer complex structures and complex derivations to complex principles. This is simply because the former tend to yield a more restrictive theory overall, and hence one to be preferred under the logic of the language-acquisition problem.

Third, we see that the alteration of a T theory is not always simply a matter of augmenting its axioms. New production rules must sometimes be included as well. The categorematic treatment of conjunctions in our new theory requires us to add production rules allowing us to go from statements containing a variable in place of a truth value ("$Val(z, S_1)$ and $Val(z', S_2)$ and $z = t$ or $z' = t$") to statements in which those variables are instantiated ("$Val(t, S_1)$ or $Val(t, S_2)$").

Finally, we see that even when syntactic and semantic investigation don't produce identical forms, the two can be made compatible in a constrained way. In light of the general situation of PC versus PC', it is conceivable that the facts of meaning and truth conditions alone might not allow us to articulate coordinations so finely as to include a ConjP. Nonetheless, even if semantic analysis brings us only to the more coarsely articulated structures in (2), semantics is clearly compatible with the structures in (6). We can give a T theory defined over such trees that preserves constraining principles like strong compositionality. Thus a certain amount of divergence is possible between syntax and semantics. What is crucial from the standpoint of systematicity is that the structures of syntax and semantics be compatible. And what is crucial from the standpoint of learnability is that they be close enough to restrict hypotheses appropriately.

In summary, then, the imposition of strong compositionality makes semantic theory highly sensitive to the syntactic configurations to which it must apply. Under strong compositionality, an apparently minor change in the syntax of coordinate and negation structures—one that assigns categorematic status to conjunctions and negations but does not affect the weak generative capacity of the grammar—forces a major revision in our semantic analysis. We are now obliged to view truth and falsity as objects associated with sentences. And we are drawn to view the semantic contributions of other elements (conjunctions, negation) in terms of such semantic objects, and in so doing, introducing a number of new axioms and production rules.

3.2.3   Must Semantic Analysis Be Exhaustive?

We can further strengthen compositionality beyond that discussed above. For example, observe that under the axioms in (36) and (37), there are no syncategorematic elements: each constituent is assigned its own independent interpretation, and the semantic value for a complex node is expressed in terms of a semantic value for each of its daughter nodes:

(50) Val(z, 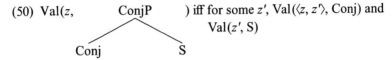) iff for some z', Val($\langle z, z' \rangle$, Conj) and Val(z', S)

This property of the axioms in (36) and (37) might be raised to the status of a general constraint on semantic rules. That is, we might consider restricting our semantic rules to ones that exhaustively analyze the constituents of a given node, assigning a semantic value to each immediate daughter.

Although **exhaustivity** is a potential constraint on semantic rules and attractive as such on familiar grounds of restricting the class of possible natural-language grammars, there are important empirical difficulties facing its adoption. First, observe that exhaustivity compels us to find a semantic contribution for every syntactic constituent, and so excludes the possibility of semantically empty elements. In point of fact, however, there do appear to be cases of contentless grammatical elements—items that occur to satisfy specific grammatical properties but do not appear to receive an independent interpretation. Consider the indicated elements in (51), for instance:

(51) a. **There** is a man in the garden.
        (Cf. A man is in the garden.)
      b. **It** is raining.
        (Cf. *What is raining?)

(52) a. The resolution **of** conflicts is desirable.
        (Cf. Resolving conflicts is desirable.)
      b. All **of** the candidates were present.
        (Cf. All the candidates were present.)

The *there* and *it* occuring in subject position in (51a, b) are standardly analyzed by grammarians as **pleonastic** elements: noun phrases that appear simply because English requires every sentence to have a formal subject. These items make no semantic contribution, as we see from the fact that they can be eliminated without loss of meaning and cannot be questioned, as contentful NPs can. Likewise, the *of* occuring in (52a, b) is generally viewed as a purely grammatical preposition, present because English requires all NPs to be governed by a case-marking element, such as a verb or preposition. Again, this *of* makes no clear semantic contribution, as we see from the fact that it can be eliminated without significant change of meaning. The apparent existence of such purely syntactic elements casts doubt on exhaustivity as a property of semantic rules.

Exhaustivity also places questionable constraints on *the way* in which meaningful elements are permitted to contribute to interpretation. Consider again the categorematic analysis of conjunction in (50) versus the syncategorematic account in (53):

(53) Val(t,   S   ) iff both Val(t, S_1) and Val(t, S_2)

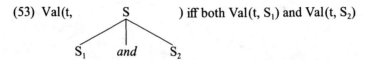

Notice that although *and* receives no independent semantic value in (53), it nonetheless makes a definite semantic contribution. The presence of *and* in the object language on the LHS of the biconditional is responsible for the presence of "and" in the metalanguage on the RHS of the biconditional. We might put this by saying that *and* contributes as part of the overall conjunction structure in (53), rather than as a discrete lexical element. Again, exhaustivity would exclude this kind of rule, in which semantic contribution is "spread over" structure. Exhaustivity requires discrete lexical elements to be assigned discrete interpretations.

As it turns out, there once again appear to be empirical reasons for thinking that structural contributions excluded by exhaustivity are available in natural languages. It's a familiar fact that in many languages of the world, the equivalent of conjunction in English is expressed by a simple juxtaposition of clauses or phrases. For example, in Kannada (a language of Southern India), structural adjacency alone typically encodes sentence conjunction:

(54) Ramaswa:mi manege   ho:daru na:nu sku:lige   ho:de.
      Ramaswami home-DAT go-PST I   school-DAT go-PST
      'Ramaswami went home, and I went to school.'

If (54) is a simple juxtaposition, as it appears, this argues that configurational structure itself can express the conjunction relation, and hence that natural language must permit rules like (55):

(55) Val(t, 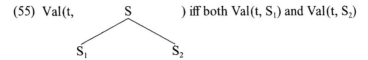) iff both Val(t, S_1) and Val(t, S_2)

But note now that if rules like (55) are allowed, it becomes plausible to view the *and* in (53) as a purely formal mark of the conjunction structure, rather than as an autonomous lexical item that actually contributes the meaning of conjunction. These results suggest that exhaustivity is overly restrictive in the way that it allows meaning to be expressed in structure, excluding syncategoremata from the grammar of natural language.

3.3   Some Syntactic Theory

We have considered the hypothesis that structural representations from semantic and syntactic theory converge, and we have discussed some general virtues of this view. For the hypothesis to yield specific results for our semantic program, however, we must evidently settle on a definite syntactic theory yielding specific structural forms.

At this point, prior to the analysis of any natural-language constructions beyond conjunction and negation, choice of syntactic theory is largely indeterminate for us. As it turns out, however, the syntactic theory that appears to fit best with the semantic theory developed here is the "principles and parameters" theory elaborated by Chomsky and numerous associates over the last decade.[13] This theory involves a variety of components and assumptions. Below we sketch some basic syntactic notions, spelling out further elements as they are needed in subsequent chapters. These remarks are intended only to supply a broad picture of the main principles by which syntactic structures are licensed and transformed. (Readers familiar with modern syntactic theory may skip to section 3.3.3.)

3.3.1   Structural Descriptions

One of the central goals of all modern syntactic theory is to characterize the **structural descriptions** (SDs) of a language *L*. The latter encode various properties of the expressions of *L*, including syntactic and phonological properties. Structural descriptions are standardly represented by **phrase markers** or **constituent-structure diagrams**, of which (56) is a simple example:[14]

(56)

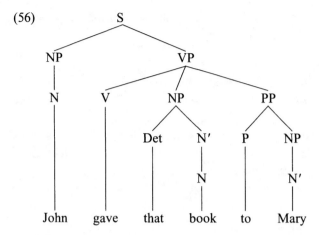

Representations like these encode three different kinds of information about a given expression *E*:

- The relative hierarchical arrangement of its subparts (if any)
- The linear ordering of its subparts (if any)
- The syntactic category or part of speech of *E* and its subparts

Thus (56) represents the sentence *John gave that book to Mary* as containing the discrete subgroupings of words *that book* and *to Mary*, which in turn are contained within a hierarchically larger subgrouping of the sentence *gave that book to Mary*, and so on. This articulation into parts is the **constituent structure** of S according to (56). Through left-right order, (56) also encodes the fact that in the sentence *John gave that book to Mary*, *John* precedes *gave*, which in turn precedes *that*, which in turn precedes *book*, etc. Finally, (56) expresses the claim that *John* is a lexical noun (N) contained within a larger noun phrase (NP); that *book* is a noun contained within a nominal category (N′), which in turn is part of a larger noun phrase along with the determiner (Det) *that*; that *to* is a preposition (P) combining with a noun phrase containing the noun *Mary* to form a prepositional phrase (PP); and so on.

Formally speaking, a phrase marker is a labeled tree in the sense of graph theory. That is, it is a collection of points or **nodes** that have relations of **dominance** and **precedence** defined over them, that have a unique root node, and that are of finite depth.[15] The nodes in (56) are the points labeled with syntactic categories or words, like "S", "NP", "V", *book*, *Mary*, etc. These nodes are connected to each other by lines or **branches** leading upward or downward.

The dominance relation in a phrase marker is read off its structure of branches and through the vertical orientation of the tree. Thus we say that a node X dominates another node Y in a phrase marker if there is a path of branches leading downward in the tree from X to Y. So, for example, the node labeled "S" (henceforth the S node) dominates every other node in (56), since it is possible to find a downward path of branches beginning at S and ending at any other node in (56). (The node that has this property in a phrase marker is said to be its **root node**.) By contrast, the node PP does not dominate the node V in (56), since it is not possible to find a downward path of branches from PP to V in the tree. Nodes that dominate other nodes (i.e., that are connected to other nodes by downward branches) are called **nonterminal nodes**. Nodes that dominate no other nodes are **terminal nodes**. In (56) and other phrase markers, the terminal nodes are labeled with words or morphemes such as *John, give, that, book*, etc.

Phrase markers allow us to capture a variety of relations between the parts of an expression. We have already made reference to some of these relations in an informal way. For example, strong compositionality constrains the amount of structure analyzed by a semantic rule to a node and its immediate daughters. We can define the notions of daughter and immediate daughter more precisely as follows:

Definition   A node α is a **daughter** of a node β in phrase marker P just in case β dominates α in P.

Definition   A node α is an **immediate daughter** of β in phrase marker P just in case α is a daughter of β in P and there is no node $\gamma \neq \alpha$ such that α is a daughter of γ and γ is a daughter of β.

We can also define the the notion of a constituent of a given expression E:

Definition   Let P be a phrase marker and $\alpha_1 \alpha_2 \ldots \alpha_k$ a string of terminal nodes of P. If there is a node of P that dominates all and only the terminal nodes $\alpha_1, \alpha_2, \ldots, \alpha_k$, then $\alpha_1, \alpha_2, \ldots, \alpha_k$ is a **constituent** of P. If the node in question is labeled with category X, then $\alpha_1 \alpha_2 \ldots \alpha_k$ is a **constituent** of P of category X.

Thus in (56), *that book* is a constituent of category NP, since there is a node labeled NP that exhaustively dominates the string *that book*. Similarly, *gave that book to Mary* is a constituent of category VP, and *to Mary* is a constituent of category PP. And so on.

3.3.2 Licensing Phrase Markers

In early versions of transformational grammar, phrase markers like (56) were assumed to be produced by a set of (context-free) rewrite rules like those in (57) or those discussed in connection with PC and PC':

(57) a. S → NP VP
     b. NP → N
     c. NP → Det N'
     d. N' → N
     e. VP → V NP PP
     f. PP → P NP
     g. N → {*John, Mary, book, fish,* ...}
     h. V → {*give, send, kiss, arrive,* ...}
     i. P → {*to, from, on, in,* ...}
     j. Det → {*that, the, every,* ...}

Such rules are understood as allowing one to rewrite a given single symbol, such as "NP," as a string of symbols, such as "Det N'." The rewriting is assumed to start from the initial symbol "S." Thus (57a) allows us to rewrite S as the string "NP VP." Using (57e), we can rewrite the "VP" symbol in the new string as "V NP PP." Using (57f), we can rewrite the "PP" symbol as the string of symbols "P NP." Ultimately this process terminates in a string of words that is a sentence:

(58) a. S
     b. NP VP
     c. NP V NP PP
     d. NP V NP P NP
     e. NP V NP P N
     f. NP V NP P Mary
     g. NP V NP to Mary
     ⋮
     q. John gave that book to Mary

Given phrase-structure rules, a phrase marker like (56) may be seen as showing the derivation of the sentence *John gave that book to Mary* from the rewrite rules in (57), with the lines of the tree diagram indicating how various categories have been rewritten in the course of the derivation.

Within more modern versions of transformational grammar, such as the "principles and parameters" theory, phrase markers still play a central role, though their formal licensing is recast. Trees like (56) are no longer viewed as being produced by a distinct set of phrase-structure rules. Rather, they are seen as licensed by very general syntactic principles organized into a number of distinct modules. These modularized principles interact with the properties of specific lexical items to yield full structural descriptions. We can illustrate this idea with the example *John gave that book to Mary*, considering three modules: *X*-bar theory, θ-theory, and case theory.

X-Bar Theory

X-bar theory is responsible for the overall organization of sentences into hierarchically arranged words and phrases. The theory does this by specifying a set of general structural templates that fix the possible phrasal forms available in a given natural language. For a phrase marker P to be a licit structural description, all sub-phrase-markers of P must match one of the licit templates. To illustrate, (59a–c) are potential templates of this kind, where parentheses around an item indicate that it is optionally present:

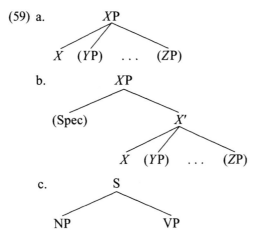

The template in (59a) admits any structure consisting of a phrasal node XP that dominates a lexical node X of matching category together with a number of additional phrasal nodes YP, ..., ZP. In this configuration, X is traditionally referred to as the **head** (or center) of the phrase XP, and YP, ..., ZP are referred to as the **complements** of *X*. The template in (59b) admits any structure consisting of a phrasal node *X*P that dominates a node *X'* (or $\bar{X}$) of matching category, which in turn dominates a matching head *X*. *X'* may optionally have a sister specifier node accompanying it (Spec), and *X* may optionally have a number of complements. Finally, the template in (59c) groups a subject phrase and a predicate phrase. This template is rather different from the previous two in that the mother node S does not dominate an expression of like category but rather dominates two nodes (NP and VP) that are categorially distinct from it and from each other. Phrases that have this property are called **exocentric**: they lack a center or head. By contrast, phrases of the form in (59a, b) are called **endocentric**: they contain a center or head.

The phrase marker (56) exemplifies all of these templates. Thus the subject in (56) instantiates (59a). In this case, *X* is *N*, and *X* has no phrasal complements, (60a). The prepositional phrase and the verb phrase also instantiate (59a); here *X* is P or V (respectively), and *X* takes one or two phrasal complements, (60b, c):·

(60) a.   NP   b.   VP   c.   PP

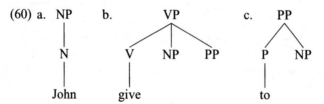

The direct object of (56) exemplifies (59b). Here *X* is N, Det is the specifier phrase, and there are no complements of N:

(61)   NP

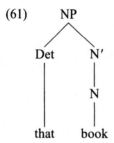

Finally, the S node of (56) exemplifies the configuration in (59c). The three templates in (59) thus jointly license all of the hierarchical organization in (56) in the sense that each node in this phrase marker is an instance of one of the three template schemes.

Theta-Theory

X-bar theory determines the general hierarchical form of (56); however, the co-occurrence of the specific phrases in this tree follows from particular facts about the lexical verb *give* interacting with principles from another module of grammar: that of θ-theory. Informally speaking, the verb *give* describes an action involving three essential participants: a giver, an object given, and a recipient. In logical terminology, this idea is expressed by saying that *give* takes three **arguments**; i.e., it corresponds to a ternary relation give(x, y, z). In grammatical terminology, the idea is expressed by saying that *give* assigns three **thematic roles**: an agent, a theme, and a goal (respectively).[16] The two NPs and the PP present in (56) serve as arguments of *give* or, alternatively, bear the thematic roles that *give* assigns. Theta-theory is concerned with the assignment of thematic roles in phrase markers. A central principle of this module, called the θ-criterion, is the following:

Theta-criterion   Every phrase appearing in subject or complement position must bear a thematic role, and every thematic role determined by a phrase must be assigned to a subject or complement phrase.

The θ-criterion insures that if an expression α assigns n thematic roles, then n expressions must co-occur in the phrase marker with α (whether overtly or covertly) to bear those roles. Furthermore, there can be no extraneous phrases in grammatical representation. This principle explains the unacceptability of (62a), which lacks an argument expression to bear the theme role, and it accounts for the unacceptability of (62b) which contains more argument expressions than *give* has roles to assign:[17]

(62) a. *John gave to Mary.
      b. *John gave that book to Mary Peter.

Similar points apply to other verbs that assign a different number of roles (for example, *fall* or *kick*); these require a correspondingly different number of accompanying argument phrases in the phrase marker.

The particular roles borne by the subject, direct object, and prepositional-phrase object in (56) are not accounted for by the θ-criterion and indeed appear to derive from a combination of principles, both general and lexically specific. For example, it seems to be a general principle relating role to structure that the thematic role of agent is never assigned internally to the verb phrase (VP). From this it follows that *John* must denote the agent in (56) since the subject is the only phrase external to VP. By contrast, it is a specific fact about the lexical items *give* and *to* that they both assign the thematic role of goal. From this it follows that the PP object (*Mary*) in (56) must denote the goal and, by process of elimination, that the direct object (*a book*) must denote the theme, the remaining thematic roles assigned by *give*.

Case Theory

Even with the hierarchical organization of a phrase marker determined by X-bar theory and the co-occurence of phrases determined by θ-theory, this still leaves some aspects of (56) unaccounted for. For instance, nothing said so far explains why the basic order of complements in this example (and in English generally) should be direct object, PP (*that book to Mary*) versus PP, direct object (*to Mary that book*). This fact is explained by case theory, the final module relevant to (56).

As is familiar from traditional grammar, verbs and prepositions typically govern a **case inflection** on argument nominals (NPs). This case inflection appears as explicit marking in highly inflected languages like Latin and Kannada. For example, the Latin sentence in (63) shows nominative (NOM), accusative (ACC), and ablative (ABL) case forms; the Kannada example in (64) shows nominative (NOM), accusative (ACC), locative (LOC), genitive/possessive (GEN), dative (DAT), and instrumental/ablative (INSTR) case marking:[18]

(63) Caesar   exercit-um   in hibern-i:s   con-lav-it.
     Caesar-NOM army-MASC.ACC.SING in winter-NEUT.ABL.PL put-PST-3SING
     'Caesar put the army in winter quarters'

(64) So:manu   santiyannu no:dalu do:niyalli nadiyannu da:ti
     Soma-NOM Shanti-ACC see-INFIN boat-LOC river-ACC cross-PST PART

     ma:vana   manege   ho:daru: durdaivadinda   avalu
     father-in-law-GEN house-DAT go-PST-CONCESS misfortune-INSTR she

     iralilla.
     be-PST-NEG

     'Although Soma crossed the river in a boat and went to his father-in-law's house to see Shanti, unfortunately, she wasn't there.'

In the principles and parameters theory, the notion of case is generalized and assumed to be present in all natural languages. Languages like Latin and

Kannada are assumed to realize this case by explicit marking, whereas other languages, such as English and Chinese, leave underlying case largely unexpressed. All lexically overt noun phrases in all languages are required to bear case marking, whether overtly expressed or not, under the so-called case filter, a principle in the module of case theory:

Case filter   If α is a noun phrase and α is phonetically nonnull, then α must be assigned case.

Again following traditional grammar, case is assumed to be assigned by a limited class of elements under rather strict conditions:

Case assignment   Case is assigned only by nonnominal elements (i.e., verbs and prepositions) to NPs that are structural sisters of the case assigner and are immediately adjacent to the case assigner.[19]

These conditions are responsible for the ordering of complements in *John gave that book to Mary*. *A book* constitutes a (phonetically nonnull) noun phrase, and so must bear case under the case filter. By contrast, *to Mary* is a PP and doesn't require case. Under the order of complements in (56), *that book* occurs adjacently and as a sister to the case-assigning verbal element *gave*. Under an alternative ordering of complements in which *to Mary* was positioned closest to the verb and *that book* at the end of the VP, the NP would fail to be adjacent to the verb, and so fail to receive case, contrary to what is required by the case filter. Nominal complements must therefore occur adjacent to the verb and before prepositional complements as a consequence of case theory.

3.3.3   Levels of Representation

Phrase markers represent a considerable amount of syntactic information. Nonetheless, an important assumption of modern syntactic theory has been that the structure of natural-language expressions is not adequately captured by one phrase marker alone. Rather a set of phrase markers is required. On this view, a given expression has a number of different representations at a number of different syntactic levels. These levels are distinct but are related one to another through a special kind of grammatical rule called a **transformation**.

The principles and parameters theory associates four different levels of syntactic representation with each linguistic form: a D-structure representation (DS; "D" stands for "deep"), an S-structure representation (SS; "S" stands for "surface"), a phonological form (PF), and a logical form (LF). These representations are related together by a single very general operation, "move α," in the way shown in (65):

(65)

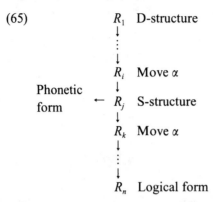

Thus a given expression E will have an initial D-structure representation R_1 expressing the thematic properties of the lexical items of E under the constraints of X-bar theory. In the D-structure, all arguments of predicates of E are realized, and realized in the canonical positions for their roles; furthermore, all structures conform to X-bar templates. This initial representation R_1 is then mapped to a series of additional representations $R_2, \ldots, R_i, R_j, R_k, \ldots, R_n$ by successive application of the rule move α. The final member of this sequence is the level of logical form. At some point in this derivational history, one member R_j of the sequence $(R_1, \ldots, R_n)$ is mapped to the phonetic form, and hence is phonologically realized. By convention, this representation constitutes the level of S-structure.

We may illustrate this picture concretely with the example (66). The latter is an interrogative variant of (56), containing the **wh- word** (or **question word**) *what* in initial position:

(66) What did [$_S$ John give to each girl]?

We noted above that the verb *give* is ditransitive, assigning three thematic roles: agent, theme, and goal. According to the θ-criterion, then, *give* requires the presence of three argument phrases to bear these roles. Now in the bracketed sentential portion of (66), no theme element appears as a counterpart to *that book* in (56). Superficially, then, (66) appears to be a counterexample to this principle. Intuitively, however, the bearer of the theme role is present: the question word *what* is associated with this role. Answers to (66), such as (56), involve removal of the question word and substitution of a theme argument. The central difference between (66) and (56) is thus that the theme element appears displaced in the former.

The relation between (56) and (66) is captured by assigning this sentence a D-structure and an S-structure related by movement. The D-structure for (66) captures the relation between the question word and the theme role straightforwardly. The *what* is taken to underlyingly occupy the object position, as shown below:

(67)

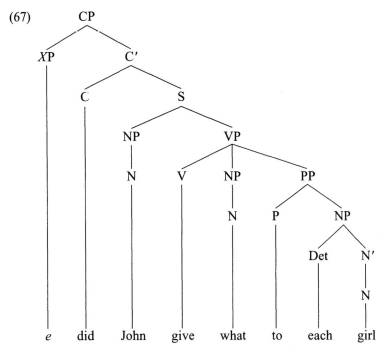

As usual, all parts of this phrase marker are licensed by the templates specified by *X*-bar theory. Furthermore, *what* inhabits the position of *that book* in (56), so providing a bearer for the theme role, as required by θ-theory. This representation thus expresses the implicit thematic relations in a direct way, with role-bearing elements all in their canonical positions.

The S-structure for this sentence, corresponding to the audible order of constituents, is derived by applying move α to relevant phrases, displacing them from their DS positions. Note that the sentential portion of (66) is taken to occur within a larger clausal phrase (CP), containing an empty specifier posi-tion *X*P. This empty position is the landing site for movement. The interroga-tive noun phrase *what* is displaced from object position to the CP specifier position. Movement leaves a structural residue or **trace** (*t*) in the site from which movement takes place. The relation between the moved item and its trace is indicated by subscript coindexing:

(68)

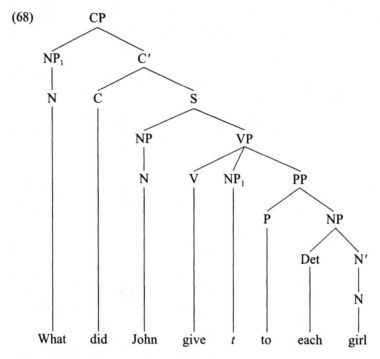

The analysis of (66) in terms of the D-structure in (67), the S-structure in (68), and the movement operation thus maps the intuitive thematic relations in the sentence to the audible arrangement of its parts. There is a representation of the thematic relations (D-structure), a representation of the audible arrange-ment of parts (S-structure), and a rule expressing their relation.

The phrase marker in (68) is not the final representation for (66). An additional movement takes place in deriving the LF for this example. Note that (66) differs from (56) not only in containing a question word in place of the demonstrative *that book* but also in containing the quantified phrase *each girl* in place of the name *Mary*. For reasons we will discuss later, quantifier phrases are viewed as analogous to question words in undergoing movement. Thus (68) is viewed as mapping to a further representation in which the quantified noun phrase moves out and occupies a structurally superior position. This movement is rather different in character than the movement encountered in (68). The movement in (68) involves **substitution** of a phrase for a vacant space. By contrast, the movement of quantifiers involves **adjunction** of the moved element to a containing phrase. In our example sentence, *each girl* moves out of prepositional-object position and attaches itself as a sister to its containing S. A copy of S is then built above it and its sister as a mother node. As usual, this movement leaves a coindexed trace (t) in the premovement site:

(69)

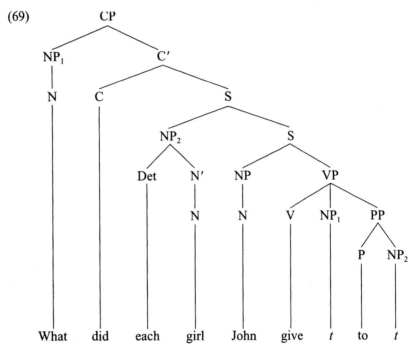

The representation in (69) is the logical form for *What did John give to each girl?*

The movements of quantifiers and question words differ not only in the matter of substitution versus adjunction but also in another significant respect. Note that the *wh-* phrase is heard in its postmovement site (clause-initial position), whereas the quantified phrase is heard in its premovement site (direct-object position). In the principles and parameters theory this difference is accounted for by the mapping of levels in the diagram in (65). Observe that since S-structure is the level that is phonologically interpreted (i.e., mapped to the phonetic form), levels of representation lying before this point (D-structure) or after this point (logical form) will be phonologically unrealized. English question movement is assumed to take place in the mapping between D-structure and S-structure, whereas quantifier movement takes place in the mapping between S-structure and logical form.[20] Accordingly, with question movement, S-structure represents the postmovement structure; hence it is the postmovement position of the *wh-* phrase that is audible. By contrast, with quantifier movement, S-structure represents the premovement structure; hence it is the premovement position of the quantifier phrase that is audible.

The Syntax-Semantics Interface

The existence of multiple levels of representation in the principles and parameters theory raises an important issue for the hypothesis that syntax and semantics converge. Since expressions are associated with a family of syntactic representations, it clearly makes no sense to speak of *the* syntactic form of a phrase aligning with its semantic form. The hypothesis is not well defined until we say *which* level of syntactic structure matches the semantic form. Just as the mapping to phonological interpretation might potentially take place at several different points in the derivation of an expression, so might the mapping to semantic interpretation.

As with the choice of syntactic theory, choice of level for semantic interpretation is largely indeterminate at this point. We will see later on, however, that there are strong reasons for taking the final level of syntactic representation, logical form, as the point of interface with semantics. A key motivation for this choice comes from sentences containing quantified phrases. As it turns out, structures like (69), in which a quantified phrase is displaced from its base position, leaving a trace at the original site, are well suited to be interpreted by simple, strongly compositional semantic rules. To interpret other, prior levels of structure requires a substantial increase in the scope and complexity of these rules.

Given these points, our proposal about the relation between syntactic and semantic structure comes down to the claim that the level of logical form is the interface between syntax and semantics. We will state this precisely in the form of the following LF hypothesis:

LF hypothesis   The level of logical form is where syntactic representation is interpreted by semantic rules.

In view of earlier discussion, it's clear that adoption of the LF hypothesis has strong consequences for semantic theory. Indeed, it implies that the truth conditions and the logical form for a given construction should be worked out in tandem. Since logical form is a level of syntactic representation, its structure is governed by, and must satisfy, the principles licensing grammatical representations generally. Accordingly, any structure proposed for a construction on the basis of semantic considerations must also be licensed by syntactic principles: it must obey X-bar theory, satisfy relevant constraints from case theory and θ-theory, derive by move α from a licit S-structure, and so on. Likewise, since logical form is a representation of semantic structure in the sense of being the form to which semantic rules apply, it must be suitable for compositional interpretation: it must provide an articulation of constituents allowing the truth-relevant contribution of the whole to be calculated from the truth-relevant contributions of its parts. The syntactician's task and the semanticist's task are closely intertwined at this level.

3.4   Concluding Methodological Remarks

The assumption that syntax and semantics converge, together with constraints on the formulation of semantic rules, provide a general framework for the task of constructing a concrete semantic theory for a range of natural-language constructions. Let us consider some points of this framework as we look to the task ahead.

3.4.1   Combining Syntax and Semantics

A guiding assumption for us will be the LF hypothesis, which identifies logical form as the level over which semantic rules are defined. This assumption allows us to proceed in either of two ways in exploring the interpretation of a given construction C. On the one hand, we may simply accept the logical form for C delivered by syntactic theory and attempt to give a compositional T theory for it. Our task would be to find appropriate axioms and interpretation rules that take the given structure as input. Alternatively, we can consider the construction independently, looking at the semantic grounds for structure assignment. Here our task is to show how making sense of someone's speech entails a certain structure for their utterances. As a matter of practice, the former is often somewhat easier, but as semanticists, we remain responsible for the latter. We are responsible for eliciting and making clear the semantic foundation of structure assignment.

In the chapters to follow, we will typically pursue both approaches, working with structures given by syntactic theory and exploring the independent semantic composition of the form. Thus in studying predication, we will first consider basic structures consisting of verbs (*agrees*) and proper names (*Chris*) (70a), and how to give a T theory that assigns them appropriate T sentences. We will also see how, in order to systematically account for the truth conditions of sentences like these, it is natural to divide the sentence semantically into object-designating terms (names) and condition-introducing terms (predicates) (70b).

(70) a.

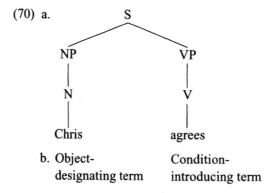

       b. Object-   Condition-
          designating term   introducing term

Thus we see not only that a T theory can be built around trees of this shape but also that the semantic task independently suggests them.

Similarly, in exploring the semantics of quantification, we will introduce structures like (71a) and see how to give an appropriate T theory for them, following proposals by Tarksi. We will then observe semantic grounds for dividing quantifications into three basic parts: a quantity expression, a restriction, and a scope (71b). In so doing, we will see that the syntactically motivated parse and the semantically motivated division of terms fit together.

(71) a.

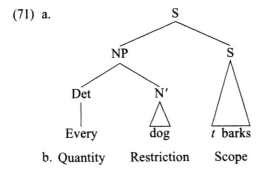

      b. Quantity   Restriction   Scope

By pursuing the interpretation of constructions from both of these perspectives, the relation between syntactic structure and semantic structure becomes clearer, as does the remarkable strength of the convergence hypothesis.

3.4.2 Analyzing Fragments of Natural Language

Since various constructions can occur in a single sentence of natural language, we clearly need our semantic rules to interact with each other in appropriate ways. We cannot, for example, accept rules yielding correct results for simple predications but wrong results for predications containing modifiers. Semantic theory must form a system. To insure that our theorizing is systematic in this way, we will follow the strategy of giving theories that analyze progressively larger and more inclusive portions or fragments of natural language.

At this point we have the theory PC analyzing that fragment of English that contains the three elementary sentences *Chris agrees, Phil ponders, Jill knows Kate* and all complex sentences that can be derived from them using negation or the conjunctions *and* and *or*. Our strategy will be to expand the scope of this theory, always retaining the coverage of previous, less-inclusive fragments. Since all rules will be part of a single theory, we will be compelled to attend to their interactions. In this way we integrate present and past results and do not lose our grasp on constructions as our investigation widens.

The format of these theories will follow that of PC. In each case we will presuppose some set of phrase markers provided by syntactic theory. We then give **lexical axioms** for the terminal elements, **phrasal axioms** for the nonterminal configurations, and **production rules** to derive appropriate interpretive T sentences. These axioms and rules provide a fully explicit statement of what precisely we are hypothesized to know when we know the semantics of a language. In general, we will also provide a number of explicit derivations of T theorems for the theory to show that it yields the desired results. T sentence derivations constitute, in effect, a check of correctness for the axioms and production rules proposed.

In proceeding, we will build on the results we have obtained with conjunction and PC. One way of framing this process is as one of working our way down through successively finer levels of structure in the clause. Thus consider sentence (72) and its logical form in figure 3.2.

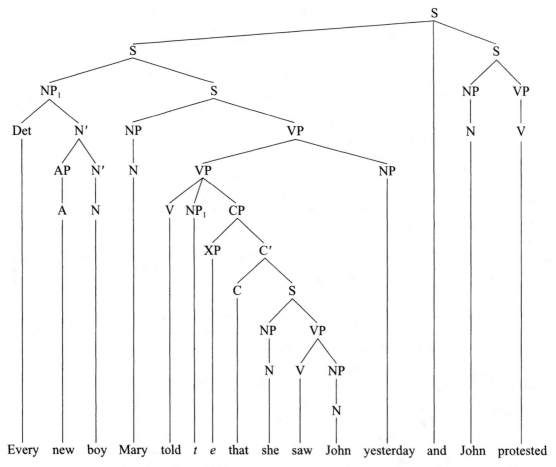

Figure 3.2 The logical form for *Mary told every new boy that she saw John yesterday, and John protested.*

(72) Mary told every new boy that she saw John yesterday, and John
    protested.

At this point we have some grasp on the rules that would take us from the
highest S node to its immediate daughter sentences: we know that the former
is true if and only if the latter are both true. Beyond this, however, the sentence is entirely opaque. We have no rules to take us down the simple right-
hand S to its terminal nodes, to say nothing of rules allowing us to move
down the far more complex left-hand branch. The task before us in part is to
discover the rules necessary to interpret sentences of whatever complexity. We
must articulate and justify the semantic contributions of each of the parts in
these structures. And we must give rules for combining them appropriately. As
discussed earlier, the rules in question must respect relevant constraints on the
syntax-semantics interface, specifically, strong compositionality. This entails
that we must have rules assigning interpretations to each of the many local
mother-daughter configurations in figure 3.2.

In the literature, syntactic forms are often classified in terms of the **semantic
constructions** they are taken to exemplify. The phrase marker in figure 3.2
provides a variety of illustrations. Elementary forms like (73a, b), for instance,
are traditionally described as **predications**. At their simplest, they involve a
predicate term ([$_{VP}$ protested], [$_{VP}$ saw John]) and some sequence of **referring
terms** ([$_{NP}$ John], [$_{NP}$ she]) functioning as their arguments:

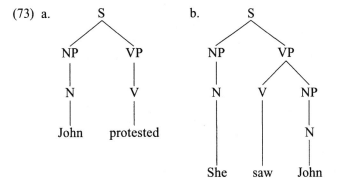

Structures like (74) are traditionally called **quantifications**. As we remarked,
their syntactic form involves a quantified expression ([$_{NP}$ every boy]) adjoined
to some phrase XP containing the coindexed trace (t) of the former:

(74)

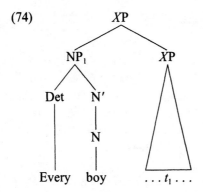

The relation between a trace and the phrase with which it is coindexed (75a) is often viewed as analogous to the relation between a pronoun and its antecedent (75b). Both are said to be **anaphoric constructions**.

(75) a.   b.

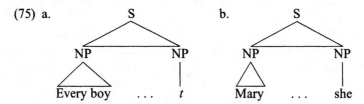

Structures like (76a, b) are called **clausal-complement constructions** or **propositional-attitude constructions**. They typically involve a verb and a sentential complement, where the former is associated with some form of utterance event or mental attitude ($[_V$ tell] or $[_V$ believe]) and where the latter gives the content of this utterance or mental attitude ($[_{CP}$ that ...]).

(76) a.   b.

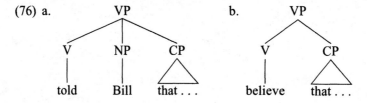

Finally, structures like (77a, b) exemplify what is termed **modification**. They involve a modifying expression ($[_{AP}$ new] or $[_{NP}$ yesterday]) adjoined to the phrase they modify ($[_{N'}$ boy] and $[_{VP}$ told ...]):

(77) a.

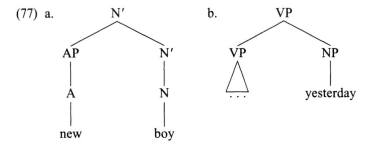

In the next chapters of this book we will proceed by semantic construction. We begin by exploring the analysis of predicates and referring terms in chapters 4 through 6. We then move on to quantification structures and the analysis of individual quantifier expressions and their properties in chapters 7 and 8. A certain class of expressions, standardly referred to as descriptions, turn out to exhibit properties reminiscent of both referring terms and quantifiers; hence we pause in chapter 9 to examine their status and analysis. We then proceed to examine anaphoric relations in chapter 10, clausal-complement constructions in chapter 11, and adverbial-modification structures in chapter 12.

Theory and Exercises

The Theory PC′ (An Alternative Propositional Calculus)

Lexical Axioms

(1) a. Val(t, *Phil ponders*) iff Phil ponders
   b. Val(t, *Chris agrees*) iff Chris agrees
   c. Val(t, *Jill knows Kate*) iff Jill knows Kate
   d. Val($\langle z, z' \rangle$, *and*) iff $z = t$ and $z' = t$
   e. Val($\langle z, z' \rangle$, *or*) iff $z = t$ or $z' = t$
   f. Val(z, *it is not the case that*) iff it is not the case that $z = t$

Phrasal Axioms

(2) a. Val(t, [$_S$ S ConjP]) iff for some z, Val(z, S) and Val(z, ConjP)
   b. Val(z, [$_{ConjP}$ Conj S]) iff for some z', Val($\langle z, z' \rangle$, Conj) and Val(z', S)
   c. Val(t, [$_S$ Neg S]) iff for some z, Val(z, Neg) and Val(z, S)

   d. Val($\langle z, z' \rangle$, [$_{Conj}$ α]) iff Val($\langle z, z' \rangle$, α) (for any conjunction α)

   e. Val(z, [$_{Neg}$ α]) iff Val(z, α) (for any negation α)

   f. Val(t, [$_S$ α]) iff Val(t, α) (for any elementary sentence α)

Production Rules

(UI)   Universal instantiation

      For any S, $F(S)$

      ―――――――――

      $F(\alpha)$

(SE)   Substitution of equivalents

      $F(\alpha)$

      α iff β

      ―――――――――

      $F(\beta)$

(CJ)   Conjunction

      ϕ iff for some x, y, Val(x, S_1), Val(y, S_2), and $x =$ t and $y =$ t

      ―――――――――――――――――――――――――――――――――――――

      ϕ iff both Val(t, S_1) and Val(t, S_2)

(DJ)   Disjunction

      ϕ iff for some x, y, Val(x, S_1), Val(y, S_2), and $x =$ t or $y =$ t

      ―――――――――――――――――――――――――――――――――――――

      ϕ iff either Val(t, S_1) or Val(t, S_2)

(Neg) Negation

      ϕ iff for some z, it is not the case that $z =$ t, and Val(z, S)

      ―――――――――――――――――――――――――――――――――――――

      ϕ iff it is not the case that Val(t, S)

Exercises

1. Give full T-sentence derivations for each of the following sentences of PC'.

   (1) It is not the case that Chris agrees.

   (2) Chris agrees and Phil ponders.

   (3) It is not the case that Jill knows Kate, or Chris agrees.

There are two possible structures for this last example. Use the one in which *it is not the case that* and *Jill knows Kate* form a constituent.

2. What must be added to the theory PC′ so that it will yield appropriate T sentences for the following?

    (1) Junko eats pizza, and Chris agrees.

    (2) It is the case that Kumiko ponders.

    (3) Chris agrees, although Jill protests.

3. In an earlier exercise, we extended PC to include the connectives *if*, *only if*, and *if and only if* (abbreviated *iff*). Do the same for PC′. That is,

    ▪ give syntactic structures introducing *if*, *only if*, and *iff*, and

    ▪ extend the semantic rules of PC′ so that sentences containing these connectives are interpreted appropriately.

   Check the correctness of your extension by showing that it assigns appropriate T sentences to the following examples:

    (1) Phil ponders only if Jill knows Kate.

    (2) Chris agrees if it is not the case that Phil ponders if and only if Chris agrees.

   Be sure to give a full derivation, with each step justified by your T theory.

4. Suppose that the structures for conjunctions are as shown in (1):

    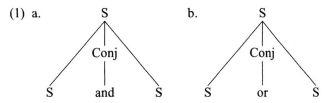

    ▪ Give a set of semantic axioms and production rules that interpret these structures and assign appropriate T sentences.

    ▪ Check your results by showing how they apply to (2) and (3):

    (2) Phil ponders or Chris agrees.

    (3) Jill knows Kate, and Phil ponders.

5. The form *if and only if* looks suspiciously like a conjunction of *if* and *only if*. That is, it appears to have composite internal structure. Consider (1):

(1)

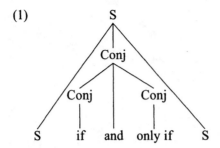

Show that it is possible to make sense of this structure semantically. More precisely, do the following:

a. Assume we have a structure of the form $[_{Conj}$ Conj$_1$ *and* Conj$_2]$. Give the axiom that we must add to the T theory to interpret this structure appropriately.

b. Show that your rule is correct by exhibiting the T sentence you generate for *Phil ponders if and only if Chris agrees.*

c. The fragment PC′, augmented with your rule in (a), would be peculiar in its treatment of conjunction. In what way is it peculiar? This peculiarity suggests further modifications of the structures for conjunction and *if and only if.* What modifications? What question does this now raise for the semantics?

4   Verbs and Predication

The fragment PC provides a compositional semantic analysis of complex sentences like *Chris agrees and Phil ponders* and *It is not the case that Jill knows Kate*. It provides no such analysis, however, of their constituent Ss: *Chris agrees*, *Phil ponders*, and *Jill knows Kate*. The latter are treated essentially as words in PC: they are given individual semantic axioms and assigned no internal structure. This represents a vast oversimplification, of course. Sentences without connectives are neither learned nor understood as unstructured blocks. Our grasp of them too is compositional and is based on a grasp of more elementary semantic constituents. A theory of semantic knowledge must identify these constituents, assign a semantic contribution to them, and state the semantic significance of their combination.

4.1   The Structure and Interpretation of Elementary Clauses

Basic sentences like *Chris agrees* and *Jill knows Kate* are widely taken to possess a syntactic structure wherein their words are divided into nouns (N) and verbs (V) and grouped into noun phrases (NP) and verb phrases (VP):

(1) a.

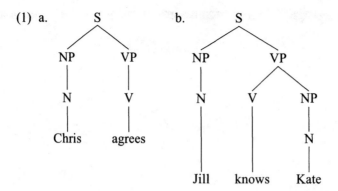

Separation of words into Ns and Vs is supported by data about inflectional form. For example, words like *ponder, know,* and *agree* inflect for tense (*Chris agreed/agrees, Chris will agree*) and have participial forms (*Chris has agreed, Chris is agreeing*), whereas words like *Kate* and *Chris* do not. Likewise, words like *Kate, Phil, Chris,* and *Jill* are intersubstitutable, preserving well-formedness (2a–c), and words like *agree, ponder, know,* and *admire* can be intersubstituted as well (2d–f).

(2) a. Phil agrees.   d. Chris ponders.
    b. Jill agrees.   e. Chris laughs.
    c. Kate agrees.   f. Chris protests.

Substitution across these classes is forbidden, however:

(3) a. *Phil Kate.
    b. *Agrees agrees.

Again, this is evidence for two distinct classes.

   The division of S into NP VP corresponds to the traditional division of the clause into a subject phase and a predicate phrase, the latter containing the verb and its complements (including objects). Again, there is substantial empirical evidence for this division. It is widely held that only syntactic constituents can be dislocated, elided, replaced by a proform, or substituted for by a single form. The examples in (4) show that a verb and its object can appear in a sentence dislocated from their standard position, whereas this is not possible with a verb and its subject:

(4) a.   Jill said that she knows Kate, and [$_{VP}$ know Kate] she does ____.
         (Cf. And she does know Kate.)
    b. *Jill said that she knows Kate, and [she know] does Kate.

The examples in (5) show that a verb and its object can be elided in a sentence as a unit, whereas this is not possible with a verb and a subject:

(5) a. Jill said that she knows Kate, and she does ____.
    b. *Jill said that she knows Kate, and ____ does Kate.

The examples in (6) show that a verb and its object can be replaced by a single proform *so*, whereas there is no equivalent proform *glarf* that can substitute for a verb and its subject:

(6) a. Jill visited Kate, and Chris did *so* too.
    b. *Jill visited Kate, and *glarf* Chris.
        (Cf. Jill visited Kate, and *Jill visited* Chris.)

Finally, the examples in (7) show that a verb and its object can be substituted for a single intransitive verb while preserving well-formedness; however, no single element can be substituted for a verb and its subject:

(7) a. Chris *agrees.*
    b. Chris *knows Kate.*
    c. __?__ Kate.

All of these contrasts are explained directly if operations like movement, ellipsis, etc., are restricted to constituents and if the verb and its object form a predicate-phrase constituent (VP).

4.1.1 The Theory PC+

If we accept the structures in (1) as empirically sound, what kind of T theory will assign them appropriate semantic interpretations? On reflection, our task is similar to the one facing us in the last chapter with structures like (8a, b):

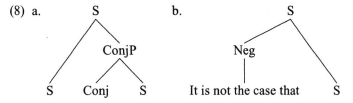

There we had to discover appropriate semantic contributions for sentences, conjunctions, conjunction phrases, and negations. Here we have to discover an appropriate contribution for sentences, verbs, verb phrases, and proper nouns.

With (8a, b) we adopted a Fregean analysis using semantic values. We understood the semantic contribution of each node in (8) in terms of some object assigned to the node. S nodes were assigned truth values, as were ConjPs and Negs and lexical negations. Conj nodes and lexical conjunctions were assigned pairs of truth values. We will adopt the same basic approach to (1), viewing Ss, VPs, NPs, Vs, etc., as taking certain objects as values and stating axioms in terms of them. However, in place of truth values, we will appeal to familiar, garden-variety objects like people, places, and things. The idea will be to express the truth conditions of sentences with proper nouns and verbs in terms of relations between such objects. The fragment of English that we will be dealing with contains all the sentences that can be constructed as in (1) from the four names *Jill, Chris, Phil*, and *Kate* and the three verbs *ponder, agree*, and *know*. In the background, we assume the analysis of conjunctions and negation from PC. We will call the resulting theory PC+ because it contains PC plus elementary predication structures.

We begin with axioms for the terminal nodes of PC+, the lexical items. Proper nouns like *Jill, Chris, Phil*, and *Kate* are analyzed as having persons as their semantic values, that is, as referring to those individuals:

(9) a. Val(x, *Jill*) iff x = Jill
    b. Val(x, *Chris*) iff x = Chris
    c. Val(x, *Phil*) iff x = Phil
    d. Val(x, *Kate*) iff x = Kate

Intransitive verbs like *agree* and *ponder* are also analyzed as having objects as their values, but intuitively they express certain general conditions that hold of those objects, for example, that they agree or ponder:

(10) a. Val(x, *ponders*) iff x ponders
     b. Val(x, *agrees*) iff x agrees

Finally, transitive verbs like *know* are analyzed as taking pairs of objects as their values. Intuitively, a transitive verb expresses a condition on a pair of individuals, here, that the first knows the second:

(11) Val($\langle x, y \rangle$, *knows*) iff x knows y

Next come the axioms for nonterminal nodes. The basic job of these rules is to relate semantic values together in such a way that the individuals designated by the nominals fall under the conditions expressed by the predicates. Take the axiom for [$_S$ NP VP] first:

(12) Val(t, [$_S$ NP VP]) iff for some x, Val(x, NP) and Val(x, VP)

We want a sentence like *Chris agrees* to be true just in case the individual identified by *Chris* meets the condition expressed by *agrees*. The correct result is obtained with (12). This says that a sentence S consisting of an NP and a VP is true if and only if there is some individual x that is a value of both NP and VP. Ultimately, x will be a value of the NP just in case x is identified by the noun (e.g., *Chris*), and x will be a value of the VP just in case x meets the condition expressed by the predicate (e.g., *agrees*).

The axiom for transitive VPs, (13), is similar to that for sentences.

(13) Val(x, [$_{VP}$ V NP]) iff for some y, Val($\langle x, y \rangle$, V) and Val(y, NP)

One simple way of understanding this rule is to view it as saying when an individual x meets a certain complex condition given by the verb phrase. According to (13), an individual x meets the condition expressed by a VP like *knows Kate* just in case there is some individual y such that the pair $\langle x, y \rangle$ is a value of *knows* and y is a value of *Kate*. That is, x is a value of *knows Kate* just in case x knows Kate.

There are also axioms for passing values between a mother node and a daughter node that it exhaustively dominates, for example, between an NP and a single daughter N, between a VP and a single daughter V, and between a lexical category node and a word it dominates. These may be stated with a series of rules like (14):

(14) a. Val(x, [$_{VP}$ V]) iff Val(x, V)
      b. Val(x, [$_V$ α]) iff Val(x, α) (where α is any lexical item)
      c. Val(x, [$_{NP}$ N]) iff Val(x, N)
      d. Val(x, [$_N$ α]) iff Val(x, α) (where α is any lexical item)

However, a more compact and general formulation can be given as in (15), where X ranges over nodes and Y ranges over nodes and lexical items:

(15) Val(x, [$_X$ Y]) iff Val(x, Y)

For brevity we will adopt (15).

Finally, as we saw in the discussion of truth values with PC′, we need a production rule to handle derivations involving objects. Our rule is substitution of identicals, (SI); this is like our rule (CJ) but is generalized here to apply to all kinds of objects x:

(SI) **Substitution of identicals**

$$\frac{\phi \text{ iff for some } x,\ F(x) \text{ and } x = \alpha}{\phi \text{ iff } F(\alpha)}$$

A Sample Derivation

We will illustrate the workings of PC+ by applying it to (1b) *Jill knows Kate.*
As usual, we start at the highest S node. Using (12) and (UI), we derive (16):

(16) Val(t, [$_S$ [$_{NP}$ [$_N$ Jill]] [$_{VP}$ [$_V$ knows] [$_{NP}$ [$_N$ Kate]]]]) iff for some x,
Val(x, [$_{NP}$ [$_N$ Jill]]) and Val(x, [$_{VP}$ [$_V$ knows] [$_{NP}$ [$_N$ Kate]]])

The semantic value of the subject NP unfolds as in (17a–e):

(17) a. Val(x, [$_{NP}$ [$_N$ Jill]]) iff Val(x, [$_N$ Jill]) (by (UI), (15))
b. Val(x, [$_N$ Jill]) iff Val(x, *Jill*) (by (UI), (15))
c. Val(x, *Jill*) iff x = Jill (9a)
d. Val(x, [$_N$ Jill]) iff x = Jill ((17b, c), (SE))
e. Val(x, [$_{NP}$ [$_N$ Jill]]) iff x = Jill ((17a, d), (SE))

The semantic value of the predicate VP spells out as in (18):

(18) Val(x, [$_{VP}$ [$_V$ knows] [$_{NP}$ [$_N$ Kate]]]) iff for some y,
Val($\langle x, y \rangle$, [$_V$ knows]) and Val(y, [$_{NP}$ [$_N$ Kate]]) (by (UI), (13))

The contribution of the verb is computed as in (19):

(19) a. Val($\langle x, y \rangle$, [$_V$ knows]) iff Val($\langle x, y \rangle$, *knows*) (by (UI), (15))
b. Val($\langle x, y \rangle$, *knows*) iff x knows y (11)
c. Val($\langle x, y \rangle$, [$_V$ knows]) iff x knows y (by (19a, b), (SE))

The contribution of the direct object NP is computed just like the subject:

(20) Val(y, [$_{NP}$ [$_N$ Kate]]) iff y = Kate (as in (17a–e))

Using (18), (19c), (20), and (SE), we derive (21a), and one application of (SI)
(where F is x *knows* y and α is *Kate*) then yields (21b):

(21) a. Val(x, [$_{VP}$ [$_V$ knows] [$_{NP}$ [$_N$ Kate]]])
iff for some y, x knows y and y = Kate
b. Val(x, [$_{VP}$ [$_V$ knows] [$_{NP}$ [$_N$ Kate]]]) iff x knows Kate

Using (16), (17e), (21b), and (SE), we derive (22a), and another application of (SI) (where *F* is *x knows Kate* and *α* is *Jill*) then gives us (22b):

(22) a. Val(t, [$_S$ [$_{NP}$ [$_N$ Jill]] [$_{VP}$ [$_V$ knows] [$_{NP}$ [$_N$ Kate]]]])
      iff for some *x*, *x* = Jill and *x* knows Kate
     b. Val(t, [$_S$ [$_{NP}$ [$_N$ Jill]] [$_{VP}$ [$_V$ knows] [$_{NP}$ [$_N$ Kate]]]]) iff Jill knows Kate

This last line is the desired result. No more rules can be applied, and the derivation ends.

PC+ represents a very small fragment of English; however, the theory is easily extended to accommodate additional classes of verbs and other predicates. We explore a wide variety of such extensions in the exercises to this chapter.

4.2   The Semantics of Predicates and Predication

Sentences like those analyzed in PC+ are often described as exhibiting two basic semantic relations: a relation of **naming** and a relation of **predication**. Certain expressions in the sentence are taken to **name**, **refer to**, or **designate** an object. Other expressions are taken to **describe**, **apply to**, or **be predicated of** those objects. The sentence is true just in case the object named **satisfies** the predicate or **falls under** the concept expressed by the predicate. The semantic categories of name and predicate are often taken to align with the syntactic categories of proper noun and verb as shown below:

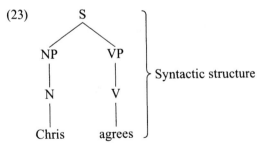

Let us set aside names for the next chapter and consider the notion of predicate and predication more closely. What are the properties that unite the semantic class of predicates and set it apart from other classes of expressions?

And what are the semantic properties that distinguish among the various categories of predicates, such as verbs, nouns, and adjectives?

4.2.1   Some Thought Experiments

The philosopher Gareth Evans (1975) has suggested an interesting set of thought experiments that shed light on the basic nature of predicates. Imagine yourself as an "astrolinguist" who has come upon a group of extraterrestrials, or as an animal-communications specialist who has encountered some hitherto unknown species of intelligent primates. These creatures have a vocal communication system. You are attempting to discover the significance of their utterances. There are two languages that you investigate in two different locales. We'll call them "language *A*" and "language *B*."

Language A

Language *A* contains a finite set of sentences or utterance types that are used to talk about various features of the local environment. In observing the utterances that speakers make and the local conditions that prevail when they make them, you jot down the correlations in (24) between simple expressions and utterance situations:

(24) Expression   Utterance situation
   a. *Rain!*   Uttered when it's raining nearby the speaker at the time of speech.
   b. *Rabbit!*   Uttered when a rabbit or rabbits are nearby the speaker at the time of speech.

Similarly for *Fog, Red, Warm, White, Hut*, etc.
   Suppose further that these expressions can be compounded, so that you also record the expressions and correlated situations shown in (25):

(25) Expression   Utterance situation
   a. *Warm hut!*   Uttered when there is warmth and a bit of a hut in the vicinity of the speaker, that is, when warmth and "hutness" overlap.
   b. *White rabbit!* Uttered when there is a bit of white rabbit stuff around the speaker, that is, when rabbithood and whiteness overlap.

And similarly for *White water, Warm rabbit*, etc. You discover that these latter, complex expressions are truly compounded and not learned one by one. Perhaps you learn this by observing patterns of acquisition or deficit of the kind discussed in chapter 2.

An important general fact you note about speakers' use of language *A* is that, although they have words like *rabbit* and *hut* that they apply when certain kinds of objects are present, they exhibit no sensitivity to the boundaries of these objects. So, for example, if any part of a nearby rabbit is white, they will assent to *White rabbit*. If a nearby rabbit is partly white and partly red, they will assent to both *White rabbit* and *Red rabbit*. If two or more nearby rabbits are white, they will assent to *White rabbit*. Nothing in their language appears to distinguish between a part of a rabbit being white, a whole rabbit being white, two rabbits being white, three rabbits being white, and so on.

Language B

The second exotic tongue, language *B*, has properties rather different than its counterpart's. Again in your capacity as explorer-linguist, you have the task of semantic analysis. In investigating, you discover that language *B* contains two fundamentally different kinds of expressions: type 1 and type 2. The first expression type is uttered when certain material objects such as men, rabbits, huts, etc., are in the vicinity. The second expression type is uttered when the environment shows certain general features, but this expression type does not require the presence of specific kinds of objects:

(26) Type	Expression	Utterance situation
1	Man	Uttered when men are nearby.
	Rabbit	Uttered when rabbits are nearby.
	Hut	Uttered when huts are nearby.
	⋮	⋮
2	White	Uttered when the local environment shows whiteness.
	Warm	Uttered when the local environment shows warmth.
	Furry	Uttered when the local environment shows furriness.
	⋮	⋮

These expressions can stand alone or can enter into compounds joining a type 2 expression with a type 1 expression. Thus you record *White rabbit*, *Warm hut*, etc.

In examining the use of compound expressions, you observe a significant fact that distinguishes this speech community from that of language *A*. For speakers of language *B* to assent to an expression like *White rabbit*, it is not enough simply for a white, rabbit-sized, rabbit-shaped bit of rabbit matter to be around. For example, suppose you arrange the white tails of a group of brown rabbits so that they combine to form a white rabbit shape. You ask language *B* speakers *White rabbit?* They shake their heads in disagreement. On further study, you find that what is required for assent to an expression like this is for the type 2 feature to be distributed over the type 1 objects in a certain way. Specifically, the type 2 feature must cover the boundaries of a single object whose presence would prompt assent to the type 1 expression. So, for example, to get speakers to assent to *White rabbit*, it is necessary that whiteness cover the boundaries of a single object that would prompt assent to *Rabbit*. To get agreement to *Warm hut*, it's necessary that warmth prevail within the volume of a single object that would prompt assent to *Hut*. And so on.

Hypothesizing Predicates

As the expedition linguist, how should you analyze the different significance of compound expressions in language *A* versus language *B*? One way you might tackle this is to reflect on whether (27) might be rendered along the lines of (28):

(27) Warm hut!

(28) Here is a warm hut!

The English sentence (28) contain expressions that we identify as predicates. What is a predicate? Well, consider the important difference between saying *This is warm* and saying *It's raining*. In the first case you can meaningfully ask, *What is warm?* But you can't meaningfully ask, *What's raining?* This is because *warm* can be used to describe objects: a rabbit or a hut can be warm, and one can use the word *warm* to express the fact. But *It's raining* merely reports on the presence of a general feature in the environment. Expressions of the latter sort are sometimes called **feature placers**. Expressions of the former sort, the ones that describe objects, are **predicates**.

Consider language *A* in this light. Given what you know about it, do you have evidence for predicates in the language? The answer is no. The term *red*, for example, applies when there is some red in the local environment. But it does not apply to objects and ascribe redness to them. Evans illustrates this point with the example of a quantity red ink dissolving in a pool of water. Speakers of language *A* might well assert *Red water*, but are they talking about some object that is water and also red? "Which object is it, even roughly, whose satisfaction of the predicate 'Red' makes the remark true? Is it the whole pool, or just the water immediately diluting the ink, or one of the indefinitely many intermediate alternatives? The language provides us with no way of answering these questions, to which we must somehow find an answer if the construction is predication" (Evans 1985, 32). What goes for water goes for rabbits. Just as there is no question of some watery object having to be red for the expression *Red water* to apply, so there is no question of any rabbitty object being white for the expression *White rabbit* to apply. So you have no evidence that the expressions of language *A* are genuine predicates. So far as the evidence shows, the expressions of *A* are merely feature placers that record the incidence and overlapping of features in the environment. The best you can really do in these circumstance is to interpret the expressions of language *A* along the lines of (29):

(29) a. Here warmth and hutness overlap!

b. Here redness and rabbithood are copresent!

Very well, then, what about language *B*? With language *B* the situation is quite different. For here it seems that to account for the significance that expressions have for speakers, you have to talk about expressions applying to objects. As we said, in the case of *White rabbit*, you have to talk about the feature of being white distributing itself over a single object that would prompt assent to *Rabbit*. Hence to capture the function of *white* when it combines with a type 1 expression, you have to say that it applies to an object just in case the object is white.

The contrast between languages *A* and *B* shows what kind of evidence would lead one to hypothesize predicates in a language. When we find expressions whose semantic contributions require us to distinguish features of objects, and hence objects themselves, we are dealing with predicates.

4.2.2 Generality and Object Independence

The thought experiments described above suggest that predicates are associated with conditions of application to objects. Each predicate is associated with a condition that an object may meet or fail to meet. If the object meets the condition, the predicate applies to the object. If not, it doesn't. This result accords naturally with the PC+ verb axioms:

(30) a. Val(x, *agrees*) iff x agrees
     b. Val($\langle x, y \rangle$, *knows*) iff x knows y

Semantic statements like these can be viewed as stating rules for determining when a given word can be applied to a given thing or pair of things. For example, (30a) can be seen as providing a rule for determining when we can apply the verb *agrees* to a given thing x: we can do so just in case x agrees, and otherwise not. Similarly, (30b) can be seen as providing a rule for determining when we can apply the verb *knows* to a pair of things $\langle x, y \rangle$: we can do so just in case the first thing knows the second, and otherwise not. Both transitive and intransitive verbs thus have an associated condition of application to objects, a condition that says when they apply to an object or pair of objects and when they don't.

Note that what is at issue here is how we are to understand the metatheory: what is the import of axioms like (30)? Our theory purports to be a theory of speakers' knowledge, specifically, knowledge in the semantic module of the language faculty. When we write down an axiom like (30a), we are saying that a speaker (unconsciously) knows that any object x is a value of *agrees* if and only if x agrees. When we say further that such a statement can be viewed as providing a rule of application, we mean that this is how speakers view such axioms (or how the cognitive systems within speakers view such axioms): speakers with axiom (30a) in their semantic module will apply the word *agrees* to an object if and only if (they believe that) the object agrees.

The notion of a condition of application to objects fits naturally with axioms for PC+ verbs. Might it also extend smoothly to proper nouns? Axiom (31) might also be viewed as stating a rule of application to objects, one that is met by a given object just in case that object is identical to Chris, and otherwise not:

(31) Val(x, *Chris*) iff x = Chris

But although proper nouns and verbs are similar in having an associated condition, on reflection it is easy to see that the kinds of rules or conditions that PC+ ascribes are markedly different.

First of all, predicates are associated with **general conditions of application**: conditions that are indifferent to the *number* of individuals that meet them. A predicate axiom like (30a, b) is compatible with many things meeting its condition, with only one thing meeting its condition, or with no things meeting its condition. And predicates do differ in the number of individuals they apply to; consider (32a–c):

(32) a. Val(x, *philosopher*) iff x is a philosopher
     b. Val(x, *moon of earth*) iff x is a moon of earth
     c. Val(x, *vampire*) iff x is a vampire

The word *philosopher* applies to many objects (Plato, Aristotle, Descartes, Donald Davidson, etc.), the phrase *moon of earth* applies to exactly one object (Luna), and the word *vampire* applies to none (we hope). But such real-world facts are in no sense crucial to these expressions meaning what they do.

By contrast, PC+ associates proper NPs with **singular conditions of application**. An axiom like (31) is not at all indifferent to the number of individuals that meet it. Rather, its formulation requires *Chris* to apply to exactly one object: the person Chris.[1]

A second feature of predicates is that they are associated with **object-independent conditions**. A predicate is not only indifferent to the number of individuals that meet its condition, it is indifferent to their *identity* as well. We see this object independence in the fact that the world could have turned out differently, with a predicate applying to different individuals but with its meaning being unaffected.

Again, this point follows from what is involved in knowing the axioms. Suppose that in the real world the philosophers are the particular individuals $a_1, \ldots, a_n$. Nevertheless, we can coherently imagine that this were not case, that the quite different individuals $b_1, \ldots, b_n$ are the philosophers. This would make no difference to what is involved in knowing that for any x, x is a value of *philosopher* if and only if x is a philosopher. Either way, the content of the knowledge is the same, and the predicate therefore has the same meaning.

Again by contrast, proper nouns in PC+ are associated with **object-dependent conditions**. The semantics of a proper noun like *Chris* crucially involves the specific individual Chris. This is because the condition of application of the proper noun, i.e., being identical with the very individual Chris, could not have been met by any individual other than Chris himself. This difference between predicates and proper nouns becomes particularly clear when we look at the truth conditions of sentences in which they appear. Whereas the truth conditions of two sentences sharing a predicate can involve different individuals —Chris, Jill, etc., (33a, b)—the truth conditions of two sentences sharing a proper noun always involve a common individual (34a, b):

(33) a. Val(t, *Chris agrees*) iff Chris agrees
     b. Val(t, *Jill agrees*) iff Jill agrees

(34) a. Val(t, *Chris agrees*) iff Chris agrees
     b. Val(t, *Chris ponders*) iff Chris ponders

The truth of a sentence with a proper noun always depends crucially on how things stand with some particular individual. And this is because the condition of application for a proper noun is always object-dependent in PC+.[2]

4.2.3   Distinguishing Predicates

Generality and object-independence are semantic properties of all predicates and distinguish them from proper nouns in PC+. But what properties distinguish among predicate types themselves? Are there regular correlations between the semantic properties of predicates and their status as verbs, common nouns, or adjectives?

Proper Nouns: Conditions on Identity

Geach (1962) argues that common nouns possess a semantic property distinguishing them from other predicate types. He begins by observing that only with nominal predicates *F* does the expression *the same F* make sense. Thus (35a–c), with concrete and abstract count nouns and a noncount noun, are all grammatically well formed and make sense, whereas (35d–f), with adjectives and a verb, are all grammatically ill formed and entirely senseless:

(35) a.   The same man
     b.   The same number
     c.   The same water
     d.   *The same tall

e. *The same happy
f. *The same agree

Geach attributes this difference to an additional condition indicated by common nouns. Along with a condition on application to objects, he suggests that nouns also have a **condition on identity**. The latter determines when two objects to which the common noun applies count as the same object or as different objects. Put another way, it is a principle for determining how to count objects falling under the common noun. Thus the common noun *man* has a (general, object-independent) condition determining whether some object is a man or not. But it also has a condition for determining whether two individuals constitute the same man or different men. That is, it has a principle allowing us to tell whether we are in the presence of one man, two men, three men, etc. Predicates that have identity conditions for their objects are sometimes said to be **sortal**.

As observed by Gupta (1980), the conditions of identity for nouns are often quite complex, and two nouns applying to the same objects may diverge sharply on their identity conditions. He illustrates this with the invalid inference in (36):

(36) National Airlines served at least 2 million passengers in 1975.
     Every passenger is a person.
     _____

     # National Airlines served at least 2 million persons in 1975.

As Gupta points out, a natural explanation for the invalidity of this reasoning is that although *passenger* and *person* apply to the same kinds of objects (human beings), the conditions on identity are different in the two cases. One individual taking two different flights on two different occasions counts as two different passengers on those occasions. However, he or she still still counts as the same person. The condition on identity for persons is the familiar one involving circumstances of birth, spatiotemporal and/or psychological continuity, and so on. The condition on identity for passengers involves the condition on identity for persons together with the condition on identity for trips.

It is important to note that our PC+ axioms do not explicitly indicate whether a predicate possesses only a condition of application or a condition of application and a condition of identity. Unlike the case with proper nouns versus predicates, we cannot simply look at the axioms for common nouns and adjectives and see what kind of predicate conditions they will possess:

(37) a. Val(x, *linguist*) iff x is a linguist
　　　 b. Val(*x, tall*) iff x is tall

At this point we leave it as an open question as to whether or how such a distinction should be drawn within the present theory.[3]

Adjectives: Gradability

Adjectives diverge from common nouns in lacking conditions on identity. But they depart semantically from nouns and verbs in another important aspect as well. As is frequently noted in grammar books, prototypical adjectives are **gradable** predicates, whereas nouns and verbs are not. This difference is seen in the fact that only adjectives take degree modifiers like *very, so, too,* etc. (38), and only adjectives come in an absolute, comparative, and superlative, form (39):

(38) a. very/so/too tall
　　　 b. *a very/so/too man
　　　 c. *Chris very/so/too agrees.

(39) a. tall/taller/tallest
　　　 b. complex/more complex/most complex
　　　 c. man/*maner/*manest
　　　 d. agree/*agreer/*agreest

One attractive approach to this difference is discussed by Klein (1991), developing a proposal by Lewis (1970). The idea is that adjectives differ from other predicates in containing an additional parameter or coordinate in their semantic values. Thus whereas a noun like *man* is a one-place predicate true of things, an adjective like *tall* is actually a two-place predicate, containing an extra parameter for **delineations**. A delineation for a predicate is a standard according to which something is judged to fall under the predicate. Thus a delineation for the adjective *tall* is a standard for determining when something is tall and when it isn't. It fixes the cut-off point between tall and not tall along the dimension of height. Under this view, axioms for nouns and adjectives can be distinguished as follows, with d ranging over delineations:

(40) a. Val(*x, man*) iff x is a man
　　　 b. Val($\langle x, d \rangle$, *tall*) iff x is at least as tall as d

As Klein points out, this formulation entails that individuals themselves possess no unique standard of tallness. If Chris meets a delineation (a cut-off point) of 6 feet for tallness, he also meets a delineation of $5^1/_2$ feet, and so on. In a given use, the value of the delineation is supplied by context.

This account of adjectives has a number of attractive features. For one thing, it permits a simple semantics for equative sentences like (41a) and comparative sentences like (42a).

(41) a. Chris is as tall as Phil.
     b. $\forall d[\text{tall(Phil, } d) \rightarrow \text{tall(Chris, } d)]$

(42) a. Phil is taller than Chris.
     b. $\exists d[\text{tall(Phil, } d) \ \& \ \neg \text{tall(Chris, } d)]$

Intuitively, (41a) is true if and only if every delineation that counts Phil as tall also counts Chris as tall. Thus if Phil is at least as tall as 6 feet and Chris is as tall as Phil, then Chris too must be at least as tall as 6 feet. Similarly, (42a) is true if and only if there is some delineation counting Phil as tall that doesn't count Chris as tall. There must be some delineation, say 6 feet 2 inches, such that Phil is at least that tall and Chris is not at least that tall. We can express these truth conditions for (41a) and (42a) using first-order logic as in (41b) and (42b).[4]

The delineation theory also correctly predicts certain logical relations between equatives and comparatives. For example, notice that (43a) entails not merely that Chris and Phil are of different heights; it entails that Phil is taller (42a).

(43) a. Chris is not as tall as Phil.
     b. $\neg \forall d[\text{tall(Phil, } d) \rightarrow \text{tall(Chris, } d)]$

This result follows straightforwardly under the delineation theory: (43b) can be proven equivalent to (42b) by standard logical reasoning with quantifiers.

Though brief, these remarks suggest that there are indeed features that semantically distinguish among the categories of predicates. We have observed that the properties of having or lacking conditions on identity ([$\pm$Sortal]) and having or lacking a delineation parameter ([$\pm$Gradable]) separate verbs, nouns, and adjectives (table 4.1). We leave it as a thought exercise for the reader to determine whether there are or could be expressions of English filling the cell in the table labeled "?". Are there, or could there be, expressions that are both sortal (and so countable) and gradable (and so degree-modifiable)?

Table 4.1 Types of predicates distinguished along the dimensions of sortal versus nonsortal and gradable versus nongradable

	Sortal	Not sortal
Gradable	?	A
Not gradable	N	V

4.3   Alternatives to the PC+ Analysis of Predicates

We have seen that in PC+, all predicates share the semantic feature of determining general, object-independent conditions on application. To see the full force of these properties, it is instructive to examine two alternative semantic theories for elementary clauses in which these properties seem to be absent, and hence theories in which predicates appear to be analyzed in a very different way.

4.3.1   PC^{set}

The first theory departs from PC+ in introducing sets into the axioms for proper nouns and verbs. In view of this, we will refer to the theory as PC^{set}. Proper nouns in PC^{set} take singleton sets as their semantic values rather than individuals:

(44) a. Val(X, *Chris*) iff $X = \{\text{Chris}\}$
    b. Val(X, *Jill*) iff $X = \{\text{Jill}\}$
    c. Val(X, *Phil*) iff $X = \{\text{Phil}\}$
    d. Val(X, *Kate*) iff $X = \{\text{Kate}\}$

Likewise, verbs take sets of individuals and sets of pairs of individuals as values, rather than individuals and pairs of individuals:

(45) a. Val(X, *agrees*) iff $X = \{x : x \text{ agrees}\}$
    b. Val(X, *ponders*) iff $X = \{x : x \text{ ponders}\}$
    c. Val(X, *knows*) iff $X = \{\langle x, y \rangle : x \text{ knows } y\}$

According to (45a), X is a value of *agrees* if and only if X is the set of agreers; according to (45c), X is a value of *knows* if and only X is the set of pairs $\langle x, y \rangle$

such that the first knows the second. In PC^{set}, the axioms for verbs are similar to those for nouns.

The phrasal axioms of PC^{set} are like those in PC+ but modified so as to allow set values to be combined appropriately. Axioms for S nodes and transitive VP nodes are given in (46a, b). The remaining axiom (46c) simply passes values between a mother node and a daughter node that it exhaustively dominates:

(46) a. $Val(t, [_S \text{ NP VP}])$ iff for some X, Y, $Val(X, \text{NP})$, $Val(Y, \text{VP})$, and $X \subseteq Y$
   b. $Val(X, [_{VP} \text{ V NP}])$ iff $X = \{x:$ for some Y, Z, $Val(Y, \text{V})$, $Val(Z, \text{NP})$ and $Z \subseteq \{z : \langle x, z \rangle \in Y\}\}$
   c. $Val(x, [_X \text{ } Y])$ iff $Val(x, Y)$

Some Sample Derivations

We illustrate the application of PC^{set} to the sentence *Chris agrees*. Axiom (46a) states that a sentence consisting of an NP and a VP is true if and only if there is a set X that is the value of the NP, there is a set Y that is the value of the VP, and X is a subset of Y:

(47) $Val(t, [_S [_{NP} [_N \text{ Chris}]] [_{VP} [_V \text{ agrees }]]])$ iff for some X, Y, $Val(X, [_{NP} [_N \text{ Chris}]])$ and $Val(Y, [_{VP} [_V \text{ agrees}]])$ and $X \subseteq Y$

As the reader can show, $Val(X, [_{NP} [_N \text{ Chris}]])$ will be equivalent to $X = \{\text{Chris}\}$, and $Val(Y, [_{VP} [_V \text{ agrees}]])$ will be equivalent to $Y = \{y : y \text{ agrees}\}$. Hence the sentence as a whole will receive the following T theorem:

(48) $Val(t, [_S [_{NP} [_N \text{ Chris}]] [_{VP} [_V \text{ agrees}]]])$ iff for some X, Y, $X = \{\text{Chris}\}$, $Y = \{y : y \text{ agrees}\}$ and $X \subseteq Y$

Applying (SI) twice, we reduce this to (49), the T theorem that PC^{set} provides for *Chris agrees*:

(49) $Val(t, [_S [_{NP} [_N \text{ Chris}]] [_{VP} [_V \text{ agrees}]]])$ iff $\{\text{Chris}\} \subseteq \{x : x \text{ agrees}\}$

Though nonhomophonic, this T theorem is at least prima facie interpretive. If we step outside PC^{set} and appeal to an elementary equivalence of set theory, we can show that (49) is equivalent to (50):[5]

(50) $Val(t, [_S [_{NP} [_N \text{ Chris}]] [_{VP} [_V \text{ agrees}]]])$ iff Chris agrees

PC^{set} applied to a transitive construction is only slightly less transparent. Consider the sentence *Jill knows Kate*. The main-sentence axiom yields (51), and the transitive-VP axiom then yields (52):

(51) Val(t, [$_S$ [$_{NP}$ [$_N$ Jill]] [$_{VP}$ [$_V$ knows] [$_{NP}$ [$_N$ Kate]]]]) iff for some X, Y,
    Val(X, [$_{NP}$ [$_N$ Jill]]) and Val(Y, [$_{VP}$ [$_V$ knows] [$_{NP}$ [$_N$ Kate]]]) and $X \subseteq Y$

(52) Val(Y, [$_{VP}$ [$_V$ knows] [$_{NP}$ [$_N$ Kate]]]) iff
    $Y = \{y$: for some Z, W, Val(Z, [$_V$ knows]),
    Val(W, [$_{NP}$ [$_N$ Kate]]) and $W \subseteq \{z : \langle y, z \rangle \in Z\}\}$

Again, as the reader can show, Val(Z, [$_V$ knows]) is equivalent to $Z = \{\langle r, s \rangle : r$ knows $s\}$, and Val(W, [$_{NP}$ [$_N$ Kate]]) is equivalent to $W = \{$Kate$\}$.[6] Hence by (SE) we have (53):

(53) Val(Y, [$_{VP}$ [$_V$ knows] [$_{NP}$ [$_N$ Kate]]]) iff
    $Y = \{y$: for some Z, W, $Z = \{\langle r, s \rangle : r$ knows $s\}$, $W = \{$Kate$\}$, and
    $W \subseteq \{z : \langle y, z \rangle \in Z\}\}$

Applying (SI) twice to (53), we derive (54):

(54) Val(Y, [$_{VP}$ [$_V$ knows] [$_{NP}$ [$_N$ Kate]]]) iff
    $Y = \{y : \{$Kate$\} \subseteq \{z : \langle y, z \rangle \in \{\langle r, s \rangle : r$ knows $s\}\}\}$

Another elementary equivalence of set theory then yields (55):[7]

(55) Val(Y, [$_{VP}$ [$_V$ knows] [$_{NP}$ [$_N$ Kate]]]) iff $Y = \{y : y$ knows Kate$\}$

This VP will combine with the subject *Jill* to yield that *Jill knows Kate* is true if and only if Jill knows Kate.

Generality and Object Independence in PC^{set}

The axioms for PC^{set} are obviously different from those of PC+. Furthermore, in PC^{set}, axioms for verbs and proper nouns have a very similar form. In both, the semantic value is identified as some particular set. On the basis of this, one might wonder what becomes of the semantic distinction between predicates and names in PC^{set}. Does this theory semantically treat verbs like proper nouns?

On careful examination, it can be seen that, despite appearances, our familiar properties of generality and object independence are still present in PC^{set}, although in a slightly different form from PC+. Take the property of generality. The axioms of PC^{set} identify the semantic value of either a verb or a proper noun with a single thing, a set. In this sense they appear to express singular conditions on objects (sets) rather than general ones. Nonetheless, there remains an important difference. Notice that the axioms for verbs are indifferent to the number of things appearing in the set, whereas the axioms for proper nouns are not. An axiom like (56a) identifies the value of *agree* with the set of individuals that agree, *however many they may be*. As such it implies nothing about whether this set contains many members, one member, or no members at all. By contrast, an axiom like (56b) is quite specific about the size of the set X with its unique member Chris. This set must contain exactly one member, neither more nor less:

(56) a. Val(X, *agrees*) iff $X = \{x : x$ agrees$\}$
     b. Val(X, *Chris*} iff $X = \{$Chris$\}$

On reflection, then, the generality property is still there but is simply transferred to the conditions on set membership. Verb axioms in PC^{set} express general conditions on membership in the sets that are their values. By contrast, proper nouns express singular conditions on membership in the sets that are their values.

A similar result holds for the property of object independence. Again, since the axioms of PC^{set} identify the value of a verb or a proper noun with a single set, they appear to express object-dependent conditions for both. The semantics of both verbs and proper nouns seems to implicate some particular object, some particular set, for each verb and proper noun. Again, however, this is largely an illusion. Notice that the axioms for verbs are indifferent to the identity of things appearing in the sets, whereas the axioms for proper nouns are not. Axiom (56a) identifies the value of *agree* with the set of individuals that agree, *whoever they may be*. As such it implies nothing about whether this set contains Jill, Phil, Chris, Kate, or anyone else. By contrast, an axiom like (56b) is quite specific about the contents of the set X. This set must contain the specific individual Chris, and no one else. The property of object dependence too is thus transferred to the conditions on set membership. Verb axioms in PC^{set} express object-independent conditions on membership in the sets that are their values. By contrast, proper nouns express object-dependent conditions on membership in the sets that are their values.

Despite surface appearances, then, PC^{set} does not really diverge from PC+ in the fundamental semantic properties it assigns to verbs and proper nouns. In both, the conditions on applying verbs and proper nouns take into consideration generality versus singularity and object independence versus object dependence. The apparent differences amount to no real difference at all.

4.3.2 PC^{prop}

The second alternative theory is PC^{prop}. This theory retains the PC+ axioms for proper nouns. However, in place of its verbal axioms, PC^{prop} includes the rules in (57):

(57) a. Val(p, *agrees*) iff p = the property of agreeing
    b. Val(p, *ponders*) iff p = the property of pondering
    c. Val(r, *knows*) iff r = the relation of knowing

The axioms for verbs are again similar to the axioms for proper nouns in the sense that the semantic value of a verb is given as some unique object. Here, however, the object is not a set but a property or a relation.

As usual, the differences in lexical axioms entail corresponding differences in the phrasal axioms. Rules for S and the transitive VP are given in (58a, b). The familiar axiom for mother and single-daughter configurations is given in (58c):

(58) a. Val(t, [$_S$ NP VP]) iff for some x, p,
        Val(x, NP), Val(p, VP), and x has p
    b. Val(p, [$_{VP}$ V NP]) iff for some r, z, Val(r, V), Val(z, NP),
        and p = the property of being an x such that x bears r to z
    c. Val(x, [$_X$ Y]) iff Val(x, Y)

We again assume (SE) and (SI) as the relevant production rules.

Some Sample Derivations

To see how this theory works and what it yields, let us work with the familiar sentence *Chris agrees*. The S axiom and (UI) give us (59):

(59) Val(t, [$_S$ [$_{NP}$ [$_N$ Chris]] [$_{VP}$ [$_V$ agrees]]]) iff for some x, p,
    Val(x, [$_{NP}$ [$_N$ Chris]]), Val(p, [$_{VP}$ [$_V$ agrees]]) and x has p

As usual, we derive the result that Val(x, [$_{NP}$ [$_N$ Chris]]) iff x = Chris. And as the reader may verify through similar steps, we derive that Val(p, [$_{VP}$ [$_V$ agrees]]) iff p = the property of agreeing. We then use (SE) to conclude (60) from (59):

(60) Val(t, [$_S$ [$_{NP}$ [$_N$ Chris]] [$_{VP}$ [$_V$ agrees]]]) iff for some x, p,
x = Chris, p = the property of agreeing, and x has p

By two applications of (SI) we then derive (61):

(61) Val(t, [$_S$ [$_{NP}$ [$_N$ Chris]] [$_{VP}$ [$_V$ agrees]]]) iff Chris has the property of agreeing

Though nonhomophonic, the final T theorem appears, prima facie, to be interpretive.

The axiom for transitive VPs works similarly. Applied to *knows Kate*, the axiom yields (62):

(62) Val(p, [$_{VP}$ [$_V$ knows] [$_{NP}$ [$_N$ Kate]]]) iff for some r, z,
Val(r, [$_V$ knows]), Val(z, [$_{NP}$ [$_N$ Kate]]) and
p = the property of being an x such that x bears r to z

We can easily prove that Val(r, [$_V$ knows]) iff r = the relation of knowing, and Val(z, [$_{NP}$ [$_N$ Kate]]) iff z = Kate. By (SE) we thus derive (63), and two applications of (SI) to (63) yield (64):

(63) Val(p, [$_{VP}$ [$_V$ knows] [$_{NP}$ [$_N$ Kate]]]) iff for some r, z,
r = the relation of knowing, z = Kate, and
p = the property of being an x such that x bears r to z

(64) Val(p, [$_{VP}$ [$_V$ knows] [$_{NP}$ [$_N$ Kate]]]) iff p = the property of being an x such that x bears the relation of knowing to Kate

When combined with a subject like *Jill*, this will give the result that *Jill knows Kate* is true if and only if Jill has the property of being an x such that x bears the relation of knowing to Kate. Although we would need a specific rule of inference to prove it, (64) is presumably true just in case Jill bears the relation of knowing to Kate. Again, this is arguably an interpretive, even if nonhomophonic, result.

Singularity and Object Dependence in PC^{prop}

In PC^{prop}, a clause has two major constituents both of which identify objects. Proper nouns identify one kind of object: familiar entities like persons, tables, chairs, etc. Verbs identify another kind of object: properties and relations.

As it turns out, under the right assumptions about properties, PC^{prop} does provide an analysis of verbs in which their semantic properties converge with proper nouns. Specifically, this is possible if we think of properties and relations as what philosophers have traditionally called **Platonic universals**.[8] Platonic universals embody a number of important features. They can exist whether they are exemplified by one individual, many individuals, or no individuals. We can have a universal BEING-THE-TWELFTH-PLANET-IN-THE-SOLAR-SYSTEM even if there is no celestial body to exemplify it. Furthermore, the identity of universals is not determined by what exemplifies them. Two universals may be distinct even when they are exemplified by exactly the same individuals. We can have the universal BEING-A-FILBERT and the universal BEING-A-HAZELNUT, and the two may be distinct even though they are exemplified by just the same nuts.[9]

With properties and relations understood in this way, PC^{prop} yields an analysis in which the conditions on applying verbs and other predicates converge with those of proper nouns. For example, notice that (65a), like (65b), has a singular condition of application.

(65) a. Val(p, agrees) iff p = the property of agreeing
     b. Val(x, Chris) iff x = Chris

The former, like the latter, is so formulated as to apply to exactly one object. In the second case it's the person Chris; in the first case it's the property of agreeing.

Similarly, (65a), like (65b), has an object-dependent condition of application. The axiom for the proper noun *Chris* involves a specific individual: Chris. As a consequence, the truth of any sentence containing the proper noun *Chris* will depend crucially on how things stand with that person (he agrees, he ponders, he knows Kate, etc.). In the just the same way, the PC^{prop} axiom for the verb *agrees* involves a specific individual: the property of agreeing. As a consequence, the truth of any sentence containing *agrees* will depend crucially on how things stand with that property (Chris has it, Jill has it, Kate has it, etc.).

PC^{prop} thus presents a very different analysis than PC^{set}. Whereas the semantic similarities between verbs and proper nouns were a surface appearance in the latter, these similarities are quite real in the former. PC^{prop} entails semantic properties for verbs (and other predicates) that are fundamentally different from those of PC^{set} or PC+. When properties and relations are understood as Platonic universals, verbs in PC^{prop} are very similar to proper nouns.

The Ineliminability of Predication

An interesting feature of PC^{prop} is its very limited use of predication in the metalanguage. Thus, whereas PC+ renders the object-language predicate *ponders* with a corresponding metalanguage predicate "ponders," PC^{prop} renders *ponders* with the nonpredicative metalanguage expression "the property of pondering":[10]

(66) a. Val(x, *ponders*) iff x ponders
    b. Val(x, *ponders*) iff x = the property of pondering

PC^{prop} does not get by entirely without metalinguistic predication, however. It uses the two-place predicates "____ = ____," "Val(_, _)," and "____ has ____" and the three-place predicate "____ bears the relation ____ to ____."

A little reflection shows that the presence of predicates in the metalanguage is not a dispensable feature, but is in fact an essential one. That is, it becomes clear that *some* predicate will always be necessary in the RHSs of the T theorems. To see why, compare the following three examples:

(67) a. Phil ponders.
    b. Phil has the property of pondering.
    c. *Phil the property of pondering.

The meaning of (67a) is given by (67b) but not by (67c). Why not? Of course, (67c) is not a sentence, but more seems to be wrong here than being syntactically ill formed. Specifically, (67c) seems to invite the question, *What* about Phil and the property of pondering? Something is needed to relate the two elements together in the right way: we need to be told that Phil *has* the property of pondering.

The need for predication in the metalanguage reveals an important point about the possibility of treating VPs and other predicative expressions as namelike: any such treatment of VPs creates a requirement that something else in each sentence take on a predicating role. Recall the composition axiom of PC^{prop}:

(58a) Val(t, [$_s$ NP VP]) iff for some x, p, Val(x, NP), Val(p, VP), and x has p

The predicating element in the RHSs of the T theorems, the word "has," derives from this axiom. The feature of the object language that licenses the metalinguistic "has" is the sentence form, the very structure [$_s$ NP VP].

According to PC^{prop}, therefore, this sentential structure provides the necessary predicating element in the object language.

Notice further that any attempt to reduce the predicating role of the sentence form to a naming one will simply recreate the problem. Thus if we treated the [$_s$ NP VP] structure as a kind of name for the "has" relation, then [$_s$ [$_{NP}$ Phil] [$_{VP}$ ponders]] would have to be seen as some sort of concatenation of three names: a name of Chris, a name of the property of pondering, and a name of the "has" relation. This would not account for the sentence's truth conditions. *Phil ponders* is true iff Phil, the property of pondering, and the having relation, well, do what? Again, we need something to relate the elements together in the right way. We need to be told that Phil stands in the relation of having to the property of pondering. Again, this further predicational element "stands in" has to be accounted for in terms of some feature of the object-language sentence. And if we tried to assimilate this feature to a name, we would run into the difficulty all over again. This is a version of what is sometimes called "Bradley's regress."[11] The moral is that predication cannot be reduced to naming. There must always be some predicating element in a sentence that does not function as a name.

4.4 Evaluating the Alternatives

Under the picture of semantic inquiry we have been pursuing, the task of giving a T theory involves articulating a sentence into parts (that is, assigning it a semantic form) and assigning semantic values to those parts. We saw earlier that this task underdetermines structure. A compositional semantics for conjunction, for example, can be defined either with a Conj phrase or without it.

Reflection on the alternatives to PC+ just discussed shows that a similar underdetermination arises with respect to semantic values, even when we assume a fixed structure. In PC+, verbs have individuals or pairs of individuals as their semantic values. But other choices of values are possible, including sets and other kinds of things.

In the case of underdetermination of semantic structure, we speculated that syntax presumably plays a deciding role, determining the finer details of structure in a clause even where semantics cannot. It is natural to ask about how underdetermination of semantic value too might be resolved. How do we chose among alternatives like PC+, PC^{set}, and PC^{prop}?

4.4.1 Ontological Commitment

So far we have uncritically assumed that both PC^{set} and PC^{prop} deliver interpretive T theorems. On further thought, however, it's not so clear that this is right. The RHSs of the T theorems in both theories appear to commit us to objects that are not clearly present in the object-language sentences they are supposed to interpret. Thus the RHS of (68) is explicitly committed to the existence of a unit set containing Chris and to a set of agreers.

(68) Val(t, [$_S$ [$_{NP}$ [$_N$ Chris]] [$_{VP}$ [$_V$ agrees]]]) iff {Chris} $\subseteq$ {$x : x$ agrees}

And the RHS of (69) is explicitly committed to the existence of the property of agreeing.

(69) Val(t, [$_S$ [$_{NP}$ [$_N$ Chris]] [$_{VP}$ [$_V$ agrees]]]) iff Chris has the property of agreeing

It is not obvious that either commitment is present in the original object-language sentence, *Chris agrees.*

To put the point slightly differently, if there are no sets, then in particular there is no set containing Chris and no set of agreers for Chris to be a member of. So "{Chris} $\subseteq$ {$x : x$ agrees}" is false. Thus if there are no sets, (68) makes *Chris agrees* false, regardless of whether Chris actually agrees or not. Equally, if there are no properties, there is no property of agreeing for Chris to have. The RHS of (69) is thus always false, whether *Chris agrees* is true or false.

Given this, if we attribute knowledge of either PC^{set} or PC^{prop} to object-language speakers, we are attributing these specific ontological commitments to them. If they know PC^{set}, then what they mean by *Chris agrees* is that {Chris} $\subseteq$ {$x : x$ agrees}. And if sets don't exist, then whenever they say *Chris agrees*, they will be saying something false, whether or not Chris agrees. Since PC^{set} brings reference to sets into all T theorems, the upshot is that, for this reason alone, all sentences would be false! Analogous remarks apply to PC^{prop}: if speakers know PC^{prop} and if properties don't exist, then all sentences turn out to be false.

One way, then, to address the issue of whether these theories are interpretive might be to examine the strength and plausibility of their ontological commitments. If the commitments of a theory are very strong and implausible, it will be implausible to attribute it to speakers, for then every time a speaker produced a sentence, however plausible it might seem, that speaker would be saying something involving a strong and implausible ontological assumption. On the other hand if the commitments of a theory are relatively mild and plausible, then it is reasonable to attribute it to speakers, for then in uttering a sentence such as *Chris agrees*, they would not automatically be saying something whose truth hinges on a strong and implausible hidden assumption.

As it turns out, such considerations do not give solid reasons to doubt PC[set] or PC[prop]. The commitment to sets apparent in PC[set] is relatively innocuous. Sets are fairly well understood both mathematically and philosophically.[12] Moreover, large parts of set theory appear indispensable to physical theories that are now widely accepted, and despite attempts to eliminate reference to sets from certain parts of physics (see Field 1980), few have found these efforts convincing.

With properties, the issue is less clear. PC[prop] is committed to a strong view of properties, namely, that for every verb phrase, there is a corresponding Platonic universal. Yet there are no very reputable arguments for this view outside semantics. And properties are perhaps not so well understood as sets, either mathematically or philosophically.[13] At the same time there are no very compelling arguments *against* the existence of properties, as required by PC[prop].

Furthermore, there is some independent evidence that speakers are committed to the existence of both sets and properties. In the former case, this evidence comes from semantics itself. As we will see in later chapters, there is considerable pressure to introduce sets in the analysis of quantifier constructions; we will argue that a promising treatment of words like *some*, *a few*, *three*, etc., is to see them as expressing relations on sets. Further, and despite appearances to the contrary, even simple PC+ turns out to be committed to sets. PC+ is committed to the existence of ordered pairs $\langle x, y \rangle$ as the values of transitive verbs, but under standard assumptions, an ordered pair just *is* a set. Following Kuratowski, the ordered pair $\langle x, y \rangle$ is defined as the set $\{\{x, y\}, \{x\}\}$. Hence even with PC+, sets are implicitly present. It thus appears that we have independent reason to suppose that speakers are indeed committed to the existence of sets.

For evidence that speakers are committed to the existence of properties, consider (70) to (75). Simple NPs like those in (70) and (71) purport to refer to properties and relations directly. And most speakers would be happy enough to accept (70) and (71) as paraphrases of *Chris is happy* and *Jill knows Kate*, respectively:[14]

(70) a. Chris has [$_{NP}$ the property of being happy]
　　 b. Chris exemplifies [$_{NP}$ happiness]
　　　 (Cf. Chris is happy.)

(71) a. Jill stands in [$_{NP}$ the relation of knowing] to Kate
　　 b. Jill and Kate exemplify [$_{NP}$ the relation of knowing]
　　　 (Cf. Jill knows Kate.)

Furthermore, as noted by Wright (1983), there is apparent anaphoric reference to properties in examples (72a, b) much like the nominal anaphoric reference in (73a, b):

(72) a. *A*: John is honest.
　　　　 B: Yes. Whatever else you can say about him, he is *that*.
　　 b. John is honest, *which* you never were.

(73) a. *A*: John will be present.
　　　　 B: Yes, whoever else is there, *he* will be.
　　 b. Jill saw John, *who* was standing nearby.

Finally, as discussed by Wright (1983) and Chierchia (1984), there is apparent quantification over properties and quantificational reasoning with properties, as in (74). This again is highly reminiscent of what occurs with nominal reference, as in (75):

(74) a. John is everything his mother wanted him to be *e*.
　　 b. John is everything that Mary is *e*.
　　　 Mary is intelligent.
　　　 _____
　　　 John is intelligent.

(75) a. John saw everything his mother wanted him to see *e*.
　　 b. John saw everyone Mary did.
　　　 Mary saw Fred.
　　　 _____
　　　 John saw Fred.

These facts do not support PC^{prop} directly, since the expressions purporting to refer to and quantify over properties are nominals or adjectives (*the property of being happy, the relation of knowing, honest, everything that Mary is, intelligent*, etc.) and not verbs. Nonetheless, they draw one naturally toward the broader conclusion that speakers do take some expressions to refer to and quantify over properties, and that speakers are therefore committed to their existence.[15]

In summary, then, ontological commitments yield no clear-cut means for deciding between PC+ and its competitors. All of the objects assumed by these theories have plausible claims to existence, and there is even some reason to suppose that ordinary speakers are committed to them.

4.4.2 Semantic Properties

A second important point of difference among our theories is in the account of semantic properties they provide. As we have seen, in PC+, proper nouns and predicates have quite different semantic properties, whereas in PC^{prop} they are basically the same. One potential way of choosing, therefore, would be to find evidence bearing on which analysis is correct.

An example of such evidence may come from neuroscience. Recent studies of **aphasia**, language loss through neural trauma and pathology, strongly suggests that knowledge about the meanings of lexical items is partitioned into a number of distinct semantic subcategories.[16] These categories appear to include abstract notions versus concrete notions, living things versus nonliving objects, animals, and fruits and vegetables. Patients have been reported as showing selective dysfunction in each of these specific domains.[17]

Interestingly, similar effects have been found with proper names. Semenza and Zettin (1989) report the case of L.S., a 41-year-old hardware-store employee who suffered head injury during a riding accident in July of 1988. As a result of this trauma, L.S. showed a marked deterioration in his ability to use proper nouns. In particular, although his aural and written comprehension of such items remained intact, his ability to produce or write them himself was severely affected. According to Semenza and Zettin,

With real persons his knowledge of names was limited to those of most members of his family, which he had relearned during the months before testing. He gave correct information, however, about other real persons ("doctor") and never experienced recognition problems. When presented with pictures of famous persons his naming performance was 2/25. Nonetheless he provided correct information and details about these people's identities in every case (for example, "prime minister").... [The] ability to retrieve geographical names was tested using a blank atlas and pictures of the sites of well-known cities. He could name only 6/15 pictures and 4/15 map sites, but he was able to match them correctly in pairs. He also gave correct information about the items.... We confronted him with several popular pieces of wordless classical music. If he demonstrated that he recognized them by singing along and continuing the melody appropriately when the music stopped, then we asked him to name the piece. He was unable to retrieve the title of any of such 12 pieces, regardless of whether their proper names were very abstract ("5th Symphony") or descriptive ("Moonlight Sonata"). He was also unable to provide the names of the composers. (1989, 678)

Semenza and Zettin analyze the deficit shown by L.S. as a semantic one. They state, "Our evidence indicates a common denominator underlying L.S.'s performances: the inability to deal (at the retrieval level) with purely referential nondescriptive semantic relations" (1989, 679). This conclusion, if correct, might be taken to bear on the choice between PC+ and PC^prop. Recall that in PC^prop the semantic analysis of predicates essentially falls in with that of proper nouns: the former, like the latter, are a species of name. Under PC^prop, then, we might expect aphasias affecting "referential nondescriptive semantic relations" to affect proper nouns, verbs, and other predicates quite generally. This was not the case with L.S., however. As described by Semenza and Zettin, L.S.'s linguistic deficit was revealed only with nominal referring expressions, and not with verbs or nominals used "descriptively" or predicatively (recall L.S.'s use of *doctor* and *prime minister*). These results with aphasia might therefore be seen as giving evidence for a more basic division of semantic roles between proper nouns and predicates than PC^prop provides. An account like PC+ would seem to fit the facts better.

Of course, we are not suggesting these results are decisive or that the data cited above are not subject to alternative interpretations. Our point here is simply that neuropsychological findings like these could potentially serve to help us chose among semantic theories that differ in their assessment of semantic properties.

4.4.3 Linguistic Predictions

PC+, PC^set, and PC^prop can also be evaluated by appeal to additional linguistic data. We can look to see which provides the simplest and most revealing account of these data, which fits in best with other aspects of the semantic theory under construction, and so on.

This point may be illustrated with coordination structures. In PC we considered conjunctions of full sentences such as *Jill ponders and Chris agrees* and *Phil ponders or Jill knows Kate*. But English allows conjunction in many other categories of phrases, including verbs and verb phrases:

(76) a. Jill [$_{VP}$ [$_V$ ponders] and [$_V$ agrees]]
    b. Jill [$_{VP}$ [$_{VP}$ ponders] or [$_{VP}$ agrees]]
    c. Jill [$_{VP}$ [$_{VP}$ ponders] and [$_{VP}$ knows Kate]]
    ˋ d. Jill [$_{VP}$ [$_V$ [$_V$ knows] or [$_V$ admires]] Kate]

One simple demand on our semantic theory is that it be able to analyze such examples and assign appropriate T sentences. An additional demand might be that it unify this account with the analysis of sentential conjunction. Speakers seem to acquire one rule when they acquire conjunction, and it seems highly doubtful that they might lose access to conjunction in one category, say through trauma, and yet still be able to interpret conjunctions in other categories. At any rate, we might expect such results on grounds of economy of design and learnability. Assuming that speakers are acquiring one general syntactic structure, we would expect them to acquire one general semantic rule as well.

As it turns out, our three theories diverge in their ability to meet these demands. With PC+, matters are easiest. It is very simple to extend PC+ so as to accommodate (76a–d), together with sentence conjunctions. The general schemes in (77a, b) give interpretive, (nearly) homophonic T theorems for both sentence and predicate conjunctions:

(77) a. $\mathrm{Val}(x, [_x\ X_1\ and\ X_2])$ iff $\mathrm{Val}(x, X_1)$ and $\mathrm{Val}(x, X_2)$
    b. $\mathrm{Val}(x, [_x\ X_1\ or\ X_2])$ iff $\mathrm{Val}(x, X_1)$ or $\mathrm{Val}(x, X_2)$ (where $X = $ S, VP, V)

By contrast, in PC^{set} and PC^{prop} things become progressively more complex.

PC^{set} will yield adequate interpretive T theorems for predicate conjunction and disjunction if we augment it with the two rules in (78).

(78) a. $\mathrm{Val}(A, [_x\ X_1\ and\ X_2])$ iff for some B, Γ, $A = B \cap \Gamma$, $\mathrm{Val}(B, X_1)$, and $\mathrm{Val}(\Gamma, X_2)$
    b. $\mathrm{Val}(A, [_x\ X_1\ or\ X_2])$ iff for some B, Γ, $A = B \cup \Gamma$, $\mathrm{Val}(B, X_1)$, and $\mathrm{Val}(\Gamma, X_2)$

According to (78a), the semantic value of a conjunction of two predicates is the intersection of their respective sets. Similarly, according to (78b), the semantic value of a disjunction of two predicates is the union of their respective sets.[18] If we want to extend (78a, b) to conjunctions of sentences, we must also make extra assumptions about the nature of the truth values. Note that with (77a, b) we are not obliged to say anything particular about the truth values t and f. It is enough that they be two distinct (if somewhat strange) objects.

With (78a, b), however, matters are not so simple. These rules require us to be able to take intersections and unions of semantic values, and such operations are defined only on sets. Accordingly, to extend the conjunction rules in (78) to sentences, it becomes necessary for us to analyze truth values as sets of some kind.[19]

With PC^{prop}, matters are more complicated still. Giving a semantic rule for conjoined predicates is already a challenge, and none of the above rules will do. For example, (77a) will always yield the truth value f if the values of *ponders* and *agrees* are properties. This is because there simply is no property *p* that is both the property of pondering and the property of agreeing:

(79) Val(p, [$_{\text{VP}}$ [$_{\text{VP}}$ ponders] and [$_{\text{VP}}$ agrees]]) iff Val(p, [$_{\text{VP}}$ ponders])
    and Val(p, [$_{\text{VP}}$ agrees])

Likewise, we cannot use (78a, b). Since properties are not sets, we cannot use rules that would perform set-theoretic operations on them, like taking intersections and unions. For predicate coordination with PC^{prop}, it seems that we require an additional theory that would allow us to combine properties in various ways, for example, a way of combining the property of pondering and the property of agreeing into a single, complex property of pondering-and-agreeing, a way of combining the property of pondering and the property of agreeing into a single property of pondering-or-agreeing, and so on. Under this idea, conjunctions would correspond to one way of producing a complex property, and disjunctions would correspond to another. Notice, however, that even if such a theory of complex property formation can be given, we still face the job of extending this analysis to sentence coordinations in PC^{prop}. Just as truth values are not naturally thought of as sets, and as subject to set-theoretic operations, it's not clear they can be naturally thought of as properties, and as subject to property-theoretic operations. But clearly, to bring S coordinations within this general picture, some property-theoretic structure will have to be introduced into t and f.[20]

Coordination thus illustrates the kind of case that might help us to choose among PC+, PC^{set}, and PC^{prop} on linguistic grounds. As we see, differences in semantic values in the analysis of elementary predication structures can yield significant advantages of simplicity and ease of generalization when we turn to slightly more complex predication structures. To handle coordination, both PC^{set} and PC^{prop} require us to introduce important additional rules and assumptions about objects, whereas PC+ does not.

Theory and Exercises

The Theory PC+ (PC + Names and Predicates)

Lexical Axioms

(1) a. Val(x, *Phil*) iff x = Phil
   b. Val(x, *Jill*) iff x = Jill
   c. Val(x, *Chris*) iff x = Chris
   d. Val(x, *Kate*) iff x = Kate
   e. Val(x, *agrees*) iff x agrees
   f. Val(x, *ponders*) iff x ponders
   g. Val($\langle x, y \rangle$, *knows*) iff x knows y

Phrasal Axioms

(2) a. Val(t, [$_S$ S_1 *and* S_2]) iff both Val(t, S_1) and Val(t, S_2)
   b. Val(t, [$_S$ S_1 *or* S_2]) iff either Val(t, S_1) or Val(t, S_2)
   c. Val(t, [$_S$ *It is not the case that* S]) iff it is not the case that Val(t, S)
   d. Val(t, [$_S$ NP VP]) iff for some x, Val(x, NP) and Val(x, VP)
   e. Val(x, [$_{VP}$ V NP]) iff for some y, Val($\langle x, y \rangle$, V) and Val(y, NP)
   f. Val(x, [$_X$ Y]) iff Val(x, Y) (where X, Y are any nodes)

Production Rules

(UI) Universal instantiation

$$\frac{\text{For any } x,\ F(x)}{F(\alpha)}$$

(SE) Substitution of equivalents

$$\frac{F(\alpha) \\ \alpha \text{ iff } \beta}{F(\beta)}$$

(SI) Substitution of identicals

$$\frac{\phi \text{ iff for some } x,\ F(x) \text{ and } x = \text{'}}{\phi \text{ iff } F(\alpha)}$$

The Theory PC^{set}

Lexical Axioms

(1) a. Val(X, *Phil*) iff $X = \{Phil\}$
    b. Val(X, *Jill*) iff $X = \{Jill\}$
    c. Val(X, *Chris*) iff $X = \{Chris\}$
    d. Val(X, *Kate*) iff $X = \{Kate\}$
    e. Val(X, *ponders*) iff $X = \{x : x \text{ ponders}\}$
    f. Val(X, *agrees*) iff $X = \{x : x \text{ agrees}\}$
    g. Val(Y, *knows*) iff $Y = \{\langle x, y \rangle : x \text{ knows } y\}$

Phrasal Axioms

(2) a. Val(t, [$_S$ S$_1$ *and* S$_2$]) iff both Val(t, S$_1$) and Val(t, S$_2$)
    b. Val(t, [$_S$ S$_1$ *or* S$_2$]) iff either Val(t, S$_1$) or Val(t, S$_2$)
    c. Val(t, [$_S$ *It is not the case that* S]) iff it is not the case that Val(t, S)
    d. Val(t, [$_S$ NP VP]) iff for some X, Y, Val(X, NP), Val(Y, VP), and
        $X \subseteq Y$
    e. Val(X, [$_{VP}$ V NP]) iff $X =$
        $\{x : \text{for some } Y, Z, \text{Val}(Y, V), \text{Val}(Z, \text{NP}), \text{ and } Z \subseteq \{z : \langle x, z \rangle \in Y\}\}$
    f. Val(x, [$_X$ Y]) iff Val(x, Y) (where X, Y are any nodes)

Production Rules

(UI) Universal instantiation

$$\frac{\text{For any } x, F(x)}{F(\alpha)}$$

(SE) Substitution of equivalents

$$\frac{\begin{array}{c} F(\alpha) \\ \alpha \text{ iff } \beta \end{array}}{F(\beta)}$$

(SI) Substitution of identicals

$$\frac{\phi \text{ iff } F(\alpha) \text{ and } \alpha = \beta}{\phi \text{ iff } F(\beta)}$$

The Theory PC^{prop}

Lexical Axioms

(1) a. Val(x, *Phil*) iff x = Phil
   b. Val(x, *Jill*) iff x = Jill
   c. Val(x, *Chris*) iff x = Chris
   d. Val(x, *Kate*) iff x = Kate
   e. Val(p, *ponders*) iff p = the property of pondering
   f. Val(p, *agrees*) iff p = the property of agreeing
   g. Val(r, *knows*) iff r = the relation of knowing

Phrasal Axioms

(2) a. Val(t, [$_S$ S$_1$ *and* S$_2$]) iff both Val(t, S$_1$) and Val(t, S$_2$)
   b. Val(t, [$_S$ S$_1$ *or* S$_2$]) iff either Val(t, S$_1$) or Val(t, S$_2$)
   c. Val(t, [$_S$ *It is not the case that* S]) iff it is not the case that Val(t, S)
   d. Val(t, [$_S$ NP VP]) iff for some x, p, Val(x, NP), Val(p, VP), and x has p
   e. Val(p, [$_{VP}$ V NP]) iff for some r, y, Val(r, V), Val(y, NP), and
       p = the property of being an x such that x bears r to y
   f. Val(x, [$_X$ Y]) iff Val(x, Y) (where X, Y are any nodes)

Production Rules

(UI) Universal instantiation

   For any x, $F(x)$
   _____
   $F(\alpha)$

(SE) Substitution of equivalents

   $F(\alpha)$
   α iff β
   _____
   $F(\beta)$

(SI) Substitution of identicals

   ϕ iff for some x, $F(x)$ and $x = \alpha$
   _____
   ϕ iff $F(\alpha)$

Exercises

1. Prove T sentences for the following examples of PC+:

   (1) Jill ponders.

   (2) Kate knows Jill.

2. State what axioms must be added to PC+ to prove interpretive T sentences for the following examples. Then prove these T sentences for each:

   (1) $[_S [_{NP}$ Rolf] $[_{VP} [_V$ ponders]]]

   (2) $[_S [_{NP}$ Chris] $[_{VP} [_V$ laughs]]]

   (3) $[_S [_{NP}$ Jill] $[_{VP} [_V$ admires] $[_{NP}$ Kate]]]

3. Sentences (1) and (2) both contain the dative or ditransitive verb *give*:

   (1) $[_S [_{NP}$ Chris] $[_{VP} [_V$ gives] $[_{NP}$ Kate] $[_{NP}$ Phil]]]

   (2) $[_S [_{NP}$ Chris] $[_{VP} [_V$ gives] $[_{NP}$ Phil] $[_{PP} [_P$ to] $[_{NP}$ Kate]]]]

   - What lexical and structural rules must be added to PC+ to interpret (1) and (2)? Give full T-sentence derivations for both sentences to illustrate your proposals.

   - Is your lexical axiom for *give* as it appears in (1) different from the axiom for *give* as it appears in (2)? Should it be?

   - Are the RHSs of the T sentences for (1) and (2) the same according to your rules? Should they be the same, or should they be different?

4. Sentence (1) below is an equative sentence; (2) is a predicational sentence containing an adjective; (3) is a predicational sentence containing a common noun:

   (1) Chris is Phil.

   (2) Chris is tired.

   (3) Chris is a linguist.

   Consider adding the rules in (4) to (7) to PC+ to treat these examples.

   (4) a. Val(x, *tired*) iff x is tired
       b. Val(x, *linguist*) iff x is a linguist

(5) $\text{Val}(x, [_{\text{NP}}\ a\ \text{N}])$ iff $\text{Val}(x, \text{N})$

(6) $\text{Val}(x, [_{\text{VP}}\ \text{V}\ X\text{P}])$ iff for some y, $\text{Val}(\langle x, y \rangle, \text{V})$ and $\text{Val}(y, X\text{P})$
     (where X is N or A)

(7) $\text{Val}(\langle x, y \rangle, is)$ iff $x = y$

Show that if (4) to (7) are added to PC+, the following T sentences can all
be derived:

(8) a. $\text{Val}(t, [_{\text{S}} [_{\text{NP}}\ \text{Chris}]\ [_{\text{VP}} [_{\text{V}}\ \text{is}]\ [_{\text{NP}}\ \text{Phil}]]])$ iff Chris = Phil
     b. $\text{Val}(t, [_{\text{S}} [_{\text{NP}}\ \text{Chris}]\ [_{\text{VP}} [_{\text{V}}\ \text{is}]\ [_{\text{AP}}\ \text{tired}]]])$ iff Chris is tired
     c. $\text{Val}(t, [_{\text{S}} [_{\text{NP}}\ \text{Chris}]\ [_{\text{VP}} [_{\text{V}}\ \text{is}]\ [_{\text{NP}}\ a\ \text{linguist}]]])$ iff Chris is a linguist

Assume that the two rules (6) and (7) are replaced by the single
rule (9), and that *be* is identified syntactically as a "pleonastic" or empty
verb ([+pleo]) that makes no semantic contribution to the sentence:

(9) $\text{Val}(x, [_{\text{VP}}\ \underset{[+\text{pleo}]}{\text{V}}\ X\text{P}])$ iff $\text{Val}(x, X\text{P})$ (where X is A or N)

Again show that the T sentences in (8) can all be derived.

Explain how the two axiom sets, though different, give the same results.
In particular, answer the following questions:

■ For each theory, what is the source of the "=" that appears in the RHS
   in (8a)? What expression in the LHS introduces it?

■ For each theory, what is the source of the "is" that appears on the RHS
   in (8b, c)? What expression in the LHS introduces it?

5. Extend PC+ to interpret sentences involving *be* and prepositional phrases
    such as the following:

    (1) a. Chris is near Kate.
         b. Phil is in Cambridge.

    Give T-sentence derivations for (1a, b) using your rules. You may use
    either (6) and (7), or (9), from problem 4 in analyzing *be*.

6. Extend the T theory PC+ to interpret sentences involving *be* and the ad-
    jectives and nouns in (1) and (2). You may use either (6) and (7), or (9),
    from problem 4 in analyzing *be*.

    (1) a. Jill is proud of Phil.
         b. Jill is angry at Chris.

(2) a. Phil is a friend of Chris.
    b. Jill is a sister of Kumiko.

7. In the text we suggested that examples like (1a–c) can be analyzed by adding the general schemes in (2) to PC+ (for all values α and $X = $ S, VP, V):

(1) a. $[_S [_S \text{ Jill ponders] and } [_S \text{ Jill agrees}]]$
    b. $[_S \text{ Jill } [_{VP} [_{VP} \text{ ponders] and } [_{VP} \text{ agrees}]]]$
    c. $[_S \text{ Phil } [_{VP} [_V [_V \text{ knows] or } [_V \text{ admires}]] \text{ Chris}]]$

(2) a. $\text{Val}(x, [_X X_1 \text{ and } X_2])$ iff $\text{Val}(x, X_1)$ and $\text{Val}(x, X_2)$
    b. $\text{Val}(x, [_X X_1 \text{ or } X_2])$ iff $\text{Val}(x, X_1)$ or $\text{Val}(x, X_2)$

■ Show that this is so. Prove T theorems for (1a–c).

■ Can the conjunction of simple noun phrases in examples like *Jill and Chris agree* be brought under your general interpretation scheme in (2a)? That is, can $[_{NP} \text{ NP } and \text{ NP}]$ be treated analogously to $[_{VP} \text{ VP } and \text{ VP}]$?

8. In problem 4 we suggested the axioms in (1) below to handle indefinite NPs occurring as predicates, as in (2). Will these axioms correctly interpret indefinite NPs occurring as arguments to Vs, as in (3)?

(1) a. $\text{Val}(x, linguist)$ iff x is a linguist
    b. $\text{Val}(x, [_{NP} a \text{ N}])$ iff $\text{Val}(x, \text{N})$

(2) Chris is a linguist.

(3) a. A linguist agrees.
    b. Jill knows a linguist.

If so, give a T-sentence derivation showing how. If not, explain why the derivation does not go through.

9. Extend PC+ to interpret sentences with depictive adjuncts like (1a, b):

(1) a. Phil arrived tired.
    b. Kumiko eats peanuts salted.

For (1b), consider the Williams-type structure (A), the Stowell-type structure (B), and the Kayne-type structure (C):[21]

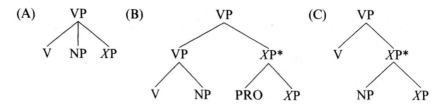

Prove your results by showing that they give interpretive T sentences for the sentences.

10. Extend PC+ to include resultative adjuncts like the following:

    (1) Jill squashes peanuts flat.

    Consider both a Williams-type structure (A) and a Kayne-type structure (C). What problems arise here beyond those involved with the depictive structures considered in the previous problem?

11. If we wish to extend PC+ to include the elements in (1), what problems arise in attempting to do so?

    (1) a. Vs that take sentential complements: *believe, expect*
        b. [$_{VP}$ V S]

12. Consider the following sentences:

    (1) a. Phil gave Fido to Kate.
        b. Jill lent Chris Fido.

    ▪ What axioms must be added to PC^{set} to interpret them correctly?
    ▪ What axioms must be added to PC^{prop}?

13. There is a similarity between the PC+ axioms for transitive sentences and the PC′ axioms for conjoined sentences. The S axiom in PC+ relates NP and VP by introducing an object that is the semantic value of both:

    (1) Val(t, [$_S$ NP VP]) iff for some x, Val(x, NP) and Val(x, VP)

    The conjoined-sentence rule of PC′ relates S and ConjP by introducing an object (t or f) that is the semantic value of both:

    (2) Val(t, [$_S$ S ConjP]) iff for some z, Val(z, S) and Val(z, ConjP)

    The VP rule of PC+ (3) and the ConjP rule of PC′ (4) are also closely parallel:

(3) Val(x, [$_{VP}$ V NP]) iff for some y, Val($\langle x, y \rangle$, V) and Val(y, NP)

(4) Val(z, [$_{ConjP}$ Conj S]) iff for some z', Val($\langle z, z' \rangle$, Conj) and Val(z', S)

A corresponding similarity exists between the semantic axioms for intransitive sentences in PC+ and those for negated sentences in PC′. These parallels suggest that the lexical conjunctions *and* and *or* are semantically similar to transitive predicates and that the lexical negation *it is not the case that* is similar to an intransitive predicate. From the standpoint of semantic properties of generality and object (in)dependence, however, is this a genuine analogy? Discuss.

14. Recall our hypothetical languages *A* and *B*. Does anything in the linguistic behavior of speakers of language *B*, as described, decide whether they can distinguish between one rabbit being white and more than one rabbit being white?

    Suppose that language *B* has a negation sign, *not*, that can be used to negate sentences (as in (1)) or to negate terms (as in (2)):

    (1) Not white rabbit!   Uttered and assented to when and only when no white rabbit is salient.

    (2) Rabbit not white!   Uttered and assented to when and only when at least one nonwhite rabbit is salient.

    Does this show anything significant about the meaning of the terms *white* and *rabbit*?

15. In chapter 3 we said that syntactic rules and principles are not construction-specific but apply to structures in a very general way. It is attractive to think that semantics too has this very general character. One natural idea is that semantic axioms for particular configurations like S, VP, etc., might ultimately be replaced with very general ones like those in (1):

    (1) a. Val(t, [$_{ZP}$ XP YP]) iff for some x, Val(x, XP) and Val(x, YP)
        b. Val(x, [$_{XP}$ X YP]) iff for some y, Val($\langle x, y \rangle$, X) and Val(y, YP)

    Here X, Y, and Z range over any phrase category. Axiom (1a) gives a very general scheme for subject-predicate configurations, and axiom (1b) for predicate-complement configurations. If this move is made, what does it imply about the status of the ill-formed strings (2a–c)?

(2) a. *[NP Jill] [NP Jill]
   b. *[VP Agrees] [VP agrees]
   c. *[VP Agrees] [VP knows [VP ponders]]

Specifically, are they predicted to be ill-formed and meaningless, or ill-formed and meaningful? Does this diagnosis seem correct? Explain your answer carefully.

16. Evans's thought experiments described in the chapter give evidence for predicates in natural language. Within clauses like *Chris agrees* and *Jill knows Kate* we can identify elements that can be securely analyzed as predicates. The word *agrees*, for example, characterizes a condition on objects that is met just in case the object agrees. Does this evidence support our distinguishing a predicate phrase? That is, are the results compatible with the structure in (1), in which no VP is posited?

(1)

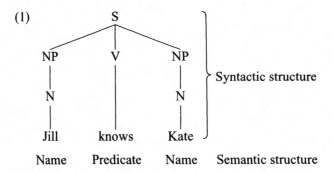

17. Consider the homophonic axioms in (1) and the nonhomophonic, dictionary-style axioms in (2):

(1) a. Val(*x, ponders*) iff *x* ponders
    b. Val(*x, agrees*) iff *x* agrees
    c. Val(⟨*x, y*⟩, *knows*) iff *x* knows *y*

(2) a. Val(*x, ponders*) iff *x* thinks quietly, soberly, and deeply
    b. Val(*x, agrees*) iff *x* gives assent or accedes
    c. Val(⟨*x, y*⟩, *knows*) iff *x* is acquainted or familiar with *y*

What T sentences do (2a–c) yield for the sentences in (3) when they are substituted for (1a–c) in PC+?

(3) a. Phil ponders.
    b. Chris agrees.
    c. Jill knows Kate.

Is there a difference in interpretivity between the T sentences yielded by (1a–c) and those given by (2a–c)?

18. Certain verbs of English alternate between an intransitive form and a causative/transitive form:

(1) a. The door opened/closed.
    b. Chris opened/closed the door.

(2) a. The mirror broke/shattered.
    b. Kumiko broke/shattered the mirror.

(3) a. The ice melted/froze.
    b. Kate melted/froze the ice.

Others do not:

(4) a. Chris laughed.
    b. *Kate laughed Chris.

(5) a. Rolf shrugged.
    b. Phil shrugged Rolf.

It is a common intuition that this pattern is not random, that the verbs that show the intransitive/transitive alternation share certain features of meaning. Consider the following dictionary-style axioms for *open, break, melt*, and *grow*:

(6) a. Val(x, *opens*) iff x comes to be in a state of having or presenting no enclosing or confining barrier
    b. Val(x, *breaks*) iff x comes to be in a state of separation into parts as a result of sudden or violent action
    c. Val(x, *melts*) iff x comes to be in a liquid state after having been in a solid state
    d. Val(x, *grows*) iff x comes to be in a state of increased size or maturity

What advantages might such axioms have over more familiar homophonic axioms in getting at the common properties of these intransitive verbs? Explain carefully.[22]

19. An alternative way of capturing relations between predicates is to state a general rule relating lexical axioms. For example, suppose that along with the separate axioms (1a, b) and (2a, b), we include the lexical rule (3), where V^{IE} is the class of intransitive verbs that have a causative counterpart and V^T is the general class of transitives:

(1) a. Val(x, *opens$_1$*) iff x opens
    b. Val($\langle x, y \rangle$, *opens$_2$*) iff x brings it about that y opens

(2) a. Val(x, *breaks$_1$*) iff x breaks
    b. Val($\langle x, y \rangle$, *breaks$_2$*) iff x brings it about that y breaks

(3) For every $\alpha \in V^{IE}$, there is an homophonous $\alpha' \in V^T$ such that Val($\langle x, y \rangle$, α') iff x brings it about that Val(y, α)

By including (3) as an axiom, we make the claim that the presence of intransitive-causative pairs is not accidental in English. Given an appropriate intransitive, this rule guarantees the presence of a corresponding causative.

In English (and many other languages) verbs of personal hygiene that are notionally transitive often show an intransitive **inherent reflexive** counterpart. The inherent reflexive form holds of its subject just in case the transitive form holds reflexively of the subject and himself or herself. Thus *Chris washes* is true (with intransitive *wash*) just in case *Chris washes Chris* or *Chris washes himself* is true (with transitive *wash*):

(4) a. Chris washed the car.
    b. Chris washed.

(5) a. Phil shaved Rolf.
    b. Phil shaved.

(6) a. Kate bathed Jill.
    b. Kate bathed.

Extend the lexical-rule approach illustrated above to handle inherent reflexives.

20. English speakers recognize an implication relation between the first and second member of each pair in (1) through (3):

(1) a. Kate pats Fido.
     b. Kate touches Fido.

(2) a. Jill sells Fido to Phil.
     b. Phil buys Fido from Kate.

(3) a. Kate chases Jill.
     b. Jill flees Kate.

Such implicational relations may be captured through statements that explicitly link the values of the verbs in question, for example, (4a–c):

(4) a. $\text{Val}(\langle x, y \rangle, pats)$ only if $\text{Val}(\langle x, y \rangle, touches)$
     b. $\text{Val}(\langle x, y, z \rangle, sells)$ only if $\text{Val}(\langle z, y, x \rangle\ buys)$
     c. $\text{Val}(\langle x, y \rangle, chase)$ only if $\text{Val}(\langle y, x \rangle, flee)$

Statements like (4a–c) are called **meaning postulates**. They give explicit constraints on relations between the meanings of words.

■ As a device for relating the meanings of expressions, meaning postulates might be seen as an alternative to or competitor with dictionary-style axioms. Why?

■ Should the relations expressed by statements like (4a–c) be analyzed as part of our knowledge of English? Are implications like those in (1), (2), and (3) semantic in nature? Discuss.

5   Proper Nouns and Reference

In the previous chapter we saw how sentences made up of proper nouns and verbs get their truth conditions. Nouns introduce individual objects. Verbs express a condition on objects. The sentence is true if and only if the objects introduced meet the conditions expressed. This sort of semantic structure is simple, basic, and intuitively very easy to understand: one type of term refers to something, the other describes it. Even so, all of the basic concepts turn out to be technically and conceptually challenging. We have already looked at some of the complexities arising with verbs and predication. In this chapter we examine proper nouns and reference more closely.

5.1   Proper Nouns in PC+

The axioms for proper nouns in PC+ are simple in form and appear simple in content. All that a rule like (1) seems to tell us about the semantics of *Jill* is that to be its value is to be the very person Jill.

(1) Val(x, *Jill*) iff x = Jill

Proper-noun axioms in PC+ seem to do no more than associate a particular word with a particular thing. Nonetheless, behind the innocent appearance of (1) lurk a number of serious complexities. We will illustrate these by considering two simple but surprisingly tough empirical questions that arise for PC+:

- How should the theory treat **coextensive proper nouns**: two or more proper nouns that are associated with the same individual?

- How should the theory treat **empty proper nouns**: proper nouns that are associated with no individual?

5.1.1   The Problem of Coextensive Proper Nouns

In day-to-day life we frequently encounter distinct proper nouns referring to the same person. Take stage names in the entertainment industry, for instance. The man whose movie billing was *Cary Grant* originally bore the name *Archie Leach*. The individual named *Judy Garland* was originally named *Frances Gumm*. Lauren Bacall originally had the name *Betty Joan Perske*. And so on. Consider also the widespread custom of wives taking their husband's names after marriage. For example, the Kleinian analyst Dr. Hanna Segal was formerly named *Hanna Poznanska*.

Coextensive proper nouns are interesting and important semantically because natural language seems to allow such proper nouns to have different significance for speakers, despite having the same reference. For example, suppose Lori is personally acquainted with the individual Archie Leach in his youth. Later she becomes familiar with the actor Cary Grant through the movies but fails to realize that Cary Grant is none other than her old friend Archie. For Lori, it is just as if *Cary Grant* and *Archie Leach* are the names of two different persons. All of her behavior, thoughts and beliefs indicate that she assigns the two terms different semantic properties. For instance, suppose that Lori suddenly notices the similarity in features between Cary Grant and her one-time acquaintance Archie Leach. She might then wonder aloud that (2):

(2) Perhaps Cary Grant is Archie Leach.

If Archie Leach and Cary Grant were identical in meaning, her utterance of (2) would mean just the same as an utterance of (3):

(3) Perhaps Archie Leach is Archie Leach.

But this seems absurd. Surely, Lori knows perfectly well that Archie Leach is Archie Leach and would hardly bother to remark on the fact. What interests her is a quite different thought that has just dawned: that perhaps the famous actor Cary Grant is her old friend Archie Leach.

In view of the clear intuition that coextensive names can have different significance, it is natural to ask how we might represent this difference in PC+. How do we assign the two distinct semantic properties? Clearly, adding a pair of axioms like (4a, b) won't do.

(4) a. Val(x, *Cary Grant*) iff x = Cary Grant
     b. Val(x, *Archie Leach*) iff x = Cary Grant

Giving identical RHSs would be tantamount to treating the two proper names *Cary Grant* and *Archie Leach* as semantically indistinguishable: their contribution would be exactly the same. For a speaker like Lori this is simply not right. Very well, then, what about an alternative pair that uses "Cary Grant" versus "Archie Leach" on the RHS:

(5) a. Val(x, *Cary Grant*) iff x = Cary Grant
    b. Val(x, *Archie Leach*) iff x = Archie Leach

On reflection, it's not clear that this will do either. After all, since Cary Grant and Archie Leach are exactly the same person, being identical to Cary Grant is exactly the same thing as being identical to Archie Leach. The conditions specified on the RHSs of the biconditionals in (4b) and (5b) appear to be the same. Even though we have used orthographically different words in the metalanguage to specify the relevant individual, the very same individual is involved.

Given this result, it's not obvious that knowledge of (4b) amounts to anything different than knowledge of (5b). In both cases we know that something is a value of the proper noun iff it is identical to a certain person, and that person is the same. But then how can PC+ axioms capture the different significance of coextensive proper nouns? How can it represent the knowledge of a speaker like Lori?

5.1.2 The Problem of Empty Proper Nouns

The proper-noun axioms of PC+ associate words with real, existing things. But alongside these there are also **empty proper nouns**: proper nouns not associated with any real, existing object. Late in the last century, observations of the planet Mercury led astronomers to postulate a new planet circling the sun within its orbit. They gave this planet the name *Vulcan* and searched the sky for it. But Vulcan was never found, and we now know that no such planet exists. The proper noun *Vulcan* refers to nothing at all.

Natural language is full of such empty proper nouns, including well-known terms from fiction, like *Pegasus* and *Rumplestiltzkin*, and nouns for entities that were thought to exist but were later discovered not to, like *Vulcan* and *El Dorado*. Furthermore, new empty proper nouns are easy to create. For example, suppose mischievous students were to enter the name *Paul R. Zwier* into the registry files of a university computer. They compile a complete bogus record to go with the name, including educational background, home address,

GPA, etc. A university official happens to read the file and comes to believe various things about the fictitious student. The official even says (6) at a meeting on student achievement:

(6) Paul R. Zwier has a GPA of 3.9.

Paul R. Zwier would be an empty term here. The proper noun refers to no one.

A strong intuition about empty proper nouns is that even though they fail to refer, they nonetheless make a meaningful contribution to the sentences in which they occur. Early twentieth-century astronomers might have questioned the truth of *Vulcan circles the Sun*, but they would not have doubted its sense. The sentence appears to state a determinate scientific claim about the solar system. In a similar way, even though the made-up name *Paul R. Zwier* fails to name a real person in the situation described, this failure seems largely irrelevant to understanding the term. Intuitively, (6) would mean the very same thing if the file data were accurate and Zwier were a real student rather than a fictitious one. To be sure, the sentence is false, but it is not meaningless.

A semantic theory of proper nouns should presumably capture the intuition that sentences with empty proper nouns are meaningful, even if usually false.[1] Accordingly, we would like to have results like (7a, b), which ascribe determinate truth-conditions for such sentences:

(7) a. Val(t, *Vulcan circles the Sun*) iff Vulcan circles the Sun
    b. Val(t, *Paul R. Zwier has a GPA of 3.9*) iff Paul R. Zwier has a GPA of 3.9

To do so, we are drawn naturally to axioms like (8a, b), which parallel our axioms for *Jill* and *Chris* and yield the desired T theorems in a parallel way:

(8) a. Val(x, *Vulcan*) iff x = Vulcan
    b. Val(x, *Paul R. Zwier*) iff x = Paul R. Zwier

Nonetheless, including rules like (8a, b) in our theory is not straightforward. After all, what exactly is the sense of (8a, b)? With an axiom like (1) matters seem clear enough.

(1) Val(x, *Jill*) iff x = Jill

The RHS expresses a precise and determinate condition on objects: being identical with Jill. If there is an individual Jill, there is such a thing as being identical to Jill. But what about (8a, b)? Since there is no Vulcan and no Paul

R. Zwier, there is no such thing as being identical to these individuals. But then what are we attributing to speakers when we say they know such a rule?[2]

5.2 Descriptive Names

The job of explaining coextensive and empty proper nouns in PC+ appears formidable. We have to say how knowing (5a) could amount to something different than knowing (5b).

(5) a. Val(x, *Cary Grant*) iff x = Cary Grant
 b. Val(x, *Archie Leach*) iff x = Archie Leach

And we have to say how knowing (8a, b) could amount to anything at all. Given this challenge, it might seem better to abandon the PC+ analysis of proper nouns and seek a different semantics entirely, one that avoids the problems. Alternative approaches are in fact available. To motivate one, let us briefly consider another thought experiment.

5.2.1 Hypothesizing Names

In the last chapter we introduced two simple, fictional languages, *A* and *B*, and we examined how you might tell from the linguistic behavior of their speakers whether the languages contained genuine predications. Consider now a third language, *C*, that raises analogous questions about names.

Language *C* is similar to *B* in containing type 1 and type 2 expressions. But you observe that it includes another sort of expression as well: type 3. These forms are like those of type 1 in that they are prompted by the presence of certain objects. But unlike type 1 expressions, each applies only when a specific individual is present. The utterance of such a term as a one-word sentence is thus correlated with the proximity or salience of a specific individual or object: *Mugar* correlates with one of the speakers (call him Mugar), Garum with another (call him Garum), *Gavag* correlates with a specific rabbit, *Jabba* with a specific hut, and so on:

(9) Type	Expression	Utterance situation
3	*Mugar*	Uttered in the presence of a specific creature (Mugar).
	Garum	Uttered in the presence of a specific creature (Garum).

Gavag	Uttered in the presence of a specific rabbit (Gavag).
Jabba	Uttered in the presence of a specific hut (Jabba).

Type 3 expressions appear in sentences along with both type 2 and type 1 expressions. Thus you find expressions like *Mugar green, Garum rabbit*, and *Jabba hut*. These complex expressions have assent conditions of a familiar kind: *Mugar green* is assented to when and only when the creature Mugar is green (assume these beings are chameleonlike and can alter their surface coloration at will). *Gavag rabbit* always elicits assent. *Mugar rabbit* always elicits dissent, and sometimes laughter.

How should you analyze the type 3 expressions? If all that you know about their usage is what is recorded in (9), then at least two possibilities are open. One simple hypothesis is that the type 3 expressions function like names in PC+; that is, they identify one specific individual. *Mugar, Garum*, etc., would be labels for some particular being or object. There is another possibility however. Suppose that each of the objects in question is the unique possessor of some property: Mugar is the tallest being in the speech community, Garum is the community's one and only doctor, Gavag is the unique mascot of the community, and Jabba the only doctor's hut. In this case it is possible that the type 3 expressions are really just type 1 expressions, that is, predicates: *Mugar* applies to an object iff it is the tallest being in the community, *Gavag* applies to an object iff it is the community mascot, *Jabba* applies to an object iff it is the doctor's hut, and so on.

How can you decide whether type 3 expressions are names or predicates? If type 3 expressions are predicates expressing the conditions we have described, then it might seem that simple tests would serve. Thus you wait until the tribe has a new tallest individual, a new mascot, a new doctor, a new doctor's hut, and so on. If they do not assent to *Gavag* in the obvious presence of a new mascot, then *Gavag* presumably does not mean mascot. Likewise, if they do not assent to *Jabba* in the presence of a new doctor's hut, then *Jabba* presumably does not mean doctor's hut.

Nonetheless, in the situation described it remains possible that for each object to which a type 3 expression applies there really is some special condition that only this object meets. And this points to an important asymmetry in the strength of evidence for predicates versus names. We saw in chapter 4 that it seems impossible to account for the significance of type 2 expressions in language *B* without analyzing them as genuine predicates. By contrast, if you don't analyze type 3 expressions in language *C* as names, then nothing much goes terribly wrong. The view that type 3 expressions are predicates expressing conditions that are uniquely tied to specific objects will account for speaker behavior. True, we must acknowledge that the predicate condition has not yet been found, so the hypothesis that type 3 expressions are predicates may be poorly motivated in these circumstances. But it is not clearly false, and hence cannot be dismissed.

5.2.2   The Theory PC+ ^{DN}

Our discussion of language C brings out the possibility that expressions superficially appearing to behave like proper nouns in PC+ might rather be predicates of a special kind, predicates designed so that each of them applies to just one specific individual. We call these special predicates **descriptive names**.

PC+ ^{DN} is a theory containing predicates of this kind. The semantics of a descriptive name is given by specifying a condition that picks out a unique individual. The semantic value of the descriptive name is then whatever individual meets this condition. PC+ ^{DN} contains familiar names from history, with the axioms given in (10):[3]

(10) a. Val(x, *Venus*) iff x is an ancient-Roman goddess of love and for all y, if y is an ancient-Roman goddess of love, then $y = x$.
   b. Val(x, *Isaac Newton*) iff x discovered gravity and for all y, if y discovered gravity, then $y = x$.
   c. Val(x, *Bucephalus*) iff x is a black, high-spirited war horse belonging to Alexander III, given to Alexander by Philip of Macedonia, and for all y, if y is a black, high-spirited war horse belonging to Alexander III, given to Alexander by Philip of Macedonia, then $y = x$
   d. Val(x, *Hesperus*) iff x is the brightest body visible in the evening sky and for all y, if y is the brightest body visible in the evening sky, then $y = x$.
   e. Val(x, *Phosphorus*) iff x is the last celestial body to shine in the morning sky and for all y, if is the last celestial body to shine in the morning sky, then $y = x$.

Note that each of these has the general form $F(x)$ and *for all y, if $F(y)$, then $y = x$*. The italicized clause guarantees uniqueness. Suppose that there is some object x, that is the ancient-Roman goddess of love. According to (10a), if there is any object y that is the ancient-Roman goddess of love, it must be identical with the original x. This means that x must be the one and only ancient-Roman goddess of love. The uniqueness clause forces descriptive names to designate a single, specific individual and distinguishes them from ordinary predicates.

PC+^{DN} differs from PC+ only in its axioms for proper nouns. The PC+^{DN} lexical rules for verbs are identical to those of PC+, as are its axioms for phrasal structures. To illustrate its results with a concrete example, consider (11):

(11)

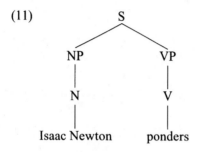

The interpretation of the S node is spelled out in the usual way in (12a). As the reader can then show, the subject NP receives the evaluation in (12b), and the verb phrase that in (12c):

(12) a. Val(t, [$_S$ [$_{NP}$ [$_N$ Isaac Newton]] [$_{VP}$ [$_V$ ponders]]]) iff for some x,
          Val(x, [$_{NP}$ [$_N$ Isaac Newton]]) and Val(x, [$_{VP}$ [$_V$ ponders]])
      b. Val(x, [$_{NP}$ [$_N$ Isaac Newton]]) iff x discovered gravity and
          for all y, if y discovered gravity, then $y = x$
      c. Val(x, [$_{VP}$ [$_V$ ponders]]) iff x ponders

(13) Val(t, [$_S$ [$_{NP}$ [$_N$ Isaac Newton]] [$_{VP}$ [$_V$ ponders]]]) iff for some x,
      x discovered gravity and for all y, if y discovered gravity, then $y = x$,
      and x ponders

According to (13), *Isaac Newton ponders* is true iff the unique individual who discovered gravity ponders. This T theorem is clearly true. It is arguably interpretive as well.

5.2.3   Semantic Properties of Descriptive Names

Descriptive names show an interesting mix of semantic properties in comparison to predicates and PC+-style proper nouns. Like the latter, descriptive names are associated with **singular conditions of application**. Furthermore, this feature is built into descriptive names in a way that distinguishes them sharply from normal predicates. We noted earlier that ordinary predicates like *is a city of more than eight million people in southern England* and *is a prime number between two and five* may apply to a single object. But when they do, this unique reference is, as it were, accidental; it does not follow from their semantic category. They remain ordinary predicates, indistinguishable in type from *is a city of less than eight million people in southern England* and *is a prime number between two and fifty*, which apply to a plurality of objects. With descriptive names the situation is different. The requirement that descriptive names apply each to a single individual is built into their axioms. The formulation for *Isaac Newton* requires the name to apply to exactly one object: the one and only discoverer of gravity.

On the other hand, descriptive names share with predicates the fact that they are associated with **object-independent conditions of application**. Recall that a predicate is indifferent not only to the number of individuals that meet its condition but to their identity as well. Predicates with different conditions and different meanings can still have the same extension. Descriptive names are also indifferent to specific individuals, as we can see by comparing (14) and (15):

(14) Val(x, *Isaac Newton*) iff x discovered gravity and for all y, if y discovered gravity, then $y = x$

(15) Val(x, *Isaac Newton*) iff $x =$ Isaac Newton

As we have seen, the former makes *Isaac Newton ponders* true iff there is some unique individual x who discovered gravity and who ponders, (13). These conditions make no reference to any particular person; all they require is that the unique individual that discovered gravity, *whoever he or she may be*, ponders. Of course, historically the individual meeting this description was Isaac Newton. But this is not reflected in (13): Isaac Newton does not directly figure in the RHS of the T sentence. By contrast, the axiom in (15) does yield object dependent truth-conditions. The latter will make *Isaac Newton ponders* true iff Isaac Newton, that very person, ponders.

Coextensive Proper Nouns and Empty Proper Nouns

Semantic differences between PC+ and PC+^{DN} also appear in the issues of coextensive and empty proper nouns. These raised serious questions for the proper-noun axioms of PC+. By contrast, they raise no difficulties at all for PC+^{DN}. Hesperus and Phosphorus are the very same planet, Venus, but the proper nouns *Hesperus* and *Phosphorus*, as defined by (10d) and (10e), respectively, are associated with different evaluation conditions, and so with different meanings. Compare (16) and (17):

(16)   Val(t, [$_S$ [$_{NP}$ [$_N$ Hesperus]] [$_{VP}$ [$_V$ circles the sun]]) iff for some x, x is the brightest body visible in the evening sky and for all y, if y is the brightest body visible in the evening sky, then $y = x$, and x circles the sun

(17)   Val(t, [$_S$ [$_{NP}$ [$_N$ Phosphorus]] [$_{VP}$ [$_V$ circles the sun]]) iff for some x, x is the last celestial body to shine in the morning sky and for all y, if y is the last celestial body to shine in the morning sky, then $y = x$, and x circles the sun

The two state very different interpretations for the sentences *Hesperus circles the sun* and *Phosphorus circles the sun*. This is clear from their different entailments. For example, (16) entails that some one thing is the brightest body visible in the evening sky and circles the sun, whereas (17) does not. By contrast, (17) entails that some one thing is the last celestial body to shine in the morning sky and circles the sun, whereas (16) does not.

These features yield a direct account of Lori and her childhood friend Archie Leach, also known as Cary Grant, within a PC+ ^{DN}-style theory. We can take Lori to possess two different axioms along the lines of (18a, b):

(18)   a.   Val(x, *Cary Grant*) iff for some x, x is a male movie actor who starred in *North by Northwest*, etc., and for all y, if y is a male movie actor who starred in *North by Northwest*, etc., then $y = x$

       b.   Val(x, *Archie Leach*) iff x is a man who went to Central High, sat behind Lori in algebra class, etc., and for all y, if y is a man who went to Central High, sat behind Lori in algebra class, etc., then $y = x$

These two are as different as any axioms applying to two different individuals. Insofar as the axioms themselves are concerned, there is no connection between them. Unlike the corresponding PC+ rules, they are not obliged by their definition to apply to the same person. It is thus fully understandable how Lori might form very different judgments with sentences involving one term versus sentences involving the other.

Finally, PC+ ^{DN} also deals straightforwardly with empty proper nouns. Like predicates, descriptive names are associated with a definite condition of application, and this provides them with a definite meaning, whether the condition happens to be met by anything or not. Axiom (10a) provides a perfectly sensible meaning for *Venus* even though no such being as the mythical Roman goddess of love exists or ever did exist. Similarly, although *Paul R. Zwier* was an entirely made-up name, it may still receive an impeccable axiom in PC+^{DN}:

(19) Val(x, *Paul R. Zwier*) iff x is a student at UC San Diego, x has a GPA of 3.9, etc., and for all y, if y is a student at UC San Diego, and y has a GPA of 3.9, etc., then $y = x$

(20) Val(t, *Paul R. Zwier is a hardworking fellow*) iff for some x, x is a student at UC San Diego, x has a GPA of 3.9, etc., and for all y, if y is a student at UC San Diego, y has a GPA of 3.9, etc., then $y = x$, and x is a hardworking fellow

Such sentences will, of course, be false. Since there is no Paul R. Zwier, the condition "for some x, ..." cannot be met. Nonetheless, they are no less meaningful than a sentence containing a referring proper noun.

5.3 Problems for PC+ ^{DN}

PC+ and PC+^{DN} are different theories of proper-noun semantics, and hence competitors. And as things stand, the second appears to have significant advantages over the first. While coextensive and empty proper nouns raise serious difficulties for PC+, PC+^{DN} handles these phenomena smoothly and in exactly the same way that it handles noncoextensive predicates, and predicates with an empty extension.

These points do not settle the contest, however. Although coextensive and empty terms raise no special problems for PC+^{DN}, there are other phenomena that do. Two of the most interesting are the rigidity of natural-language proper nouns and the problem of descriptive conditions.

5.3.1 Rigidity of Proper Nouns

Rigidity is an important feature of proper nouns that needs to be taken into consideration by any semantic theory. To understand this feature, we need to consider a certain rather special kind of judgment about the truth conditions of sentences. Take sentence (21):

(21) Isaac Newton was made Warden of the Mint.

We know that this sentence is true iff Isaac Newton was made Warden of the Mint. But we can also ask, Under what possible circumstances would this sentence have been true? One possibility, of course, is that the sentence might have meant something else. Suppose that *Isaac Newton* was the name of Johannes Kepler, and that *was made Warden of the Mint* had meant, discovered the elliptical motion of the planets. Then the sentence would have been true, since Kepler did in fact discover the elliptical motion of the planets. But this is not the sort of possibility that is important. Rather, we want to know under what possible circumstances (21) would have been true, given what it actually means. The answer to this question is that it would have been true in any circumstance in which the individual Isaac Newton was made Warden of the Mint.

Now consider (22) by way of contrast:

(22) The person who discovered gravity was made Warden of the Mint.

Under what possible circumstances is (22) true, given what it means? As it happens, Isaac Newton, the person who who discovered gravity, was made Warden of the Mint in 1696 and supervised the recasting of all English coinage. Does this mean that (22) is true in any circumstance in which Isaac Newton was made Warden of the Mint? No. There are possible circumstances in which someone other than Newton discovered gravity. Suppose that Robert Hooke, a contemporary scientist, had been the discoverer. Then, relative to this possible circumstance, (22) is true if and only if Robert Hooke had been made Warden of the Mint. Likewise, if Leibniz had discovered gravity, then (22) is true in this possible circumstance if and only if Leibniz had been made Warden of the Mint.

These examples reveal an important distinction between the proper noun *Isaac Newton* and the descriptive phrase *the person who discovered gravity*. When the proper noun appears in a sentence and we consider the truth value of the sentence relative to various possible circumstances, we always need to consider the state and doings of the same individual, Newton himself. But when the descriptive phrase appears in a sentence and we consider the truth value of the sentence relative to various possible circumstances, there is no unique individual whose state and doings the matter depends on.

The reason for this difference can be traced back to a difference between the semantics of the two phrases. There is no possible circumstance in which *Isaac Newton* could have referred to some other individual unless it also changed its meaning. We can put this point by saying that proper nouns, like *Isaac*

Newton, are **rigid designators**. (The expression is from Kripke 1972, though we depart from his official definition.) The phrase *the person who discovered gravity* works differently. Even if we keep its meaning fixed, it can pick out different individuals in different possible circumstances. Its semantics, like that of a predicate, doesn't tie it to any one individual. The descriptive phrase is a nonrigid designator.

Whether a term of natural language is a rigid designator is a matter to be decided by our intuitions, our judgments about the truth of sentences in various possible circumstances. These judgments provide data to which a semantic theory is answerable. Such judgments with nearly all natural-language proper nouns show that they are indeed rigid. Hence uniform rigidity is a property that we want our semantic theory to capture. How do PC+ and PC+^{DN} square with respect to rigidity? To answer this we must look closely at the axioms they provide for proper nouns. Compare the PC+ axiom for *Isaac Newton*, (23), with its PC+^{DN} counterpart (10b):

(23) Val(x, *Isaac Newton*) iff x = Isaac Newton

(10b) Val(x, *Isaac Newton*) iff x discovered gravity and for all y, if y discovered gravity, then $y = x$

We need to look at the RHSs of these axioms, which specify the valuation conditions of the proper noun, to see if these conditions tie the proper noun to a particular individual in all possible circumstances or leave room for variation. More specifically, we look at the RHS to see whether the condition can be met by only one individual or whether, had the world been different in certain ways, the condition could have been met by any of a plurality of individuals. If the former, then the axiom renders the proper noun rigid. If the latter, then it renders it nonrigid.

The results with PC+ and PC+^{DN} are obvious. The condition specified by the RHS of (23) is the condition of being identical with Isaac Newton. Nobody other than Isaac Newton himself could possibly have met this condition. Thus (23) treats *Isaac Newton* as a rigid designator. But the condition specified by the RHS of (10b) could have been met by various individuals. Had Robert Hooke been the unique discoverer of gravity, then the condition would have met by him; likewise for Leibniz. So (10b) renders *Isaac Newton* nonrigid.

This result generalizes in the following way. PC+-style axioms associate proper nouns with the condition of being identical with some specific individual. Any such condition can be met only by the one individual that actually meets it, if any individual does. Therefore, PC+ correctly treats all proper nouns as rigid designators. With PC+^{DN}, the issue is somewhat more complicated. In (10b) the noun was rendered nonrigid. But this needn't happen in all cases. Recall the mathematical fact that 2 is the only even prime number.[4] Mathematics being what it is, this is so in any possible circumstance. Nothing other than 2 can possibly be an even prime number, no matter how different the universe might have been. In view of this, the descriptive name given by (24) is a rigid designator:

(24) Val(x, *Mr. Even Prime*) iff x is even and x is prime and for all y, if y is even and y is prime, then $y = x$

More generally, whenever the valuation condition of a descriptive name is one that can be met only by one thing under any possible circumstance, that name will be rigid. The upshot is that PC+^{DN} does not treat proper nouns as uniformly rigid. And indeed, many proper nouns we judge to be rigid (e.g., all the proper nouns appearing in (10)) PC+^{DN} incorrectly treats as nonrigid.

5.3.2 Making Descriptive Names Rigid

Given these results, PC+^{DN} is clearly in need of revision. Specifically, we must find some way of insuring that the descriptive conditions in its proper-noun axioms are rigid, that they pick out the same unique individual across any set of circumstances. As it turns out, descriptive names can be made rigid by adding a special semantic stipulation of a certain kind. To see how this might work, consider the following claim:

(25) If Hooke, rather than Newton, had first noted the universal attraction of bodies, then the actual discoverer of gravity would not have discovered gravity.

Sentence (25) describes a possible circumstance in which the person who discovered gravity in the real world did not end up discovering gravity. The important point to note is how the expression *the actual discoverer of gravity functions*. This picks out the person who discovered gravity in the real world (Newton), not the person who did so in the described circumstance (Hooke). *Actual* thus works like a rigidifier: it ensures that when one considers the interpretation of a term relative to an imagined, nonfactual circumstance, one still thinks of the individual who meets the condition of evaluation in the real world, irrespective of whether that individual meets the condition in the non-factual world.

We can use the word *actually* in this way, as a stipulative rigidifier, in the RHS defining a descriptive name. Consider the new descriptive name *Isaac Newton@*, defined as in (26), and contrast this with the old descriptive name *Isaac Newton*, defined as in (10b):

(26)   Val(x, *Isaac Newton@*) iff x actually discovered gravity and for all y, if y actually discovered gravity, then $y = x$

(10b) Val(x, *Isaac Newton*) iff x discovered gravity and for all y, if y discovered gravity, then $y = x$

The truth conditions of *Isaac Newton ponders* and *Isaac Newton@ ponders* are the same in the actual world. Both are true if Isaac Newton, the discoverer of gravity, ponders, and both are false if he does not. But consider their truth conditions in the hypothetical situation in which Hooke first discovered gravity. *Isaac Newton ponders* would be true in that circumstance iff Hooke (the discoverer in the imagined circumstance) ponders in that circumstance. By contrast, *Isaac Newton@ ponders* would be true in that circumstance iff Isaac Newton (the discoverer in the actual world) ponders in that circumstance. Their truth conditions in this counterfactual situation are quite different.

We see, then, that by adding an element like "actual(ly)" to the RHS of the biconditionals for descriptive names, it is possible to insure that they will be uniformly rigid. Thus if natural-language proper nouns are assigned descriptive axioms of this kind, they will be rigid, as required.

5.3.3   The Problem of Descriptive Conditions

Making descriptive names rigid overcomes one serious challenge for them. But the problems do not end here. There is another, more serious difficulty facing PC+ ^{DN}. If proper nouns are descriptive names, then for each proper noun in a speaker's language there must be some descriptive condition that uniquely picks out the noun's bearer and that gives the meaning of the noun for the speaker. However, in practice it seems nearly impossible to come up with the right evaluation conditions on the RHS. A number of difficulties have been raised for the suggestion that names have associated descriptive conditions of the requisite kind, particularly by Kripke (1972). We will consider two of these problems, one that is troublesome and one that is decisive in our view.

Inadequate Conditions

The first problem is that frequently a speaker makes competent use of a proper noun without knowing enough about the bearer to uniquely pick it out from among all the other objects in the world. In such a case it seems impossible that the speaker could have in mind a descriptive condition sufficiently rich to specify the bearer. Many people, for example, have heard of William Gladstone and can use and understand the name. But surely lots of speakers don't know anything more about him than that he was a British prime minister in the nineteenth century. This doesn't distinguish Gladstone from Benjamin Disreali or Robert Peel. Yet these speakers can use the proper noun to refer to Gladstone. Or, to give another example, someone might know that Manet and Monet are both French impressionists, and be able to distinguish French impressionist paintings from those of other styles quite easily, without knowing anything that distinguishes Manet from Monet. Yet this person could use both proper nouns to say, for example, that Manet and Monet were both French impressionists. Examples of this sort are not difficult to think of. Indeed, quite likely some speakers know that Isaac Newton was a famous British scientist from some previous century but know no more than this. Such speakers can use and understand the name but have no way of uniquely identifying its bearer by description.

One might answer that in all of these cases there is something further that speakers know, and this will distinguish the bearer of the name from others. This further information is precisely knowledge of the bearer's name. The speakers just described *do* know something more about the British scientist: they know that he was called *Isaac Newton*. And this is something that sets him apart from other British scientists of some past century.[5] Nonetheless, the response does not seem to get to the root of the difficulty that Kripke observes. Whether or not speakers in fact have descriptions that are rich enough to pick out the bearers of proper nouns, it is not at all clear that this is a necessary condition for competence with those nouns. Here is a test case for your intuitions. Imagine that there are two British scientists of previous centuries both called *Isaac Newton*. One of them, Newton$_1$, discovered gravity, while the other, Newton$_2$, was a nineteenth-century physicist who made a great breakthrough in the study of electrical resistance. Suppose that Peter reads an article in a newspaper about Isaac Newton, the discoverer of gravity, but has never heard anything about Newton$_2$. After a couple of years Peter forgets everything he read about Newton$_1$, except that he was a British scientist of some past century. He remains entirely ignorant of the existence of Newton$_2$. Peter now has no uniquely identifying knowledge of Newton$_1$. He knows nothing that would distinguish him from Newton$_2$. The question is, Can Peter use and understand the name *Newton* as a name of Newton$_1$? Or does the lack of identifying knowledge of Newton$_1$ somehow take away the speaker's ability to understand the name? We leave further consideration of this issue as an exercise for the reader.

Inaccurate Conditions

The most serious difficulty that Kripke observes is that sometimes the only description that a person associates with a proper noun that is sufficiently rich to pick out a single individual is not actually true of the real bearer of the proper noun. For example, many people would associate the name *Galileo Galilei* with one, several, or perhaps all of the following historical activities or discoveries:

- Dropped a cannon ball from the Leaning Tower of Pisa
- First proved that light and heavy bodies fall at the same speed
- Explained the parabolic motion of projectiles
- Invented the telescope
- Discovered that the moon's surface is rough and irregular, like the surface of the Earth
- Discovered the moons of Jupiter (the so-called "Galilean moons")
- Discovered the phases of Venus
- Discovered the great Spiral Nebula in Andromeda
- First observed sun spots
- Was tortured by the Inquisition for promulgating the Copernican worldview
- Said "Eppur si muove" ('And yet it moves') when forced to recant his views

Accordingly, such individuals might be taken to have an axiom involving some combination of these predicates in their semantic theory:

(27) Val(x, *Galileo*) iff x dropped a cannon ball from the Leaning Tower
        of Pisa, x proved that light and heavy bodies fall at the same speed,
        x explained the parabolic motion of projectiles, etc., and for all y,

> if *y* dropped a cannon ball from the Leaning Tower of Pisa, *y* proved
> that light and heavy bodies fall at the same speed, *y* explained the
> parabolic motion of projectiles, etc., then $y = x$

As it turns out, however, and despite his own claims to the contrary, none of the above is really true of Galileo. Galileo dropped no cannon balls from the famous tower in Pisa. An earlier proof that light and heavy bodies fall with equal speed was given by Jan de Groot in 1586. The demonstration that projectiles follow a parabolic arc was appropriated by Galileo from one of his students, B. Cavalieri, and so on. Because of this, an axiom like (27) would not succeed in picking out Galileo at all. Indeed, sentences involving the name *Galileo* and an axiom like (27) would invariably end up false.

A similar example is given Kripke. Most users of the name *Peano* associate it with the person who discovered the Peano axioms for arithmetic. Accordingly, one might suggest (28) as the correct axiom for this noun:

(28) Val(*x*, *Peano*) iff *x* discovered the Peano axioms and for all *y*, if *y* discovered the Peano axioms, then $y = x$

As it happens, however, Peano did not discover the Peano axioms. They were initially discovered by the mathematician Dedekind (whom Peano himself apparently credited in a footnote). If the descriptive-name theory were correct, then, assuming that (28) is the correct axiom for *Peano*, the proper noun *Peano* ought to have Dedekind as its value, not Peano, for it is the former, not the latter, who meets the valuation condition.

It is surely plausible that for some speakers the only descriptive condition that singles out a unique bearer for *Peano* is the one appearing in (28). Accordingly, the descriptive-name theory gives (28) as their axiom for the name. However, if (28) were the case, then *Peano*, in their mouths, would refer not to Peano but to Dedekind. And this conclusion is surely false. When they say *Peano*, they refer to Peano not to Dedekind. If this does not seem clear, reflect on what they would mean by (29):

(29) Peano discovered the Peano axioms.

If *Peano* in their mouths referred to the individual who discovered the Peano axioms, then when they utter (29), they are saying something true about Dedekind. But they are not. They are saying something false about Peano.

Again it might be pointed out that the speakers would also know of Peano that he was called *Peano*. But this extra information does not help. Since no one individual both discovered the Peano axioms and was called *Peano*, (29) fails to be true of any individual at all. Similarly for *Galileo*. At this point one might attempt to refine the descriptive-name theory by suggesting that the bearer of a proper noun need not satisfy all of a speaker's associated descriptions. Rather, the value should be whatever satisfies the majority of them, or perhaps a weighted majority, with some descriptions being privileged over others.[6] But this more sophisticated proposal is still vulnerable to Kripke's objection. It seems that a speaker can use a proper noun to refer to its bearer even when most of the descriptions the speaker associates with the noun don't apply to the bearer.[7]

5.4   Knowing the Axioms of a Semantic Theory

The results above show that PC+^{DN} is not a viable alternative to PC+. We cannot appeal to it in the hopes of avoiding the original challenges for PC+: to explain how *Cary Grant* and *Archie Leach* can carry different meanings for a speaker, given the identity of their referent, or to explain how *Vulcan* and *Paul R. Zwier* can have significance, given their failure to refer.

In this section we will sketch the direction in which we think a successful account of these phenomena lies and the consequences that it has for semantic theorizing generally. To introduce our proposal, we begin with a little historical background.

5.4.1   Mill and Frege

The question of coextensive proper nouns encountered with PC+ is one version of a problem noted over a century ago in connection with the work of the philosopher John Stuart Mill. In his *System of Logic* (1843), Mill proposed that the semantics of a proper noun is exhausted by the fact that it stands for the individual that is its bearer. On this idea, *Jill* is a name for Jill, and that's it. Mill's view had the important consequence that coextensive proper nouns have the same semantic properties, and so are synonymous. This outcome runs into the problem we have seen.

About fifty years after *A System of Logic* appeared, the philosopher Gottlob Frege advanced a very different view. In considering the question of whether coextensive proper nouns could differ in meaning, Frege was led to conclude that the semantics of proper nouns cannot be exhausted by their reference. He pointed out that an identity statement featuring two occurrences of the same proper noun is a tautology, while one involving two different proper nouns could express genuine information. Consider, for example, (30a, b):

(30) a. Hesperus is Hesperus.
     b. Hesperus is Phosphorus.

Both of these sentences are true. *Hesperus* is a name for a heavenly body that is visible in the west on certain evenings. The name comes from the Greek and literally means "of the evening." *Phosphorus* is a name for a heavenly body that is visible in the west on certain mornings. It comes from the Greek meaning "bringer of light." It turned out that in both cases the heavenly body is the planet Venus. Frege observed that (30a) is a tautology, while (30b) expresses an important astronomical discovery. Thus the two sentences say different things; they have different "information value" or "cognitive content."

To account for the cognitive difference between (30a) and (30b), Frege proposed that proper nouns have semantic features that extend beyond reference. On his view, they also express what he called **senses**. Intuitively, a sense is like an idea or a concept: it is a "way of thinking about" or a "mode of presentation of" an object. The sense of *Hesperus* presents Venus as a body that appears in the evening. The sense of *Phosphorus* presents Venus as something that appears in the morning and brings light. The informativeness of (30b) is accounted for by the fact that one might not know that an object thought of as Hesperus is the same as an object thought of as Phosphorus. To be told that Hesperus is Phosphorus is therefore to be told something informative.

Frege applied his distinction between sense and semantic value to all meaningful expressions, including predicates and whole sentences. Thus every meaningful expression had for him both a sense and a semantic value, and the sense was a particular mode of presentation of the semantic value. Frege went on to develop a sophisticated theory of sense in which sense accounted not only for the cognitive content of expressions but also for the semantic value. Thus the fact that the word-form *Hesperus* took Venus as its value, as opposed to some other object (or no object at all), is to be explained by its sense. For Frege, sense suffices to fix what the term refers to. It follows that if two expressions have the same sense, they have the same semantic value as well.

Sense in Modern Guise

Frege himself professed little interest in natural languages or in the psychology of speakers. His concern was more with what we called, in chapter 3, the "logician's project," the study of logical relations among sentences or propositions. For that reason we cannot expect a fully fledged Fregean theory of sense to have application within a theory of speakers' knowledge. Nonetheless, certain aspects of Frege's theory can be used in such a theory. Indeed, we believe that PC+ ultimately must appeal to senselike entities to accommodate coextensive proper nouns.

As we said, Fregean senses are intuitively somewhat like ideas or **concepts**. It is these that will be our analogue of senses. Some general reflection on the nature of knowledge and certain other kinds of psychological states will help explain and motivate the idea.

For our example, consider Lori at a time before she notices any similarity between her childhood friend Archie and the actor Cary Grant. At this stage she believes that Cary Grant is an actor, but she does not believe that Archie Leach is an actor. Lori can entertain different psychological states—such as desires, hopes, fears, and wonderings—with respect to the same individual. For example, Lori might desire or hope or fear that Cary Grant will give up acting without desiring or hoping or fearing that Archie Leach will give up acting, even though Archie Leach and Cary Grant are the same. Psychological states of this kind are often called **propositional attitudes**, since they seem to involve a psychological attitude (e.g., belief, fear, hope, desire, etc.) toward a proposition (e.g., the proposition that Cary Grant will give up acting).

When a person has a propositional attitude, it is natural to analyze their psychological state into two parts. On the one hand, there is the attitude: the belief, desire, or whatever. On the other hand, there is some mental representation or mode of presentation of the proposition. This second component is sometimes called a "thought," a term that originated with Frege. Thus if one can formulate the thought that, say, Archie Leach is an actor, one can then believe or hope or desire that it is true. It is also natural to analyze thoughts themselves into constituent concepts. If one has the thought that Archie Leach is an actor, one has the concepts of Archie Leach and of being an actor, and these somehow form the thought.

Looking at propositional attitudes in this way explains how it is possible for Lori to believe that Cary Grant is an actor without believing that Archie Leach is an actor. Lori has two different concepts of the single individual Archie Leach (= Cary Grant), and only one of these is in play when she believes that Cary Grant is an actor. These reflections apply equally to knowledge. Lori knows that Cary Grant is an actor, but she does not know that Archie Leach is an actor. This is because her knowledge that Cary Grant is an actor involves her Cary Grant concept, not her Archie Leach concept.

We can import these results directly into our semantic theory. When we write down our semantic theory, we seek to say what speakers know about the semantics of their language, we seek to give the contents of this knowledge. When we write an axiom like (31), we are attributing to the speaker (unconscious) knowledge of the thought expressed by (31).

(31) Val(x, *agrees*) iff x agrees

We are claiming precisely that the speaker knows that for any x, x is a value of *agrees* if and only if x agrees. Since we are attributing knowledge to a speaker, we are also attributing concepts, precisely the concepts required for the piece of knowledge expressed by (31): the concept of semantic valuation, the concept of agreeing, and so on. In the context of a theory of speakers' knowledge, we can thus understand axioms like (31) as a particular version of the traditional and natural idea that to understand a word is to associate a concept with it. The association is achieved precisely because the concept features in a piece of semantic knowledge like (31).

Concepts and the Subjects of Semantic Theory

Introducing concepts into semantic theory in this way immediately raises a question. We said that we are constructing a theory of speakers' knowledge. The question is, Which speakers? Evidently, we are not trying to provide a complete account of any specific individual. This would be an impossible project, and one of little interest. Consider, by way of a rough analogy, a physicist wishing to assess the extent to which Newton's laws apply to middle-sized objects and the extent to which the effects of general relativity would spoil Newtonian predictions. The physicist wouldn't try to construct a theory of, say, the motions of balls on a particular pool table in a specific pub located in a specific city, etc. There would be many factors affecting the way the particular balls rolled: imperfections in their shape, worn patches on the cloth, the level of humidity in the room. It would be impossible to take all these into account, and the whole business would detract from the point of the exercise. What the physicist might do instead is construct a theory of a paradigmatic, or ideal, billiard table and calculate what would happen on the basis of laws arrived at by considering an array of evidence from different quarters.

Our project is roughly analogous. Our theory is a model of the semantics module of a paradigmatic, or idealized, speaker. The idea is that by providing such a theory, we can illustrate all the general features of semantic modules that we are concerned with. Much of the theory will actually be true of many people: universal features will apply to all humans (the composition axioms, for example), and many others will apply to many speakers in the United States and England. But it probably won't apply in its entirety to any actual individual, not even the authors of this book.

When we talk of a paradigmatic, or ideal, speaker, we do not mean that the speaker is in some sense special or perfect (in the way an ideal pool table might be perfect from the point of view of Newtonian physics). The point is merely that, given the general nature of our project, we can abstract away from many of the details of the particular concepts of individuals. For example, suppose that Jill thinks of a fruit as any product of plant growth useful to humans or animals, while Chris thinks of a fruit as the developed ovary of a seed plant with its contents and accessory parts. This would be a matter of interest to a psychologist studying the nature and sources of individual variation among concepts. But it is not something that has any direct relevance to a theory of the general nature of the speakers' semantic modules. Axiom (32) would apply to both of Jill and Chris:

(32) Val(x, *fruit*) iff x is a fruit

It doesn't particularly matter that Jill's concept of a fruit differs from Chris's. Our theory applies to them both in roughly the same way that a theory of an ideal pool table applies to a real pool table in a pub. They both have a concept more or less similar to that expressed by the word "fruit" in our metalanguage.

5.4.2   Coextensive Proper Nouns Again

Although individual differences will often be irrelevant, the case we illustrated with Lori, who doesn't know that Cary Grant is Archie Leach, suggests that some kinds of conceptual variation are directly pertinent to our project. Specifically, we need to explain how an individual (or an idealized individual) can associate the same semantic value with two proper nouns and yet exhibit completely different judgments with respect to them.

The model of individual concepts and their relation to semantic theory provides a simple way to address the problem.[8] Consider Lori at a time prior to any thought that her childhood friend might be the famous movie star. We might hypothesize that Lori has two different axioms in her semantic theory, each involving a particular individual concept. The first axiom involves her concept of Archie Leach. Presumably, this concept is associated with the information that this individual was a childhood friend, that he was named *Archie Leach*, that he went to the same high school as Lori, that he had dark hair, etc. The second axiom involves her concept of Cary Grant. The latter is associated with the information that this individual is a famous movie star, that he appeared in *North by Northwest*, that he spoke with a peculiar (and rather affected) English accent, etc. Suppose now that Lori hears the sentence *There's a new Cary Grant movie due out next month*. Lori's language faculty will generate an interpretation for this sentence that involves her *Cary Grant* axiom and hence her Cary Grant concept. Her *Archie Leach* axiom and her Archie Leach concept will remain uninvolved.

If this picture is right, then we have a genuine difference between the semantic rules that Lori has internalized for the two names. She uses her Cary Grant concept in the valuation clause for the name *Cary Grant*, and she uses her Archie Leach concept in her valuation clause for the name *Archie Leach* (figure 5.1). In our capacity as semantic theorists modeling Lori's internalized T theory, we need to mark the fact that she has two separate axioms involving two separate concepts. We can do this by writing two different PC+ axioms with two different metatheoretic names:

(5) a. Val(x, *Cary Grant*) iff x = Cary Grant
     b. Val(x, *Archie Leach*) iff x = Archie Leach

Thus we select (5a, b) as part of our theory of Lori on the understanding that *different metatheoretic names are used for marking different concepts in the mind of the object-language speaker*.

To elaborate the story of Lori slightly, we might suppose that even after Lori has learned that Cary Grant is Archie Leach, she might still retain two

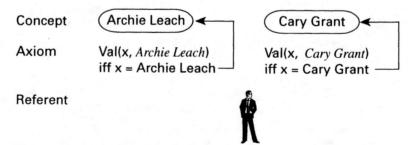

Figure 5.1 The relation among semantic axioms, concepts, and real-world referents.

different concepts. This would be a wise move on Lori's part if she was less than completely certain of the identity. The concepts would, of course, be linked by the identity belief, and a revision in beliefs involving the one would lead to a revision in those inolving the other. So if, at this stage, she hears that a new Cary Grant movie is due to be released shortly, she will infer that her friend Archie Leach will be appearing in a movie due to be released shortly. However, she will retain the knowledge that what she actually heard involved the name *Cary Grant*, and she will keep the two pieces of information separate. This will allow her to revise beliefs involving her Archie Leach concept without revising beliefs involving her Cary Grant concept. If she revises her belief in the identity, the information about Cary Grant's new movie will remain in place, but the information that Archie Leach will be in a movie will be removed.

Consider now a second subject, Peter. Peter has never come across the name *Archie Leach* but is familiar with *Cary Grant* as the name of the movie star. Peter is perusing a book on Hollywood stars and he comes across the information that Cary Grant was originally named *Archie Leach*. It is reasonably plausible that Peter will simply regard this as information about Cary Grant and not form any new concept to go with the name *Archie Leach*. For Peter, then, there is only one concept available to formulate valuation clauses for the two different names. The names are therefore synonymous for him. And we can register this fact in our theory of him by using (4a, b):

(4) a. Val(x, *Cary Grant*) iff x = Cary Grant
    b. Val(x, *Archie Leach*) iff x = Cary Grant

The general lesson that emerges with coextensive proper nouns is that the axioms of a semantic theory must be understood within the broader context of a theory of speaker knowledge. In and of themselves, the axioms for *Archie Leach* and *Cary Grant* do not tell us that the two proper nouns may, and for many speakers do, have different significance. To capture these facts, we must see them as part of a more general theory of speaker cognition. We must understand the role of our metalinguistic expressions in a model of the cognitive system of an idealized, or paradigmatic, speaker. The expressions we use correspond to concepts deployed by the speaker's cognitive systems. Only when a speaker has two different concepts can we use different axioms for the two proper nouns to register the different significance that these proper nouns have for the individual speaker.

5.4.3   Empty Proper Nouns Again

The question of how to understand empty-proper-noun axioms in PC+ can also be clarified through the notion of a concept. Consider the three rules in (33):

(33) a. Val(x, *Bucephalus*) iff x = Bucephalus
    b. Val(x, *Pegasus*) iff x = Pegasus
    c. Val(x, *Trub Neberd*) iff x = Trub Neberd

The first is an axiom for *Bucephalus*, the name of the horse ridden by Alexander the Great. The second is a rule for *Pegasus*, the name of the mythical white winged horse of Greek mythology. The third is a rule for *Trub Neberd*, an entirely made-up name that (to our knowledge) refers to nothing at all.

Most speakers of English would agree that the first two proper nouns are significant, whereas the third is not. *Bucephalus* and *Pegasus* make a meaningful contribution to any sentence in which they occur, but not so with *Trub Neberd*. Our problem is to say what is lacking in the third case but present in the first two. Evidently, there is no difference in the "shape" of these rules: all three rules of (33) have the form of legitimate PC+ axioms. Nonetheless, (33c) does not succeed in providing a semantics for the made-up proper noun *Trub Neberd*, any more than (34) succeeds in giving a semantics for the made-up predicate *blurks*:

(34) Val(x, *blurks*) iff x blurks

Furthermore, existence of a referent cannot be the relevant factor. Only the first rule (33a) associates a proper noun with a real individual, yet *Pegasus* is still a contentful term. What, then, distinguishes *blurks* and *Trub Neberd* on the one hand from *Bucephalus* and *Pegasus* on the other?

It might be replied that there is no difficulty explaining what's wrong with (33c) and (34). Since "Trub Neberd" and "blurks" are not words of the metalanguage, the language in which we frame our theories, the axioms themselves are meaningless. There is, then, no more problem in explaining why a semantic theory should not include these axioms than there is in explaining why a physical theory should not include the hypothesis that an electron's negative charge causes it to blurk. This point is correct as far as it goes, but it really only pushes the problem back a stage. For we need to know why "Trub Neberd" and "blurks" are not meaningful words of the metalanguage. This is exactly the kind of question that a semantic theory must deal with.

Informally, what seems to separate (33c) and (34) from (33a) and (33b) is the existence of a definite concept in the latter cases. Whereas we have no concept of what blurking is, or who or what Trub Neberd might be, we do have concepts of Bucephalus and Pegasus. Bucephalus was the fiery, black war horse given to Alexander III by his father, Philip of Macedonia: the horse that Alexander mastered when he was only twelve, that accompanied Alexander on his Persian expedition, and that later perished in the long retreat. Pegasus was the white, flying horse of Greek mythology: the beautiful creature that rose from the blood of the gorgon Medusa, that was captured by Bellerophon and ridden into battle against the Chimera, and that later found sanctuary in the stalls of Olympus. It is association with an individual concept that seems to give the axiom for the empty proper noun its content: (33b) is sensible, even in the absence of a real Pegasus, because the metalanguage term appearing to the right of the equal sign is supported by an individual concept of the kind described (figure 5.2).

If this general proposal is correct, then an important aspect of deciding when a semantic theory applies to a given speaker will lie in deciding whether an axiom may truly be associated with a concept in the speaker's mind (as with *Pegasus*) and when it may not (as with *Trub Neberd*). Although there is no easy general rule for making this decision, in many particular cases it is not too difficult to judge. For example, we can usually tell when a child is simply repeating words heard somewhere and when he or she has genuinely come to understand something. Suppose Timmy, age 6, comes home from school and says (35):

(35) Newton discovered gravity.

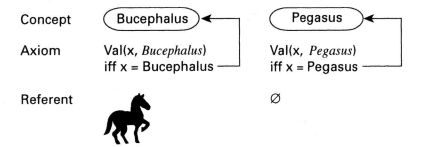

Figure 5.2 The relation among semantic axioms, concepts, and real-world referents when a referent doesn't exist.

"What's gravity?" you ask. Timmy turns red and looks down at the floor. It becomes clear that he knows nothing whatever about gravity. He has no idea whether it is a distant planet, a disease, a country. Here it would obviously be a mistake to give a semantic theory for Timmy that included the word *gravity* in his vocabulary with a rule like (36):

(36) Val(x, *gravity*) iff x is gravity

By contrast, suppose Gwendolyn, aged 14, comes home and says (35). In response to your question she says, "It's what makes objects fall down. The earth attracts objects to it. In fact, all objects attract each other. With small objects you can't really tell. But because the earth is so big, it exerts a huge gravitational force, and everything goes toward it." Gwendolyn does understand the word *gravity*, and so a semantic theory for her should take this into account.

Analogous remarks apply to proper nouns. Suppose that Timmy comes home and says, "Berlin is in Germany." You say, "Tell me more about Berlin." Timmy looks at the floor. It appears that Timmy doesn't know if Berlin is a person, a city, a theme park, a river. Gwendolyn comes home and says "Berlin is in Germany. To your question she responds, "It's a big city. It used to have a big wall in the middle, dividing the east part from the west part." Again, it's easy enough to see that we should find an axiom for *Berlin* for Gwendolyn but not for Timmy.

Concepts and Dossiers

The above points suggest the kind of theory of concepts that might underwrite PC+ axioms for proper nouns. Recall that the problem with *Trub Neberd* was that we had no idea who or what he or she or it was supposed to be. Similarly, the problem with Timmy and *Berlin* is that he has no idea who or what this name is supposed to refer to. By contrast, we knew who Pegasus was supposed to be, and Gwendolyn knows what kind of thing *Berlin* refers to. This implies that possession of a concept involves possession of information. More exactly, one might think of individual concepts as associated with something like a dossier containing data of various kinds.[9] When a person understands a name, they have a dossier that includes everything they know about, or believe to be true about, the referent of the name. When you learn a new name, you create a dossier. Every time you come to believe something new about the bearer of the name, you add this piece of information to the dossier (figure 5.3). If

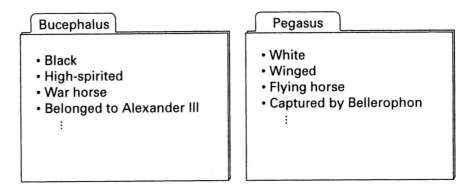

Figure 5.3　Dossiers for the names *Bucephalus* and *Pegasus*.

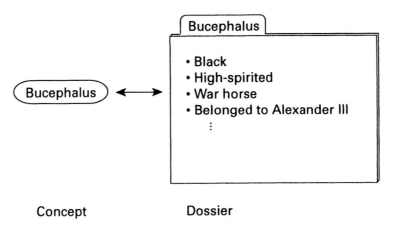

Concept　　　　　　　Dossier

Figure 5.4　The relation between dossiers and concepts.

you change your mind about something, you delete a piece of information (or misinformation) from the dossier.[10]

　In this picture, dossiers are linked to, or associated with concepts. They are thus something different from concepts themselves (figure 5.4). On reflection, it's easy to see why this must be so. When you think about an individual, your concept of that individual is a component of your thought. So when you think to yourself, "I'd like to play Julius Caesar in Shakespeare's play," your concept of Julius Caesar is a component of the thought. But your Julius Caesar dossier is not itself a component of the thought. Your knowledge that Caesar was an epileptic, that he was afraid of death, that his wife was called *Calpurnia*, and so on, does not explicitly feature. You do not think to yourself,

"I'd like to play Julius Caesar, who was an epileptic, who was afraid of death, whose wife was called *Calpurnia*, etc., in Shakespeare's play." The process of thinking is not a matter of stringing dossiers together. Rather, what the dossier does is condition the way you deploy the concept in thought. The reason that you want to play Caesar in the play might be because you think he was an interesting character. And you think this because of the information in your dossier. Thus the dossier is responsible for the concept playing its particular role in your psychology.

A fully worked out theory of concepts, dossiers, and proper nouns would involve an array of issues, including what kind of information must be in a dossier and how much information is required to ground a genuine concept. This theory would have to connect with the vast and complex topic of the general nature of concepts, a topic that currently engages many psychologists and philosophers and involves such lively issues as the relation of mind to brain.[11] We cannot attempt to provide a full theory of concepts, dossiers, and their relations to proper nouns here. What is important here is only that an empty name can be associated with a dossier, and hence a concept, in just the same way as a nonempty name. Your concept of Caesar could be just as it is even if Caesar were a mythical character and all the "history" you read and all of Shakespeare's play were fiction. The dossier would have the same contents, and the concept would play the same role in your psychology.

To summarize, then, on the view of PC+ we've sketched, a speaker's grasp of a name consists in the speaker's knowing things of this sort:

(33) a. Val(x, *Bucephalus*) iff x = Bucephalus
      b. Val(x, *Pegasus*) iff x = Pegasus

To possess such pieces of knowledge, the speaker must possess the relevant concepts to formulate the thoughts that Val(x, *Bucephalus*) iff x = Bucephalus and that Val(x, *Pegasus*) and iff x = Pegasus. Therefore, we must attribute concepts of Bucephalus and Pegasus to the speaker. Furthermore, the notion of a concept employed here must allow for the possibility of having a concept even in the absence of a real object that the concept corresponds to. We have outlined a small prototheory making use of concepts of this kind.

5.4.4 Linking Names and Things

It is important to realize that PC+, with its background theory of concepts, does not suffer from the problem of descriptive conditions noted by Kripke.

According to PC+, what appears on the RHS of an axiom for a proper noun is an individual concept. This concept is associated with a dossier of information, and the information in the dossier might be false of the individual designated by the proper noun. For example, the only information in a person's dossier for *Peano* might be that he discovered the Peano axioms. But this does *not* yield the false prediction that *Peano*, in this person's language, takes Dedekind as value. The reason is, as we mentioned before, that the information in the dossier is not what determines the reference of the noun. It determines only how the speaker thinks of the object in question, not what object the thought is about.

Kripke himself suggests that rather than being fixed by descriptive conditions, the values of proper nouns are usually fixed by historical chains of usage that link the speaker to the bearer of the name. One might envisage the name initially getting attached by a baptismal ceremony. After that, other speakers, the second generation, acquire the name by hearing it spoken by those familiar with the bearer. On acquiring the name, they continue to use it with the specific intention of picking out the same individual referred to by those from whom they acquired the name. Other speakers can acquire the name from this second generation, again continuing to use it with the intention of preserving its reference: they too intend to refer to whomever the second generation use the name to refer to. And so on. As the name is passed from speaker to speaker, various pieces of information and misinformation may become associated with the name. But the reference of the name is determined by the causal links from speaker to speaker and the common intention to preserve the reference. Kripke's sketch of what determines the reference of a name is, of course, no more than a sketch, and much work would have to be done to develop a complete theory.[12] Nevertheless, it appears to be on the right track, and so casts further doubt on PC+ [DN].

PC+ is thus perfectly compatible with a Kripke-style theory of what determines reference for a proper noun. Indeed, a complete theory of speaker knowledge would have to include such a theory as a proper part. For Kripke's point about descriptive conditions is really a point about speaker's judgments. At issue are our judgments about what fixes the value of a proper noun. We judge that in the case where the only specific information a speaker associates with the name *Peano* is that its referent discovered Peano's axioms, the noun still takes Peano as its value, rather than Dedekind. Even the subject involved must make this judgment. For when the subject is told (37), he or she will find the story perfectly intelligible:

(37) Peano did not discover Peano's axioms. He borrowed them from
     Dedekind, whom he credited in a footnote.

If the speaker took the original information to be responsible for determining
the value of the name, then (37) wouldn't make sense. If being the value of
Peano is just being the discoverer of the axioms, then (37) would be a contradiction. But it is not a contradiction. Rather, the speaker realizes that the
value of the name is fixed in some other way, knows about baptisms and other
ways in which proper nouns get attached to individuals, knows about how the

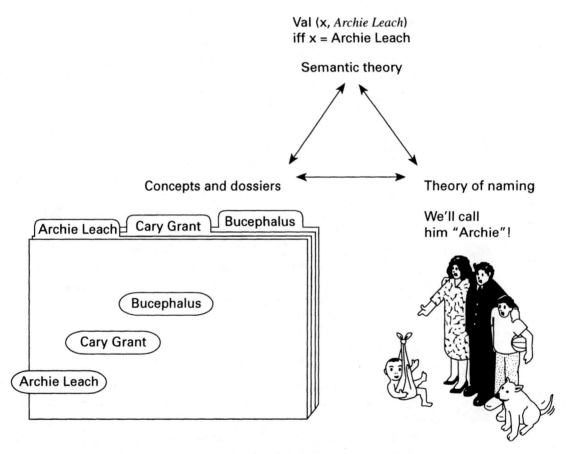

Figure 5.5 A complete theory of speaker knowledge, including semantic theory, concepts and dossiers, and a theory of naming.

name can pass from generation to generation while preserving its value, and so on. And this knowledge accounts for the judgments about what the value of the name is or might be.

A full theory of speaker knowledge should thus include a theory of what we take to be responsible for fixing the value of proper nouns. This information is presumably not within the T theory itself, nor is it closely tied to individual concepts. Rather, it must belong to some other module, perhaps a theory of naming or a theory of how semantic relations between lexical items and the world get determined. Figure 5.5 presents one possibility for what a full theory of speaker knowledge might look like.

Theory and Exercises

The Theory PC+^{DN} (PC+ with Descriptive Names)

Lexical Axioms

(1) a. Val(x, *Venus*) iff x is the ancient-Roman goddess of love and for all y, if y is the ancient-Roman goddess of love, then $y = x$

    b. Val(x, *Isaac Newton*) iff x discovered gravity and for all y, if y discovered gravity, then $y = x$

    c. Val(x, *Hesperus*) iff x is the brightest body visible in the evening sky and for all y, if y is the brightest body visible in the evening sky, then $y = x$

    d. Val(x, *Phosphorus*) iff x is the last celestial body to shine in the morning sky and for all y if y is the last celestial body to shine in the morning sky, then $y = x$

    e. Val(x, *ponders*) iff x ponders

    f. Val(x, *agrees*) iff x agrees

    g. Val($\langle x, y \rangle$, *knows*) iff x knows y

Phrasal Axioms

(2) a. Val(t, [$_S$ S$_1$ *and* S$_2$]) iff both Val(t, S$_1$) and Val(t, S$_2$)

    b. Val(t, [$_S$ S$_1$ *or* S$_2$]) iff either Val(t, S$_1$) or Val(t, S$_2$)

    c. Val(t, [$_S$ *It is not the case that* S]) iff it is not the case that Val(t, S)

d. Val(t, [$_s$ NP VP]) iff for some x, Val(x, NP) and Val(x, VP)
e. Val(x, [$_{VP}$ V NP]) iff for some y, Val($\langle x, y \rangle$, V) and Val(y, NP)
f. Val(x, [$_X$ Y]) iff Val(x, Y) (where X, Y are any nodes)

Production Rules

(UI) Universal instantiation

$$\frac{\text{For any } x, F(x)}{F(\alpha)}$$

(SE) Substitution of equivalents

$$\frac{\begin{array}{l} F(\alpha) \\ \alpha \text{ iff } \beta \end{array}}{F(\beta)}$$

(SI) Substitution of identicals

$$\frac{\phi \text{ iff for some } x, F(x) \text{ and } x = \alpha}{\phi \text{ iff } F(\alpha)}$$

Exercises

1. Prove T theorems for the following sentences using the theory PC+^{DN} (together with the axioms for *be* from chapter 4):

    (1) a. Isaac Newton ponders.
        b. Venus knows Isaac Newton.
        c. Hesperus is Hesperus.
        d. Hesperus is Phosphorus.

2. Consider the following alternative axioms for proper nouns:

    (1) a. Val(x, *Isaac Newton*) iff x is called "Isaac Newton"
        b. Val(x, *Venus*) iff x is called "Venus"
        c. Val(x, *Hesperus*) iff x is called "Hesperus"
        d. Val(x, *Phosphorus*) iff x is called "Phosphorus"

    Assume that other rules of PC+ are left unchanged. Then what T theorems can you derive for the following sentences? Give derivations.

(2) a. Isaac Newton ponders.

    b. Venus knows Hesperus.

The axioms in (1) appear circular at first. Axiom (1a) says that x is a value of the proper noun *Isaac Newton* if x is called "Isaac Newton." Are these axioms circular? What is involved in an individual being called "Isaac Newton"?

3. In the text we suggested that natural-language proper NPs like (1a–c) are semantically rigid: in any circumstance in which their meaning remains the same, they refer to the same individual:

(1) a. Mr. Arnold Schwarzenegger

    b. Ms. Vanessa Williams

    c. Mr. Bob Uecker

Consider now (2a–c). These have a similar syntactic form to (1a–c) but are associated with a certain title. In view of this we might call them **title names**:

(2) a. Mr. Olympia

    b. Miss America

    c. Mr. Baseball

- Suggest plausible semantic axioms for some of the title names in (2) (or any other title names you can think of). Justify your proposals.

- Are title names singular referring terms? Are title names semantically rigid?

4. In chapter 4 we gave an alternative theory to PC+, PC^{set}, in which verb axioms like (1a) were replaced with axioms referring to sets, as in (1b):

(1) a. Val(x, *ponders*) iff x ponders
    b. Val(X, *ponders*) iff $X = \{x : x \text{ ponders}\}$

This change in the axioms for terminal nodes required corresponding changes in the composition axioms for S and VP. It also obliged us to import some reasoning principles from set theory in order to be able to prove familiar T sentences like (2):

(2) Val(t, [$_S$ [$_{NP}$ Phil] [$_{VP}$ [$_V$ ponders]]]) iff Phil ponders

Suppose now that the axioms of PC+ for verbs are left intact but that the axioms for proper nouns are replaced with the following axioms involving sets:

(3) a. Val(x, *Jill*) iff Jill $\in X$
    b. Val(x, *Kate*) iff Kate $\in X$
    c. Val(x, *Chris*) iff Chris $\in X$
    d. Val(x, *Phil*) iff Phil $\in X$

What changes in the composition axioms must we make, and what reasoning principles must we import from set theory (if any) in order to prove (2)? State your answer in terms of a full theory that gives the axioms for all terminal and nonterminal nodes, and all production rules. Give a full derivation for [$_S$ [$_{NP}$ Phil] [$_{VP}$ [$_V$ ponders]]] using your theory.

Do the axioms in (3) attribute different semantic properties to proper nouns than the corresponding axioms of PC+? More precisely, if we assume axioms like (3a–d),

- are proper nouns rigid?
- do two proper nouns that have the same semantic value have the same significance?
- can there be empty proper nouns?

We saw earlier that the PC+ axioms for proper nouns do not permit us to analyze conjoined proper nouns like those in (4) using a general scheme like (5):

(4) [$_{NP}$ Phil and Kate] ponder

(5) Val(α, [$_X$ X_1 *and* X_2]) iff Val(α, X_1) and Val(α, X_2)

Is this also true for the axioms in (3)? That is, if we employ (3a–d) together with (5), do we assign the correct truth conditions to (4)? Justify your answer by giving a T-sentence derivation for (4).

6   **Pronouns and Demonstratives**

Proper nouns are prominent members of the class **singular referring expressions** or **singular terms**: items whose semantic properties constrain them to refer to a single object. Other members of this class include the personal pronouns *I, me, you, he, him, she, her,* and *it,* and demonstrative phrases such as *this, that, this cat,* and *that building.* Thus if Jill utters (1a), addressing herself to Arnold Schwarzenegger, then the second-person personal pronoun *you* designates the single individual Arnold Schwarzenegger. Likewise, if Jill says (1b–d), gesturing at the famous bodybuilder, then the demonstrative terms refer to him.

(1) a. *You* must like vitamins.
    b. *He* is big.
    c. *This physical culturist* is impressive.
    d. *That actor* is famous.

As with proper nouns, sentences containing these terms are true just in case the individual referred to meets the condition expressed by the predicate. Thus (1a–d) are true if and only if the individual Arnold Schwarzenegger must like vitamins, is big, is impressive, or is famous, just as with (2a–d).

(2) a. Arnold must like vitamins.
    b. Arnold is big.
    c. Arnold is impressive.
    d. Arnold is famous.

6.1   Introducing Contexts

Although pronouns and demonstratives are similar to proper nouns, they also depart from them in an important way. Whereas proper nouns refer to the same individual on any occasion of use, pronouns and demonstratives have **variable reference**. If Jill addresses Arnold Schwarzenegger with the pronoun *you*, then *you* refers to Arnold. But if Jill addresses Lou Ferrigno with *you*, then *you* refers to Lou. Similarly if Jill utters the first-person singular pronoun *I*, the term designates Jill. But if Arnold says *I*, the term designates Arnold. The same holds with *this*, *that*, *he*, *she*, and *it*. These terms can pick out a certain object on one occasion of use and a certain other object on another occasion.

Referential variability introduces a significant and very interesting problem for the semantic-value relation as we have understood it up to this point. In particular, it challenges the idea that Val holds simply between an expression and a thing. To see why, consider first a simple sentence, like *Arnold is big*, containing no variable terms. On any occasion of use the reference of the subject term is constant: *Arnold* refers to Arnold. Furthermore, on any occasion of use the truth conditions remain the same: the sentence is true iff Arnold is big.[1]

(3) Logical form

[$_S$ [$_{NP}$ Arnold] [$_{VP}$ [$_V$ is] [$_{AP}$ big]]]

Utterances

- "Arnold is big" uttered by Jill at 3:00 P.M. 23 Mar. 1989 and referring to Arnold
- "Arnold is big" uttered by Kumiko at 9:00 A.M. 8 Dec. 1992 and referring to Arnold
- "Arnold is big" uttered by Phil at 1:00 A.M. 24 July 1990 and referring to Arnold

Because the semantic values don't change, no problems arise if our axiom for the proper noun *Arnold* assigns a constant semantic value or if we have constant truth conditions for the sentence as a whole:

(4) a. Val(x, *Arnold*) iff x = Arnold
     b. Val(t, [$_S$ [$_{NP}$ Arnold] [$_{VP}$ [$_V$ is] [$_{AP}$ big]]]) iff Arnold is big

Contrast this with the situation for a sentence like *He is big*, containing a variable reference term. On different occasions of use, the reference of *he* may vary. And on such occasions the truth conditions of the sentence may vary as well. Thus in the first setting of (5), *he* refers to Arnold, and the sentence is true iff Arnold is big. In the second setting, *he* refers to Lou, and the sentence is true iff Lou is big. And so on:

(5) Logical form

$$[_S [_{NP} He] [_{VP} [_V is] [_{AP} big]]]$$

Utterances

- "He is big" uttered by Jill at 4:00 P.M. 23 Mar. 1989 and referring to Arnold
- "He is big" uttered by Kumiko at 10:00 A.M. 8 Dec. 1992 and referring to Lou
- "He is big" uttered by Phil at 2:00 A.M. 24 July 1990 and referring to Franco

Given the behavior of *he*, we clearly cannot give it an axiom that fixes its reference once and for all, (6a). Indeed, in itself, *he* doesn't really seem to have a reference; only in the context of a specific use does the pronoun assume a definite semantic value. Correlatively, we don't want a theory that will prove fixed truth conditions for *He is big*, (6b). In isolation, the sentence doesn't really seem to have truth conditions; only in the context of a specific utterance does it seem proper to speak of the sentence as being true or false.

(6) a. Val(x, *he*) iff $x = ?$
     b. Val(t, $[_S [_{NP} He] [_{VP} [_V is] [_{AP} big]]]$) iff?

These results suggest that if we are to retain the goal of proving definite truth conditions for sentences using axioms that state definite semantic values for their parts, then we must modify our view of how those truth conditions and values are assigned. In particular, the presence of variable-reference terms shows that we cannot assign values to expressions simpliciter; rather, we must assign them *with respect to a context of use or a context of utterance*.

How should we incorporate these observations within our T theory? How should we reconstruct the notion of assigning values relative to a context of utterance. One simple step in this direction is to extend our basic semantic-value relation. Rather than taking Val to be a two-place relation holding between an expression α and a semantic value x, (7), we might instead analyze it as a three-place relation holding between an expression α, a semantic value x, and a context c, (8):

(7) Val(x, α) iff ...

(8) Val(x, α, c) iff ...

This move directly expresses the context relativity of value assignments. Furthermore, it offers us an approach to the semantics of variable-reference terms and sentences that contain them. For example, suppose that we analyze *he* as taking the value x in context c iff x is the object demonstrated in c, (9a). Then, given some extrasemantic information about the objects demonstrated in particular contexts c^* and c', we can know the reference for the term in those contexts, (9b, c).

(9) a. For any c, Val(x, *he*, c) iff x = the object demonstrated in c
    b. i. The object demonstrated in c^* = Arnold
       ii. Val(x, *he*, c^*) iff x = Arnold
    c. i. The object demonstrated in c' = Lou
       ii. Val(x, *he*, c') iff x = Lou

Similarly, suppose that we can prove that for any context c, *He is big* is true iff the object demonstrated in c is big, (10a). Then once again, given extrasemantic information about the specific contexts c^* and c', we can know the truth conditions for *He is big* in c^* and c', (10b, c). The semantic behavior of *he* and *He is big* is accounted for across speech situations.

(10) a. Val(t, [$_S$ [$_{NP}$ He] [$_{VP}$ [$_V$ is] [$_{AP}$ big]]], c) iff the object demonstrated in c is big
    b. i. The object demonstrated in c^* = Arnold
       ii. Val(t, [$_S$ [$_{NP}$ He] [$_{VP}$ [$_V$ is] [$_{AP}$ big]]], c^*) iff Arnold is big
    c. i. The object demonstrated in c' = Lou
       ii. Val(t, [$_S$ [$_{NP}$ He] [$_{VP}$ [$_V$ is] [$_{AP}$ big]]], c') iff Lou is big

Expanding the Val relation offers a promising approach to variable-reference terms. Bringing this idea within the formal T theory involves considerably more than the sketch given above, however. We need to clarify the nature of contexts and show exactly how they fix the values of pronouns and demonstratives. We also need to reformulate our semantic rules so that they include the context parameter c and manipulate it correctly for all syntactic configurations in which variable-reference terms occur. Finally, we must show precisely how semantic statements like (8), which concern any context of utterance, combine with extralinguistic information about particular contexts to yield determinate truth conditions for an utterance. As we will see, spelling out these details brings important changes. We'll call the T theory that incorporates them "VRT," where "VRT" stands for "variable-reference terms."

6.2   Contexts, Sequences, and Indices

We have spoken informally about pronouns and demonstratives getting their semantic values in contexts of utterance. To sharpen our understanding of the notion of a context of utterance, let us consider how this occurs in real discourse. How is reference determined in real speech contexts?

Sometimes it is accomplished as a matter of deduction. Suppose you are at a party where a noisy individual has just exited the room. You hear someone say, "I'm glad he's left" or "That guy really gets on my nerves." Through a chain deductive reasoning based on who is present, what has transpired, and various background assumptions about social conduct at gatherings like this, you may come to conclude that *he* or *that guy* refers to the person who has just departed. Here determination of reference for these terms is inferential and quite indirect.

In other cases, however, the contextual values of pronouns and demonstratives are fixed in a much more direct and perspicuous way. Suppose someone utters, "He is crazy" or "That guy might hurt himself," pointing to a man standing upon a ledge who is about to execute a spectacular bungee dive. Through this gesture of pointing or **ostension**, the speaker indicates reference to you explicitly. The ostensive gesture fixes the value of the pronoun or demonstrative as that very man on the ledge. Likewise, suppose you are attending to the seating at a dinner party. You might say, "He should sit between her and him," gesturing successively at three of the guests. Once again your three gestures set the values of the three pronouns as the three individuals pointed to.

These observations suggest a simple way of thinking about contextual determination of semantic values and how we might model it within our theory. We might look at contexts as something like generalized situations of pointing, where someone utters a term and gestures at someone or something. Such situations involve two principal components. First, there is a collection of individuals that are the objects pointed at. In the cases described above, this is the man on the ledge or the various dinner guests. Second, there is a method for associating a given individual with a specific variable-reference term. Here

He is crazy.

He should sit between her and him.

Figure 6.1 Contextual determination of semantic values for variable-reference terms involves a collection of individuals that serve as referents and a method of associating a given individual with each variable-reference term.

the method is an outstretched arm, serving as a pointer (figure 6.1). The individuals together with the method of association fix the reference.

An elegant formalization of this picture is provided by the work of the mathematician-logician Alfred Tarski, whose name has come up previously. We noted in chapter 2 that Tarski was the originator of the T-sentence format. He was also the first to give a formally explicit T theory for certain logical languages, making use of something like the pointing idea. Corresponding to our set of individuals and method of association, Tarski employs the formal notions of a sequence and an index. A sequence σ is just an infinite set of objects $\langle a_1, a_2, a_3, \ldots, a_k, \ldots \rangle$ arranged in a linear order, for example,

(11) $\sigma = \langle$ Arnold S., King's College, Eiffel Tower, ..., Myrna Loy, ...$\rangle$
        1st place   2nd place   3rd place   ... kth place   ...

Here σ contains Arnold Schwarzenegger in its first place (the actual, physical person, not the name), the institution King's College (London) in its second place, the Eiffel Tower in its third place, ..., the actress Myrna Loy in its kth place, and so on. A sequence is defined entirely by its elements and their order. Thus it makes no sense of talk of two sequences with all the same elements arranged in the same order. Furthermore, any variation in either the elements or the order makes for a different sequence. So if sequence σ has Kings College in its second place and sequence σ' has the Sistine Chapel in its second place, then σ and σ' are different sequences, even if they are identical in every other position.

Along with the sequence, there is also a method of associating pronouns and demonstratives in a sentence with objects in a sequence. The method is as follows:

- Subscript each variable-reference term with a numerical index.

- Associate any term bearing the index i with the ith object in the sequence.

Thus pronouns and demonstratives now appear with numerical subscripts: $that_1$, he_5, $it_{2,002}$, etc. Furthermore, if a term bears the index 1 and is evaluated with respect to a sequence σ, then that term gets associated with the first object in σ. If it bears the index 2 and is evaluated with respect to σ', then it is associated with the second element in σ'. And so on. These proposals are made concrete in the following axiom schemata for variable-reference terms (here "$\sigma(i)$" stands for the ith object in the series σ):[2]

(12) a. $\mathrm{Val}(x, he_i, \sigma)$ iff $x = \sigma(i)$ for all $i \geq 1$
     b. $\mathrm{Val}(x, she_i, \sigma)$ iff $x = \sigma(i)$ for all $i \geq 1$
     c. $\mathrm{Val}(x, it_i, \sigma)$ iff $x = \sigma(i)$ for all $i \geq 1$
     d. $\mathrm{Val}(x, that_i, \sigma)$ iff $x = \sigma(i)$ for all $i \geq 1$

According to (12), x is a value of the pronoun he_i with respect to sequence σ if and only if x is the ith element of σ. So if we have the indexed pronoun it_3 and the sequence σ in (11), for example, then x will be the value of it_3 with respect to σ if and only if x is the Eiffel Tower:

(13) $\mathrm{Val}(x, it_3, \sigma)$ iff $x = \sigma(3) = $ the Eiffel Tower

6.2.1 Relativizing the T Theory to Sequences

Under the axioms in (12), pronouns and demonstratives become dependent on
sequences for their semantic values. Since these expressions can in turn occur
inside all sorts of other constituents—Ss, VPs, PPs, other NPs, etc.—it follows
that the latter too become potentially dependent on sequences: their values
may depend on the values of items that depend on sequences. We must take
account of this sequence relativity, which spreads itself from the values of terms
of variable reference to the values of expressions that may contain them. That
is, just as we introduce sequences into the axioms for pronouns, so we must
now introduce them into the axioms for categories that can contain pronouns.
From a formal point of view, it turns out to be simplest to introduce a sequence parameter uniformly into all of the axioms, that is, to reanalyze the
predicate Val as uniformly determining a relation among semantic values,
expressions, and sequences. This involves revising our axioms along the lines
illustrated in (14) through (18):

(14) *Replace* Val(t, [$_s$ NP VP]) is true iff for some x,
        Val(x, NP) and Val(x, VP)
        with Val(t, [$_s$ NP VP], σ) iff for some x, Val(x, NP, σ) and Val(x, VP, σ)

(15) *Replace* Val(x, [$_{vp}$ V NP]) is true iff for some y,
        Val($\langle x, y \rangle$, V) and Val(x, NP)
        with Val(x, [$_{vp}$ V NP], σ) is true iff for some y,
        Val($\langle x, y \rangle$, V, σ) and Val(x, NP, σ)

(16) *Replace* Val(x, [$_x$ Y]) iff Val(x, Y)
        with Val(x, [$_x$ Y], σ) iff Val(x, Y, σ)

(17) *Replace* Val($\langle x, y \rangle$, *knows*) iff x knows y
        with Val($\langle x, y \rangle$, *knows*, σ) iff x knows y

(18) *Replace* Val(x, *Kate*) iff $x =$ Kate
        with Val(x, *Kate*, σ) iff $x =$ Kate

And so on. Notice that with certain expressions—including most lexical verbs,
(17), and proper names, (18)—the semantic value will not depend on the sequence: σ doesn't figure on the RHS of their biconditionals, and hence the
contribution of σ in these axioms is vacuous. In view of this property we will

call such expressions **sequence-independent** or **sequence-insensitive**. Other expressions will be called **sequence-dependent** or **sequence-sensitive.**

A Sample Derivation

The axioms for variable-reference terms in (12) together with (14) to (18) allow us to evaluate sentences with respect to any sequence and prove sequence-relative T theorems. Let's illustrate this with the sentence $[_S [_{NP} [_N she_1]] [_{VP} [_V knows] [_{NP} Kate]]]$. We begin by using the revised composition axiom (14):

(19) Val(t, $[_S [_{NP} [_N She_1]] [_{VP} [_V knows] [_{NP} Kate]]]$, σ) iff for some x,
       Val(x, $[_{NP} [_N she_1]]$, σ) and Val(x, $[_{VP} [_V knows] [_{NP} Kate]]$, σ)
       (by (14), (UI))

The interpretation of the pronominal subject goes as in (20); by (SE) we derive (21):

(20) a. Val(x, $[_{NP} [_N she_1]]$, σ) iff Val(x, $[_N she_1]$, σ) (by (16), (UI))
      b. Val(x, $[_N she_1]$, σ) iff Val(x, she_1, σ) (by (16), (UI))
      c. Val(x, she_1, σ) iff $x = \sigma(1)$ (by (12b))
      d. Val(x, $[_N she_1]$, σ) iff $x = \sigma(1)$ (by (20b, c), (SE))
      e. Val(x, $[_{NP} [_N she_1]]$, σ) iff $x = \sigma(1)$ (by (20a, d), (SE))

(21) Val(t, $[_S [_{NP} [_N She_1]] [_{VP} [_V knows] [_{NP} Kate]]]$, σ) iff for some x,
       $x = \sigma(1)$ and Val(x, $[_{VP} [_V knows] [_{NP} Kate]]$, σ) (by (19), (20e), (SE))

The interpretation of the VP proceeds just as in PC+, but with the sequence-relative rules:

(22) Val(x, $[_{VP} [_V knows] [_{NP} Kate]]$, σ) iff x knows Kate

Another application of (SE) then yields (23):

(23) Val(t, $[_S [_{NP} [_N She_1]] [_{VP} [_V knows] [_{NP} Kate]]]$, σ) iff for some x,
       $x = \sigma(1)$ and x knows Kate (by (21), (22), (SE))

Since every sequence does have a first member that is some object, the existential quantifier on the RHS can drop out by (SI). Thus we derive (24):

(24) Val(t, $[_S [_{NP} [_N She_1]] [_{VP} [_V knows] [_{NP} Kate]]]$, σ) iff $\sigma(1)$ knows Kate

This says that $[_S [_{NP} [_N She_1]] [_{VP} [_V knows] [_{NP} Kate]]]$ is true with respect to any sequence σ iff the first member of σ knows Kate.

This derivation illustrates how indices and sequences execute the informal notion of contextual pointing introduced earlier. The index provides the pointer and the sequence gives the individuals we may point to. Between them, the reference of the pronoun is fixed:

(25) She knows Kate.

$\langle \;,\ldots\rangle$

6.2.2 Absolute Truth

The introduction of sequences has the important conceptual result that sentences are no longer simply true or false simpliciter, but true or false only with respect to a sequence. Intuitively, the idea of sequence-relative truth seems appropriate for sentences containing pronouns and demonstratives like *She$_1$ agrees* or *That woman$_1$ knows Kate*, since without knowing what *she$_1$* or *that woman$_1$* refer to, that is, without a sequence, we cannot determine the truth conditions for these examples. However, the idea does not seem appropriate for a sentence like *Chris agrees*. This sentence contains only sequence-independent expressions. No words or phrases of the sentence depend on sequences for their values. Consequently, it seems that we should be able talk about this sentence as being true or false absolutely without reference to a sequence.

We can satisfy this intuition by defining the notion of **absolute truth** in addition to the notion of sequence-relative truth. Observe that any sentence containing only sequence-independent items will be true with respect to a given sequence σ if and only if it is true with respect to every sequence σ.[3] This in turn suggests a simple definition of absolute truth:

Definition   Val(t, S) iff Val(t, S, σ) for every sequence σ.

That is, a sentence is true simpliciter just in case it is true with respect to any sequence you chose.

6.3 Conditionalized T Sentences

Our amended T theory delivers theorems that state the truth conditions of sentences relative to any sequence σ. On our view, these theorems make up part of the knowledge that allows speakers to understand sentences containing variable-reference terms. Nonetheless, sequence-relative truth conditions cannot be the whole story. Knowledge about pronouns and demonstratives gives speakers the ability to take an utterance event in which various objects are demonstrated and referred to and to infer from it the truth-conditions of that utterance. For example, if you hear Phil utter, *She₁ knows Kate*, (26a), and you know Phil is referring to Jill with his use of the pronoun *she₁*, (26b), then some knowledge enables you to infer (26d):

(26) a. Phil utters, *She₁ knows Kate.*
　　 b. Phil uses *she₁* in his utterance to refer to Jill.
　　 c. [Speaker knowledge]
　　 ───────────────────────────────────
　　 d. Phil's utterance of *She₁ knows Kate* is true iff Jill knows Kate.

If we are interested in explaining this ability, our theory should license such an inference. The results in (24) do not provide enough to do this, however:

(27) a. Phil utters, *She₁ knows Kate.*
　　 b. Phil uses *she₁* in his utterance to refer to Jill.
　　 c. Val(t, [$_S$ [$_{NP}$ [$_N$ She₁]] [$_{VP}$ [$_V$ knows [$_{NP}$ Kate]]]], σ) iff $\sigma(1)$ knows Kate
　　 ───────────────────────────────────
　　 d. #Phil's utterance of *She₁ knows Kate* is true iff Jill knows Kate.

To get from (27a, b) to (27d), we need more than the sequence-relative truth conditions of *She₁ knows Kate*. We need a way to link up information about utterance circumstances, the contents of sequences, and the truth of utterances. We need to know that given (27b), *She₁ knows Kate* should be evaluated with respect to sequences having Jill in first position. And we need to know that given the truth of *She₁ knows Kate* with respect to the relevant sequences, Phil's utterance is true as a consequence.

　　To complete our account of the interpretation of pronouns and demonstratives, we now supply the two missing parts. First, to link an utterance of a sentence containing variable-reference terms to appropriate sequences, we introduce a **selection relation** Σ holding between utterances and sequences. All utterances will select a particular set of sequences relative to which evaluation can be made; that is, (28) will be true:

(28) For any u, for some σ', $\Sigma(u, \sigma')$

Σ will link facts about the utterance situation with the content of sequences. For example, (29) will hold of Σ for any utterance u of a sentence containing a variable-reference term α_i and for any sequence σ:

(29) If a speaker uses α_i in u to refer to x, then $\Sigma(u, \sigma)$ only if $\sigma(i) = x$

So if Phil utters *She₁ knows Kate*, his utterance will select some sequence σ (that is, for some σ', Σ(Phil's utterance, σ')). And if Phil uses *she₁* in his utterance of *She₁ knows Kate* to refer to Jill, then all the sequences that Phil's utterance selects will have Jill in first position; that is, Σ(Phil's utterance, σ) only if $\sigma(1) = $ Jill.

Second, we introduce a general rule for relating the truth of an utterance to the truth of the uttered sentence relative to the sequences that the utterance selects. The rule is the following:

(30) If u is an utterance of S and $\Sigma(u, \sigma)$, then u is true iff Val(t, S, σ)

Thus if u is any utterance of *She₁ knows Kate* and $\Sigma(u, \sigma)$, then u is true if and only if Val(t, *She₁ knows Kate*, σ). We call such instances of (30) **conditionalized T sentences**. The "if" part is the **antecedent** of the conditional; it relates utterance to sentence and utterance to sequence. The "then" part is the **consequent** of the conditional; it relates the truth of the utterance to the truth value of the sentence.

These additions will now support inferences of the kind we want. Suppose that $u*$ is Phil's utterance of *She₁ knows Kate* and that Phil has used *she₁* in $u*$ to refer to Jill. Our inference proceeds as in (31), where "SQR" is short for "standard quantificational reasoning":

(31) a. $u*$ is an utterance of *She₁ knows Kate* (premise)
  b. Phil uses *she₁* in $u*$ to refer to Jill (premise)
  c. If a speaker uses α_i in u to refer to x, then $\Sigma(u, \sigma)$ only if $\sigma(i) = x$ (by (29))
  d. If Phil uses *she₁* in $u*$ to refer to Jill, then $\Sigma(u*, \sigma)$ only if $\sigma(1) = $ Jill (by (31c), (UI))
  e. $\Sigma(u*, \sigma)$ only if $\sigma(1) = $ Jill (by (31b, d), SQR)
  f. If $u*$ is an utterance of *She₁ knows Kate* and $\Sigma(u*, \sigma)$, then $u*$ is true iff Val(t, *She₁ knows Kate*, σ) (by (30), (UI))
  g. Val(t, *She₁ knows Kate*, σ) iff $\sigma(1)$ knows Kate (24)

h. If u^* is an utterance of *She$_1$ knows Kate* and $\Sigma(u^*, \sigma)$, then u^* is true iff $\sigma(1)$ knows Kate (by (31f, g), (SE))

i. If $\Sigma(u^*, \sigma)$, then u^* is true iff $\sigma(1)$ knows Kate (by (31a, h), SQR)

j. If $\Sigma(u^*, \sigma)$, then u^* is true iff Jill knows Kate (by (31e, i), SQR, (SI))

k. For some σ', $\Sigma(u^*, \sigma')$ (by (28), (UI))

l. u^* is true iff Jill knows Kate (by (31j, k), SQR)

This inference illustrates how the three core parts of our theory work together. The axioms in (12) and (14) through (18) generate truth conditions for sentences relative to all sequences. In addition, we have the relation Σ, which relates an utterance to a certain specific set of sequences. Finally, we have the conditional (30), which pools these results, defining the truth of an utterance in terms of the sequence-relative truth conditions of the sentence uttered and the particular sequences selected by the utterance.[4]

It is important to observe that (31) draws on deductive resources and information not provided by the T theory alone. For example, the last step in (31), in which we take the conditional (31j) and **detach the consequent**, (31l), to derive utterance truth conditions, draws on rules of quantificational inference that are not part of our T theory. It is likely, furthermore, that such rules cannot be included without generating unwanted uninterpretive results. Accordingly, we must assume them to come from an extrasemantic logic module, containing general reasoning principles of the required kind.

Likewise, the two premises (31a, b) represent extrasemantic information that presumably comes from some other components. This kind of information is potentially very complex, and establishing it may involve a great variety of cognitive faculties. In the particular case just discussed, one might need to follow Phil's gesture to establish that the pronoun refers to Jill. On other occasions, quite different abilities might be required. For instance, suppose that Sherlock Holmes and Dr. Watson have just arrived back at their Baker Street apartment after a full day in pursuit of a certain criminal. Suppose Holmes knows that while they were out, the criminal concealed himself in the room with a gun. Holmes has laid a trap to catch him. The detective enters the room, positions himself carefully out of range and utters (32):

(32) You can put that gun away now, you won't be needing it.

To derive the reference of *you* and *that gun* for this utterance, and hence to relate it to the proper sequences, Watson needs to know who is being addressed and the referent of the demonstrative. If Holmes has been his usual

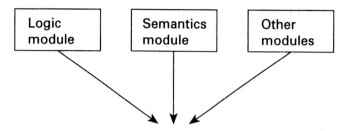

Phil's utterance of *She knows Kate*
is true iff Jill knows Kate.

Figure 6.2 To determine the truth conditions of a particular utterance, one must draw on knowledge from various modules. The semantic module provides axioms relating terms to sequences ((14) to (18)) and utterances to sequences ((28) to (30)). Other modules give the phonetics and syntax of the sentence uttered and the referents of referring terms. And the logic module provides rules for inferring the truth conditions of the given utterance.

self and has not informed Watson of any part of his plan, the good doctor will need to go through a long chain of reasoning to derive the required knowledge. To know that the criminal is the addressee and that the referent of *that gun* is the weapon in the criminal's hand, Watson will need to work out a whole intricate story for himself. If he cannot do this, he will not be able to derive absolute truth conditions for the utterance.

What we see, then, is that deductions like (31) determining the truth conditions of particular utterances must be viewed as a joint cognitive enterprise. The semantics module provides sequence-relative axioms, together with the information in (28) and (29) and the general conditional scheme in (30). Other modules provide the extrasemantic information about what sentence has been uttered and what objects have been referred to in the process. Finally, the logic module provides rules applying to this information and allowing us to derive statements about the truth of a given utterance (figure 6.2).

6.4 Complex Demonstratives

The analysis given so far accomodates various features of pronouns and demonstratives. But it also appears incomplete in important ways. Although we have axioms for simplex demonstratives like *this* and *that*, there are no rules for **complex demonstratives** like *this woman* or *that student*, which contain a nominal in addition to the proform. Furthermore, the axioms we do have make no apparent provision for the gender and distance information associated with English pronouns and demonstratives. *He/him, she/her,* and *it* are typically used to refer to objects that are male, female, and inanimate, respectively. Likewise, *this* is generally used to pick out something proximate to the speaker and the hearer, whereas *that* is typically used to refer to something more distant. This information does not figure in the axioms for these terms, and so does not figure in the truth conditions of the sentences containing them.

As it turns out, the issue of how to handle the nominal in complex demonstratives and how to accommodate gender and distance in simplex forms are closely linked. In both cases the question is how and where to treat certain information within the theory.

6.4.1   Truth Conditions versus Sequence Conditions

Our theory permits the nominal in complex demonstratives like (33) to be analyzed in a number of different ways.

(33) $[_{\text{NP}} [_{\text{Det}} \text{that}_1] [_{\text{N}'} \text{student}]]$

The nominal may contribute to the truth conditions of its containing sentence. It may constrain the reference for *that student*. It may do both. Or it may do neither and contribute nothing at all.

Compare the axioms in (34) and (35):

(34) $\text{Val}(x, [_{\text{NP}} \underset{[+\text{demo}]}{\text{Det}} \; \text{N}'], \sigma)$ iff $\text{Val}(x, \underset{[+\text{demo}]}{\text{Det}}, \sigma)$ and $\text{Val}(x, \text{N}', \sigma)$

(35) $\text{Val}(x, [_{\text{NP}} \underset{[+\text{demo}]}{\text{Det}} \; \text{N}'], \sigma)$ iff $\text{Val}(x, \underset{[+\text{demo}]}{\text{Det}}, \sigma)$

According to (34), an object x is a value of a complex demonstrative just in case it is a value of the demonstrative proper (*that$_i$*) and of the nominal (*student*). Both daughters of the NP thus figure in semantically. By contrast, under (35), an object is a value of the complex demonstrative just in case it is a value of the demonstrative alone. The nominal places no conditions on the object; it is essentially ignored. This difference in NP semantics is directly reflected in truth conditions. Under (34) the sentence *That$_1$ student agrees* receives the truth conditions in (36), whereas under (35) it receives the ones in (37):

(36) Val(t, *That₁ student agrees*, σ) iff σ(1) is a student and σ(1) agrees

(37) Val(t, *That₁ student agrees*, σ) iff σ(1) agrees

The nominal makes a contribution to the former but none to the latter. Indeed, the RHS of the biconditional is identical to that for *He₁ agrees*, (38), which contains no nominal at all:

(38) Val(t, *He₁ agrees*, σ) iff σ(1) agrees

A decision between (34) versus (35) in our theory thus amounts to a decision to analyze the nominal as truth-conditionally active versus truth-conditionally inert.

 Next compare the two sequence-condition statements in (39) and (40), where in both cases *that* is a demonstrative determiner:

(39) If a speaker uses [$_{NP}$ [Det   that$_i$] N'] in *u* to refer to *x*, then Σ(*u*, σ)
      _[+demo]
         only if σ(*i*) = *x* and Val(*x*, N', σ)

(40) If a speaker uses *that$_i$* in *u* to refer to *x*, then Σ(*u*, σ) only if σ(*i*) = *x*

According to (39), it is the full complex demonstrative [$_{NP}$ *that$_i$* N'] that is used to refer to an object, and its use constrains a sequence in two ways: the object must appear in the *i*th position in the sequence, and N' must be true of the object. By contrast, according to (40), it is only the demonstrative determiner *that$_i$* in a complex demonstrative that is used to refer to an object, and its use constrains a sequence in only one way: the object must appear in the *i*th position. The nominal places no conditions on the sequence at all; it is ignored. These differences in sequence conditions entail a difference in referential possibilities. With (39), we can successfully refer to an object with *that₁ student* only if the object is in fact a student; otherwise, reference simply fails:

(41) If a speaker uses [$_{NP}$ *that₁ student*] in *u* to refer to *x*, then Σ(*u*, σ) only if
         σ(1) = *x* and *x* is a student

By contrast, with (40) the presence of the nominal in no way constrains the reference of *that₁ student*. It is only the demonstrative *that₁* that is used to refer, and it can be used to refer to students and nonstudents alike:

(42) If a speaker uses *that₁* in *u* to refer to *x*, then Σ(*u*, σ) only if σ(1) = *x*

A decision between including (39) versus (40) in our theory thus amounts to a decision to analyze the nominal as referentially active versus referentially inert.

These candidate axioms and sequence conditions can be combined to yield various analyzes of complex demonstratives. For example, if we adopt (34) and (39), then we are saying that the nominal contributes to the truth conditions and also constrains referential possibilities. If we adopt (34) and (40), we're saying that it contributes to the truth conditions but does not constrain reference. And so on.

Which of these analyses is correct? As an empirical test, consider the following situation. You and a friend come home late one night to find a badger rummaging through your garbage bin, spreading trash all over the yard. You mistake it (the badger, not the bin) for a fox and say (43), gesturing at the animal.

(43) That fox is making a terrible mess.

What (if anything) did you refer to with your utterance of *that fox*? And was what you said true or false? Our intuitions are not entirely clear on this point, but they tend toward the judgment that in uttering *that fox*, you referred to the badger. Even though the animal in question was not a fox, you still succeeded in picking it out with your utterance. Furthermore, your utterance of (43) was true. Although the animal was not a fox, the state of your yard was enough to verify the sentence.

If these (admittedly tentative) intuitions match your own, then they argue for the weakest possible analysis of the contribution of N′ in a complex demonstrative. That is, they support the idea that N′ does enter into the truth conditions of the containing sentence, (35), and that it does not constrain reference, (40). On this view, the contribution of N′ can be at most a pragmatic one: it functions as an often helpful "information pointer" to the object that the utterer is getting at. But this role is completely nonsemantic, and when the information is incorrect, it can be ignored.

6.4.2 Gender Information in Pronouns

The analysis of gender in pronouns presents us with options very similar to those of complex demonstratives. For example, with the pronoun *she* we have the choice of bringing gender information into the pronoun axiom, and hence into the truth conditions of sentences containing *she*. Under (44) this information figures in; under (45) (= (12b)) it doesn't:

(44) $\text{Val}(x, she_i, \sigma)$ iff $x = \sigma(i)$ and x is female for all $i \geq 1$

(45) $\text{Val}(x, she_i, \sigma)$ iff $x = \sigma(i)$ for all $i \geq 1$

Likewise, we have the option of bringing gender information into the sequence conditions for pronouns, and hence into the determination of reference. Under (46) this information does figure in; under (47) it doesn't:

(46) If a speaker uses she_i in u to refer to x, then $\Sigma(u, \sigma)$ only if $\sigma(i) = x$ and x is female

(47) If a speaker uses she_i in u to refer to x, then $\Sigma(u, \sigma)$ only if $\sigma(i) = x$

Once again, there are four possible analyses of *she* corresponding to the four possible combinations of (44) through (47). And once again, empirical tests yield results similar to those in the case of complex demonstratives. Suppose that King's College (London) is going to be closed over the Christmas period. You are walking with Alan, who points to King's College and utters (48):

(48) She is going to be closed over the Christmas period.

Alan's utterance is clearly a peculiar one. He evidently has some reason for thinking of King's College as female. If we treat the fact that *she* refers to a female object as semantic information, as in (44) or (46), then we must regard this utterance of (48) in one of two ways. Either we must view it as attributing femininity to King's, and hence as false, or else we must deny that the pronoun refers to King's College at all. Neither option seems right, however. On the one hand, the utterance doesn't seem straightforwardly false in the situation described; King's will be closed over the Christmas interval. But neither does it seem that *she* couldn't possibly refer to King's College. The pointing and the intention behind it are clearly aimed at King's. And Alan does appear to succeed in fixing the referent of *she* by making the pointing gesture. Thus since the pronoun does seems to refer to King's and since the utterance doesn't seem to be false, we conclude that (48) does not literally say or require that the referent of *she* be female. Rather, it truly says of King's that it will be closed over the Christmas period, and it also contributes some kind of additional non-truth-conditional information to the effect that King's is female.

The upshot, then, is that with pronouns, the weakest theory of gender contribution appears to hold. The relevant axiom is (45), and the relevant sequence condition is (47), which together treat gender as semantically inert, even if pragmatically useful in many cases.

6.5   Indexical Pronouns and the Relation Σ

The utterance-sequence relation Σ can be extended in an interesting way to deal with a rather special group of pronouns called **indexicals**. This group includes the singular personal pronouns *I* and *you*, as well as the proadverbs *here* and *now*. Like other proforms, these items are referentially variable: different people can be designated with *you*, and different places can be referred to by *here*. Unlike other proforms, however, the individual they refer to always plays a constant role in the speech situation. In any utterance containing *I*, the pronoun refers to the person who makes that utterance, and in any utterance containing *here*, the proadverb refers to the site where the speech event occurs.

One simple way to accommodate indexicals is to constrain the Σ relation to associate fixed utterance roles with fixed sequence positions. For example, suppose that Σ has the following properties for any utterance u and sequence σ:

(49) a. $\Sigma(u, \sigma)$ only if $\sigma(1) =$ the utterer of u
  b. $\Sigma(u, \sigma)$ only if $\sigma(2) =$ the addressee of u
  c. $\Sigma(u, \sigma)$ only if $\sigma(3) =$ the place of u
  d. $\Sigma(u, \sigma)$ only if $\sigma(4) =$ the time of u

Then corresponding axioms for *I*, *you*, *here* and *now* can be given as in (50):

(50) a. $\mathrm{Val}(x, I, \sigma)$ iff $x = \sigma(1)$
  b. $\mathrm{Val}(x, you, \sigma)$ iff $x = \sigma(2)$
  c. $\mathrm{Val}(x, here, \sigma)$ iff $x = \sigma(3)$
  d. $\mathrm{Val}(x, now, \sigma)$ iff $x = \sigma(4)$

Thus Σ introduces a certain constant structure into all sequences σ, and indexicals take advantage of this constant structure to find their values.

To illustrate the interaction of (49) and (50), consider a partial derivation of the truth conditions for an utterance of the sentence *I ponder*. Using the apparatus introduced above, we have the conditionalized T sentence (51a). With the sequence-relative rules and the new axiom (50a), it is then easy to show (51b):

(51) a. If u is an utterance of $[_S\ [_{NP}\ I]\ [_{VP}\ [_V\ \text{ponder}]]]$ and $\Sigma(u, \sigma)$,
   then u is true iff $\mathrm{Val}(t, [_S\ [_{NP}\ I]\ [_{VP}\ [_V\ \text{ponder}]]], \sigma)$
  b. $\mathrm{Val}(t, [_S\ [_{NP}\ I]\ [_{VP}\ [_V\ \text{ponder}]]], \sigma)$ iff $\sigma(1)$ ponders

Finally, since (51a) holds for any utterance u and sequence σ, we can put these results together as in (52):[5]

(52) If u is an utterance of $[_S [_{NP} \text{I}] [_{VP} [_V \text{ponder}]]]$, then u is true iff the utterer of u ponders

This is intuitively the correct result.

The Σ approach to indexicals, in which certain utterance roles are tied to fixed positions in a sequence, requires a change in our indexing conventions for nonindexical pronouns. To see why, consider the truth conditions our rules now assign to utterances of the pairs in (53) and (54):

(53) a. I ponder.
      b. He$_1$ ponders.

(54) a. You ponder.
      b. She$_2$ ponders.

On reflection, the truth conditions will be the same. Both (53a) and (53b) will be true if and only if the utterer ponders. Both (54a) and (54b) will be true iff the addressee ponders. Clearly, this is not a desirable result. English *I* and *he* are never semantically equivalent, nor are sentences that contain them. We would never use (53b) to express what we would normally express by (53a), for example. Similarly for *you* and *she*. The problem arises here because the nonindexical pronouns have derived their values from the same sequence positions as *I* and *you*, namely from $\sigma(1)$ and $\sigma(2)$. And they have done so because of the indices they bear, namely 1 and 2. To prevent this situation, we must block the relevant indexings. More generally, we must ensure that nonindexical pronouns never bear an index that Σ can associate with a fixed utterance role.

Our solution to the numbering problem with indexicals will be to adjust the notation for sequences in a somewhat nonstandard way. As things now stand, a sequence is an ordered collection of individuals, where position in the order is given strictly by a numerical index (55a).[6] We propose to adjust the definition of a sequence to include two different kinds of indices: alphabetic letters $(a, b, \ldots, z)$ and numerals $(1, 2, \ldots)$. The first r positions (for some r) will be indexed with letters under their alphabetic ordering. Subsequent positions in the sequence will be indexed with positive natural numbers under their usual ordering (55b):[7]

(55) a. $\sigma = \langle \sigma(1), \sigma(2), \sigma(3), \ldots, \sigma(i), \ldots \rangle$

b. $\sigma = \langle \underbrace{\sigma(a), \sigma(b), \ldots, \sigma(r)}_{\text{letter indices}}, \underbrace{\sigma(1), \sigma(2), \ldots, \sigma(i), \ldots}_{\text{number indices}} \rangle$

The idea is to associate the first r positions in a sequence with individuals playing a fixed utterance role and to refer to them by a different set of indicies than we use for referring to individuals with a nonfixed utterance role.

How many sequence positions r will Σ associate with fixed utterance roles? In (50) and in our formal theory with variable-reference terms, VRT, this number is 4, but 4 may not be large enough. There are indexicals that we have not considered yet, such as the plural pronouns *us*, *we*, and *you*, the adjectives *actual*, *former*, *present*, and *local*, and the adverbs *actually*, *previously*, *currently*, and *locally*. While many of these will draw on established utterance roles for their reference, others (like *actual* and *actually*) may require us to introduce new roles and hence require new sequence positions to be set aside.

Just how many different utterance roles can play a part in human language interpretation, and thus what kinds of indexicals and indexicality are possible, is clearly an empirical matter, to be established by investigation of the facts. In advance of such investigation, all we can really say is that Σ will determine some definite number of sequence positions to be linked to fixed utterance roles. For our purposes it is enough to chose an r sufficiently large:

(56) a. Val(x, I, σ) iff $x = \sigma(a)$

b. Val(x, you, σ) iff $x = \sigma(b)$

c. Val$(x, here, \sigma)$ iff $x = \sigma(c)$

d. Val(x, now, σ) iff $x = \sigma(d)$

$\vdots$

r. Val(x, α, σ) iff $x = \sigma(r)$

After we choose such an r, we can leave the conditions of Σ for pronouns and demonstrative determiners (α_i) in the simple form in (57):

(57) If a speaker uses α_i in u to refer to x, then $\Sigma(u, \sigma)$ only if $\sigma(i) = x$

Likewise, we can leave our axiom schemata for nonindexical pronouns and demonstrative determiners as in (58):

(58) a. $\text{Val}(x, he_i, \sigma)$ iff $x = \sigma(i)$ for all $i \geq 1$

   b. $\text{Val}(x, she_i, \sigma)$ iff $x = \sigma(i)$ for all $i \geq 1$

   c. $\text{Val}(x, it_i, \sigma)$ iff $x = \sigma(i)$ for all $i \geq 1$

   d. $\text{Val}(x, that_i, \sigma)$ iff $x = \sigma(i)$ for all $i \geq 1$

In both cases, i is understood to range over the natural numbers. These changes will insure that if someone utters a sentence containing the nonindexical pronoun he_1 and uses this pronoun to refer to the individual x, then this utterance will select only sequences having x, not in the first position but in the $(r + 1)$th position. Correlatively, the semantic value of he_1 will be the first element in the sequence σ following all the positions associated with indexical elements:

(59) pronouns: *I*   *you* he_1

   sequence: $\langle \sigma(a), \; \sigma(b), \ldots, \; \sigma(r), \; \sigma(1), \ldots, \sigma(i), \ldots \rangle$

   indexical positions

With this change in indexing conventions, a nonindexical pronoun will never be associated with a constant utterance role.

6.6 The Semantic Properties of Pronouns and Demonstratives

We earlier considered the semantic nature of proper nouns, looking at issues concerning empty nouns, coextensive nouns, and rigidity. Let us consider these issues with respect to the pronouns and demonstratives of VRT.

Are empty pronouns and demonstratives meaningful? This question makes sense, of course, only when applied to particular utterances. Abstracted from particular utterances, the demonstrative *that* is neither empty nor nonempty. So the question really is, Are particular utterances of empty pronouns and demonstratives meaningful? Interestingly, the answer turns out to be yes and no. In one sense they are meaningful, and in another they are not.

Let us consider an example. Suppose that it's a dark night and I am walking along Long Island Sound. I believe I see a boat in the distance, point to it, and say (60):

(60) That is the ferry from Port Jeff.

It may turn out that I was wrong, that it was just a trick of the light and where I took the boat to be there was nothing at all. But it surely seems that I've said something meaningful, even if my demonstrative *that* referred to nothing. The utterance is meaningful at least in the following sense. It is an utterance of a sentence with perfectly cogent semantic features: our theory explains how (60) interacts with contexts of utterance to derive truth conditions. The T theory, along with appropriate nonsemantic resources, will deliver the conditional in (61) (various details suppressed):

(61)   If u is an utterance of [$_S$ [$_{NP}$ That] [$_{VP}$ is the ferry from Port Jeff]] and x is the object demonstrated by the utterer of u, then u is true iff x is the ferry from Port Jeff

The utterance was therefore a perfectly intelligible piece of discourse: the conditions (as specified by Σ) under which *that* would have referred are perfectly clear, and the truth conditions (as specified by the T theory plus other resources) that the utterance would have had if *that* had received a value are also clear.

However, there is also clearly something amiss with the utterance. There is a sense in which it lacks a complete and determinate meaning. Since there is no object demonstrated by the utterer in the example described, there is no way of detaching the consequent to derive a statement of the utterance's truth conditions. Thus there is an important sense in which my utterance of (60) lacks content: it has no truth conditions, and so fails to say anything true or false.

Adopting some convenient terminology from Kaplan 1990, we can distinguish two senses of "meaning" in order to allow us to express the idea that (60) and similar cases are both meaningful and meaningless. The utterance is meaningful because it is an utterance of a sentence type with fully determinate semantic features. These features, as we said earlier, constitute a sort of recipe that allows us to calculate the truth conditions of a propitious utterance once we know the relevant details of the context. We can call these semantic features the sentence's **character**. The character specifies a mapping from contexts of utterance to truth conditions: given a context of utterance as input, the character will provide the utterance's truth conditions as output. Thus we can say that utterances of sentences containing empty pronouns are meaningful in that they have characters but that they nevertheless lack truth conditions.

What about different but coextensive pronouns and demonstratives? Do they have the same meaning or different meanings? Here again we must confine our attention to particular utterances, since only for such does the question of extension arise. And here again, the answer is yes and no. Utterances of different types of pronouns referring to the same object differ in character but yield the same truth conditions. An example will make this clear.

Katherine Hepburn might utter (62), thereby saying something about herself, and Cary Grant might utter (63), saying the same thing about Katherine Hepburn.

(62) I need a haircut.

(63) She needs a haircut.

Evidently, the fixed semantic features of (62) and (63) are different. One contains *I* where the other contains *she*, and Σ provides a different way for evaluating these terms.

However, the truth conditions of the two utterances are identical. The conditionalized truth conditions are as follows (again with irrelevant details suppressed):

(64) If u is an utterance of $[_S [_{NP} I] [_{VP}$ need a haircut$]]$ and x is the utterer of u, then u is true iff x needs a haircut

(65) If u is an utterance of $[_S [_{NP}$ She$] [_{VP}$ needs a haircut$]]$ and x is the object demonstrated by the utterer of u, then u is true iff x needs a haircut

What are the actual truth conditions of the particular utterances (62) and (63)? In both cases the RHSs of the conditionals is "x needs a haircut." Who is x? In both cases it is Katherine Hepburn, the utterer of (62) and the object demonstrated by the utterer of (63). As far as our theory is concerned, it is this object x that enters into the truth conditions. No particular way of specifying that object is given, no descriptive content enters into the truth conditions. All we have is the variable x marking the spot where the object goes. Of course, hearers may have their own way of specifying the relevant object ("Katherine Hepburn," "the elegant woman standing in the corner," "that actress," or whatever), and when they detach the consequent of the conditionals, they can fill in the place occupied by x with such as specification. But on our theory, these are not present in the truth conditions of the utterance itself. They are best thought of not as part of what is actually said but rather as elaborations of what is actually said.

Finally, let us consider the issue of rigidity. Think about (65). It is true, of course, that if Cary Grant had gestured at someone else when speaking (63) (say Audrey Hepburn), then his utterance would have had different truth conditions. But nonrigidity is not a matter of this particular kind of variable reference. Rather, it is a question of whether the truth conditions that the utterance actually did have could have been met in some counterfactual circumstance because someone other than Katherine Hepburn needed a haircut. The answer to that question is evidently no. As we have just said, it's Katherine Hepburn herself who enters into these truth conditions.

What this shows is that evaluating an utterance under different counterfactual circumstances is a three-step process:

1. We take the sentence uttered and determine its fixed semantic features, its character. At this stage we get a conditionalized T theorem.

2. We determine how these features interact with the context of utterance to fix truth conditions. Here we use nonlinguistic knowledge and extra-semantic logical resources to detach the consequent of the conditionalized T theorem.

3. We consider under what counterfactual circumstances the truth conditions would have been met.

Rigidity enters the picture only at step 3: a term is nonrigid just when at step 3 different objects are relevant to the truth value of the utterance in different counterfactual circumstances. This is not case with the utterance of (63): only the state of Katherine Hepburn's hair is relevant to whether the truth conditions of this utterance would have been met in any given counterfactual circumstance. The variation of values that we find with demonstratives occurs at step 2: their character allows them to have different values in different contexts of utterance. But this is quite different from nonrigidity.

Theory and Exercises

The VRT Theory (Variable-Reference Terms)

Lexical Axioms

(1) a. Val(x, *Kate*, σ) iff x = Kate
   b. Val(x, *Chris*, σ) iff x = Chris
   c. Val(x, *Phil*, σ) iff x = Phil
   d. Val(x, *Jill*, σ) iff x = Jill

    e.   Val(x, *ponders*, σ) iff x ponders
    f.   Val(x, *agrees*, σ) iff x agrees
    g.   Val(x, *protests*, σ) iff x protests
    h.   Val($\langle x, y \rangle$, *knows*, σ) iff x knows y
    i.   Val($\langle x, y \rangle$, *admires*, σ) iff x admires y
    j.   Val($\langle x, y \rangle$, *instructs*, σ) iff x instructs y
    k.   Val(x, *I*, σ) iff $x = \sigma(a)$
    l.   Val(x, *you*, σ) iff $x = \sigma(b)$
    m.   Val(x, *here*, σ) iff $x = \sigma(c)$
    n.   Val(x, *now*, σ) iff $x = \sigma(d)$
    o.   Val(x, *he$_i$*, σ) iff $x = \sigma(i)$ for all $i \geq 1$
    p.   Val(x, *she$_i$*, σ) iff $x = \sigma(i)$ for all $i \geq 1$
    q.   Val(x, *him$_i$*, σ) iff $x = \sigma(i)$ for all $i \geq 1$
    r.   Val(x, *her$_i$*, σ) iff $x = \sigma(i)$ for all $i \geq 1$
    s.   Val(x, *it$_i$*, σ) iff $x = \sigma(i)$ for all $i \geq 1$
    t.   Val(x, *this$_i$*, σ) iff $x = \sigma(i)$ for all $i \geq 1$
    u.   Val(x, *that$_i$*, σ) iff $x = \sigma(i)$ for all $i \geq 1$

Phrasal Axioms

(2) a. Val(t, [$_S$ S$_1$ *and* S$_2$], σ) iff both Val(t, S$_1$, σ) and Val(t, S$_2$, σ)
    b. Val(t, [$_S$ S$_1$ *or* S$_2$], σ) iff either Val(t, S$_1$, σ) or Val(t, S$_2$, σ)
    c. Val(t, [$_S$ *It is not the case that* S], σ) iff it is not the case that Val(t, S, σ)
    d. Val(t, [$_S$ NP VP], σ) iff for some x, Val(x, NP, σ) and Val(x, VP, σ)
    e. Val(x, [$_{VP}$ V NP], σ) iff for some y, Val($\langle x, y \rangle$, V, σ) and Val(y, NP, σ)
    f. Val(x, [$_X$ Y], σ) iff Val(x, Y, σ) (where X, Y are any nodes)
    g. Val(x, [$_{NP}$ Det N'], σ) iff Val(x, Det, σ)
             [+demo]   [+demo]

Production Rules

(UI) Universal instantiation

    For any x, $F(x)$
    ―――――――
    $F(\alpha)$

(SE) Substitution of equivalents

    $F(\alpha)$
    α iff β
    ―――――――
    $F(\beta)$

(SI) Substitution of identicals

$$\frac{\phi \text{ iff for some } x, F(x) \text{ and } x = \alpha}{\phi \text{ iff } F(\alpha)}$$

The Conditionalized T Scheme

(3) If u is an utterance of S and $\Sigma(u, \sigma)$, then u is true iff Val(t, S, σ)

Definition   Let Σ be a relation between utterances and sequences such that

- for any utterance u, for some sequence σ, $\Sigma(u, \sigma)$,
- for any utterance u, sequence σ, individual x, nonindexical pronoun and demonstrative determiner α_i,
    a. $\Sigma(u, \sigma)$ only if $\sigma(a) =$ the utterer of u,
    b. $\Sigma(u, \sigma)$ only if $\sigma(b) =$ the addressee of u,
    c. $\Sigma(u, \sigma)$ only if $\sigma(c) =$ the place of u,
    d. $\Sigma(u, \sigma)$ only if $\sigma(d) =$ the time of u,
    e. If a speaker uses α_i in u to refer to x, then $\Sigma(u, \sigma)$ only if $\sigma(i) = x$,

Then Σ is a **selection relation**.

Definition   For any sequence σ, $\sigma(a)$, $\sigma(b)$, $\sigma(c)$, $\sigma(d)$ are the first, second, third, and fourth elements of σ, respectively. For any natural number i, $\sigma(i)$ is the $(i + 4)$th element of σ.

Exercises

1. The following are sentences of VRT:

    (1) He_2 ponders.

    (2) She_3 knows her_1.

    (3) I ponder.

    - Prove the sequence-relative truth conditions for (1) to (3).
    - If these sentences are evaluated with respect to the sequence in (4), what are their absolute (i.e., non-sequence-relative) truth conditions?

    (4) ⟨Jill, Phil, King's College, 4 December 1993, Kate, Kumiko, the Eiffel Tower, 7, the *USS Enterprise*, ...⟩

- Suppose that Jill utters each of (1) to (3) at King's College on 4 December 1993. What are the truth conditions of her utterances? Give a conditionalized T theorem and state what its detached consequent should be. (You don't need to prove these results; you would need logical rules not stated here.)

2. In the text it was suggested that axioms can be given for pronouns and demonstratives only if Val is relativized to sequences. Is this really true? If so, what is wrong with the following axioms, which do not invoke sequences at all:

   (1) Val(x, *that*) iff x = the thing demonstrated

   (2) Val(x, *you*) iff x = the addressee

   (3) Val(x, *you*) iff x = you

   Discuss your answer carefully.

3. Consider the situation where someone is addressing a group of individuals and utters (1) nodding to three different persons in turn:

   (1) You, you, and you know Phil.

   - What problems do cases like this present for the analysis of *you* given in the text?
   - What analysis can you suggest to solve the problem?

4. The pronoun *we* can have an **inclusive use,** where its reference includes the speaker and the addressee. For instance, Phil may say (1) to Jill, intending to indicate that the two of them (Phil and Jill) should leave:

   (1) We should leave.

   We can also have an **exclusive use,** where its reference includes the speaker and some other contextually salient individuals but excludes the addressee. For instance, Phil may use (2) to report to Jill that he and Kate went shopping:

   (2) We went shopping.

   How might the difference between the inclusive and exclusive *we* be analyzed semantically? It might be useful to think about plural NPs like *we* as having sets X as their semantic values:

(3) Val(X, *we*, σ) iff $X = \{\ldots\}$

What set should X be in the two cases?

5. Fillmore (1971) notes that the verbs *come* and *go* contain indexical information in that the former indicates motion toward the speaker (or utterance location) and the latter indicates motion away from the speaker (or utterance location).

(1) Chris is going (to New York).

(2) Chris is coming (to New York).

- Give axioms for *come* and *go* that capture this hidden indexicality.
- Consider the verbs *bring* and *take* from the same perspective and suggest appropriate axioms for them.

6. Here is a simple children's joke:

A: I can prove that you are not here.
B: How?
A: Are you in London?
B: No.
A: Are you in New York?
B: No.
A: If you're not in London and not in New York, then you must be someplace else, right?
B: Yes.
A: Well, if you're someplace else, then you're not here!

Why does this proof appear to hold? And why in fact doesn't it hold?

7. In the text we judged that one might successfully refer to an animal that was not a fox using the demonstrative *that fox* and go on to say something truthful about it. From this we tentatively concluded that the nominal in a complex demonstrative neither constrains reference nor contributes to the truth conditions of the sentence containing it.

Reconsider the example situation in the case where someone had said (1b) instead of (1a):

(1) a. That fox is messing up your yard.
    b. That elephant is messing up your yard.

The judgments that there is successful reference and that the utterance is true seem more difficult in this case. We seem more inclined to judge that reference fails in (1b) and hence that the sentence fails to say anything at all, or else that (1b) is simply false. What account might be given of this extra degree of difficulty?

8. In the text we suggested that there is a three-step process in the interpretation and evaluation of utterances. We described this process for an utterance of a sentence containing a pronoun and showed that it was rigid. Go through the three-step process for a sentence involving a descriptive name and show at what point nonrigidity arises.

7   Quantification

As constructed so far, our theory is adequate for simple sentences involving singular referring terms and predicates, such as *Chris agrees* and *Jill knows Kate*. However, this leaves out a large number of examples, like the following, whose subjects and objects do not appear to refer:

(1) a. No man agrees.
    b. Every man admires some woman.

Such sentences are often called **quantified** or **quantificational**, since they purport to describe how many things of a certain sort are such and such: how many men are also agreers, how many men admire how many women, and so on. Formatives like *every*, *no*, *some*, *two*, etc., are called **quantifiers**, and the noun phrases that contain them, such as *every man* and *no woman*, are called **quantified noun phrases**.

In this chapter we extend our semantic theory to provide an analysis of quantified sentences and their parts. The extended theory, PredC, furnishes a general account of quantification and yields interpretations for sentences containing indefinitely many quantified noun phrases. It sheds light on various relationships between the syntax of quantified sentences and their interpretation. It also suggests a useful characterization of the broader class of **operators** to which quantified phrases belong.

7.1   The Syntactic Form of Quantification

In analyzing basic predications like *Phil ponders* and *Jill knows Kate*, we began with their surface syntactic forms as provided by grammatical theory and showed how such forms could be directly interpreted by means of the semantic theory PC+. With quantified sentences, the picture becomes more complicated.

As noted in chapter 3, modern syntactic theory takes quantified sentences like (1a, b) to possess a number of different grammatical representations. Beginning with Chomsky (1976) and May (1977), it has been argued that quantified sentences possess two very different kinds of forms. One is a surface form (or S-structure), in which the quantified NPs occupy positions like those occupied by proper nouns. The other is a logical form (or LF), in which quantified elements have undergone movement and are raised. This raising adjoins the moved phrase to a containing S and leaves an indexed structural residue or "trace" (*t*) in the premovement site.

To illustrate, (1a) receives the S-structure representation in (2a), where the quantified NP *no man* occupies the subject position, like the proper noun in *Chris agrees*. The sentence also receives the LF representation in (2b), where the quantified NP is raised and adjoined to the S node, leaving a coindexed trace (t_1):

(2) a.   b.

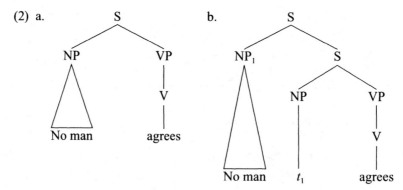

Similarly, (1b) receives the S-structure representation in (3a), where *every man* and *some woman* occur in subject and object positions, respectively. It further receives the two LFs in (3b, c), which are derived by raising the object NP first, followed by the subject, (3b), and by raising the subject NP first, followed by the object, (3c):

(3) a.

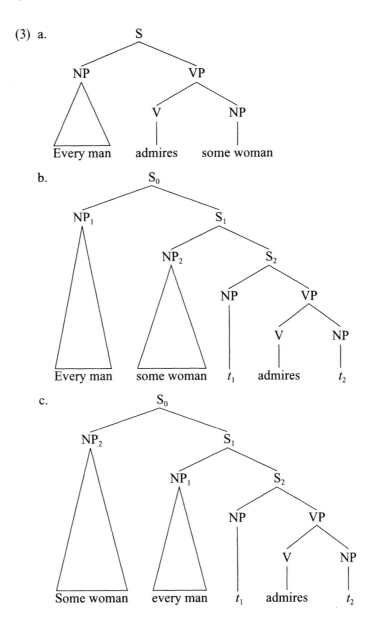

Since (2b) and (3b, c) diverge from their associated surface sentences, LFs are evidently a covert or inaudible class of syntactic representations.[1]

The idea that quantificational sentences possess LFs like those in (2) and (3) is a natural one on our previous assumptions. Recall our suggestion in chapter 2 that ambiguity is fundamentally a syntactic matter and that multiplicity of meaning like that found in (4) and (5) should be analyzed as arising from a multiplicity of form, as shown in (4a, b) and (5a, b):

(4) Pedro jumped from the bank.
    a. Pedro jumped from the bank$_1$.
    b. Pedro jumped from the bank$_2$.

(5) Mad dogs and Englishmen go out in the noonday sun.
    a. [[Mad dogs] and [Englishmen]] go out in the noonday sun.
    b. [Mad [dogs and Englishmen]] go out in the noonday sun.

Sentences with multiple quantified NPs, like (1b), also show ambiguities. These arise according to the order in which these NPs are understood. Thus (1b) has a reading in which every man admires at least one woman (possibly a different one for each man), (6a). It also has a reading on which there is some one woman whom all the men admire, (6b):

(6) a. For every man x, for some woman y, x admires y (every, some)
    b. For some woman y, for every man x, x admires y (some, every)

LFs like (3b, c) provide the distinct representations that we expect if ambiguity in interpretation follows from ambiguity in form. These structures differ precisely in the relative order of the two quantifiers. It is natural to associate (3b) with (6a), where the subject NP is understood with broadest scope, and to associate (3c) with (6b), where the object NP is understood with broadest scope.

The view that quantificational sentences have LFs in which certain phrases are moved from base positions is a claim not about English in particular but about all languages generally. And indeed in other languages the quantifier raising hypothesized for English actually seems to be visible in surface form. Kiss (1986, 1991) offers Hungarian as a case in point. Kiss proposes that the Hungarian sentence is underlyingly verb-initial, with arguments and modifiers of the verb following it in free order. To achieve various focusing or topicalization effects, these elements may be preposed, as we illustrate schematically with English words in (7):

(7) a. See Janos Maria

    b. [$_S$ See [$_{NP}$ Janos] [$_{NP}$ Maria]]

    c. [$_S$ [$_{NP}$ Janos] [$_S$ see t [$_{NP}$ Maria]]]

Such preposing is available with a range of phrases and appears to be the standard option with quantified NPs and other scopal elements. Kiss argues that the sentence in (8a), for example, has essentially the surface grammatical form in (8b), where the scopal elements (*X*Ps) have been extracted from the minimal sentential category and have been adjoined to it and have left traces:[2]

(8) a. János   többször is   mindent   világosan el   magyarázott
       John-NOM several-times everything-ACC clearly   PREF explained
       'As for John, on several occasions he explained everything clearly.'

    b.

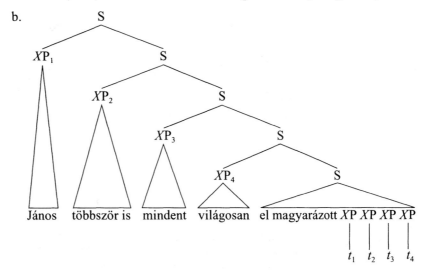

Kiss observes that such sentences are unambiguous with respect to their scopal interpretation. The order in which the scopal elements appear is the order in which they must be understood. To obtain a different interpretation of the scopal elements, they must be preposed in the appropriate order. Thus the interpretation of (8a) contrasts with that of (9a) and (9b), in which the *X*Ps have been extracted from S in different orders:

(9) a. János$_1$ mindent$_2$ többször is$_3$ világosan$_4$ [$_S$ el magyarázott t_1 t_2 t_3 t_4].
       'As for John, everything was several times explained by him clearly.'

    b. Többször is$_1$ mindent$_2$ János$_3$ [$_S$ magyarázott el világosan t_1 t_2 t_3].
       'On several occasions, everything John explained clearly.'

The scopal relations that can be overtly observed in Hungarian appear closely analogous to the quantifier relations we have hypothesized for English. In English, quantified NPs originate within a minimal domain of predication (S) and subsequently move out to various adjoined positions that determine their scope. That this movement is "audible" in Hungarian makes it clear that such derived representations must be available in principle for English. The assumption that such representations are present in English allows us to capture both important similarities and differences between the two languages. Hungarian and English can be understood as fundamentally similar in their treatment of quantificational elements in that both languages prepose these elements to fix their scope. Where they differ is simply in whether the movement is present at a phonologically interpreted level or at a covert level. English sentences with multiple quantified NPs are ambiguous because these NPs have not been assigned audible scope, whereas the corresponding Hungarian sentences are unambiguous because they have been.

Further arguments have been given for LF representations. We will not rehearse them here but will simply take the existence of LFs to be reasonably motivated at this point. We turn now to the semantics of quantification and the interpretation of quantificational structures.

7.2   The Semantics of Quantification

We observed that quantified sentences do not appear to be basic predications, since quantified NPs are not singular referring terms. Nonetheless, while quantified sentences are not themselves basic predications, it is natural to try to relate them to the latter. There are a number of different ways of drawing this connection. Here we will consider two approaches: one involving proper nouns and one involving terms of variable reference.

7.2.1   Quantification and Proper Nouns

One attractive idea about the truth conditions of quantified sentences is that they derive from the truth conditions of simple sentences in which a proper noun replaces the quantified NP. On this kind of view, the truth conditions of a quantified sentence like *No man agrees* or *Every man agrees* would be spelled out in terms of the truth conditions of elementary predicational sentences like

Chris agrees, *Bill agrees*, *Phil agrees*, etc., where *Chris*, *Bill*, *Phil*, etc., are proper nouns for men.

We can execute this general proposal in various ways, depending on what we see ourselves as counting or quantifying over in quantified sentences. One idea is that quantified sentences implicitly count or quantify over names. This notion can be illustrated for *Some man agrees* and *Every man agrees* as in (10a, b):

(10) a. Val(t, *Some man agrees*) iff for some proper noun α such that
        Val(x, α) only if Val(x, *man*), Val(t, α *agrees*)
     b. Val(t, *Every man agrees*) iff for every proper noun α such that
        Val(x, α) only if Val(x, *man*), Val(t, α *agrees*)

Here *Some man agrees* is true just in case for some proper noun that is the name of a man (say *John*), the sentence formed by replacing the quantified NP with that proper noun is true (i.e., *John agrees* is true). Similarly, *Every man agrees* is true just in case for every proper noun that is the name of a man (*Chris, Rolf, Phil, Hiroaki*, etc.), the sentence formed by replacing the quantified NP with the proper noun is true, (i.e., *Chris agrees* is true, *Rolf agrees* is true, *Hiroaki agrees* is true, etc.). In both cases the relevant quantity being evaluated is a *quantity of proper nouns*, and the truth of the quantified sentences depends on the truth of the elementary sentences in which these proper nouns appear.[3]

An alternative execution of this general approach is to take quantified sentences as counting or quantifying over the individuals designated by some proper noun. This second idea is illustrated in (11a, b), again for the sentences *Some man agrees* and *Every man agrees*.

(11) a. Val(t, *Some man agrees*) iff for some x such that Val(x, *man*), for
        some proper noun α such that Val(x, α), Val(t, α *agrees*)
     b. Val(t, *Every man agrees*) iff for every x such that Val(x, *man*), for
        some proper noun α such that Val(x, α), Val(t, α *agrees*)

Here *Some man agrees* is true just in case for some man (say John), we can find a proper noun (say *John*) such that the sentence formed by replacing the quantified NP with this name is true (i.e., *John agrees* is true). And *Every man agrees* is true just in case for every man (Chris, Rolf, Phil, Hiroaki, etc.), we can find a proper noun (*Chris, Rolf, Phil, Hiroaki*, etc., respectively) such that the sentence formed by replacing the quantified NP with this proper noun is true (i.e., *Chris agrees* is true, *Rolf agrees* is true, *Phil agrees* is true, etc.)

For (11a, b), the relevant quantity being evaluated is a *quantity of persons*, and truth of the quantified sentences depends on the truth of the elementary sentences in which the proper nouns naming those persons appear.[4]

These approaches might look equivalent at first sight; however, there are interesting and subtle differences involved and problems that arise with each. For example, notice, that if we analyze quantification in terms of quantifying over proper nouns, then we will run into problems if the fit between things in the world and proper nouns in our language is inexact, for example, if a given thing has more than one name or if some things are nameless. Consider the truth conditions for *Many men agree* and *Few grains of sand are small* under this view:

(12) Val(t, *Many men agree*) iff for many proper nouns α such that Val(x, α) only if Val(x, *man*), Val(t, α *agrees*)

(13) Val(t, *Few grains of sand are small*) iff for few proper nouns α such that Val(x, α) only if Val(x, *grains of sand*), Val(t, α *is small*)

In a situation where few men agree but where one of the male agreers has a great many different names, (12) makes the false prediction that *Many men agree* will be true. This is because what counts for the truth of (12) is numbers of names and not numbers of persons. Similarly, although *Few grains of sand are small* is false in reality, (13) predicts it to be true. This is because few (and perhaps no) grains of sand have names in English (or any other language). Hence there are few names for sand grains α that make α *is small* true.[5]

The problem of fit between proper nouns and objects also arises in the approach that involves quantifying over things, although in a reduced form. The situation of one individual having many names produces no difficulty for the account, since it is not names that are being counted but individuals. However, the problem of nameless individuals still arises, since truth conditions like those in (11) still require the existence of *some* name for a given individual. Consider the truth conditions for *No grain of sand is small* (14) under this view:

(14) Val(t, *No grain of sand is small*) iff for no x such that Val(x, *grain of sand*), for some proper noun α such that Val(x, α), Val(t, α *is small*)

Although *No grain of sand is small* is false in fact, it comes out true according to (14). The problem here is the same as before: no grain of sand has a name in English. Hence the requirement is met that there be no sand grain having a proper noun α such that α *is small* is true.

As it turns out, the problem of nameless individuals can be resolved technically by considering local or global extensions of the language in which every individual does in fact have a name. That is, we can deal with the shortage of proper nouns in English by providing truth conditions for its quantified sentences in terms of truth conditions for sentences of an extended language, English[+], in which every individual really does possess a name.[6] Through this artifice we can formulate a workable (even if rather complex) formal implementation that approaches natural-language quantification through elementary predications involving proper nouns. Nonetheless, from our perspective, there remains a serious metatheoretical drawback to the general approach. The problem is most easily appreciated by looking at a candidate axiom based on the LF syntax for quantification discussed earlier. For simplicity, we will suppose that English contains proper nouns for every entity so that the issue of nameless individuals does not arise:[7]

(15) Val(t, [$_S$ [$_{NP_i}$ *every* N'] S*]) iff for every x such that Val(x, N'), for some proper noun α such that Val(x, α), Val(t, S'), where S' is the result of substituting α for t_i in S*

As in our informal exposition (11b), this axiom spells out the interpretation of a quantified sentence in terms of the truth of simple sentences involving proper names. In (15), the trace of quantifier raising (t_i) is used to mark the point where the appropriate proper noun (α) is to appear.

Now observe that although (15) interprets the structure in (16), it does not do so by giving the semantic value of the highest S in terms of the semantic values of its subconstituents: NP and S*. Rather, it gives the semantic value of the highest S in terms of the semantic values of *every*, N', and a new syntactic object S', derived from S* through substitution.[8]

(16)

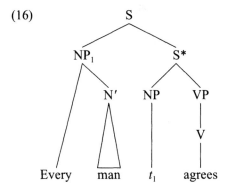

Axiom (15) thus fails to be strongly compositional in the sense discussed in chapter 3. It fails to give an interpretation of (16) that is *strictly local*: one stated in terms of immediate mother-daughter nodes (S, NP, S*). Rather, it appeals to a more extended family, including mothers, daughters, and grand-daughters (S, *every*, N', S*). Furthermore, it fails to give a semantics for (16) that is *purely interpretive*: (15) does not assign a value to S based solely on the values of its parts. Instead, it relies crucially on a new structure in which a proper noun appears in place of the trace. The rule in (15) actually produces (part of) the structure that it interprets.

The departure from compositionality involved with axioms like (15) will clearly arise under all approaches to quantification involving elementary predications with proper nouns, since all such approaches require us to interpret structures in which proper nouns appear. Under the program pursued here, which adopts strong compositionality as a methodological principle, this is sufficient to motivate our considering alternative approaches. As it turns out, there is indeed another way.

7.2.2 Quantification and Variable-Reference Terms

In attempting to explicate quantification in terms of elementary predications with proper nouns, we encountered a simple problem of linguistic resources: such an approach requires a proper noun for every object, but the language being interpreted may not contain that many proper nouns. This outcome suggests an interestingly different approach to quantifier semantics through a different class of terms, one for which the problem of linguistic resources will not arise. Suppose that instead of trying to analyze quantification in terms of elementary predications with proper nouns, we appeal to elementary predications containing terms of variable reference, such as pronouns or demonstratives. On this approach, for example, we might try to state the truth of *Some man agrees* in terms of the truth of a sentence like *He agrees*, where *he* refers to some man. Similarly, we might try to state the truth of *Every man agrees* in terms of the truth of *He agrees*, where *he* refers (successively) to every man. Such an account would explicate the truth of quantified sentences in terms of the truth of elementary predications. However, it would not require different names for each distinct individual, and hence it would not strain linguistic resources. The same term (a pronoun or demonstrative) would simply be re-used, spreading its reference across all the objects in question. To spell out this idea, we will use the semantics of variable-reference terms developed in the last chapter.[9]

We observed that pronouns and demonstratives often have their reference fixed explicitly through a gesture of pointing or ostension, as when I say *He is crazy* or *That guy might hurt himself*, pointing to a man standing on a roof. My gesture of pointing fixes the reference of the pronoun or demonstrative as the man on the roof. This general line of thinking extends to quantified sentences as well. Consider a sentence like *Every man in the class agrees*. Notice that this sentence will be true if (and only if) the sentence *He agrees* is true, where you speak it and point successively to each man in the class. That is,

(17) Val(t, *Every man in the class agrees*) iff for each pointing π to a man in the class, Val(t, *He agrees*) with respect to π

On this view, the counting or quantification in a quantified sentence is not over names or over individuals, as in previous axioms, but rather it is over pointings. *Every man in the class agrees* is true if and only if every pointing of a certain kind makes the sentence *He agrees* true.

This approach to quantifier semantics has a number of promising features. For one thing, it can be applied not only to simple examples with a single quantifier but to multiply quantified sentences as well. Consider *Every man in the class knows some woman in the class*. This sentence will be true if (and only if) the sentence *He knows her* is true, where each time you speak it pointing to a man in the class, you can also point to a woman in the class that he knows. That is,

(18) Val(t, *Every man in the class knows some woman in the class*) iff for each pointing π to a man in the class and (simultaneously) to a woman in the class, Val(t, *He knows her*) with respect to π

If we abstract away from practical constraints on the number of fingers and toes you have to point with, sentences containing any number of quantified NPs can be handled in this way.

The idea of pronouns and pointing also offers a way of escaping some of the compositionality problems that arose with the analyses employing proper nouns. Recall the structure of *Every man agrees* in (16) (repeated below), where the subject NP has undergone movement, leaving a trace in subject position:

(16)

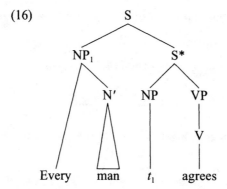

Notice that if we analyze the trace as semantically analogous to a pronoun, assuming different values with respect to different pointings, we can then treat the little sentence S* as equivalent to *He agrees*. We are not forced to appeal to other syntactic structures in our interpretation rules but can assign values to the structures actually present.

7.2.3   Sequence Variants

Most of the technical apparatus required to formalize the variable-reference-term approach is already on hand at this point. We have sequences as a formal way to spell out pointings; hence quantification over pointings can be recast as quantification over sequences. Likewise, traces can be treated like pronouns by giving them similar axioms in the T theory, ones that make them sensitive to sequences. There is, however, one new notion that we must introduce before giving our formal theory of quantified sentences. This is the notion of a **sequence variant**. Sequence variants are needed for analyzing sentences containing more than one quantifier.

To motivate the basic idea, consider the sentence *Every woman at the meeting knows three men at the meeting*, which contains two quantified NPs. Under the general approach sketched above, this sentence will be true just in case we can assert *She knows him* and point appropriately. What kind of pointings are appropriate for such a sentence? On reflection, they will be ones in which we point to each woman and then, holding one finger fixed on that woman point successively with the other hand to three different men at the meeting in turn, each time asserting the sentence *She knows him*. If each assertion so made is true, then the original quantified sentence will be true. That is, (19) will be true just in case for each woman, you can make a family of three related pointings,

She knows him. She knows him. She knows him.

She knows him. She knows him. She knows him.

Etc.

Figure 7.1 The truth conditions of *Every woman at the meeting knows three men at the meeting* given in terms of the more elementary sentence *She knows him* and appropriate pointings.

where each member of the family is a pointing that keeps one finger fixed on a given woman and varies the men pointed to with the other hand (figure 7.1).

(19) Every woman at the meeting knows three men.

Notice that when we evaluate the sentence, pointing to a given woman, it is crucial to keep one finger fixed on her as we point to the three men at the meeting that she knows. It would not verify the truth of (19) if we freely altered our gestures, pointing at women and men indiscriminately.

These reflections motivate the informal notion of a pointing variant: a pointing that leaves part of some original gesture fixed but allows other parts to vary. We may capture this notion precisely with the counterpart concept of a **sequence variant**. A variant of a sequence σ is one that leaves certain positions in σ fixed but allows other positions in σ to vary (that is, allows them to be filled with different individuals). More precisely, we define an *i*-variant of a sequence σ as follows:[10]

Definition   A sequence σ' is an *i*-variant of a sequence σ ($\sigma' \approx_i \sigma$) if and only if σ' differs from σ at most in its *i*th place.

Thus the sequences σ_1, σ_2, and σ_3 in table 7.1 are all 27-variants of σ, since the only place where they differ from σ is in their 27th place. Notice that by the definition, σ is in fact a 27-variant of itself, since σ doesn't differ from itself at all, and hence differs from itself at most in its 27th position. Henceforth we will use the notation "$\sigma' \approx_i \sigma$" to abbreviate the statement that σ' is an *i*-variant of σ (and vice versa).

7.3   The Theory PredC

We now collect our informal observations together into a formal semantic theory for quantified sentences. We will call this theory "PredC," since it embodies a semantics similar to that of the logical language called the predicate calculus. PredC is an extension of VRT, containing all the elements of the latter together with new axioms for traces and the various parts of quantifier adjuncts.

The PredC axioms for traces are directly analogous to those of pronouns. Traces are analyzed as elements whose values are fixed by sequences together with their numerical subscript:

Table 7.1   Examples of 27-variants of the sequence σ

Sequence	Place					
	1st	2nd	3rd	...	27th	...
σ	⟨John,	SUNY-SB,	Eiffel Tower,	...,	Barry,	...⟩
σ_1	⟨John,	SUNY-SB,	Eiffel Tower,	...,	Felix,	...⟩
σ_2	⟨John,	SUNY-SB,	Eiffel Tower,	...,	Berlin,	...⟩
σ_3	⟨John,	SUNY-SB,	Eiffel Tower,	...,	3,	...⟩

(20) $\mathrm{Val}(x, t_i, \sigma)$ iff $x = \sigma(i)$ for all $i \geq 1$

This incorporates our idea of treating traces as variable-reference terms.

The PredC axioms for the quantifier adjuncts have the general form anticipated in our pointing analysis. We observed that quantified statements like *Every man in the class agrees* are true iff for each pointing π to a man in the class, *He agrees* is true. Intuitively, then, our formal rule for quantification will involve the counterparts of three things:

1. How many pointings are involved: every, some, two, etc.

2. Who or what is being pointed to: men in the class, women at the meeting, etc.

3. What is true of the individual pointed to: he agrees, she knows him, etc.

We also saw that we had to talk of the variants of a given pointing in order to accommodate sentences containing more than a single quantifier.

Using sequences as the formal counterpart of pointings, we can state the PredC axioms for quantification in (21) and (22). These capture the basic elements of (1) to (3) and employ the notion of a sequence variant:

(21) $\mathrm{Val}(t, [_{S} [_{NP_i} \textit{every } N'] S], \sigma)$ iff
    1. for every σ', $\sigma' \approx_i \sigma$ such that
    2. $\mathrm{Val}(\sigma'(i), N', \sigma)$,
    3. $\mathrm{Val}(t, S, \sigma')$

(22) $\mathrm{Val}(t, [_{S} [_{NP_i} \textit{some } N'] S], \sigma)$ iff
    1. for some σ', $\sigma' \approx_i \sigma$ such that
    2. $\mathrm{Val}(\sigma(i), N', \sigma)$,
    3. $\mathrm{Val}(t, S, \sigma')$

Thus the rule for *every* in (21), spelled out, states that a sentence of the form [$_S$ [$_{NP_i}$ *every* N'] S] will be true with respect to a sequence σ iff for every *i*-variant σ' of σ whose *i*th position is occupied by an individual satisfying N', the sentence S is true with respect to σ'.

Finally, PredC contains axioms for nominals like *man, woman, fish*, etc., that appear in quantificational NPs like *every man, no woman, three fish*, etc. We analyze nominals by means of the lexical axioms in (23), which treat them as simple predicates:

(23) a. Val(x, *man*, σ) iff x is a man
   b. Val(x, *woman*, σ) iff x is a woman
   c. Val(x, *fish*, σ) iff x is a fish

A Sample Derivation

To illustrate the operation of these axioms, consider our example sentence *Every man agrees*, assuming it to receive the LF given earlier in (16). We interpret this structure as follows, using axiom (21) and (UI):

(24) Val(t, [$_S$ [$_{NP_i}$ *Every* [$_{N'}$ [$_N$ *man*]]] [$_S$ [$_{NP}$ t_1] [$_{VP}$ [$_V$ *agrees*]]]], σ) iff
   for every σ', $\sigma' \approx_1 \sigma$ such that Val($\sigma'(1)$, [$_{N'}$ [$_N$ *man*]], σ),
   Val(t, [$_S$ [$_{NP}$ t_1] [$_{VP}$ [$_V$ *agrees*]]], σ')

Applying the axioms for nonbranching nodes, the axioms for nominals in (23), and (SE), we derive (25a–e):

(25) a. Val($\sigma'(1)$, [$_{N'}$ [$_N$ *man*]], σ) iff Val($\sigma'(1)$, [$_N$ *man*], σ)
   b. Val($\sigma'(1)$, [$_N$ *man*], σ) iff Val($\sigma'(1)$, *man*, σ)
   c. Val($\sigma'(1)$, *man*, σ) iff $\sigma'(1)$ is a man
   d. Val($\sigma'(1)$, [$_N$ *man*], σ) iff $\sigma'(1)$ is a man
   e. Val($\sigma'(1)$, [$_{N'}$ [$_N$ *man*]], σ) iff $\sigma'(1)$ is a man

Using (24), (25e), and (SE) yields (26):

(26) Val(t, [$_S$ [$_{NP_i}$ *Every* [$_{N'}$ [$_N$ *man*]]] [$_S$ [$_{NP}$ t_1] [$_{VP}$ [$_V$ *agrees*]]]], σ) iff for every
   σ', $\sigma' \approx_1 \sigma$ such that $\sigma'(1)$ is a man, Val(t, [$_S$ [$_{NP}$ t_1] [$_{VP}$ [$_V$ *agrees*]]], σ')

The interpretation of the smaller S can then be unpacked using the sequence-relative axioms for sentences, traces, and VPs (respectively):

(27) Val(t, [$_S$ [$_{NP}$ t_1] [$_{VP}$ [$_V$ *agrees*]]], σ') iff for some x, Val(x, [$_{NP}$ t_1], σ') and
   Val(x, [$_{VP}$ [$_V$ *agrees*]], σ')

(28) a. $\text{Val}(x, [_{\text{NP}} \, t_1], \sigma')$ iff $\text{Val}(x, t_1, \sigma')$

    b. $\text{Val}(x, t_1, \sigma')$ iff $x = \sigma'(1)$

    c. $\text{Val}(x, [_{\text{NP}} \, t_1], \sigma')$ iff $x = \sigma'(1)$

(29) a. $\text{Val}(x, [_{\text{VP}} \, [_{\text{V}} \, \textit{agrees}]], \sigma')$ iff $\text{Val}(x, [_{\text{V}} \, \textit{agrees}], \sigma')$

    b. $\text{Val}(x, [_{\text{V}} \, \textit{agrees}], \sigma')$ iff $\text{Val}(x, \textit{agrees}, \sigma')$

    c. $\text{Val}(x, \textit{agrees}, \sigma')$ iff x agrees

    d. $\text{Val}(x, [_{\text{V}} \, \textit{agrees}], \sigma')$ iff x agrees

    e. $\text{Val}(x, [_{\text{VP}} \, [_{\text{V}} \, \textit{agrees}]], \sigma')$ iff x agrees

(30) a. $\text{Val}(t, [_{\text{S}} \, [_{\text{NP}} \, t_1] \, [_{\text{VP}} \, [_{\text{V}} \, \textit{agrees}]]], \sigma')$ iff for some x, $x = \sigma'(1)$ and x agrees

    b. $\text{Val}(t, [_{\text{S}} \, [_{\text{NP}} \, t_1] \, [_{\text{VP}} \, [_{\text{V}} \, \textit{agrees}]]], \sigma')$ iff $\sigma'(1)$ agrees

Using (26), (30b), and (SE), we then derive (31), the final T theorem for the sentence:

(31) $\text{Val}(t, [_{\text{S}} \, [_{\text{NP}_1} \, \textit{Every} \, [_{\text{N}'} \, [_{\text{N}} \, \textit{man}]]] \, [_{\text{S}} \, [_{\text{NP}} \, t_1] \, [_{\text{VP}} \, [_{\text{V}} \, \textit{agrees}]]]], \sigma)$ iff for every σ', $\sigma' \approx_1 \sigma$ such that $\sigma'(1)$ is a man, $\sigma'(1)$ agrees

The results in (31) may appear odd at first, since a sentence that intuitively speaks of every man is assigned a T sentence that speaks of every sequence of a certain kind. As we noted earlier, quantification in this theory is spelled out in terms of quantification over sequences and not directly over individuals. Nonetheless, on reflection, it is not hard to see that quantification over individuals is implicit in these results. Recall that sequences are distinguished by the individuals that they contain in their various positions. If σ_1 and σ_2 are sequences containing the same objects in the same positions, then σ_1 and σ_2 are the same sequence. Recall also that, by definition, the i-variants of a given sequence σ will differ from σ by at most the single individual appearing in the ith position. As a consequence, there is a natural correspondence between individuals and the i-variant sequences of a given sequence σ. For each individual α, there will be a unique i-variant of σ with α appearing in the ith place (table 7.2). In view of this, quantification over i-variants of σ is tantamount to quantification over the individuals appearing in their ith positions. Thus in stating the T sentence for a quantified sentence, we are justified in switching from talk of quantifying over sequences σ', as in (31), to talk of quantification over the individuals appearing in their ith positions. That is, we are justified in rewriting (31) as (32):

Table 7.2 Correspondence between individuals and i-variants of the sequence σ

Individual	Sequence	ith place
Barry	$\sigma\ = \langle$John, SUNY-SB, Eiffel Tower, ..., Bary, ...$\rangle$	
Felix	$\sigma_1 = \langle$John, SUNY-SB, Eiffel Tower, ..., Felix, ...$\rangle$	
Berlin	$\sigma_2 = \langle$John, SUNY-SB, Eiffel Tower, ..., Berlin, ...$\rangle$	
3	$\sigma_3 = \langle$John, SUNY-SB, Eiffel Tower, ..., 3, ...$\rangle$	

(32) Val(t, [$_S$ [$_{NP_1}$ *Every* [$_{N'}$ [$_N$ *man*]]] [$_S$ [$_{NP}$ t_1] [$_{VP}$ [$_V$ *agrees*]]]], σ) iff for every x such that x is a man, x agrees

This result, like that in (31), is interpretive.

7.3.1 Quantified Sentences as True or False Absolutely

In discussing context-relative truth conditions, we saw that the notion of truth with respect to a sequence seemed appropriate for certain sentences but not for others. *He$_1$ agrees* is a sentence that is only true or false with respect to a sequence, since it only appears to have determinate truth conditions when we know the semantic value of the pronoun *he$_1$*. By contrast, *Arnold Schwarzeneggar agrees* appears to be sequence-independent, in the sense that we can apparently determine its truth conditions independent of context and ostensive gestures.

Intuitively, it seems that quantified sentences containing no unbound traces and no free pronouns or demonstratives should also be sequence-independent, since the values that any t_i can assume are wholly specified through the interpretation of the adjoined quantified NP that binds it. That is, it seems that such sentences, if true, should be true absolutely.

The axioms for quantification given above do in fact entail that quantified Ss with no unbound traces or free pronouns, if true, are true independently of sequence choice. A formal proof of this claim is possible, but for our purposes it will be enough to give an informal idea of why the result holds.[11] First, notice that if a sentence S contains the sequence-sensitive elements ζ_i, ζ_j, ..., ζ_n, then the semantic value of S with respect to a given sequence σ will depend only on the objects appearing in the ith, jth, ..., nth positions of σ. The identity of objects appearing in the other positions will be irrelevant. For example, the sentence t_1 *agrees* contains the single sequence-sensitive expression t_1. The semantic value of t_1 *agrees* with respect to σ will thus depend only on the identity of $\sigma(1)$; the identity of $\sigma(2)$, $\sigma(2,002)$ etc., will be irrelevant. The reason for this is clear: t_1 is the only expression in t_1 *agrees* whose value depends on the sequence choice, and under (20), the semantic value of t_1 is determined strictly by what appears in the first position of σ. Hence the semantic value of t_1 *agrees* with respect to σ depends (at most) on the identity of $\sigma(1)$. Notice further that since the semantic value of a sentence S with respect to σ depends only on those positions in σ corresponding to the sequence-sensitive elements in S, it also follows that whenever σ and σ^* agree in all positions corresponding to the sequence-sensitive elements in S, the semantic value of S with respect to σ and σ^* will be identical. Thus if σ and σ^* contain the same object in first position, the semantic value of t_1 *agrees* with respect to σ and σ^* will be the same.

With these points in mind, consider now the evaluation of *Every man agrees* with respect to two different starting sequences σ and σ^*. Our axioms yield the results in (33) (with irrelevant syntactic details suppressed):

(33) a. Val(t, [$_S$ *Every man$_1$ t_1 agrees*], σ) iff for every σ', $\sigma' \approx_1 \sigma$ such that $\sigma'(1)$ is a man, $\sigma'(1)$ agrees
      b. Val(t, [$_S$ *Every man$_1$ t_1 agrees*], σ^*) iff for every σ'', $\sigma'' \approx_1 \sigma^*$ such that $\sigma''(1)$ is a man, $\sigma''(1)$ agrees

Observe that in both (33a) and (33b), what is required for the truth of the sentence is stated not in terms of σ and σ^* but in terms of their 1-variants σ' and σ''. By (33a), t_1 *agrees* must be true with respect to specific 1-variants of σ, and by (33b), t_1 *agrees* must be true with respect to specific 1-variants of σ^*. What are these 1-variants of σ and σ^* that make t_1 *agrees* true? They are all of the sequences just like σ and σ^* but possibly differing from their originals in containing a man in 1st position (table 7.3). Notice that for every 1-variant of σ containing man α in its first position, there will be a 1-variant of σ^* containing α in its first position. Recall also that the truth of t_1 *agrees* with respect to any sequence depends only on the object appearing in the first position of that sequence. These points together entail that t_1 *agrees* will be true with respect to every σ' whose first position contains a man just in case t_1 *agrees* is true with respect to every σ'' whose first position contains a man. But then by (33a, b), *Every man t_1 agrees* will be true with respect to σ just in case it is true with respect to σ^*. Since σ and σ^* were chosen arbitrarily, we can further conclude that if *Every man t_1 agrees* is true with respect to one sequence σ,

Table 7.3 Some 1-variants of σ and σ^* that make t_1 *agrees* true

$\sigma = \langle$ Paris, 3, Eiffel Tower, Berlin, $\ldots \rangle$	$\sigma^* = \langle$ NYC, Oscar, Moscow, Flipper, 74, $\ldots \rangle$
$\sigma' \approx_1 \sigma$ such that $\sigma'(1)$ is man	$\sigma'' \approx_1 \sigma^*$ such that $\sigma''(1)$ is man
$\langle$ Phil, 3, Eiffel Tower, Berlin, $\ldots \rangle$	$\langle$ Phil, Oscar, Moscow, Flipper, 74, $\ldots \rangle$
$\langle$ Rolf, 3, Eiffel Tower, Berlin, $\ldots \rangle$	$\langle$ Rolf, Oscar, Moscow, Flipper, 74, $\ldots \rangle$
$\langle$ Hiroaki, 3, Eiffel Tower, Berlin, $\ldots \rangle$	$\langle$ Hiroaki, Oscar, Moscow, Flipper, 74, $\ldots \rangle$
$\langle$ Bill, 3, Eiffel Tower, Berlin, $\ldots \rangle$	$\langle$ Bill, Oscar, Moscow, Flipper, 74, $\ldots \rangle$
$\langle$ Chris, 3, Eiffel Tower, Berlin, $\ldots \rangle$	$\langle$ Chris, Oscar, Moscow, Flipper, 74, $\ldots \rangle$
$\vdots$	$\vdots$

then it is true with respect to every sequence; that is, if *Every man t_1 agrees* is true at all, then it is true absolutely. This reasoning can be applied to any closed quantified sentence, any quantified sentence containing no unbound traces or free pronouns. All such sentences, if true, are true absolutely.

7.3.2 Residual Noncompositionality in PredC

Axioms (21) and (22) do not rely on proper nouns in any way; hence they do not encounter the problem of linguistic resources observed earlier with approaches to quantification based on proper nouns. Nonetheless, it is important to observe that like axiom (15), (21) and (22) still exhibit an element of noncompositionality. Noncompositionality arises in one particular place: (21) and (22) assign no semantic value to the quantified NP that has been raised and adjoined to S. Instead, they essentially ignore the NP node and look directly at its constituents: the determiners *every* and *some*, and N'.

The departure from compositionality in the sequence-based theory is arguably less serious than that found in theories based on proper nouns, since it does not involve the introduction of syntactic elements not present in the LF but rather depends only on the interpretation and arrangement of syntactic elements that are present. One way of appreciating this point is to observe that we could restore strict compositionality to our theory *without altering its basic semantics* if we were to reanalyze the underlying syntax of quantificational sentences so that the quantificational NP nodes were eliminated and the determiners were treated as a syntactic feature of an adjoined nominal. For example, with (21') (and analogously for *some*), strict compositionality is restored within the framework of a sequence-based approach to quantification. Note that the right-hand side of the biconditional in (21′) is identical to that in (21):

(21′) $\text{Val}(t, [_\text{S} \ \underset{[+every]}{N'_i} \ \text{S}], \sigma)$ iff for every σ', $\sigma' \approx_i \sigma$ such that $\text{Val}(\sigma'(i), N', \sigma)$,
      $\text{Val}(t, \text{S}, \sigma')$

No such move is possible with name-based theories of quantification, however. The latter appeal *essentially* to the interpretation of structures containing new syntactic elements, names, and there appears to be no way of reanalyzing the constituents of the logical forms to get around this fact. These theories are thus irreducibly noncompositional in our sense.

We will not actually attempt to reanalyze the LF syntax of quantified sentences along the lines of (21′) but instead will simply accept this element of noncompositionality for the time being. In chapter 8 we will argue that it is not only methodologically useful but also empirically necessary to eliminate this residual noncompositionality in quantified structures.

7.4   Quantification and the LF Hypothesis

The axioms we have given for quantified sentences apply to LF representations, in which quantified NPs appear in adjoined positions and bind a trace in their sister S. They do not apply to surface forms, in which the quantified NPs occupy subject and object positions directly. On reflection, it is easy to see that this is not an accidental result. Our axioms apply naturally to LFs because the division of parts provided by LF syntax closely tracks the division of parts induced by our quantificational semantics. We noted earlier that our semantic analysis articulates quantification into three basic components:[12]

1. A **quantification** stating how many (*i*-variant) sequences are involved (every, some, two, etc.)

2. A **restriction** on the individuals appearing in the *i*th positions of the sequence (the men in the class, the women at the meeting, etc.)

3. A **scope** stating what is true of these individuals (he agrees, she knows him, etc.)

In the LFs we have adopted from modern syntactic theory, these three components of the semantic structure correspond to three main syntactic constituents in the phrase marker. The quantification corresponds to the determiner: *every* or *some* in the case of PredC. The restriction corresponds to the nominal N'. And the scope corresponds to the S to which NP is adjoined:

(34)

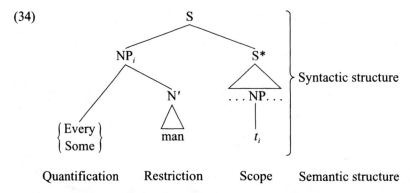

Quantification   Restriction   Scope   Semantic structure

With surface forms, of course, there is no such direct correspondence between components of quantificational semantics and pieces of quantificational syntax. The quantifier and its restriction are actually contained within the constituent S that is intuitively the scope.

The close correspondence between units of syntax at LF and units of compositional semantic interpretation lends support to what we earlier termed the "LF hypothesis":

LF hypothesis   LF is the level of syntactic representation that is interpreted by semantic rules.

Recall that the LF hypothesis is an empirical conjecture about the relation between meaning and form. Under the hypothesis, if our best syntactic theories imply a certain LF, then semantic theory must accept the task of providing axioms for that LF. Likewise, if our best compositional semantic theories entail a certain syntactic structure, then syntactic theory must accept the job of justifying that structure as an LF.

With quantification, we see a clear convergence of syntactic and semantic results. As noted above, syntactic representations with quantifier raising have been advanced by syntacticians on grounds independent of quantifier semantics. Correlatively, our reflections on the semantics of quantification arose without consideration of the form of quantified sentences. That the two should come together neatly is surely more than an accident. And indeed, there are other points where we can observe a strong interaction between our T theory and syntactic form.

7.4.1 Proper Binding

Early in the analysis of syntactic movement it was proposed that structures resulting from movement obey a very general constraint on well-formedness. This constraint, called "proper binding," is standardly stated in terms of the structural relation of c-command (constituent-command):

Proper-binding constraint A referentially variable expression α can be interpreted as a variable bound by an quantified expression Q only if Q c-commands α at LF.

Definition A phrase X **c-commands** a phrase Y iff neither of X or Y dominates the other and the first branching node dominating X dominates Y.

The proper-binding constraint, or some analog of it, is widely assumed in many purely syntactic theories.[13] In such theories, the constraint has the status of a basic axiom or assumption, not a theorem following from further principles. In PredC, however, the proper-binding constraint is not an independent assumption or tenet but rather a *consequence* of the way in which meaning is related to form. In particular, it follows from the way in which referentially variable elements, such as traces, get interpreted as bound variables and from the way in which sequence variation is introduced and propagated.

When an element behaves as a variable bound by a quantified NP, it assumes a range of different semantic values determined by that NP. In PredC, a trace receives different values by being interpreted with respect to different sequences of the right kind; specifically, sequences that vary in a position corresponding to the index on the trace. Under the axioms for adjunction structures like (35a), the truth of S* is interpreted with respect to *i*-variant sequences determined by the quantified noun phrase NP_i. The latter tells us how many such sequences S* is true with respect to, and also what kind of object is in their *i*th position. These sequences "pass down" the tree to the constituents of S*, so that if S* is interpreted with respect to a particular σ', then the parts and subparts of S* are interpreted with respect to σ' as well. Furthermore, *only* S* is interpreted with respect to *i*-variant sequences σ'. If the adjunction structure is part of some larger construction (X in (35b)), then no variation in sequences is induced in any structure outside S* (for example, no sequence variation is induced in Y):

(35) a.

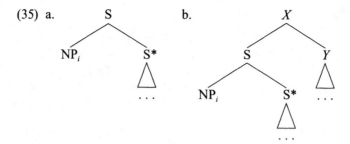

b.

From these results the proper-binding constraint follows. Since only S* and its constituents are evaluated with respect to different sequences determined by NP$_i$, only traces within S* will be interpreted with respect to different sequences determined by NP$_i$. Hence only traces within S* can be interpreted as variables bound by NP$_i$. Since the traces within S* are precisely the ones c-commanded by NP$_i$, it follows that only traces c-commanded by NP$_i$ can be interpreted as bound variables.

7.4.2   Quantifier-Scope Ambiguity

We have observed that multiply quantified sentences like (1b) appear to be ambiguous between the interpretations represented informally in (6a, b) (repeated below):

(1b) Every man admires some woman.

(6)   a. For every man x, for some woman y, x admires y
      b. For some woman y, for every man x, x admires y

The representations in (6a) and (6b) establish two different sorts of truth conditions for the sentence. On the former (*every-some*), the sentence is true if and only if every man admires some woman, with possibly a different woman admired by each different man. On the latter (*some-every*), the sentence is true if and only if there is one woman who is universally admired by the men (figure 7.2).

    We further observed that under modern syntactic theory (Chomsky 1981, 1986a, 1986b), this ambiguity of meaning is matched by an ambiguity of form. The surface sentence (1b) is actually associated with two distinct LFs that differ in the relative attachment heights of the quantified NPs:

These structures correlate with the meanings in (6) in that the relative structural prominence of the NPs in the syntactic trees reflects the scope of their associated quantifiers. Thus structure (36a), in which the universally quantified NP_1 has structural prominence over the existentially quantified NP_2, corresponds to meaning (6a), in which the universal quantifier has scope over the existential quantifier. Likewise, structure (36b), in which the existentially quantified NP_2 has structural prominence over the universally quantified NP_1, corresponds to meaning (6b), in which the existential quantifier has scope over the universal quantifier.

The correlation between form and meaning assumed for (1b) and other multiply quantified sentences is often expressed in the form of a scope principle, in which the syntactic notion of c-command spells out the idea of structural prominence:[14]

Scope principle   An expression α is interpreted as having scope over an expression β just in case α c-commands β.

Thus in the structure (36a) above, NP_1 c-commands NP_2, since the first branching node dominating NP_1 (namely S_0) also dominates NP_2. On the other hand, NP_2 fails to c-command NP_1, since the first branching node dominating NP_2 (namely S_1) does not dominate NP_1. Given these c-command relations, the scope principle correlates (36a) with a reading in which *every man* is understood with scope over *some woman*, that is, with reading (6a). Similarly, the scope principle applied to (36b) entails the scopal interpretation (bb).

Like the proper-binding constraint, the scope principle is widely assumed in purely syntactic theories and generally given the status of an unanalyzed axiom or assumption.[15] But once again, in PredC the scope principle follows as a consequence of the way the theory relates meaning to form. The reason can be seen by reflecting on the general adjunction structure (37a) (where α is *every* or *some*) and the two PredC axioms below it:

(37) a.

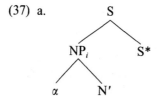

b. Val(t, [$_S$ [$_{NP_i}$ *Every* N'] S], σ) iff for every $\sigma' \approx_i \sigma$ such that
Val($\sigma'(i)$, N', σ), Val(t, S*, σ')

c. Val(t, [$_S$ [$_{NP_i}$ *Some* N'] S], σ) iff for some $\sigma' \approx_i \sigma$ such that
Val($\sigma'(i)$, N', σ), Val(t, S*, σ')

When the highest S node in (37a) is interpreted by either of (37b) or (37c), a quantification over sequence variants is introduced, and the smaller-sentence node S* is then evaluated within the scope of this quantification. This smaller sentence may be a simple clause containing a trace, such as t_1 *agrees*. But it may itself also be a quantifier-adjunction structure, as in (36a), in which case the quantificational axioms will apply recursively, introducing another quantification over sequence variants and another smaller-sentence node. This will then in turn be evaluated within the scope of the two higher quantifications. The result will be an embedded series of quantifications in the T sentence that tracks the relative embeddings of the quantified noun phrases in the syntactic tree.

We can see this embedding clearly in the T sentences assigned by PredC to the structures in (36). These are displayed in (38), where brackets have been added on the RHS to show the stage at which a given portion of the T sentence was added in:

(38) a. Val(t, [*Every man*$_1$ [*some woman*$_2$ [t_1 *admires* t_2]]], σ) iff
[for every $\sigma' \approx_1 \sigma$ such that $\sigma'(1)$ is a man
[for some $\sigma'' \approx_2 \sigma'$ such that $\sigma''(2)$ is a woman
[$\sigma''(1)$ admires $\sigma''(2)$]]]

b. Val(t, [*Some woman*$_2$ [*every man*$_1$ [t_1 *admires* t_2]]], σ) iff
[for some $\sigma' \approx_2 \sigma$ such that $\sigma'(2)$ is a woman
[for every $\sigma'' \approx_1 \sigma'$ such that $\sigma''(1)$ is a man
[$\sigma''(1)$ admires $\sigma''(2)$]]]

Evidently, parts of the LF appearing on the left-hand side of the biconditional closely correlate with parts of the T sentence appearing on the right-hand side of the biconditional. This correlation is a simple outcome of the way in which the semantics uses the object-language syntax to construct the T sentence, compositionally building parts of the latter using the "skeleton" provided by the former.

PredC thus applies recursively to multiple adjunction structures, like those in (36), associating a scopal interpretation with an LF tree in the way described by the scope principle. That is, it correlates increased structural prominence with broader semantic scope. As a result, PredC allows us to deduce the scope principle, and thus to explain why it holds. Under PredC, it is no accident that the scope principle holds but a consequence of the way in which form is mapped to meaning.

7.5   Variable-Binding Operators

The semantic apparatus developed to account for quantification can be extended to accommodate a variety other structures involving moved elements and traces that they bind. That is, it provides a general approach to what we might term **operator-variable structures**.

7.5.1   Topicalization

We noted earlier that English (unlike Hungarian) does not allow raising of quantifier phrases in surface form. Nonetheless, other, analogous kinds of movement are observable in English. Consider (39) and (40), illustrating **topicalization**:

(39) a. Jill knows Kate.
     b. Kate, Jill knows.

(40) a. Jill gave that to Chris.
     b. That, Jill gave to Chris.
     c. Chris, Jill gave that to.

Under current syntactic proposals, (39b) and (40b, c) derive by a movement operation that raises and adjoins the referring phrase to its containing sentence, similarly to what occurs with quantifier raising:[16]

(41)

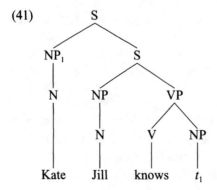

Apart from differences of focus and emphasis, topicalized examples appear fully synonymous with their nontopicalized counterparts. Our T theory should therefore assign the two examples equivalent T sentences. Consider the following axiom for referring terms ([+ref]) adjoined to S:

(42) $\mathrm{Val}(t, [_S \underset{[+\mathrm{ref}]}{\mathrm{NP}_i} S], \sigma)$ iff for the $\sigma' \approx_i \sigma$ such that $\mathrm{Val}(\sigma'(i), \mathrm{NP}, \sigma)$,
$\mathrm{Val}(t, S, \sigma')$

This rule specifies that a sentence of the form $[_S \mathrm{NP}_i\, S]$ is true with respect to a sequence σ just in case the interior S is true with respect to a specific i-variant of σ, namely the one whose ith position is occupied by the individual that is the value of NP. We do not evaluate the smaller S with respect to a range of i-variants, as in our quantification rules, but rather with respect to a single, specific i-variant.

As the reader can show, when (42) is applied to the example *Kate, Jill knows*, the result is (43).

(43) $\mathrm{Val}(t, [_S [_{\mathrm{NP}_1} \mathrm{Kate}] [_S [_{\mathrm{NP}} [_\mathrm{N} \mathrm{Jill}]] [_{\mathrm{VP}} [_\mathrm{V} \mathrm{knows}] [_{\mathrm{NP}} t_1]]]], \sigma)$ iff for the
$\quad\quad\quad {}_{[+\mathrm{ref}]}$
$\sigma' \approx_1 \sigma$ such that $\sigma'(1) = \mathrm{Kate}$, Jill knows $\sigma'(1)$

And (43) is equivalent to (44).

(44) $\mathrm{Val}(t, [_S [_{\mathrm{NP}_1} \mathrm{Kate}] [_S [_{\mathrm{NP}} [_\mathrm{N} \mathrm{Jill}]] [_{\mathrm{VP}} [_\mathrm{V} \mathrm{knows}] [_{\mathrm{NP}} t_1]]]], \sigma)$ iff
$\quad\quad\quad {}_{[+\mathrm{ref}]}$
Jill knows Kate

Note that although the topicalization rule invokes sequence variants, the central device in quantification, it does not analyze the adjoined NP as a quantificational phrase in any way. This is clear from the clause "$\mathrm{Val}(\sigma'(i), \mathrm{NP}, \sigma)$," which analyzes NP in the usual way, as a referring expression whose semantic value is a specific individual, $\sigma'(i)$. The quasi-quantificational semantics of topicalization arises not with the adjoined element but rather with the larger adjunction structure:

(45)

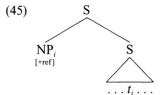

It is the presence of this configuration that prompts appeal to i-variants of σ.

7.5.2   Restrictive Relative Clauses

Another place in the grammar of English where we see movement whose semantics arguably involves variable binding is in restrictive-relative-clause constructions. Examples are (46a, b):

(46) a. [$_{NP}$ Every woman [who$_1$ Jill knows t_1]] agrees
      b. [$_{NP}$ Every woman [O$_1$ (that) Jill knows t_1]] agrees

In both cases, the transitive verb *knows* lacks a surface direct object. In (46a), this missing object is associated with the relative pronoun *who*, which is standardly analyzed as having moved to the front of the subordinate clause from direct-object position. In (46b), the missing object is associated with an unpronounced counterpart of *who*, the empty operator O, which is once again analyzed as having started out as a direct object.[17]

    Stowell (1981), McCawley (1981b), and numerous others have argued that restrictive relative clauses like those in (46) have a structure as in (47), where the modifying clausal phrase (CP) is adjoined to an N' and the relative pronoun or empty operator moves to the specifier position of CP:

(47)

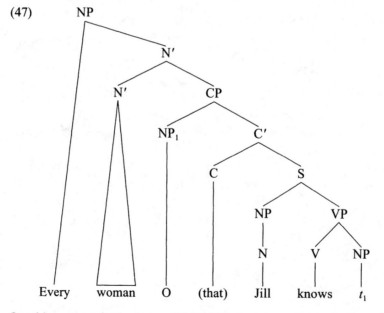

On this proposal, the larger N' in (47) functions semantically as a complex predicate true of things that are both women and known by Jill.

Using sequence variants, we can state axioms that deliver a general complex-predicate analysis of relative clauses:

(48) a. $\text{Val}(x, [_{N'} \text{ N}' \text{ CP}], \sigma)$ iff $\text{Val}(x, \text{N}', \sigma)$ and $\text{Val}(x, \text{CP}, \sigma)$
  b. $\text{Val}(x, [_{CP} \text{ NP}_i \text{ C}'], \sigma)$ iff for the $\sigma' \approx_i \sigma$ such that $\sigma'(i) = x$,
      $\text{Val}(\text{t}, \text{C}', \sigma')$
  c. $\text{Val}(\text{t}, [_{C'} \text{ C S}], \sigma)$ iff $\text{Val}(\text{t}, \text{S}, \sigma)$

Here the relative clause CP is treated semantically as a predicate taking things as its values, that is, we have "$\text{Val}(x, [_{CP} \ldots], \sigma)$." Axiom (48a) states that x is a value of a complex nominal just in case it is a value of the daughters N′ and CP (with respect to σ). Axiom (48b) states that x is a value of a relative CP with respect to σ just in case the C′ contained in CP is true with respect to a certain sequence σ'. This σ' is the i-variant of σ having x in its ith position, where i is the index of the moved operator—the relative pronoun or the empty operator. Finally, axiom (48c) states that a C′ containing a C and an S is true with respect to a sequence just in case the S is true with respect to that sequence.

Applying these rules to the larger N′ in (47), it is straightforward to prove the result in (49):

(49) $\text{Val}(x, [_{N'} [_{N'} [_{N} \text{ woman}]]$
    $[_{CP} \text{O}_1 [_{C'} [_{C} \text{ that}] [_{S} [_{NP} \text{ Jill}] [_{VP} [_{V} \text{ knows}] [_{NP} t_1]]]]]], \sigma)$ iff x is a woman and for the $\sigma' \approx_1 \sigma$ such that $\sigma'(1) = x$, Jill knows $\sigma'(1)$

And (49) is equivalent to (50):

(50) $\text{Val}(x, [_{N'} [_{N'} [_{N} \text{ woman}]]$
    $[_{CP} \text{O}_1 [_{C'} [_{C} \text{ that}] [_{S} [_{NP} \text{ Jill}] [_{VP} [_{V} \text{ knows}] [_{NP} t_1]]]]]], \sigma)$ iff x is a woman and Jill knows x

This is the desired result: x is a value of the complex predicate woman-that-Jill-knows if and only if x is a woman and Jill knows x.

The relative-clause axioms show an interesting feature that we've seen before: they are nonexhaustive. As we move down from C′ to S in (48c), no semantic value is assigned to the C node, nor to the complementizer it dominates. Likewise, as we move from CP down to C′ in (48b), no semantic value is assigned to NP_i, nor to the relative pronoun or empty operator that it dominates. In the case of the complementizer, the material is simply ignored. In the case of the moved NP, only its index enters into the semantic rule. It is this index that tells us which position in the sequence variant to constrain. In effect, then, under the semantic account of relatives in (48), relative pronouns and empty operators in a restrictive relative clause are nothing more than index bearers. They have no other semantic content.

7.5.3 Variable Binding, Sequence Variants, and Compositionality

The axioms for quantification, topicalization, and relative clauses share a common form. All three introduce sequence variants and evaluate some expression X with respect to these variants:

(51) ... iff for ____ $\sigma' \approx_i \sigma$ such that ... $\sigma'(i)$ ..., Val(α, X, σ')

The three sets of rules differ only according to which variants are to be considered, what holds of $\sigma'(i)$, and what expression are to be evaluated with respect to them.

The quantification axioms

- count i-variants (the slot "____" is filled with "every" or "some"),
- require $\sigma'(i)$ to be a value of the nominal N′,
- evaluate the contained S with respect to the i-variants.

The topicalization axiom

- identifies a particular i-variant (the slot "____" is filled with "the"),
- requires $\sigma'(i)$ to be the value of the adjoined NP,
- evaluates the contained S with respect to the i-variant.

The relative-clause axiom

- identifies a particular i-variant (the slot "____" is filled with "the"),
- requires $\sigma'(i)$ to be the value x inherited from the containing N′,
- evaluates the contained C′ with respect to the i-variant.

This common form reflects the general role of sequences in interpreting these constructions. In all three, we have one element that is syntactically distant from another element, where the former must determine the value of the latter. Given compositionality constraints, this situation poses a challenge: How can one expression determine the value of another that it is not in local construction with? How can the two "communicate" semantically in the tree?

Sequences answer this question. In each of the constructions, one element—the higher, c-commanding one—imposes a value or a range of values on some position in the sequence. This sequence is compositionally propagated down the tree. The second element—the lower, c-commanded one—then extracts the value from the sequence, which secures the link between the two:

(52)

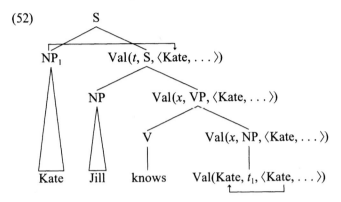

The index plays a crucial coordinating role in this communication. The shared index tells us, at the higher point in the tree, where to put a particular value in the sequence variants (first position, second position, etc.). And the index tells us where to draw the value out again once we pass down to the lower point in the tree. In the relative-clause construction, this function is particularly clear. As we have noted, the moved operator serves no semantic purpose beyond bearing an index up to the CP, where it allows us to coordinate the values of N' and the trace.

Theory and Exercises

The Theory PredC (Predicate Calculus)

Lexical Axioms

(1) a. Val(x, *Kate*, σ) iff x = Kate
   b. Val(x, *Chris*, σ) iff x = Chris
   c. Val(x, *Phil*, σ) iff x = Phil
   d. Val(x, *Jill*, σ) iff x = Jill

(2) a. Val(x, *man*, σ) iff x is a man
 b. Val(x, *woman*, σ) iff x is a woman
 c. Val(x, *fish*, σ) iff x is a fish

(3) a. Val(x, *I*, σ) iff $x = \sigma(a)$
 b. Val(x, *you*, σ) iff $x = \sigma(b)$
 c. Val(x, *here*, σ) iff $x = \sigma(c)$
 d. Val(x, *now*, σ) iff $x = \sigma(d)$

(4) a. Val(x, *he$_i$*, σ) iff $x = \sigma(i)$ for all $i \geq 1$
 b. Val(x, *she$_i$*, σ) iff $x = \sigma(i)$ for all $i \geq 1$
 c. Val(x, *him$_i$*, σ) iff $x = \sigma(i)$ for all $i \geq 1$
 d. Val(x, *her$_i$*, σ) iff $x = \sigma(i)$ for all $i \geq 1$
 e. Val(x, *it$_i$*, σ) iff $x = \sigma(i)$ for all $i \geq 1$
 f. Val(x, *this$_i$*, σ) iff $x = \sigma(i)$ for all $i \geq 1$
 g. Val(x, *that$_i$*, σ) iff $x = \sigma(i)$ for all $i \geq 1$
 h. Val(x, *t$_i$*, σ) iff $x = \sigma(i)$ for all $i \geq 1$

(5) a. Val(x, *ponders*, σ) iff x ponders
 b. Val(x, *agrees*, σ) iff x agrees
 c. Val(x, *protests*, σ) iff x protests

(6) a. Val($\langle x, y \rangle$, *knows*, σ) iff x knows y
 b. Val($\langle x, y \rangle$, *admires*, σ) iff x admires y
 c. Val($\langle x, y \rangle$, *instructs*, σ) iff x instructs y

Phrasal Axioms

(7) a. Val(t, [$_S$ S$_1$ *and* S$_2$], σ) iff both Val(t, S$_1$, σ) and Val(t, S$_2$, σ)
 b. Val(t, [$_S$ S$_1$ *or* S$_2$], σ) iff either Val(t, S$_1$, σ) or Val(t, S$_2$, σ)
 c. Val(t, [$_S$ *It is not the case that* S], σ) iff it is not the case that Val(t, S, σ)

(8) a. Val(t, [$_S$ NP VP], σ) iff for some x, Val(x, NP, σ) and Val(x, VP, σ)
 b. Val(x, [$_{VP}$ V NP], σ) iff for some y, Val($\langle x, y \rangle$, V, σ) and Val(y, NP, σ)
 c. Val(x, [$_X$ Y], σ) iff Val(x, Y, σ) (where X, Y are any nodes)
 d. Val(x, [$_{NP}$ Det N'], σ) iff Val(x, Det, σ)
                [+demo]   [+demo]

(9) a. Val(t, [$_S$ [$_{NP_i}$ *every* N'] S], σ) iff for every $\sigma' \approx_i \sigma$ such that Val($\sigma'(i)$, N', σ), Val(t, S, σ')

b. $\mathrm{Val}(t, [_S [_{NP_i} \; some \; N'] \; S], \sigma)$ iff for some $\sigma' \approx_i \sigma$ such that $\mathrm{Val}(\sigma'(i), N', \sigma)$, $\mathrm{Val}(t, S, \sigma')$

(10) $\mathrm{Val}(t, [_S \; NP_i \; S], \sigma)$ iff for the $\sigma' \approx_i \sigma$ such that $\mathrm{Val}(\sigma'(i), NP, \sigma)$,
      [+ref]
      $\mathrm{Val}(t, S, \sigma')$

(11) a. $\mathrm{Val}(x, [_{N'} \; N' \; CP], \sigma)$ iff $\mathrm{Val}(x, N', \sigma)$ and $\mathrm{Val}(x, CP, \sigma)$
      b. $\mathrm{Val}(x, [_{CP} \; NP_i \; C'], \sigma)$ iff for the $\sigma' \approx_i \sigma$ such that $\sigma'(i) = x$, $\mathrm{Val}(t, C', \sigma')$
      c. $\mathrm{Val}(t, [_{C'} \; C \; S], \sigma)$ iff $\mathrm{Val}(t, S, \sigma)$

(Utt) If u is an utterance of S and $\Sigma(u, \sigma)$, then u is true iff $\mathrm{Val}(t, S, \sigma)$.

Production Rules

(UI), (SE), (SI) as in PC+

Definition   Let Σ be a relation between utterances and sequences such that

- for any utterance u, for some sequence σ, $\Sigma(u, \sigma)$,
- for any utterance u, sequence σ, individual x, and nonindexical pronoun and demonstrative determiner α_i,
  a. $\Sigma(u, \sigma)$ only if $\sigma(a) = $ the utterer of u,
  b. $\Sigma(u, \sigma)$ only if $\sigma(b) = $ the addressee of u,
  c. $\Sigma(u, \sigma)$ only if $\sigma(c) = $ the place of u,
  d. $\Sigma(u, \sigma)$ only if $\sigma(d) = $ the time of u,
  e. if a speaker uses α_i and u to refer to x, then $\Sigma(u, \sigma)$ only if $\sigma(i) = x$.

Then Σ is a **selection relation**.

Definition   For any sequence σ, $\sigma(a)$, $\sigma(b)$, $\sigma(c)$, $\sigma(d)$ are the first, second, third, and fourth elements of σ, respectively. For any positive integer i, $\sigma(i)$ is the $(i + 4)$th element of σ.

Definition   For any sequences σ, σ', $\sigma \approx_i \sigma'$ iff σ' differs from σ at most at $\sigma'(i)$.

Definition $\mathrm{Val}(t, S)$ iff $\mathrm{Val}(t, S, \sigma)$ for all sequences σ.

Exercises

1. Prove T sentences for the following sentences of PredC:

(1) a. Chris admires some woman.
     b. Every woman admires some fish. (Wide scope for *some fish*.)

2. Extend PredC to interpret quantificational sentences involving *no, most, two,* and *three.* Give T-sentence derivations for the following sentences:

(1) a. No woman knows Jill.
    b. Phil instructs most fish.
    c. Three men admire two women. (Wide scope for *three men.*)

3. The quantificational axioms in (1) and (2) (and the ones you arrived at in exercise 2 above) appear to simply pass quantification from the object language to the metalanguage:

(1) Val(t, [$_S$ [$_{NP_i}$ *Every* N′] S], σ) iff for every $\sigma' \approx_i \sigma$ such that Val($\sigma'(i)$, N′, σ), Val(t, S, σ')

(2) Val(t, [$_S$ [$_{NP_i}$ *Some* N′] S], σ) iff for some $\sigma' \approx_i \sigma$ such that Val($\sigma'(i)$, N′, σ), Val(t, S, σ')

This suggests that we might dispense with separate disquotational rules for quantifiers in favor of one simple, general scheme like (3):

(3) Val(t, [$_S$ [$_{NP_i}$ Q N′] S], σ) iff for Q $\sigma' \approx_i \sigma$ such that Val($\sigma'(i)$, N′, σ), Val(t, S, σ')

Are matters really so simple?
    Consider the following statements:

(4) a. *Cats* has four letters.
    b. Cats have four paws.

Can these be combined together into the following single, general statement?

(5) For some *x*, *x* has four letters, and *x* has four paws.

What is the problem with trying to do so? How does this bear on the question of whether (1) and (2) can be combined as in (3)?
    The German determiner *jeder* has essentially the same interpretation as the English determiner *every*; furthermore, German quantified NPs occur in the same LF structure. Given this, we might propose the following axiom for interpreting German LFs involving *jeder*:

(6) Val(t, [$_S$ [$_{NP_i}$ *Jeder* N′] S], σ) iff for every $\sigma' \approx_i \sigma$ such that Val($\sigma'(i)$, N′, σ), Val(t, S, σ')

Can (6) be assimilated into the general scheme in (3)? If so, how? If not, what's the problem?

What general conclusions can you draw from the above about replacing (1), (2), and similar axioms with (3)?

4. Consider the words *only* and *even* as they occur in sentences like the following:

(1) a. Only Chris protests.
    b. Even Chris protests.

Assume that these elements combine with (referring) NPs to create other NPs and involve quantifier-raised LFs like (2):

(2)

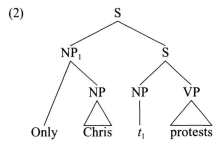

Extend PredC to interpret these structures. Do *only* and *even* raise any issues not involved with *every* and *some*?

5. Using the axioms for topicalization and restrictive relative clauses, give complete T-sentence derivations for the following:

(1) Kate, Jill admires.

(2) Every woman who Jill knows agrees.

6. Nonrestrictive relatives are often held to have a structure different from restrictives, one in which the relative is adjoined to an NP rather than an N′:

(1) a. Kate, who admires Jill, protests.

    b.

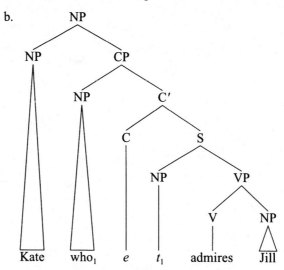

It is generally believed that nonrestrictives involve an anaphoric relation between the head NP (*Kate*) and the *wh-* operator in view of the fact that nonrestrictives require an actual relative pronoun and are not licit with a simple complementizer:

(2) Kate, $\left\{ \begin{array}{c} \text{who} \\ \text{*that} \end{array} \right\}$ admires Jill, protests.

Can you give axioms for the nonrestrictive structure that capture the anaphoric relation between the head NP and the *wh-* phrase? (This is a challenge because presumably the relative *who admires Jill* must also be suitable to appear in a restrictive relative like *every man who admires Jill*.)

7. In "On Wh-Movement" (1977), Chomsky proposes that the structure for topicalizations like (1a) is essentially as shown in (1b):

(1) a. Jill, Kate admires e

b.

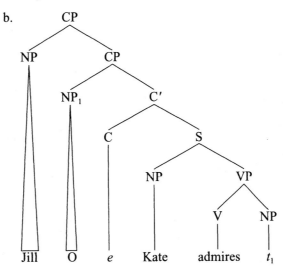

On this view, the topic is generated in clause-initial position, and it is an empty operator that undergoes movement.

Give the axioms necessary to interpret topicalizations under this theory. Show that they assign an appropriate T sentence to (1a).

Consider so-called left-dislocation structures like (2):

(2) Jill, Kate admires her.

Given our results with topicalization, what new axioms are necessary to interpret them?

It is frequently observed that quantified NPs cannot undergo topicalization or left dislocation:

(3) a. # Every fish, Kate admires *e*.
     b. # No fish, Kate admires it.

Assume that these judgments are correct. Do your interpretation rules above capture this result? If not, can they be adjusted to do so?

8. Stowell (1981) and May (1985) propose that quantifier raising can adjoin quantified NPs not only to S but to any maximal projection. On this view, sentence (1a), for example, may receive the LF shown in (1b), where *every woman* is adjoined to a VP:

(1) a. Phil admires every woman

   b.

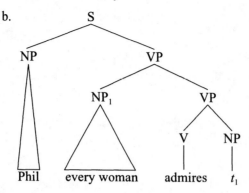

Show that this idea makes sense semantically. More precisely, extend PredC to include structures like (1b). Add an axiom that will interpret the following:

(2) $[_{VP} [_{NP_i} every\ N'] VP]$

Show that the extension you propose assigns an appropriate T sentence to the LF in (1).

9. Fiengo and Higginbotham (1980) observe that examples like (1) appear to be scopally ambiguous, showing the two readings given informally in (2):

(1) $[_{NP}$ Every picture of two persons] developed

(2) a. For two persons x, y, every picture of x and of y developed.
    b. Every two-person picture developed.

Assume the D-structure for (1) shown in (3) (together with your earlier results for quantified sentences with *two*).

(3)

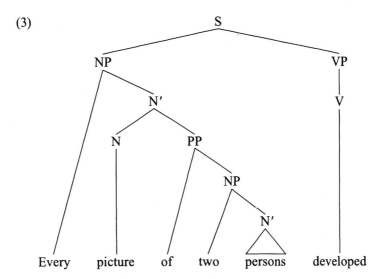

Every   picture   of   two   persons   developed

Can these two readings be captured in PredC (with the obvious additions for *picture*, *develop*, etc.)? If not, extend PredC to obtain the missing reading(s). For purposes of this exercise, assume that *of* is syncategorematic and that *two persons* is an argument of *picture*.

10. May (1985) proposes quantifier-raising structures in which a quantified NP adjoins another quantified NP. For example, on his account, (1a) can receive the LF in (1b):

(1) a. Some delegate from every city attended.

    b.

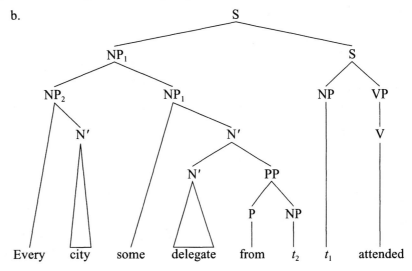

Every   city   some   delegate   from t_2 t_1 attended

What problems arise in attempting to extend PredC to (1b)? Can you add an axiom that will interpret the following:

(2) $[_{NP} [_{NP_i} \textit{every } N'] \text{ NP}]$

Why not? What would we have to do to interpret structures like (1b) in PredC? (Ignore the obvious additions we would have to make to the lexical categories.)

8 Quantifiers and Quantifier Properties

The PredC theory provides insight into important aspects of natural-language quantification and assigns plausible truth conditions to sentences containing any number of quantified NPs. At the same time, however, the theory also involves a number of peculiarities, particularly with regard to its syntax-semantics mapping. In this chapter we will see how these motivate a richer, more articulated view of quantification, one that allows the syntax-semantics mapping to become simpler and more transparent. The central insight underlying this view is the so-called **relational analysis of determiners**.

8.1 Noncompositionality in PredC

The PredC theory interprets quantificational structures like (1) by means of the axioms in (2), where α is either *every* or *some*:

(1)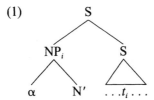

(2) a. $\text{Val}(t, [_S [_{NP_i} \textit{Every } N'] S], \sigma)$ iff for every $\sigma' \approx_i \sigma$ such that $\text{Val}(\sigma'(i), N', \sigma)$, $\text{Val}(t, S, \sigma')$

    b. $\text{Val}(t, [_S [_{NP_i} \textit{Some } N'] S], \sigma)$ iff for some $\sigma' \approx_i \sigma$ such that $\text{Val}(\sigma(i), N', \sigma)$, $\text{Val}(t, S, \sigma')$

As we have already noted, these rules are not strongly compositional. The axioms in (2) assign no semantic value to the quantified NP adjoined to S: no clauses of the form "Val(α, NP, σ)" appears on the right-hand side of the biconditionals. Instead, the axioms look past the NP node to the determiner and N' contained within. The implicit claim of PredC is thus that whatever syntactic justification there may be for grouping determiners and N's under an NP node, this structure has no semantic significance.

The fact that quantified NPs receive no semantic value is a serious drawback for PredC, given the presence of certain simple recursive NP structures. To see the problem, consider (3a) and its LF in (3b):

(3) a. Every man and some woman ponders.

   b. [$_S$ [$_{NP}$ [$_{NP}$ Every man] and [$_{NP}$ some woman]] [$_S$ t ponders]]

Observe that this structure does not fall under the axioms (2a, b): neither can be used to interpret it. To accommodate the new sentence, we must augment PredC to include an axiom like (4a). More generally, to handle conjoined quantified NPs containing pairs of determiners α and β, we must add axioms of the form in (4b) for every possible pairing:

(4) a. Val(t, [$_S$ [$_{NP_i}$ *Every* N$'_1$] *and* [$_{NP}$ *some* N$'_2$]] S], σ) iff
      for every $\sigma' \approx_i \sigma$ such that Val($\sigma'(i)$, N$'_1$, σ), Val(t, S, σ'), and
      for some $\sigma'' \approx_i \sigma$ such that Val($\sigma'(i)$, N$'_2$, σ), Val(t, S, σ'')
   b. Val(t, [$_S$ [$_{NP_i}$ α N'] *and* [$_{NP}$ β N']] S], σ) iff ...

Recall now that NP conjunction is recursive. We not only get pairs of conjoined NPs but arbitrarily large sequences of them:

(5) a. Every man and some woman and three girls ponder.
   b. Every man and some woman and three girls and five boys ponder.
   c. Every man and some woman and three girls and five boys and four accountants ponder.
      $\vdots$

In view of this, it's clear that we cannot rest after providing axioms for *pairs* of conjoined NPs. We must consider triples, quadruples, quintuples, etc., as well. And just as conjoined NPs like (3a) force us to add axioms for each possible pair of determiners, conjoined NPs like those in (5) will force us to add axioms as in (6), for each $n = 2, 3, 4, \ldots$, and for various determiners $\alpha, \beta, \ldots, \zeta$:

(6) Val(t, [$_S$ [$_{NP_i}$ [$_{NP_1}$ α N'] *and* [$_{NP_2}$ β N'] *and* ... *and* [$_{NP_n}$ ζ N']] S], σ) iff ...

Clearly, there is an infinite number of axioms of this form (indeed, there will be many such axioms for each choice of *n*). PredC requires an infinite set of axioms to interpret conjunctions of quantified NPs.

It is natural to suspect that the need for an infinite set of axioms arises precisely because PredC assigns no semantic value to the node NP. If PredC had a rule of the general form in (7a), then we could presumably handle the recursive growth of NPs under conjunction with an axiom like (7b). Taken together, (7a) and (7b) would suffice to interpret all of the examples in (5).

(7) a. Val(t, [$_S$ NP$_i$ S], σ) iff ... Val(α, NP, σ) ... Val(t, S, σ) ...
    b. Val(α, [$_{NP}$ NP$_1$ *and* NP$_2$], σ) iff Val(β, NP$_1$, σ) and Val(γ, NP$_2$, σ)

Because PredC assigns no semantic values to simple quantified NPs, it does not allow recursive evaluation of complex quantified NPs, and so must appeal to separate axioms.

An analogous result holds with determiners. Alongside examples like (8a), we also get conjunctions like (8b), (8c), etc.:

(8) a. One man pondered.
    b. One or two men pondered.
    c. One or two or three men pondered.
       $\vdots$

As in the NP case, determiner recursion forces PredC to include infinite additional axioms. Since PredC does not assign determiners an interpreted category Det as in (9a), it does not allow recursive evaluation of conjoined Dets as in (9b):

(9) a. Val(α, [$_{NP}$ Det N'], σ) iff ... Val(β, Det, σ) ... Val(x, N', σ) ...
    b. Val(β, [$_{Det}$ Det$_1$ *or* Det$_2$], σ) iff Val(γ, Det$_1$, σ) or Val(δ, Det$_2$, σ)

Once again we need an infinite axiom set.

As was discussed in chapter 2, infinite axiom sets are more than a formal inelegance for any semantic theory whose task is to describe linguistic knowledge. Since the acquisition period is of finite length, we could not learn such axioms on an individual basis, nor could we be exposed to an infinite number of semantically distinct conjunctions as data. Furthermore, since human brains are finite objects with finite storage capacity, we could not accommodate an infinite set of axioms in any case. Results like these therefore cast serious doubt on PredC as a theory of what speakers of English know about natural-language quantification. PredC does not appear to yield a learnable, knowable semantic theory when confronted with simple recursive NP constructions, which any adequate theory must accommodate. These difficulties suggest the need for an alternative, more fully compositional approach to quantification.

8.2   The Relational Analysis of Determiners

The philosopher Gottlob Frege is well known for having introduced the analysis of quantification adopted in modern logic. This analysis is similar to that embodied in PredC. However, Frege also spoke in terms of an alternative and interestingly different way of analyzing quantification, one that introduces additional semantic structure into quantified NPs. In *The Foundations of Arithmetic* (1953, sec. 47), Frege suggests that examples like (10a) might be analyzed as having the semantic form in (10b), where the terms *whale* and *mammal* are taken to express the concepts 'whalehood' and 'mammalhood' respectively and the determiner *all* is taken to express a binary relation between concepts, ALL:

(10) a. All whales are mammals.
     b. ALL('whalehood')('mammalhood')

Frege describes ALL intuitively as the "subordination relation." Thus (10a) is true if and only if the concept of 'whalehood' is subordinate to the concept of 'mammalhood', that is, if and only if every object that falls under the former concept (and hence is a whale) also falls under the latter concept (and hence is a mammal).[1]

A similar view is available for other determiners, for instance, *some* in (11a). The logical form of this sentence can also be taken to involve a binary relation between concepts:

(11) a. Some whales are mammals.
     b. SOME('whalehood')('mammalhood')

On this view, SOME would be the nonexclusion relation. That is, (11b) would assert that 'whalehood' and 'mammalhood' are nonexclusive concepts: some object falling under the former also falls under the latter.

This general proposal can be elaborated and made more precise by borrowing a bit of apparatus from elementary set theory. The notion of a concept can be spelled out using the notion of a set, and the notion of a relation between concepts can be spelled out in terms of set relations. We begin by equating the concept 'ϕ-hood' with the set of things that are ϕ:

(12) 'whalehood' $= \{y : y \text{ is a whale}\}$
      'mammalhood' $= \{x : x \text{ is a mammal}\}$

We then analyze ALL, SOME, and NO as the following relations between sets:

(13) ALL$(Y)(X)$ iff $Y \subseteq X$
      SOME$(Y)(X)$ iff $Y \cap X \neq \varnothing$
      NO$(Y)(X)$ iff $Y \cap X = \varnothing$

Here the notion of subordination between concepts is captured with the subset relation, the notion of nonexclusive concepts is captured in terms of the non-empty intersection of sets, and the notion of exclusive concepts is captured in terms of a null intersection.

These assumptions yield truth conditions for quantified sentences. Putting (12) and (13) together, we get the following results:

(14) a. *All whales are mammals* is true iff
          $\{y : y \text{ is a whale}\} \subseteq \{x : x \text{ is a mammal}\}$
      b. *Some whales are mammals* is true iff
          $\{y : y \text{ is a whale}\} \cap \{x : x \text{ is a mammal}\} \neq \varnothing$
      c. *No whales are mammals* is true iff
          $\{y : y \text{ is a whale}\} \cap \{x : x \text{ is a mammal}\} = \varnothing$

Thus *All whales are mammals* is true if and only if the set of mammals contains the set of whales, that is, if and only if all whales are mammals. Similarly, *Some whales are mammals* is true if and only if the sets X and Y above have a nonnull intersection, that is, if and only if something is both a whale and a mammal. And so on.

Quantified NPs as Predicates of Sets

The relational analysis of determiners suggests a natural way of assigning semantic values to quantified NPs. Consider the syntactic-adjunction structure corresponding to *All whales are mammals*, (15a), and its semantic structure on the relational view, (15b):

(15) a.

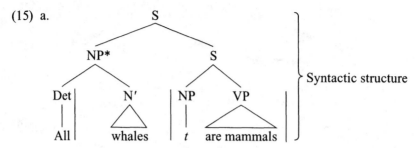

b. ALL ({*y:y* is a whale})({*x:x* is a mammal})   Semantic structure

Notice that ALL has roughly the status of a transitive predicate, in the sense that it relates two arguments. The N′ *whales* functions rather like the object argument of ALL—it is the immediate complement of Det. And the smaller sentence *t are mammals* functions like the subject argument of ALL.

This analogy becomes clearer on comparing (15) with the explicitly transitive sentence (16), where we have inverted the subject-predicate ordering to highlight the resemblance. Notice that NP* in (15) comes out as analogous to the VP node in (16):

(16) a.

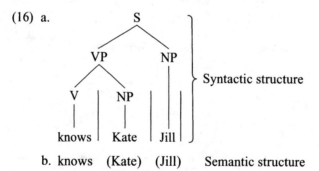

b. knows   (Kate)   (Jill)   Semantic structure

This analogy suggests that we might give rules for interpreting quantified sentences that mimic those for elementary transitive sentences. Recall that in the latter, the VP *knows Kate* takes as its values those individuals standing in the know relation to the individual Kate:

(17) Val(x, [$_{VP}$ knows Kate], σ) iff x knows Kate

If we follow the analogy, a natural idea is to let the quantified NP *all whales* take as its values those sets standing in the ALL relation to, that is, containing, the set of whales:

(18) Val(X, [$_{NP}$ all whales], σ) iff $\{y : y$ is a whale$\} \subseteq X$

Furthermore, recall that in *Jill knows Kate*, the entire sentence receives the value t just in case there is some individual that is a value of both the NP and the VP:

(19) Val(t, [$_S$ Jill knows Kate], σ) iff for some x, Val(x, [$_{NP}$ Jill], σ) and
        Val(x, [$_{VP}$ knows Kate], σ)

Again following the analogy, this suggests that we might let the entire quantified sentence in (15) be true just in case there is some set that is a value of NP and is derived through S:

(20) Val(t, [$_S$ *All whales t are mammals*], σ) iff for some X,
        Val(X, [$_{NP}$ *all whales*], σ) and $X = \{x : x$ is a mammal$\}$

In effect, such axioms would analyze quantificational structures as predications. In place of subjects (NPs) that refer to individuals and predicates (VPs) that are true of individuals, we would have subjects (Ss) that are associated with sets and predicates (quantified NPs) that are true of sets.

8.3   The Theory GQ

We now gather up these informal observations into a new theory that adopts the relational view of determiner semantics. This theory includes lexical axioms for the determiners, as well as a general compositional analysis of the quantifier-adjunction structure. We will call this theory "GQ," for "generalized quantifiers," since the interpretations in (14) and (18) embody ideas closely similar to those arising in so-called **generalized quantification theory** in modern logic.[2]

   In accord with the discussion above, our lexical rules for determiners in GQ will analyze Dets as expressing binary relations between sets. GQ includes the following axioms:[3]

(21) a. Val($\langle X, Y \rangle$, *every*, σ) iff $|Y - X| = 0$
     b. Val($\langle X, Y \rangle$, *some*, σ) iff $|Y \cap X| > 0$
     c. Val($\langle X, Y \rangle$, *no*, σ) iff $|Y \cap X| = 0$

    d. $Val(\langle X, Y \rangle, two, \sigma)$ iff $|Y \cap X| = 2$

    e. $Val(\langle X, Y \rangle, most, \sigma)$ iff $|Y \cap X| > |Y - X|$

    f. $Val(\langle X, Y \rangle, the\ one, \sigma)$ iff $|Y - X| = 0$ and $|Y| = 1$

    g. $Val(\langle X, Y \rangle, the, \sigma)$ iff $Val(\langle X, Y \rangle, the\ one, \sigma)$

    h. $Val(\langle X, Y \rangle, the\ two, \sigma)$ iff $|Y - X| = 0$ and $|Y| = 2$

    i. $Val(\langle X, Y \rangle, both, \sigma)$ iff $Val(\langle X, Y \rangle, the\ two, \sigma)$

    j. $Val(\langle X, Y \rangle, neither, \sigma)$ iff $|Y \cap X| = 0$ and $|Y| = 2$

These rules are regularized in two ways. First, (21a–j) are all stated in terms of cardinality or number. Thus, whereas we previously interpreted *every* by means of the subset relation, here we adopt a logically equivalent formulation in terms of cardinality. According to (21a), the *every* relation holds between sets X and Y just in case the number of things that are Y and that are not X is zero. This is just another way of saying that Y is a subset of X. Similarly, whereas we previously interpreted *some* as expressing the "nonempty intersection" relation, in (21) we employ an equivalent statement about cardinality: the *some* relation holds between sets X and Y just in case the number of things that are both Y and X is greater than zero. By expressing things this way we get a more uniform form for our rules and also make clear their status as relations of quantity.

    Axioms (21a–j) also adopt the ordered-pair notation for relations familiar from transitive verbs. Recall that when a pair $\langle x, y \rangle$ is a value of a transitive verb, x corresponds to the subject argument, and y corresponds to the object argument. Accordingly, our axioms specify that when a pair $\langle X, Y \rangle$ is the value of a determiner, X corresponds to the subject argument, the set contributed by S, and Y corresponds to the object argument, the set contributed by the nominal N′.

    The phrasal axioms for quantified NPs and for the quantificational-adjunction structure follow the analogy with transitive-verb sentences suggested above. Axiom (22) analyzes quantified NPs as predicates of sets, on analogy with VPs, which are predicates of individuals:

(22) $Val(X, [_{NP}$ Det N′$], \sigma)$ iff for some Y, $Val(\langle X, Y \rangle,$ Det$, \sigma)$ and
       $Y = \{y : Val(y,$ N′$, \sigma)\}$

Axiom (23) for the quantificational-adjunction structure identifies the value of a quantified NP with a set derived from the S that is its scope:

(23) $Val(t, [_S$ NP$_i$ S$], \sigma)$ iff for some X, $Val(X,$ NP$, \sigma)$ and
       $X = \{\sigma'(i) : Val(t,$ S$, \sigma'),$ for some $\sigma' \approx_i \sigma\}$

A Sample Derivation

We illustrate these axioms with the sentence *Every man ponders*, which has the LF syntax in (24):

(24)

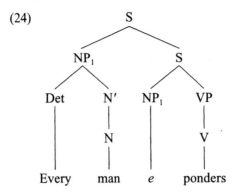

The interpretation of the highest S node is given in (25):

(25) Val(t, [$_S$ [$_{NP_1}$ [$_{Det}$ Every] [$_{N'}$ [$_N$ man]]] [$_S$ [$_{NP_1}$ e] [$_{VP}$ [$_V$ ponders]]]], σ)
       iff for some X, Val(X, [$_{N'}$ [$_{Det}$ every] [$_{N'}$ [$_N$ man]]], σ) and
       $X = \{\sigma'(1) : \text{Val}(t, [_S [_{NP_1} e] [_{VP} [_V \text{ponders}]]], \sigma'), \text{for some } \sigma' \approx_1 \sigma\}$
       (by (23), (UI))

we derive the interpretation of the adjoined NP in (26):

(26) a. Val(X, [$_{NP}$ [$_{Det}$ every] [$_{N'}$ [$_N$ man]]], σ) iff for some Y,
           Val($\langle X, Y \rangle$, [$_{Det}$ every], σ) and $Y = \{y : \text{Val}(y, [_{N'} [_N \text{man}]], \sigma)\}$
           (by (22), (UI))
       b. Val($\langle X, Y \rangle$, [$_{Det}$ every], σ) iff Val($\langle X, Y \rangle$, *every*, σ) (by PredC)
       c. Val($\langle X, Y \rangle$, *every*, σ) iff $|Y - X| = 0$ (21a)
       d. Val($\langle X, Y \rangle$, [$_{Det}$ every], σ) iff $|Y - X| = 0$ (by (26b, c), (SE))
       e. Val(y, [$_{N'}$ [$_N$ man]], σ) iff . . . iff y is a man (by PredC)
       f. Val(X, [$_{NP}$ [$_{Det}$ every] [$_{N'}$ [$_N$ man]]], σ) iff for some Y,
           $|Y - X| = 0$ and $Y = \{y : y \text{ is a man}\}$ (by (26a, d, e), (SE))
       g. Val(X, [$_{NP}$ [$_{Det}$ every] [$_{N'}$ [$_N$ man]]], σ) iff
           $|\{y : y \text{ is a man}\} - X| = 0$ (by (26f), (SI))

The interpretation of the lower S is derived as in (27) by reasoning familiar from PredC:

(27) Val(t, [$_S$ [$_{NP_1}$ e] [$_{VP}$ [ponders]]], σ') iff $\sigma'(1)$ ponders (by PredC)

Taking these results together, we derive (28):

(28) Val(t, [$_S$ [$_{NP_1}$ [$_{Det}$ Every] [$_{N'}$ [$_N$ man]]] [$_S$ [$_{NP_1}$ e] [$_{VP}$ [$_V$ ponders]]]], σ)
        iff for some X, $|\{y : y \text{ is a man}\} - X| = 0$ and
        $X = \{\sigma'(1) : \sigma'(1) \text{ ponders, for some } \sigma' \approx_i \sigma\}$ (by (25), (26g), (27), (SE))

Since $\{\sigma'(i) : \sigma'(i) \text{ ponders, for some } \sigma' \approx_i \sigma\}$ is just the set $\{x : x \text{ ponders}\}$, (28) yields the final T sentence by (SI):

(29) Val(t, [$_S$ Every man e ponders], σ) iff
        $|\{y : y \text{ is a man}\} - \{x : x \text{ ponders}\}| = 0$

That is, *Every man ponders* is true if and only if the number of members of the set of men that are not members of the set of ponderers is zero.

The result in (29) is nonhomophonic: whereas the object language sentence speaks of every man, the rules of GQ deliver a T sentence that speaks of sets and their cardinalities. The situation is similar to that encountered with PredC in the last chapter, where the sentence *Every man agrees* was assigned a T sentence that spoke of every sequence of a certain kind, and not of every man.

As it turns out, we can derive natural, set-free T sentences if we assume that other, extrasemantic modules contribute the set-theoretic equivalences in (30):

(30) a. $|Y - X| = 0$ iff $Y \subseteq X$
        b. $Y \subseteq X$ iff for every x such that $x \in Y$, $x \in X$
        c. $x \in \{x : x \text{ is a man}\}$ iff x is a man
        d. $x \in \{x : x \text{ ponders}\}$ iff x ponders

Applying these to the result in (29), we derive (31), which is equivalent to the T sentence ultimately yielded by PredC:

(31) Val(t, [$_S$ Every man e ponders], σ) iff for every x such that x is a man,
        x ponders

We can usually reduce our results to a final T sentence that does not mention sets or their cardinalities if we assume that extrasemantic modules make available principles like those in (30).[4] Thus although we appeal to sets and their relations to interpret quantified sentences in a fully compositional way, reference to these elements can potentially be dropped out in the end.

GQ versus PredC

The GQ theory retains the positive empirical features of the PredC theory. Its axioms yield interpretations for sentences like (32a–c) containing multiple quantifiers. And it correctly predicts scopal ambiguities for these sentences:

(32) a. Every man met two friends.
     b. Some patient visited every doctor.
     c. No girl sent five presents to three friends.

At the same time, however, GQ avoids the compositionality problem observed earlier with PredC.

Because GQ assigns values to quantified NPs, it can easily be extended to include conjoined NPs. We can do this by adding the recursive axioms in (33):

(33) a. $\mathrm{Val}(X, [_{\mathrm{NP}}\ \mathrm{NP}_1\ and\ \mathrm{NP}_2], \sigma)$ iff $\mathrm{Val}(X, \mathrm{NP}_1, \sigma)$ and $\mathrm{Val}(X, \mathrm{NP}_2, \sigma)$
     b. $\mathrm{Val}(X, [_{\mathrm{NP}}\ \mathrm{NP}_1\ or\ \mathrm{NP}_2], \sigma)$ iff $\mathrm{Val}(X, \mathrm{NP}_1, \sigma)$ or $\mathrm{Val}(X, \mathrm{NP}_2, \sigma)$

Taken together with the general axiom for the adjunction structure, (33) will correctly interpret all of the examples in (3) and (5) discussed earlier. For example, *Every man and some woman ponders* will be assigned the same T sentence as *Every man ponders, and some woman ponders*.

Similarly, because GQ interprets determiners, it can easily be extended to include conjoined determiners by means of the recursive axioms in (34):

(34) a. $\mathrm{Val}(\langle X, Y \rangle, [_{\mathrm{Det}}\ \mathrm{Det}_1\ and\ \mathrm{Det}_2], \sigma)$ iff
       $\mathrm{Val}(\langle X, Y \rangle, \mathrm{Det}_1, \sigma)$ and $\mathrm{Val}(\langle X, Y \rangle, \mathrm{Det}_2, \sigma)$
     b. $\mathrm{Val}(\langle X, Y \rangle, [_{\mathrm{Det}}\ \mathrm{Det}_1\ or\ \mathrm{Det}_2], \sigma)$ iff
       $\mathrm{Val}(\langle X, Y \rangle, \mathrm{Det}_1, \sigma)$ or $\mathrm{Val}(\langle X, Y \rangle, \mathrm{Det}_2, \sigma)$

The axioms in (34), taken together with the general axiom for quantified NPs, will correctly interpret all of the examples in (8). For example, *One or two men ponder* will be assigned the same T sentence as *One man ponders or two men ponder*. For both noun phrases and determiners, then, we avoid the need for infinite axioms sets, and its negative consequences for knowability and learnability.

There is also a subtle but interesting difference between GQ and PredC with respect to the role played by sequences. Recall that in PredC, sequences fulfill two important but conceptually quite different functions. First, they are the objects of quantification in the metalanguage: in PredC, quantifying over things is captured by quantifying over sequences in which things appear. Second, sequences fix the semantic values of referentially variable elements. In PredC, the semantic values of traces and pronominals are determined by sequences. Interestingly, in GQ only one of these two roles for sequences is preserved: reference fixing. In GQ, sequences still serve to determine the values of traces and pronouns, which in turn serve to determine the set of individuals associated with a given clause (see (25), (27), (28) above). However, quantification is not over sequences in GQ but rather over objects. In GQ, determiners express relative quantities of *objects* in two sets.[5]

One way to appreciate the independence of quantification from sequences in GQ is to observe that its resources will allow us to evaluate certain quantified structures without appeal to sequences at all. Consider once again the example sentence *Every man ponders*. Above we interpreted this example under the LF in (24), involving (string-vacuous) movement from subject position.[6] Note, however, that with the resources of GQ, we could have accepted a different syntactic analysis for this sentence—one involving no movement, (35a), and hence no trace, and hence no sequence-dependent element—and still have provided an appropriate interpretation via the rule in (35b):

(35) a.

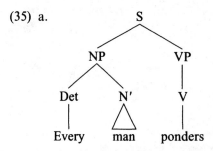

b. Val(t, [_S NP VP]) iff for some X, Val(X, NP) and $X = \{x : \text{Val}(x, \text{VP})\}$

Working through the example, we can easily see that (35b), together with the rules for quantified NPs and predicates, will yield the same result as in (29) (minus the sequence parameter). This kind of traceless account is simply not available in PredC, where quantification is over sequences, and where we thus require the presence of a sequence-dependent item in syntax (a trace or formal variable) in order to get a quantificational interpretation.

Although sequence-free axioms like (35b) are clearly available in GQ, we will not appeal to them, for simple reasons of parsimony. In the syntactic theory we are adopting, movement as in (24) is assumed to be freely available. Furthermore, we independently require an axiom like (23) to deal with object quantifiers and to predict scope ambiguities. Thus, since the grammar will generate and correctly interpret sentences with raised subject quantifiers in any case, an axiom like (35b) would be redundant at best.

8.4   Quantifier Properties

The quantification axioms of PredC are not strongly compositional, in that they fail to give a strictly local interpretation. They are also not exhaustive: (2a, b) assign no semantic value to the determiners *every* and *some*. Determiners do make a semantic contribution to quantification, fixing a quantity of sequences, but they do so simply as part of the interpretation of the larger quantification structure. The implicit claim of the PredC theory is that, despite their apparent status as independent words, *every* and *some* are not genuine lexical items with independent interpretation. Rather, they are syncategoremata: syntactic features or "diacritics" of the adjunction structure.

In sharp contrast to PredC, the GQ analysis treats determiners as independently contentful elements. They are thus grouped with other lexical items having their own specific interpretation and individual semantic properties. This change not only allows us to surmount the problem of conjoined determiners noted above, it also permits us to talk about certain lexicosemantic properties that appear to inhere in individual determiners and in certain classes of determiners.

8.4.1   Affectivity and Directional Entailment

The grammar of English contains an interesting class of expressions called **negative-polarity items** or **negpols**. These include words and phrases such as *anyone, anything, ever, budge an inch, give a hoot in hell*, etc. Their salient property is that they only appear smoothly when licensed by an appropriate **affective** item, typically, a negative element of some kind. Affectivity, the ability to license a negative-polarity item, appears to be a property inhering in specific words. Certain verbs, prepositions, and adverbs have this property, while others don't:

(36) a. John $\left\{\begin{array}{l}\text{denies}\\ \text{*claims}\end{array}\right\}$ that *anyone* was misbehaving.

b. John $\left\{\begin{array}{l}\text{doubts}\\ \text{*believes}\end{array}\right\}$ that he *ever* visited Paris.

(37) a. $\left\{\begin{array}{l}\text{Without}\\ \text{*With}\end{array}\right\}$ *anyone* signed up, we have no chance for a prize.

b. John visited Paris $\left\{\begin{array}{l}\text{before}\\ \text{*after}\end{array}\right\}$ *anyone* else did.

(38) a. John $\left\{\begin{array}{l}\text{rarely}\\ \text{*often}\end{array}\right\}$ will *budge an inch* on such matters.

b. John $\left\{\begin{array}{l}\text{never}\\ \text{*usually}\end{array}\right\}$ appreciates *anyone* else using his name in examples.

Interestingly, this property also appears to distinguish among determiners. As shown by (39), the determiner *no* licenses negpols in both its N′ (shown in brackets) and in the predicate:

(39) a. No [person who has *ever* visited Boston] has returned to it.
    b. No [person who has visited Boston] has *ever* returned to it.

In the analogous example (40), *some* licenses negpols neither in its N′ nor in the predicate:

(40) a. *Some [person who has *ever* visited Boston] has returned to it.
    b. *Some [person who has visited Boston] has *ever* returned to it.

And in (41), *every* licenses negpols in its N′ but not in the predicate:

(41) a. Every [person who has *ever* visited Boston] has returned to it.
    b. *Every [person who has visited Boston] has *ever* returned to it.

Since affectivity characterizes a group of elements that are formally quite disparate—including verbs, adverbs, prepositions, and determiners—it is plausible to think that this property is a semantic one. If so, then we clearly want to speak about the semantics of individual determiners in order to speak about which ones are or are not affective. Furthermore, we'd like our theory to shed light on the source of affectivity, to allow us to predict when a determiner will be affective and when it won't.

As it turns out, affectivity does indeed appear to have a semantic source, illuminated by the theory GQ. Let us begin by considering the inference paradigms in (42):

(42) a. Every man left.

   Every tall man left.

 b. Every tall man left.

   # Every man left.

 c. Every man left.

   # Every man left at 3:00 P.M.

 d. Every man left at 3:00 P.M.

   Every man left.

(The crosshatch, recall, marks unacceptable inferences.) As (42a) shows, the determiner *every* yields a valid inference when a less restrictive nominal (*man*) is replaced with a more restrictive one (*tall man*); *Every man left* entails *every tall man left*. However, (42b) shows that the converse is not true. We cannot infer from a more restrictive nominal term to a less restrictive one. This pattern inverts itself when we switch our attention from the nominal to the predicate. Thus we get a valid inference when a more restrictive verbal predicate (*leave at 3:00 P.M.*) is replaced with a less restrictive one (*leave*) (42d), but we get an invalid inference with the converse (42c).

The determiners *some* and *no* show different inference patterns from *every*:

(43) a. Some man left.

   # Some tall man left.

 b. Some tall man left.

   Some man left.

 c. Some man left.

   # Some man left at 3:00 P.M.

 d. Some man left at 3:00 P.M.

   Some man left.

(44) a. No man left.

   No tall man left.

 b. No tall man left.

   # No man left.

 c. No man left.

   No man left at 3:00 P.M.

 d. No man left at 3:00 P.M.

   # No man left.

With *some* it seems that we are always allowed to infer from a more restrictive to a less restrictive term in both the nominal and the predicate. But we can never infer from a less restrictive to a more restrictive term. By contrast, with *no* we can always infer from a less restrictive to a more restrictive term in both the nominal and the predicate, but we can never infer from more restrictive to a less restrictive term.

Ladusaw (1979) refers to the property singled out by inference paradigms like those in (42) to (44) as "directional entailingness." An environment where we can infer from a less restrictive to a more restrictive term is called a **downward entailing environment**, and an environment where we can infer from a more restrictive to a less restrictive term is called an **upward entailing environment**. More formally,

Definitions   Let X, $Y \subseteq E$, where E is the universe of discourse and α a determiner. Then

(i) a. α is **downward entailing in its first argument** iff
$\text{Val}(\langle X, Y \rangle, \alpha, \sigma)$ and $X' \subseteq X$ imply $\text{Val}(\langle X', Y \rangle, \alpha, \sigma)$,

 b. α is **downward entailing in its second argument** iff
$\text{Val}(\langle X, Y \rangle, \alpha, \sigma)$ and $Y' \subseteq Y$ imply $\text{Val}(\langle X, Y' \rangle, \alpha, \sigma)$,

(ii) a. α is **upward entailing in its first argument** iff
$\text{Val}(\langle X, Y \rangle, \alpha, \sigma)$ and $X \subseteq X'$ imply $\text{Val}(\langle X', Y \rangle, \alpha, \sigma)$,

 b. α is **upward entailing in its second argument** iff
$\text{Val}(\langle X, Y \rangle, \alpha, \sigma)$ and $Y \subseteq Y'$ imply $\text{Val}(\langle X, Y' \rangle, \alpha, \sigma)$.

By these definitions, *every* is downward entailing in its second argument (the set contributed through N$'$), but is upward entailing in its first argument (the set contributed through the predicate). *Some* is upward entailing in both of its arguments, and *no* is downward entailing in both of its arguments.

The directional entailment properties of *every*, *some*, and *no* follow directly under their interpretations as assigned by GQ.[7] For example, the fact that *every* is downward entailing in its second argument follows by elementary set-theoretic reasoning as in (45a). The fact that it is upward entailing in its first argument follows as in (45b):

(45) a. $\text{Val}(\langle X, Y \rangle, \textit{every}, \sigma)$ iff $|Y - X| = 0$
For all X, Y, Y', if $|Y - X| = 0$ and $Y' \subseteq Y$, then $|Y' - X| = 0$
$|Y' - X| = 0$ iff $\text{Val}(\langle X, Y' \rangle, \textit{every}, \sigma)$
___
$\text{Val}(\langle X, Y \rangle, \textit{every}, \sigma)$ and $Y' \subseteq Y$ imply $\text{Val}(\langle X, Y' \rangle, \textit{every}, \sigma)$

 b. $\text{Val}(\langle X, Y \rangle, \textit{every}, \sigma)$ iff $|Y - X| = 0$
For all X, Y, Y', if $|Y - X| = 0$ and $X \subseteq X'$, then $|Y - X'| = 0$
$|Y - X'| = 0$ iff $\text{Val}(\langle X, Y' \rangle, \textit{every}, \sigma)$
___
$\text{Val}(\langle X, Y \rangle, \textit{every}, \sigma)$ and $X \subseteq X'$ imply $\text{Val}(\langle X', Y \rangle, \textit{every}, \sigma)$

Similar reasoning allows us to deduce the relevant directional entailment properties of *some* and *no*.

Interestingly, directional entailment also appears to be what lies behind affectivity, the property of being able to license negative-polarity items. Recall from (39) to (41) (repeated below) that *every* permits a negative-polarity item in its associated nominal but not in the predicate; *some* allows a negative-

Table 8.1   The correlation between negative-polarity items and directional entailingness

Det	First argument	Second argument
no	↓ np	↓ np
some	↑	↑
every	↑	↓ np

Note: ↑ = upward entailing; ↓ = downward entailing; np = "allows a negative-polarity item."

polarity item in neither its nominal nor in the predicate; and *no* permits negative-polarity items both in its nominal and in the predicate:

(39) a.   No [person who has *ever* visited Boston] has returned to it.
      b.   No [person who has visited Boston] has *ever* returned to it.

(40) a.   *Some [person who has *ever* visited Boston] has returned to it.
      b.   *Some [person who has visited Boston] has *ever* returned to it.

(41) a.   Every [person who has *ever* visited Boston] has returned to it.
      b.   *Every [person who has visited Boston] has *ever* returned to it.

This correlates with the upward and downward entailment properties of the determiners (table 8.1). The correlation that emerges is clearly the following (due to Ladusaw [1979] and Fauconnier [1979]):

Correlation   Negative polarity items are licensed in downward entailing environments.

Thus in (41a), *ever* is contained in the phrase (N′) that provides the second argument of *every*, and *every* is downwardly entailing in its second argument. Hence *ever* is in a downward entailing environment, and the sentence is acceptable. By contrast, in (41b) *ever* is contained in the phrase that provides the first argument of *every*, and *every* is upward entailing in its first argument. Hence *ever* is not in a downward entailing environment, and the sentence is unacceptable.

   The correlation between negpol acceptability and downward entailment extends beyond determiners to the entire class of expressions licensing these items. Recall that the prepositions *before* and *after* differ in that the first permits negative-polarity items in its complement, whereas the second does not, (37b). Likewise, recall that the frequency adverbs *rarely* and *often* differ in that the first permits negative-polarity items in its scope, whereas the second does not, (38a). This result correlates with the fact that *before* is downwardly entailing in its complement, whereas *after* is not, (46), and *rarely* is downwardly entailing in its scope, whereas *often* is not, (47):[8]

(46) a. John visited Paris before a meeting was arranged.

   John visited Paris before an afternoon meeting was arranged.

   b. John visited Paris after a meeting was arranged.

   #John visited Paris after an afternoon meeting was arranged.

(47) a. John rarely will talk to a stranger.

   John rarely will talk to a curious stranger.

   b. John often will talk to a stranger.

   #John often will talk to a curious stranger.

Other expressions permitting and forbidding negative-polarity items pattern similarly. In each case, those allowing negpols also license downward entailments in the environments where the negpols appear. And those excluding negative-polarity items also exclude downward entailments in the relevant positions.

These results support the general view suggested earlier that affectivity, the ability to license negpols, is a semantic property inhering in specific lexical items. We see that in virtue of their particular interpretations, various items either are or are not downward entailing, and that downward entailment appears to be the key to negpol distribution. These results also support the specific interpretations assigned in the GQ theory, since these appear to predict downward entailment in the appropriate way. What these remarks leave unsettled is the issue of *why* negative-polarity items should be sensitive to the direction of entailment in just this way, and indeed why there should even be a class of expressions showing distributional sensitivities of this kind. These questions are in fact open ones at present and a subject of continuing research.

8.4.2 The Definiteness Effect

Certain "existential environments" involving the verbs *have* and *be* allow only a limited class of noun phrases to appear. The permissible noun phrases are often termed **indefinite NPs,** and status of a noun phrase as indefinite seems to depend on the determiner that it contains. Thus, NPs with determiners like *a,* *some*, *many*, *no*, and numeral determiners like *two*, *five*, etc., count as indefinite noun phrases with respect to such environments. By contrast, NPs with determiners such as *the*, *every*, *most*, *both*, and *neither* count as definite noun phrases, since they yield unacceptable results in these existential environments (where Pred is a predicate and *there* is the existential *there*, not the demonstrative *there*):

(48) have NP Pred
    a. Mary has ⎡ a friend   ⎤ in Cleveland.
    b.   ⎢ many friends   ⎢
    c.   ⎢ no friends   ⎢
    d.   ⎨ two friends   ⎬
    e.   ⎢ *the friend   ⎢
    f.   ⎢ *every friend   ⎢
    g.   ⎣ *most friends   ⎦

(49) There is/are NP Pred
    a. There is/are ⎡ a problem   ⎤ in Cleveland.
    b.   ⎢ many problems ⎢
    c.   ⎢ no problems   ⎢
    d.   ⎨ two friends   ⎬
    e.   ⎢ *the problem   ⎢
    f.   ⎢ *every problem ⎢
    g.   ⎣ *most problems ⎦

Once again, there are no obvious formal features that account for what unites *a*, *many*, and *some* together and divides this group from *the*, *every*, and *most*. Accordingly, it is plausible to think that the ability to create an indefinite NP is a semantic property inhering in specific determiners. Again, to speak of the semantic properties of determiners, we need a theory that assigns a semantics to determiners.

There are a number of proposals under debate within the general GQ approach as to just how the semantic property of definiteness should be characterized. Here we will consider two such proposals: one due to Barwise and Cooper (1981) and one due to Keenan (1987).

Weak versus Strong Determiners

Barwise and Cooper (1981) suggest an account of indefiniteness based on the properties of sentences of the general form in (50):

(50) a. Det N′ is an N′
     b. Det N′s are N′s

Specifically, they observe that when different determiners are substituted in for Det, one of two semantic results occurs. With some determiners, the sentences obtained are either always true or always false, regardless of the choice of N′. For example, with *every* and *the*, sentences of the paradigmatic form are always true (51a–d).[9] With *neither*, sentences of the paradigmatic form are always false (51e, f). In neither case does it matter whether the N′ selected is true of some objects (such as *man*) or is true of no objects (such as *unicorn*):

(51) a. Every man is a man.
     b. Every unicorn is a unicorn.
     c. The man is a man.
     d. The unicorn is a unicorn.
     e. Neither man is a man.
     f. Neither unicorn is a unicorn.

However, with other determiners, including *some, few,* and *no*, sentences of the form in (50) are sometimes true and sometimes false, depending on whether the N′ in question is or is not true of some objects. Thus (52a) is true, but (52b) is false; (52c) is false, but (52d) is vacuously true. Similarly, (52e) is false, but (52f) is true:

(52) a. Some man is a man.
     b. Some unicorn is a unicorn.
     c. No man is a man.
     d. No unicorn is a unicorn.
     e. Few men are men.
     f. Few centaurs are centaurs.

Determiners that are uniformly true or uniformly false in the paradigmatic frame are called **strong determiners** by Barwise and Cooper (1981), and NPs containing strong determiners are called **strong NPs**. Determiners that are true or false in the paradigmatic frame, depending on the extension of N′, are termed **weak determiners**, and NPs containing weak determiners are called **weak NPs**.

Being a weak or strong determiner is a semantic property that follows directly under the GQ determiner axioms. Observe that for a given choice of determiner α and N′ β, the truth or falsity of the paradigm sentence (50) will depend on the truth or falsity of (53):

(53) $\mathrm{Val}(\langle X, X\rangle, \alpha, \sigma)$, where $X = \{x : \mathrm{Val}(x, \beta, \sigma)\}$

The status of *every* as a strong determiner follows from the fact that $\langle X, X\rangle$ is a value of *every* for any set X (i.e., for every choice of N′) (54a). The status of *some* as a weak determiner follows from the fact that $\langle X, X\rangle$ is a value of *some* when X is a nonempty set (i.e., when N′ is true of some objects), and $\langle X, X\rangle$ is not a value of *some* when X is the empty set $\varnothing$ (i.e., when N′ is true of no objects) (54b). And the status of *no* as a weak determiner follows from the fact that $\langle X, X\rangle$ is a value of *no* when X is the empty set (i.e., when N′ is true of no objects), and $\langle X, X\rangle$ is not a value of *no* when X is nonempty (i.e., when N′ is true of some objects) (54c):

(54) a. $\mathrm{Val}(\langle X, X\rangle, every, \sigma)$ iff $|X - X| = 0$
     b. $\mathrm{Val}(\langle X, X\rangle, some, \sigma)$ iff $|X \cap X| \neq 0$
     c. $\mathrm{Val}(\langle X, X\rangle, no, \sigma)$ iff $|X \cap X| = 0$

Similarly for other determiners.

Barwise and Cooper propose that the weak/strong distinction is precisely the property determining the distribution of postverbal NPs in existential constructions of the general form in (55):

(55) There $\begin{Bmatrix} \text{is an NP.} \\ \text{are NPs.} \end{Bmatrix}$

As the sentences in (56) show, only NPs containing determiners that we have independently identified as weak may appear in this construction:

(56) a. There is no beer.
     b. There are few possibilities.
     c. There are some peanuts.
     d. *There is every person.
     e. *There is neither boy.
     f. *There is the answer.

Existential versus Nonexistential Determiners

Keenan (1987) suggests an alternative semantic characterization of the class of indefinite noun phrases, based on a different semantic property. For simple lexical determiners, this property can be characterized by means of the paradigm in (57):

(57) Det N′ VP iff Det N′ that $\begin{Bmatrix} \text{is a VPer exists} \\ \text{are VPers exist} \end{Bmatrix}$

For some determiners, including *a, some, no, many, few, a few, several, at least n* and numerals like *one, two, three,* etc., the paradigm in (57) always yields a truth, regardless of which N′ or VP is chosen. Thus the sentences in (58), involving *no,* are all true:

(58) a. No man flies iff no man that is a flier exists.
      b. No fish loves Mary iff no fish that is a lover of Mary exists.
      c. No flights from Heathrow go directly to Durbin iff no flights from Heathrow that go directly to Durbin exist.

For other determiners, including *every, the, the n, all, both, neither, most,* the paradigm sentence in (57) is always false, whatever the choice of N′ or VP. Thus the sentences with *every,* in (59) are all false:

(59) a. Every man flies iff every man that is a flier exists.
      b. Every fish loves Mary iff every fish that is a lover of Mary exists.
      c. Every flight from Heathrow goes directly to Durbin iff every flight from Heathrow that goes directly to Durbin exists.

Keenan (1987) refers to lexical determiners that are true in the paradigmatic frame as **basic existential determiners**, and he refers to lexical determiners that are false in the paradigmatic frame as **basic nonexistential determiners**. Keenan defines a series of operations by which complex determiners can be built from basic ones, and he goes on to define an **existential determiner** as either a basic existential determiner or a complex determiner constructed from basic existential determiners by means of the specified operations.[10]

As with the weak/strong distinction, status as an existential or nonexistential determiner is a semantic property that follows directly from the GQ axioms. For a given lexical determiner α, truth or falsity of the paradigm sentence (57) amounts to the truth or falsity of (60) for all sets X and Y (where E is the set of all entities):

(60) $\text{Val}(\langle X, Y \rangle, \alpha, \sigma)$ iff $\text{Val}(\langle E, X \cap Y \rangle, \alpha, \sigma)$

The fact that *some* is a basic existential determiner then follows by the elementary set-theoretic reasoning in (61a). The fact that *every* is nonexistential follows from the nonequivalence of the right-hand side of (61b) (which is trivially true) with the right-hand side of (61c) (which is not trivially true):

(61) a. Val($\langle X, Y \rangle$, *some*, σ) iff $|Y \cap X| > 0$ iff $|E \cap X \cap Y| > 0$ iff
          Val($\langle E, X \cap Y \rangle$, *some*, σ)
      b. Val($\langle E, X \cap Y \rangle$, *every*, σ) iff $|X \cap Y - E| = 0$
      c. Val($\langle X, Y \rangle$, *every*, σ) iff $|Y - X| = 0$

Similarly for the other determiners.

Keenan proposes that existentiality is the key semantic property relevant to the existential construction. More precisely, he suggests that only existential constructions containing existential NPs can have what he terms an "existence interpretation," one that asserts the existence or nonexistence of objects satisfying the nominal. Thus (62a–c) (which repeat (56)) permit an existence interpretation because they contain NPs with existential determiners (and given the semantic interpretation Keenan assigns to the existential construction). By contrast, (62d–f) simply lack an existence interpretation, given that the relevant determiners are not existential:

(62) a. There is no beer.
      b. There are few possibilities.
      c. There are some peanuts.
      d. *There is every person.
      e. *There is neither boy.
      f. *There is the answer.

The set of weak determiners appears to coincide with the set of existential determiners for basic lexical members like *a*, *some*, *no*, *many*, *few*, *every*, *the*, *the n*, *all*, *both*, *neither*, *most*, etc. However, the two sets come apart when more complex determiners are considered. Thus, as Keenan (1987) points out, three-place determiner relations such as *more . . . than* (as in *More men than women are bald*), *fewer . . . than* (as in *Fewer women than men are bald*), and *as many . . . as* (as in *As many men as women are bald*) are existential determiners that are also strong determiners under Barwise and Cooper's paradigm. (They are strong because *Fewer N' than N' are F* is always false, and *As many N' as N' are F* is always true.) As such, they are predicted to be licit in existential constructions under Keenan's account but illicit under Barwise and Cooper's. Keenan observes that NPs formed from these complex determiners can in fact occur smoothly in existential constructions with an existence interpretation:

(63) There are $\begin{cases} \text{more men than women} \\ \text{fewer women than men} \\ \text{as many men as women} \end{cases}$ in the army.

Hence these examples appear to give evidence that it is the existential/nonexistential distinction, rather than the weak/strong distinction, that is relevant to whether these complex determiners can occur in the existential construction.

Syntactic versus Semantic Explanation

The results in either Barwise and Cooper 1981 or Keenan 1987 can easily be fitted into a syntactic account of NP distribution in existential *be* and *have* constructions (although none of these authors actually propose to do so themselves). Suppose that members of the class of weak (or existential) determiners are all marked in the lexicon with the syntactic feature [−Definite], and suppose that members of the class of strong (or nonexistential) determiners are all marked in the lexicon with the syntactic feature [+Definite]. Suppose further that, by convention, any NP directly dominating an [α Definite] determiner is itself marked [α Definite] (that is, suppose that definiteness is inherited upward from determiner to NP). Then a formal constraint on NPs appearing in existential *be* and *have* constructions can be stated straightforwardly as follows:[11]

Indefinite NP constraint $*\dots \begin{Bmatrix} have \\ be \end{Bmatrix}$ [NP Pred], where NP is [+Definite]

That is, the structure *have* [NP Pred] or *be* [NP Pred], where NP is [+Definite], is ungrammatical. On this account, the unacceptability in sentences like (62d–f) is analyzed as a *syntactic* one: such examples are *ungrammatical* in virtue of violating a formal constraint on existential constructions.

Barwise and Cooper (1981) suggest an alternative, *semantic* account of the unacceptability in (62d–f), that is, one under which (62d–f) are not syntactically ill formed but rather semantically anomalous. Their account attempts to trace the anomaly of existential constructions containing strong NPs to a particular fact about the interpretation of these constructions.

Barwise and Cooper's account of the interpretation of existential constructions with strong NPs hinges on an interesting formal result. They show that such sentences are equivalent to sentences of another kind. Specifically, any sentence of the form (64a) is truth-conditionally equivalent to a corresponding sentence of the form (64b) (that is, (50) above):[12]

(64) a. There $\begin{Bmatrix} is \\ are \end{Bmatrix}$ [NP Det N′]

b. Det $\begin{Bmatrix} [\text{N}' \text{ is an N}'] \\ [\text{N}'\text{s are N}'\text{s}] \end{Bmatrix}$

Thus we can derive all the equivalences in (65a–c):

(65) a. Val(t, [$_\text{S}$ There is [$_\text{NP}$ [$_\text{Det}$ every] [$_{\text{N}'}$ man]]]) iff
      Val(t, [$_\text{S}$ [$_\text{NP}$ [$_\text{Det}$ Every] [$_{\text{N}'}$man]] is a man])[13]

    b. Val(t, [$_\text{S}$ There are [$_\text{NP}$ [$_\text{Det}$ some] [$_{\text{N}'}$ men]]]) iff
      Val(t, [$_\text{S}$ [$_\text{NP}$ [$_\text{Det}$ Some] [$_{\text{N}'}$ men]] are men])

    c. Val(t, [$_\text{S}$ There are [$_\text{NP}$ [$_\text{Det}$ no] [$_{\text{N}'}$ men]]]) iff
      Val(t, [$_\text{S}$ [$_\text{NP}$ [$_\text{Det}$ No] [$_{\text{N}'}$ men]] are men])

As we have already seen, sentences of the paradigmatic form (64b) are either trivially true or trivially false with strong NPs. Thus *Every man is a man* is trivially true, and *Neither man is a man* is trivially false. By contrast, such sentences are informative with weak NPs: they may be either true or false, depending on whether the particular N' happens to apply to anything or not. For example *Some man is a man* happens to be true, because *man* applies to some things, but *Some unicorn is a unicorn* happens to be false, because the N *unicorn* is not true of anything. Given the equivalence between existential sentences of the form (64a) and sentences of the form (64b), these results carry over from the latter to the former. Thus an existential construction of the form (64a) with a strong NP would be either trivially true or trivially false, but one with a weak NP would be informative.

Barwise and Cooper propose that the anomalous character of existential constructions with strong NPs versus their acceptability with weak NPs follows directly from this difference of informativeness in the two cases. They suggest that existential sentences with strong NPs are uninformative because they are either trivially true or trivially false. And this uninformativeness is the source of their anomalous character. By contrast, existential sentences with weak NPs are true or false, depending upon the existence or nonexistence of the relevant individuals. Hence they are informative, and hence acceptable.

Barwise and Cooper's semantic account is interesting in that it not only attempts to characterize semantically the class of NPs appearing in existential constructions but also tries to explain *why* this class of NPs is allowed to appear and not some other. Nonetheless, despite these virtues, the account is clearly inadequate as it stands. For many trivially true sentences are perfectly acceptable, as are many sentences that are trivially false. Indeed, we find examples among the very equivalences that Barwise and Cooper use to generate their results. Thus (56d) (*There is every person*) is held to be anomalous because it has the same truth conditions as the trivially true (66):

(66) Every person is a person.

But (66) is perfectly acceptable! If the anomalous character of (56d) were to follow merely from the tautological character of its truth conditions, (66) should be unacceptable for the very same reason. Analogous remarks apply to all the other examples. Barwise and Cooper's account therefore fails as it stands: every existential construction with a strong NP is, by their own account, truth-conditionally equivalent to another sentence that is not anomalous. So even if strong NPs in existential constructions are uninformative, we still require some additional idea about why uninformativeness should lead to deleterious consequences only in the latter cases.

8.4.3 The Partitive Constraint

Partitive noun phrases, such as *each of the pencils* or *all of the stew*, are said to allow only **definite** NPs in the position following *of* (NP* in (67)). Again, status as a definite NP in this paradigm seems to depend on the determiner that appears within it. Plural NPs containing the definite determiner *the* or the demonstratives *these* or *those* are permitted in the position following *of* and thus count as definite with respect to the paradigm. NPs containing other determiners are not allowed and count as indefinite:[14]

(67) [NP Det *of* NP*]
    a. One/all/each of   the men   was seated.
    b.   these men
    c.   those men
    d.   *some men
    e.   *all men
    f.   *no men
    g.   *most men

Here again, given the lack of formal features distinguishing acceptable and unacceptable cases, it is plausible to think that the property of being definite is semantic.

The issue of which NPs can appear in the partitive construction appears to turn on the answer to a second, more general question raised by partitives for

GQ. Note that partitive and nonpartitive pairs like those in (68) are quite similar in interpretation, the chief difference being that in the case of partitives, quantification appears to be over some specific, contextually fixed set, here a particular set of fish:

(68) a. some of the fish
         some fish
     b. few of the fish
         few fish
     c. each of the fish
         each fish

Recall now that we have taken determiners to express binary relations between sets, one of which is derived from the nominal complement of Det and one of which is derived from the remainder of the sentence. In the case of NPs of the standard [Det N'] form, the set Y corresponding to the nominal complement is just the set of things that are values of N':

(69) $Y = \{y : \mathrm{Val}(y, \mathrm{N}', \sigma)\}$

However, in the case of partitive NPs, which have the form [Det *of* NP], the nominal complement of Det is not N' but rather NP, an expression whose values are not individuals but sets. Forming a set of values from an NP would thus not yield a set of individuals—an appropriate value for Det—but rather a family of sets:

(70) $Z = \{X : \mathrm{Val}(X, \mathrm{NP}, \sigma)\}$

The question that arises is thus the following: How is the appropriate combination of semantic values achieved with partitives? How do we fit together the semantics of Det and NP?

The solution to this more general question appears to lie with certain formal differences among the predicates of sets assigned to NPs in GQ. Consider, for example, the predicates that GQ assigns to *every fish* and *the fish*. We can represent them graphically with Venn diagrams as in figure 8.1, where $Y = \{y : y$ is a fish$\}$. For a set X to be a value of *every fish*, X must contain Y, the set of fish. For a set X to be a value of *the fish*, X must contain Y, and furthermore, Y must be a singleton. In both cases the sets that are values of the NP, the sets of which NP is true, share a common core. That is, there is a set contained in every set that is a value. With *every fish* and *the fish*, the common core is the set of fish Y.

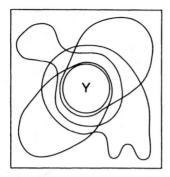
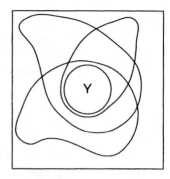

every fish
Val(X, *every fish*) iff |Y − X| = 0

the fish
Val(X, *the fish*) iff |Y − X| = 0
and |Y| = 1

Figure 8.1   Some of the sets that GQ assigns to *every fish* and to *the fish*.

Not all NPs correspond to predicates of sets of this kind. The noun phrases *some fish* and *no fish*, for example, are associated with families of values like those shown in figure 8.2, where again $Y = \{y : y$ is a fish$\}$. With *some fish*, the sets that are values of the NP must intersect Y, but they needn't share any common core. And with *no fish*, the sets that are values of the NP are actually excluded from sharing a common core in Y.

The semantic property possessed by *every fish* and *the fish*, but not by *some fish* and *no fish*, is the property of being a **principal filter**. We may define it precisely as follows:

Definition   A predicate of sets Φ is a **principal filter** iff there is some Y such that for any X, Val(X, Φ, σ) iff $Y \subseteq X$.

The set Y forming the core of a principal filter Φ is referred to as the **generator of** Φ. Among principal filters, we can distinguish ones that are proper and ones that are not. Intuitively, proper principal filters are principal filters that never degenerate in a certain way. Recall the axioms for *every* and *the*:

(71) a. Val($\langle X, Y \rangle$, *every*, σ) iff $|Y - X| = 0$
     b. Val($\langle X, Y \rangle$, *the*, σ) iff $|Y - X| = 0$ and $|Y| = 1$

As noted earlier, the two determiners differ only in that *the* requires its nominal set to contain a unique member. This requirement has the effect of keeping NPs with *the* from reducing semantically to predicates true of all sets, that is

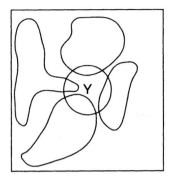
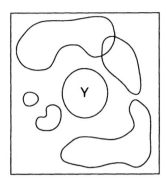

some fish   no fish
Val(X, *some fish*) iff |Y ∩ X| > 0   Val(X, *no fish*) iff |Y ∩ X| = 0

Figure 8.2   Some of the sets that GQ assigns to *some fish* and to *no fish*.

true of all members of E^*, the set of all subsets of E. To see this, consider the interpretation of the NP *every unicorn*, (72a). Since there are no unicorns, $Y = \{y : \text{Val}(y, \textit{unicorn}, \sigma)\} = \varnothing$, and hence (72a) reduces to (72b):

(72) a. Val(X, [$_{\text{NP}}$ *every unicorn*], σ) iff $|Y - X| = 0$,
         where $Y = \{y : \text{Val}(y, \textit{unicorn}, \sigma)\}$
     b. Val(X, [$_{\text{NP}}$ *every unicorn*], σ) iff $|\varnothing - X| = 0$

But $|\varnothing - X| = 0$ is true for any set X, and hence the predicate of sets corresponding to *every unicorn* is true of all members of E^*, the set of all subsets of entities. Such a result cannot occur with NPs containing *the*. In virtue of the uniqueness requirement, the nominal must apply to at least one object, and hence NPs of the form [*the* N′] cannot degenerate into a predicate true of all sets. We will call principal filters that do not degenerate in this way, **proper principal filters**. And we will call determiners that always yield NPs corresponding to proper principal filters **definite determiners**. More formally:

Definition   A predicate of sets Φ is a **proper principal filter** iff Φ is a principle filter and it is not the case that for all $X \in E^*$, Val(X, Φ, σ).

Definition   A determiner α is **definite** iff for every N′, [$_{\text{NP}}$ [$_{\text{Det}}$ α] N′] is a proper principal filter.

Barwise and Cooper (1981) propose that status as a proper principal filter provides an answer to the two central questions raised by partitives:

- How can Det and NP be semantically combined in an appropriate way?
- Why are the NPs following *of* in partitives restricted to definites?

NPs that are principal filters are generated by a core set Y, and this Y is just the set of the values of the nominal heading NP. In view of this, with NPs that are principal filters, we can always recover the set associated with their nominal head. We can do this by taking the intersection of the sets that are values of the NP. For example, the NP *every fish*, takes as its values the sets X containing the set $Y = \{y : \text{Val}(y, \textit{fish}, \sigma)\}$, the set of values of the N'. To recover the set associated with N', we take the intersection of all these Xs, (73a). Similarly, the NP *the fish* takes as its values sets X containing the singleton $\{f\}$ (f a fish). To recover the set associated with N', $\{f\}$, we take the intersection of all the Xs, (73b):

(73) a. $\bigcap \{X : \text{Val}(X, [_{\text{NP}} \textit{every fish}], \sigma)\} = \{y : \text{Val}(y, \textit{fish}, \sigma)\}$
    b. $\bigcap \{X : \text{Val}(X, [_{\text{NP}} \textit{the fish}], \sigma)\} = \{y : \text{Val}(y, \textit{fish}, \sigma)\} = \{f\}$

Notice that with definite NPs—NPs that are proper principal filters—we are assured of a certain further result: when we take intersections like those in (73), the outcome will be nonnull. With principal filters that are not proper, the intersection of all values can be the empty set, $\varnothing$. However, with proper principal filters, the intersection is always nonempty.

Barwise and Cooper (1981) suggest this as the source of the definite NP restriction in partitives. They propose that the only NPs that can appear in the frame [Det *of* NP] are those whose semantics (a) ensures recovery of the set of values of N' and (b) ensures recovery of a nonempty set of values. In view of requirement (a), NP must be a principal filter. In virtue of requirement (b), NP must be a proper principal filter. These proposals are embodied in the following axiom for the partitive *of* phrase:

(74) $\text{Val}(Z, [_{\text{N'}} \textit{of} \text{NP}], \sigma)$ iff $Z = \bigcap \{X : \text{Val}(X, \text{NP}, \sigma)\}$, where NP is a proper principal filter

Since NP must be a proper principal filter, it must contain a definite determiner, which accounts for the definite NP restriction with which we began.

8.4.4 Conservativity and "Possible Determiners"

Properties like directional entailment in first argument position and determiner strength characterize specific determiners and appear to shed light on specific facts about the grammar of English. There are other semantical properties, however, that characterize determiners generally and seem to shed light on the notion of a possible human determiner.

One such property that has been studied in some detail is that of **conservativity**. Consider the following determiner relations:

(75) a. $\text{Val}(\langle X, Y \rangle, \textit{every}, \sigma)$ iff $|Y - X| = 0$
      b. $\text{Val}(\langle X, Y \rangle, \textit{some}, \sigma)$ iff $|Y \cap X| > 0$
      c. $\text{Val}(\langle X, Y \rangle, \textit{no}, \sigma)$ iff $|Y \cap X| = 0$

Under (75a), the truth of *Every man runs* requires that the set of men be a subset of the set of runners. Under (75b), the truth of *Some man runs* requires that a subset of men constitute a subset of the runners. Finally, under (75c), the truth of *No man runs* requires that no subset of men constitute a subset of the runners. Notice that in each case we are working with members of the nominal set Y in checking whether the determiner relation holds. We are looking at men in all cases. The nominal uniformly "sets the scene": it specifies the collection of individuals on which the truth of the sentence depends.

This regularity observed with *every*, *some*, and *no* is not found in all quantifierlike relations. Consider the relations expressed by *all but* and *everyone except* as they occur in examples like (76a, b):

(76) a. All but boys received a prize.
      b. Everyone except mothers attended.

Intuitively, the situation described above does not hold with these two quantifiers. In evaluating (76a), we are not concerned with boys and whether some quantity of them are prize recipients; rather, we are concerned with nonboys. Similarly, in evaluating (76b) we look not at mothers but instead at nonmothers.

The intuitive property of setting the scene or fixing the the collection of individuals on which the truth of the sentence depends—a property that is present with *every*, *some*, and *few* but absent with *all but* and *everyone except* —is in essence the property of conservativity. We may define it more precisely as follows:

Definition   A determiner α is **conservative** if for any X, Y, $\text{Val}(\langle X, Y \rangle, \alpha, \sigma)$ iff $\text{Val}(\langle X \cap Y, Y \rangle, \alpha, \sigma)$.

A conservative determiner relation is one that holds between two sets X, Y just in case it holds between the intersection of the first with the second and the second. Since $X \cap Y$ and Y are both subsets of Y, this means that the truth of Val($\langle X, Y \rangle, \alpha, \sigma$) with a conservative determiner depends only on individuals in the nominal set Y. Y sets the scene.

Interestingly, conservativity is a property that appears to characterize all human language determiner relations—not just *every*, *some*, and *no* but also *few, many, most, two, three, several*, etc., and their many counterparts in the world's languages. It is what might be called a "semantic universal." This result is quite surprising on reflection, since there is no clear a priori motivation for it. Nonconservative determiner relations are neither conceptually inaccessible nor somehow unnatural or unuseful. We have noted informally that *all but* and *everyone except* are not conservative: their nominal does not specify the range of quantification. Note now that while these expressions are not themselves determiners in English (and indeed are not even syntactic constituents), there is no difficulty in defining a hypothetical determiner *nall* having exactly their semantics:

(77) Val($\langle X, Y \rangle, nall, \sigma$) iff $|(E - Y) - X| = 0$, where $E = \{x : x \text{ exists}\}$

Under this definition, a sentence like (78a) would be true, and presumably useful, in exactly the same situations as (78b) or (78c) (figure 8.3).

(78) a. Nall squares are striped.
    b. All but squares are striped.
    c. Everything except squares is striped.

Figure 8.3 A situation in which the sentence *Nall squares are striped* is true, where NALL(X, Y) iff $|(E - Y) - X| = 0$.

On general grounds, *nall* is thus a perfectly reasonable candidate for a natural-language determiner. Nonetheless, no such element occurs in English, or in any other human language so far as we know.

A similar result holds with the element *only*, which occurs in examples like *Only birds fly*. On reflection, *only* can be seen to have a semantics that is the inverse of *every*:

(79) Val($\langle X, Y \rangle$, *only*, σ) iff $|X - Y| = 0$

Thus, whereas *Every bird flies* is true just in case the birds are a subset of the fliers, *Only birds fly* is true if and only if the fliers are a subset of the birds. Given this, it is easy to show that *only* is not conservative. Superficially, this would seem to contradict the view that natural-language determiners are always conservative. In fact, however, there is no contradiction, for *only* is not a determiner, as it turns out. Instead, it is a quantity adverb with a distribution very different from that of genuine determiners, as the following data show:

(80) a. $\left\{ \begin{array}{l} \text{Only} \\ \text{*Every} \\ \text{*Few} \end{array} \right\}$ the president sneezed.

    b. The president $\left\{ \begin{array}{l} \text{only} \\ \text{*every} \\ \text{*few} \end{array} \right\}$ sneezed.

The prohibition on nonconservative determiners is thus observed. But whereas *nall* is simply absent from the language, *only* is present but housed in another category: that of adverb.

Why conservative determiners should be singled out by natural language is an interesting question that we cannot pursue here. However, results by Keenan and Stavi (1986) suggest that this may arise from natural-language-determiner relations being typically composed out of certain basic, atomic parts. It can be formally shown that if one begins with elementary determiner relations such as "every," "the (one)," and "possessor" and augments this set with more complex determiner interpretations constructed by elementary operations like intersection and complementation, the result will include only conservative determiners. This is because the atomic determiners are all conservative and elementary set-theoretic operations preserve conservativity. The ubiquity of conservative determiners may thus reflect a deep fact about how our space of determiner concepts is structured: that it forms a Boolean algebra over certain elementary determiner relations.

8.5   What Is a Quantifier?

In GQ, many of the elements we would informally refer to as "quantifiers" are realized syntactically in the category Det. Familiar items like *every, some,* and *no* are cases in point. At the same time, however, our results with *nall* and *only* show that the correspondence between quantifiers and determiners is not exact. While *nall* and *only* are intuitively quantificational, they are not determiners. Indeed, under the conservativity restriction, *nall* and *only* are not even possible natural-language determiners. Given that conservativity is the semantic criterion for determiner relations and that quantifiers and determiners do not coincide, we are led to ask if there is a corresponding semantic criterion for quantifiers. More simply, we would like to know what a quantifier is semantically.

8.5.1   Permutation

Looking at the axioms for quantificational determiners in GQ, we can see that a salient property is that they express *relations of quantity between sets*: they concern the quantity of things satisfying the nominal, the quantity of things satisfying the predicate phrase, and the relation between these two quantities. Intuitively, a relation of quantities is one that is sensitive to *numbers* of things but not to identities of things. Putting things slightly differently, a quantificational relation has the property that if we were to change the identities of the individuals in X and Y in a consistent way, preserving the numbers in each and their relative proportions, then the relation would continue to hold. A relation that holds only in virtue of the relative numbers of Xs and Ys, and not their identities, is a quantificational relation.

We can capture this idea precisely by appeal to another concept from set theory: the notion of an automorphism, or **permutation**. A permutation is a consistent change of identities. If A is a set, a permutation π on A is a 1-1 mapping from A onto A itself. With this notion, the idea of a quantifier as a relation holding across changes of identities can be defined as follows:

Definition   If α is a relation on subsets of A, then α is a **quantifier** on A just in case for any X, $Y \subseteq A$ and any permutation π on A (and any σ), $\text{Val}(\langle X, Y \rangle, \alpha, \sigma)$ iff $\text{Val}(\langle \pi(X), \pi(Y) \rangle, \alpha, \pi(\sigma))$.

This definition states that quantifiers are relations between sets that respect permutations of their members. If we call the property of respecting permutations the **permutation property**, then we may rephrase this definition as saying that a quantifier is a set relation having the permutation property.

We can illustrate the content of this definition by contrasting two example relations. Consider the axiom for *every*, repeated in (81a), and a plausible axiom for the (complex) determiner *John's*, given in (81b). The latter treats *John's* N as equivalent to *the* N *of John*. That is, it treats *John's* N as a definite NP:

(81) a. $\text{Val}(\langle X, Y \rangle, \textit{every}, \sigma)$ iff $|Y - X| = 0$
      b. $\text{Val}(\langle X, Y \rangle, \textit{John's}, \sigma)$ iff $|Y - X| = 0$, $|Y| = 1$,
          and for all $x \in Y$, John has x

Suppose that $A = \{a, b, c, d, e, f\}$, let $Y = \{x : x \text{ is a fish}\} = \{a\}$, and let $X = \{x : x \text{ swims}\} = \{a, b, d, e\}$. And suppose further that John owns a but doesn't own any of $\{b, c, d, e, f\}$. Notice that under these assumptions, *Every fish swims* is true, since $|\{a\} - \{a, b, d, e\}| = 0$. Furthermore, *John's fish swims* is also true, since $|\{a\} - \{a, b, d, e\}| = 0$, $|\{a\}| = 1$, and John has a.

Now let π be the permutation shown below in figure 8.4, which maps members of A uniquely onto other members of A. Under this permutation, $\pi(Y) = \{\pi(a)\} = \{c\}$, and $\pi(X) = \{\pi(a), \pi(b), \pi(d), \pi(e)\} = \{c, f, e, a\}$. Notice that under the permutation π, *Every fish swims* is still true because $|\pi(Y) - \pi(X)| =$

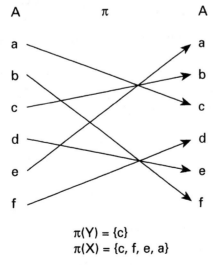

$$\pi(Y) = \{c\}$$
$$\pi(X) = \{c, f, e, a\}$$

Figure 8.4 The permutation π, which maps members of A uniquely onto other members of A.

$|\{\pi(a)\} - \{\pi(a), \pi(b), \pi(d), \pi(e)\}| = |\{c\} - \{c, f, e, a\}| = 0$. In fact, it can be shown that *Every fish swims* will continue to hold true for *any* permutation π of *A*. Hence *every* is classified as a quantifier by the definition given above, since *every* is interpreted by a set relation that has the permutation property. By contrast, *John's fish swims* does not hold under the permutation, that is, we don't have Val($\langle \pi(X), \pi(Y) \rangle$, *John's fish*, σ). For although it is true that $|\{c\} - \{c, f, e, a\}| = 0$, and that $|\{c\}| = 1$, it is not true that John has c. This result will hold with any permutation failing to map a to itself. Accordingly, *John's* is not classed as a quantifier by the above definition, since it is interpreted by a set relation that lacks the permutation property. This example shows clearly how truth under permutation captures the sense in which a relation must be indifferent to identities of the members of the sets it relates. Because *every* does not invoke member identities, *Every fish swims* holds true under π and other permutations. And because *John's* does invoke member identities (John must possess the unique member of the nominal set), *John's fish swims* fails to hold true under π.

Quantifier Status and Weak Crossover

Our semantic criterion for quantifier status, invariance under permutation, appears to converge in an interesting way with a syntactic criterion for quantifier status widely assumed in the principles and parameters theory of syntax (see chapter 3, section 3.3). Consider the example in (82), which involves an interrogative *wh*- NP, a quantified NP, and a simple name. In terms of superficial form, (82b) and (82c) pattern together against (82a), since (82a) contains a *wh*- NP, *which boy*, that has undergone surface movement, leaving a trace (*t*) in the object position of *love*. By contrast, (82b) and (82c) show no movement. In both cases, the understood direct object of *love* appears in the object position:

(82) a. Which boy does his mother love *t*?
     b. His mother loves every boy.
     c. His mother loves John.

Interestingly, this patterning changes when we consider meanings. Chomsky notes that with (82a) and (82b), there is an apparent constraint against construing the pronoun *his* with the *wh*- NP or the quantified NP. Thus, it is quite difficult to understand (82a) as expressing the question in (83a), where the individual who is loved and the individual referred to by *his* are the same. And it is quite difficult to understand (82b) as expressing the assertion in (83b), where again the individual who is loved and the individual referred to by *his* are the same. This constraint is not present with example (82c), involving a name. Apart for the minor exertion required with "backward anaphora," there is no difficulty in understanding this sentence along the lines represented in (83c), where the individual who is loved (John) and the individual referred to by *his* are the same:

(83) a. *For which x, x a boy, does x's mother love x?
     b. *For every x, x a boy, x's mother loves x.
     c. John's mother loves John.

Chomsky proposes that the constraint on interpretation in (83a) reflects the formal constraint on binding stated in (84), which forbids a moved operator element from simultaneously binding its trace (t_i) and a pronoun (*pronoun$_i$*) embedded within another constituent:[15]

(84) *XP_i [[... pronoun$_i$ ...] ... t_i ...]

This so-called **weak crossover constraint** excludes the relevant interpretation of (82a) by excluding the syntactic configuration that represents this interpretation, (85a):

(85) a. *Who$_i$ [$_S$ [$_{NP}$ his$_i$ mother] love t_i]
     b. *Every boy$_i$ [$_S$ [$_{NP}$ his$_i$ mother] love t_i]

Chomsky observes that if this explanation is correct, it argues that (82b) must also involve a movement structure like (85b) at some level of representation. That is, given the parallel interpretive constraints on (82a, b) and the account of this constraint as structural, it follows that (82a) and (82b) must be structurally similar. More precisely, it argues that quantified NPs must be similar to *wh-* NPs in undergoing movement and producing an operator-trace structure at some level of representation.

Under Chomsky's analysis, examples like (82) give us a diagnostic for whether a given element undergoes obligatory LF movement like quantifiers. If we see a pattern of reference possibilities like that shown by (82a, b), then we have a quantificational element. By contrast, if we see a pattern like (82c), then we have a nonquantificational item. Interestingly, the syntactic property of obligatory LF movement appears to correlate quite closely with semantic status as a quantifier. That is, the class of NPs showing the weak-crossover effects diagnostic of LF movement is also the class of NPs containing a specifier element that has the permutation property. Weak-crossover effects are found with NPs containing quantificational determiners like *every*, *some*, *no*, *two*, (86), and with the quantificational adverb *only*, (87):[16]

(86) a.   Her mother loves $\left\{ \begin{array}{l} \text{every} \\ \text{some} \\ \text{no} \\ \text{two} \end{array} \right\}$ girl(s).

b.   *For $\left\{ \begin{array}{l} \text{every} \\ \text{some} \\ \text{no} \\ \text{two} \end{array} \right\}$ x, x's mother loves x.

(87) a.   Her mother loves only Jill.
b.   *For only x = Jill, x's mother loves x.

By contrast, sentences involving determiners like *Jill's*, *this*, and *that* exhibit no weak-crossover effects (88). These determiners also lack the permutation property; that is, they are nonquantificational:

(88) a.   His mother loves Jill's brother.
b.   Her mother loves this/that girl.

The semantic and syntactic characterizations of quantifiers thus seem to converge.

To summarize our results, we have seen that although status as a determiner and status as a quantifier coincide in many cases, the two classes are distinct, both syntactically and semantically. Syntactically, determiners are constituents of noun phrases, appearing in configurations of the form [$_\text{NP}$ Det N']. Semantically, they are conservative. By contrast, quantifiers induce movement in their phrases at the level of logical form, a behavior revealed by the presence of weak-crossover effects. Semantically, they are characterized by the permutation property (table 8.2). This independence permits (actual and potential) English expressions in all four possibilities according to whether the expression is or is not a determiner and is or is not a quantifier ([$\pm$ Determiner], [$\pm$ Quantifier]). That is, we admit expressions that are both determiners and quantifiers, expressions that are determiners but not quantifiers, expressions that are not determiners but are quantifiers, and, of course, many expressions

Table 8.2 Syntactic and semantic criteria of determiners and quantifiers

	Determiners	Quantifiers
Syntactic criterion	Constituents of NPs	Obligatory LF movement
Semantic criterion	Conservative	Permutation property

Table 8.3 Examples of English expressions that are or are not determiners and are or are not quantifiers

	[+ Determiner]	[− Determiner]
[+ Quantifier]	*every, some, no, two*, etc.	*only, nall*, etc.
[− Quantifier]	*John's, that, this*, etc.	*Fred, run, to*, etc.

(including the vast majority of nouns, verbs, prepositions, adjectives, etc.) that are neither (table 8.3).

8.5.2 Quantifiers as Cardinality Functions

The analysis of quantifiers as expressing relations of quantity between sets can be given a useful formal characterization in terms of cardinality functions.[17] (This section is technical and may be skipped on a first reading.)

Consider a sentence of the general form in (89), where Q is a quantifier, N′ is a nominal that restricts the quantifier, and S is the scope of the quantifier:

(89) $[_s \ Q \ N' \ S]$

Example sentences of this form include *Every bird t flies*, *Most candy Max likes t*, and so on. In the relational analysis of determiners, the nominal and the scope correspond to subsets of the universe of discourse E (figure 8.5). When we consider a Venn diagram of the two sets, we see that they divide E into four regions (figure 8.6). First there are the entities in N′ but not in S (that is, N′ − S). Then there are the entities that are in S, but not in N′ (S − N′). There are the entities that are in both N′ and S (N′ ∩ S). And finally, there are the entities in neither N′ nor S (E − (N′ ∪ S)). Together these four regions sum to E, which entails that (90) will be true for any N′, S, and E:

(90) $|N' - S| + |S - N'| + |N' \cap S| + |E - (N' \cup S)| = |E|$

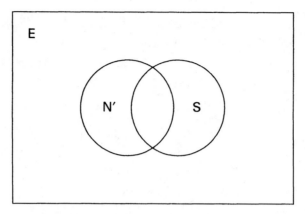

Figure 8.5 The nominal N′ and the scope S as subsets of the universe of discourse E.

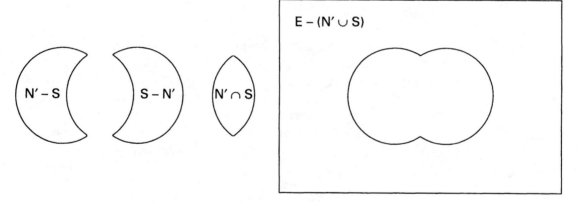

Figure 8.6 N′ and S divide E into four regions: N′ − S, S − N′, N′∩S, and E − (N′∪S).

We spoke earlier of quantifiers Q as expressing relations of quantity between sets. In terms of figure 8.6, a quantifier may be viewed a function relating the sizes of N′ − S, S − N′, N′∩S, and E − (N′∪S). More generally, a quantifier in a universe of discourse of size ε can be analyzed as a **cardinality function** from quadruples of numbers that sum to ε to the truth values t and f:

(91) $f_\varepsilon : \{\langle \alpha, \beta, \gamma, \pi \rangle : \alpha + \beta + \gamma + \pi = \varepsilon\} \rightarrow \{t, f\}$

Intuitively, $\alpha = |N′ − S|$, $\beta = |S − N′|$, $\gamma = |N′ \cap S|$, and $\pi = |E − (N′ \cup S)|$.

The idea is that a sentence of the form [$_S$ Q N' S] is true just in case the cardinality function associated with the quantifier maps the relevant quadruple to true.

To illustrate, consider the universal quantifier *every*. What cardinality function $f_\varepsilon^\forall$ will allow us to define Val($\langle X, Y\rangle$, *every*, σ) appropriately along the lines in (92)?

(92) Val($\langle X, Y\rangle$, *every*, σ) iff
$$f_{|E|}^\forall(|Y - X|, |X - Y|, |Y \cap X|, |E - (Y \cup X)|) = \text{t}$$

Given our earlier discussion of *every*, it's clear that $f_\varepsilon^\forall$ should be the following function:

(93) $f_\varepsilon^\forall(\alpha, \beta, \gamma, \pi) = \begin{cases} \text{t} & \text{if } \alpha = 0 \\ \text{f} & \text{otherwise} \end{cases}$

Every holds of $\langle X, Y\rangle$ just in case Y is a subset of X, that is, just in case $\alpha = |Y - X| = 0$.

We can define all of the quantifiers considered in the GQ theory, and indeed all binary quantifiers, by these means. Consider the cardinality functions given below in (94a) to (98a), which are defined for any ε and for quadruples $\langle \alpha, \beta, \gamma, \pi\rangle$ such that $\alpha + \beta + \gamma + \pi = \varepsilon$. These functions can be used to give the axioms for English quantifiers shown in (94b) to (98b), respectively:[18]

(94) a. $f_\varepsilon^{66}(\alpha, \beta, \gamma, \pi) = \begin{cases} \text{t} & \text{if } 2\alpha = \gamma \\ \text{f} & \text{otherwise} \end{cases}$

b. Val($\langle X, Y\rangle$, *66% of the*, σ) iff
$$f_\varepsilon^{66}(|Y - X|, |X - Y|, |Y \cap X|, |E - (Y \cup X)|) = \text{t}$$

(95) a. $f_\varepsilon^M(\alpha, \beta, \gamma, \pi) = \begin{cases} \text{t} & \text{if } \gamma > \alpha \\ \text{f} & \text{otherwise} \end{cases}$

b. Val($\langle X, Y\rangle$, *most*, σ) iff
$$f_\varepsilon^M(|Y - X|, |X - Y|, |Y \cap X|, |E - (Y \cup X)|) = \text{t}$$

(96) a. $f_\varepsilon^O(\alpha, \beta, \gamma, \pi) = \begin{cases} \text{t} & \text{if } \beta = 0 \\ \text{f} & \text{otherwise} \end{cases}$

b. Val($\langle X, Y\rangle$, *only*, σ) iff
$$f_\varepsilon^O(|Y - X|, |X - Y|, |Y \cap X|, |E - (Y \cup X)|) = \text{t}$$

(97) a. $f_\varepsilon^{O*}(\alpha, \beta, \gamma, \pi) = \begin{cases} \text{t} & \text{if } \beta \neq 0 \\ \text{f} & \text{otherwise} \end{cases}$

b. $\mathrm{Val}(\langle X, Y \rangle, \textit{not only}, \sigma)$ iff
$$f_\varepsilon^{\mathrm{O}^*}(|Y - X|, |X - Y|, |Y \cap X|, |E - (Y \cup X)|) = \mathrm{t}$$

(98) a. $f_\varepsilon^{\mathrm{F}}(\alpha, \beta, \gamma, \pi) = \begin{cases} \mathrm{t} & \text{if } \alpha + \gamma < \beta + \gamma \\ \mathrm{f} & \text{otherwise} \end{cases}$

b. $\mathrm{Val}(\langle X, Y \rangle, \textit{there are fewer \dots than objects that}, \sigma)$ iff
$$f_\varepsilon^{\mathrm{F}}(|Y - X|, |X - Y|, |Y \cap X|, |E - (Y \cup X)|) = \mathrm{t}$$

The approach to quantification through cardinality functions gives us a general way of characterizing quantifiers and a way of calculating how many possible quantifiers there will be for a universe of given size. For a domain of size ε, there will be as many quantifiers as there are functions from quadruples of cardinals $(\alpha, \beta, \gamma, \pi)$ such that $\alpha + \beta + \gamma + \pi = \varepsilon$ to the truth values $\{\mathrm{t}, \mathrm{f}\}$. For universes of any appreciable size ε, the number of possible quantifiers will be extremely large. But, evidently, only a small proportion of these are realized either as simple lexical quantifiers (e.g., *every*, *some*, *only*, etc.) or as complex quantifiers constructed through the combinatory resources of the language (*not only*, *more than finitely many*, etc.). In view of this, it is an interesting and important question what further properties (if any) constrain the class of natural-language quantifiers to those routinely found. This question has received considerable attention in current work in formal semantics but remains an open one at present.

Theory and Exercises

The Theory GQ (Generalized Quantifiers)

Lexical Axioms

(1) a. $\mathrm{Val}(x, \textit{Kate}, \sigma)$ iff $x = \mathrm{Kate}$
   b. $\mathrm{Val}(x, \textit{Chris}, \sigma)$ iff $x = \mathrm{Chris}$
   c. $\mathrm{Val}(x, \textit{Phil}, \sigma)$ iff $x = \mathrm{Phil}$
   d. $\mathrm{Val}(x, \textit{Jill}, \sigma)$ iff $x = \mathrm{Jill}$

(2) a. $\mathrm{Val}(x, \textit{man}, \sigma)$ iff x is a man
   b. $\mathrm{Val}(x, \textit{woman}, \sigma)$ iff x is a woman
   c. $\mathrm{Val}(x, \textit{fish}, \sigma)$ iff x is a fish

(3) a. Val(x, *ponders*, σ) iff x ponders
 b. Val(x, *agrees*, σ) iff x agrees
 c. Val(x, *protests*, σ) iff x protests

(4) a. Val($\langle x, y \rangle$, *knows*, σ) iff x knows y
 b. Val($\langle x, y \rangle$, *admires*, σ) iff x admires y
 c. Val($\langle x, y \rangle$, *instructs*, σ) iff x instructs y

(5) a. Val($\langle X, Y \rangle$, *every*, σ) iff $|Y - X| = 0$
 b. Val($\langle X, Y \rangle$, *some*, σ) iff $|Y \cap X| > 0$
 c. Val($\langle X, Y \rangle$, *no*, σ) iff $|Y \cap X| = 0$
 d. Val($\langle X, Y \rangle$, *most*, σ) iff $|Y \cap X| > |Y - X|$
 c. Val($\langle X, Y \rangle$, *two*, σ) iff $|Y \cap X| = 2$
  (And similarly for other numeral determiners.)
 f. Val($\langle X, Y \rangle$, *the two*, σ) iff $|Y - X| = 0$ and $|Y| = 2$
 g. Val($\langle X, Y \rangle$, *both*, σ) iff Val($\langle X, Y \rangle$, *the two*, σ)
 h. Val($\langle X, Y \rangle$, *neither*, σ) iff $|Y \cap X| = 0$ and $|Y| = 2$
 i. Val($\langle X, Y \rangle$, *the*, σ) iff Val($\langle X, Y \rangle$, *the one*, σ)

Phrasal Axioms

(6) a. Val(t, [$_S$ S$_1$ *and* S$_2$], σ) iff both Val(t, S$_1$, σ) and Val(t, S$_2$, σ)
 b. Val(t, [$_S$ S$_1$ *or* S$_2$], σ) iff either Val(t, S$_1$, σ) or Val(t, S$_2$, σ)
 c. Val(t, [$_S$ *It is not the case that* S], σ) iff it is not the case that Val(t, S, σ)

(7) a. Val(t, [$_S$ NP VP], σ) iff for some x, Val(x, NP, σ) and Val(x, VP, σ)
 b. Val(x, [$_{VP}$ V NP], σ) iff for some y, Val($\langle x, y \rangle$, V, σ) and Val(y, NP, σ)
 c. Val(x, [$_X$ Y], σ) iff Val(x, Y, σ) (where X, Y are any nodes)

(8) a. Val(X, [$_{NP}$ Det N'], σ) iff for some Y, Val($\langle X, Y \rangle$, Det, σ) and
  $Y = \{y : \text{Val}(y, \text{N}', \sigma)\}$
 b. Val(x, [$_{NP_i}$ e], σ) iff $x = \sigma(i)$ for $i \geq 1$
 c. Val(t, [$_S$ NP$_i$ S], σ) iff for some X, Val(X, NP, σ) and
  $X = \{\sigma'(i) : \text{Val}(t, \text{S}, \sigma'), \text{ for some } \sigma' \approx_i \sigma\}$

Production Rules

(UI), (SE), (SI) as in PC+

Definition For any sequence σ, $\sigma(a)$, $\sigma(b)$, $\sigma(c)$, $\sigma(d)$ are the first, second, third, and fourth elements of σ, respectively. For any positive integer i, $\sigma(i)$ is the $(i + 4)$th element of σ.

Definition For any sequences σ, σ', $\sigma \approx_i \sigma'$ iff σ' differs from σ at most at $\sigma'(i)$.

Definition Val(t, S) iff Val(t, S, σ) for all sequences σ.

Exercises

1. Give GQ T sentence derivations for each of the following sentences, reducing them to set-free forms wherever you can:

   (1) a. No student knows Jill.
       b. Max likes most fish.
       c. Three boys admire two girls. (Wide scope for *three boys*.)

2. In chapter 4, we considered an axiom for indefinite NPs occurring as predicates. According to this rule (reproduced in (1)) the determiner *a* is syncategorematic. We further saw that this axiom could be extended to argument NPs. When it is so extended, the quantificational force of indefinites arises from the composition axioms for clauses.

   (1) Val(x, [$_{NP}$ a N$'$]) iff Val(x, N$'$)

   This general nonquantificational view of indefinites can be captured in a categorematic analysis of the indefinite determiner. Assume that NPs of the form [$_{NP}$ a N$'$] take individuals as their values:

   (2) Val(x, [$_{NP}$ Det N$'$], σ) iff for some Y, Val($\langle x, Y \rangle$, Det, σ) and
        $Y = \{y : \text{Val}(y, N', \sigma)\}$

   Assume further that the indefinite determiner *a* expresses a relation between an individual x and a set Y:

   (3) Val($\langle x, Y \rangle$, a, σ) iff $x \in Y$

   Show that these axioms assign appropriate truth conditions to the sentence *A woman ponders*.

      Definite NPs are widely held to differ from indefinites in imposing a uniqueness condition. On this view, the truth conditions of *The man ponders* require that there be a single man and that this man ponder. Show that the nonquantificational view of indefinites can be extended to definites as well. Propose an axiom (4) for the definite determiner *the* that imposes a uniqueness condition on Y:

(4) Val($\langle x, Y \rangle$, *the*, σ) iff ...

Show that this axiom (together with (2)) assigns appropriate truth conditions to *The man ponders*.

3. May (1985) proposes that quantifier raising can adjoin a quantified NP not only to S but to any maximal projection. On this view, (1a), for example, may receive the logical form shown in (1b), where *every woman* is adjoined to a VP:

(1) a. John admires every woman.

    b.

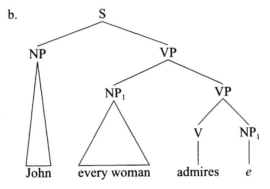

Show that this idea makes sense semantically. More precisely, extend GQ to include structures like (1b). Add an axiom that will interpret the following:

(2) [$_{VP}$ NP$_i$ VP]

Show that the extension you propose assigns an appropriate T sentence to the logical form (1b).

4. Recall that examples like (1) are scopally ambiguous, having the two readings given informally in (2):

(1) [$_{NP}$ Every picture of two persons] developed

(2) a. For two persons *x*, every picture of *x* developed.

    b. Every two-person picture developed.

Assume the D-structure for (1) shown in (3). Can the two readings in (2) be captured in GQ as it stands?

(3)

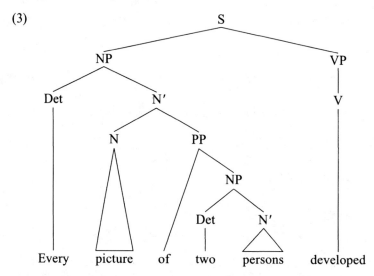

If not, extend GQ to obtain the missing reading(s). Show that your extension gives the relevant readings by providing T-sentence derivations where necessary. (For purposes of this exercise, assume that *of* is syncategorematic and that *two persons* is an argument of *picture*.)

5. Recall that May (1985) proposes quantifier-raising structures in which a quantified NP adjoins another quantified NP, so that (1a) receives the LF in (1b):

(1) a. Some delegate from every city attended.

b.

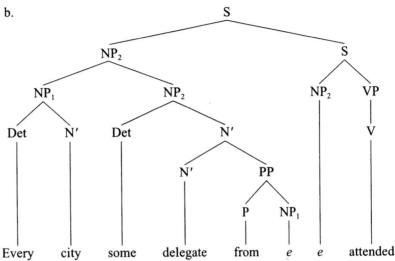

Show that this idea makes sense semantically in GQ. More precisely, extend GQ to include structures like (1b). Add an axiom that will interpret the following:

(2) [$_{NP}$ NP$_i$ NP]

Show that the extension you propose assigns an appropriate T sentence to the LF in (1b). (For purposes of this exercise, assume that *from* is a relation on individuals and that [$_{N'}$ N' PP] is a copredication structure.)

6. Generalize your results in problems 2 to 4 to provide a cross-categorial rule for quantifying-in. That is, give an axiom of the following form, where *x* ranges over semantic values and *X* ranges over syntactic categories:

(1) Val(x, [$_X$ NP$_i$ X], σ) iff ...

Explain how this axiom can replace the three separate axioms derived in problems 3 to 5.

7. Using inference paradigms like (42) to (44) in the chapter, investigate the following determiners with respect to upward and downward entailment: *few, many, three, exactly seven*, and *the*. Check your results with respect to the distribution of negative-polarity items.

8. Consider the partitive noun phrases in (1), assuming the judgments shown:

(1) a.   each of the two fish
           *each of both fish
     b.   each of the fish
           *each of the one fish
     c. *each of Max

Discuss their relevance for the analysis of the partitive constraint in section 8.4.3.

9. In view of the definition of conservativity, one simple way to check whether a given determiner Det is conservative is to consider the validity of sentences of the following general form, for any N′ and VP:

(1) Det N′ VP iff Det N′ $\left\{ \begin{matrix} \text{is an N}' \\ \text{are N's} \end{matrix} \right\}$ that VP

(For instance, *Both men run iff both men are men that run.*) If the scheme always yields a true sentence, then the determiner is conservative. If the scheme yields a false sentence, then it isn't. Using this scheme, investigate whether *every, some,* and *exactly two* are conservative.

10. In the text we claimed that natural-language determiners are uniformly conservative. Yet consider sentence (1) (due to Westerstahl).

(1) Many Scandinavians have won the Noble Prize.

On reflection, this example is ambiguous. What are its truth conditions? Do any of its readings raise problems for conservativity?

11. Conservativity (together with a couple of other properties) allows us to represent the space of possible determiner concepts graphically by means of a **number-theoretic tree.**[19] Let Y and X be sets, let $a = |Y - X|$ (the number of Ys that aren't Xs), and let $b = |Y \cap X|$ (the number of Ys that are Xs). Then we can construct a **tree of determiners** corresponding to the possible pairs $\langle a, b \rangle$:

$a+b=0$				0, 0			
$a+b=1$			1, 0		0, 1		
$a+b=2$		2, 0		1, 1		0, 2	
$a+b=3$	3, 0		2, 1		1, 2		0, 3
$\vdots$			$\vdots$				

To illustrate, the determiner *neither* is represented by the point $\langle 2, 0 \rangle$ on the tree, since in any sentence of the form "Neither N′ VPs" the number of N′s that don't VP is 2, and the number of N′s that VP is 0. Conversely, the determiner *both* is represented by $\langle 0, 2 \rangle$, since in any sentence of the form "Both N′s VP," the number of N′s that don't VP is 0, and the number of N′s that VP is 2.

If the following determiners can be represented on the tree of determiners, show how they are represented. If they cannot be represented, indicate why this is so:

(1) a. the, the *n*
    b. every
    c. most
    d. at most two
    e. exactly one or exactly three
    f. only

Define a **symmetric determiner** as follows:

Definition   A determiner Det is **symmetric** just in case Val($\langle X, Y \rangle$, Det, σ) iff Val($\langle Y, X \rangle$, Det, σ).

If symmetric determiners can be represented on the tree of determiners, show how they are represented. If they cannot be represented, indicate why this is so.

9   Definite Descriptions

In examining noun phrases, we have encountered **singular referring NPs** like *Chris* and *Jill* (1a) and **quantified NPs** like *every man* and *no woman* (1b):

(1) a. Chris agrees.
    b. Every man agrees.

These two classes differ significantly in semantic properties. Hence one might think it would be a straightforward matter to distinguish their members. This naive view is refuted by **definite descriptions**, which comprise NPs of the general form [$_{NP}$ the . . .] and [$_{NP}$ NP's . . .]:

(2) a. The man agrees.
    b. Jill's brother agrees.

The proper semantic analysis of definite descriptions has been a subject of continuing debate for over a century, and the accounts that have been proposed span the range of logical possibilities. Definite descriptions have been claimed to be quantified NPs, to be referring NPs, to be both quantified and referring (and hence ambiguous), and to be neither quantified nor referring (and hence members of a wholly different semantic category). Furthermore, the arguments advanced in this debate draw on an interesting mixture of semantic, pragmatic, and methodological considerations.

9.1   Definite Descriptions as Quantifiers

The most popular theory of definite descriptions originates with the philosopher Bertrand Russell (1905, 1919), who analyzed them as quantified phrases.

On Russell's account, a sentence of the form (3a) is true if and only if there is exactly one F and every F Gs (3b):

(3) a. [The F] Gs

   b. At least one thing is F, and at most one thing is F, and whatever is F Gs.

So (4) is true just in case there is exactly one last Pharaoh and he pondered:[1]

(4) The last Pharaoh pondered.

The Russellian analysis is embodied in the GQ axiom for *the*.[2] Recall that GQ includes an array of numerical quantifiers that share a combination of existential commitment and universal quantification. Among them are *the one*, *the two*, ..., *the n*. The truth of $[_S [_{NP}$ *the k* N'$]$ VP$]$ requires the existence of exactly k individuals that are values of N', and it requires that each individual that is a value of N' also be a value of VP. In GQ the definite determiner is interpreted identically to the determiner *the one*:

(5) Val($\langle X, Y \rangle$, *the*, σ) iff $|Y - X| = 0$ and $|Y| = 1$

This yields the GQ interpretation for (4) as in (6) (with syntactic details suppressed):

(6) Val(t, $[_S$ The last Pharaoh pondered], σ) iff
$|\{y : y \text{ is a last Pharaoh}\} - \{x : x \text{ pondered})| = 0$ and
$|\{y : y \text{ is a last Pharaoh}\}| = 1$

The RHS of (6) is equivalent to Russell's truth conditions. It requires all last Pharaohs to have pondered, and it requires there to be exactly one last Pharaoh.

9.1.1 Reference versus Denotation

In analyzing definite descriptions as quantified NPs, the GQ theory claims that their semantic values are not specific individuals but sets. Thus the value of $[_{NP}$ the last Pharaoh] is not the person who was the last Pharaoh, Nekhtharheb, but rather any set X that meets a certain condition, namely the one in (7):

(7) Val(X, $[_{NP}$ the last Pharaoh], σ) iff $|\{y : y \text{ is a last Pharaoh}\} - X| = 0$
and $|\{y : y \text{ is a last Pharaoh}\}| = 1$

(In English, "X is a value of *the last Pharaoh* with respect to σ if and only if there is no last Pharaoh that is not in X and the number of last Pharaohs is exactly 1.") Under this analysis, then, we must distinguish between the semantic value of a definite NP and the object that it intuitively refers to (if there is one). The semantic values are sets, but the intuitive referent is the individual that is the unique value of the embedded N'. Following Russell, we will call this unique individual (if he, she, or it exists) the **denotation** of the description. Thus we will say that *the last Pharaoh* denotes Nekhtharheb, the last Pharaoh, and that Nekhtharheb is the denotation of *the last Pharaoh*.

The relation between a definite description and its Russellian denotation differs sharply from the relation between a proper noun and its referent. This difference is reflected in truth conditions. Compare (7) with (8):

(8) Val(x, [$_{NP}$ Nekhtharheb], σ) iff x = Nekhtharheb

The latter yields truth conditions that depend crucially on how things stand with the particular individual Nekhtharheb. *Nekhtharheb pondered* is true just in case that very individual, Nekhtharheb, pondered:

(9) Val(t, [$_S$ Nekhtharheb pondered], σ) iff Nekhtharheb pondered

Thus the truth conditions of (9) are object-dependent in the sense discussed in 4.2.2. Use of a proper noun produces a sentence that is *about* a specific individual. By contrast, the truth conditions yielded by (7) lack this sort of object dependence. The RHS of (6) does not specify how things stand with a fixed, specific individual but rather specifies a general condition: that there is some object or other—it doesn't matter which—that is the one and only last Pharaoh and that pondered.

9.1.2 Some Virtues of the Quantificational Account

The GQ analysis of definite descriptions is attractive in many respects. The Russellian truth conditions it assigns to definites seem to capture important uses of these expressions. Furthermore, the analysis can be extended to cover a variety of phenomena involving definite NPs.

Truth Conditions

We have noted that Russell's semantics makes definite descriptions object-independent. This result seems correct in many cases and to distinguish definites appropriately from proper nouns and other referring terms. To test your intuitions on this, suppose I say (10) to you, intending to communicate something about Mr. John Major, who I assume is the prime minister.

(10) The prime minister of England is a Conservative.

Suppose further that, unknown to us, in the interval since we last listened to the news, Mr. Major has been replaced as prime minister by another member of his party, who is also conservative. Does what I say continue to be true? Many would hold that it does. Despite my intention to speak about Mr. Major, what I said does continue to be literally true. If correct, this result shows that the truth of (10) does not depend on the factual circumstances of any particular individual or on the speaker's intentions to communicate about a particular individual. It is object-independent, concerned only with whatever individual meets the description.

The existence assertion entailed by Russell's truth conditions for definites also appears correct in a great many cases. As Neale (1990a) observes, examples like (11a–c), involving definite descriptions that fail to denote any individual, seem to be straightforwardly false:

(11) a. This morning my father had breakfast with the king of France.
      b. The king of France was interviewed on *The Tonight Show* last night.
      c. The king of France shot my cat.

Examples (12a–12c) are analogous:

(12) a. The first Russian to land on the moon visited me today.
      b. The largest even number is greater than 5.
      c. The village of Monrovia is two miles west of Port Jefferson, N.Y.

Although judgments are admittedly less clear with famous cases like (13) (from Strawson 1950), which contains a predicate that attributes a stable, relatively time-independent property, clearly for many examples with definite descriptions, existence appears to be asserted.

(13) The present king of France is bald.

Finally, the uniqueness assertion contained in Russell's truth conditions also seems to capture an important fact about definites. Certainly a strong and common intuition about the use of (14a) versus (14b) is that the former is appropriate for cases where there was a unique contest winner, whereas the latter is appropriate where there was more than one:

(14) a. The winner of the contest was featured in the news.
      b. A winner of the contest was featured in the news.

This intuition receives further support from examples like (15a–c), where the superlative adjective independently entails that there be only one individual satisfying the predicate in question (that is, there can be but one strongest man, one tallest mountain, one fastest plane). As we see, the superlative mandates the presence of the definite determiner and strongly resists indefinites:[3]

(15) a. The/#a/#some strongest man in the world was on TV.
    b. Sir Edmund Hilary climbed the/#a/#some tallest mountain in the world.
    c. The/#a fastest plane in the world flew at better than Mach 5.

Interestingly, there are cases where we appear to be able to use definites smoothly, even in the presence of more than one individual that meets the description. "Pick up *the newspaper*," "Put out *the cat*," etc., are familiar cases in point. We will return to them directly.

Scope

Russell's theory deals straightforwardly with interactions between definite descriptions and various scopal items, such as negations and modal verbs. Consider (16):

(16) The king of France is not bald.

Russell (1905) observes that this sentence permits two readings. On one reading, (16) is true, since there is no king of France to be bald. On the other reading, (16) is false, since it attributes being not bald to the king of France, and there is no king of France around to be hirsute. On the quantificational account, this ambiguity can be analyzed as a matter of scope. Movement at logical form will yield the two structures in (17a) and (17b):

(17) a. [$_S$ It is not the case that [$_S$ [$_{NP_1}$ the king of France] [$_S$ t_1 is bald]]]
    b. [$_S$ [$_{NP_1}$ The king of France] [$_S$ it is not the case that [$_S$ t_1 is bald]]]

Under GQ, (17a) will be true if and only if the embedded quantified sentence is false, i.e., if and only if it is not the case that the number of kings of France is one and every king of France of bald. By contrast, (17b) will be true just in case the number of kings of France is one and every King of France is not bald, or, more idiomatically, just in case there is exactly one king of France and he is not bald.

    Similarly, consider the ambiguous (18) (due to Quine (1960)):

(18) The number of planets might have been even.

On one reading, this sentence is true, since it might have been the case that the number of planets was an even number, rather than the number it actually is (nine). On the other reading, (18) is false, since the number of planets that there actually are, namely nine, could not possibly have been even; that is, the number nine could not possible have been even, mathematics being what it is. Again this ambiguity can be seen as arising by scopal movement at LF. The logical forms in (19) give relevant structures for the two readings:[4]

(19) a. $[_S\ e$ might have been $[_S\ [_{NP_1}$ the number of planets$]\ [_S\ t_1$ even$]]]$
b. $[_S\ [_{NP_1}$ The number of planets$]\ [_S\ t_1$ might have been $[_S\ t_1$ even$]]]$

Complex Descriptions

The GQ analysis can be extended to handle possessive noun phrases, which are widely held to be a species of definite description. These include NPs like *Jill's book* or *that man's picture of Phil*, with structures as in (20). The phrases *Jill's* and *that man's* are analyzed here as complex determiners, and the element *'s* is treated as a lexical item of category Poss.

(20) a.
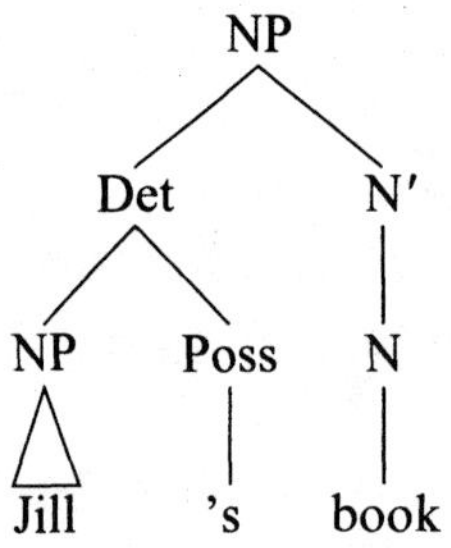

b.
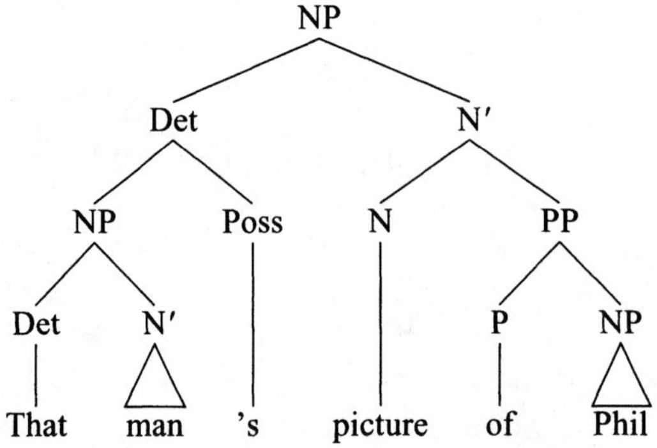

Complex possessive determiners can be interpreted via the axiom in (21):

(21) $\text{Val}(\langle X, Y \rangle, [_{\text{Det}} \text{ NP Poss}], \sigma)$ iff for some z, $\text{Val}(z, \text{NP}, \sigma)$ and $\text{Val}(\langle X, Y, z \rangle, \text{Poss}, \sigma)$

The possessive element itself (*'s*) may be analyzed as a three-place determiner-like relation taking an individual and two sets as arguments (22):

(22) $\text{Val}(\langle X, Y, z \rangle, 's, \sigma)$ iff $|(Y \cap \{w : z \text{ has } w\}) - X| = 0$ and $|Y \cap \{w : z \text{ has } w\}| = 1$

Note that (22) incorporates the familiar Russellian semantics and is very similar to the axiom for *the*, (5). The main difference is that in place of the simple set Y, we have $(Y \cap \{w : z \text{ has } w\})$. This modification restricts the nominal set to objects possessed by the individual that is picked out by the NP in the possessive phrase (*Jill*, *that man*, etc.). In effect, *'s* is analyzed as if it meant *the . . . that z has*, where z is the value of that NP.

As the reader can easily verify, (21) and (22) (together with obvious additions for the noun and verb) yield the following T sentence for *Jill's book opened* in GQ:

(23) $\text{Val}(t, [_{\text{S}} \text{ Jill's book opened}], \sigma)$ iff
$|(\{y : y \text{ is a book}\} \cap \{w : \text{Jill has } w\}) - \{x : x \text{ opened}\}| = 0$ and
$|\{y : y \text{ is a book}\} \cap \{w : \text{Jill has } w\}| = 1$

These truth conditions are Russellian. For *Jill's book opened* to be true, there must be a book that Jill has, there must be a unique book that Jill has, and every book that Jill has must have opened. These are the same truth conditions as would be assigned to *The book that Jill has opened*, containing a definite NP with the determiner *the*.

Predicate Descriptions

Definite descriptions occur not only in argument positions, as subjects and objects, (24), but also in predicate positions, (25) and (26):

(24) The president of the United States got a haircut.

(25) a. Bill Clinton is $\Big\{$ $[_{\text{AP}} \text{ tall}]$
      b. $[_{\text{NP}} \text{ the president of the United States}]$
      c. $[_{\text{NP}} \text{ Hilary Rodham's husband}]$

(26) a. We consider him $\left\{\begin{array}{l} [_{AP} \text{ tall}] \\ [_{NP} \text{ the president of the United States}] \\ [_{NP} \text{ Hilary Rodham's husband}] \end{array}\right.$

    b.

    c.

It is often suggested that these **predicate descriptions** should also be treated as Russellian quantifiers, just like argument descriptions. Suppose we analyze the *be* in (25) and its null variant in (26) as the *be* **of identity**, with the semantics in (27):

(27) Val($\langle x, y \rangle$, *be*, σ) iff $x = y$

Then if the predicate descriptions are assigned scope in the usual way at LF (28a, b), *Bill Clinton is the president of the United States* will be true if and only if the unique individual that is president of the United States is identical to Bill Clinton. Likewise, *Bill Clinton is Hilary Rodham's husband* will be true just in case the unique individual that is the husband of Hilary Rodham is Bill Clinton.

(28) a. $[_S [_{NP_1} \text{ The president of the United States}] [_S \text{ Bill Clinton is } t_1]]$

    b. $[_S [_{NP_1} \text{ Hilary Rodham's husband}] [_S \text{ Bill Clinton is } t_1]]$

   This proposal is attractive in that it requires no special additions for predicate descriptions, but still assigns plausible truth conditions. However, McCawley (1981a) notes an interesting problem for the general view that predicate descriptions are uniformly quantifiers co-occurring with the *be* of identity. To set up the point, consider first example (29) (from McCawley). Observe that this sentence is ambiguous with respect to Mr. Moskowitz's desires. On one reading, there is an individual satisfying the description and M.M. wants to meet him, (29a). On the second reading M.M. wants to meet whoever satisfies the description, (29b):

(29) Michael Moskowitz wants to meet the mayor of Heppleworth, Iowa.

    a. There is a unique mayor of Heppleworth, Iowa, such that Michael Moskowitz wants to meet him, that very person.

    b. Michael Moskowitz wants to meet the mayor of Heppleworth, Iowa, whoever that individual may turn out to be.

This kind of ambiguity is widely taken to arise through scope. The underlying structure of (29) contains an embedded infinitival sentence whose inaudible subject (PRO) refers back to the main-clause subject (M.M.). The first reading corresponds to an LF in which the description raises and has scope outside the embedded infinitive, (30a). The second reading corresponds to an LF in which the description raises and has scope within the embedded S, (30b).

(30) a. $[_S [_{NP_1}$ The mayor of H]
        $[_S$ Michael Moskowitz wants $[_S$ PRO to meet $t_1]]]$
    b. $[_S$ Michael Moskowitz wants
        $[_S [_{NP_1}$ the mayor of H] $[_S$ PRO to meet $t_1]]]$

With these points in mind, consider now example (31), which is similar to (29) except that it contains *be* instead of *meet*. McCawley states that this example contrasts with the previous one in having *three* distinct readings (31a–c):

(31) Michael Moskowitz wants to be the mayor of Heppleworth, Iowa.

    a. There is a certain unique mayor of Heppleworth, Iowa, such that Michael Moskowitz wants to be that individual.
    b. Michael Moskowitz wants to be the individual who is mayor of Heppleworth, Iowa, whoever that individual may turn out to be.
    c. Michael Moskowitz wants to be mayor of Heppleworth, Iowa.

The first two readings express desires about identity. On the first, there is a certain person matching the description that M.M. wants to be. On the second, M.M. wants to be whatever person matches the description. The third reading, however, does not concern identity. Rather, M.M. simply wants to be mayor of Heppleworth, to hold that office. Intuitively, this reading differs from the other two.

As McCawley points out, a uniform, quantificational analysis of descriptions will furnish LFs for the two readings that express desires about identity: (32a) will correspond to (31a), and (32b) to (31b). But this analysis leaves no distinct structure for the third, predicational reading. What is the LF for it?

(32) a. $[_S [_{NP_1}$ the mayor of H] $[_S$ Michael Moskowitz wants $[_S$ PRO to be $t_1]]]$
    b. $[_S$ Michael Moskowitz wants $[_S [_{NP_1}$ the mayor of H] $[_S$ PRO to be $t_1]]]$
    c. ?

A natural idea is that this reading matches a structure in which the definite description is not a quantifier at all, and so does not undergo scopal movement. The LF for (31c) would therefore be (33):

(33) $[_S$ Michael Moskowitz wants $[_S$ PRO to be $[_{NP}$ the mayor of H]]]$

So if we assume that there are both quantified and predicational occurrences of definite descriptions, we will have LFs for each of the three readings of (31).

This proposal may seem incompatible at first with Russell's semantics for definites. After all, the latter requires quantificational truth conditions for sentences with definite descriptions. Doesn't this mean that definites have to be quantified NPs, as in GQ? In fact, it does not. Russell's truth conditions and definites-as-quantified-NPs are really two quite independent things.[5] The easiest way to see this is to consider some actual rules. Suppose that we take (34) and (35) as our axioms governing definite descriptions when they occur as predicates.[6]

(34) Val(x, [$_{NP}$ Det N'], σ) iff for some Y, Val($\langle x, Y\rangle$, Det, σ) and
$Y = \{y : \text{Val}(y, \text{N'}, \sigma)\}$

(35) Val($\langle x, Y\rangle$, *the*, σ) iff $x \in Y$ and $|Y| = 1$

Notice that (34) analyzes these NPs as taking *individuals* as their values, like other predicates, not as taking sets as values, like quantifiers. An individual x is a value of the NP just in case the pair $\langle x, Y\rangle$ is a value of the determiner, where Y is the set of objects that are values of N'. According to the second rule, (35), a pair $\langle x, Y\rangle$ is a value of the definite determiner if and only if x is a member of Y and Y has only one member.

As the reader can easily show, these rules assign *Chris is the mayor* the truth conditions in (36a), which is equivalent to (36b) (by (SI)):

(36) a. Val(t, [$_S$ Chris is the mayor], σ) iff for some x, $x = $ Chris and
x is a mayor and $|\{y : y \text{ is a mayor}\}| = 1$
  b. Val(t, [$_S$ Chris is the mayor], σ) iff Chris is a mayor and
$|\{y : y \text{ is a mayor}\}| = 1$

The truth conditions in (36a) reveal why the predicate description can be associated with quantificational truth conditions even when it is not analyzed as a quantifier itself. The existential-quantificational force of the sentence arises from the composition axioms ("for some x") and not from the definite phrase. These truth conditions are Russellian in requiring a mayor to exist and in requiring there to be a unique mayor.

Predicate descriptions illustrate the considerable flexibility of Russell's basic account. Russell's truth conditions can be associated uniformly with sentences containing definite descriptions without our being obliged to analyze definites themselves as quantified in all occurrences. Definites can also be analyzed as predicates while still preserving the fundamental Russellian view.

9.1.3 Improper Descriptions

We noted earlier the requirement of uniqueness associated with Russellian definites. One interesting question for this requirement is posed by what are called **incomplete** or **improper descriptions**. These are definite descriptions that clearly fail to denote a single object but rather contain nouns satisfied by many objects. Examples of incomplete descriptions are easy to come by. We often say things like *Shut the door, Open the window, The baby is crying, I'm off to the office, Switch the radio off*, etc., when we know that there is more than one door, window, baby, office, radio, etc., in the universe. Indeed, there is often more than one in the immediate perceptual environment. Incomplete descriptions create a simple, prima facie difficulty for the Russellian account. Since an utterance of *The F Gs* is true only if there is exactly one *F*, utterances of incomplete descriptions turn out to be false.

Three responses to improper descriptions have been offered in the literature. These appeal to pragmatics, to ellipsis, and to what is sometimes called **domain selection**. Supporters of the Russellian treatment can deploy more than one of these responses, adopting different measures for different cases.

Pragmatics

The pragmatic response accepts that utterances of incomplete descriptions are false, literally speaking. But it holds that even though they are false, utterances of incomplete descriptions can be used pragmatically to convey the propositions that we understand them to be expressing. Thus when someone says (37) to you, what they are claiming is something false, namely that there is a unique door in the universe and that you have left it open.

(37) You left the door open.

But in saying (37), this person still gets across to you the idea that you have left open the particular door through which you entered. The person says something false but conveys something different and more plausible. The main difficulty with the proposal is that it is hard to see why speakers should be forced to thus speak falsely in these situations. Generally, one uses a clear falsehood to convey what one believes to be a truth only for some definite reason: out of politeness, coyness, a sense of drama, or, at the very least, for want of a better option. But in these cases there is no such motive: speakers are not being ironic or arch or coy. Moreover, as Millican (1990) points out, there are perfectly acceptable alternatives that do not require one to utter evident falsehoods. Thus instead saying *The door is open*, one might use (38) or (39):

(38) That door is open.

(39) A door is open.

Sentence (38) is available if the speaker is in a position to refer demonstratively to the door (by pointing, for example). And (39), along with elementary pragmatics, would work perfectly well. Hearing (39), you would know the speaker is not merely conveying that some door located somewhere or other was open. More must be meant. So you could infer that the relevant door was open. In view of these difficulties, the pragmatic response does not seem to be a forceful one.

Ellipsis

The ellipsis response holds that so-called incomplete descriptions really aren't incomplete after all, that there is additional material implicit in the description that completes it. The idea is that when someone utters (37), this is simply an abbreviated or elliptical version of something fuller, such as (40):

(40) You left the door through which you have just entered open.

A person saying (37) would thus be committed not to there being a unique door in the universe but only to there being a unique door through which you have just entered. The real, underlying utterance would then not be false. One simple challenge for the ellipsis response is noted by Donnellan (1968) and Wettstein (1981): typically there are countless different ways in which the description could be completed, but there appears to be no way of determining which of these completions is actually present. Thus suppose that Boris comes in, leaving the door open, and Natasha produces (41):

(41) The door is open.

Then each of the bracketed phrases in (42) is a suitable candidate for the missing material:

(42) a. The door [through which you just entered] is open.
       b. The door [that I am now pointedly looking at] is open.
       c. The door [to this room] is open.

> d. The door [that is immediately behind you] is open.
> e. The door [that is adjacent to that window] is open.

It seems unlikely that Natasha has some particular candidate in mind, to the exclusion of the others. It is not as if we would expect her to be able to tell us if we asked her. Moreover, even if Natasha herself did have a particular completion in mind, there is no way that Boris could tell what it was, nor indeed is there any need for him to do so. This last point seems particularly troublesome for the ellipsis account. For surely if there were a complete description implicit in the utterance of (41), then for Boris to really understand what Natasha had said, he would need to know which description she had intended. But this doesn't seem right. All he seems to have to know is which door she is talking about, and this is something he can discover without knowing which particular descriptive material Natasha might use to single it out.

The ellipsis response encounters another difficulty as well. In general, material that is semantically significant but phonetically unpronounced is treated in discourse as if it were nonetheless overt. Consider the dialogue in (43):

(43) *Chris*: Kiwis [$_{VP}$ fly].
    Kate: No, they don't [$_{VP}$ *e*].
    Phil: I agree with Kate: Kiwis don't fly.

Kate's response is elliptical, involving an elided VP [$_{VP}$ fly]. However, Phil's continuation makes it clear that he treats this missing material just as if it were part of Kate's spoken words. Similarly for the deleted *N'* in (44):

(44) *Chris*: Whose [$_{N'}$ picture of Kumiko] is that?
    Kate: It's Jill's [$_{N'}$ *e*].
    Phil: It is not Jill's picture of Kumiko; it's mine.

Given this result, if (41) were elliptical for one of (42a–e), we might expect an utterance of the first to be discourse-equivalent to an utterance of the second. But this doesn't seem to be so. Compare the dialogues in (45). Although the first is natural, the second is decidedly odd:

(45) a. *Natasha*: The door through which you just entered is open.
       Boris: Actually, I entered through the door some time ago.
       You've only just now noticed, that's all.
    b. *Natasha*: The door is open.
       Boris: #Actually, I came in through the door some time ago.
       You've only just now noticed, that's all.

The source of oddness in (45b) seems clear enough: while Natasha's utterance of *The door is open* commits her to the door being open, she is not committed to Boris's having just entered. This is not part of what she said, and hence is not something that can be overtly disputed or agreed with. If the definite description did contain an elliptical *through which you just entered*, we might expect such material to be on the table for discussion, as it is in (43) and (44). But that doesn't seem to be true. Since this result can be duplicated for any of the bracketed phrases in (42), it undermines the idea that incomplete descriptions involve ellipsis, at least as ellipsis is normally understood.

Domain Selection

The final and most promising response involves what may be called "domain selection." The proposal here is that when we use definites, the domain of quantification is not the universe at large but rather a subdomain of it that is small enough to allow just one thing to satisfy the nominal. So when someone says *The door is open*, the relevant domain might be objects in the immediate vicinity. The domain for (46) might be objects in the house.

(46) The baby is crying again. I'll see to it while you put the cat out, empty the trash, and put the kettle on.

   This proposal has an advantage over the previous one in that there is no need to search for any particular specification of the relevant domain. It doesn't matter how speaker or hearer conceive of the domain; it simply has to be clear what the domain is. Nonetheless, appeal to domain selection is not completely straightforward, since incompleteness often recurs within the smaller domain. Suppose, for example, that Boris has entered a room containing several doors. Natasha might well utter *The door is open* and successfully tell Boris that he has left open the door through which he has just entered. But if we operate with an unsophisticated, intuitive conception of domains of discourse, the other doors are in the domain as well: they are right there in the room, perceptually salient and easily available as objects of discussion. Somehow they have to be excluded.

   Of course, the domain-selection theory is not compelled to operate with the ordinary, intuitive conception of a domain of discourse. It may make use of a more technical conception. But then the burden is on that theory to come up with such a conception, and the relevant notion is, one must admit, none too clear. The only thing clear about the alleged domain for the utterance of *The door is open* is that the door through which Boris entered is in it, and no other doors are. Is the domain exhausted by that door, then, or are there other objects in it as well? If so, which objects? We are not aware of any principled answers to these questions.

Definite Descriptions and Standard Quantifiers

It is often suggested that Russell's quantificational account *must* be able to handle incomplete definites, since other quantifiers encounter the same problem.[7] After all, people say things like (47a–d) without intending something about the total number of persons in the entire universe who had a great time last night:

(47) a. Everyone had a great time last night.
     b. Nobody had a great time last night.
     c. Most people had a great time last night.
     d. Only three people had a great time last night.

Since the incompleteness problem is widespread among quantifiers, it appears to pose little threat to the quantificational treatment of definite descriptions in particular. Some analysis must be available for these other cases, and whatever analysis is available there will carry over to definite descriptions treated as quantifiers. So the argument goes.

This argument is attractive in assimilating incomplete definite descriptions to a larger, more general issue. Before accepting it, however, we should make sure that the incompleteness found with other quantifiers is genuinely similar to that facing quantificationally treated definite descriptions. Are the two cases really parallel? In fact, it's not so clear. To return to our earlier example, suppose that Boris enters the hall twice through different doors, each time leaving the door open. Suppose that there are five doors in the room, and consider (41) (repeated below) versus (48):

(41) The door is open.

(48) Every door is open.

Whereas Natasha could say something true by uttering (41) in this situation, it certainly doesn't seem that she could do so by uttering (48). But if the mechanisms governing domains are the same in the two cases, then this is mysterious. If the domain of quantification can shrink small enough to exclude all doors but the one Boris left open, which thereby allows Natasha to say something true with (41), one would expect the same possibility in the case of Natasha's saying (48). Evidently in the latter case the domain does *not* shrink to exclude all the doors except the two through which Boris entered, but why is this? The examples and situations appear parallel in relevant respects. If this is right, it weakens the simple claim of a parallel between definites and true quantifiers. The former may have to appeal to mechanisms not available in the latter case.

The upshot of these remarks is that incomplete or improper descriptions appear to remain an open question for the Russellian analysis. Although a number of responses have been proposed, in truth none looks completely satisfactory. Furthermore, the presence of incomplete standard quantifiers may not entirely lift the burden from the Russellian account. To do so, quantifiers and definites must be incomplete in a way that is fully parallel, but it is not entirely clear that this is so.

9.2 Definite Descriptions as Referring Terms

The Russellian analysis is broad, powerful, and widely held. However, it is not universally accepted. It has been argued that the Russellian account alone does not fully capture the semantics of definites and that alongside a quantificational interpretation there must also be a separate, referential interpretation in which definites behave as namelike terms that rigidly designate a particular object. On this view, *the last Pharaoh* would actually be ambiguous, receiving two interpretations. One is the familiar quantificational interpretation in (49):

(49) Val(X, [$_{NP}$ the last Pharaoh], σ) iff $|\{y : y$ is a last Pharaoh$\} - X| = 0$ and $|\{y : y$ is a last Pharaoh$\}| = 1$

The second is a referential interpretation, roughly along the lines of (50):

(50) Val(x, [$_{NP}$ the last Pharaoh], σ) iff $x = $ Nekhtharheb

This ambiguity in the NP would presumably arise from an ambiguity in the determiner *the*: English would contain two forms both pronounced [ðə].

The idea that English contains a definite determiner that is ambiguous in just this way is plausible on a number of grounds. For one thing, there are languages that seem to display the same ambiguity directly. Examples are German, modern Greek, and spoken colloquial Spanish. These languages exhibit the definite determiner in quantificational uses parallel to those found in English, (51a) to (53a). In addition, however, they also allow (and typically require) the definite determiner to co-occur with proper nouns in normal referring uses, (51b) to (53b):

(51) a. Der letzten Pharaoh ist weggegangen. (German)
        'The last Pharaoh is gone.'
     b. Der Hans ist weggegangen.
        'Hans is gone.'

(52) a. O teleutaios Faraw efuge. (Greek)
        'The last Pharaoh is gone.'
     b. O Kostis efuge.
        'Kostis is gone.'

(53) a. El ú'ltimo faraó'n se fue. (Spanish)
        'The last pharaoh is gone.'
     b. El Juan se fue.
        'John is gone.'

For languages like these, an ambiguity analysis seems nearly inescapable. Since the object of semantic theory is not English semantic competence but semantic competence generally, even if a strict Russellian analysis could be upheld for English, the question of quantificational/referential ambiguity would remain unsettled. We are responsible, in the end, for all that the human language faculty makes possible semantically, and whether this faculty countenances a quantificational/referential ambiguity in definite determiners cannot be decided from English data alone.

A second point is that English itself seems to show this general ambiguity in other parts of its grammar. Unlike German, Spanish, and Greek, English definite determiners do not co-occur productively with proper nouns. Examples like (54a–d) appear to be "frozen forms"—items that look like definites but are no longer syntactically analyzed that way by native speakers.

(54) a. the United Nations
     b. the Danube
     c. the Empire State Building
     d. Pike's Peak

However, determiner ambiguity of the relevant kind *does* seem to be present with the determiner *this*. As we know, canonical, demonstrative utterances of

[$_{NP}$ *this* N′] are referential. When used with an appropriate gesture or pointing, *this book*, *this problem*, *this man*, etc., refer rigidly to a specific individual:

(55) a. This book is interesting. (Said while raising the book.)
    b. I solved this problem. (Said while pointing.)
    c. Give this man a drink! (Said while gesturing.)

However, modern English also shows a second wide-spread use of [$_{NP}$ *this* N′] in which the phrase is neither demonstrative nor (it seems) referential. Rather, it behaves very much like an indefinite, existentially quantified expression:[8]

(56) a. There is this book I'm reading. (It's pretty long, but it has a lot of pictures.)
    b. I have this problem with my cat Cleo. (She keeps clawing the sofa.)
    c. This man went into a bar and ordered a drink. (The bartender brought him iced tea.)

What is possible with *this* is surely possible with *the*: the English definite determiner might be similarly ambiguous between a referential and a quantificational interpretation.

9.2.1   Referential Cases

The primary grounds for a referential analysis of the definite determiner have come neither from the behavior of definites in other languages nor from the behavior of other determiners in English but rather from semantic judgments. The argument has been made that in certain cases Russell's analysis does not seem to deliver the correct truth conditions and that in these cases, definites appear to be functioning as referring terms.

Incomplete Descriptions Again

We have already noted one class of this kind. Recall examples that raise the problem of incomplete or improper descriptions:

(57) a. The window is open.
    b. The kettle is boiling.
    c. The dog wants out.
    d. The car is making funny noises.

Such sentences can be uttered felicitously even when there is more than one object of the relevant kind in the immediate perceptual environment. We saw that in the absence of additional moves, Russell's account entailed that such utterances were simply false. We reviewed suggestions for countering this prediction by appeal to pragmatics, ellipsis, and domain selection. But we saw that none of these responses straightforwardly handled the problem.

By contrast, a referential analysis of definites appears to handle the matter well. On the occasions described, *the window, the kettle, the dog, the car*, etc., would be analyzed as referring directly to the relevant individuals and as saying something true about them. There is thus no question of justifying false speech, of having to find some missing material that completes a description, or of having to narrow down some putative domain of quantification. The definite picks out the relevant individual directly, with no mediation of descriptive material at all. This result accords well with our earlier judgment about (41) (repeated below) in a situation with multiple doors:

(41) The door is open.

We noted that if a complete description were implicit in Natasha's utterance of (41), then for Boris to understand Natasha, he would have to know which description she had used. But all he really has to know is which door she is talking about. This is all that is involved under a referential account.

Donnellan's Examples

The referential analysis also seems well suited to certain cases discussed by Donnellan (1966, 1978). In these, a definite description is used to pick out an object that turns out to be different from the description's Russellian denotation. To illustrate, suppose that we are at a party and you and I are speaking about the various people present. You turn to me and say (58), nodding at a man across the room.

(58) The man who is holding a martini is Albanian.

Suppose we later learn that although the individual in question is indeed Albanian, he was actually holding not a martini but rather a martini glass containing water and an olive. Suppose further that there was only one genuine martini drinker present at the party and that man was French. Given the domain as the individuals in the room, the Russellian account entails that when you uttered (58), you said something false about the Frenchman. However, a common intuition is that, on the contrary, when you uttered (58), you said something true about the Albanian. Many people would judge that you didn't say something general holding of the unique individual that satisfies the descriptive material *who is holding a martini.* Rather, you said something about the particular man indicated.

Donnellan calls this sort of use of a definite description a **referential use** and contrasts it with what he calls an **attributive use**. To illustrate the difference, consider (59), uttered in two different circumstances.

(59) Smith's murderer is insane.

In the first circumstance, Mr. Jones has been charged with the murder of Smith. We are at the trial, where Jones is ranting, raving, and behaving very strangely. Noting this behavior, you say (59) with a clear intention to talk about Jones. In the second circumstance, you are a coroner called in to view the remains of poor Mr. Smith. Seeing the shocking state of his body, you utter (59) without having any idea about who, in particular, murdered the unfortunate man.

In the first circumstance, if we later found that although Jones was indeed insane, he wasn't really Smith's murderer, we would still be strongly inclined to judge that you had said something true on the occasion. Whatever the mental state of Smith's true murderer, the fact is that Jones *was* insane. This is a referential use. By contrast, in the second case, the truth of what you said depends crucially on how things turn out with Smith's real murderer. Whoever that individual may be, he or she must be insane if you are to have spoken truly. The latter is an attributive use.

Donnellan argues that while Russell's quantificational treatment may suffice for attributive uses, it cannot account for the referential uses. This argument has some force in our view. Note that the judgments and reasoning employed by Donnellan are similar to those we employed earlier with proper nouns. In chapter 5 we considered whether a proper noun like *Peano* should be analyzed descriptively, as in (60):

(60) Val(x, *Peano*, σ) iff x is the discoverer of the Peano axioms for arithmetic

We rejected this proposal on the grounds that failure to meet the putative description did not block reference. Recall that even though Dedekind was the true discoverer of the Peano axioms for arithmetic, and not Peano, we do not judge (61) to be a true statement about Dedekind (the satisfier of the description in (60)). Rather, it is a false statement about Peano:

(61) Peano discovered the Peano axioms for arithmetic.

The situation is analogous with (58) and (59) on their referential uses. Failure to meet the descriptive condition is not enough to block reference. In both examples, the NP appears to pick out the individual in question, without regard to the descriptive material that appears.

9.2.2 Definite Descriptions As Demonstratives

Suppose we accept that definite descriptions do indeed refer in certain cases. How might this be captured formally in our semantic theory? One attractive proposal (due to Peacocke [1975]) is that when definite descriptions refer, they are behaving semantically as demonstrative expressions. So when a speaker utters a sentence containing a referring definite description as the subject, $[_S [_{NP}$ *The* N'] VP], this NP serves to pick out a particular object in the context, and the utterance is true just in case this object is a value of VP.

This suggestion may be implemented formally in our theory VRT, which includes demonstratives and other referentially variable terms. Recall that VRT factors the analysis of demonstratives into three components. There is Σ theory, which relates utterances of expressions in particular contexts to sequences of objects. Σ theory includes statements (62a, b), for example:

(62) a. For any u, for some σ', $\Sigma(u, \sigma')$
    b. If a speaker uses α_i in u to refer to x, then $\Sigma(u, \sigma)$ only if $\sigma(i) = x$

In addition, there are semantic rules that provide sequence-relative evaluation conditions for expressions. For complex demonstratives, these included the phrasal rule in (63) and the lexical rule in (64):

(63) $\mathrm{Val}(x, [_{NP} \ \underset{[+\text{demo}]}{\mathrm{Det}} \ \mathrm{N'}], \sigma)$ iff $\mathrm{Val}(x, \ \underset{[+\text{demo}]}{\mathrm{Det}}, \sigma)$

(64) $\mathrm{Val}(x, that_i, \sigma)$ iff $x = \sigma(i)$

Finally, there is the axiom in (65), which pools the results of Σ theory and the semantic rules and allows us to prove conditionalized T theorems:

(65) If u is an utterance of S and $\Sigma(u, \sigma)$, then u is true iff $\mathrm{Val}(t, S, \sigma)$.

To assimilate definite descriptions to demonstratives, we must add rules allowing us to prove conditionalized T theorems. As it turns out, with the apparatus already in place, it is enough to add the one lexical axiom (66) for demonstrative *the*. This rule is completely analogous to the one for *that*.

(66) $\text{Val}(x, \textit{the}_i, \sigma)$ iff $x = \sigma(i)$ for all $i \geq 1$

The rules for referential definites will apply to structures different from those found in the quantificational case: there must be an ambiguity in logical form corresponding to the ambiguity of meaning. Consider an example like *The baby protests*. On a quantificational interpretation, this sentence receives the LF in (67a): *the* is a quantifier, and the description moves to take scope. On a referential interpretation, the sentence gets the LF in (67b): here the determiner is an indexed, referentially variable term, and the description remains in situ.

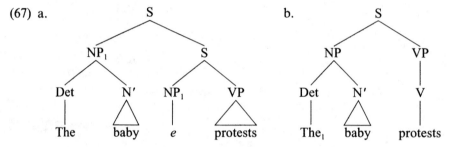

As the reader may verify, when we apply (62) through (66) to (67b), we derive a conditionalized T sentence of the desired form:

(68) If *u* is an utterance of $[_S [_{NP} \text{ The}_1 \text{ baby}] \text{ protests}]$, then
       u is true iff $\sigma(1)$ protests

These are object-dependent truth conditions; the truth of the sentence depends crucially on how things stand with the particular individual $\sigma(1)$.

Demonstratives and Referential Use

A demonstrative analysis of referential *the* accords well with Donnellan's examples noted above. We saw that the nominal in a definite description need not contribute to the truth conditions of an utterance, nor need it block reference to an individual that it fails to describe. Thus *The man who is holding a martini is Albanian* might be true without the individual referred to being a man holding a martini. Likewise, *Smith's murderer is insane* might be true without Jones's having murdered Smith.

Under a demonstrative analysis of *the*, these results assimilate directly to those discussed in chapter 6 in connection with example (69):

(69) That fox is making a terrible mess.

Recall that if someone comes home to find a small mammal rummaging through their garbage can and utters (69), then even if this animal should turn out to be a badger and not a fox, what they say is not thereby made false, nor is reference impeded. The demonstrative still picks out the relevant individual. Our analysis of demonstratives entails this result. The rule for complex demonstratives in (63) ignores N′ and gives the semantic value of $[_{NP}$ Det N′$]$ solely in terms of the contribution of Det. Furthermore, Σ theory allows the designated individual to appear in the appropriate sequence position regardless of whether it satisfies the nominal. Σ theory does *not* specify something like (70), for example:

(70) If a speaker uses $[_{NP}\ [_{Det}\ the_i\ ]\ N']$ in u to refer to x, then
$[+demo]$

$\Sigma(u, \sigma)$ only if $\sigma(i) = x$ and Val(y, N′, σ)

Because of this, the (conditionalized) truth conditions for (69) do not require the individual to be a fox. Likewise, the conditionalized truth conditions for *The₁ man who is holding a martini is an Albanian* do not require the relevant individual to be a man holding a martini.

Of course, we did not claim, and do not claim now with definites, that the nominal makes no contribution at all. In a use of *the baby* there is some kind of implied, pragmatic understanding that what is referred to is a baby. This information is analogous to gender in pronouns, where the use of *he* suggests, but does not require, that what is being referred to is male. The appeal to pragmatics with definites presumably applies to certain other kinds of information as well. Definite descriptions differ somewhat from other demonstratives in the way that reference is determined. Suppose, for example, that a group of managers is having lunch in a pub. One of them, Kate, begins to feel that she should be getting back to work. Clearly, (71) is a more natural sentence for Kate in this context than (72):

(71) I'd better be getting back to the office.

(72) I'd better be getting back to that office.

In the absence of any act of demonstration, (72) begs the question "Which office?" in a way that (71) does not. Demonstratives with *this* and *that* seem to require some act of demonstration, or at least a special sort of perceptual salience on the part of their referent, if they are to refer. A definite description, by contrast, seems to automatically pick out the most salient object in the context that is a value of its embedded noun. Thus Kate's utterance of (71) is naturally interpreted as being about the office most salient to the assembled party. On a demonstrative analysis too, this additional information is presumably a pragmatic matter. Use of *that* and *this* implies that the referent is a perceptually salient satisfier of the nominal, while use of demonstrative *the* implies that the referent is the contextually most salient satisfier of the nominal.

9.3   A Pragmatic Alternative

The account sketched above entails the existence in English of two definite determiners, both pronounced [ðə], associated with two different semantic axioms and appearing in two different kinds of structures.

This ambiguity account of *the* has been challenged in an influential article by Kripke (1977). Kripke suggests that the phenomena motivating a referential analysis of *the* are not really semantic phenomena at all, and that a strict Russellian analysis supplemented by an independently motivated pragmatics yields a better account. Kripke's challenge thus raises an important question about the proper division of labor between semantics and pragmatics in explaining these facts.

9.3.1   Referential Interpretation versus Referential Use

Kripke's counterproposal is based on a simple and familiar fact about speech and communication, namely that we can use statements that mean something quite general to convey information about specific individuals. Everyday examples of this are easy to find. Suppose that we are waiting in a checkout line and a person cuts in front of us. You turn to me and utter (73):

(73) Some people have no manners.

Literally speaking, what you have said is that there exist mannerless people in the world. But in this context, you've clearly conveyed something more specific than that. You have conveyed that a *particular person*, the individual who cut in, is without manners. You have used a statement about people in general to convey something about him or her in particular.

This phenomenon occurs widely with quantifiers. Suppose a group of anxious students come to my office to ask about their results on a recent exam. I might use (74), a general, quantified statement, to convey something about the specific individuals gathered in the room:

(74) Every student currently in my office did very well on the test.

Similarly, suppose we are at a party and see Bloggs and Spratt, the well-known convicted embezzlers, lurking around. I might use the quantified sentence (75) to convey the information that the particular persons Bloggs and Spratt are flirting with your sister:[9]

(75) Two convicted embezzlers are flirting with your sister.

Finally, suppose that Bloggs is the only person standing in the corner holding a champagne glass, and that this is apparent to both you and me. I might utter (76) or even (77) to convey that Bloggs is flirting with your sister:

(76) Exactly one person is drinking champagne in that corner, and he is flirting with your sister.

(77) Not everyone in that corner is abstaining from champagne, and any such nonabstainer is flirting with your sister.

In accounting for such phenomena, we could assume an ambiguity in the determiners in question. We could suppose that along with its quantificational axioms for *some*, *all*, *two*, *exactly one*, etc., English contains referential axioms as well, perhaps demonstrative axioms along the lines suggested above for *the*. Then, together with their quantificational structures and object-independent truth conditions, examples like (73) to (77) would also have referential structures and object-dependent truth conditions. Example (73), for instance, would have a structure and interpretation in which it was literally about the person who had cut in front of us, etc.

While such a view is clearly possible, it seems to miss something important. It seems to miss the distinction between what we literally *say* with our words and what they *convey* or *suggest* in a given context. Put differently, it misses the difference between the literal interpretation of a word or phrase and what it can be used to say on a given occasion. The difference is a familiar one that we have already touched upon in chapter 1. This seems to be what is operative in (73) to (77). In each of these cases, we are saying one thing but conveying something stronger. We are making a general, quantified statement that, in itself, doesn't concern any particular individuals but, taken in the context, conveys something stronger, something about specific individuals. Given this, it seems a mistake to propose a new referential interpretation of the quantifiers involving new axioms. What's involved here is not a *referential interpretation* of *some*, *all*, *two*, *exactly one*, etc., but rather a *referential use*.

Kripke suggests that this phenomenon is also what is behind the referential readings of definite descriptions. The idea is that these are not independent referential interpretations of the definites but rather referential uses of the one Russellian quantificational interpretation. So in the case of (59) (repeated below), you intend to make a claim about Jones and succeed in getting me, your audience, to take you to be talking about Jones.

(59) Smith's murderer is insane.

But the words you used do not strictly and literally express that claim. What you said, strictly and literally, is that Smith's murderer is insane. The reference to Jones is thus a pragmatic fact, not a semantic one. Semantically, Jones is out of the picture.

Notice an important empirical claim about this proposal: if Smith's real murderer is not insane, then what you've said is literally false. For example, if someone other than Jones murdered Smith, Brown, say, and Brown is sane, then your utterance of (59) is false, and it is false even if Jones is as mad as a hatter. You may believe that Jones murdered Smith, and so believe that *Smith's murderer* denotes Jones. When you use the expression *Smith's murderer*, you may take yourself to be using an expression that denotes Jones. I, your audience, may be aware of all this, and so take your utterance to be an attempt to express a belief about Jones. But none of this makes your statement semantically about Jones. What you actually said is something general and Russellian, so the Kripkean argument goes.

9.3.2 A Pragmatic Typology

Kripke's pragmatic account of referential readings for definites is attractive on general grounds. The account simplifies our semantic theory: rather than multiplying axioms, we can instead appeal to a pragmatic explanation that is well motivated on independent grounds. Furthermore, the general approach can be extended to handle a wide range of cases involving quantifiers.

Ludlow and Neale (1991) provide a helpful typology of quantifier uses based on Kripke's account. Their typology is constructed around a three-fold distinction that is largely implicit in what we've observed so far:

- What a speaker literally says with his or her words. This is the **proposition expressed** (PE).
- What a speaker intends to convey with his or her words. This is the **proposition meant** (PM).
- The evidence or beliefs that the speaker has for making the statement that he or she makes. These are the **speaker's grounds** (SG).

With these notions Ludlow and Neale distinguish between a **pure quantificational use** of a quantifier, a **referential use**, and a **specific use**.

The Pure Quantificational Use

A pure quantificational use is one in which the proposition expressed, the proposition meant, and the speaker's grounds are all general. To give an example with a definite description, suppose a recent general election has taken place in Britain. Jill and I know the names of the parties involved, but we know nothing about the individuals who lead them. Jill sees a newspaper announcing that the Conservative Party has won a substantial majority in parliament. On the basis of this, she utters (78) to me, attempting to convey the upshot of the election:

(78) The prime minister of England is a Conservative.

On the Russellian analysis, Jill would be expressing a completely general proposition, namely that there is a unique prime minister of England and this person is a Conservative. Furthermore, her intention was to say something general. Under this circumstance, she could have also used the sentence *The prime minister of England, whoever he is, is a Conservative*, where the nonspecific character of the definite description is made explicit. Finally, her grounds for making the assertion are general as well. She doesn't know anything about specific individuals, only about parties and the overall election results.

Adapting from Ludlow and Neale 1991, we might represent the pure quantificational use of a definite description as follows:

(79) The pure quantificational use of a definite

    PE: There is exactly one F, and it is G.
    PM: There is exactly one F, and it is G.
    SG: There is exactly one F, and it is G.

In each case we have a general Russellian proposition. In our particular example, F is *prime minister of England* and G is *a Conservative.*

The Referential Use

A referential use is one where the proposition expressed is general but the proposition meant and the speaker's grounds for making the assertion are both singular, that is, about specific individuals. Again suppose that the general election has just taken place. But suppose now that Jill and I are very familiar with the British political scene. Jill sees a newspaper announcing that John Major has become prime minister, and she knows that I too will have have heard the news. Having a dim view of Mr. Major's political abilities, she utters (80) to me, intending to point out one of his faults:

(80) The prime minister of England is an ineffective politician.

Jill has asserted the general proposition that there is a unique prime minister of England and this person is an ineffective politician. But in virtue of our shared background knowledge, she has conveyed the stronger, singular proposition that Mr. John Major is an ineffective politician. Furthermore, the grounds for her assertion are singular as well: she said what she did on the basis of her beliefs about the specific individual John Major. The referential use of the definite description would therefore be represented as in (81):

(81) The referential use of a definite

    PE: There is exactly one F, and it is G.
    PM: $G(a)$
    SG: $G(a)$

While the proposition expressed is a general, Russellian one, the proposition meant and the speaker's grounds are a singular proposition about a specific individual a. Here F is *prime minister of England* and G is *an ineffective politician*, and a is *John Major*.

The Specific Use

A specific use is one where the proposition expressed and the proposition meant are general but the speaker's grounds for making the assertion are singular. Again suppose the election has taken place, but in this case Jill is an expert on British politics, and I am not. Jill knows that I am a novice in these matters. She sees a newspaper announcing that Mr. Major has become prime minister. Again she utters (80) to me, this time intending to communicate that Britain's highest elected official has serious faults

(80) The prime minister of England is an ineffective politician.

Jill has asserted the general proposition that there is a unique prime minister of England and this person is an ineffective politician. And knowing my weak knowledge of British politics, she intended only to convey something general. Nonetheless, the grounds for her assertion are singular. Her assertion was based on beliefs about the particular individual John Major. We represent this specific use of a definite description as in (82):

(82) The specific use of a definite

     PE: There is exactly one F, and it is G.
     PM: There is exactly one F, and it is G.
     SG: $G(a)$

The values of F, G, and a are the same as in (81).

The Ludlow and Neale typology is applicable to many quantifiers, and it suggests useful ways of understanding their differences. For example, we noted earlier that phrases of the form [*this* N′] can be used similarly to phrases of the form [*an* N′] in American English. *This Egyptian* in (83b) can function like the indefinite, existential phrase *an Egyptian* in (83a):

(83) a. There is an Egyptian in my department.
      b. There is this Egyptian in my department.

Even though (83a) and (83b) are close in meaning, there is still an intuitively felt difference between the two. Roughly speaking, (83b) implies that the speaker is actually acquainted with the individual in question or has a particular individual in mind, whereas (83a) does not. In terms of the typology above, one simple way of phrasing this is to say that *this* N′ as an indefinite is conventionally associated with a specific use. Use of *this* N′ versus *a(n)* N′ implicates that the speaker has singular grounds for his or her assertion.

9.3.3 Semantics or Pragmatics?

We have considered two accounts of referential phenomena with definite descriptions. One, a semantic account, proposes that definite descriptions are ambiguous between a quantificational and a demonstrative interpretation. It entails two separate axioms and two different structural configurations. The second, a pragmatic account, proposes that definite descriptions are unambiguous, with a strict Russellian quantificational interpretation and a single structural realization. Referential phenomena are analyzed as nonsemantic—something that can be conveyed by use of a description but not literally expressed. Which account is right? Is *the* ambiguous or not?

Initially, the Kripkean pragmatic account seems more attractive. It involves fewer semantic axioms for English. Furthermore, it appeals to notions about what is said and what is conveyed that are both plausible and independently motivated. On this basis, some, including Kripke himself, have argued that the pragmatic analysis is preferable on methodological grounds. It appears to yield the simpler theory.

For our part, we don't find these points decisive. First, nearly all of the apparatus necessary for the semantic account is also independently motivated and available. This account assimilates definite descriptions to (complex) demonstrative expressions, and both the syntax and the semantics for the latter is independently required and already in place. The only genuine addition that has to be made under the semantic account of referential definites is the one axiom (66). The difference in simplicity thus amounts at most to a single lexical rule.

Second, while the pragmatic account provides genuine insight into the use of quantifiers to express particular propositions, and while it might explain some of the referential readings of definites, it appears to offer no account of the apparent quantificational readings with *this* phrases noted earlier. There is no sense, then, in which the analysis furnishes a way of eliminating determiner ambiguity in English as a whole, even ambiguity that is intuitively of a very similar kind.

Third, it's not at all clear that the pragmatic account can deal with incomplete descriptions, as we argued in section 9.1.3

Fourth and perhaps most telling, it is not so clear that the pragmatic account is really simpler after all, even taken on its own terms. Recall our earlier point that the aim of semantic theory is not a theory of English semantic competence but of human semantic competence in general. Although we explore and construct theories for particular languages, our goal is to discover what the human language faculty makes possible for all languages. We have already observed that a referential/quantificational ambiguity with definite determiners seems inescapable in other languages. If this is correct, there really is no sense in which the pragmatic account offers a simpler general solution. To put the point somewhat differently, given our goal, evaluations of simplicity do not apply at the level of individual grammars for individual languages. Rather, they apply at the level of the theory of grammar. If the pragmatic analysis is going to save us anything, it has to be able to obviate a referential analysis of *the* everywhere. This looks dubious for other languages, and if it cannot be avoided there, there is no particular advantage in avoiding it in English.

Some Empirical Points

If the question of the ambiguity with *the* cannot be decided on narrow methodological grounds, then the criteria that remain to us are just the usual ones: we must look for further empirical arguments. There are additional facts that seem worth noting in this context.

Kripke's account predicts certain judgments about truth and falsity for Donnellan's cases. For example, when it turns out that Smith's murderer is a perfectly sane person, we should judge (59) to be false, even if Jones (the person intended) is insane:

(59) Smith's murderer is insane.

While many people do get Kripke's predicted intuition, in our experience there is always a firm residue of people that do not. Those that do not get the Kripke intuition typically react as speakers do with any ambiguous string, such as (84):

(84) Old men and women are vulnerable.

That is, they hold that, like (84), (59) may be true on one way of taking the words (here, when *Smith's murderer* refers to Jones) and false on the other way of taking the words (that is, when *Smith's murderer* denotes Brown).

Second, there are phenomena showing a parallel between pronouns, demonstratives, and definite descriptions that excludes other quantifiers. Consider the "*such that* relative" construction in (85a). This is similar to the more familiar *wh-* relative clause in (85b), except that it involves *such that* in place of the *wh-* operator and a pronoun (*him*) in place of the trace (t_1):

(85) a. Every boy [such that you gave him an A on the exam] will get a prize.
     b. Every boy [whom$_1$ you gave t_1 an A on the exam] will get a prize.

Interestingly, the range of forms for *such that* relatives is broader than what is shown. In place of the pronoun, one can also have a demonstrative (*that boy*) and a definite description (*the boy*) and preserve the same reading. Other quantified NPs, including ones that are intuitively similar to definite descriptions on the Russellian account (*a unique boy*, *exactly one boy*) are flatly excluded however:

(86) every boy [such that you gave
$\left\{\begin{array}{l}\text{him} \\ \text{that boy} \\ \text{the boy} \\ \text{*a boy} \\ \text{*a unique boy} \\ \text{*exactly one boy}\end{array}\right\}$
an A on the exam]

A similar parallelism is seen with (87), which involves a quantified possessive determiner and a pronoun in object position. In place of the pronoun we can also have a demonstrative and a definite description, which preserve the initial reading. Other quantified NPs are not permitted, however, without a shift in reading:

(87) Every boy's mother loves
$\left\{\begin{array}{l}\text{him.} \\ \text{that boy.} \\ \text{the boy.} \\ \text{*a boy.} \\ \text{*a unique boy.} \\ \text{*exactly one boy.}\end{array}\right\}$

The force of these examples is considerable. In each we seem to be dealing with elements that are functioning as bound variables. As we will discuss more fully in the next chapter, such readings are possible only if the bound element is sequence-sensitive. In the case of pronouns and demonstratives, this sequence-sensitivity is immediate: it follows directly from their semantic axioms. The fact that definite descriptions too can function as bound variables suggests that they too are sequence-sensitive. This is just what is predicted under the demonstrative analysis.

These remarks show that the issue of ambiguity with definite descriptions is a largely unsettled question. While many would agree that Russell's analysis is necessary, it is not clear that the account is sufficient or that an independent referential definite is not required. While many referential phenomena with definite descriptions can perhaps be handled by pragmatic means, without appeal to referential interpretations, it is not clear that this buys us a simpler account either within English or beyond its narrow confines. Furthermore, some phenomena suggest that definites parallel pronouns and complex demonstratives in certain cases, all of which is compatible with a referential semantics and hence with the ambiguity hypothesis.

9.4   Proper NPs as Referential Definites

The demonstrative analysis of definite descriptions has the interesting auxiliary consequence of allowing us to return to the analysis of proper nouns from a new angle and to shed light on an important semantic feature of proper nouns touched on only briefly in chapter 5.

We noted earlier that although our fragments have typically contained only a single proper noun *Chris*, a single proper noun *Jill*, a single proper noun *Kate*, etc., proper nouns in natural language typically seem to apply to more than one individual. Many people are called *Chris, Jill, Kate, Kumiko,* and so on. A natural way to analyze this phenomenon in PC+ is to analogize it to our account of *bank* in chapter 1. Recall we proposed that the spoken form [bæŋk] actually collapses two different English words, with two different meanings and two different underlying syntactic representations: $bank_1$ and $bank_2$. PC+ might treat ambiguous proper nouns in the same way, with distinct underlying syntactic representations: $Kate_1, Kate_2, \ldots, Kate_n$, etc.

Burge (1973) proposes an interesting alternative account of proper nouns that asserts exactly the reverse of PC+: instead of there being many syntactically different items sharing the same spoken and written form, there is only one syntactic element *Kate* with one meaning that applies to all the many Kates. On Burge's view, proper nouns are just ordinary predicates. Like other predicates, they can, and typically do, apply to a plurality of individuals. They have predicative axioms roughly like those in (88):

(88) a. Val(x, *Aristotle*, σ) iff x is called Aristotle
     b. Val(x, *Kate*, σ) iff x is called Kate

These rules may look either circular or trivial at first: (88a), for example, says that something is a value of the name *Aristotle* just in case its named *Aristotle*, and this does not seem to tell us much. However, as is so often the case with T theorems, the triviality or circularity is only apparent. To understand axioms like these requires knowing what's involved in coming to be called *Aristotle* or *Kate*, and this is far from a trivial matter. To be competent in using the predicate *Aristotle*, an object-language speaker has to know what is involved in baptisms, birth certificates, deed-polls, and so on, as we discussed in chapter 5.[10] This further knowledge is presumably not itself part of the internalized T theory. To understand how one gets to be a Kate or an Aristotle, we must look beyond language out into the world.

The ordinary predicate account is attractive, since proper nouns clearly do have predicative uses. Consider (89a–e), for instance, and compare them to the parallel examples in (90a–e):

(89) a. There are two Aristotles.
     b. Which Aristotle did you mean?
     c. I meant that Aristotle.
     d. The Aristotle standing over there by the expensive yacht.
     e. I meant the other Aristotle, the one that wrote *De Anima*.

(90) a. There are two cats.
     b. Which cat did you mean?
     c. I meant that cat.
     d. The cat standing over there by the expensive yacht.
     e. I meant the other cat, the one that wrote *De Anima*.

If proper nouns are fundamentally predicates applying equally to a multitude of individuals, then how are we to analyze their use in argument positions? We noted earlier that proper NPs that are arguments depart sharply from predicates in having singular conditions of application and in being object-dependent and rigid. How does this behavior arise?

Burge's proposal is that proper NPs in argument positions do not consist solely of a predicative proper noun. Rather, they are underlyingly made up of a proper-noun predicate and an unspoken demonstrative element equivalent to *that* (THAT). On this hypothesis, proper NPs are underlyingly complex demonstratives. *Kate ponders*, for example, would have the structure in (91), and would be understood as similar to *That woman ponders*:[11]

(91)

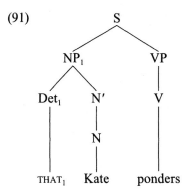

This proposal derives the semantic behavior of proper NPs in a straightforward way: Proper NPs have singular conditions of application because demonstratives have singular conditions of application. Proper NPs are object-dependent because demonstratives are object-dependent. Proper NPs are rigid because demonstratives are rigid. And so on.

Burge's analysis has a nice consequence with respect to a point made earlier about complex demonstratives. Recall the situation in which we come home to find a badger rummaging through the trash bin. You utter (92), intending to refer to the troublesome animal:

(92) That fox is making a terrible mess.

We observed that it did not seem necessary for the animal demonstrated to be a fox in order for reference to succeed, that one might point to badger, successfully refer to it, and go on to say something true about it, using (92).

Parallel cases seem available with proper nouns. Suppose I am at a professional conference listening to an interesting presentation by a curly-haired individual dressed all in black. I believe this individual is Steven S., but in reality it is Jason N. I point to the individual in question and utter (93) to the person sitting beside me:

(93) Steven is really giving a nice presentation.

It seems that I have successfully referred to Jason, the speaker, in this circumstance and have gone on to say something truthful about him, even though he is in fact not named Steven. If this judgment is correct, the case is similar to what occurs with complex demonstratives: the predicate *Steven* would neither constrain reference nor contribute to the truth conditions of the containing sentence.

The complex-demonstrative analysis of proper NPs is clearly attractive. However, on one interesting point it does not seem entirely accurate, namely in its identifying the hidden-demonstrative element in proper NPs with the demonstrative *that*. The differences between the two are brought out clearly in an example from Higginbotham 1988. Suppose you see a woman coming out of a seafood restaurant and take her for your friend Mary. Suppose further that the woman you see is *a* Mary—that is, she is named *Mary*—but is not your friend Mary. Then (95) is true if the woman in question had fish for lunch, but (94) might still be false:

(94) Mary had fish for lunch.

(95) That Mary had fish for lunch.

Since (94) and (95) differ in truth conditions, we cannot assign them identical (conditional) T sentences. On reflection, the contrast between *Mary* and *that Mary* appears similar to the one between *the cat* (taken as a referential definite) and *that cat* in (96) and (97):

(96) The cat wants in.

(97) That cat wants in.

Suppose that I see a cat scratching at my back door and take it for my cat Cleo, whereas in reality it is a stranger from elsewhere in the neighborhood. Then (97) is true of the cat in question, but (96) might still be false. Examples (96) and (97) have distinct truth conditions. Moreover, (97) requires some act of demonstration or special perceptual salience on the part of the object referred to, whereas (96) does not. All that seems required for a referential definite description is that the entity in question be the most salient object in the context that is a value of the embedded noun, in this case, the most salient cat. Likewise, *that Mary* appears to require some demonstration of the person in question, whereas *Mary* simply refers to the most salient individual in the context that is a Mary.

These points suggest that a more accurate version of the complex-demonstrative analysis of proper NPs would assimilate the covert determiner to referential *the* rather than to demonstrative *that*:

(98)

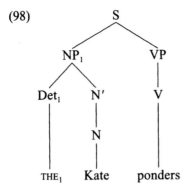

This revision would correctly account for the contrast between (94) and (95). It would also bring the analysis of proper nouns in English in line with that found in other languages. Recall that in Greek and German, proper NPs routinely take the form of definite descriptions. The analysis in (98) would give us a handle on this: in English and these other languages, a proper NP would be a species of complex demonstrative containing a referential definite determiner. The difference would reduce to surface syntax: in Greek and German this definite determiner is audible, whereas in English it is simply covert.

We will not attempt to develop the complex-demonstrative account of proper NPs further here but will simply leave it as a promising alternative to the traditional PC+ line developed earlier in the text, one that deserves further study.

Theory and Exercises

Axioms for Definite Descriptions

GQ Axioms

(1) $\text{Val}(\langle X, Y \rangle, \textit{the}, \sigma)$ iff $|Y - X| = 0$ and $|Y| = 1$

(2) $\text{Val}(\langle X, Y, z \rangle, \textit{'s}, \sigma)$ iff $|(Y \cap \{w : z \text{ has } w\}) - X| = 0$ and $|Y \cap \{w : z \text{ has } w\}| = 1$

(3) $\text{Val}(\langle X, Y \rangle, [_{\text{Det}} \text{ NP Poss}], \sigma)$ iff for some z, $\text{Val}(z, \text{NP}, \sigma)$ and $\text{Val}(\langle X, Y, z \rangle, \text{Poss}, \sigma)$

Demonstrative Axioms

(4) $\text{Val}(x, \textit{the}_i, \sigma)$ iff $x = \sigma(i)$ for all $i \geq 1$

Predicate Axioms

(5) $\text{Val}(\langle x, Y \rangle, \textit{the}, \sigma)$ iff $x \in Y$ and $|Y| = 1$

(6) $\text{Val}(\langle x, Y, z \rangle, \textit{'s}, \sigma)$ iff $x \in (Y \cap \{w : z \text{ has } w\})$ and $|Y \cap \{w : z \text{ has } w\}| = 1$

(7) $\text{Val}(\langle x, Y \rangle, [_{\text{Det}} \text{ NP Poss}], \sigma)$ iff for some z, $\text{Val}(z, \text{NP}, \sigma)$ and
$\text{Val}(\langle x, Y, z \rangle, \text{Poss}, \sigma)$

Exercises

1. The following examples all involve definite NPs:

   (1) a. The man protests.
       b. Jill knows the man.
       c. Jill's friend protests.

   ▪ Give full T-sentence derivations for sentences (1a–c), using the GQ axioms and appropriate syntactic structures. (Add obvious lexical axioms where necessary.)

   ▪ Give full T-sentence derivations for sentences (1a–c), using the demonstrative axioms and appropriate syntactic structures.

2. It is possible to apply the axioms for predicate descriptions to cases of descriptions in argument positions like (1a–c) above.

   ▪ Show that this is so by giving T-sentence derivations for (1a–c), using the predicate axioms (and whatever related rules you need from GQ).

   ▪ How do the T sentences you derive here compare to those derived in question 1?

   ▪ What does this show about the relation between assigning Russell's truth conditions to a sentence containing a definite description and analyzing the definite description as a quantifier? (For more on this, see Kaplan 1972.)

3. In the previous chapter we saw that quantifier phrases show weak-crossover effects. We noted that with the examples in (1), the interpreta-

tions in (2) are unavailable:

(1) His cabinet members will obey $\begin{Bmatrix} \text{no} \\ \text{every} \\ \text{some} \\ \text{neither} \end{Bmatrix}$ prime minister.

(2) For no/every/some/neither x such that x is prime minister, x's cabinet members will obey x.

Compare (1) with (3), where the quantifier expressions are replaced with a definite description:

(3) His cabinet members will obey the prime minister.

This sentence can be interpreted as in (4):

(4) For the x such that x is prime minister, x's cabinet members will obey x.

What do you conclude from this?

Example (3) shows the range of readings typical of definite descriptions. First, there is a reading where it is about a particular individual. Suppose that Bloggs and Spratt are two personal private secretaries of former prime minister Harold Wilson. They are discussing whether Wilson will manage to get a controversial bill through parliament. Bloggs says (5). In this case Bloggs conveys a proposition about the individual Wilson.

(5) Well, the backbenchers might revolt, but his cabinet members always obey the prime minister.

Equally, (3) can be used to express a purely general proposition, namely that there is a unique prime minister and this prime minister's cabinet members obey him. On this reading, (3) is synonymous with (6), where no particular individual is intended:

(6) His cabinet members will obey the prime minister, whoever he is.

How do these facts bear on your answer above?

4. Using the axioms for complex descriptions given in the text (and whatever related rules you need from GQ), prove the following T sentence:

(1) Val(t, [$_s$ Jill's book opened], σ) iff
$|(\{y : y \text{ is a book}\} \cap \{z : \text{Jill has } z\}) - \{x : x \text{ opened})| = 0$ and
$|\{y : y \text{ is a book}\} \cap \{z : \text{Jill has } z\}| = 1$

What problems do NPs like (2) and (3) present for our analysis of possessive constructions?

(2) Jill's brother

(3) Chris's picture

What further analysis can we give to cases like these to capture the relevant readings?

5. One problem noted for the ellipsis response to incomplete definite descriptions was that there are many ways of completing the description in the context. Hence it would seem to be impossible for an interpreter to tell which completion was implicit in the NP. Suppose a Russellian claims that the implicit material is always the same, in particular, it is always *that is most salient in this context*. On this proposal, an utterance with the surface form of (1) would have the LF (2):

(1) The door is open.

(2) The door [that is most salient in this context] is open.

Does this solve the problem? (Recall the point made in the text about the discourse properties of elliptical material.)

6. Consider the following examples adapted from Klein 1980:

(1) (Leo took George Bush to lunch yesterday, and Jude took George Jetson to dinner.) Leo thought George had a good time, and Jude did [$_{VP}$ e] too.

(2) (Leo took a troop of boy scouts to lunch yesterday, and Jude took a troop of girl scouts swimming.) Leo thought everyone had a good time, and Jude did [$_{VP}$ e] too.

Examples (1) and (2) each give a context followed by a conjoined sentence with VP ellipsis. Notice that in (1), the George referred to in the elided material must be the same as the one referred to by the overt proper noun in the first conjunct (George Bush). By contrast, in (2) the *everyone* appearing in the first conjunct can be understood as ranging over the boy scouts, while the elided *everyone* understood in the second conjunct can be understood as ranging over the girl scouts. The judgement with (1) reflects a familiar constraint on VP ellipsis across conjunctions: an elided element that is formally identical to an overt element must also refer identically. The elided *George* is formally identical to the overt *George*, so it must refer to the same person. Example (2) shows that this constraint does not apply to quantificational domains: quantifiers can switch domains of quantification across conjuncts in VP deletion.

Now compare (3), where two different presidents are introduced in the context and definite descriptions appear in the conjoined sentence. Does (3) behave analogously to (1) or to (2)? Must *the president* be associated with the same individual in the two conjuncts (the president of the Kiwanis Club), or can it be associated with different individuals (the president of the Kiwanis Club in the first and the president of the Rotary Club in the second)?

(3) (Leo took the president of the Kiwanis Club to lunch yesterday, and Jude took the president of the Rotary Club to dinner.) Leo thought the president had a good time, and Jude did [$_{VP}$ *e*] too.

What do you conclude from this?

7. In section 9.2.1 we suggested that the referential analysis of definites accounts smoothly for incomplete descriptions such as *the dog* and *the baby*. However, Peacocke (1975) points out that some uses of incomplete descriptions do not appear to be referential. For example, suppose you and I happen to see a very dirty Rolls Royce and I say (1):

(1) The owner must be rich and lazy.

Here it does not seem I'm in a position to refer directly to the owner of the car, since I have never met the individual and don't know who he or she is.

- Find three other cases of incomplete, nonreferential descriptions.
- How should our semantic theory account for cases like these?

10 Anaphora

The analysis of quantification introduced in PredC and developed in GQ rests crucially on a semantics for terms of variable reference, such as pronouns and traces. Hence it comes as no surprise that these theories suggest a natural approach to anaphora of various kinds. In the semantics literature, three different types of anaphoric relations between nominal and pronominal expressions have been widely recognized: **bound-variable anaphora**, as exemplified in (1a), **argument anaphora**, as exemplified in (1b), and **unbound anaphora** as exemplified in (1c):[1]

(1) a. *Every man* agreed with *his* neighbor.
    b. *Chris* agreed with *his* neighbor.
    c. If Max agrees with *a neighbor*, then Bill always disagrees with *him*.

In this chapter we will examine these anaphoric relations and their syntactic features, and explore how they may be accommodated within our semantic theory.

10.1 Bound-Variable Anaphora

Bound-variable anaphora is the relation holding between a quantified phrase and a referentially variable expression, where the reference of the latter varies systematically with the choice of individual determined by the quantifier. The canonical case of bound-variable anaphora is the relation between a quantified NP (*every man*) and a trace that it binds (*t*), (2a); in logical representations, the trace is spelled out as a variable (x) bound by the quantifier (2b):

(2) a. *Every man* [*t* agrees].
    b. [For every *x* such that *x* is a man] [*x* agrees]

Traces are not the only instances of bound-variable anaphors, however; pronouns can also behave in this way, as shown by the examples in (3a) to (6a):

(3) a. *Every woman* loves *her* car.
    b. [For every *x* such that *x* is a woman] [*x* loves *x*'s car]

(4) a. Alice introduced *many girls* to *their* sponsors.
    b. [For many *x* such that *x* is a girl] [Alice introduced *x* to *x*'s sponsor]

(5) a. Someone from *every city* despises *it*.
    b. [For every *x* such that *x* is a city] [for some person *y* such that *y* is from *x*] [*y* despises *x*] (May 1985)

(6) a. We will sell *no wine* before *its* time.
    b. [For no *x* such that *x* is a wine] [we will sell *x* before *x*'s time] (Ludlow 1985b)

For each of these sentences there is a reading in which the pronoun is understood as a variable (*x*) bound by the quantifier, and hence where the reference of the pronoun varies systematically with the choice of individual determined by the quantifier, (3b) to (6b).

10.1.1 Syntactic Constraints on Bound-Variable Anaphora

Bound-variable anaphora exhibits the same dependence on syntactic structure observed earlier between a quantifier and its trace:

Proper-binding constraint A referentially variable expression α can be interpreted as a variable bound by a quantified expression Q only if Q c-commands α at LF.

Recall that under this constraint, bound-variable anaphora is possible in the general configurations shown in (7a, b), where the quantified expression (Q) c-commands the pronoun (α). On the other hand, bound-variable anaphora is excluded in (7c, d), where Q is embedded within a constituent *Z*, and hence fails to c-command the pronoun:

(7) a.   b.

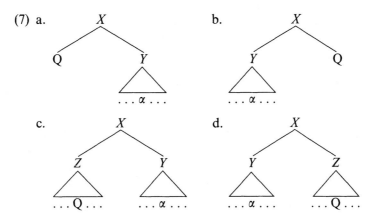

    c.   d.

We will illustrate the proper-binding constraint as it applies to pronouns in two contexts: one involving interrelationships between scope and anaphora and one involving extraction constraints. Consider first example (8), due to Higginbotham (1979):

(8) Every musician will play some piece that you ask him to play.

As Higginbotham observes, this sentence can be read with either the universally quantified noun phrase (*every musician*) or the existentially quantified noun phrase (*some piece you ask him to play*) taking widest scope. Importantly, however, only on the former reading can the pronoun *him* be understood as a variable bound by the universal quantifier. Thus (8) has the interpretation represented in (9a) (where *him* corresponds to a bound variable), and it has the interpretation represented in (9b) (where *him* has independent reference). But it has no reading as in (9c), where the universal NP takes narrower scope than the existential NP and the pronoun is still understood as bound; that is, it has no reading where there is some piece of music such that if you ask any musician to play it for you, then he will do so:

(9) a. [For every x such that x is a musician] [for some y such that y is a piece of music that you ask x to play] [x will play y]

    b. [For some y such that y is a piece of music that you ask him to play] [for every x such that x is a musician] [x will play y]

    c. #[For some y such that y is a piece of music] [for every x such that x is a musician] [if you ask x to play y, then x will play y]

This result follows from the proper-binding constraint. Example (8) contains two quantified NPs and is thus associated with two LFs differing in relative scope. (10a) is the LF corresponding to the reading in which *every musician* takes widest scope, and (10b) is the LF corresponding to the reading in which *some piece you ask him to play* takes widest scope:

(10) a.

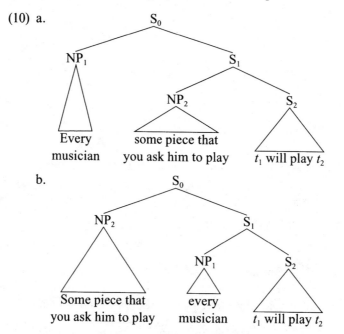

In (10a) the universally quantified NP c-commands the pronoun *him*; in (10b) it does not. The proper-binding constraint thus predicts that only structure (10a), the structure corresponding to wide scope for *every musician*, will allow the pronoun to be interpreted as a variable bound by the universal NP. This is just the result observed in (9).

Consider next the contrast between (3) to (6) and (11) to (14). Observe that in the latter, the bound-variable readings for the pronouns are difficult or impossible:

(11) a.   A person who knows *every woman* loves *her* car.
      b.   #[For every x such x is a woman] [for some person y such that y knows x] [y loves x's car]

(12) a.   The fact that Alice introduced *many girls* impressed *their* sponsors.
      b.   #[For many x such x is a girl] [the fact that Alice introduced x impressed x's sponsor]

(13) a.   Someone who is from *every city* despises *it*.

   b.   #[For every x such that x is a city] [for some person y such that y is from x] [y despises x]

(14) a.   If we sell *no wine*, then *it* will be drunk.

   b.   #[For no x such that x is a wine] [if we sell x then x will be drunk]

This fact about the meanings of (11) to (14) correlates with a fact about their structure. In each, the quantified NP occurs within a syntactic domain that can be seen to block extraction of elements internal to it. Look at (11) and (13), where the quantified NP is inside a relative clause, and (12), where it is within an NP-complement construction. Both of these constructions have the general form in (15a), a configuration that blocks extraction of *wh-* phrases, (15b), as seen in (16):

(15)

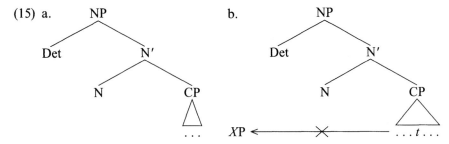

(16) a.   *Who does [$_{NP}$ a [$_N$ person [$_{CP}$ who knows t]]] love Bill's car?

   b.   *Who does [$_{NP}$ the [$_N$ fact [$_{CP}$ that Alice introduced t]]] impress them?

   c.   *What does [$_{NP}$ someone [$_{CP}$ who is from t]] despise it?

On the assumption that blocking holds not only for the overt movement of *wh-* phrases but also for the covert movement of quantified noun phrases at LF, the proper-binding constraint explains the unavailability of bound-variable readings. Such syntactic representations as in (17) will be unavailable, since they too involve extraction of a phrase out of an NP like (15):

(17) a.   [Every woman] [$_{NP}$ a person who knows t] loves her car

   b.   [Many girls] [$_{NP}$ the fact that Alice introduced t] impressed their sponsors

   c.   [Every city] [$_{NP}$ someone who is from t] despises it

The only possible representations will be ones in which the quantified expressions move and adjoin internally to the subject noun phrase:

(18) a. [NP A person who knows [every woman]] loves her car
     b. [NP The fact that Alice introduced [many girls]] impressed their
        sponsors
     c. [NP Someone who is from [every city]] despises it

But adjoined internally to the subject NPs, the quantified expressions in (11) to (13) fail to c-command their associated pronouns at LF. Hence the bound-variable constraint forbids the pronouns from being interpreted as bound variables.

The explanation for why (14) lacks a bound-variable reading is similar. Example (14) has the general structure shown in (19a), and this structure is one that blocks the surface extraction of *wh-* phrases, (19b), as seen in (20):

(19) a.   b.

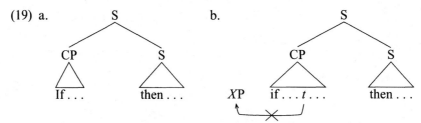

(20) *John wonders [what [CP if we sell *t*] then it will be drunk]

If this blocking also holds for the movement of quantified noun phrases, then a syntactic representation as in (21a) will be unavailable. The only possible representation will be one where the quantified NP attaches inside the preposed CP, (21b):

(21) a. #[No wine] [CP if we sell *t*] [S then it will be drunk]
     b.   [CP If we sell [no wine]] [S then it will be drunk]

Adjoined internally to the preposed CP, *no wine* fails to c-command the pronoun *it* at LF. Hence the proper-binding constraint correctly blocks the pronoun from being interpreted as a bound variable.

10.1.2 Bound-Variable Anaphora in GQ

An adequate semantics for quantification should provide an analysis of how pronouns can behave as bound variables. It should also explain why the availability of bound-variable anaphora is governed by syntactic c-command relations as stated in the proper-binding constraint.

The semantics for quantification developed earlier satisfies both of these requirements, yielding a simple account of the phenomena discussed above. In introducing quantification in chapter 7, we considered pronouns as a canonical case of variable-reference terms, and we assimilated traces to them. Pronouns and traces were given referential indices and were interpreted via axioms that assigned them values relative to their indices i and sequences σ:

(22) a. $\text{Val}(x, he_i, \sigma)$ iff $x = \sigma(i)$ for all $i \geq 1$
    b. $\text{Val}(x, she_i, \sigma)$ iff $x = \sigma(i)$ for all $i \geq 1$
    c. $\text{Val}(x, her_i, \sigma)$ iff $x = \sigma(i)$ for all $i \geq 1$
    d. $\text{Val}(x, it_i, \sigma)$ iff $x = \sigma(i)$ for all $i \geq 1$

This yields an immediate account of (3) to (6) with readings in which the pronoun (*her*, *he*, *it*) functions as a variable bound by the quantified NP, with its value changing for each choice of woman, girl, wine, city, etc.

We briefly illustrate with (3a). For simplicity, we will assume that the possessive NP is interpreted using nonquantificational axioms for definites as introduced in the last chapter, and we will assume that the possessive pronoun *her*, is underlyingly $[_{\text{Det}} [_{\text{NP}} her_1] [_{\text{Poss}} \text{'s}]]$:[2]

(23) a. $\text{Val}(\langle x, Y, z \rangle, \text{'s}, \sigma)$ iff $x \in (Y \cap \{w : z \text{ has } w\})$ and
      $|Y \cap \{w : z \text{ has } w\}| = 1$
    b. $\text{Val}(\langle x, Y \rangle, [_{\text{Det}} \text{NP Poss}], \sigma)$ iff for some z, $\text{Val}(z, \text{NP}, \sigma)$ and
      $\text{Val}(\langle x, Y, z \rangle, \text{Poss}, \sigma)$

Example (3a) receives the LF in (24), where the definite remains in situ and the trace and possessive pronoun bear the same referential index:

(24)

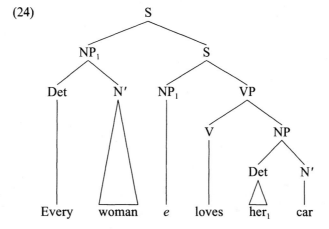

Under GQ, the highest node is interpreted as in (25):

(25) Val(t, [$_S$ [$_{NP_1}$ Every woman]
        [$_S$ [$_{NP_1}$ e] [$_{VP}$ [$_V$ loves] [$_{NP}$ [$_{Det}$ her$_1$] [$_{N'}$ car]]]]], σ) iff
        for some X, Val(X, [$_{NP}$ every woman], σ) and
        $X = \{\sigma'(1) : \text{Val}(t, [_S [_{NP} t_1] [_{VP} [_V \text{loves}] [_{NP} [_{Det} \text{her}_1] [_{N'} \text{car}]]]], \sigma')\}$

As the reader may verify, familiar calculations (and appeal to the equivalences of set theory mentioned in chapter 8) ultimately yield the T sentence in (26):

(26) Val(t, [$_S$ [$_{NP_1}$ every woman]
        [$_S$ [$_{NP_1}$ e] [$_{VP}$ [$_V$ loves] [$_{NP}$ [$_{NP}$ her$_1$] [$_{N'}$ car]]]]], σ) iff
        $|\{x : x$ is a woman$\}$ $-$
        $\{\sigma'(1) :$ for some y, $\sigma'(1)$ loves y and y is a car and $\sigma'(1)$ has y and
        $|\{w : w$ is a car$\} \cap \{w : \sigma'(1)$ has $w\}| = 1\}| = 0$

In prose this says that *Every woman loves her car* is true (on the relevant indexing) just in case the set of women minus the set of individuals that possess a unique car that they love is zero, that is, just in case every woman loves the unique car she has. Note carefully that in these final results, *her$_1$* has been assigned the same value as the trace t_1, namely $\sigma'(1)$, and hence it is being interpreted as a variable bound by the quantifier, as desired.

The Naturalness of C-Command

The analysis of variable binding adopted here explains the syntactic constraint on quantifier-bound-variable relations that we observed:

Proper-binding constraint   A referentially variable expression α can be interpreted as a variable bound by a quantified expression Q only if Q c-commands α at LF.

As we noted in chapter 7, an element behaves as a variable bound by a quantified NP because it receives different semantic values in a manner determined by that NP, in particular, through sequences that vary in the position corresponding to the index i on the bound element. The quantificational axioms that we have adopted ensure that only the sister of an adjoined quantifier (S*) will have its sequences systematically varied. Accordingly, only items contained within this sister S* can be interpreted with respect to i-variant sequences σ', (27a). If the adjunction structure is part of some larger construction (*X* in (27b)), then no variation in sequences is induced in the structure outside S* (for example, no sequence variation is induced in *Y*):

(27) a.   b.

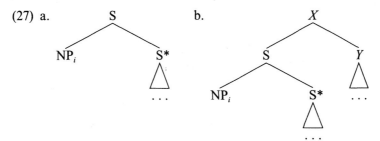

Since the traces and pronouns within S* are precisely the ones c-commanded by NP$_i$, it follows that only traces and pronouns c-commanded by NP$_i$ can be interpreted as bound variables.

10.2   Argument Anaphora

Referentially variable elements show anaphoric relations not only with quantified expressions but with names as well. In (28a, b), for instance, the pronouns *her* and *she* may be understood as coreferring with the name *Kate*:

(28) a. Kate loves her car.
      b. Kate eats peanuts when she is nervous.

We would like to know what kind of anaphoric relation is involved in such cases and how it is to be analyzed.

10.2.1   Names and Pronouns: Variable Binding

One natural idea about (28a, b) is that they involve variable binding, just as with quantified expressions. A simple way of implementing this view (following Geach 1962 and Montague 1974) is for us to treat proper names as operators, letting them undergo quantifier raising at LF. Under this proposal, (28a), for example, would be assigned the LF representation in (29):

(29)

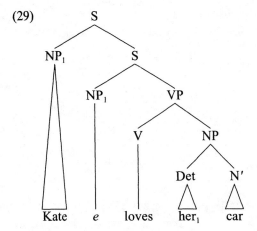

The structure in (29) can then be interpreted via our axiom for topicalization structures from chapter 7:

(30) Val(t, [ₛ NP$_i$ S], σ) iff for the σ' ≈$_i$ σ such that Val(σ'(i), NP, σ),
     [+ref]
     Val(t, S, σ')

With (30) it is not hard to prove the (sequence-free) T sentence given in (31):

(31) Val(t, [ₛ Kate *t* loves her car]) iff for some *x*, Kate loves *x* and
     x is a car and Kate has *x* and |{*w* : *w* is a car} ∩ {*w* : Kate has *w*}| = 1

This T sentence yields the desired result that Kate is both the lover and owner of some unique car.

Problems for a Bound-Variable Analysis

Variable binding provides one account of sentences with an anaphoric relation holding between a name and pronoun. And perhaps for certain cases, structures like (29) and an axiom like (30) may indeed be appropriate. Nonetheless, there are a number of difficulties with the view that anaphoric relations between referring expressions and pronouns can be reduced to variable binding in all cases.

We noted that bound-variable anaphora is sensitive to syntactic configuration. Under our axioms, only pronouns and traces that are c-commanded by a quantified NP at LF can be bound by it. We also saw how certain structures seem to block syntactic movement, forbidding *wh-* phrases and quantifiers from being extracted. The result is bound-variable readings are blocked as well. Thus with (11a) (repeated as (32a)), the NP structure blocks extraction of the quantified NP at LF, (32b). This excludes the bound-variable reading in (32c):

(32) a.   A person who knows every woman loves her car.

   b.   [Every woman] [$_{NP}$ a person who knows *t*] loves her car.

   c.   #[For every *x* such *x* is a woman]
         [for some person *y* such that *y* knows *x*] [*y* loves *x*'s car]

Interestingly, anaphora between referential expressions and pronouns does not show this sensitivity to syntactic islands (that is, to structures that block extraction). Consider (33) and (34). Sentence (33a) is similar to (32a) but with a name replacing the quantified expression. Here, however, there is no problem in reading the name and the pronoun as anaphoric, (32b):

(33) a. [A person who knows *Mary*] loves *her* car.

   b. A person who knows Mary loves Mary's car.

The same result holds in (34), where the proper NP is embedded in two relative clauses, a configuration that would typically block quantifier raising to the main sentence:

(34) a. [A person who spoke to everyone that knows *Mary*] loves *her* car.

   b. A person who spoke to everyone that knows Mary loves Mary's car.

This divergence between names and quantified expressions evidently gives us two choices: Either we can say that names still move and bind variables like quantified NPs but that somehow they are immune to syntactic islands. Or else we must reject the view that the names variable-bind the pronouns in (33) and (34), and seek some other account of the anaphoric relation between them.

Anaphoric relations between quantifiers, referring terms, and pronouns also diverge with respect to so-called weak crossover (WCO) effects, discussed in chapter 8. Recall that with (35a) and (36a) it is very difficult to understand the *wh-* phrase *which boy* and quantified NP *every boy* as binding the possessive pronoun (see (35b) and (36b) respectively):

(35) a.   Which boy does *his* mother love *t*?

     b.   # For which boy x, x's mother loves x?

(36) a.   His mother loves every boy.

     b.   # For every boy x, x's mother loves x.

The suggestion was that this semantic limitation reflects a general syntactic constraint proscribing configurations of the form in (37):

(37) $*XP_i$ [[... pronoun$_i$ ...] ... t_i ...], where pronoun$_i$ does not c-command t_i (for all i)

This constraint rules out the relevant readings of (35) and (36) by ruling out the structures that would yield them. Interestingly, the WCO effect found with quantifiers is not observed with proper NPs. Thus consider (38a). There is no problem in understanding this sentence so that the proper name *John* and the pronoun *his* corefer, (38b). But if this anaphoric interpretation is derived by variable binding, then it must appeal to a structure that violates the WCO constraint, namely (38c):

(38) a.   His mother loves John.

     b.   John's mother loves John.

     c.   John$_1$ [$_S$ [$_{NP}$ his$_1$ mother] love t_1]

Here again, we may retain the variable-binding analysis of proper NPs for (38) and specifically exempt them from the WCO constraint. Or else we must reject the view that the name and pronoun in (38a) stand in a variable-binding relation.

   The proper-binding constraint and WCO facts offer a similar choice between retaining the variable-binding analysis and making specific stipulations for names or else finding a new analysis of the name-pronoun relation. Given the ad hoc nature of the stipulations required, it seems reasonable to explore the latter course and recognize a nonquantificational anaphoric relation. We will refer to this new anaphoric relation between names and pronouns as **argument anaphora** and explore some approaches to it.

10.2.2   Names and Pronouns: Sequence Constraints

The bound-variable analysis makes *Every girl$_1$ loves her$_1$ car* and *Kate$_1$ loves her$_1$ car* alike in being sequence-independent with respect to their truth or falsity. Both sentences appeal to sequence variants, and so both are either absolutely true or absolutely false. This result suggests an alternative approach to argument anaphora in which the anaphoric relation between names and pronouns does not appeal to sequence variation. The idea is to use the original sequence of evaluation to form the anaphoric connection, letting nonreferentially variable elements place constraints on it.

Up to this point, we've been treating proper NPs as sequence-insensitive expressions: elements whose interpretation does not interact with σ in any way. However, suppose we alter this view for NPs bearing referential indices. In particular, suppose we let a proper NP α with index i place the following condition on any sequence of evaluation σ: the ith element of σ must be the individual designated by α. This would force any pronoun bearing the same index and evaluated with respect to the same sequence to designate the same individual. That is, it would force the pronoun to corefer with the proper NP as a condition of truth. This would create a sequence-sensitive anaphoric connection between the name and pronoun, but one that does not appeal to variable binding or sequence variation.

We can make this proposal precise by means of the axiom in (39) for NP nodes bearing a referential index:

(39) $\mathrm{Val}(x, \mathrm{NP}_i, \sigma)$ iff $x = \sigma(i)$ and $\mathrm{Val}(x, \mathrm{NP}, \sigma)$

This axiom is similar to the ones for lexical pronouns. It identifies the value of a name with a certain object in a sequence by means of the referential index. The difference between names and pronouns is that with the former we get an additional sequence-independent specification of reference. Thus contrast the following:

(40) $\mathrm{Val}(x, [_{\mathrm{NP}_i} \textit{Kate}], \sigma)$ iff $x = \sigma(i)$ and $x = \mathrm{Kate}$

(41) $\mathrm{Val}(x, \textit{her}_i, \sigma)$ iff $x = \sigma(i)$

These are identical except that, along with its sequence-sensitive conjunct, $[_{\mathrm{NP}_i} \textit{Kate}]$ also has the independent specification of reference that $x = \mathrm{Kate}$.

We can illustrate this analysis of argument anaphora by means of the example sentence *Kate₁ loves her₁ car*. Under the present proposal, this sentence receives the LF in (42), where no quantifier raising occurs:

(42)

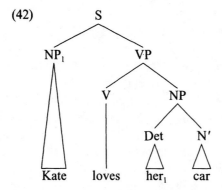

Under familiar axioms, the highest node is interpreted as in (43):

(43) Val(t, [$_S$ [$_{NP_1}$ Kate] [$_{VP}$ [$_V$ loves] [$_{NP}$ [$_{Det}$ her$_1$] [$_{N'}$ car]]]], σ) iff
for some x, Val(x, [$_{NP_1}$ Kate], σ) and
Val(x, [$_{VP}$ [$_V$ loves] [$_{NP}$ [$_{Det}$ her$_1$] [$_{N'}$ car]]], σ)

The first conjunct is then interpreted as in (44) under our axiom for indexed proper names, and the second conjunct is interpreted as in (45):

(44) a. Val(x, [$_{NP_1}$ Kate], σ) iff $x = σ(1)$ and Val(x, [$_{NP}$ Kate], σ)
b. Val(x, [$_{NP}$ Kate], σ) iff … iff x = Kate
c. Val(x, [$_{NP_1}$ Kate], σ) iff $x = σ(1)$ and x = Kate

(45) Val(x, [$_{VP}$ [$_V$ loves] [$_{NP}$ [$_{Det}$ her$_1$] [$_{N'}$ car]]], σ) iff
for some y, x loves y and y is a car and $σ(1)$ has y and
$|\{w : w \text{ is a car}\} \cap \{w : σ(1) \text{ has } w\}| = 1$

Collecting results (and suppressing details), we thus get (46):

(46) Val(t, [$_S$ *Kate$_1$ loves her$_1$ car*], σ) iff $σ(1)$ = Kate and
for some y, Kate loves y and y is a car and $σ(1)$ has y and
$|\{w : w \text{ is a car}\} \cap \{w : σ(1) \text{ has } w\}| = 1$

This T sentence relates the semantic values of *Kate* and *her* through σ. The index 1 on *Kate* requires $σ(1)$ to be Kate. The index 1 on *her* requires $σ(1)$ to be the value of *her*. Hence *Kate* and *her* together must have the same reference for the sentence to be true.

Properties of the Sequence-Constraint Analysis

The analysis embodied in axiom (39) does not appeal to movement and variable binding. Hence it correctly entails that argument anaphora should show no WCO effects, since the configuration relevant to the WCO constraint simply does not come up. In addition, anaphoric relations between names and pronouns are independent of c-command on this view. This result is seen concretely by working through the T sentence for an example like *Her₁ car pleases Kate₁*. As the reader may verify, the outcome is (47), where, despite the fact that the name fails to c-command the pronoun, the two are related through the sequence σ, just as in (46):

(47) Val(t, [ₛ *Her₁ car pleases Kate₁*], σ) iff for some y, y is a car and
$\sigma(1)$ has y and $|\{w : w \text{ is a car}\} \cap \{w : \sigma(1) \text{ has } w\}| = 1$ and
y pleases Kate and $\sigma(1) =$ Kate

This result follows from the way that coreference between proper NPs and pronouns is determined. As we noted, the presence of an indexed name α_i simply adds a condition in the T sentence to the effect that the referent of α is $\sigma(i)$ (where σ is the sequence of evaluation). In the T sentence, the pronoun is then interpreted with respect to this constrained σ. Hence the name and pronoun must corefer as a condition of truth. On this picture, it evidently does not matter *where* the relevant constraint on σ is added in the derivation of the T sentence; all that is important is that it is added. Hence it does not matter where the name occurs in the syntactic structure vis-à-vis the pronoun.

The analysis also yields *sequence-dependent* truth conditions. Unlike the case with variable binding, reference to σ on the right-hand side of biconditionals like (46) is not eliminable by further formal manipulations. Hence under this account a sentence like *Kate₁ loves her₁ car* is never true or false absolutely but true or false only with respect to a particular choice of sequence σ. This result makes understanding a sentence involving argument anaphora essentially context-dependent: to judge whether the sentence is true, we have to know the context in which it is uttered, in the form of a sequence σ. Following Evans (1980), we might call this a **pragmatic theory of argument anaphora**, since the reference of *her* in *Kate loves her car* is determined in the same way as for *her* in *Jill admires her*—in both cases through context in the form of σ.

Finally, the notion of anaphoric connection in this analysis is a very weak one. In talking informally about a sentence like *Kate loves her car* on its reading where *Kate* and *her* corefer, it is commonplace to speak of the name as determining the reference of the pronoun, or of the pronoun as picking up its reference from the name. Under the analysis embodied in (39), however, this way of speaking is not accurate. On this account, pronouns (and other referentially variable elements) do not receive their values through other expressions, such as names. Rather, they receive their values through a sequence σ. Other expressions may place conditions on this sequence, dictating what objects must occupy various positions for the sentence to be true, but whether the sequence actually has the relevant objects in the relevant positions is not (and cannot be) determined by these constraints. Thus, suppose that we evaluate *Kate₁ loves her₁ car* with respect to the sequence σ^* containing Jill in its first position. Then note that according to (46), the sentence will be true with respect to σ^* just in case Kate is Jill and Kate loves Jill's car. Evidently, *Kate₁ loves her₁ car* will be false under this σ^* if Kate and Jill are different people, but the important point to observe is that the semantic value of *her₁* is the individual $\sigma^*(1)$ determined by σ^*, regardless of the constraints placed on σ^*. This individual is Jill, even if Kate and Jill turn out to be nonidentical.

The Wrong-Sequence Problem

The sequence-constraint analysis likens indexed proper NPs to variable-reference terms in making them sensitive to sequences. As it turns out, this feature raises an interesting problem that we will call the **wrong sequence problem**.

Suppose that someone asserts the simple sentence in (48) and that the individual Phil named by *Phil* does in fact ponder.

(48) Phil₁ ponders.

Suppose further that we happen to evaluate this sentence with respect to a sequence σ that does not have Phil in its first position. Perhaps surprisingly, (48) comes out false in these circumstances. Suppressing irrelevant details, the T sentence for (48) will be as in (49):

(49) Val(t, *Phil₁ ponders*, σ) iff Phil ponders and Phil = $\sigma(1)$

Since one of the conjuncts on the RHS of the biconditional is not met in these circumstances (Phil = $\sigma(1)$), the sentence evaluates as false. This is a counterintuitive result. Since the sentence contains no referentially dependent expressions, we might expect the index on *Phil* to do no semantic work, and the truth conditions of *Phil ponders* to simply be a matter of whether Phil ponders or not. But under the sequence-constraint analysis, the index does in fact entail a semantic contribution, even when no dependent elements are present. Hence the possibility of the case above.

This problem can be resolved by further strengthening the analogy between indexed proper NPs and variable-reference terms, in particular, by extending our account of sequences and the Σ relation to names. Recall that in this account, sentences containing indexed pronouns and demonstratives are not evaluated freely with respect to sequences. Rather, they are evaluated with respect to *relevant sequences* selected by the Σ relation. If a speaker uses an indexed pronoun in an utterance to refer to an object o, then Σ selects those sequences having o in the position given by the index, (50). The conditionalized T schema in (51) then ensures that sentences containing variable-reference terms are evaluated only with respect to the sequences selected by Σ:

(50) If a speaker uses α_i in u to refer to x, then $\Sigma(u, \sigma)$ only if $\sigma(i) = x$

(51) If u is an utterance of S and $\Sigma(u, \sigma)$, then u is true iff Val(t, S, σ)

Suppose now that we simply remove the requirement in (50) that the indexed item be a pronoun or demonstrative.[3] Then the use of *any* indexed expression to refer, including a proper NP, will be reflected in Σ. Σ will select only sequences with the right object in the relevant position. In the case of the example sentence with $Phil_1$, we will have the result in (52):

(52) If a speaker uses $Phil_1$ in u to refer to x, then $\Sigma(u, \sigma)$ only if $\sigma(1) = $ Phil

The conditionalized T schema will then ensure that the truth of $Phil_1$ *ponders* is only evaluated with respect to the right sequences, in this case, ones with Phil in the first position:

(53) If u is an utterance of $Phil_1$ *ponders* and $\Sigma(u, \sigma)$, then u is true iff
        Val(t, $Phil_1$ *ponders*, σ)

Thus by making the selection relation Σ sensitive to the use of indexed proper NPs, the wrong-sequence problem is avoided.

Coreference and Coindexation

The sequence-constraint analysis implies an important semantic distinction between expressions that are coindexed (i.e., bear identical indices) and expressions that are contraindexed (i.e., bear distinct indices). Consider the example in (54a) and its T sentence (54b):

(54) a. She$_1$ saw her$_1$ car.
   b. Val(t, *She$_1$ saw her$_1$ car*, σ) iff for some y, $\sigma(1)$ saw y and
      y is a car and $\sigma(1)$ has y and $|\{w : w$ is a car$\} \cap \{w : \sigma(1)$ has $w\}| = 1$

The latter shows that the semantic effect of coindexing is coreference. The fact that *she* and *her* bear the same numerical subscript entails that (54a) is true if and only if the seer and the car owner in question are the same person. Now compare (55a) and its T sentence (55b):

(55) a. She$_1$ saw her$_2$ car.
   b. Val(t, *She$_1$ saw her$_2$ car*, σ) iff for some y, $\sigma(1)$ saw y and
      y is a car and $\sigma(2)$ has y and $|\{w : w$ is a car$\} \cap \{w : \sigma(2)$ has $w\}| = 1$

T sentence (55b) shows that the effect of contraindexing is *not* disjoint reference. Rather, it is simply the weaker nonrequirement of coreference. The fact that *she* and *her* bear the subscripts 1 and 2 (respectively) entails that (55b) is true if and only if the first object in σ saw the car owned by the second object in σ. But this implies nothing about whether $\sigma(1)$ or $\sigma(2)$ are the same individual or not. Contraindexing is simply neutral on this score.

This interpretation of co- and contraindexing accords with the intuitive interpretation of indices assumed in current versions of the binding theory developed by Chomsky (1981, 1986a) and others. Binding theory governs the distribution of indices within a clause, specifying when expressions must, can, and cannot bear the same index. These indexing possibilities show when expressions must and can refer to the same individuals or when they normally would be taken to refer to different individuals. For example, consider (56a–c). As it applies to reflexives, pronouns, and names, binding theory entails that the indices i and j must be identical in (56a), distinct in (56b), and distinct in (56c):

(56) a. John$_i$ loves himself$_j$.
   b. John$_i$ loves him$_j$.
   c. He$_i$ loves John$_j$.

These results correspond to the semantic fact that the name and reflexive are understood as coreferring in (56a) but the name and pronoun are not naturally understood as coreferring in either (56b) or (56c).

It has sometimes been suggested that the interpretation of identical indices in examples like (56a–c) should involve obligatory coreference, and that the interpretation of distinct indices should involve obligatory disjoint reference.[4] However, various authors have forcefully argued that this view cannot be sustained. In particular, they argue that even though contraindexing fails to entail coreference, it cannot entail disjoint reference. Thus Evans (1980) cites example (57) as showing that the reference of the name and pronoun in the final sentence can be taken as identical, despite the fact that binding theory requires their indices to be distinct (compare (56c)).

(57) What do you mean John loves no one? He loves John.

Similarly in the discourse in (58), it appears possible to take the name and pronoun as coreferring even though binding theory requires their indices to be different (compare (56b)).

(58) What do you mean John loves no one? John loves him (indicating John).

A similar point is made by Higginbotham (1985) with the respect to example (59). Binding theory requires the indices of the pronoun and the name to be distinct. However, there are discourses in which the two expressions can clearly be understood as coreferring. Suppose that we are debating the identity of a certain individual, where I maintain that the individual is none other than John. As an argument in support of my view, I might utter (59):

(59) He$_i$ put on John$_j$'s coat.

In making this utterance, I clearly intend, and would be taken to intend, that the reference of *John* and *he* are the same. So again it appears that distinct indices cannot require disjoint reference. The distribution and interpretation of indices predicted under binding theory thus appears compatible with the sequence-constraint semantics of argument anaphora. Under binding theory and under this semantics, coindexing implies obligatory coreference, and contraindexing implies lack of obligatory coreference.

10.2.3 Names and Pronouns: Antecedence

We noted above that the sequence-constraint analysis of argument anaphora supports only a very weak notion of antecedence. The interpretation of *Kate loves her car* in which *Kate* and *her* corefer does not involve the name supplying or determining the semantic value of the pronoun. Instead, the pronoun's value comes from a sequence whose content is merely constrained by the name as a condition of truth. We also saw that the account entails sequence-dependent truth conditions with argument anaphora. A sentence like *Kate loves her car* is true only relative to a sequence, even when *her* and *Kate* corefer. Hence the account implicitly claims that sentences containing a pronoun and a coreferring name are as contextually dependent for their understanding as a sentence containing a free pronoun, such as *Her car is green*. On reflection, it is easy to see that these two properties are closely related. Because we use the device of sequences to fix the values of pronouns, a name can affect the value of a pronoun only through the mediation of sequences. And because we use the sequence of evaluation to link the values of names and pronouns, this parameter cannot be eliminated in the final T sentence.

Evans (1977, 1980) proposes an interesting alternative account of argument anaphora in which these two properties of the sequence-constraint analysis are absent. On Evans's analysis, a name directly determines the semantic value of an anaphorically related pronoun, without mediation of sequences. Furthermore, the semantics of argument anaphora yields absolute, context-independent conditions of truth. The core of Evans's proposal is the introduction of a new formal syntactic relation of **antecedence**.[5] Antecedence is a binary relation holding between a referentially variable expression and some other phrase. By means of this relation, the semantic value of one element (the anaphoric expression) is fixed by the value of the other.

We can illustrate Evans's proposal using the sentence *Kate loves her car*, on the interpretation where *her* and *Kate* are anaphorically related. This interpretation is represented formally with a phrase marker containing a directed arrow whose head (signified by the arrowhead) is the name and whose tail is the pronoun.

(60)

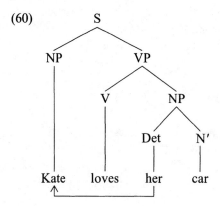

The arrow represents the antecedence relation. We will call the phrase at the head of the arc ($[_{NP}$ Kate]) the **antecedent** of the phrase at the tail of the arc ($[_{Det}$ her]). And we will call an arrow with its two endpoint nodes a **chain** (following Evans 1977).[6] Such representations can be viewed as derived from an underlying chainless phrase marker. Slightly reformulating proposals in Evans 1977, 1980, we may state the chaining rule as follows, where an **argument phrase** is a phrase appearing in the position of a singular term (subject position, object position, etc.):

Chaining rule   Chain a pronoun β to any argument phrase α that is not c-commanded by β.

The formal semantics for argument anaphora involves revising the axioms for pronouns so that they depend on antecedents rather than sequences for their values. Candidate axioms are those in (61) (essentially following Evans 1977):

(61) a. Val(x, *she*, σ) iff Val(x, NP*, σ), where NP* is the antecedent of *she*.
  b. Val(x, *her*, σ) iff Val(x, NP*, σ), where NP* is the antecedent of *her*.
  c. Val(x, *he*, σ) iff Val(x, NP*, σ), where NP* is the antecedent of *he*.
  d. Val(x, *it*, σ) iff Val(x, NP*, σ), where NP* is the antecedent of *it*.

According to these axioms, the semantic value of a pronoun is simply the semantic value of its antecedent, whatever the latter may be.

As the reader may show, in the T sentence derivation for (60), the subject NP $[_{NP}$ Kate] will receive the usual interpretation in (62):

(62) Val(x, $[_{NP}$ Kate], σ) iff ... iff x = Kate

However, the interpretation of the pronoun *her* in the object NP will be as in (63a), which reduces to (63b) by (SE):

(63) a. Val(z, $[_{Det}$ her], σ) iff Val(z, *Kate*, σ) (by (61b))
  b. Val(z, $[_{Det}$ her], σ) iff z = Kate (by (62), (63a), (SE))

Note that no sequences are involved in the latter. Ultimately, we derive the sequence-independent T sentence in (64), which is the desired result:

(64) Val(t, $[_S$ Kate loves her car], σ) iff for some y, Kate loves y and y is a car and Kate has y and $|\{w : w$ is a car$\} \cap \{w : $ Kate has $w\}| = 1$

In appealing to antecedent phrases, the axioms in (61) might initially seem to violate strong compositionality in a serious way. Under (61b), for example, the semantic value of *her* is given not through its immediate constituents but rather through its antecedent. On reflection, however, the matter is really not so clear. Up to this point we've been concerned with phrase markers of a standard kind, which involve the two relations of precedence and dominance. However, under Evans's account of argument anaphora, this simple notion of a phrase marker no longer applies. Antecedence adds a new relation into the picture that involves neither dominance nor precedence between its relata. Since this analysis involves an extended notion of a phrase marker, it seems reasonable to allow an extended notion of compositionality as well. For example, for antecedence structures, strict locality might permit semantic rules to look at the constituents of a node *and* their antecedents. In effect, this revision would treat the antecedents of the daughters of a node *X* essentially as daughters of *X* themselves. On this amended understanding, the rules for pronoun interpretation in (61) would in fact be fully compositional.

Sequences versus Antecedence

The sequence-constraint and antecedence theories converge on a number of important points. According to Evans 1977, 1980, an antecedent need not c-command a pronoun in a chain. Hence argument anaphora is independent of c-command here, just as in the sequence-constraint analysis. Furthermore, antecedence does not involve operator-trace structures; hence no weak-cross-over effects are predicted to occur. Finally, it can be shown that the antecedence analysis requires a pronoun to be c-commanded by a quantified NP if it is to be interpreted as a variable bound by NP. Hence this analysis also accounts for the bound-variable constraint discussed earlier.[7]

The sequence-constraint and antecedence theories also diverge in important ways. We have already noted that the latter produces sequence-independent truth conditions for argument anaphora, whereas the former does not. This entails very different analyses of an example like (65a). On the sequence-constraint view, the relation between *John* and *his* in (65a) is no closer than, and no different from, the relation between *John* and *his* in (65b). By contrast, on the antecedence theory, the relation between *John* and *his* in (65a) can be a context-independent one established purely internally to the sentence:[8]

(65) a. John agrees with his neighbor.
     b. John is wrong. Mary agrees with his neighbor.

Evans's account also yields a view of bound-variable pronouns that is inter-estingly different from the one discussed earlier. Reconsider the example *Every woman loves her car*. Under earlier proposals, this sentence received the LF in (66a), which involves variable binding. Under Evans's proposals, the sentence gets the LF in (66b), which involves both binding and antecedence:

(66) a.

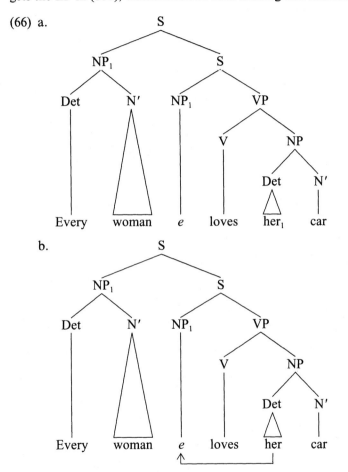

b.

As the reader may verify, the T sentences assigned to these representations by the two approaches are actually identical (up to object-language syntax). For both, the result is (67):

(67) Val(t, [$_S$ Every woman$_1$ t_1 loves her car]) iff
$|\{x : x$ is a woman$\} - \{x :$ for some y, x loves y and y is a car and x has y and $|\{w : w$ is a car$\} \cap \{w : x$ has $w\}| = 1\}| = 0$

Nonetheless, the route by which this result is obtained is quite different in the two cases. In the variable-binding analysis, the trace and pronoun in *Every woman t loves her car* are *both* semantically dependent upon the adjoined NP, and they are semantically independent of each other. *Every woman* induces sequence variation in the evaluation of the lower S; this in turn determines identical values for *t* and *her*. By contrast, in the chain analysis the trace is semantically dependent on the adjoined NP, and the pronoun is semantically dependent on the trace. *Every woman* induces sequence variation in the lower S, determining a value for *t*. This value then gets picked up by the pronoun through antecedence. The values of *her* and *t* come out identical not by being related to *every woman* but by being related to each other via antecedence.

This last result underlines the important distinction drawn in Evans's account between the binding relation, which holds between a trace and its adjoined quantifier, and the antecedence relation, which holds between a pronoun and its antecedent. The binding relation is represented by coindexing, and its semantics involves sequences, (68a). By contrast, the antecedence relation is represented by a chain, and its semantics appeals to a direct identity of values between expressions in the tree, (68b):[9]

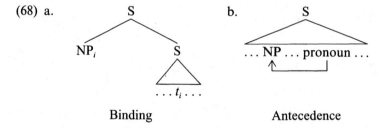

Both the sequence-constraint analysis of argument anaphora and Evans's antecedence-based account remain under active discussion in the literature. Indeed, it has been argued that *both* analyses are required to account for the full range of anaphoric phenomena in natural language.[10] We will leave the question of argument anaphora open at this point, noting that either (or both) appear(s) to be incorporable within our general framework.

10.2.4 Bound-Variable Anaphora with Proper Names?

Earlier we gave some reasons to doubt that anaphora between a proper name and a pronoun could always be reduced to variable binding. Nonetheless, Lasnik (1976) and Reinhart (1983) observe certain cases in which the anaphoric relations between proper names and pronouns do appear to show the earmarks of variable binding. These cases involve the **sloppy identity** phenomenon, illustrated in (69) to (71):

(69) John likes his teachers, and Bill does too.

(70) Alice introduced Jill to her new neighbors, and Penelope did too.

(71) Alice introduced Jill to her new neighbors, and Penelope, Ann.

These are all understood as having deleted or elliptical VP material in their second conjuncts. Thus (69) is understood as "John likes his teachers, and Bill *likes his teachers* too," and so on. Furthermore, notice that each sentence is ambiguous according to how the pronoun in the elided material is understood. Thus the pronoun may be understood as preserving its reference from the first conjunct, as in (72a) to (74a). Alternatively it may be understood as coreferring with an NP in the second conjunct, as in (72b) to (74b):

(72) a. John likes John's teachers, and Bill also likes John's teachers.
      b. John likes John's teachers, and Bill likes Bill's teachers.

(73) a. Alice introduced Jill to Alice's new neighbors, and Penelope also introduced Jill to Alice's new neighbors.
      b. Alice introduced Jill to Alice's new neighbors, and Penelope introduced Jill to Penelope's new neighbors.

(74) a. Alice introduced Jill to Jill's new neighbors, and Penelope introduced Ann to Jill's new neighbors.
      b. Alice introduced Jill to Jill's new neighbors, and Penelope introduced Ann to Ann's new neighbors.

The former readings, in which pronominal reference is rigidly preserved across the two conjuncts, are usually referred to as **strict readings** of the elided pronoun. The latter readings, in which pronominal reference changes between the two conjuncts, are usually referred to as **sloppy readings** of the elided pronoun.

Lasnik (1976) and Reinhart (1983) argue that sloppy readings, like (72b) to (74b), are available only in restricted circumstances. Specifically, they are possible only when the configurational relation between the pronoun and coreferring NP in the first conjunct is one that would also support bound-variable anaphora. Observe first that if we replace the relevant proper NP with a quantified noun phrase in the first conjunct of each of (69) to (71), then the resulting sentence is one permitting the pronoun to be understood as a variable bound by the quantifier:

(75) *Every boy* likes *his* teachers.

(76) *Every girl* introduced Jill to *her* new neighbors.

(77) Alice introduced *every girl* to *her* new neighbors.

Thus when the configurational relation between the name and pronoun permits sloppy identity, it permits variable binding as well. Now consider the examples in (78) to (80). In each of (78a) to (80a), the elided pronoun in the second conjunct cannot readily receive a sloppy reading (78b) to (80b). And correlatively, when the proper name in the first conjunct is replaced by a quantified NP, (78c) to (80c), the pronoun cannot be understood as a variable bound by the quantifier, (78d) to (80d):

(78) a.   Three people that knew *Mary* greeted *her*, and three people that knew Alice did too.
      b.   #Three people that knew Mary greeted Mary, and three people that knew Alice greeted Alice.
      c.   Three people that knew *every girl* greeted *her*.
      d.   #For every x such that x is a girl, three people that knew x greeted x.

(79) a.   The fact that we neglected *John* angered *him*, and the fact that we neglected Bill did too.
      b.   #The fact that we neglected John angered John, and the fact that we neglected Bill angered Bill.
      c.   The fact that we neglected *every boy* angered *him*.
      d.   #For every x such that x is a boy, the fact that we neglected x angered x.

(80) a.   If Jill approved *Chris*, then we will admit *him*, and if Jill approved Rolf, then we will too.
      b.   #If Jill approved Chris, then we will admit Chris, and if Jill approved Rolf, then we will admit Rolf.
      c.   If Jill approved *every boy*, then we will admit *him*.
      d.   #For every x such that x is a boy, if Jill approved x then we will admit x.

Thus when the configurational relation between the name and pronoun excludes sloppy identity, it excludes variable binding as well. The fact that sloppy readings for a pronoun seem to demand the same structural configuration required for bound-variable anaphora suggests that sloppy readings involve bound-variable anaphora. More precisely, it suggests that the semantic relation between the proper name and pronoun in (72) to (74) involves sequence alternation. If this conclusion is correct—if sloppy identity involves variable binding between the NP and pronoun in the antecedent VP—then clearly it must be possible for proper names to function as variable binders.[11]

Sloppy-identity phenomena can be brought within a bound-variable analysis of the name-pronoun relation with a copying analysis of ellipsis. Under this analysis, examples like (81a), which contain missing VP elements in surface form, are actually fully explicit at the point when they are semantically interpreted. Such fully explicit representations are derived by means of a syntactic copying operation that operates on LFs and reconstructs missing elements from explicit ones. Thus with (81a), the explicit VP in S_1 is literally copied into the empty VP in S_2, (81b), yielding the fully explicit conjunction (81c):

(81) a. John could see Mary, and Bill could too.
  b. $[_{S_1}$ John could $[_{VP}$ see Mary$]]$ and $[_{S_2}$ Bill could $[_{VP}$ *e*$]$ too$]$
    └──────copy──────────────↗
  c. $[_{S_1}$ John could $[_{VP}$ see Mary$]]$ and $[_{S_2}$ Bill could $[_{VP}$ see Mary$]$ too$]$

On this view, VP ellipsis is merely a surface phenomenon—one not present at the level where syntactic structures are submitted to semantic rules.

Consider now what this view of ellipsis yields in cases like (82a), where the elliptical material contains a pronoun and the pronoun can be understood either strictly or sloppily. The strict reading of (82a) is obtained straightforwardly with our analysis of argument anaphora as sequence conditions. We simply assign *John* and *his* the same index (say 1) and *Bill* a distinct index (say 2). VP copying at LF then yields the representation in (82b):

(82) a. John likes his teachers, and Bill does too.
  b. $[_{S_1}$ John$_1$ $[_{VP}$ likes his$_1$ teachers$]]$ and
    $[_{S_2}$ Bill$_2$ does $[_{VP}$ like his$_1$ teachers$]$ too$]$

Since *John* and the two instances of *his* bear the same index, the conjoined sentence will be true with respect to a given sequence σ only if *John* and the two instances of *his* have the same individual as their value (where this individual is the first object in σ).

The sloppy reading of (82a) is a bit trickier. What we want for this reading is a fully explicit conjunction in which the first *his* can be interpreted as anaphoric with *John* and the second *his* can be interpreted as anaphoric with

Bill. However, if the proper names and pronouns are only related via sequence conditions, then there is no way to achieve this result. *John* and *his* in the first conjunct must bear the same index in order to corefer, and the two instances of *his* must also bear the same index, since one is copied from the other. But this means that we can coindex *Bill* and the second *his* only by letting the two names have the same index. Under our semantics for argument anaphora, this will force *John* and *Bill* to denote the same individual, which is clearly the wrong result.

Consider, however, an alternative view of the anaphoric relation between the names and pronouns in (82a). Suppose that the names are allowed to undergo quantifier raising and participate in variable binding. Then (82a) will have an additional structure in which the two names are raised and all of the NPs are coindexed. After VP copying, this structure will be the one in (83):

(83) $[_{S_1}$ John$_1$ $[_{S_1}$ t_1 $[_{VP}$ likes his$_1$ teachers]]] and
      $[_{S_2}$ Bill$_1$ $[_{S_2}$ t_1 $[_{VP}$ likes his$_1$ teachers]]]

Interestingly, despite the fact that all the NPs bear the same index here, *John* and *Bill* are *not* forced to refer to the same individual. In fact, this structure will yield precisely the sloppy reading we desire. The evaluation sequence σ for the conjunction (83) will pass down into each of its conjuncts S_1 and S_2, but when we encounter the conjuncts S_1 and S_2, we appeal to sequence variants of σ. According to (30), the larger S_1 will be true with respect to σ iff the smaller S_1 is true with respect to a 1-variant σ' containing John in its first position. And the larger S_2 will be true with respect to σ iff the smaller S_2 is true with respect to a 1-variant σ'' containing Bill in its first position. There is no conflict in these requirements: σ' and σ'' are simply two different 1-variants of the original σ. Under these distinct sequences, the conjunction will be true just in case John likes John's teachers and Bill likes Bill's teachers. This is the sloppy interpretation.

This account is attractive in that it not only obtains the desired strict and sloppy readings for the examples in question but also suggests *why* the latter should require variable binding, and hence exhibit the familiar dependence on c-command found with bound-variable anaphora. If ellipsis involves copying pieces of syntax and indices are part of the syntactic form of pronouns, then copied pronouns will always bring along their indices. This means that in order for pronouns bearing the same index to take different values in different conjuncts, they must be interpreted with respect to different sequences. Now in our semantics for quantification, the sequence of evaluation for a given node is typically also the sequence of evaluation for its parts. With conjunction, for instance, if S is evaluated with respect to σ, then S_1 and S_2 are evaluated with respect to σ as well:

(84)

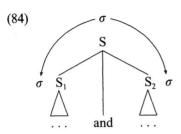

The only structures that induce a change of sequence in the evaluation of their parts are variable-binding structures: the latter require interpreting one of their parts with respect to an *i*-variant of the original sequence of evaluation. This entails that the only way for pronouns bearing the same index (pronoun$_i$) to take different values in different conjuncts is to be interpreted within the scope of different variable binders (α_i, β_i) in the two conjuncts:

(85)

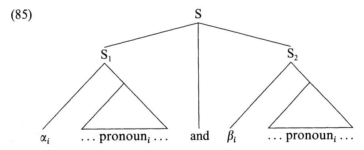

Thus only when the pronouns are interpreted as variable-bound by the names in the two conjuncts will a sloppy reading be possible.

10.3 Unbound Anaphora

Our final anaphora type is **unbound anaphora**, illustrated by (86a–c):

(86) a. If Max agrees with *a waiter*, then Bill always disagrees with *him*.
  b. No person who owns *a car* insures *it*.
  c. When you purchase *a chess set*, you get a board with *it*.

These examples show a dependence between the indicated indefinite expression (*a waiter, a car, a chess set*) and the pronoun. Semantically, this dependence appears similar to variable binding. Sentences (86a–c) have been widely held to have the interpretations represented in (87a–c), respectively, where the indefinite corresponds to a universal quantifier and the pronoun corresponds to a bound variable:

(87) a. [For every x such that x is a waiter and Max agrees with x]
       [Bill disagrees with x]
    b. [For no x such that x is a car] [for no y such that y is a person
       that owns x] [y insures x]
    c. [For every x such that x is a chess set and you purchase x]
       [you get a board along with x]

Nonetheless, these examples also diverge from more familiar cases of variable binding in at least two important ways, one semantic and one syntactic.

Semantically, there is the issue of *quantificational force*. The examples in (86a–c) all involve a pronoun whose antecedent is an indefinite expression. And very typically, indefinites are interpreted as existentially quantified phrases, as illustrated in (88) through (90):

(88) a. Max found a waiter.
    b. [For some x such that x is a waiter] [Max found x]

(89) a. A car drove up.
    b. [For some x such that x is a car] [x drove up]

(90) a. Chris sent a chess set to Kumiko.
    b. [For some x such that x is a chess set] [Chris sent x to Kumiko]

However, in (86a–c) the quantification associated with the indefinite is not existential but universal in each case. The informal glosses in (87) all involve "for every" or "for no," and not "for some." The semantic question raised by unbound anaphora is thus the following: Why does an expression whose quantificational force is typically existential come to have universal force in unbound-anaphora constructions? How is this result achieved?

Syntactically, there is the important issue of *scope*. We saw earlier that certain structural configurations appear to block movement of quantifiers at LF. In particular, relative-clause structures and preposed adverbial constructions present strong barriers to movement. Nonetheless, the unbound-anaphora examples in (86) appear to require scopal movement of exactly the prohibited kind. In (86a, c) the indefinite is embedded within a preposed adverbial (CP), and in (86b) the indefinite occurs inside a relative clause. Yet the glosses suggest that the quantification associated with the indefinite obtains widest scope in the clause. This result seems to imply that the indefinite escapes from the blocking configuration and adjoins to the highest clause (S), where it can c-command the pronoun and bind it:

(91) a.

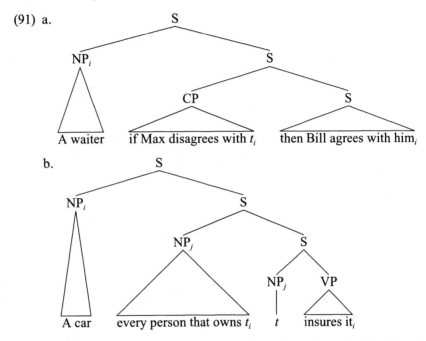

b.

Hence the syntactic question raised by unbound anaphora is this: How is the proper scope for quantifiers obtained in unbound-anaphora constructions? Why is the syntactic blocking effect observed in other cases apparently lifted in structures of this kind?

Current research has explored two quite different approaches to unbound anaphora. The basic difference between the approaches roughly corresponds to where the special properties of unbound anaphora are taken to arise. On one account—the **nonquantificational-indefinite theory** of Lewis (1975), Kamp (1981), and Heim (1982)—the special properties of unbound anaphora arise with the indefinite expression: how it is interpreted and how it receives scope.

By contrast, on the second analysis—the **descriptive-pronoun theory** of Evans (1977), Parsons (1978), and Cooper (1979)—the special properties of unbound anaphora arise with the pronominal expression: how it is interpreted and how it refers back to its quantificational antecedent.

10.3.1   The Nonquantificational Indefinite Theory

The nonquantificational-indefinite theory (NQI theory) approaches unbound anaphora through the question of how the quantificational force in examples like (86a–c) is to be explained. The central proposal is that constructions with indefinites involve a different association of syntactic and semantic form than we have encountered to this point.

The Basic Analysis

We noted above that the general view of quantification embodied in PredC and GQ assumes a tripartite division of logical form into a quantifier, a restriction, and a scope. We further observed that under the rules for either theory, the first two of these three components are associated with a single element, the quantified noun phrase, whereas the third is associated with the sentence S. This yields the correspondence of syntactic and semantic structure in (92):

(92)

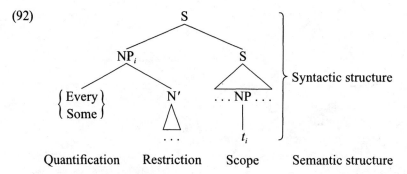

The leading idea of the NQI theory is that for indefinite expressions there is a different mapping of syntactic to semantic constituents. In place of the partition in (92), we have the one in (93), where NP$_i$ is an indefinite such as *a donkey* or *a chess set*:

(93)

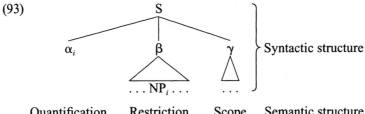

Quantification   Restriction   Scope   Semantic structure

On this view, indefinite constructions involve a quantifier falling *outside* the indefinite noun phrase. That is, indefinite NPs are viewed as nonquantificational and as semantically analogous to the N′ in a quantified NP such as *every man* or *no beagle*. Indefinites contribute only to the restriction on the quantification, not to the quantification itself.

We can make these points clearer with a concrete example, for instance, the conditional construction in (86a): *If Max agrees with a waiter, then Bill always disagrees with him.* Under the NQI theory, this sentence receives the LF in (94), where the frequency adverb *always* appears in a superordinate position, the indefinite NP *a waiter* is raised within the conditional clause, and the index borne by the indefinite "percolates" up to *always*:[12]

(94)

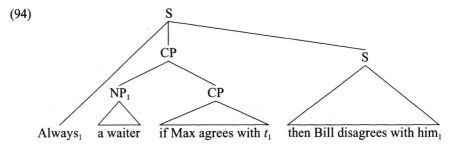

This structure can be interpreted by means of the axioms in (95) to (97):

(95) $\mathrm{Val}(t, [_S \ \textit{Always}_i \ CP \ S], \sigma)$ iff
$|\{\sigma'(i): \mathrm{Val}(t, CP, \sigma')\} - \{\sigma'(i): \mathrm{Val}(t, S, \sigma')\}| = 0$ (where $\sigma' \approx_i \sigma$)

(96) $\mathrm{Val}(t, [_{CP} \ NP_i \ CP], \sigma)$ iff $\mathrm{Val}(\sigma(i), NP, \sigma)$ and $\mathrm{Val}(t, CP, \sigma)$

(97) $\mathrm{Val}(\sigma(i), [_{NP} \ a \ N'], \sigma)$ iff $\mathrm{Val}(\sigma(i), N', \sigma)$

Axiom (95) is similar to the familiar rule for quantifier structures with *every*; *always* expresses a subset relation between sets. One set is given by CP and corresponds to the restriction on the quantification. The other is given by S and corresponds to the scope. Axiom (96) unpacks the interpretation of a clause containing an adjoined indefinite; it says that the whole construct is true with respect to σ' if the smaller sentence is true with respect to σ' and the ith element of σ' is a value of the indefinite NP. Finally, axiom (97) interprets indefinite NPs as semantically identical to the N's they contain. With these axioms it is easy to prove the T sentence for (94):

(98) Val(t, [$_S$ Always if Max agrees with a waiter,
         then Bill disagrees with him], σ) iff
       $|\{\sigma'(1) : \sigma'(1) \text{ is a waiter and Max agrees with } \sigma'(1)\} -$
       $\{\sigma'(1) : \text{Bill disagrees with } \sigma'(1)\}| = 0$

Under familiar equivalences of set theory, this reduces to (99), the desired result (compare (87a)):

(99) Val(t, [$_S$ If Max agrees with a waiter,
         then Bill always disagrees with him])
       iff for every x such that x is a waiter and Max agrees with x,
       Bill disagrees with x

This example shows the association of syntactic and semantic form discussed above in (93). We see that although the interpretation of the indefinite involves quantification, this quantification issues not from the indefinite itself but rather from an external element, in this case a frequency adverb. The indefinite contributes to the restriction on this quantifier as a simple predicate, with the determiner a treated as a purely grammatical element making no semantic contribution of its own.

Extending the Account

The basic NQI analysis can be extended to examples with multiple indefinites and to examples with other kinds of quantificational elements. It can also accommodate the general existential character of indefinite expressions noted earlier in connection with (88a) to (90a). We will briefly sketch the extensions involved here without trying to justify all details.

Multiple indefinites

Sentences with multiple indefinites, such as (100a–c), are treated in the NQI account by allowing quantificational elements like *always* to bind a number of variables simultaneously, and not just a single variable, as in the more familiar case.

(100) a. If a boy sees a dog, he always pets it.
     b. If a girl gives a boy a present, he always thanks her for it.
     c. If a delivery boy leaves a package for a customer at a place, she always picks it up from him there.

We can illustrate with (100b). Suppose this example is assigned the LF in (101), where the three indefinite NPs have all adjoined and their indices have all percolated to *always*:

(101)

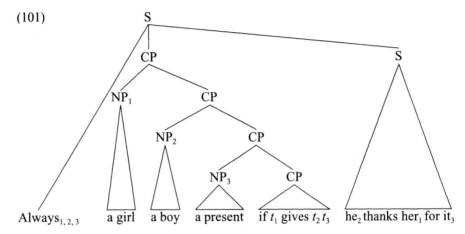

Always$_{1,2,3}$ a girl   a boy   a present   if t_1 gives $t_2 t_3$ he$_2$ thanks her$_1$ for it$_3$

Suppose further that we generalize our basic quantificational axiom to handle such multiple indices and extend our definition of sequence variance appropriately:

(102) $\text{Val}(t, [_S \ Always_{i,j,\ldots,n} \ CP \ S], \sigma)$ iff
$|\{\langle \sigma'(i), \sigma'(j), \ldots, \sigma'(n)\rangle : \text{Val}(t, CP, \sigma')\} -$
$\{\langle \sigma'(i), \sigma'(j), \ldots, \sigma'(n)\rangle : \text{Val}(t, S, \sigma')\}| = 0$ (where $\sigma' \approx_{i,j,\ldots,n} \sigma$)

Definition A sequence σ' is a $(i, j, \ldots, n)$**-variant** of a sequence σ just in case σ' differs from σ at most in its $i, j, \ldots, n$ positions.

With these revisions, (101) will receive the T sentence in (103) (where $\sigma' \approx_{1,2,3} \sigma$):

(103) $\text{Val}(t, [_S \ \text{If a girl gives a boy a present, he always thanks her for it}], \sigma)$ iff
$|\{\langle \sigma'(1), \sigma'(2), \sigma'(3)\rangle : \sigma'(1) \text{ is a girl and } \sigma'(2) \text{ is a boy and}$
$\sigma'(3) \text{ is a present and } \sigma'(1) \text{ gave } \sigma'(2) \ \sigma'(3)\} -$
$\{\langle \sigma'(1), \sigma'(2), \sigma'(3)\rangle : \sigma'(2) \text{ thanks } \sigma'(1) \text{ for } \sigma'(3)\}| = 0$

By the familiar homology between sequences and individuals, (103) is tantamount to quantifying over triples of individuals $\langle x, y, z \rangle$. Hence we are justified in rewriting this T sentence as in (104):

(104) Val(t, [$_S$ If a girl gives a boy a present, he always thanks her for it], σ) iff for every triple $\langle x, y, z \rangle$ such that x is a girl, y is a boy, z is a present, and x gives y z, y thanks x for z

Other quantificational elements

Examples with other kinds of quantificational elements, like (105a, b), or with missing quantificational elements, like (106a, b), can be treated similarly to *always*:

(105) a. If Max agrees with a waiter, then Bill sometimes disagrees with him.
       b. No person who owns a car insures it.

(106) a. When you purchase a chess set, you get a board with it.
       b. A person who owns a car insures it.

In the case of (105a), we may simply assume an LF like (94), but with the existential frequency adverb *sometimes* appearing in place of *always*. This structure will have a corresponding semantic axiom like (95) but stating that there is a nonempty intersection of the relevant sets of n-tuples. With (105b), we postulate an LF in which the determiner contributes the quantification analogously to a frequency adverb and the relative clause contributes the restriction analogously to the preposed adverbial:[13]

(107)

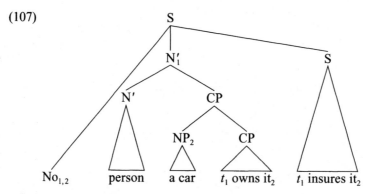

This structure can then be interpreted via axioms like those given for (101):

(108) Val(t, [$_S$ $No_{i,j,...,n}$ N'_k S], σ) iff
$|\{\langle\sigma'(i), \sigma'(j), \ldots, \sigma'(n)\rangle : \mathrm{Val}(\sigma'(k), N', \sigma')\} \cap$
$\{\langle\sigma'(i), \sigma'(j), \ldots, \sigma'(n)\rangle : \mathrm{Val}(t, S, \sigma')\}| = 0$ (where $\sigma' \approx_{i,j,...,n} \sigma$)

(109) Val(x, [$_{N'}$ N' CP], σ) iff Val(x, N', σ) and Val(t, CP, σ)

As the reader may show, these will yield a T sentence as in (110), which is equivalent to the quantification over pairs given in (111):

(110) Val(t, [$_S$ No person who owns a car insures it], σ) iff
$|\{\langle\sigma'(1), \sigma'(2)\rangle : \sigma'(1)$ is a person and $\sigma'(2)$ is a car and $\sigma'(1)$ owns $\sigma'(2)\} \cap$
$\{\langle\sigma'(1), \sigma'(2)\rangle : \sigma'(1)$ insures $\sigma'(2)\}| = 0$ (where $\sigma' \approx_{i,j,...,n} \sigma$)

(111) Val(t, [$_S$ No person who owns a car insures it]) iff for no pair $\langle x, y\rangle$ such that x is a person, y is a car, and x owns y, x insures y

The LFs for (106a, b) are the counterparts of (105a, b) but with an inaudible universal quantifier, an unpronounced version of *always*. Representing this unpronounced quantifier by "∀", we have the following:[14]

(112)

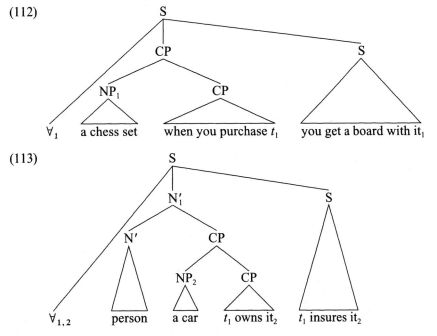

These structures will be interpreted analogously to (94) and (107).

Existential closure

Finally, the NQI analysis can accommodate the general existential character of indefinite expressions in most uses, such as (88a) to (90a) (repeated):

(88a) Max found a waiter.

(89a) A car drove up.

(90a) Chris sent a chess set to Kumiko.

Assume that in simple sentences involving no preposed adverbial clauses there is a default existential quantifier adjoined to S. The latter may be thought of as an implicit frequency adverb equivalent to *once*. If we represent this element by "∃", (88a), for example, will receive the LF in (114):

(114)

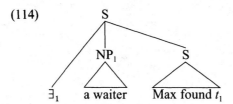

This structure can then be interpreted as in our earlier examples with "∃" providing the (existential) quantification, the indefinite *a waiter* providing the restriction, and the sentence *Max found* t_1 providing the scope. Adjunction of a default existential quantifier as in (114) is sometimes referred to as **existential closure**.[15]

   These results illustrate clearly how the NQI account answers the basic semantic and syntactic questions raised by unbound anaphora. On the NQI theory, the quantificational force shown by an indefinite derives entirely from some quantifier with which it is in construction—either an explicit frequency adverb or determiner, or their implicit, inaudible counterparts. The variation shown by indefinites is thus a natural consequence of being in construction with quantifiers of different kinds. Furthermore, since the binding of pronouns in the matrix clause is accomplished by this external quantificational element, the indefinite has no problem obtaining broad scope. It is not the indefinite that must have scope over the pronominal element at LF but rather the independent quantifier occurring elsewhere in the tree, and this quantifier always has scope broad enough to bind the relevant pronoun, even when the indefinite itself is confined to the adverbial or relative clause.

The Proportion Problem

The NQI theory evidently handles a variety of phenomena involving unbound anaphora, assigning T sentences that appear to capture central aspects of the meaning of these constructions. Nonetheless, the theory also encounters an interesting problem that has been much discussed in recent literature on unbound anaphora.[16] Consider (115):

(115) Most women who talked to a waiter commended him.

Under the NQI analysis, this sentence receives the LF in (116a) and the (equivalent of the) T sentence in (116b), involving quantification over pairs:

(116) a.

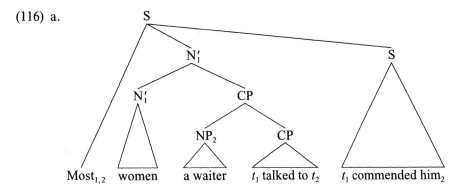

b. Val(t, [$_S$ Most women who talked to a waiter commended him]) iff for most pairs $\langle x, y \rangle$ such that x is a woman, y is a waiter, and x talked to y, x commended y

Consider now the following situation:

- There are five women.
- There are ten waiters.
- One woman, Jill, talked to and commended all ten waiters.
- The other four women talked to one waiter each but did not commend any of them.

For the majority of the women (that is, for four of them), the number of waiters who were talked to and not commended was greater than the number of waiters who were talked to and commended. Hence our intuition is that in this situation (115) is false. It is not true that most women who talked to a waiter commended him. Nonetheless, on careful inspection, the T sentence in

(116b) actually predicts the sentence to be true. To see this, simply notice that the number of pairs $\langle x, y \rangle$ where x is a woman and y is a commended waiter that x talked to is ten (i.e., there are ten pairs where x is Jill) but the number of pairs $\langle x, y \rangle$ where x is a woman and y is a noncommended waiter is four (i.e., there is one pair $\langle x, y \rangle$ for each of the four women besides Jill):

(117) $\langle x, y \rangle$ such that x is a woman and
y is a waiter such that x talked to y and x commended y:
$\langle$Jill, $W_1\rangle$, $\langle$Jill, $W_2\rangle$, ..., $\langle$Jill, $W_{10}\rangle$

$\langle x, y \rangle$ such that x is a woman and
y is a waiter such that x talked to y and x did not commend y:
$\langle$Betty, $W_2\rangle$, $\langle$Sue, $W_5\rangle$, $\langle$Judy, $W_8\rangle$, $\langle$Jo, $W_{10}\rangle$,

According to (116b), the sentence should be true if the number of pairs of the first sort exceeds the number of pairs of the second sort, and this is indeed the case here. Hence we incorrectly predict (115) to be true.

On reflection, it can be seen that this problem, referred to as the **proportion problem**, is not a superficial one but arises from a fundamental feature of the NQI theory, namely from the proposal that indefinites lack inherent quantificational content. Since *a waiter* is taken to have no quantificational force of its own, it must be seen as bound by the quantifier *most*. Accordingly, *most* must be analyzed as quantifying over pairs of women and waiters, and not over women alone. But this then raises the problem just noted: our intuition about the truth or falsity of examples like (115) tracks proportions of women of a certain kind, and not proportions of women-waiter pairs. Hence when the two proportions diverge, as in the example situation given, the NQI analysis gets the truth conditions wrong.

A number of proposals have been made in the literature on how to resolve the proportion problem with the NQI account. For example, Reinhart (1987) suggests that the general analysis can be saved if the pairs quantified over in (116) consist of an individual and a set rather than two individuals. Suppose that rather than pairing women and the individual waiters they talked to and commended or did not commend, the truth conditions instead pair women with sets of the appropriate waiters:

(118) $\langle x, Y \rangle$ such that x is a woman and
$Y = \{y : y$ is a waiter, x talked to y, and x commended $y\}$:
$\langle$Jill, $\{W_1, ..., W_{10}\}\rangle$

$\langle x, Y \rangle$ such that x is a woman and
$Y = \{ y : y$ is a waiter, x talked to y, and x did not commend $y \}$:
$\langle$ Betty, $\{W_2\} \rangle$, $\langle$ Sue, $\{W_5\} \rangle$, $\langle$ Judy, $\{W_8\} \rangle$, $\langle$ Jo, $\{W_{10}\} \rangle$

Then the number of such pairs collapses dramatically. Rather than being associated with ten pairs, Jill is associated with only a single pair, and similarly for each of the other women. In effect, the number of pairs simply collapses to the number of women, and hence the proportion of *pairs* consisting of women and sets of waiters talked to and commended or not commended collapses to the proportion of *women* who talked to and commended waiters versus those who talked to but did not commend them.

It is easy to see that if we quantify over pairs of this kind then the proportion problem will not arise. In (118) there are more pairs of women and waiters not commended (four) than of women and waiters commended (one). This is what we want for the situation in question. We will not attempt to further spell out Reinhart's proposal here but will simply refer interested readers to Reinhart 1987.

10.3.2   The Descriptive-Pronoun Theory

The descriptive-pronoun (DP) theory approaches unbound anaphora from a very different perspective than the NQI analysis. It does not reanalyze the quantificational force of the antecedent; rather, it reassesses the relation between the antecedent and the pronoun.

The Basic Analysis

The leading idea of the descriptive-pronoun analysis is that an unbound pronoun that is anaphoric on a quantified antecedent goes proxy for a definite description. To illustrate, the indicated pronoun in (119a) is understood as going proxy for the definite description in (119b), where the definite description is understood as a Russellian quantifier:

(119) a. *A man* came in. *He* sat down.
   b. *A man* came in. *The man who came in* sat down.

On this view, the anaphoric connection between the antecedent and the pronoun arises neither through binding nor through sequence constraints. Rather, the shared descriptive material and the uniqueness condition on the definite description conspire to insure that the two NPs denote the same person:

(120) For some x, x is a man, and x came in. For some x, for all y, y is a man and y came in iff $y = x$, and x sat down.

The general DP analysis is attractive on a number of counts. The descriptive-pronoun analysis achieves the connection between pronoun and antecedent in (119) without special assumptions about scope. By contrast, a variable-binding analysis can only capture the connection between the existential quantifier and the pronoun by finding means to extend the scope of the existential quantifier across two clauses:

(121) $\exists x[x$ is a man & x came in & x sat down$]$

Also, the descriptive-pronoun analysis achieves the connection between pronoun and antecedent without requiring the latter to be a referring term or the speaker to have specific grounds for his or her utterance. For example, suppose that Sherlock Holmes returns to his Baker Street apartment and finds evidence of an unknown intruder. He says (119a) in the process of deducing the intruder's movements about the room. Evidently, the pronoun *he* can be anaphoric on *a man* without there being a specific individual referred to and without Holmes knowing who the man was. The descriptive-pronoun analysis accommodates this result smoothly, since, as we saw in chapter 9, descriptions analyzed as quantifiers do not induce object-dependent truth conditions. By contrast, a sequence-constraint analysis can capture anaphoric connections across sentences only when the antecedent is a referring expression and the speaker has singular grounds for his or her assertion. It does not extend to cases where the antecedent is nonreferring and the speaker does not have singular grounds.

Finally, as noted by Evans (1977), the DP account extends naturally to cases that a binding analysis does not handle correctly. Evans observes that examples like (122a–c) are not rendered properly by the bound-variable formulas in (123a–c) respectively, since the latter lose the implication that Harry vaccinates *all* of the sheep that John owns, that *all* of the (small number of) MPs who attended the party had a marvellous time, and that *all* of the (many) boys that Mary danced with found her interesting:

(122) a. John owns *some sheep*, and Harry vaccinates *them*.
       b. *Few MPs* came to the party, but *they* had a marvellous time.
       c. Mary danced with *many boys*, and *they* found her interesting.

(123) a. For some x, x a sheep, John owns x, and Harry vaccinates x.
       b. For few x, x is an MP, x came to the party, and x had a marvellous time.

   c. For many x, x is a boy, Mary danced with x, and x found her interesting.

By contrast, these implications are preserved under the DP analysis. Sentences (122a–c) are analyzed as (124a–c), which do carry the entailment of universality:

(124) a. John owns *some sheep*, and Harry vaccinates *the sheep that John owns*.
     b. *Few MPs* came to the party, but *the MPs that came to the party* had a marvellous time.
     c. Mary danced with *many boys*, and *the boys that Mary danced with* found her interesting.

Spelling Out the Descriptive Pronoun

In the formulation of the DP theory above, the notion that "the pronoun … goes proxy for a definite description" is left vague, and indeed there are a number of ways of technically spelling out the idea. One possibility is that the pronoun is literally replaced by the appropriate description at the level of logical form. Under this view, (124a) represents, in effect, the LF of (122a), and unbound anaphora is fundamentally a syntactic matter. No change in our pronoun-interpretation rules are required, because, at the relevant syntactic level, pronouns are simply not present.[17]

An alternative is to take the pronouns to be lexically ambiguous, so that in addition to their normal, sequence-relative axioms, (125a), they have axioms parallel to those of definite descriptions, and part of their content (the restriction $\{x : \Phi(x)\}$) is fixed in the process of interpretation, (125b):

(125) a. $\text{Val}(x, he_i, \sigma)$ iff $x = \sigma(i)$
     b. $\text{Val}(X, he_i, \sigma)$ iff $|\{x : \Phi(x)\} - X| = 0$ and $|\{x : \Phi(x)\}| = 1$

In the case of (119), for example, we have $\{x : \Phi(x)\} = \{x : x \text{ is a man \& } x \text{ came in}\}$. On this idea, unbound anaphora is fundamentally an interpretive phenomenon. No replacement of the pronoun occurs.

The issue of how the relevant definite description (or its descriptive content) is reconstructed can also be executed in different ways. Recovery might be understood as a pragmatic matter, determined by general contextual cues.[18] Alternatively it may be a matter of specific rules for calculating the content. For example, there is the following rule for reconstructing a descriptive pronoun, based on proposals by Davies (1981a) and Neale (1990a, 1990b):[19]

(126) If α is a pronoun anaphoric on a quantified $[_{NP_1}$ Det N′], where the latter is adjoined to an S clause, and if S is interpreted with respect to sequence σ, then for any σ″, Val(X, α, σ″) iff $|(Y \cap Z) - X| = 0$ and $|(Y \cap Z)| = 1$, where

$$Y = \{\sigma'(1) : \mathrm{Val}(\sigma'(1), \mathrm{N'}, \sigma), \sigma' \approx_1 \sigma\},$$

$$Z = \{\sigma'(1) : \mathrm{Val}(\sigma'(1), \mathrm{S}, \sigma'), \sigma' \approx_1 \sigma\}.$$

This rule reconstructs the descriptive content of the pronoun as the set of individuals satisfying the N′ in the quantified antecedent and the open sentence given by S. Applied to (119), for example, this rule correctly projects the descriptive content of *he* in terms of the N′ $[_{N'}$ *man*] together with the clause $[_S t_1$ came in]:[20]

(127)

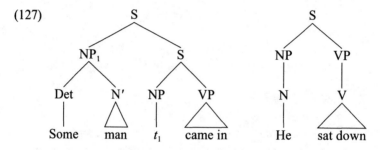

Val(X, *he*, σ″) iff $|\{\sigma'(1) : \sigma'(1) \text{ is a man \& } \sigma'(1) \text{ came in}\} - X| = 0$ and $|\{\sigma'(1) : \sigma'(1) \text{ is a man \& } \sigma'(1) \text{ came in})\}| = 1$

Val(X, *he*, σ″) iff $|\{x : x \text{ is a man \& } x \text{ came in}\} - X| = 0$ and $|\{x : x \text{ is a man \& } x \text{ came in})\}| = 1$

These values for *he* are the same result as yielded by GQ (with respect to σ″) for *the man that came in*.

The exact nature of the reconstructive rules is, of course, an empirical matter, and Neale (1990a) notes cases where the equivalent of (126) does not predict the correct result. Consider examples like (128a, b), where the antecedent is what Neale terms a "maximal quantifier" (roughly, a quantifier carrying a universality implication):

(128) a. *The inventor of bifocals* was a genius; *he* ate a lot of fish.
      b. *Both recipients of the prize* were geniuses; *they* ate a lot of fish.

As Neale observes, the pronouns in the second clauses are correctly interpreted not by the paraphrases in (129) but rather by the simpler ones in (130):

(129) a. *The inventor of bifocals* was a genius; *the inventor of bifocals who was a genius* ate a lot of fish.

   b. *Both recipients of the prize* were geniuses; *both recipients of the prize who were geniuses* ate a lot of fish.

(130) a. *The inventor of bifocals* was a genius; *the inventor of bifocals* ate a lot of fish.

   b. *Both recipients of the prize* were geniuses; *both recipients of the prize* ate a lot of fish.

Evidently, in the case where the quantified antecedent is maximal, only the N' contributes to the descriptive content of the anaphoric pronoun. Hence the rule in question must be relativized according to the quantifier type of the antecedent.

The Problem of Uniqueness

The DP analysis is attractive and natural in many respects. Nonetheless, it appears to encounter an immediate problem with our initial set of examples of unbound anaphora. Compare (86a–c) (repeated below) with (131a–c) respectively, where the pronoun has been replaced by a definite description:

(86) a. If Max agrees with *a waiter*, then Bill always disagrees with *him*.
   b. No person who owns *a car* insures *it*.
   c. When you purchase *a chess set*, you get a board with *it*.

(131) a. If Max agrees with *a waiter*, then Bill always disagrees with *the waiter that Max agrees with*.
   b. No person who owns *a car* insures *the car that he owns*.
   c. When you purchase *a chess set*, you get a board with *the chess set you purchase*.

As various authors have noted, there is an apparent uniqueness implication in the latter examples that is not present in the former. Whereas (131a) implies that Bill disagrees with *one* unique waiter, (86a) does not; whereas (131b) implies that car owners possess a *single* car, (86b) does not; and so on. The readings of (131) are expected under the Russellian analysis, which takes a definite description to denote a unique individual. However, the divergence between (86) and (131) is unexpected. If the pronoun is a Russellian quantifier, then we would expect it to carry a uniqueness implication too. But this doesn't appear to be so.[21]

In general terms, there are two different lines by which we might accommodate failure of uniqueness implications under the DP analysis. On the one hand, we might weaken the semantics of the descriptive pronoun so that the uniqueness requirement is lifted. Broadly speaking, this is the approach proposed in Davies 1981a and developed in detail in Neale 1990a, 1990b. Consider the NPs in (132):

(132) a. [Whoever broke the window] must pay for it.
      b. Mary saw [what(ever) Fred saw].

Following a suggestion by G. E. Moore, Neale (1990a, 1990b) proposes that the indicated phrases are what he calls "numberless descriptions." That is, they have essentially the same semantics as the corresponding phrases in (133), which contain a definite description denoting one or more individuals.

(133) a. [The person or persons who broke the window] must pay for it.
      b. Mary saw [the thing or things that Fred saw].

On this view, the semantic value of *whoever broke the window* works out as in (134):

(134) Val(X, [$_{NP}$ whoever broke the window], σ) iff
      $|\{x : x \text{ is a person} \ \& \ x \text{ broke the window}\} - X| = 0$ and
      $|\{x : x \text{ is a person} \ \& \ x \text{ broke the window}\}| \geq 1$

Neale (1990a, 1990b) then argues that unbound pronouns that are anaphoric on a quantifier should be analyzed in parallel with (132a, b). That is, they are interpreted not as singular definite descriptions but rather as numberless definite descriptions.[22] The counterparts of (86a–c) are thus not the examples in (131) but rather the examples in (135):

(135) a. If Max agrees with *a waiter*, then Bill always disagrees with *the waiter or waiters that Max agrees with*.
      b. No person who owns *a car* insures *the car or cars that he owns*.
      c. When you purchase *a chess set*, you get a board with *the set or sets that you purchase*.

These deliver the correct truth conditions for (86a–c) while avoiding the unwanted uniqueness implications.

An alternative strategy for dealing with uniqueness is to strengthen the content of the descriptive pronoun so that uniqueness of denotation is restored. Broadly speaking, this is the approach taken in recent work that relativizes the content of the descriptive pronoun to an additional parameter of events.[23] We will not introduce events formally until chapter 12, but the relevant notions can be made clear in informal terms. Following the exposition in Ludlow 1994a, let us assume that conditionals are fundamentally quantificational constructions that quantify over events; for example, (136a) is approximately spelled out as in (136b):

(136) a. If Chris leaves, then Phil leaves too.
      b. $\forall e[\text{leaves}(\text{Chris}, e) \rightarrow \exists e'[e' Re \ \& \ \text{leave}(\text{Phil}, e')]]$

The idea behind this is that (136a) is true just in case for every event e in which Chris leaves, there is a related event e' in which Phil leaves.[24]

Suppose we now apply this idea to the conditional in (86a) (repeated as (137a)), spelling the pronoun out as a definite quantified phrase, (137b):

(137) a. If Max agrees with *a waiter*, then Bill always disagrees with *him*.
      b. $\forall e[\exists x[\text{waiter}(x) \ \& \ \text{agrees-with}(\text{Max}, x, e)] \rightarrow$
         THE $x[\text{waiter}(x) \ \& \ \text{agrees-with}(\text{Max}, e)]$
         $\exists e'[e' Re \ \& \ \text{disagrees-with}(\text{Bill}, x, e')]]$

The latter makes (137a) true just in case for every event in which Max agrees with a waiter, there is a related event e' in which Bill disagrees with the unique waiter that Max agreed with in e. The crucial point to notice here is that by enriching the content of the pronoun and making it relative to events, we no longer require simply a unique waiter that Max agreed with but instead require a unique waiter that Max agreed with *in the event e*. The conditions under which a violation of uniqueness would occur have become much tighter. Hence the description can remain singular. Note furthermore that the truth conditions imposed by (137b) seem to track our natural picture of this example in which whenever there is an event of Max agreeing with a waiter, it is always followed by an event of Bill disagreeing with that very same man.

Both of these analyses—numberless pronouns and event relativization—are under active investigation at present, and we will not attempt to pursue them further here. We simply note that with either analysis, we get a fundamentally different resolution of the problems of unbound anaphora than with the nonquantificational-indefinite theory. We observed truth conditions for (86a–c) where the pronoun appeared to behave as a bound variable (recall (87a–c)):

(87) a. [For every x such that x is a waiter and Max agrees with x]
[Bill disagrees with x]

b. [For no x such that x is a car] [for no y such that y is a person
that owns x] [y insures x]

c. [For every x such that x is a chess set and you purchase x]
[you get a board along with x]

These in turn raised questions of scope and of quantificational force: How can *a waiter* obtain sufficiently broad scope to bind the pronoun? Why does its quantificational force apparently change from existential to universal? Under the descriptive-pronoun analysis (fleshed out either with numberless pronouns or event-relative quantification), *a waiter* does not bind the pronoun. Rather, the pronoun is interpreted as a quantifier. Furthermore, the indefinite does not change its quantificational force from existential to universal. Rather, the universal force that we detect in (86a–c) is the effect of interpreting the pronoun as a definite description, which is itself a species of universal phrase. The resulting truth conditions end up very similar to (87a–c), but the latter do not reveal the true nature of the construction under the descriptive theory.

Theory and Exercises

Axioms for Anaphoric Expressions

(1) $Val(t, [_S \ NP_i \ S], \sigma)$ iff for the $\sigma' \approx_i \sigma$ such that $Val(\sigma'(i), NP, \sigma)$,
$[+ref]$
$Val(t, S, \sigma')$

(2) $Val(x, NP_i, \sigma)$ iff $Val(x, NP, \sigma)$ and $x = \sigma(i)$

(3) a. $Val(x, him, \sigma)$ iff $Val(x, NP*, \sigma)$, where NP* is the antecedent of *him*
b. $Val(x, her, \sigma)$ iff $Val(x, NP*, \sigma)$, where NP* is the antecedent of *her*
c. $Val(x, it, \sigma)$ iff $Val(x, NP*, \sigma)$, where NP* is the antecedent of *it*

Exercises

1. Give derivations in GQ for (1) and (2).

(1) Every woman admires her fish. (With *her* bound by *every woman*.)

(2) No woman admires her fish. (With the trace of *no woman* in a chain with *her*.)

2. Give a T-sentence derivation in GQ for the LF below, which violates the WCO constraint:

(1) [s [NP₁ Every [N′ boy]] [s [NP [Det his₁] [N′ mother]] [VP [V admires] [NP₁ *e*]]]]

Is there anything semantically odd about this derivation or its result?

3. Three prominent analyses of reflexive anaphors have been advanced in the syntactic literature:

Obligatory binding/coreference   A reflexive is an item obligatorily coindexed with another element (its antecedent) within some specified syntactic domain:

(1)
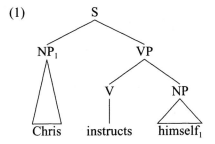

On this view, *Chris instructs himself* is a transitive clause; the reflexive is an argument and receives its own semantic value.

Valence reduction   Reflexives mark a predicate as having undergone a reduction in its valence or polyadicity:

(2)
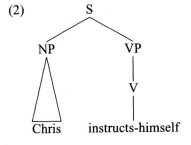

On this view, *Chris instructs himself* is an intransitive clause; the reflexive is not an argument but rather indicates that values of the predicate are identical. *Instructs-himself* is a complex (lexically derived) intransitive predicate.

Operator   Reflexives are operators having scope within a major predicate projection:

(3)

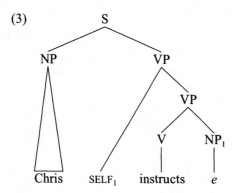

Here *Chris instructs himself* is once again transitive, but the reflexive is not referential. Rather, it is an operator (similar to that occurring in relatives) that adjoins the immediate domain of its antecedent.

Give three extensions of GQ that interpret reflexives according to the three different proposals in above. Prove your results showing that *Chris instructs himself* is interpreted appropriately.

4. It has been widely observed that sentences like (1) are ambiguous between interpretations of the kind given informally in (2):

(1) Only Satan admires his mother.

(2) a. Only for x = Satan, x admires x's mother
    b. Only for x = Satan, x admires Satan's mother

Evans (1977) proposes that the interpretations in (2) are respectively associated with the two distinct representations in (3) involving chains:

(3) a.

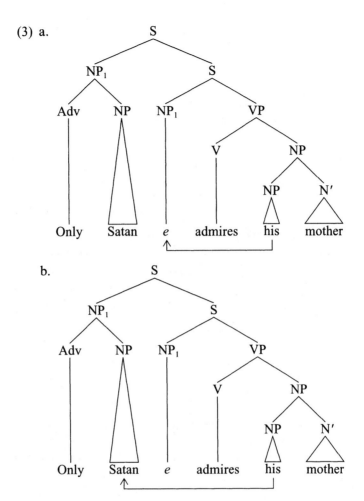

b.

Using the axioms in (4) for the adverb *only*, together with the axioms for interpreting trees with chains given in the text, show that (3a, b) do in fact yield appropriate T sentences. That is, show that (3a) is associated with a T sentence corresponding to (2a) and that (3b) is associated with a T sentence corresponding to (2b).

(4) a. Val(X, [$_{NP}$ Adv NP], σ) iff for some Y, $Y = \{x : \mathrm{Val}(x, \mathrm{NP}, \sigma)\}$ and
    Val($\langle X, Y \rangle$, Adv, σ)
  b. Val($\langle X, Y \rangle$, *only*, σ) iff $|X - Y| = 0$

5. The sentence in (1), containing two pronominal subjects, admits both a strict and a sloppy reading:

(1) He likes his teachers, and he does too.

What problems arise in extending the analysis of sloppy identity suggested in the text to accommodate this example? More generally, discuss what such a case suggests about the indices born by quantifier-raised expressions.

6. Dahl (1972) notes certain complex examples like (1) in which sloppy and strict readings are mixed in a single sentence:

(1) John likes his teachers, and Bill does too, but his mother doesn't.

This example has the fully strict reading in (2a) and the fully sloppy reading in (2b). But it also appears to have a mixed reading as in (2c), where the elided pronoun in the second conjunct is understood sloppily while the elided pronoun in the third conjunct is understood strictly:

(2) a. John likes John's teachers, and Bill likes John's teachers, but Bill's mother doesn't like John's teachers.
   b. John likes John's teachers, and Bill likes Bill's teachers, but Bill's mother doesn't like Bill's mother's teachers.
   c. John likes John's teachers, and Bill likes Bill's teachers, but Bill's mother doesn't like Bill's teachers.

On the analysis suggested in the text, readings (2a, b) can be obtained through structures (3a, b), respectively, with appropriate choice of sequence. The former involves in situ names in each conjunct, and the latter involves quantifier raising in each conjunct:

(3) a. $[_{S_1}$ John$_1$ $[_{VP}$ likes his$_1$ teachers]] and
      $[_{S_2}$ Bill$_2$ $[_{VP}$ likes his$_1$ teachers]] but
      $[_{S_3}$ his$_2$ mother$_3$ doesn't $[_{VP}$ like his$_1$ teachers]]
   b. $[_{S_1}$ John$_1$ $[_{S_1}$ t_1 $[_{VP}$ likes his$_1$ teachers]]] and
      $[_{S_2}$ Bill$_1$ $[_{S_2}$ t_1 $[_{VP}$ likes his$_1$ teachers]]] but
      $[_{S_3}$ his$_2$ mother$_1$ $[_{S_3}$ t_1 doesn't $[_{VP}$ like his$_1$ teachers]]]

Suggest a structure and an appropriate choice of sequence that will obtain the mixed sloppy-strict reading in (2c).

7. The following sentence is an example of unbound anaphora:

(1) If I have a dollar, I will give it you.

- How would (1) be analyzed under the NQI theory of unbound anaphora?
- How would (1) be analyzed under a DP theory of unbound anaphora in which we assumed numberless pronouns?
- How would (1) be analyzed under a DP theory of unbound anaphora in which we assumed event relativization?
- Does one of these approaches handle the facts better than the others?

8. What problems do the following examples pose for the DP theory of unbound anaphora (the second of which is due to Heim [1982]):

(1) *A*: A man fell in front of a train.
      B: *He* didn't fall, he was pushed.

(2) If a man buys a sage plant, he buys nine others along with it.

11   Clausal Complements and Attitude Reports

A very important class of constructions not yet within the scope of our semantic theory includes sentences with clausal complements like (1a–c):

(1) a. Chris says Jill agrees.
     b. Kate believes Rumplestiltzkin ponders.
     c. Kumiko hopes Kate admires Phil.

In the philosophical literature such examples are often called **propositional-attitude reports**, since they purport to convey some individual's attitude—saying, believing, hoping—toward the proposition expressed by the embedded sentence (that Jill agrees, that Rumplestiltzkin ponders, etc.).

Clausal complement constructions have received enormous attention in the semantics literature for over a century.[1] One reason is that embedded clauses seem to require a different semantics from their unembedded counterparts. As a way of introducing the issues, let us begin by seeing why complementation rules of the kind we've developed so far do not extend directly to embedded Ss.

11.1   Clausal Complements and Truth Values

Clausal complements occur in structures very similar to those involving NP objects. Indeed, they often co-occur with the very same predicates.[2]

(2) a. $[_{VP} \text{ V NP}]$ (e.g., *Chris says* $[_{NP}$ *those words*$]$)
     b. $[_{VP} \text{ V S}]$ (e.g., *Chris says* $[_{S}$ *Jill agrees*$]$)

(3) a. $[_{VP} \text{ V NP NP}]$ (e.g., *Chris told Phil* $[_{NP}$ *that story*$]$)
     b. $[_{VP} \text{ V NP S}]$ (e.g., *Chris told Phil* $[_{S}$ *Jill agrees*$]$)

Given this parallel distribution, it's natural to try to analyze the two in a semantically parallel way. We've taken simple NPs (like *that story*) to refer to things, and we've analyzed verbs that select NP objects (like *say*) as expressing relations between things (4a, b). The rules that analyze structures like (2a) bind together the semantic values of the component V and NP, (4c):

(4) a. Val(x, [$_{NP}$ that$_i$ story], σ) iff $x = \sigma(i)$
  b. Val($\langle x, y \rangle$, *says*, σ) iff x says y
  c. Val(x, [$_{VP}$ V NP], σ) iff for some y, Val($\langle x, y \rangle$, V, σ) and Val(y, NP, σ)

A parallel analysis of embedded clauses would take Ss as referring to certain things, here truth values, and would take verbs that select clauses as expressing relations between things, (5a, b). The rules that analyze structures like (3a) would again bind together the semantic values of the component V and S, (5c):

(5) a. Val(t, [$_S$ Jill agrees], σ) iff Jill agrees
  b. Val($\langle x, y \rangle$, *says*, σ) iff x says y
  c. Val(x, [$_{VP}$ V S], σ) iff for some y, Val($\langle x, y \rangle$, V, σ) and Val(y, S, σ)

As natural as these rules may look, they very quickly encounter problems when we try to apply them. As the reader may verify, (5a–c) (together with other familiar axioms) will not allow us to prove anything like (6a). The furthest they will carry us in analyzing *Chris says Jill agrees* is what appears in (6b):

(6) a. Val(t, [$_S$ Chris says Jill agrees], σ) iff Chris says Jill agrees
  b. Val(t, [$_S$ Chris says Jill agrees], σ) iff for some y, Chris says y and
    Val(y, [$_S$ Jill agrees], σ)

The crucial stumbling block here is the clause "Val(y, [$_S$ Jill agrees], σ)." Our rules only tell us under what conditions a sentence has the specific value t; they provide clauses like (5a). But (6b) requires much more than this. To proceed beyond (6b) in the derivation, we need to know under what conditions *any arbitrary thing y* is a value of the S *Jill agrees*. A T theory simply does not give us this. Hence we can go no further.[3]

  It is tempting to think that the difficulty here is merely technical, one to be solved by revising axioms or adding new production rules. For example, consider the revised axiom for [$_{VP}$ V S] in (5c′), which doesn't employ the general variable y but rather appeals to the specific value t. This rule will allow us to prove the result in (7):[4]

(5c′) Val(x, [$_{VP}$ V S], σ) iff Val($\langle x, t \rangle$, V, σ) and Val(t, S, σ)

(7)   Val(t, [$_S$ Chris says Jill agrees], σ) iff Chris says t and Jill agrees

It's easy to see that this is unsatisfactory, however. For one thing, it's unclear how we are to understand something like "Chris says t." This is not an acceptable sentence of day-to-day English. And even if we decide to assign it some special rendering along the lines of "Chris says the truth" or "Chris speaks truly," it's plain that this will not capture the truth conditions of the sentence in question:

(8) Val(t, [$_S$ Chris says Jill agrees], σ) iff Chris speaks truly and Jill agrees

Contra (8), it is not necessary for Chris to speak truly in order for *Chris says Jill agrees* to be true. Also, it's not necessary for Jill to agree. Furthermore, (8) fails to capture the fact that for *Chris says Jill agrees* to be true, what Chris must say is precisely that Jill agrees. T sentence (8) requires Chris to say something—indeed, to say something true—but it doesn't require him to say that Jill agrees.

We believe the difficulty here is not merely a technical one but one that results from a deep problem with the attempt to regard the relation between a sentence and a truth value as wholly analogous to the relation between a referring NP and its semantic value. What lies at the root of the problem is a crucial difference between

- the general form of an appropriate specification for an NP or predicate expression and
- the general form of an appropriate specification of the truth conditions for sentences.

In the former case we can state outright what the conditions are under which any arbitrary object is a value of the singular term or predicate; (9a, b) are typical examples:

(9) a. Val(x, *Chris*, σ) iff x = Chris
     b. Val($\langle x, y \rangle$, *says*, σ) iff x says y

In the latter case, however, we do not give the general conditions under which any arbitrary thing is a value of the sentence. Rather, we give the conditions under which the sentence has the particular value t. The general form is thus given by (10a). This result is not a mere artifact of our theory. We cannot simply replace (10a) by something apparently more general, such as (10b):

(10) a. Val(t, S, σ) iff p

  b. Val(x, S, σ) iff $x = $ t and p, or $x = $ f and it is not the case that p

It's easy to show that (10b), combined with the axioms in (5), also fails to give extensionally correct truth conditions for a sentence like *Chris says Jill agrees.* Evidently, this is because (10b) is not interpretive. What appears on the RHS of specifications like (10b) does not intuitively give the meaning of the object-language sentence in question.

What these reflections suggest is that the relation of a sentence to a truth value simply isn't very similar to that between a referring term or predicate and its value or values. A sentence doesn't name or describe a truth value in the way that a proper noun or predicate names or describes its value or values. A sentence expresses a truth condition. And what this means is that a sentence specifies a condition under which it has the specific object t as its value. Given all this, it comes as no surprise that we fail in our attempt to treat [$_{VP}$ V S] as exactly analogous to [$_{VP}$ V NP], with S playing the same role as an ordinary NP.

11.2   Words, Worlds, and Propositions

The idea of treating clausal-complement VPs on the general model of [$_{VP}$ V NP] appears natural. However, the results of the last section strongly imply that we cannot take clausal-complement verbs to express relations to truth values. If not t or f, what should these values be then? This question was first raised by Frege (1893), and it has been discussed in a vast amount of literature since. It would be impossible to survey this literature in any detail. Nonetheless, it is possible to sketch some basic ideas behind the main proposals. These ideas suggest themselves rather naturally when we consider specific verbs taking clausal complements.

Consider the verb *say* in (11a). Canonically, people say things by uttering sentences or other linguistic expressions, and in fact, *say* occurs not only in indirect or reported speech constructions like (11a) but also in direct or quoted speech constructions like (11b):

(11) a. Chris says Jill agrees.

  b. Chris says "Jill agrees."

The close link between direct and indirect speech suggests an analysis in which the semantic objects of clausal-complement verbs are sentences or linguistic expressions. Such theories are often called **quotational** because of the connection they draw to directly quoted speech.

For a different approach, consider (12a). A common metaphor about dreams is that they involve entering into a "world" where circumstances may diverge considerably from reality. Examples like (12a) can even be paraphrased as in (12b), where worlds are mentioned explicitly.

(12) a. Chris dreams Jill agrees.
 b. Chris dreams of a world in which Jill agrees.

The paraphrase relation here suggests a semantics in which clausal-complement verbs relate an individual to a world or set of worlds of some kind. Such theories may be called **modal**, because they appeal to a notion of a world (or possible world) that also arises prominently in the analysis of modal expressions like *must*, *can*, *necessarily*, and *possibly*.

Finally, consider (13a). Logicians often use the term **proposition** to describe the things that are believed, asserted, conjectured, rejected, etc. Propositions are normally conceived of as the content of a sentence—what the sentence expresses, means, or is about. Even in nonphilosophical speech we can often paraphrase talk about belief, assertion, conjecture, etc., in terms of talk about propositions:

(13) a. Chris believes Jill agrees.
 b. Chris believes the proposition that Jill agrees.

This suggests that clausal-complement verbs might be analyzed as relating an individual to a proposition or set of propositions—the proposition(s) expressed by the complement clause. For obvious reasons, such theories are called **propositional**.

The three approaches just sketched are evidently based on different metaphors and different intuitions. But each has its own attractive features. Let us examine them a little further and consider how each might be worked out within a T-theoretic framework.

11.2.1 Quotational Theories

Quotational theories take the semantic objects of attitude reports to be linguistic entities, that is, sentences or some other kind of linguistic expression. One simple way of executing this idea formally is as in (14):

(14) a. Val($\langle x, y \rangle$, *says*, σ) iff x says y
    b. Val(x, [$_{VP}$ V S], σ) iff for some y, Val($\langle x, y \rangle$, V, σ) and $y = $ S

Under these axioms, our T theory would prove results like (15), where the object of an attitude verb is just the complement phrase maker itself:

(15) Val(t, [$_S$ Chris says Jill agrees], σ) iff Chris says

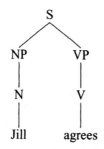

In a full theory, this proposal would be extended beyond *say* to all verbs taking clausal complements including *think*, *believe*, *dream*, *hope*, etc. In all cases the object of the attitude verb is a structured piece of language.

The quotational theory embodied in (14) makes a number of attractive predictions. In current syntactic theory, phrase markers encode a variety of information about an expression, including the constituent structure of its words and phrases, the phonological content of its lexical forms, and the various binding and antecedence relations that hold within it. The quotational theory predicts that all of this information is potentially relevant to distinguishing the truth conditions of attitude-report sentences. Whenever we have different phrase markers, the prediction is that we'll have different truth conditions.

This prediction looks correct, as Larson and Ludlow (1993) discuss across a broad range of cases. For example, phrase markers can differ in the lexical forms they contain. Where (16a) contains the proper NP *Cary Grant*, (16b) contains *Archie Leach*:

(16) a. Peter believes [Lori met Cary Grant]
    b. Peter believes [Lori met Archie Leach]

The quotational theory predicts different truth conditions here, even though the two names refer to the very same individual. For (16a) to be true, Peter must stand in a belief relation to the phrase marker for *Lori met Cary Grant*. For (16b) to be true, Peter must stand in a belief relation to the phrase marker for *Lori met Archie Leach*. Since these are different phrase markers, they create different truth conditions. The prediction is clearly correct. Suppose Peter knows that *Cary Grant* refers to the famous actor but not that *Archie Leach* does. Then we can easily imagine one of (16) being true and the other false.

Phrase markers also encode constituent structure, so the quotational theory predicts that this too can be relevant to distinguishing truth conditions. Examples confirming this prediction are easy to find. For instance, the complement clause in (17) can be understood as having either of the structures in (18):

(17) Max believes old men and women are vulnerable.

(18) a. Max believes [[[old men] and women] are vulnerable]
     b. Max believes [[old [men and women]] are vulnerable]

In the first *old* applies to men alone, and in the second it applies to men and women both. This difference of structure clearly correlates with a difference in truth-conditions for the larger sentence. Max may surely believe one thing but not the other.

A similar case, but with word structure, is found in (19):

(19) Kathrin believes this bottle is uncorkable.

The word *uncorkable* is ambiguous according to how its three constituent morphemes *un-*, *cork*, and *-able* are taken together. On one construal, it applies to things that cannot be corked, (20a); on the other, it applies to things that can be uncorked, (20b):

(20) a. Kathrin believes [this bottle is [un[corkable]]]
     b. Kathrin believes [this bottle is [[uncork]able]]

The quotational theory predicts that this difference of word structure should yield different truth conditions, and this is surely correct. Clearly, one of (20) might be true and the other false: Kathrin might believe one thing and not the other.

Finally, phrase markers encode information about binding and antecedence. The quotational theory predicts that this will be relevant to distinguishing truth conditions. Consider (21):

(21) Mary believes Max loves his mother.

The pronoun *his* can be understood to have *Max* as its antecedent. Alternatively, *his* may refer to some other individual whose identity is determined from context. As discussed in chapter 10, this difference is indicated syntactically by means of indices. On the first reading, *Max* and *his* are coindexed, (22a); on the second they are not, (22b):

(22) a. Mary believes [Max$_1$ loves his$_1$ mother]
    b. Mary believes [Max$_1$ loves his$_2$ mother]

Under the quotational theory, this difference of syntactic diacritics in the phrase markers implies different truth conditions. Again this prediction is obviously correct. Mary may believe that Max loves his own mother without believing that he loves some other person's mother, and vice versa.

Samesaying

The quotational theory in (14) assimilates indirect speech to direct speech. It analyzes (11a) identically to (11b) (repeated):

(11) a. Chris says Jill agrees.
    b. Chris says "Jill agrees."

Making such an assimilation is not plainly right, however. For (11b) to be true, Chris must have uttered the very English sentence *Jill agrees*. However, for (11a) to be true, this isn't necessary. Suppose Chris and I both know Jill to be his upstairs neighbor, and suppose Chris says (23) to me:

(23) My upstairs neighbor agrees.

Then I could truly report what Chris said as in (11a), at least in the same conversational contexts. But I couldn't report what he said as in (11b).
    Another, slightly different way of making the point is with the three sentences in (24):

(24) a. Caesar said "Carthago delenda est."
    b. Caesar said "Carthage must be destroyed."
    c. Caesar said Carthage must be destroyed.

Caesar was an ancient Roman, and hence a speaker of Latin; he didn't speak modern English. Accordingly, while (24a) is true, (24b) is surely false. On the other hand, notice that (24c) is true, even though its complement clause is in English. The indirect-speech construction doesn't require the complement clause to give the exact words used by the subject. All that's necessary is that the complement clause have the same content as what the speaker said, that they say the same thing. Given these points, it seems that we should draw some distinction between direct- and indirect-speech constructions so that the relation between the speaker and the complement clause is relaxed in the latter case.

One simple way of doing this, following Davidson (1968), is to introduce the notion of similarity or "samesaying" directly into the truth conditions for indirect-speech verbs.[5] The idea is that for a speech report to be true, the reporter needs to choose a complement sentence that is in some appropriate sense similar in semantic content to the sentence produced by the person whose speech is being reported. For example, suppose we amend our rules in (14) as in (25):

(25) a. $\text{Val}(\langle x, y \rangle, \textit{says}, \sigma)$ iff x says y
b. $\text{Val}(x, [_{\text{VP}} \text{ V S}], \sigma)$ iff for some y, $\text{Val}(\langle x, y \rangle, \text{V}, \sigma)$ and
y is similar to S

Then we can prove results like (26):

(26) $\text{Val}(t, [_{\text{S}} \text{ Chris says Jill agrees}], \sigma)$ iff for some y, Chris says y and y is
similar to

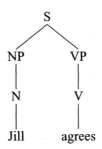

These truth conditions no longer require an individual to use precisely the words given by the complement clause. Rather, (26) demands only that Chris say something suitably similar to [$_{\text{S}}$ Jill agrees]. Likewise, Caesar need not actually have said "Carthage must be destroyed" in order for (24c) to be true. It is enough that he said something similar to this in Latin.

The introduction of similarity has the interesting feature of making propositional-attitude reports sensitive to pragmatic context. Note that similarity is a three-place relation: an object x is similar to another object y *with respect to some feature(s) F*. In axiom (25b), the metalanguage predicate "similar" is left vague with respect to the similarity features. These are to be determined by context. And indeed, context does often seem to figure importantly in the relation between what someone actually says, thinks, believes, etc., and the truth of a report about what that person says, thinks, believes, etc. For example, it's clear that (24c) can serve as a good report of what Caesar actually said in Latin. The reason is that *Carthago delenda est* and *Carthage must be destroyed* are similar in content.

For other cases, similarity of referential content may be less important than similarity of what in chapter 6 we called "character," For example, suppose that Jill's favorite movie actress is Ms. Smith and she says "My favorite actress will win an Oscar this year." Suppose Phil's favorite movie actress is Ms. Jones and he says the very same words: "My favorite actress will win an Oscar this year." Suppose you want to know whether Jill and Phil made the same claim. From a certain standpoint they didn't make the same claim: one said something about Smith; the other said something about Jones. From another standpoint, however, they did make the same claim: they both made a similar claim about their favorite actresses. Given this, I could potentially report what Phil said to you in either of two ways:

(27) a. Phil said that Ms. Jones will win an Oscar this year.
     b. Phil said that his favorite actress will win an Oscar this year.

Whether I choose the one or the other depends a lot on whether I think you are interested in specifics about persons or broader issues about their general ideas. But plainly in certain circumstances, (27b), which is more similar in character to Phil's original assertion, might be better than (27a). Thus whether we allow that two sentences are similar often depends on context. That is, how we report other people's sayings, thoughts, beliefs, etc., often depends pragmatically on our goals and our assumptions about what the listener is trying to find out.

Problems

While the quotational theory correctly distinguishes a range truth conditions of clausal-complement sentences, certain distinctions still escape it.[6] Consider (28), for example.

(28) a. Jill is a philosopher. Phil thinks [she_1 ponders].
     b. Kate is a philosopher. Phil thinks [she_1 ponders].

It is clearly possible for the bracketed sentence to be true in the one example and false in the other. The reason is simply that in the one case *she* refers to Jill, and so the sentence has Phil believing something about Jill. In the other, *she* refers to Kate, and so the sentence has Phil believing something about Kate. Surely, one can be true while the other is false. Interestingly, the quotational theory does not predict this result. Since the form of the complement clause is the same in the two cases, Phil stands in relation to the same linguistic object in both. The quotational theory thus incorrectly assigns the very same truth conditions.

It is tempting to think that this problem can be avoided by appeal to enriched syntactic representations. For example, one might claim that the two readings correspond to two distinct indexings, as in (29a, b):

(29) a. Jill is a philosopher. Phil thinks [she$_1$ ponders].
     b. Kate is a philosopher. Phil thinks [she$_2$ ponders].

The problem with this suggestion is that there is nothing in our theory that blocks the very same pronoun, *with the very same index*, from referring to different individuals on different occasions of use. If we employ different sequences, the one form [she$_1$ ponders] can still be used with *she$_1$* referring to Jill at one time and *she$_1$* referring to Kate at another. Given this, it follows that we will be able to reproduce our original problem with (30), where the indices are the same:

(30) a. Jill is a philosopher. Phil thinks [she$_1$ ponders]. (*She$_1$* refers to Jill.)
     b. Kate is a philosopher. Phil thinks [she$_1$ ponders].
        (*She$_1$* refers to Kate.)

Cases like (28) thus raise a significant problem for the quotational theory, since they seem to show that the syntax of the complement is not always rich enough to mark all the distinctions in truth conditions that we need. More generally, these cases motivate the following basic observation:

Observation 1 The truth conditions of clausal-complement constructions are discriminated at least as finely as the objects referred to in the embedded clauses.

The fact that identical forms can refer to different objects causes problems for quotational theories.

11.2.2   Modal Theories

Modal theories take the semantic objects of attitude reports to be worlds or sets of worlds: the worlds relative to which the complement sentence is true. To work out this idea, we evidently need to introduce worlds and the idea of truth relative to a world.

Worlds and Truth

As it turns out, the basic ideas needed are already available from the study of modal notions like necessity and possibility. Indeed, the notions of a world and truth relative to a world arises very directly in this context. One common way of explaining what it is for something to be necessary is that it couldn't have been any other way. For example, if I said (31a) to you and you asked for clarification of what I meant, I could go on to say that there is no alternative scenario for the world in which objects lack either mass or energy, that is, that there is no alternative world relative to which (31b) is false:

(31) a. Objects necessarily have mass or energy.
     b. Objects have mass or energy.

Similarly, if I said (32a) to you and you asked me to explain further, I might go on by saying that there is a conceivable alternate course of events in which Earth's orbit had a circular shape, that there is an alternative world relative to which (32b) is true:

(32) a. Earth's orbit could have been circular.
     b. Earth's orbit is circular.

In both cases, we appeal to the absence or presence of alternative possible worlds.

When we invoke alternative worlds in explaining necessity and possibility, we are, of course, not simply talking about an alternative planet Earth, or even an alternative Solar System. Rather, we mean an entire alternative universe: an alternative to everything that is. In the philosophical literature there has been considerable debate and discussion about what exactly possible worlds are and how they are to be conceived. For present purposes, it will be enough to introduce them as primitive entities whose elucidation is to be given by continuing empirical investigation. So, along with concrete objects like tables and chairs and abstract objects like numbers and the gross national product of France, there are now all the objects that are possible worlds.

Once worlds are introduced, we can straightforwardly relativize truth to worlds in our T theory by extending the "Val" relation to include a world parameter. So in place of (33a), we would adopt (33b):

(33) a. Val(x, α, σ) iff . . .
     b. Val(x, α, σ, w) iff . . .

The new valuation relation is read in the expected way: "x is a value of α relative to sequence σ and world w if and only if," and so on. As we said, a world must provide a complete specification of how things are in the universe. There will be a huge set of sentences that are true relative to each world and hence describe it:

- w_1 : {*Jill walks, Kate walks, It is not the case that Phil walks,* . . .}
- w_2 : {*Jill walks, Phil walks, It is not the case that Kate walks, Chris knows Kate, Kate agrees,* . . .}
- w_3 : {*Jill walks, Phil walks, Kate walks, It is not the case that Jill agrees, Chris knows Kate, It is not the case that Rolf walks,* . . .}
- w_4 : {*Jill agrees, Chris knows Kate, Rolf walks,* . . .}
- w_5 : {*Jill walks, Chris walks, Jill agrees, It is not the case that Chris knows Kate, Rolf protests,* . . .}

         ⋮

As usual, introducing a new parameter into the Val predicate entails adjusting our phrasal rules so that worlds are manipulated in the right way, and also adjusting lexical rules so that basic terms are made sensitive to worlds. Below is a small sample theory W showing how such changes might go.

(34) a. Val(x, *Phil*, σ, w) iff x = Phil
     b. Val(x, *Jill*, σ, w) iff x = Jill
     c. Val(x, *Chris*, σ, w) iff x = Chris
     d. Val(x, *Kate*, σ, w) iff x = Kate

(35) a. Val(x, *walks*, σ, w) iff x walks in w
     b. Val(x, *ponders*, σ, w) iff x ponders in w
     c. Val(x, *arrives*, σ, w) iff x arrives in w
     d. Val($\langle x, y \rangle$, *kisses*, σ, w) iff x kisses y in w
     e. Val($\langle x, y \rangle$, *admires*, σ, w) iff x admires y in w

f. Val($\langle x, y, z \rangle$, *gives*, σ, w) iff x gives y to z in w

g. Val$\langle x, y, z \rangle$, *buys*, σ, w) iff x buys y from z in w

(36) a. Val(t, [$_s$ NP VP], σ, w) iff for some x, Val(x, NP, σ, w) and
Val(x, VP, σ, w)

b. Val(x, [$_{VP}$ V NP], σ, w) iff for some y, Val($\langle x, y \rangle$, V, σ, w) and
Val(y, NP, σ, w)

c. Val(x, [$_{VP}$ VP NP$_1$ NP$_2$], σ, w) iff for some y, z,
Val($\langle x, y, z \rangle$, V, σ, w) and Val(z, NP$_1$, σ, w) and Val(y, NP$_2$, σ, w)

d. Val(x, [$_X$ Y], σ, w) iff Val(x, Y, σ, w)
(where X, Y are any nodes and x is any value)

Note that (34) through (36) generate an important difference between predicates and proper nouns: whereas the former are sensitive to the world coordinate w, the latter are world-insensitive. This answers to an observation we made earlier in chapter 5. Recall that proper nouns are **rigid**, picking out the same individual across different possible circumstances; thus *Chris* designates the same man Chris in w_1, w_2, w_3, ... By contrast, predicates are **nonrigid**, applying to different individuals in different possible worlds; *walk* may designate one set of walkers in w_1 ({Jill, Kate}), a different set of walkers in w_2 ({Jill, Phil}), yet a different set of walkers in w_3 ({Jill, Phil, Kate}), and so on. This set of circumstances is presented in figure 11.1 and is formally stated in (37):

(37) a. Val(x, *Chris*, σ, w) iff x = Chris

b. Val(x, *walks*, σ, w) iff x walks in w

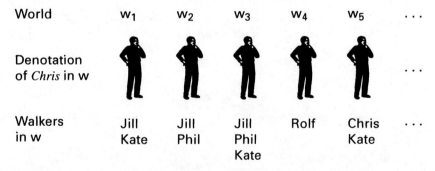

World	w_1	w_2	w_3	w_4	w_5	$\cdots$
Denotation of *Chris* in w						$\cdots$
Walkers in w	Jill Kate	Jill Phil	Jill Phil Kate	Rolf	Chris Kate	$\cdots$

Figure 11.1 A proper name like *Chris* is rigid in that it designates the same individual in any world. In contrast, a predicate like *walks* is nonrigid in that it applies to different individuals in different worlds.

As the reader can easily show, theory W yields formal results like (38):

(38) Val(t, [$_S$ Chris agrees], σ, w) iff Chris agrees in w

We read this sentence as saying that [$_S$ Chris agrees] is true (with respect to sequence σ) in world w if and only if Chris agrees in w. Once armed with the notion of truth relative to a world, we can go on to define the notion of truth simpliciter. We designate one of the worlds w^* as the actual world. A sentence is then true (with respect to sequence σ) if and only if it is true relative to w^* (with respect to σ).

We noted that the notion of possible worlds receives independent motivation from the study of necessity and possibility. The late-seventeenth-century philosopher G. W. Leibniz is usually credited with the suggestion that necessity be analyzed in terms of truth in all possible worlds, although the formal notions of a possible world and truth relative to a world were worked out much more recently by Hintikka (1969), Kanger (1957), Kripke (1963), Lewis (1968), Montague (1974). The adverbs *necessarily* and *possibly* can be introduced into theory W by means by GQ-style axioms like (39) and (40):

(39) a. Val(X, *necessarily*, σ, w) iff $|W - X| = 0$
          (where W is the set of all worlds)
      b. Val(X, *possibly*, σ, w) iff $|X \cap Y| > 0$

(40) a. Val(t, [$_S$ AdvP S], σ, w) iff for some X, Val(X, AdvP, σ, w) and
          $X = \{w' : \text{Val(t, S, } \sigma, w')\}$
      b. Val(X, [$_{AdvP}$ Adv], σ, w) iff Val(X, Adv, σ, w)
      c. Val(X, [$_{Adv}$ α], σ, w) iff Val(X, α, σ, w) (for any lexical adverb α)

Axioms for notionally related words like *can*, *may*, and *must* are similar. Again as the reader may show, these additions yield (41a, b):

(41) a. Val(t, [$_S$ Necessarily Chris agrees], σ, w) iff for all worlds w',
          Chris agrees in w'
      b. Val(t, [$_S$ Possibly Chris agrees], σ, w) iff for some world w',
          Chris agrees in w'

We are not committed to the correctness of this analysis of modality, and we will not pursue it further here. Our main point is simply that although the introduction of worlds represents a significant formal step, worlds are not a special construct required only for the analysis of clausal complements. They appear to have more general utility.

Clausal Complements

Having introduced worlds and truth relative to a world, we can now formally reconstruct the idea that the semantic object of a verb taking a clausal complement is the set of worlds relative to which the complement is true. We retain the simple transitive analysis of verbs like *dreams*, *thinks*, *believes*, etc., (42a), but introduce the new phrasal axiom in (42b):

(42) a. $\text{Val}(\langle x, y \rangle, dreams, \sigma, w)$ iff x dreams y in w
  b. $\text{Val}(x, [_{VP} \text{ V S}], \sigma, w)$ iff for some y, $\text{Val}(\langle x, y \rangle, \text{V}, \sigma, w)$ and
    $y = \{w' : \text{Val(t, S}, \sigma, w')\}$

Our T theory derives results like (43):

(43) $\text{Val(t, } [_{S} \text{ Chris dreams Jill agrees]}, \sigma, w)$ iff
  Chris dreams $\{w' : \text{Jill agrees in } w'\}$ in w

Thus *Chris dreams Jill agrees* is true with respect to sequence σ and world w just in case Chris stands in the dream relation in w to the set of worlds in which Jill agrees. This approach is extended by adopting axioms parallel to (42a) for all of the verbs taking clausal complements.

Sets of worlds and linguistic expressions are fundamentally different kinds of objects. Unsurprisingly, then, the modal and the quotational theories of the semantics of clausal complements make different predictions. For example, recall (28a, b) (given below in slightly modified form):

(44) a. Jill is a philosopher. *Phil thinks [she$_1$ ponders].*
  b. Kate is a philosopher. *Phil thinks [she$_1$ ponders].*

This pair makes trouble for the quotational theory, since it assigns them the same truth conditions when they surely should be different. By contrast, the modal approach discriminates the truth conditions appropriately. As the reader may easily calculate, the modal theory assigns to the italicized sentence the truth conditions in (45):

(45) $\text{Val(t, } [_{S} \text{ Phil thinks [she}_1 \text{ ponders]]}, \sigma, w)$ iff
  Phil thinks $\{w' : \sigma(1) \text{ ponders in } w'\}$ in w

If this sentence is evaluated with respect to a sequence in which Jill is the first member, then the worlds in question are those in which Jill ponders. If the sentence is evaluated with respect to a sequence in which Kate is the first member, then the worlds are those in which Kate ponders. The modal theory thus correctly predicts that the truth conditions of *Phil thinks she₁ ponders* depends on whom the pronoun *she₁* refers to.[7]

Problems

Although the modal theory has advantages over the quotational theory with cases like (28), it encounters its own problems in other data. For example, consider our earlier pair (16) (repeated below):

(16) a. Peter believes [Lori met Cary Grant]
     b. Peter believes [Lori met Archie Leach]

The modal theory assigns these examples the truth-conditions in (46):

(46) a. Val(t, [$_S$ Peter believes [Lori met Cary Grant]], σ, w) iff
        Peter believes $\{w' :$ Lori met Cary Grant in $w'\}$ in w
     b. Val(t, [$_S$ Peter believes [Lori met Archie Leach]], σ, w) iff
        Peter believes $\{w' :$ Lori met Archie Leach in $w'\}$ in w

The proper nouns *Cary Grant* and *Archie Leach* refer to the very same individual. Hence the worlds where Lori meets Cary Grant are the same as the worlds where Lori meets Archie Leach. That is,

(47) $\{w' :$ Lori met Cary Grant in $w'\} = \{w' :$ Lori met Archie Leach in $w'\}$

In view of this, the modal theory incorrectly assigns the same truth conditions to (16a, b). It doesn't allow for the possibility of one being true and the other false.

A similar kind of problem is encountered in relation to pairs like (48a, b):

(48) a. Peter believes [2 is a prime number]
     b. Peter believes [5 is a prime number]

Although our theory W doesn't currently accommodate mathematical propositions like these, it's easy to see that if it were extended to them, the results would be as in (49):

(49) a. Val(t, [$_S$ Peter believes [2 is a prime number]], σ, w) iff
        Peter believes $\{w' :$ 2 is a prime number in $w'\}$ in w
     b. Val(t, [$_S$ Peter believes [5 is a prime number]], σ, w) iff
        Peter believes $\{w' :$ 5 is a prime number in $w'\}$ in w

Mathematics being universally true, if 2 is a prime number in some world, then it is a prime number in every world. Likewise, if 5 is a prime number in some world, then it is a prime number in every world. This entails that the sets of worlds in which the two complement sentences are true are just the same. That is,

(50) $\{w' : 2 \text{ is a prime number in } w'\} = \{w' : 5 \text{ is a prime number in } w'\}$

But then the modal theory assigns the same truth conditions to (48a,b). It fails to capture the intuition that Peter might believe one mathematical proposition but not another, and hence that the two reports might have different truth values.

The difficulty we meet with modal theory is essentially opposite to the one encountered with the quotational theory. The latter had a problem with examples where syntactic form was constant but reference was not—where we had the same pronouns referring to different things. By contrast, pairs like (16) and (48) represent cases where reference is constant but form is not. In both pairs the complement clauses pick out the same set of worlds, but evidently this is too coarse-grained; it doesn't discriminate finely enough. Not just whom we refer to but also *how* we refer to them—whether we use *Cary Grant* or *Archie Leach*—seem to yield a difference in truth conditions. Once again, we may summarize matters in the form of an observation:

Observation 2 The truth conditions of clausal-complement constructions are discriminated at least as finely as the forms used in the embedded clauses.

The fact that different forms can refer to the same objects causes problems for modal theories.

11.2.3 Propositional Theories

Finally, let's consider propositional theories of the semantics of clausal complements. The situation here is somewhat more diffuse than with quotational or modal theories, simply because the notion of a proposition has no standard interpretation or formalization. Indeed, propositions are often defined derivatively in other theories using their own constructs. For example, modal theories will often define propositions as sets of possible worlds.

Not all approaches attempt to reduce propositions to other constructs (like sets of possible worlds). One such approach derives from the early work of

Bertrand Russell, who suggested that propositions are a kind of abstract structured object consisting of a property or relation along with other familiar, garden-variety kinds of individuals.[8] For example, the proposition that Jill agrees consists of the property of agreeing (P_{agree}) together with the person Jill, (51a). The proposition that Jill knows Kate consists of the relation of knowing (R_{know}) along with the person Jill and the person Kate, (51b). The proposition that Jill agrees and Jill knows Kate is compounded of the two subpropositions through the conjunction relation (R_{and}), (51c).

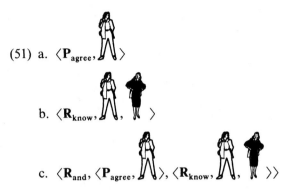

(51) a. $\langle P_{agree}, \text{ } \rangle$

b. $\langle R_{know}, \text{ }, \text{ } \rangle$

c. $\langle R_{and}, \langle P_{agree}, \text{ } \rangle, \langle R_{know}, \text{ }, \text{ } \rangle \rangle$

A Russellian theory of the semantics of clausal complements would draw upon such objects. More precisely, the truth conditions of sentences like *Chris thinks Jill agrees* or *Phil believes Jill knows Kate* would involve relations to propositions. Candidate axioms are given in (52), where "$\langle S \rangle$" is the proposition corresponding to S:

(52) a. Val($\langle x, y \rangle$, *thinks*, σ) iff x thinks y
b. Val(x, [$_{VP}$ V S], σ) iff for some y, Val($\langle x, y \rangle$, V, σ) and $y = \langle S \rangle$

Assuming the propositions given above for *Jill agrees* and *Jill knows Kate*, we get the results in (53):

(53) a. Val(t, [$_S$ Chris thinks Jill agrees], σ) iff Chris thinks $\langle P_{agree}, \text{ } \rangle$
b. Val(t, [$_S$ Phil believes Jill knows Kate], σ) iff

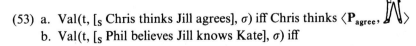

Phil believes $\langle R_{know}, \text{ }, \text{ } \rangle$

The propositional theory shares some features with the quotational account and, because of this, handles certain empirical challenges in a similar way. Like a sentence, a proposition is a structured object. Hence truth-conditional differences ascribed to linguistic structure in the one account can often be captured in propositional structure in the other. For example, (54a) is ambiguous according to whether the grouping of the complement parts is understood as in (54b) or (54c):

(54) a. Chris thinks Jill agrees or Kate protests and Phil ponders.
     b. Chris thinks (Jill agrees or Kate protests) and Phil ponders
     c. Chris thinks Jill agrees or (Kate protests and Phil ponders)

The quotational theory would trace this to a syntactic ambiguity in the complement clause; Chris stands in the think relation to two phrase markers differing in the relative scope of *or* and *and*. In a similar way, the propositional theory would trace the ambiguity to a structural difference in the propositions expressed by the complement clause; Chris stands in the think relation to two propositions that differ in the relative scope of R_{and} and R_{or}:

(55) a. $\langle R_{and}, \langle R_{or}, \langle P_{agree}, \text{🧍} \rangle, \langle P_{protest}, \text{🧍} \rangle \rangle, \langle P_{ponder}, \text{🧍} \rangle \rangle$

     b. $\langle R_{or}, \langle P_{agree}, \text{🧍} \rangle, \langle R_{and}, \langle P_{protest}, \text{🧍} \rangle, \langle P_{ponder}, \text{🧍} \rangle \rangle \rangle$

A propositional theory can also capture certain differences in truth conditions that the quotational theory ascribes to lexical form. For example, the verbs *xerox* and *photocopy* in (56) are coextensive and closely related in meaning:[9]

(56) a. Chris believes Jill xeroxed *War and Peace*.
     b. Chris believes Jill photocopied *War and Peace*.

Nonetheless, it seems the two belief sentences might differ in truth value, for example, if Chris doesn't know that the two words mean the same. The quotational theory captures this by putting Chris in relation to two different phrase markers: one containing *xerox* and the other containing *photocopy*. By contrast, the propositional theory might account for this by recognizing two different relations, $\mathbf{R}_{xerox}$ and $\mathbf{R}_{photocopy}$, and hence two different propositions:

(57) a. $\langle \mathbf{R}_{xerox},$ 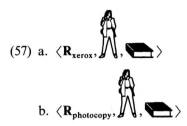 $\rangle$

   b. $\langle \mathbf{R}_{photocopy},$ $\rangle$

The two relations apply to the same pairs of objects, of course, but this might be no barrier to our distinguishing them. Perhaps one individuates relations and properties more finely than the individuals or sequences that they are true of.

   The propositional theory cannot mimic all aspects of the quotational theory. For example, the propositions corresponding to the complements in (16) (repeated) will contain the same individuals (Lori, Cary Grant/Archie Leach) standing in the same relation ($\mathbf{R}_{met}$). Hence the theory will incorrectly assign the same truth conditions to (16a, b):[10]

(16) a. Peter believes [Lori met Cary Grant]
   b. Peter believes [Lori met Archie Leach]

On the other hand, the propositional theory does capture results that the quotational theory misses. The propositions corresponding to the complements in (28) (repeated) will contain different individuals (Jill and Kate) possessing the ponder property ($\mathbf{P}_{ponder}$) (58).

(28) a. Jill is a philosopher. Phil thinks [she$_1$ ponders].
   b. Kate is a philosopher. Phil thinks [she$_1$ ponders].

(58) a. $\langle \mathbf{P}_{ponder},$ 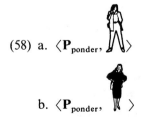 $\rangle$

   b. $\langle \mathbf{P}_{ponder},$ $\rangle$

Hence the theory correctly distinguishes the truth conditions of the pair in (28).

Semantic Innocence

Implementing Russellian propositions is not straightforward in our T theory, given that it does not invoke properties like $\mathbf{P}_{\text{ponder}}$ or relations like $\mathbf{R}_{\text{photocopy}}$. We simply do not have such objects as semantic values. To introduce propositions, we would therefore have to do one of two things:

- Introduce properties and relations in addition to the semantic values already present.

- Go back and revise our basic theory, using properties and relations from the very start.

Neither of these options is very attractive, however.

Adding properties and relations to our current semantic theory means supplementing rules for unembedded clauses, like (59a, b), with rules for embedded clauses, like (59c, d):

(59) a. Val(x, *ponders*, σ) iff x ponders
    b. Val($\langle x, y \rangle$, *knows*, σ) iff x knows y
    c. Val^{emb}(p, *ponders*, σ) iff $p = \mathbf{P}_{\text{ponder}}$
    d. Val^{emb}(r, *knows*, σ) iff $r = \mathbf{R}_{\text{know}}$

This move would introduce considerable duplication and redundancy into the lexicon. Every lexical item would now get a pair of semantic values under a pair of semantic-value relations (Val and Val^{emb}). More than this, however, by proceeding as in (59), we are assuming a fundamental divorce between the semantics of embedded and unembedded structures. In essence, we have one semantics for one kind of context and a different semantics for the other.[11]

As Davidson (1968) has noted, prima facie, we would prefer an "innocent" semantics: one that assumes the same values for phrases wherever they occur. Such a theory is preferable on grounds of conceptual simplicity, but there is also an advantage in terms of language learnability. On an innocent theory, a child acquiring language has only one semantic-valuation statement to learn for any given lexical item. Since that axiom is valid for all contexts, evidence for it will be available from the simplest parts of the grammar, including elementary unembedded sentence constructions like *Chris agrees* and *Jill know Kate*. By contrast, on a noninnocent semantics, a learner is obliged to acquire a number of valuation statements for a given item, mastering the context where each applies. Furthermore, the data motivating this multiplication of values will become available only in syntactically complex contexts: clausal-complement constructions.

It is possible to avoid the duplication of semantic values in the propositional theory by going back and reworking the semantics for the unembedded parts of the grammar so that they too invoke properties and relations. Indeed, we have already encountered a theory of this kind in PC^{prop}, which employed axioms much like (59c, d). In this case, properties and relations would be involved from the very start, so nothing new would arise when we encountered clausal complements. Nonetheless, it's important to see that even if we proceed in this way, Davidson's point about semantic innocence still applies. For we would not be motivating the semantic analysis of the simpler parts of the grammar from data available in those simpler parts. Rather, we would be motivating the analysis of the simple parts from data concerning the more complex parts. This seems implausible as a theory of how the learner would proceed, revising backwards, as it were. In any case, it seems preferable to seek an alternative that avoids such backward revision. We summarize these points in the form of an observation.

Observation 3   We prefer the semantics of clausal-complement constructions to be **innocent**: the values assigned in embedded and unembedded contexts should be the same; furthermore, the analysis of the unembedded parts should not depend on evidence from the embedded parts.

Stated in this strong form, innocence is clearly a problem for propositional theories.

11.3   Interpreted Logical Forms

We now turn to a theory of the semantics of clausal complements that shares some features with the accounts sketched above but also avoids a number of their problems. This theory is called "interpreted logical forms" (ILFs), because its basic element, the ILF, is a treelike object that resembles a syntactic logical form. We begin by introducing ILFs informally.[12]

11.3.1   Introducing ILFs

We saw earlier that the truth conditions of clausal-complement constructions are rather fine-grained. They are as finely discriminated as the words used in the clausal complements: using different words yields different truth conditions. And they are as finely discriminated as the objects referred to in the complements: reference to different objects yields different truth conditions.

This result implies that *both* kinds of information should figure in the semantic object of verbs selecting clausal complements. ILFs take this implication to heart. The main idea of the ILF theory is that verbs taking clausal complements express relations between individuals and phrase markers whose terminal and nonterminal nodes are annotated with semantic values. For example, consider sentence (60):

(60) Lori met Cary Grant.

In the course of a standard T-sentence derivation for (60), we prove a series of iff statements like (61a–e):

(61) a. $\text{Val}(t, [_S \text{ Lori met Cary Grant}], \sigma)$ iff for some x,
           $\text{Val}(x, [_{NP} \text{ Lori}], \sigma)$ and $\text{Val}(x, [_{VP} \text{ met Cary Grant}], \sigma)$
      b. $\text{Val}(x, [_{NP} \text{ Lori}], \sigma)$ iff $x = \text{Lori}$
      c. $\text{Val}(x, [_{VP} \text{ met Cary Grant}], \sigma)$ iff for some y,
           $\text{Val}(\langle x, y \rangle, [_V \text{ met}], \sigma)$ and $\text{Val}(y, [_{NP} \text{ Cary Grant}], \sigma)$
      d. $\text{Val}(\langle x, y \rangle, [_V \text{ met}], \sigma)$ iff x met y
      e. $\text{Val}(y, [_{NP} \text{ Cary Grant}], \sigma)$ iff $y = \text{Cary Grant}$

Notice now that if (60) is true, then S and its subexpressions actually have the values in question. That is, if *Lori met Cary Grant* is true, then the following hold:

(62) a. $\text{Val}(t, [_S \text{ Lori met Cary Grant}], \sigma)$
      b. $\text{Val}(\text{Lori}, [_{NP} \text{ Lori}], \sigma)$
      c. $\text{Val}(\text{Lori}, [_{VP} \text{ met Cary Grant}], \sigma)$
      d. $\text{Val}(\langle \text{Lori}, \text{Cary Grant} \rangle, [_V \text{ met}], \sigma)$
      e. $\text{Val}(\text{Cary Grant}, [_{NP} \text{ Cary Grant}], \sigma)$

Suppose that we now take the syntactic tree for *Lori met Cary Grant* and annotate its nodes with the semantic values they would need to have if the sentence were true. The result is (63), where values appear in square brackets to the right of each node:

(63)

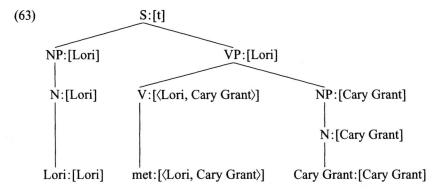

This object is the **interpreted logical form** (or ILF) for *Lori met Cary Grant.* It is an amalgam of syntactic and referential material.

In the ILF theory, we prove T sentences for clausal-complement constructions that relate individuals to ILFs. For example, *Peter believes Lori met Cary Grant* receives the T sentence in (64):

(64)   Val(t, [$_S$ Peter believes [$_S$ Lori met Cary Grant]], σ) iff Peter believes

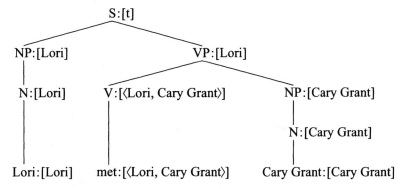

11.3.2   The Empirical Adequacy of ILFs

ILFs contain both linguistic and nonlinguistic material. As a result, the ILF theory discriminates truth conditions for clausal-complement sentences at least as finely as either the quotational or modal accounts. Thus it answers to our two observations made earlier:

- The truth conditions of clausal-complement constructions are discriminated at least as finely as the forms used in the embedded clauses.

■ The truth conditions of clausal-complement constructions are discriminated at least as finely as the objects referred to in the embedded clauses.

To illustrate the first point, consider (16) (repeated below):

(16) a. Peter believes [Lori met Cary Grant]
      b. Peter believes [Lori met Archie Leach]

The parts of the two complement clauses refer to the same object but use different expressions in doing so. The truth conditions for (16a) were given in (64). By contrast, the truth conditions for (16b) are as in (65):

(65) Val(t, [$_S$ Peter believes [$_S$ Lori met Archie Leach]], σ) iff Peter believes

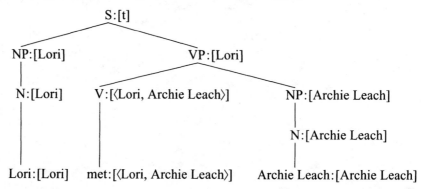

Note carefully that (64) and (65) place Peter in the belief relation to *different* ILFs: the first contains the lexical item *Cary Grant*, whereas the second contains the lexical item *Archie Leach*. Since these are different ILFs, they are different, nonequivalent truth conditions. We get the same result for the other examples in (17) to (22): in each case we have different syntactic forms; these yield different ILFs, which in turn yield different truth conditions.

To illustrate how ILFs answer to the second observation, consider (28) (repeated below with details suppressed):

(28) a. Jill is a philosopher. Phil thinks [she ponders].
      b. Kate is a philosopher. Phil thinks [she ponders].

Here the two complement clauses contain exactly the same expressions but refer to different objects. The truth conditions for (28a) and (28b) are given in (66) and (67), respectively:

(66) Val(t, [$_S$ Phil thinks [$_S$ she ponders]], σ) iff Phil thinks

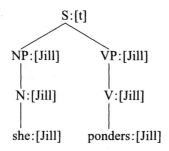

(67) Val(t, [$_S$ Phil thinks [$_S$ she ponders]], σ) iff Phil thinks

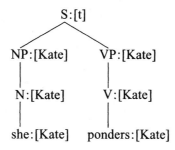

Once again, these truth conditions place the subject in a belief relation with different ILFs: the first contains the person Jill, whereas the second contains the person Kate. Since these are different ILFs, they give different, nonequivalent truth conditions. The same reasoning will apply to other cases where linguistic form remains constant but reference does not: in virtue of containing distinct referents, the ILFs will correctly discriminate these cases.

Finally, consider our point that it is desirable to have an innocent theory of the semantics of clausal complements.

- We prefer the semantics of clausal-complement constructions to be innocent: the values assigned in embedded and unembedded contexts should be the same; furthermore, the analysis of the unembedded parts should not depend on evidence from the embedded parts.

The ILF theory meets this desideratum. As simple amalgams of words, phrases, and the objects they refer to, ILFs invoke no entities not already required for giving the semantics of the simplest parts of the grammar. No new, special entities like propositions, relations, or properties are introduced.

The ILF theory is thus semantically innocent in a way not matched by propositional accounts.

Are ILFs Too Fine-Grained?

The ILF theory is a fine-grained one in the sense that small details of form and reference can affect truth conditions. Cases like (68a, b), for instance, are assigned distinct truth conditions in the ILF theory.

(68) a. Kate believes that Kumiko will finish her book in a fortnight.
    b. Kate believes that Kumiko will finish her book in two weeks.

Some might argue that the theory is in fact too fine-grained in this prediction —that (68a) and (68b) really are truth-conditionally equivalent. For, they might say, believing that Kumiko will finish her book in a fortnight is just the same thing as believing that Kumiko will finish her book in two weeks. There is just one belief there, which could be reported by either of the two sentences. Others, such as Burge (1978), would deny this, arguing that it's quite possible in principle for Kate to believe that Kumiko will finish her book in a fortnight without believing that Kumiko will finish her book in two weeks. This could happen if, for example, Kate thought that a fortnight is ten days.

The ILF theory has the advantage of being able to accommodate both views. By providing different RHSs in the T theorems for (68a, b), it leaves open the possibility that Burge's view is correct and that the two reports could in principle differ in truth value. But the ILF theory also leaves open the possibility that the two reports are necessarily equivalent. This is because the theory is compatible with the truth of (69):

(69) Necessarily, if Kate believes the ILF of Kumiko will finish her book in a fortnight, then she believes the ILF of Kumiko will finish her book in two weeks.

Whether or not (69) is true is an interesting question. But it is one that lies largely outside of the semantics of attitude reports. It is at least in part a question of what is involved in possessing a concept and the relation of concept possession to language.

Suppose Kate has been heard to claim *A fortnight is a period of ten days*, and we know that she is sincere is saying this. Suppose further that Kate is otherwise competent in the use of the phrase *a fortnight*: she uses it appropriately in contexts where one normally would. On some views of concept possession, this suffices for her to have the concept of a fortnight, even though she has an importantly false belief about what a fortnight is. If this view is correct, then it should be possible for Kate to believe that Kumiko will finish her book in a fortnight without also believing that Kumiko will finish her book in two weeks. And so the conditional (69) will be false. On other views of concept possession, the mere fact that Kate agrees to *A fortnight is ten days* suffices to show that she does not use *a fortnight* to express the concept of a fortnight. Rather, *her* use of this word expresses a different concept, a concept of a period of ten days. On such views there is no room for a difference between the concept of a fortnight and the concept of two weeks: it is simply impossible for these concepts to apply to periods of different lengths. The concept of a fortnight and the concept of two weeks are the same concept, one that can be expressed by either *a fortnight* or *two weeks*. In this case (69) is true.

Evidently, the question of what is involved in possession of a concept and its relation to language is not one for the semantics of attitude reports but rather is one for other areas of psychology or philosophy.[13] As far as semantics goes, either answer is perfectly compatible with the ILF theory. If there are two beliefs that Kate might have, one with a 'fortnight' concept, the other with a distinct 'two weeks' concept, the ILF theory shows how we can use attitude reports with different truth conditions to distinguish them. On the other hand, if there is only one possible belief corresponding to the two reports, this too is perfectly compatible with the ILF theory. There is no reason why a single belief of Kate's could not be reported by reference to either of two distinct ILFs. This would be analogous to reporting on the temperature using Fahrenheit or Centigrade measures. A single temperature can be described as either 212 degrees F or 100 degrees C.

The ILF theory therefore allows us to provide different T theorems for sentences that intuitively have different truth conditions. And it leaves open the question of whether attitude reports with syntactically distinct embedded Ss can ever be truth-conditionally equivalent.

11.3.3   The Intuitive Adequacy of ILFs

Even if ILFs do serve the purpose of tracking differences among the truth conditions of propositional-attitude reports, one might still worry that they are not intuitively right as the objects of such reports. Consider the fact that

Caesar said "Carthago delenda est." When we report on this in English, we say (70):

(70) Caesar said that Carthage must be destroyed.

According to the ILF theory, the semantic object of *say* is the ILF of an English sentence, something that contains English words. But this seems to be the wrong object. Caesar didn't speak English. The same goes for the belief that Caesar voiced when he uttered his words. We use (71) to report his belief:

(71) Caesar believed that Carthage must be destroyed.

The ILF theory delivers the result that the semantic object of *believe* is, again, the English ILF. But surely Caesar didn't stand in any direct belief relation (a so-called **doxastic relation**) to an ILF containing English words. How could he have believed something he didn't understand?

We believe this problem is illusory. The intuitive idea behind the ILF theory can be understood via the notion of **expression**. Words and sentences can express attitudes. Thus when Caesar uttered "Carthago delenda est," he expressed himself in Latin. If he had spoken English, he might have produced the words "Carthage must destroyed." Thus we can use English words to express what Caesar expressed in Latin. In general, propositional attitudes—sayings, beliefs, desires, doubts, and so on—can be expressed in language. ILFs are linguistic objects: they have a syntactic structure, and they contain words. They are therefore appropriate to give expression to attitudes. The ILF partially depicted in (72) is an object one can use to express what Caesar said and believed:[14]

(72)

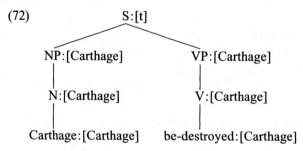

Consider now the T theorem (73) (details omitted):

(73) Val(t, *Caesar said that Carthage must be destroyed*, σ) iff Caeser said

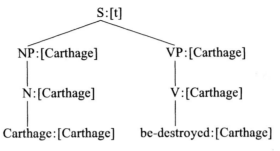

We can intuitively understand the RHS as something like (74):

(74) Caeser performed an utterance expressed by

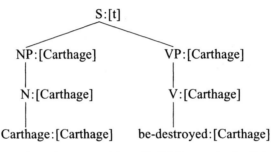

So even though Caesar himself didn't speak English, it is still reasonable to have an English ILF as the object of the verb *say* in (70). On this proposal, to say an ILF is to perform an utterance expressed by the ILF. Analogously for belief and the other attitudes: to believe an ILF is to have a belief expressed by it, to desire an ILF is to have a desire expressed by it, and so on.[15]

Note that the explication of relations like saying and believing in terms of expression is not intended as part of the actual semantic theory. It is meant only to explain in intuitive terms what these relations involve. By way of analogy, suppose someone is unsure what the word *knows* means in English. As part of the semantic theory PC +, we prove T theorems like (75):

(75) Val(t, *Kumiko knows Chris*, σ) iff Kumiko knows Chris

Not knowing exactly what *knows* means, the person asks for an explanation. We might explain, to say that Kumiko knows Chris is to say that she is acquainted with him: she has probably met him and is aware of at least some aspects of his character. The explanation here is not part of the content of PC + itself. It is not even a lexical analysis of *knows*. It is just a way of helping someone understand what has been written down in PC+. In the case of knowing, there is no need for us to offer this sort of intuitive explication, since the concept is familiar. However, as we said above, the case of attitude verbs is different. Since it is not immediately obvious what it means to say that someone says or believes an ILF, we need to provide an intuitive explanation of the relation.

11.4   The Theory ILF

Having introduced ILFs in an informal way, we now provide a formal theory that integrates them into the truth conditions of clausal-complement sentences. Our theory is a version of that presented in Larson and Ludlow (1993) and contains two basic parts:

- Lexical and phrasal axioms for the relevant items and structures
- An algorithm for generating ILFs

The lexical axioms for verbs that select clausal complements are straightforward: we analyze them as transitive predicates relating a subject argument to an object argument:

(76) a. Val($\langle x, y \rangle$, *says*, σ) iff x says y
      b. Val($\langle x, y \rangle$, *believes*, σ) iff x believes y
      c. Val($\langle x, y \rangle$, *thinks*, σ) iff x thinks y

The phrasal axiom (77) introduces the ILF of the complement clause (abbreviated "$\llbracket S \rrbracket \sigma$") at the point where VP is encountered:

(77) Val(x, [$_{VP}$ V S], σ) iff for some y, Val($\langle x, y \rangle$, V, σ) and $y = \llbracket S \rrbracket \sigma$

This insures that the semantic object of a verb taking a clausal complement will be an ILF.

The recursive algorithm for generating ILFs with respect to a given sequence σ is given below:

Algorithm for generating ILFs   Let α be a phrase marker with root S, let σ be a sequence, and for each β, a subtree of α, let x be the unique value assigned to β, assuming that Val(t, S, σ). Then

1. a. if β is a terminal node, $\llbracket \beta \rrbracket \sigma = \beta : [x]$;

    b. if $\beta = [_\gamma \, \delta_1 \, \delta_2 \ldots \delta_n]$ for $n \geq 1$ and $\mathrm{Val}(x, [_\gamma \, \delta_1 \, \delta_2 \ldots \delta_n], \sigma)$,
       $⟦\beta⟧\sigma = [_{\gamma \, : \, [x]} \, ⟦\delta_1⟧\sigma \; ⟦\delta_2⟧\sigma \ldots ⟦\delta_n⟧\sigma]$;

2. if $\mathrm{Val}(x, \beta, \sigma)$ is not unique or not defined, then
    a. if β is a terminal node, $⟦\beta⟧\sigma = \beta : [\;\;]$;
    b. if $\beta = [_\gamma \, \delta_1 \, \delta_2 \ldots \delta_n]$ for $n \geq 1$, $⟦\beta⟧\sigma = [_{\gamma \, : \, [\;\;]} \, ⟦\delta_1⟧\sigma \; ⟦\delta_2⟧\sigma \ldots ⟦\delta_n⟧\sigma]$.

This algorithm has the general structure alluded to earlier. If S is true, its constituent phrases and lexical items receive definite values. Words are paired with their values under clause 1a, and phrases are compositionally paired with their values under clause 1b. Clause 2 in the definition covers cases where a phrase receives no unique semantic value with respect to a given S, or receives no value at all. In such a case the ILF for the phrase is just the phrase itself. Examples are discussed in section 11.4.2. We will call $⟦\alpha⟧\sigma$ the **interpreted logical form of α with respect to σ.**

A Sample Derivation

We illustrate our new rules with an abbreviated sample derivation. Consider (78), which we can give the simple syntax in (79) for present purposes:

(78) Chris says Jill agrees.

(79)

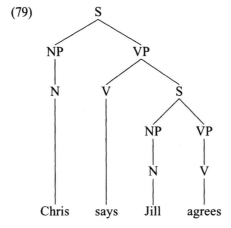

Together with familiar rules and axioms, (76) and (77) yield the following partial result:

(80) $\mathrm{Val}(t, [_S \, [_{NP} \, [_N \, \text{Chris}]] \, [_{VP} \, [_V \, \text{says}] \, [_S \, [_{NP} \, [_N \, \text{Jill}]] \, [_{VP} \, [_V \, \text{agrees}]]]]], \sigma)$ iff
     for some y, Chris says y and $y = ⟦ \, [_S \, [_{NP} \, [_N \, \text{Jill}]] \, [_{VP} \, [_V \, \text{agrees}]]] \, ⟧\sigma$

We need to derive the ILF ⌐ [$_S$ [$_{NP}$ [$_N$ Jill]] [$_{VP}$ [$_V$ agrees]]] ⌐σ in order to complete this T sentence. Using our T theory, we calculate the usual biconditionals for each of the parts of [$_S$ [$_{NP}$ [$_N$ Jill]] [$_{VP}$ [$_V$ agrees]]]. Assuming this sentence is true, the parts actually have the values in question; furthermore these values are unique with respect to the given tree:

(81) a. Val(t, [$_S$ Jill agrees], σ)
    b. Val(Jill, [$_{NP}$ Jill], σ)
    c. Val(Jill, [$_N$ Jill], σ)
    d. Val(Jill, *Jill*, σ)
    e. Val(Jill, [$_{VP}$ agrees], σ)
    f. Val(Jill, [$_V$ agrees], σ)
    g. Val(Jill, *agrees*, σ)

Using the ILF algorithm, we compositionally pair nodes and their values, constructing the interpreted phrase marker. The result is (82):

(82)

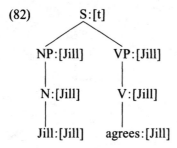

This object is then substituted into (80), after which (SI) yields the final T sentence:

(83) Vat(t, [$_S$ [$_{NP}$ [$_N$ Chris]] [$_{VP}$ [$_V$ says] [$_S$ [$_{NP}$ [$_N$ Jill]] [$_{VP}$ [$_V$ agrees]]]]], σ) iff Chris says

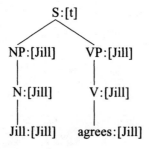

The latter is the desired result.

11.4.1   ILFs and Variable-Reference Terms

The ILF algorithm given above interacts with other parts of our theory in the appropriate way. For example, consider variable-reference terms, which appeared in the earlier pair (28a, b):

(28) a. Jill is a philosopher. Phil thinks [she$_1$ ponders].
     b. Kate is a philosopher. Phil thinks [she$_1$ ponders].

We saw that *she$_1$ ponders* can differ in truth value when the pronoun *she$_1$* refers to different individuals. The utterances of this subsentence must therefore be able to receive different truth conditions.

  The theory ILF correctly derives this result. Recall from chapter 6 that every sentence type has sequence-relative truth conditions. And every utterance selects a particular set of sequences via the selection relation Σ. An utterance is then true iff the sentence uttered is true relative to the particular sequences selected by the utterance. It is easy to show that *Phil thinks she$_1$ ponders* receives the T sentence in (84) under our new rules:

(84) Vat(t, [$_S$ [$_{NP}$ [$_N$ Phil]] [$_{VP}$ [$_V$ thinks] [$_S$ [$_{NP}$ [$_N$ she$_1$]] [$_{VP}$ [$_V$ ponders]]]]], σ)
     iff Phil says

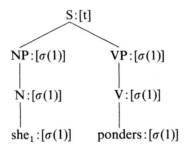

Recall now the conditionalized T scheme from VRT, repeated here as (85):

(85) If u is an utterance of S and $\Sigma(u, \sigma)$, then u is true iff Val(t, S, σ)

Suppose that we are dealing with Kate's utterance of (28a), with Kate using *she$_1$* to refer to Jill. The method of calculating conditionalized T sentences is exactly parallel to the one we deployed earlier for utterances of ordinary VRT sentences (compare the inference in (31) from chapter 6):

(86) a. u^* is an utterance of *Phil thinks she$_1$ ponders* (premise)
     b. Kate uses *she$_1$* in u^* to refer to Jill (premise)

c. If a speaker uses α_i in u to refer to x, then $\Sigma(u, \sigma)$ only if $\sigma(i) = x$

d. If Kate uses *she*₁ in u^* to refer to Jill, then $\Sigma(u^*, \sigma)$ only if $\sigma(1) = $ Jill

e. $\Sigma(u^*, \sigma)$ only if $\sigma(1) = $ Jill

f. If u^* is an utterance of *Phil thinks she₁ ponders* and $\Sigma(u^*, \sigma)$, then u^* is true iff Val(t, *Phil thinks she₁ ponders*, σ)

g. Val(t, *Phil thinks she₁ ponders*, σ) iff Phil thinks

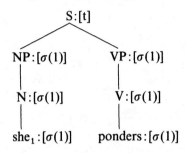

h. If u^* is an utterance of *Phil thinks she₁ ponders* and $\Sigma(u^*, \sigma)$, then u^* is true iff Phil thinks

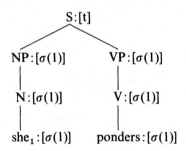

i. If $\Sigma(u^*, \sigma)$, then u^* is true iff Phil thinks

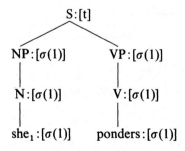

j. If $\Sigma(u^*, \sigma)$, then u^* is true iff Phil thinks

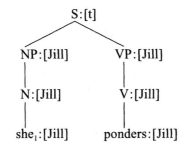

k. For some σ', $\Sigma(u^*, \sigma')$ (by (85))
l. u^* is true iff Phil thinks

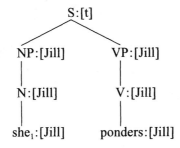

This last, (86*l*), is the desired result.

11.4.2   Purely Syntactic ILFs

ILFs, as generated by our algorithm, are syntactic forms annotated with specific real-world entities: people, tables, cities, etc. As such, an interesting question arises when we come to sentences like (87a), whose semantics doesn't involve specific entities, or sentences like (87b), whose semantics doesn't involve any real-world objects at all:

(87) a. Phil thinks [some woman ponders]
     b. Phil thinks [Aphrodite ponders]

The valuation predicate assigns no unique object to phrases like *some woman*. So no object can be paired with this expression in an ILF. Likewise, although our theory countenances true axioms like (88), its free logical character does not allow us to deduce the existence of an individual (let alone a unique individual) who is Aphrodite.

(88) Val(x, *Aphrodite*, σ) iff x = Aphrodite

So there is no object to associate with *Aphrodite* or the N and NP nodes that dominate it. What, then, is the ILF in such cases?

Our answer is given in clause 2 in the ILF-generation algorithm. In brief, this clause simply stipulates that whenever a phrase fails to have an object or a unique object as its semantic value, the ILF for the phrase is just the phrase annotated with the empty list "[ ]". This is a purely syntactic object: the ILF is essentially identical to the phrase marker itself.

To illustrate concretely, consider (87a) under a PredC semantics for quantifiers and where the quantifier has scope within the embedded clause. Recall that *some* and *some woman* are assigned no semantic values in the PredC theory (they are syncategorematic). Furthermore, traces of quantifiers receive varying (and hence nonunique) semantic values with each choice of sequence variant. The ILFs of both phrases are thus provided under clause 2: they include only linguistic material and no objectual content. The resulting truth conditions are as in (89):

(89) Val(t, [$_S$ Phil thinks [$_S$ [$_{NP_1}$ some woman] [$_S$ t$_1$ ponders]]], σ) iff
      Phil thinks

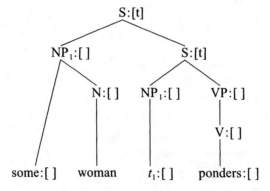

A similar result obtains for (87b). Although axiom (88) is true, from this we (correctly) fail to infer the existence of a real Aphrodite. Since the lexical item *Aphrodite* is paired with no value, none of the noun nodes that dominate it inherit a value. Likewise, the verb, V node, and VP do not get associated with a unique value. The result is an ILF denuded of objects, in other words, a syntactic tree:

(90) Val(t, [$_S$ Phil thinks [$_S$ Aphrodite ponders]], σ) iff Phil thinks

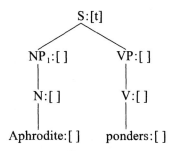

Since the semantic object of the attitude verb contains no referential material, we might call such ILFs **purely syntactic**.[16]

11.4.3   What's in an ILF?

Thus far we have argued that the objects of attitude reports, ILFs, are syntactic objects with certain semantic properties. Specifically, we have represented them as phrase markers with semantic values attached to certain of their nodes. But information beyond this seems to be relevant to the semantics of clausal complements. Consider (91), observed by Ludlow (1985b):

(91) Jason believes Harvard is a fine school.

The truth of (91) can depend on the pronunciation of the word *Harvard.* Suppose that Jason is an individual from New York and is unfamiliar with the unique pronunciation patterns of Bostonians. Then (92a) could be true without (92b) being true:

(92) a. Jason believes [[harverd] is a fine school]
     b. Jason believes [[hahvahd] is a fine school]

This indicates that the objects of attitude reports have more properties than those described by the purely syntactic theory of LF and the semantic algorithm we provided to build up ILFs.[17]

Still other properties might be relevant as well. Consider the following story. Jason attends a philosophy lecture, which he considers to be a complete fiasco. He expresses his view by uttering (93), with heavy sarcasm:

(93) I'm, like, really impressed.

Later, someone asks Kathrin what Jason thought of the lecture, and she utters (94), mimicking Jason's sarcasm as she utters the complement sentence:

(94) Jason said he was, like, really impressed.

It is at least arguable that the tone of Kathrin's utterance is relevant to the truth value of (94). Had she uttered the complement sentence without a hint of sarcasm, she might reasonably be held to have said something false. This suggests that the verb *said* is sensitive to more than just the strict and literal content of people's utterances. Rather, what people are held to say encompasses their pragmatic, communicative intentions. If this is right, then we should think of the objects of attitude reports as including pragmatic properties as well.

If they include more than just syntax and semantics, it is clearly inadequate to view ILFs as phrase markers interpreted only by the semantic component; other components of grammar are relevant as well. Here we will not present a more refined theory of ILFs. However, the basic ideas on which the refinement would be built are straightforward. When someone utters a speech report, the embedded clause is built up by various different modules: From within the language faculty proper it receives a syntactic form, a semantics, and a phonological form. From the pragmatics module, outside the language faculty proper, it receives an array of pragmatic properties. It is this complex, totally interpreted form that would be the true object of an attitude report. These revised ILFs would differ from what we currently have only in being more complex. They are tree structures with nodes consisting of clusters of properties. Each terminal node will possess phonological and orthographic properties, as well as semantic ones. And at least the S node will be annotated with pragmatic properties, assigned by the pragmatics module in the specific context of utterance. These souped-up ILFs would naturally retain the virtues of those produced by our current ILF theory. We would expect the revised theory to be empirically and intuitively adequate. Furthermore, it would be semantically innocent: all the work that needs to be done to construct an ILF can be carried out by the modules normally responsible for linguistic understanding.

11.5   ILFs and Inference

We noted earlier that attitude reports have received great attention in the philosophical literature since Frege (1893). The focus of discussion has been the inferential relations among attitude reports. We have already argued that the question of when two attitude reports that refer to different ILFs are necessarily equivalent is not a question for semantics. Rather, it is a question for a theory of the attitudes themselves. There is a further issue concerning inferential relations among attitude reports that is closer to linguistic semantics but is still distinct from it. This is the question of what accounts for speakers' judgments about the equivalences and nonequivalences among attitude reports. The question is not about whether, for example, (95a) could be true while (95b) was false, or whether (95c) could be true while (95d) was false:

(95) a. Chris believes that Cary Grant agrees.
     b. Chris believes that Archie Leach agrees.
     c. Chris believes that a fortnight is a fortnight.
     d. Chris believes that a fortnight is two weeks.

Rather, it is a question of what accounts for an individual's judgments on these matters. A complete answer to this question would require a great deal of work. For it lies at the intersection of semantics with at least three further areas of enquiry.

The first area of enquiry concerns humans' intuitive conceptions of the attitudes themselves. This is the theory of what is sometimes called "folk psychology." Normal human beings are themselves commonsense psychologists. Humans attribute desires, beliefs, and other propositional attitudes to one another and predict and explain each others' actions on the basis of such attributions. This competence is itself a subject for scientific psychology to study. What is the basis of the competence? How is it acquired? How is it put to use in practice?

It is not unreasonable to hypothesize that we owe our competence in commonsense psychology to a special purpose psychology module. The psychology module is similar to the language faculty, but its business is the learning and use of psychology, rather than of language. Thus we might suppose that the module contains a body of knowledge that takes the form of a psychological theory. Perhaps much of the theory is innate, the remainder being acquired rapidly in the first few years of life.[18]

The psychology module will have its own way of representing propositional attitudes. These representations may well not involve ILFs. ILFs are represented within the semantics module of the language faculty. They are therefore involved in our understanding of the linguistic representation of attitudes— how we represent the attitudes in language. But different modules can and often do represent, or conceptualize, things in different ways. For us, it is an open question how the psychology module represents attitudes.

Evidently, a full theory of our judgments about the inferential relations among attitude reports would require a theory of the psychology module and an account of its relation to the semantics module. Suppose, for example, that Kate is considering whether (95b) follows from (95a) and decides that it does. Abstracting from a variety of complicating factors, her judgment is presumably based on some inference like (96), where

□ [$_S$ [$_{NP}$ [$_N$ Cary Grant]] [$_{VP}$ [$_V$ agrees]]] □σ   and
□ [$_S$ [$_{NP}$ [$_N$ Archie Leach]] [$_{VP}$ [$_V$ agrees]]] □σ

are ILFs, as provided by the T theory, "*F*(Chris)" stands for the way Kate's psychology module represents the proposition that Chris believes that Cary Grant agrees, and the transitions from (96b) to (96c) and (96c) to (96d) take place at some interface between the language faculty and the psychology module:

(96) a. Val(t, *Chris believes that Cary Grant agrees, σ*) iff
Chris believes □ [$_S$ [$_{NP}$ [$_N$ Cary Grant]] [$_{VP}$ [$_V$ agrees]]] □σ
   b. Chris believes □ [$_S$ [$_{NP}$ [$_N$ Cary Grant]] [$_{VP}$ [$_V$ agrees]]] □σ iff *F*(Chris)
   c. *F*(Chris) iff Chris believes □ [$_S$ [$_{NP}$ [$_N$ Archie Leach]] [$_{VP}$ [$_V$ agrees]]] □σ
   d. Val(t, *Chris believes that Archie Leach agrees, σ*) iff
Chris believes □ [$_S$ [$_{NP}$ [$_N$ Archie Leach]] [$_{VP}$ [$_V$ agrees]]] □σ
   e. Val(t, *Chris believes that Cary Grant agrees, σ*) iff
Val(t, *Chris believes that Archie Leach agrees, σ*) (by (96a–d), (SE))

That is to say, the way in which Kate's psychology module represents the information that her language faculty represents as "Chris believes □ [$_S$ [$_{NP}$ [$_N$ Cary Grant]] [$_{VP}$ [$_V$ agrees]]] □σ" is the very same way that it represents the information that the language faculty represents as "Chris believes □ [$_S$ [$_{NP}$ [$_N$ Archie Leach]] [$_{VP}$ [$_V$ agrees]]] □σ."

The second area of enquiry relevant to our judgments about attitude reports is pragmatics. Attitude reporting shows a certain kind of sensitivity to conversational contexts. Sometimes we are rather liberal in our judgments of the truth of, say, a belief report: we judge the report to be true even if it is couched in terms that do not give a very exact expression to the believer's belief. At other times our judgments are more restrictive. Consider the following example. In Roman times, biology had not developed to the point of distinguishing fish from aquatic mammals. Consequently, let us suppose, Caesar had no word or concept corresponding exactly to our word *fish*—his closest equivalent covering both fish and aquatic mammals. Consider now the belief report (97):

(97) Caesar believed that fish swim.

Is (97) true or false? In most conversational contexts, we would allow that (97) is true. However, if we were engaged in a precise study of Caesar's psychology, we might reasonably hold that (97) is false, strictly speaking. He didn't believe that fish swim, because he had no concept of fish.

In the strict cases we only count a report as good if the elements in the ILF correspond very closely in their semantic properties to the semantic properties of the attitude. The English word *fish* does not exactly match Caesar's concept in extension. Therefore, when we are being strict, we do not count it as appropriate to express Caesar's belief. When we are being liberal, the slight mismatch of extension is allowed. In our view, the best way to account for this is within pragmatics. There is a pragmatically determined set of constraints that fixes the amount of slack allowed between the semantic properties of the attitude and the semantic properties of the ILF. Or, to put it in terms of the notion of expression, introduced above, pragmatic constraints determine which ILFs express which beliefs in a given context.

The contextual sensitivity of attitude reporting relates to our judgments about equivalences among them. For, evidently, in slack contexts we will be inclined to allow certain inferences to go through that we would not allow in stricter contexts. Suppose, for example, that Bill and Ted, two old friends of Archie Leach, are in conversation. Bill has recently heard Alfred Hitchcock say (98):

(98) Jimmy Stewart said that Cary Grant is a great actor.

Bill says (99) to Ted:

(99) Jimmy Stewart said that Archie Leach is a great actor.

In context, this report might be perfectly acceptable. It doesn't matter to Bill and Ted what name or description Jimmy Stewart used to refer to Archie. All that matters in this context is that Jimmy Stewart said, of their old friend Archie, that he is a great actor. Given this, (99) counts as equivalent to (98) in this particular context.

The kind of contextual sensitivity present in attitude reports is not unusual. It seems to be of the same general sort as we find in judgments of many other kinds: whether Olga Korbutt was a better gymnast than Nadia Comaneci, whether the Beatles had long hair in 1963, whether London is like New York. In each of these cases our judgments will vary from context to context, depending on pragmatically determined parameters: the relevant qualities of gymnasts, the comparison class for hair length, the respects in which cities are judged to be like one another.

A full theory of our judgments about the inferential relations among attitude reports therefore needs to take into account not only the semantics module and the psychology module, but also pragmatics and the relationship among all three. And it doesn't end here. There are still further factors involved. Psychologists and philosophers, for example, have, in addition to their folk-psychological conception of attitudes, a theoretical conception. We already saw this in section 11.3.2, where we considered how one's theory of concept possession determines one's views about the relation of the concept expressed by *a fortnight* to that expressed by *two weeks*. To make the general point clearer with an analogy, consider a linguist studying English. The linguist will have both unconscious knowledge of English in his or her language faculty and a theoretical conception of English, which may well be different in various ways. The linguist's judgment about, say, the grammaticality of a given sentence might well involve some interaction of both unconscious knowledge in the language faculty and explicit scientific knowledge. This is one reason why it is a good idea for linguists to have a good supply of lay informants. In parallel fashion, when a philosopher or a psychologist makes a judgment about an inference involving attitude reports, their philosophical or scientific theory will also play a role. The third area of inquiry that is relevant here is thus a theory of explicit theories of attitudes, as opposed to the innately determined theory in the psychology module.

In summary, the semantics of belief reporting intersects with a variety of other areas of inquiry in accounting for our judgments about attitude reports. Not until all these areas and their (no doubt complicated) interrelationships are understood will there be a complete theory of these judgments. Given the variety and complexity of all the factors involved, it is not surprising that attitudes and attitude reports continue to be a flourishing topic in philosophy and psychology.

Theory and Exercises

The Theory ILF (Interpreted Logical Forms)

Lexical Axioms

(1) a. Val(x, *Kate*, σ) iff x = Kate
    b. Val(x, *Chris*, σ) iff x = Chris
    c. Val(x, *Phil*, σ) iff x = Phil
    d. Val(x, *Jill*, σ) iff x = Jill
    e. Val(x, *Kumiko*, σ) iff x = Kumiko

(2) a. Val(x, *man*, σ) iff x is a man
    b. Val(x, *woman*, σ) iff x is a woman
    c. Val(x, *fish*, σ) iff x is a fish

(3) a. Val(x, *ponders*, σ) iff x ponders
    b. Val(x, *agrees*, σ) iff x agrees
    c. Val(x, *protests*, σ) iff x protests

(4) a. Val($\langle x, y \rangle$, *knows*, σ) iff x knows y
    b. Val($\langle x, y \rangle$, *admires*, σ) iff x admires y
    c. Val($\langle x, y \rangle$, *instructs*, σ) iff x instructs y

(5) a. Val($\langle x, y \rangle$, *says*, σ) iff x says y
    b. Val($\langle x, y \rangle$, *believes*, σ) iff x believes y
    c. Val($\langle x, y \rangle$, *thinks*, σ) iff x thinks y

(6) a. Val($\langle X, Y \rangle$, *every*, σ) iff $|Y - X| = 0$
    b. Val($\langle X, Y \rangle$, *some*, σ) iff $|Y \cap X| > 0$
    c. Val($\langle X, Y \rangle$, *no*, σ) iff $|Y \cap X| = 0$
    d. Val($\langle X, Y \rangle$, *most*, σ) iff $|Y \cap X| > |Y - X|$
    e. Val($\langle X, Y \rangle$, *two*, σ) iff $|Y \cap X| = 2$
       (And similarly for other numeral determiners)
    f. Val($\langle X, Y \rangle$, *the two*, σ) iff $|Y - X| = 0$, where $|Y| = 2$
    g. Val($\langle X, Y \rangle$, *both*, σ) iff Val($\langle X, Y \rangle$, *the two*, σ)
    h. Val($\langle X, Y \rangle$, *neither*, σ) iff $|Y \cap X| = 0$, where $|Y| = 2$
    i. Val($\langle X, Y \rangle$, *the*, σ) iff Val($\langle X, Y \rangle$, *the one*, σ)

Phrasal Axioms

(7) a. Val(t, [$_S$ S$_1$ *and* S$_2$], σ) iff both Val(t, S$_1$, σ) and Val(t, S$_2$, σ)

   b. Val(t, [$_S$ S$_1$ *or* S$_2$], σ) iff either Val(t, S$_1$, σ) or Val(t, S$_2$, σ)

   c. Val(t, [$_S$ *It is not the case that* S], σ) iff it is not the case that Val(t, S, σ)

(8) a. Val(t, [$_S$ NP VP], σ) iff for some x, Val(x, NP, σ) and Val(x, VP, σ)

   b. Val(x, [$_{VP}$ V NP], σ) iff for some y, Val($\langle x, y \rangle$, V, σ) and Val(y, NP, σ)

   c. Val(x, [$_X$ Y], σ) iff Val(x, Y, σ) (where X, Y are any nodes)

(9) a. Val(X, [$_{NP}$ Det N$'$], σ) iff for some Y, Val($\langle X, Y \rangle$, Det, σ) and $Y = \{y : \text{Val}(y, \text{N}, \sigma)\}$

   b. Val(x, [$_{NP_i}$ e], σ) iff $x = \sigma(i)$ for all $i \geq 1$

   c. Val(t, [$_S$ NP$_i$ S], σ) iff for some X, Val(X, NP, σ) and $X = \{\sigma'(i) : \text{Val}(t, \text{S}_1, \sigma'), \text{where } \sigma' \approx_i \sigma\}$

(10) Val(x, [$_{VP}$ V S], σ) iff for some y, Val($\langle x, y \rangle$, V, σ) and $y = \square$S$\square\sigma$

Production Rules

(UI), (SE), (SI) as in PC+

Definition For any sequence σ, $\sigma(a)$, $\sigma(b)$, $\sigma(c)$, $\sigma(d)$ are the first, second, third, and fourth elements of σ, respectively. For any positive integer i, $\sigma(i)$ is the $(i + 4)$th element of σ.

Definition For any sequences σ, σ', $\sigma \approx_i \sigma'$ iff σ' differs from σ at most at $\sigma'(i)$.

Definition Val(t, S) iff Val(t, S, σ) for all sequences σ.

Algorithm for generating ILFs Let α be a phrase marker with root S, let σ be a sequence, and for each β, a subtree of α, let x be the unique value assigned to β, assuming that Val(t, S, σ). Then

1. a. if β is a terminal node, $\square\beta\square\sigma = \beta : [x]$;

   b. if $\beta = [_\gamma\ \delta_1\ \delta_2 \ldots \delta_n]$ for $n \geq 1$ and Val(x, [$_\gamma\ \delta_1\ \delta_2 \ldots \delta_n$], σ), $\square\beta\square\sigma = [_{\gamma\,:\,[x]}\ \square\delta_1\square\sigma\ \square\delta_2\square\sigma \ldots \square\delta_n\square\sigma]$;

2. if Val(x, β, σ) is not unique or not defined, then

   a. if β is a terminal node, $\square\beta\square\sigma = \beta : [\ ]$;

   b. if $\beta = [_\gamma\ \delta_1\ \delta_2 \ldots \delta_n]$ for $n \geq 1$, $\square\beta\square\sigma = [_{\gamma\,:\,[\ \ ]}\ \square\delta_1\square\sigma\ \square\delta_2\square\sigma \ldots \square\delta_n\square\sigma]$.

Exercises

1. Discuss what problems arise with the following candidate axiom for clausal-complement constructions:

   (1) Val(x, [$_{VP}$ V S], σ) iff Val($\langle x, t \rangle$, V, σ) and Val(t, S, σ), or
   Val($\langle x, f \rangle$, V, σ) and it is not the case that Val(t, S, σ)

2. What T sentences does the ILF theory assign to the following examples:

   (1) Phil thinks Chris admires Kate.
   (2) Phil thinks Chris admires every woman.

3. Consider the alternative axioms (1) and (2) for the ILF theory:

   (1) a. Val($\langle x, y \rangle$, *says*, σ) iff x says $\llbracket y \rrbracket$
       b. Val($\langle x, y \rangle$, *believes*, σ) iff x believes $\llbracket y \rrbracket$
       c. Val($\langle x, y \rangle$, *thinks*, σ) iff x thinks $\llbracket y \rrbracket$

   (2) Val(x, [$_{VP}$ V S], σ) iff for some y, Val($\langle x, y \rangle$, V, σ) and y = S

   Call the theory that includes them (together with the ILF generation algorithm) ILF′. Do ILF and ILF′ assign the same T sentence to (3)?

   (3) Chris says Jill agrees.

   Compare ILF and ILF′. Consider the fact noted earlier that verbs taking clausal complements also frequently select NP objects:

   (4) a. Chris says Jill agrees.
       b. Chris says those words.

   (5) a. Kate believes Phil ponders.
       b. Kate believes that story.

4. Example (1) has been held to have a syntax in which the quantified expression *every woman* has scope inside the complement clause, (2a), and a syntax in which it has scope outside the complement clause, (2b):

   (1) Phil thinks every woman ponders.

   (2) a. [$_S$ Phil thinks [$_S$ [$_{NP_1}$ every woman] [$_S$ t_1 ponders]]]
       b. [$_S$ [$_{NP_1}$ every woman] [$_S$ Phil thinks [$_S$ t_1 ponders]]]

- Compute T sentences for the structures in (2). (You may use either the PredC or GQ axioms for quantification.)

- Are different truth conditions assigned to these two structures? If yes, describe situations in which their truth values might diverge.

5. The ILF algorithm is applied in the text to examples with one level of sentence embedding. However, much more complex examples are possible in English:

(1) Phil thinks Chris believes Jill ponders.

(2) Phil thinks Chris believes Kate says Jill ponders.

What T sentences does the ILF theory assign to these examples? Be explicit in your answer.

6. Rocky Balboa was a fictional character introduced by the creators of the movie *Rocky*. Rocky J. Squirrel was a fictional character introduced by the creators of the *Rocky and Bullwinkle* cartoon show. Consider the following example:

(1) Peter believes Rocky was very courageous.

Clearly this sentence might have different truth conditions, depending on *which* fictional Rocky Peter holds his belief about.

- What problem does this raise for the ILF theory?

- Can you suggest a way to accommodate such examples in the ILF theory?[19]

7. The following scenario is adapted from Kripke 1979: Jones's upstairs neighbor is a man named "Paderewski." Jones knows him as the retiring tenant who walks his dog on Sunday mornings. The symphony conductor in Jones's town is also named "Paderewski." Jones knows him as an extravagant music impresario. As it turns out, the two Paderewskis are one and the same individual. Consider now the following pair of sentences:

(1) Jones believes Paderewski is shy.

(2) Jones does not believe Paderewski is shy.

- Under the circumstances described, is it possible to assert both (1) and (2) without being guilty of self-contradiction?

- If so, what problem does this raise for the ILF theory?
- Can you suggest a way to accommodate such examples in the ILF theory?[20]

8. The propositional theory stated in the text gives no explicit procedure for generating propositions. Try to give such an algorithm, noting the associated changes you must make in the semantic-valuation rules.

9. Suppose that Kathrin utters (1), where *but she doesn't* appears outside the scope of *says* but *she* is nevertheless intended to refer back to Kate:[21]

    (1) Kumiko says that Kate agrees, but she doesn't.

    - What is the syntactic structure of (1), on this reading?
    - Prove an interpretive T theorem for your structure.
    - What problems might a semantically noninnocent theory face with (1)?

10. We objected to quotational theories on the grounds that the syntax of complement clauses is not always rich enough to mark truth-conditional differences. Does the fact that the ILF theory allows for purely syntactic ILFs render it vulnerable to the same objection?

11. We suggested in the text that (1) and (2) pose a problem for quotational theories:

    (1) Jill is a philosopher. Phil thinks she$_1$ ponders. (*She$_1$* refers to Jill.)

    (2) Kate is a philosopher. Phil thinks she$_1$ ponders. (*She$_1$* refers to Kate.)

    The problem is that the syntactic form of the embedded clause *she$_1$ ponders* is identical in (1) and (2). Hence quotational theories are obliged to assign the same truth conditions to *Phil thinks she$_1$ ponders* in both cases.

    Assess the following response on behalf of quotational theories:

    Examples (1) and (2) do not create a problem for quotational theories. The sentences at issue involve the demonstrative pronoun *she$_1$*. As with all sentences containing demonstratives, one needs to distinguish their character from their content (in the sense of chapter 6). It's true that quotational theories must assign identical characters to *Phil thinks she$_1$ ponders* in both cases. But it does not follow that such theories must assign them identical contents. For content is determined by character together with the context of utterance. And the contexts are different in (1) and (2).

Points to consider: (a) Would the pronoun *she*$_1$ in (1) and (2) be appropriately treated by VRT from chapter 6, or by the axioms for argument anaphora from chapter 10? (b) Would it be consistent with a theory being a **quotational theory** that it appeal to extralinguistic factors in the way suggested?

12   Events, States, and Times

The ontology of our semantic theory—the collection of objects that names and demonstratives refer to, that predicates are true of, and that quantifiers count over—has so far been of a familiar and largely uncontroversial kind. Semantic values for phrases have included people, places, and various day-to-day kinds of things, and sequences constructed out of them. Even the introduction of ILFs for complement clauses brought nothing very new in this regard: ILFs are simple compounds of expressions and normal things—words or category nodes paired up with people, songs, etc.

In this chapter we will see evidence for expanding our ontology to include entities of a new and less familiar kind. These include events, states, and time points. Our goal is to illustrate how these new entities make their way into semantic theory and propagate through it, and to raise the kinds of conceptual questions that they bring in their wake.

12.1   Analyses of Adverbs

Our encounter with the new objects starts with the analysis of adverbs and adverbial constructions like those in (1):

(1) Chris arrived $\begin{cases} [_{AP} \text{ late}] \\ [_{AdvP} \text{ recently}] \\ [_{NP} \text{ that day}] \\ [_{PP} \text{ on Thursday}] \\ [_{CP} \text{ when you were away}] \end{cases}$

The bracketed items are called **VP adverbs** (or **VP adverbials**) because they occur adjoined to a VP in the phrase marker, (2a), or leave a trace in that position in the case of quantificational VP adverbs that move at the level of logical form, (2b):[1]

(2) a.

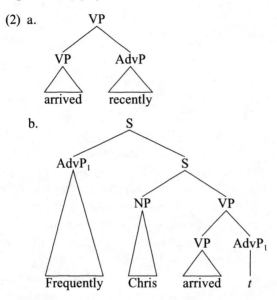

b.

As usual, the task of the semanticist is to determine their semantic mode of combination in clauses and provide compositional rules for their interpretation. And as with other structures that we have encountered to this point, a limited number of possibilities present themselves. If we concentrate on the central [$_{\text{VP}}$ VP *X*P] structure, two natural conjectures arise:

- Adverbs are arguments, and so function similarly to other argument expressions, like *Chris*.

- Adverbs are predicates, and so function similarly to other predicate expressions, like *arrived*.

Both of these possibilities raise interesting points.

12.1.1 Adverbs as Arguments

In our fragments, verbs and other predicates have been assigned an argument structure based on the number of NPs or clauses they require. For example, *walks* was analyzed as a one-place predicate because it requires a subject NP, *believe* was analyzed as a two-place predicate because it requires a subject and a complement clause, and so on:

(3) a. Val(x, *walks*, σ) iff x walks
     b. Val($\langle x, y \rangle$, *believes*, σ) iff x believes y

To treat adverbs as arguments, we might extend the relational structure of predicates to include coordinates ρ, λ, τ, etc., for notions like rate, location, time, reason, etc.—the sort of information typically provided by adverbial elements. For example, we might extend the lexical axiom for *walks* as in (4), allowing for possible occurrences of adverbs with it:

(4) a. Val($\langle x, \rho, \lambda, \tau \rangle$, *walks*, σ) iff x walks at rate ρ at location λ at time τ

Adverbial elements would then be given axioms in which they refer to rates, places, times, and so on, as in (5) (for simplicity, we ignore the internal constituency of the PPs):

(5) a. Val(ρ, *at 5 mph*, σ) iff ρ = 5 mph
     b. Val(λ, *in Paris*, σ) iff λ = Paris
     c. Val(λ, *here*, σ) iff $\lambda = \sigma(c)$
     d. Val(τ, *on 24 March 1998*, σ) iff τ = 24 March 1998

The two would be brought together by means of composition rules for [$_{\mathrm{VP}}$ VP XP] (XP an adverbial category) that treat the adverbs like other argument phrases, (6b):

(6) a.

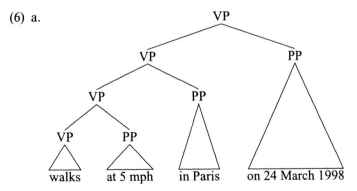

     b. i. Val(x, [$_{\mathrm{VP}}$ VP XP], σ) iff for some τ,
             Val($\langle x, \tau \rangle$, VP, σ) and Val(τ, XP, σ)

ii. Val($\langle x, \tau \rangle$, [$_\text{VP}$ VP XP], σ) iff for some λ,
    Val($\langle x, \lambda, \tau \rangle$, VP, σ) and Val(λ, XP, σ)

iii. Val($\langle x, \lambda, \tau \rangle$, [$_\text{VP}$ VP XP], σ) iff for some ρ,
    Val($\langle x, \rho, \lambda, \tau \rangle$, VP, σ) and Val(ρ, XP, σ)

$\vdots$ (where X is A, Adv, or P)

As the reader may show, such rules allow us to prove the T sentence in (7), which seems to state the truth conditions of *Chris walks at 5 mph in Paris on 24 March 1998* correctly:

(7) Val(t, [$_\text{S}$ Chris walks at 5 mph in Paris on 24 March 1998], σ) iff
    Chris walks at rate 5 mph at location Paris at time 24 March 1998

Challenges for the Argument Analysis

Executing the argument analysis in a full way turns out to involve a number of technical and empirical difficulties. Most of them stem from the fact that adverbs show rather different syntactic and semantic behavior from typical arguments. This disrupts attempts at assimilating the one to the other.

For example, the argument analysis assumes that the number and identity of adverbial arguments for a given predicate can be exactly specified. But exactly which ones a given predicate should have is often far from clear. It's obvious that arguments for rate, place, and time will not be enough for *walk*. In view of examples like (8), we would at least need to expand its lexical entry to allow for phrases of manner, purpose, and reason, (9):

(8) a. Chris walked [clumsily] [because he was tired]
    b. Chris walked [clumsily] [in order not to arrive too early]

(9) Val($\langle x, \mu, \rho, \lambda, \tau, \pi \rangle$, *walks*, σ) iff x walks in manner μ at rate ρ at location λ at time t for purpose π

But are these then enough? It seems difficult to say. This problem intensifies in the presence of an important distributional property of adverbs that distinguishes them from typical nominal arguments: the fact that adverbs are generally iterable. Example (10) (from Bresnan 1982) shows that we can have any number of adverbs of manner (MANNER), of time (TEMP), and of location (LOC):

(10) Fred *deftly* [MANNER] handed the toy to the baby *by reaching behind his back* [MANNER] *over lunch* [TEMP] *at noon* [TEMP] *in a restaurant* [LOC] *last Sunday* [TEMP] *in Back Bay* [LOC] without interrupting the discussion.

By contrast, (11) shows that adding extra nominal arguments (objects) leads to ungrammaticality:[2]

(11) a. *Jill admires Chris the student.
   b. *Phil gave Fido this dog to Kumiko.
   c. *Fred handed Barney this toy to the baby Alice.

It is not entirely clear how to deal with multiple manner, temporal, or locative phrases, given that multiple subjects, direct objects, indirect objects, etc., are disallowed. One proposal might be to expand lexical entries still further, allowing for multiple adverbial arguments of a given type:

(12) $Val(\langle x, y, z, \mu, \mu' \rangle, hands, \sigma)$ iff x hands y to z in manner μ, in manner μ', etc.

However, this move injects a serious element of indefiniteness into the lexicon. Since it simply isn't clear how many iterations of a given adverb type are possible for a given lexical item, it is correspondingly unclear how many variant axioms for a given form (*walks*, *hands*, etc.) will be required.

The argument analysis also encounters problems with the important fact that adverbs are typically optional in a sentence. Whereas arguments generally cannot be omitted, as illustrated by (13), adverbial elements are commonly omissible without loss of well-formedness, as seen in (14):

(13) a. Kumiko admires *(Jill).
   b. Phil instructed *(Chris).
   c. Kate put Phil in *(the refrigerator).

(14) a. Chris walked (quickly) (along the river) (to the store).
   b. The enemy's destruction of the city (with rockets) horrified us.
   c. Kate left Phil (in the refrigerator).

Since the argument analysis assumes that adverbial coordinates are part of the basic relational structure of the predicate, adverbial information must be regarded as implicit even when it is not overtly expressed. For example, even though (15a) appears to say nothing about the rate, manner, place, time, reasons, purposes, etc., of the walking, this information must nonetheless be present, since it is required by axiom (9); (15a) must imply (15b), much as (16a) implies (16b), given that *eat* is transitive:

(15) a. Chris walks.
  b. Chris walks at some rate in some manner at some location at some
   time along some path for some reason with some purpose, etc.

(16) a. Chris ate.
  b. Chris ate something.

As observed by Parsons (1990), this consequence appears problematic for
many pairs like (17) and (18), which differ by the presence of an adverbial:

(17) a. Chris threatened Phil with a cleaver.
  b. Chris threatened Phil.

(18) a. Chris baked a cake for Jill.
  b. Chris baked a cake.

Threatening does not necessarily imply threatening with some sort of instrument, such as a cleaver. Likewise, baking doesn't necessarily imply baking for
someone (even oneself). Given this result, an approach using a single axiom
that encompasses all possible adverbial modifiers seems headed for trouble.
Including all adverbs makes them necessary parts of the predicate relation,
and this requires an explicit or implicit adverbial contribution whenever the
predicate is present. It simply doesn't appear that the adverbial information
need be present or implied in all cases.

12.1.2   Adverbs as Predicates

An alternative to treating adverbs as arguments is to analyze them as a species
of predicate. However, the question immediately arises as to what kind of
predicates they are and what they apply to. The question is a sharp one because adverbs don't seem to apply to the same kinds of things that other predicates do. The easiest way to see this is through an example like (19):

(19) Chris arrived [$_{AP}$ late]

This sentence is ambiguous between two quite different understandings of the
adjective *late*. The first is what we'll call the **copredicational reading**. On the
copredicational reading, both the adjective *late* and the verb *arrived* apply to
the individual Chris. The sentence is thus true iff Chris arrived and Chris was
late.[3] On this reading, Chris's actual arrival time needn't have been late; it

could have occurred early in the day. Roughly speaking, it was Chris that was late, not his arriving.

The second reading is what we'll call the **adverbial interpretation**. On this reading, *late* applies not to Chris but rather to Chris's arrival. It is the arrival that is late (e.g., 1:00 A.M. in the morning) not Chris himself: Chris may have been on time for an engagement scheduled at a late hour. Since the adverbial reading is precisely one in which *late* does *not* apply to Chris, what the verb applies to, it is clear that verb and adverb are predicated of different things.[4]

The challenge for the predicational analysis of adverbs is thus more basic and immediate than any challenges facing the argument account: if adverbs and adverbials semantically are predicates, what are they predicates of?

12.2 Davidson's Event Analysis

Davidson (1967a) has proposed an analysis of adverbs as predicates that answers this basic question in an interesting way. Let us reconsider the example *Chris arrived late*. We saw that on one reading of this sentence, *arrive* and *late* are copredicates, true of people:

(20) Copredicate analysis

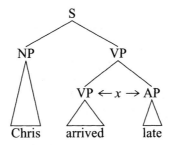

The verb and adjective are semantically bound together in the VP by sharing such objects as their values:

(21) $\mathrm{Val}(x, [_{\mathrm{VP}}\ \mathrm{VP}\ \mathrm{AP}], \sigma)$ iff $\mathrm{Val}(x, \mathrm{VP}, \sigma)$ and $\mathrm{Val}(x, \mathrm{AP}, \sigma)$

Davidson's proposal is that modification relates verbs and adverbs in a very similar way. Verbs and adverbs are copredicates true of *events*. The verb and adverb are bound together semantically in the VP by sharing events *e* as their values:

(22) Adverb analysis

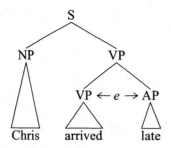

12.2.1   The Theory EC

We will instantiate Davidson's proposal in a new theory EC (short for "event calculus"). The new technical element in EC is the introduction of event variables e and axioms that manipulate them appropriately.

We begin with the lexical axioms for verbs, whose relations are expanded to accommodate an additional event argument, (23a–c). Thus former one-place verbs become two-place, two-place verbs become three-place, and so on:

(23) a. $\text{Val}(\langle x, e \rangle, \textit{walks}, \sigma)$ iff x walks in e

 b. $\text{Val}(\langle x, e \rangle, \textit{ponders}, \sigma)$ iff x ponders in e

 c. $\text{Val}(\langle x, e \rangle, \textit{arrives}, \sigma)$ iff x arrives in e

 d. $\text{Val}(\langle x, y, e \rangle, \textit{kisses}, \sigma)$ iff x kisses y in e

 e. $\text{Val}(\langle x, y, e \rangle, \textit{admires}, \sigma)$ iff x admires y in e

 f. $\text{Val}(\langle x, y, z, e \rangle, \textit{gives}, \sigma)$ iff x gives y to z in e

Adverbs, on the other hand, are interpreted as one-place predicates of events:

(24) a. $\text{Val}(e, \textit{late}, \sigma)$ iff e was late

 b. $\text{Val}(e, \textit{quickly}, \sigma)$ iff e was quick

 c. $\text{Val}(e, \textit{locally}, \sigma)$ iff e was local

The phrasal rules of EC are arranged so as to manipulate event variables appropriately. For example, (25) states that a sentence consisting of an NP and a VP is true with respect to σ just in case there is some individual x and some event e such that x is a value of the NP and the pair is a value of the VP:

(25) $\text{Val}(t, [_S \text{ NP VP}], \sigma)$ iff for some x, e, $\text{Val}(x, \text{NP}, \sigma)$ and
      $\text{Val}(\langle x, e \rangle, \text{VP}, \sigma)$

This new event variable is then passed down by the rules that interpret the verb phrase, as in (26):

(26) a. $\text{Val}(\langle x, e \rangle, [_{VP} V], \sigma)$ iff $\text{Val}(\langle x, e \rangle, V, \sigma)$
    b. $\text{Val}(\langle x, e \rangle, [_{VP} V\ NP], \sigma)$ iff for some y, $\text{Val}(\langle x, y, e \rangle, V, \sigma)$ and
       $\text{Val}(y, NP, \sigma)$
    c. $\text{Val}(\langle x, e \rangle, [_{VP} V\ NP_1\ NP_2], \sigma)$ iff for some y, z,
       $\text{Val}(\langle x, y, z, e \rangle, V, \sigma)$ and $\text{Val}(z, NP_1, \sigma)$ and $\text{Val}(y, NP_2, \sigma)$

Finally, we introduce axioms for adverbial elements. Axioms (27a, b) analyze the internal structure of adjunct AP and AdvP:

(27) a. $\text{Val}(e, [_{AP} A], \sigma)$ iff $\text{Val}(e, A, \sigma)$
    b. $\text{Val}(e, [_{AdvP} A], \sigma)$ iff $\text{Val}(e, Adv, \sigma)$

Axioms (28a, b) analyze adverbial modification as copredication of events:

(28) a. $\text{Val}(\langle x, e \rangle, [_{VP} VP\ AP], \sigma)$ iff $\text{Val}(\langle x, e \rangle, VP, \sigma)$ and $\text{Val}(e, AP, \sigma)$
    b. $\text{Val}(\langle x, e \rangle, [_{VP} VP\ AdvP], \sigma)$ iff $\text{Val}(\langle x, e \rangle, VP, \sigma)$ and
       $\text{Val}(e, AdvP, \sigma)$

Note that the latter are formally parallel to our earlier copredication axiom (21).

A Sample Derivation

We illustrate these rules with *Chris arrives late*, on its adverbial reading. As usual, we start at the highest S node. Using (25) and (UI), we derive (29):

(29) $\text{Val}(t, [_S [_{NP} [_N \text{Chris}]] [_{VP} [_{VP} [_V \text{arrives}]] [_{AP} [_A \text{late}]]]], \sigma)$ iff for some x, e,
    $\text{Val}(x, [_{NP} [_N \text{Chris}]], \sigma)$ and $\text{Val}(\langle x, e \rangle, [_{VP} [_{VP} [_V \text{arrives}]] [_{AP} [_A \text{late}]]], \sigma)$

The subject NP is interpreted, via familiar rules, as in (30):

(30) $\text{Val}(x, [_{NP} [_N \text{Chris}]], \sigma)$ iff $x = \text{Chris}$

The interpretation for the verb phrase is expanded using the rule for adverbial modification (28) (and (UI)):

(31) $\text{Val}(\langle x, e \rangle, [_{VP} [_{VP} [_V \text{arrives}]] [_{AP} [_A \text{late}]]], \sigma)$ iff
    $\text{Val}(\langle x, e \rangle, [_{VP} [_V \text{arrives}]], \sigma)$ and $\text{Val}(e, [_{AP} [_A \text{late}]], \sigma)$

The VP interpretation proceeds as in (32), and the AP interpretation as in (33):

(32) a. $\text{Val}(\langle x, e \rangle, [_{\text{VP}} [_{\text{V}} \text{ arrives}]], \sigma)$ iff $\text{Val}(\langle x, e \rangle, [_{\text{V}} \text{ arrives}], \sigma)$

   b. $\text{Val}(\langle x, e \rangle, [_{\text{V}} \text{ arrives}], \sigma)$ iff $\text{Val}(\langle x, e \rangle, \textit{arrives}, \sigma)$

   c. $\text{Val}(\langle x, e \rangle, \textit{arrives}, \sigma)$ iff x arrives in e

   d. $\text{Val}(\langle x, e \rangle, [_{\text{VP}} [_{\text{V}} \text{ arrives}]], \sigma)$ iff x arrives in e (by (SE) twice)

(33) a. $\text{Val}(e, [_{\text{AP}} [_{\text{A}} \text{ late}]], \sigma)$ iff $\text{Val}(e, [_{\text{A}} \text{ late}], \sigma)$

   b. $\text{Val}(e, [_{\text{A}} \text{ late}], \sigma)$ iff $\text{Val}(e, \textit{late}, \sigma)$

   c. $\text{Val}(e, \textit{late}, \sigma)$ iff e is late

   d. $\text{Val}(e, [_{\text{AP}} [_{\text{A}} \text{ late}]], \sigma)$ iff e is late (by (SE) twice)

Applying (SE) in (31) and (29) yields (34), which reduces to (35) by (SI):

(34) $\text{Val}(\tau, [_{\text{S}} [_{\text{NP}} [_{\text{N}} \text{ Chris}]] [_{\text{VP}} [_{\text{VP}} [_{\text{V}} \text{ arrives}]] [_{\text{AP}} [_{\text{A}} \text{ late}]]]], \sigma)$
iff for some x, e, $x = $ Chris and x arrives in e and e is late

(35) $\text{Val}(\tau, [_{\text{S}} [_{\text{NP}} [_{\text{N}} \text{ Chris}]] [_{\text{VP}} [_{\text{VP}} [_{\text{V}} \text{ arrives}]] [_{\text{AP}} [_{\text{A}} \text{ late}]]]], \sigma)$ iff for some e,
Chris arrives in e and e is late

Thus *Chris arrives late* is true iff there is some event in which Chris arrives that is late. This is the adverbial reading.

12.2.2 Virtues of the Event Analysis

The event analysis accounts smoothly for the properties of adverbs we've seen. As adjunct predicates (of events), adverbs are not required by the semantic properties of any other sentence elements, and hence are optional. The optionality of the adverb in (36a) is exactly counterpart to the optionality of the adjective in (36b):

(36) a. Kate ran (quickly).

   b. Kate ran (barefoot).

Similarly, the iterability of adverbs can be attributed to the fact that once we've adjoined a copredicate of events, there is nothing in principle to block additional copredicates of the same event. The iterability of adverbs in (37a) is parallel to the iterability of adjuncts in (37b):

(37) a. Chris arrived (yesterday) (at two o'clock).

   b. Chris arrived (tired) (in a complete daze).

The event-predicate analysis goes further in predicting a variety of interesting entailment relations that arise with adverbial modification. Consider the set of sentences in (38):

(38) a. Jones buttered the toast with a knife at midnight.
   b. Jones buttered the toast with a knife and Jones buttered the toast at midnight.
   c. Jones buttered the toast with a knife.
   d. Jones buttered the toast at midnight.
   e. Jones buttered the toast.

As noted by Davidson, these examples show the asymmetric pattern of entailments in (39) (where higher items entail lower items, but not conversely):[5]

(39)

On the event analysis, this pattern is explained by the logical entailment relations holding among (38a–e). Thus if there is an event ($\exists e$) of buttering by Jones (j) of the toast (t) and this buttering is with a knife and this buttering is at midnight, then there is an event of buttering by Jones of the toast that is with a knife, and there is an event of buttering by Jones of the toast that is at midnight; that is, (40a) implies (40b). Similarly, if there is an event of buttering by Jones of the toast that is with a knife and there is an event of buttering by Jones of the toast that is at midnight, then there is an event of buttering by Jones of the toast that is with a knife; that is, (40b) implies (40c). And so on.

(40) a. $\exists e[\text{buttering}(j, t, e) \;\&\; \text{with-a-knife}(e) \;\&\; \text{at-midnight}(e)]$
   b. $\exists e[\text{buttering}(j, t, e) \;\&\; \text{with-a-knife}(e)] \;\&\;$
      $\exists e[\text{buttering}(j, t, e) \;\&\; \text{at-midnight}(e)]$
   c. $\exists e[\text{buttering}(j, t, e) \;\&\; \text{with-a-knife}(e)]$
   d. $\exists e[\text{buttering}(j, t, e) \;\&\; \text{at-midnight}(e)]$
   e. $\exists e[\text{buttering}(j, t, e)]$

The analysis also explains why the reverse entailments do not go through. If there is an event of buttering by Jones of the toast that is with a knife and there is an event of buttering by Jones of the toast that is at midnight, it doesn't follow that there is some single event of buttering by Jones of the toast that is both with a knife and at midnight; that is, (40b) does not entail (40a). Under the event analysis, all of these implications (and nonimplications) are simple matters of quantifier logic.

Semantic Theory and Inference Again

These last points illustrate how semantic theory can sometimes help explain judgments concerning entailment relations among object-language sentences. They also illustrate an interesting contrast between the following two cases:

- The semantic theory correctly helps to predict that speakers will judge a certain class of inferences to be valid.

- The semantic theory correctly fails to predict that speakers will judge a certain class of inferences to be valid.

Recall chapter 2, section 3.1, where we said that entailment relations constituted a "mixed case": we expect some entailments to be captured by semantic theory and others to be captured by other, neighbouring cognitive theories. The general structure of an explanation of why speaker's judge that a sentence S entails another sentence S′ is thus as in (41):

(41) a. S is true iff *p*   Semantic module
     b. If *p*, then *q*   Other module
     c. S′ is true iff *q*   Semantic module

The T theory provides interpretations for the sentences, and some other module of the mind calculates an entailment relation between these interpretations. If the sentences concern mathematics, for example, then the module responsible for our mathematical competence will be responsible for step (b). We have also posited, somewhat speculatively, a special logic module. This module is responsible for entailments that are matters of pure logic and involve no content drawn from other specific domains.

There is thus a division of labor among different modules, and consequently among theories of these modules. In different cases, the relative amount of work done will vary: sometimes most of the work will be done by the T theory; other times it will be done by some other module. For the specific entailments we have just considered, much of the work is done by the semantic module. The interpretations it provides, such as those in (40), are already suitable for the application of very simple rules of quantifier logic.

To bring this point out, suppose that instead of providing interpretations in terms of events, the semantic module had delivered relatively less structured interpretations, as illustrated in (42):

(42) a. Val(t, *Jones buttered the toast at midnight*) iff Jones buttered the toast at midnight
　　 b. Val(t, *Jones buttered the toast*) iff Jones buttered the toast

In such a case, the logic module would have to consider the inference (43):

(43) Jones buttered the toast at midnight.
───────────────────────────────
　　 Jones buttered the toast.

But no straightforward logical rules apply to this candidate inference. For the semantic structure of the two propositions involved is not transparent. To make it transparent, the logic module would have to do some analysis of its own. For example, it might contain rules that license the inference in (44):

(44) a. If Jones buttered the toast at midnight, then there is an event e and e is a buttering and e is by Jones and e is at midnight.
　　 b. If there is an event e and e is a buttering and e is by Jones and e is at midnight, then there is an event e and e is a buttering and e is by Jones.
　　 c. If there is an event e and e is a buttering and e is by Jones, then Jones buttered the toast.

However, since the semantic theory already provides suitable representations for the logic module, we do not need such resources in the logic module to prove (44a) and (44c).

The flipside case is where the semantic theory correctly fails to predict that speakers will judge a class of inferences to be valid. Take (45) as an example:

(45) Jones buttered the toast with a knife, and
　　 Jones buttered the toast at midnight.
───────────────────────────────
　　 Jones buttered the toast with a knife at midnight.

Speakers do not judge this inference to be valid. It is thus very important that the semantic theory does not assign interpretations to the sentences that, given deduction rules that speakers abide by, would license the inference (45). For if it did, it is very hard to see what could prevent speakers from making the corresponding inference. There is a possibility that the failure is some kind of performance error, a processing limitation, or some such. But this seems very unlikely. There is also a possibility that some other module overrides the inference. This would result in the very strange position that one component of the speaker's mind delivers the verdict that the inference is valid and some other component then prevents the speaker from being aware that of this inner psychological result and causes him to judge the inference to be invalid. This is logically possible but empirically implausible.

The cases of predicting an inference that speakers do make and failing to predict an inference that they do not are therefore not symmetrical from the point of view of semantic theory. In the first case there is always the possibility that some nonlinguistic module accounts for the judgments. But in the second, there is no corresponding realistic possibility. It is not likely that some nonlinguistic module can, as it were, invalidate an inference that the semantic module would count as valid.

12.3 Thematic Roles

In writing out the logical notation in (40), we made use of expressions like "with-a-knife(e)" and "at-midnight(e)" to describe the adverbial contribution. On reflection, however, it may not be so clear what such expressions mean. Expression (46) seems to say that there exists some kind of "with-a-knife event":

(46) $\exists e[\ldots \text{with-a-knife}(e)\ldots]$

Consider also Davidson's (1967a) treatment of the sentence *I flew my spaceship to the morning Star*:

(47) $\exists e[\text{flying}(I, \text{my spaceship}, e)\ \&\ \text{to}(\text{the morning star}, e)]$

This seems to imply that there is an event e standing in the 'to' relation to the morning star. Again, it's not clear that this is sensible.

One proposal for resolving these unclarities is to see prepositions like *with* and *to* as expressing certain very general parts or *roles* that can be played by participants in events. For example, the preposition *with* in (40a) functions to introduce the means or *instrument* through which an action or activity is accomplished. This same use is observed in (48) and (49):

(48) Phil opened the door with this key.

(49) Kate excavated the tomb with a shovel.

Likewise, the preposition *to* in *I flew my spaceship to the morning star* functions to relate the motion of flying to the point that the flying is directed toward, the *goal* of the flying. The same use is found in (50) and (51)

(50) Jill walked to Kendall Square.

(51) Chris sent a message to Kumiko.

Event roles like Instrument and Goal are typically referred to as **thematic roles** (θ-roles).

A variety of thematic roles have been proposed in semantic theory, including at least the list in table 12.1 (drawn largely from Haegeman 1990). We provide typical, informal descriptions of these notions. Thematic roles allow us to make better sense of (46) and (47). Suppose we take the prepositions *with* and *to* to express the thematic relations of Goal and Instrument respectively. Then our examples may be revised along the lines in (46') and (47'):

(46') $\exists e[\ldots \text{Instrument}(a \text{ knife}, e)\ldots]$

(47') $\exists e[\ldots \text{Goal}(\text{the morning star}, e)\ldots]$

It is now clearer what is being expressed by the adverbs: the knife is an instrument in the buttering event, the morning star is the goal of the flying event, etc.

It is not the case, of course, that every preposition will have its own specific thematic role. Even if *at* expresses the role of Location, the fact is that there

Table 12.1   Thematic roles and their descriptions

Role	Description
Goal	Individual toward which the event is directed
Source	Object or individual from which something is moved by the event, or from which the event originates
Experiencer	Individual experiencing some event
Beneficiary	Object or individual that benefits from the event
Location	Place at which the event is situated
Instrument	Secondary cause of event; the object or individual that causes some event that in turn causes the event to take place

are many different locative prepositions, including at least *on, in, under, over, between, near,* and *past.* For these we must presumably assume distinct individual relations. *I flew my spaceship near the morning star* and *I flew my spaceship past the morning star* will thus involve truth conditions like those in (46″) and (46‴), in which the specific event-object relations 'near' and 'past' appear:

(46″) $\exists e[\dots \text{near(the morning star, } e) \dots]$

(46‴) $\exists e[\dots \text{past(the morning star, } e) \dots]$

Some prepositions will thus correspond to "pure" thematic relations, while others will correspond to relations that are semantically more complex and more differentiated.

12.3.1   Decomposing the Verb

The use of thematic roles can be given a further, somewhat more radical extension into the semantics of verbs. On the general picture sketched above, thematic roles express various relationships that individuals can bear to events. One elegant idea would be to generalize this view to encompass *all* relationships between individuals and events, to let all such relations be mediated by thematic roles. In the case of verbs, we would reanalyze the latter as simple unary-predicate of events whose participants are related to them via thematic roles.

To illustrate, consider (52):

(52) Romeo kissed Juliet.

As analyzed in EC, *kiss* expresses a three-place relation between an event and its two participants. The EC truth conditions of the sentence are thus (53a). By contrast, under the expanded thematic-role proposal, the truth conditions would be reanalyzed along the lines of (53b): the sentence is true just in case a certain kind of event took place, a kissing event, in which Romeo played the role of Agent and Juliet played the role of Patient. We might abbreviate the latter as in (53c), using the symbolism of logic:[6]

(53) a. For some *e*, Romeo kissed Juliet in *e*.
      b. For some *e*, *e* is a kissing & Romeo is the Agent of *e* & and Juliet is the Patient of *e*
      c. $\exists e[\text{kissing}(e) \ \& \ \text{Agent(Romeo, } e) \ \& \ \text{Patient(Juliet, } e)]$

Table 12.2   Thematic roles and their descriptions

Role	Description
Agent	Volitional initiator of action
Patient	Object or individual undergoing action
Theme	Object or individual moved by action
Goal	Individual toward which event is directed

Once again, a variety of roles have been proposed in the literature that link verbs to their participants. A sampling, with informal descriptions, is given in table 12.2. On this general view, the meaning of a verb would be decomposed into its primary event predicate, and a family of satellite roles would serve to relate that event to its crucial participants.

12.3.2   The Theory ECΘ

Thematic roles can be incorporated directly as a revision of the theory EC. The main changes come in the introduction of new, decompositional lexical axioms for verbs and new axioms for prepositions as expressing thematic roles. There are also two new rules to accommodate adjunct PPs. We will call the resulting ammended theory ECΘ, for "event calculus + thematic roles":

(54) a. $\mathrm{Val}(\langle x, e \rangle, walks, \sigma)$ iff e is an event of walking and $\mathrm{Agent}(x, e)$

     b. $\mathrm{Val}(\langle x, e \rangle, ponders, \sigma)$ iff e is an event of pondering and $\mathrm{Experiencer}(x, e)$

     c. $\mathrm{Val}(\langle x, e \rangle, arrives, \sigma)$ iff e is an event of arriving and $\mathrm{Theme}(x, e)$

     d. $\mathrm{Val}(\langle x, y, e \rangle, kisses, \sigma)$ iff e is an event of kissing and $\mathrm{Agent}(x, e)$ and $\mathrm{Patient}(y, e)$

     e. $\mathrm{Val}(\langle x, y, e \rangle, admires, \sigma)$ iff e is an event of admiring and $\mathrm{Experiencer}(x, e)$ and $\mathrm{Patient}(y, e)$

     f. $\mathrm{Val}(\langle x, y, z, e \rangle, gives, \sigma)$ iff e is an event of giving and $\mathrm{Agent}(x, e)$ and $\mathrm{Theme}(y, e)$ and $\mathrm{Goal}(z, e)$

(55) a. $\mathrm{Val}(\langle x, e \rangle, to, \sigma)$ iff $\mathrm{Goal}(x, e)$

     b. $\mathrm{Val}(\langle x, e \rangle, from, \sigma)$ iff $\mathrm{Source}(x, e)$

     c. $\mathrm{Val}(\langle x, e \rangle, with, \sigma)$ iff $\mathrm{Instrument}(x, e)$

     d. $\mathrm{Val}(\langle x, e \rangle, by, \sigma)$ iff $\mathrm{Agent}(x, e)$

     e. $\mathrm{Val}(\langle x, e \rangle, in, \sigma)$ iff $\mathrm{Location}(x, e)$

(56) a. Val($\langle x, e \rangle$, [$_{VP}$ VP PP], σ) iff Val($\langle x, e \rangle$, VP, σ) and Val(e, PP, σ)
     b. Val(e, [$_{PP}$ P NP], σ) iff for some x, Val($\langle x, e \rangle$, P, σ) and
         Val(x, NP, σ)

We leave it to the reader to show that these rules, together with ones given
earlier for PC, allow us to prove the T sentence (57):

(57) Val(t, [$_S$ [$_{NP}$ [$_N$ Chris]] [$_{VP}$ [$_{VP}$ [$_V$ arrives]] [$_{PP}$ [$_P$ in] [$_{NP}$ Paris]]]], σ) iff
      for some e, e is an event of arriving and Theme(Chris, e) and
      Location(Paris, e)

12.3.3 Virtues of the Thematic-Role Analysis

The introduction of thematic roles allows us to capture various semantic relations in a natural way. It also suggests a means of relating the argument structure of a predicate to the syntactic forms that realize it.

Thematic Parallelisms

Recall triples of examples like (58), discussed in chapter 1.

(58) a. The train traveled from London to Paris.
     b. The inheritance passed from Jill to Kate.
     c. The substance changed from a liquid to a gas.

These sentences exhibit a clear semantic parallelism: all involve the idea of an
object undergoing a change of some kind, whether a change of location, possession, or properties.[7] With more traditional truth conditions, the relation
between these examples is not directly expressed.[8] But with a thematic-role
analysis, the source of the parallelism is captured in a very explicit way. With
irrelevant detail suppressed, the truth conditions of (58a–c) are as in (59a–c),
respectively:

(59) a. $\exists e$[traveling(e) & Theme(train, e) & Source(London, e) &
         Goal(Paris, e)]
     b. $\exists e$[passing(e) & Theme(inheritance, e) & Source(John, e) &
         Goal(Mary, e)]
     c. $\exists e$[changing(e) & Theme(substance, e) & Source(liquid, e) &
         Goal(gas, e)]

We have a different event predicate in each of the three cases: *traveling* versus *passing* versus *changing*. However, the constellation of roles relating the participants to the events is the same in all three: Theme, Source, and Goal. This tracks our intuition that though the three examples involve different activities, the relevant individuals participate in these activities in parallel ways.

A similar result obtains with pairs like (60a, b), also introduced in chapter 1.

(60) a. Ernie is buying a block from Kermit.
     b. Kermit is selling a block to Ernie.

Recall that although the three NPs occur in different positions, the semantic parts played by their referents are very similar. On the thematic-role analysis, these similarities are captured using thematic roles. Logical formulas (61a, b) give their respective truth conditions (again with irrelevant detail ignored):

(61) a. $\exists e$[buying(e) & Agent(Ernie, e) & Theme(block, e) & Source(Kermit, e) & Goal(Ernie, e)]
     b. $\exists e$[selling(e) & Agent(Kermit, e) & Theme(block, e) & Source(Kermit, e) & Goal(Ernie, e)]

The bearers of the Source, Theme, and Goal roles are constant across the buying and the selling. This corresponds to what we judge as similar in the two events: the same object goes from the same person to the same recipient. In contrast, the agent changes across the two sentences. This corresponds to what we judge as different in the two events: Ernie is the initiator of action in (60a), whereas Kermit is the initiator in (60b).[9]

Thematic roles thus allow us to capture a number of interesting semantic patterns across lexical items, and do so in a way that follows our intuitions about the source of these patterns.

Thematic Roles and Grammatical Roles

The examples in (60) raise another attraction of the thematic-role analysis, one that has already been anticipated to some extent. Earlier we observed that pairs like those in (60) describe what are by and large the same real-world situations: any circumstance in which Ernie buys a block from Kermit is also one in which Kermit sells a block to Ernie. The same was true with *Ernie gave a block to Kermit* versus *Kermit received a block from Ernie* and *Bert is chasing*

Fozzy versus *Fozzy is fleeing Bert* and so on. Given this, the question arose as to how children decide that the verb *sell* means to sell and not to buy, how they decide that *chase* means to chase and not to flee, etc.

One answer we considered was that children might deploy universal "linking rules" specifying that in a structure of roughly the form [$_s$ NP$_1$ V NP$_2$ P NP$_3$], the subject noun phrase (NP$_1$) must always refer to the individual playing a specific part in the action, the part of Agent. This would allow them to distinguish *buy* and *sell* correctly in terms of the environmental data and the syntactic forms that accompany its presentation. Hearing *Ernie is buying a block from Kermit*, viewing the relevant situation, and knowing the Agent linking rule, the child might reason that *buy* denotes events of commercial exchange in which the recipient of the object exchanged is also the agent; i.e., *buy* denotes buyings.

These remarks suggest that thematic roles might play an important general part in relating meaning to its regular grammatical expression, particularly in the course of language acquisition. And indeed, there is evidence for such a view. A number of strong and persistent correlations have in fact been observed between thematic roles and the grammatical relations of the argument expressions that bear them: subject, direct object, indirect object, oblique object, etc. For example, it is an overwhelming generalization that with transitive verbs involving both an Agent and a Patient, the individual bearing the Agent relation will be expressed by the subject, whereas the the individual bearing the Patient relation will be expressed by the object. Indeed, when a verb assigns the Agent thematic role, this role never seems to be assigned internally to the VP. Likewise, in verbs involving both an Experiencer and a Theme (e.g., *like*), the former is typically assigned to the subject, and the latter is assigned to an object. And it has been argued that when this ordering is superficially contravened (as, e.g., with *please*), there is evidence that the surface subject is an object at some underlying level of representation.[10] Again, if a predicate assigns both an Instrument and a Patient, very typically the former will be realized as subject, and the latter as object.

Thematic roles thus show promise as a theory of the cognitive categories through which children view the world and organize the projection of semantic knowledge into syntactic structure. They would constitute an underlying general theory of the parts that individuals play in actions and events. And these parts would be linked in a regular and perhaps language-independent way to positions (or relative positions) in syntactic phrase markers.[11]

12.3.4   Uniqueness and Identity of Thematic Roles

The introduction of thematic roles brings a number of important conceptual questions about how these relations are to be understood vis-à-vis their associated events and also how they are to be identified and elaborated.

The Uniqueness Requirement on Thematic Roles

Consider the truth conditions for *Romeo kissed Juliet*, as expressed in (62):

(62) $\exists e[\text{kissing}(e) \ \& \ \text{Agent(Romeo, } e) \ \& \ \text{Patient(Juliet, } e)]$

We want (62) to insure that in the event of kissing, Romeo was the kisser, and Juliet was the one kissed. On reflection, however, it's not clear that (62) actually delivers this result. For instance, (62) might be understood as requiring Romeo to be *an* agent in the kissing event—he must have been doing something—but that is still compatible with someone else having done the actual kissing. For example, to mix Shakesperean plays a bit, consider a scenario in which Romeo pays Hamlet, the Prince of Denmark, to kiss Juliet. Arguably, Romeo is an agent in this scenario, since he intentionally intiates the event of kissing. But clearly we don't want these circumstances to count as ones described by *Romeo kissed Juliet*. Likewise, (62) might be understood as requiring Juliet to be *a* patient in the kissing event—she must have undergone something in it—but this is still compatible with someone else having been kissed. Suppose that Juliet observes Romeo kissing Ophelia and is humiliated as a result. Then plausibly Juliet is a patient. But clearly we don't want this scenario to be one truthfully described by *Romeo kissed Juliet*.

Evidently, for (62) to express what we want it to express, we must somehow insure that Romeo and Juliet are understood as the *relevant* agent and patient in each case. One simple way of achieving this is to require that if an individual bears a thematic role in an event, then no other individual bears the same role in that event. We might call this the uniqueness requirement on thematic roles (following Carlson 1982):[12]

Uniqueness requirement on thematic roles (URTR)   For all thematic roles θ, $\forall e \forall x[\theta(x, e) \rightarrow \forall y[\theta(y, e) \rightarrow x = y]]$.

Since every kissing event must have a kisser, and since an event can have at most one Agent by URTR, it follows that (62) can be true only if Romeo was the one who did the kissing. Likewise, since every kissing involves a person kissed and since no event can have more than a single Patient by URTR, it follows that if (62) is true, Juliet must have been the one kissed.

The adoption of URTR has strong consequences for our understanding of events and how they are individuated. For example, in our scenario of Romeo paying Hamlet to kiss Juliet, where both Romeo and Hamlet appear to be Agents, the uniqueness requirement obliges us to distinguish two distinct events: roughly speaking, a paying event, in which Romeo was Agent, and a separate kissing event, in which Hamlet was Agent. Similarly, our second scenario must be resolved into a kissing event, in which Ophelia was Patient, and a distinct humiliation event, in which Juliet was Patient. URTR thus forces us to individuate events in a rather fine way.[13]

Which Thematic Roles Are There?

Our account of thematic roles is largely informal at this point. Our list of them is not exhaustive, nor are our definitions final in any sense. In further elaborating a theory like ECΘ, we would clearly need to say more on what thematic roles there are and how they are to be specified. Our ultimate task would be to articulate a set of well-discriminated roles $\theta_1, \theta_2, \ldots, \theta_n$ so that the arguments of any predicate of English could be expressed in terms of them. Given the points made above about language acquisition, we might expect this set to be small in number and its members to have cross-linguistic validity.

These requirements on a full-fledged theory of thematic roles are formidable, and no current account comes close to meeting them. We know neither how many thematic roles are required for lexical description nor, correlatively, what their precise definitions are. We can see the kinds of problems that arise by considering the relations of Theme and Patient, whose informal definitions we repeat below:

Patient: object or individual undergoing action

Theme: object or individual moved by action

An individual who undergoes an act of hitting doesn't necessarily move as a result. Apparently, then, one can be a patient without being a theme. Similarly, a ball may roll, and hence move, without undergoing some action. This suggests that one can be a theme without being a patient. Nonetheless, in a large number of cases the two notions overlap. If Chris throws Fido to Jill, then Fido is moved and also undergoes the actions of some Agent. Is Fido a Theme or a Patient or both? Alternatively, should Patient and Theme be collapsed into some single, more inclusive thematic role Object that somehow embraces both notions? Similar points arise with the notion of Agent, as noted by Lakoff (1970) and Dowty (1989, 1991):

Agent: volitional initiator of action

When closely examined across a variety of verbs, the notion of Agent seems to fragment itself into a number of subnotions like Actor, Causer, etc. Thus it is hard to know whether one is dealing with a single role or a family of roles.

Worries like these have led some researchers to be skeptical about thematic roles altogether. For our part, we do not find their arguments decisive. For example, it seems to us that the fragmentation problem noted with the notion of Agent arises with equal force in the definition of many predicates of natural language. Any detailed dictionary will give entries for prepositions like *to*, *by*, and *with* that show equal fragmentation into subentries, with divergence in meaning at least as great as that attributed to Agent. For example, consider the following sample entry from *Webster's Nineth New Collegiate Dictionary* for *to*:

¹**to** \tə, tù, (')tü; *before vowels usu* tə *also* təw; *after* t (*as in* 'want') *often* ə; *sentence-final usu* (') tü*prep* [ME, fr. OE *tō*; akin to OHG *zuo* to, L *do*nec as long as, until] (bef. 12c)

1 a —used as a function word to indicate movement or an action or condition suggestive of movement toward a place, person, or thing reached (drove *to* the city) (went back *to* his original idea)

  b —used as a function word to indicate direction (a mile *to* the south) (turned his back *to* the door) (a tendency *to* silliness)

  c —used as a function word to indicate contact or proximity (applied polish *to* the table) (stood there with her hands *to* her eyes)

  d (1)—used as a function word to indicate the place or point that is the far limit (100 miles *to* the nearest town) (2)—used as a function word to indicate the limit of extent (stripped *to* the waist)

  e —used as a function word to indicate relative position (perpendicular *to* the floor)

2 a —used as a function word to indicate purpose, intention, tendency, result, or end (came *to* our aid) (drink *to* his health)

  b —used as a function word to indicate the result of an action or a process (broken all *to* pieces) (go *to* seed) (*to* their surprise, the train left on time)

  c —used as a function word to indicate a determined condition or end (sentenced *to* death)

3 —used as a function word to indicate position or relation in time: as

  a : BEFORE (five minutes *to* five)

  b : TILL (from eight *to* five)

4   —used as a function word to indicate addition, attachment, connection, belonging, possession, accompaniment, or response (the key *to* the door) (danced *to* live music) (comes *to* his call)

5   —used as a function word (1) to indicate the extent or degree (as of completeness or accuracy) (loyal *to* a man) or the extent and result (as of an action or a condition) (beaten *to* death) (2) to indicate the last or an intermediate point of a series (moderate *to* cool temperatures)

6 a —used as a function word (1) to indicate a relation to one that serves as a standard (inferior *to* his earlier works) (2) to indicate similarity, correspondence, dissimilarity, or proportion (compared him *to* a god)

  b —used as a function word to indicate agreement or conformity (add salt *to* taste) (*to* my knowledge)

  c —used as a function word to indicate a proportion in terms of numbers or quantities (400 *to* the box)

7 a —used as a function word (1) to indicate the application of an adjective or a noun (agreeable *to* everyone) (attitude *to* friends) (title *to* the property) (2) to indicate the relation of a verb to its complement or to a complementary element (refers *to* the traditions) (refers him *to* the traditions) (3) to indicate the receiver of an action or the one for which something is done or exists (spoke *to* his father) (gives a dollar *to* the man) (the total effect was a gain *to* reading—Joseph Trenaman) and often used with a reflexive pronoun to indicate exclusiveness (as of possession) or separateness (had the house *to* themselves) (thought *to* himself)

  b —used as a function word to indicate agency (falls *to* his opponent's blows)

8   —used as a function word to indicate that the following verb is an infinitive (wants *to* go) and often used by itself at the end of a clause in place of an infinitive

If fragmentation is grounds for saying that there is no single Agent role, then it would seem to be grounds for concluding that there is no single preposition *to*. Lexicographers evidently reject this conclusion: they give it a single entry. We believe the same conclusion is warranted with Agent, but our point here is not so much whether there is a single Agent role, or whether there is a single preposition *to*. It's rather that the problems raised seem to be the same. There seems to be nothing special about thematic roles in this regard.

A similar response can be given, we believe, to the claim that having a well-defined set of thematic roles means having necessary and sufficient conditions for their application. Some researchers have held that we need stringent criteria of these kinds to ground thematic roles properly. It is hard to see why such strictures should apply to thematic roles only. A rule like (63) states the conditions under which the predicate *hit* applies to a pair $\langle x, y \rangle$:

(63) $\text{Val}(\langle x, y \rangle, \textit{hit}, \sigma)$ iff x hits y

It applies just in case the first member of the pair hits the second. Compare this to (64), where *laugh* applies to a pair $\langle x, e \rangle$ just in case the first member of the pair is the Agent of the laughing and the second is a laughing:

(64) Val($\langle x, e \rangle$, *laugh*, σ) iff e is an event of laughing and x is the agent of e

There seems to be no crucial difference here. The relation "is the Agent of" is a perfectly respectable predicate of the metalanguage (English). It's true that we don't always know when to call the relation between an individual and a given circumstance "agency" (as opposed to "instrumency," "causation," etc.). We lack necessary and sufficient conditions for its use. But it's equally true that we don't always know whether to call a relation between two individuals "hitting" (as opposed to "tapping," "poking," etc.). Notions like Agent do not seem to involve any special conceptual problem requiring them to be accompanied by more stringent definitions: necessary and sufficient conditions for their application. As elsewhere in science, concepts need to be precise enough to advance the subject matter, but that is all.

The upshot is that we regard the questions of which thematic roles there are and how they are defined as empirical ones, to be resolved in the usual way: by investigations that construct specific theories making detailed and specific predictions. Preliminary theories of this kind have been proposed; however, it is likely that resolving thematic roles precisely will require a great deal of investigation, involving domains beyond linguistics. It is worth remembering that fully 22 centuries ellapsed between the first suggestion of the atomic theory of matter, in which all substances were factored into earth, water, air, and fire, and the elaboration of atomic theory by John Dalton, in which a more complete and satisfactory set of atomic constituents was proposed. Finding elementary constituents can evidently be a long-term project.

12.4 States

According to the main-S rule of ECΘ, sentences involve an implicit quantification over events:

(65) Val(t, [$_s$ NP VP], σ) iff for some x, e, Val(x, NP, σ) and
       Val($\langle x, e \rangle$, VP, σ)

This looks natural enough for examples like *Juliet kissed Romeo* or *Rolf traveled from Rome to Paris*, which are intuitively felt to describe actions or events

—things that *happen* or *occur*. Not all sentences of English are like this, however. Consider (66a–e):

(66) a. Chris knows Kate.
     b. This road extends to Canada.
     c. Jill likes sugar.
     d. Kumiko is happy.
     e. Rolf is in Paris.

These do not seem to describe happenings or occurences. Rather, they describe circumstances or **states** in which something obtains or holds true.

There are a variety of linguistic phenomena, usually discussed under the heading of **aspect** or **Aktionsart**, that support the intuitive distinction between events and states, and between the predicates that express them. For example, it has been widely noted that eventive verbs occur smoothly in the progressive (*-ing*) form, whereas stative verbs do not (here "#" indicates unacceptability):[14]

(67) a.   Juliet is kissing Romeo.
     b.   Rolf is traveling to Paris.

(68) a.   #Chris is knowing Kate.
     b.   #This road is extending to Canada.
     c.   #Jill is liking sugar.

Eventive verbs occur smoothly in imperatives, but statives do not:

(69) a.   Kiss Romeo!
     b.   Travel to Paris!

(70) a.   #Know Kate!
     b.   #Extend to Canada!
     c.   #Like sugar!

Eventives occur in the pseudocleft construction; however, statives are peculiar in this context:

(71) a.   What Juliet did was kiss Romeo.
     b.   What Rolf did was travel to Paris.

(72) a.   #What Chris did was know Kate.
     b.   #What the road did was extend to Canada.
     c.   #What Jill did was like sugar.

Eventives can be modified by adverbs like *deliberately* and *carefully*, whereas statives cannot:[15]

(73) a.   Juliet deliberately/carefully kissed Romeo.
       b.   Rolf deliberately/carefully traveled to Paris.

(74) a.   #Chris deliberately/carefully knew Kate.
       b.   #The road deliberately/carefully extended to Canada.
       c.   #Jill deliberately/carefully liked sugar.

Finally, eventives can occur in the complements of verbs like *force* and *persuade*, but statives are unnatural here:

(75) a.   Mercucio forced Juliet to kiss Romeo.
       b.   Chris forced Rolf to travel to Paris.

(76) a.   #Kumiko persuaded Chris to know Kate.
       b.   #Phil forced the road to extend to Canada.
       c.   #Kate forced Jill to like sugar.

12.4.1   Accommodating the Event/State Distinction in ECΘ

Facts like these support the linguistic reality of the event/state distinction. The natural question arises, then, as to how to express it within our theory ECΘ.

Parsons (1990) proposes to capture the dichotomy between events and states using two predicates **Cul** and **Hold**.[16] The basic idea is that some kinds of circumstances have an internal structure in which they develop over an interval and then culminate at a certain point, whereas other don't. Think, for example, of the event described by *Jefferson built Monticello*. House building follows a development that includes securing the foundation, putting up the walls, raising the roof, etc. At a certain point, the event culminates in a completed house. When a sentence with an eventive verb is true at a given time, we are either in the development portion of the event or at its climax. These are the kinds of circumstances that we call "events" in day-to-day speech (figure 12.1). Other kinds of situations lack this structure of development and culmination. Instead, they simply hold or do not hold at any point. Consider the circumstance described by *Juliet loved Romeo*, for example. At any point in time we are either in the interval where the state of loving obtains or we are not. Situations that have this undifferentiated internal structure are the ones we normally speak of as "states" (figure 12.2). Parsons' proposal is to let the variable *e* range neutrally over circumstances. When the predicate "Cul" is

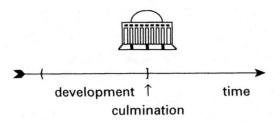

Figure 12.1 The event described by *Jefferson built Monticello*. This sentence is true when it is about either the development or the culmination of the event.

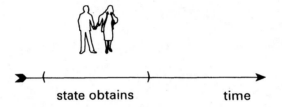

Figure 12.2 The state described by *Juliet loved Romeo*. This sentence is true when it is about a time when the state holds.

added to the truth conditions, as in (77), we are dealing with events:

(77) Val(t, *Jefferson built Monticello*, σ) iff for some *e*, building(*e*) & Agent(Jefferson, *e*) & Patient(Monticello, *e*) & Cul(*e*)

When the predicate "Hold" is added to the truth conditions, as in (78), we are dealing with states:[17]

(78) Val(t, *Juliet loved Romeo*, σ) iff for some *e*, loving(*e*) & Experiencer(Juliet, *e*) & Theme(Romeo, *e*) & Hold(*e*)

Obtaining results like (77) and (78) in our formal theory is a matter of introducing Cul and Hold into our axioms at an appropriate point. Since status as an eventive or a stative appears to be a lexical matter holding of individual predicates, the simplest idea is to introduce Cul and Hold directly into our lexical axioms. For example, suppose we modify the ECΘ predicate axioms in (54) to be as in (79):

(79) a. Val(⟨*x*, *e*⟩, *walks*, σ) iff *e* is a walking and Agent(*x*, *e*) and Cul(*e*)
      b. Val(⟨*x*, *e*⟩, *ponders*, σ) iff *e* is a pondering and Experiencer(*x*, *e*) and Hold(*e*)

    c. Val($\langle x, e \rangle$, *arrives*, σ) iff e is an arriving and Theme(x, e) and Cul(e)

    d. Val($\langle x, y, e \rangle$, *kisses*, σ) iff e is a kissing and Agent(x, e) and Patient(y, e) and Cul(e)

    e. Val($\langle x, y, e \rangle$, *admires*, σ) iff e is an admiring and Experiencer(x, e) and Patient(y, e) and Hold(e)

    f. Val($\langle x, y, z, e \rangle$, *gives*, σ) iff e is a giving and Agent(x, e) and Theme(y, e) and Goal(z, e) and Cul(e)

Then, as the reader can easily verify, these revisions will produce appropriate T sentences for eventives like *Chris gives Kate Fido* and for statives like *Phil admires Kumiko.*

For convenience, we will continue to speak of all objects that e ranges over in our semantic axioms and theorems as "events." However, when it's necessary to avoid confusion, we will distinguish between events proper, those es of which "Cul" is true, and states, those es of which "Hold" is true.

12.4.2 States and Events in AP and PP

We introduced events into the semantics of verbs in order to handle adverb modification. The fact that our sentence-interpretation rules apply to all types of sentences then pushes us to bring in states for other kinds of verbs. That is, the **generality** of our semantic rules exerts a pressure for ontological elements introduced in one part of the grammar to spread themselves to other parts.

A similar pressure arises from the **interdependence** of our rules. The introduction of events and states into one class of predicates, verbs, also drives events and states into the analysis of adjectives, PPs, and the constructions that feature them.

Copular Constructions

Consider copular constructions with AP and PP predicates like those in (80):

(80) a. Kumiko is happy.
    b. Rolf is in Paris.

In Chapter 4, exercise 4, we explored the proposal that the verb *be* is pleonastic, making no semantic contribution of its own. Semantically, the copular construction simply passes a value *x* from VP to the postcopular predicate phrase (*X*P):

(81) Val(*x*, [$_{VP}$ V$_{[+pleo]}$ *X*P]) iff Val(*x*, *X*P)

Generalizing this proposal to ECΘ in the most direct way, it seems we should pass a pair of values $\langle x, e \rangle$ from VP to *X*P:

(82) Val($\langle x, e \rangle$, [$_{VP}$ V$_{[+pleo]}$ *X*P]) iff Val($\langle x, e \rangle$, *X*P)

But, of course, if our rules pass an $\langle x, e \rangle$ pair to an AP or PP, then the AP or PP must take these kinds of objects as values. Relativization to events must spread from V to the other predicate categories.

The introduction of states gives us a way to bring events into adjectives and prepositional phrases. If we generalize on our analysis of verbs, a natural idea is that the truth conditions of APs and PPs involve states having Kumiko and Rolf, for example, as participants. The immediate question arises, then, as to just what roles these participants play in the relevant states. With psychological predicates like *happy*, it is plausible to see Kumiko as bearing the familiar Experiencer role: when Kumiko is happy, she experiences happiness, etc. With Rolf's being in Paris, the situation is less clear, however. Rolf is not a Theme, since he doesn't undergo movement; similarly, Rolf is not a Patient.

We will leave the question of role in *Rolf is in Paris* and many other AP and PP constructions as an open one to be answered by future research. Accordingly, in relevant cases we will simply use "θ" as a variable to stand for a role to be determined later. The truth conditions for (80a, b) thus come out as in (83a, b), respectively:

(83) a. $\exists e$[happiness(*e*) & Experiencer(Kumiko, *e*) & Hold(*e*)]
   b. $\exists e$[Loc(Paris, *e*) & Θ(Rolf, *e*) & Hold(*e*)]

According to (83a), *Kumiko is happy* is true iff there is a state of happiness in which Kumiko is the Experiencer. Under (83b), *Rolf is in Paris* is true if and only if there is a state of being located in Paris in which Rolf bears some role θ, whose precise identity is left open at this point.

Given our pleonastic analysis of *be*, more or less all of the various semantic contributions represented in (83) must be contributed by the lexical adjective and preposition. Adjectives and PPs will be analyzed as intransitive predicates of events that assign the Theme role to their subject and assert "Hold" of *e*:

(84) a. Val($\langle x, e \rangle$, *happy*, σ) iff e is a happiness and Experiencer(x, e) and Hold(e)

   b. Val($\langle x, y, e \rangle$, *in*, σ) iff Loc(y, e) and $\theta(x, e)$ and Hold(e)

Furthermore, the general PP rule must be adjusted to accommodate events and the lexical assignments in (85):

(85) Val($\langle x, e \rangle$, [$_{PP}$ P NP], σ) iff for some x, Val($\langle x, y, e \rangle$, P, σ) and Val(x, NP, σ)

These proposals yield the T sentences in (83), as the reader may show.

Secondary Predicate and Adverbial Constructions

Reanalysis of APs and PPs as applying to individual-state pairs carries its own further consequences, compelling us to introduce e values into other phrases and to quantify over e positions in other rules.

For example, consider secondary-predicate constructions. Earlier we looked at examples like *Chris arrives happy* and *Chris arrives late*, on the reading where the sentence-final adjective modifies the subject. Axiom (86) was proposed to account for this reading:

(86) Val($\langle x, e \rangle$, [$_{VP}$ VP AP], σ) iff Val($\langle x, e \rangle$, VP, σ) and Val(x, AP, σ)

The truth conditions for *Chris arrives happy* under this rule might be symbolized as in (87):

(87) $\exists e$[arrival(e) & Theme(Chris, e) & Cul(e) & happy(Chris)]

Evidently, with adjectives reanalyzed as holding of event-individual pairs, this rule won't work anymore. We must revise it to handle the new event position in AP.

The revisions are not completely trivial. For instance, we can't simply revise (86) as in (88):

(88) Val($\langle x, e \rangle$, [$_{VP}$ VP AP], σ) iff Val($\langle x, e \rangle$, VP, σ) and Val($\langle x, e \rangle$, AP, σ)

The result would be (89):

(89) $\exists e$[arrival(e) & Theme(Chris, e) & Cul(e) & happiness(e) & Experiencer(Chris, e) & Hold(e)]

Although Chris's bearing multiple roles in the same event seems harmless, the predication "happiness(e)" is not. We want Chris to be in a state of happiness, not the arrival event. Furthermore, note that the event e is asserted both to hold and to culminate—to be both an event and a state. It's not clear that this is even a coherent situation.

For things to work out properly, we must distinguish the events of arriving and being happy by introducing a new event associated with the AP:[18]

(90) Val($\langle x, e \rangle$, [$_{VP}$ VP AP], σ) iff Val($\langle x, e \rangle$, VP, σ) and for some e', Val($\langle x, e' \rangle$, AP, σ)

(91) $\exists e$[arrival(e) & Theme(Chris, e) & Cul(e)] & $\exists e'$[happiness(e') & Experiencer(Chris, e') & Hold(e')]

Thus once APs include events, our rules must be arranged to inject *new* events into the truth conditions at appropriate points.

The consequences of adding events also spread themselves to adverbs. To obtain the adverbial reading of *Chris arrived late* (where the arrival is late), we must allow the adjective in (90) to predicate of the main clause event. Furthermore, since we seek a general scheme for adverb interpretation, we are drawn to generalize the rule so that it applies to AdvP:

(92) Val($\langle x, e \rangle$, [$_{VP}$ VP XP], σ) iff Val($\langle x, e \rangle$, VP, σ) and for some e', Val($\langle e, e' \rangle$, XP, σ), where X is A, Adv, or P

And having once generalized to AdvP, we are obliged to adjust the interpretation of its lexical items to accommodate events and states. The result is that adverbs also become predicates of events in which individuals participate:

(93) a. Val($\langle x, e \rangle$, *quickly*, σ) iff e is quick and $\theta(x, e)$ and Hold(e)
    b. Val($\langle x, e \rangle$, *locally*, σ) iff e is local and $\theta(x, e)$ and Hold(e)
    c. Val($\langle x, e \rangle$, *recently*, σ) iff e is recent and $\theta(x, e)$ and Hold(e)

12.4.3 States and Events in Nominals

The propagation of new entities through the grammar can result not only from the generality and interdependence of semantic rules but also from the structure of our arguments used to introduce them. If a phenomenon found in one place in the grammar can be found elsewhere as well, then entities introduced to account for the former will appear natural in an account of the latter. Again, events and states provide a good example of this point.

Adjectival Modification

We motivated our event analysis of adverbs with example (94):

(94) Chris arrived late.

We observed that this example is ambiguous. On one reading the sentence entails that Chris was late (but his arrival needn't have been). On a second reading, it entails that the arrival was late (but Chris needn't have been). We took the source of this ambiguity to lie with the verb *arrived*. *Arrive* takes an individual-event pair $\langle x, e \rangle$ as its semantic value. The adjective *late* can apply to either x or e, yielding the one reading or the other:

(95)

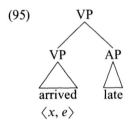

Consider now (96), a well-known example from the literature on adjectival modification:

(96) Olga is a beautiful dancer.

Example (96) is also ambiguous. On one reading, the sentence entails that Olga is beautiful (but her dancing needn't be); on the other, it entails that Olga's dancing is beautiful (but she needn't be). In the semantics literature, the source of this ambiguity has standardly been attributed to the adjective *beautiful*.[19] For example, suppose *beautiful* is analyzed as relational, having both an individual argument x and an argument for a standard of comparison C, (97a). Roughly speaking, the former gives the object that is beautiful; the latter gives the standard according to which beauty is assessed. The ambiguity of (96) is taken to arise according to whether Olga is beautiful as a person, (97b), or beautiful as a dancer, (97c):[20]

(97) a. beautiful(x, C)
     b. beautiful(Olga, Person)
     c. beautiful(Olga, Dancer)

On the former interpretation, the inference from (96) to *Olga is beautiful* goes through. On the latter, it doesn't.

The event analysis of (94) suggests a very different approach to (96).[21] Rather than locating the ambiguity in the adjective, we might instead locate it in the noun. Suppose that *dancer* is relational, taking an individual-event pair $\langle x, e \rangle$ as its semantic value; the latter is the event of dancing, the former is the individual who dances:

(98) Val($\langle x, e \rangle$, *dancer*, σ) iff dancing(e) & Agent(x, e)

Suppose further that *beautiful* is free to apply to either x or e in the modification structure:

(99)

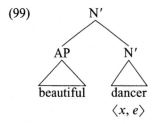

Then we derive exactly the right results. When *beautiful* applies to x, (99) will entail that the dancer is beautiful; when *beautiful* applies to e, (99) will entail that the dancing is beautiful.

The parallelism between adjectival and adverbial modification under this proposal appears significant and extends beyond cases like (96). Notice that adjunct predicates in the VP include ones that apply unambiguously to the subject NP (pure secondary predicates), (100); ones that apply unambiguously to the event (pure adverbials), (101); and ones that apply to either the subject or to event, (102):

(100) a. Chris ran away [tired].
       b. Chris arrived [barefoot].

(101) Chris ran away [fast].

(102) Chris arrived [late].

Similar facts are found with nouns and adjectives. Thus there are adjectives that lack what we've identified as an event-modifying reading. These so-called **pure intersective adjectives** have a simple predicative use but no counterpart adverbial forms or adverbial paraphrases:

(103) a. i.   That is a yellow kitchen.
    ii.   That is yellow, and that is a kitchen.
    iii. #That is yellowly a kitchen.
  b. i.   This is a white house.
    ii.   This is white, and this is a house.
    iii. #This houses whitely.

There are also adjectives that seem to have only an event reading. These **pure attributive adjectives** lack the simple predicative use but do have counterpart adverbial forms or paraphrases:

(104) a. i.   Marya is a former dancer.
    ii.   #Marya is former, and Marya is a dancer.
    iii.   Marya was formerly a dancer.
  b. i.   Chris is a future doctor.
    ii.   #Chris is future, and Chris is a doctor.
    iii.   Chris will be a doctor in the future.
  c. i.   He is a mere boy.
    ii.   #He is mere, and he is a boy.
    iii.   He is merely a boy.

Finally, there are adjectives that allow either the predicative reading or the adverbial reading, and hence create ambiguity:

(105) a. i.   Olga is a beautiful dancer.
    ii.   Olga is beautiful, and Olga is a dancer.
    iii.   Olga dances beautifully.
  b. i.   Alex is a careful painter.
    ii.   Alex is careful, and Alex is a painter.
    iii.   Alex paints carefully.

Given this parallelism in distribution, a parallel event analysis for adjectives looks highly attractive.

Relativizing Nouns to Events

Extending ECΘ to accommodate events in nouns and noun-modification structures involves many of the same changes introduced earlier with adjectives. We adjust our semantics for lexical common nouns so that they express stative relations between events and nonevent individuals:

(106) a. Val($\langle x, e \rangle$, *man*, σ) iff e is a being-a-man and $\theta(x, e)$ and Hold(e)

b. Val($\langle x, e \rangle$, *president*, σ) iff e is a being-president and $\theta(x, e)$ and Hold(e)

c. Val($\langle x, e \rangle$, *dancer*, σ) iff e is a dancing and Agent(x, e) and Hold(e)

d. Val($\langle x, e \rangle$, *gift*, σ) iff e is a being-a-gift and Theme(x, e) and Hold(e)

The rules that introduce common nouns must be also ammended to introduce events and pass them appropriately between mother and daughter nodes; for example, the GQ axioms for quantificational NPs and simple N's would be revised as follows:

(107) Val(X, [$_{NP}$ Det N'], σ) iff for some Y, Val($\langle X, Y \rangle$, Det, σ) and
$Y = \{ y : \text{for some } e, \text{Val}(\langle y, e \rangle, \text{N}', \sigma) \}$

(108) Val($\langle y, e \rangle$, [$_{N'}$ N], σ) iff Val($\langle y, e \rangle$, N, σ)

Finally, we introduce rules parallel to those for secondary predicates and adverbs to handle the adjectival-modification facts discussed above:

(109) Val($\langle x, e \rangle$, [$_{N'}$ AP N'], σ) iff Val($\langle x, e \rangle$, N', σ) and for some e',
Val($\langle x, e' \rangle$, AP, σ)

(110) Val($\langle x, e \rangle$, [$_{N'}$ AP N'], σ) iff Val($\langle x, e \rangle$, N', σ) and for some e',
Val($\langle e, e' \rangle$, AP, σ)

In the exercises to this chapter, we explore the effects of these additions and the T sentences they yield.

Verb-Noun Parallelisms in Complements and Adjuncts

The introduction of events into nouns has many attractive results beyond those of adjectival modification. For example, consider the verbal paradigm in (111) and the nominal paradigm in (112):

(111) a. Someone wrote a letter.
b. Someone wrote a letter to Chris.
c. Kumiko wrote a letter to Chris.

(112) a. a [$_{N'}$ letter]
b. a [$_{N'}$ letter to Chris]
c. a [$_{N'}$ letter to Chris by Kumiko]

The two are clearly analogous. In ECΘ, the examples in (111) are analyzed as event quantifications in which the complements and adjuncts are "glued together" by predicating of a single event e:

(113) a. Theme(letter, e)
      b. Theme(letter, e) & Goal(Chris, e)
      c. Theme(letter, e) & Goal(Chris, e) & Source(Kumiko, e) & Agent(Kumiko, e)

The event analysis of nouns allows us to give a highly parallel account for (112). By a straightforward extension to nouns of the rules for verbal complements and adjuncts, we can prove valuation statements like those in (114):

(114) a. Val($\langle x, e \rangle$, [$_{N'}$ letter], σ) iff e is a state of being a letter and Theme(x, e) and Hold (e)
      b. Val($\langle x, e \rangle$, [$_{N'}$ letter to Chris], σ) iff e is a state of being a letter and Theme(x, e) and Goal(Chris, e) and Hold(e)
      c. Val($\langle x, e \rangle$, [$_{N'}$ letter to Chris from Kumiko], σ) iff e is a state of being a letter and Theme(x, e) and Goal(Chris, e) and Source(Kumiko, e) and Agent(Kumiko, e) and Hold(e)

Here the Goal, Source, and Theme phrases relate to a single event, exactly as they do in the verbal predication.

Facts like (111) and (112) lend further support to the basic idea of ECΘ that verbal predications should be decomposed into an event predication and a family of satellite thematic predications like Theme(x, e), Source(x, e), etc. Under a more traditional treatment, like the one in EC, relations among arguments are established directly through the verb, (115a); there is no decomposition as in (115b):

(115) a. Val($\langle x, y, z, e \rangle$, *write*, σ) iff x writes y to z in e
      b. Val($\langle x, y, z, e \rangle$, *write*, σ) iff e is a writing and Agent(x, e) and Source(x, e) and Theme(y, e) and Goal(z, e)

But in (112) there simply is no verb present. Hence under the traditional view there is nothing relating arguments together in the required way. By contrast, with the analysis in (115b), where the verbal semantics is distributed among a basic event predication and a family of satellite thematic predications, the parallelism can be captured through the latter.

12.4.4   The Nature of States and Events

As we saw in chapter 4 in discussing PC^{prop}, the introduction of new entities into our semantic theory carries with it an important commitment. Our T theorems now explicitly quantify over events and states, and even a simple sentence like *Fraser walks* now asserts the existence of an event:

(116)   Val(t, [$_S$ Fraser walks], σ) iff for some e, walking(e) and
          Agent(Fraser, e) and Cul(e)

Hence if there is no event in which Fraser walks, *Fraser walks* is false on our analysis. But this conclusion is not credible if there is any possibility that the sentence *Fraser walks* could be true in the absence of an event of Fraser walking. It is crucial to our theory that events of the appropriate kinds actually happen.

The same point applies to states. The T theorem for *Fraser is happy* is now (117):

(117)   Val(t, [$_S$ Fraser is happy], σ) iff for some e, happiness(e) and
          Experience(Fraser, e) and Hold(e)

If there are no such things as states of happiness, then the RHS of (117) could be false while the LHS was true, and our analysis would be incorrect.

What, then, are events and states? In our view, the difference between ordinary physical objects like Fraser or the planet Venus, on the one hand, and events and states, on the other, has to do with how they are individuated with respect to time. Ordinary physical objects are three-dimensional things that persist through time. At any given moment during an object's existence, the entire object is present. The whole of Venus existed in 1895, and the very same thing, in its entirety, still exists right now. Events and states are not like this, however. At any given moment during the duration of an event or state, it is not true that the entire event or state is present. At this moment France is in a state of being a member of the European Economic Community (EEC). But the entirety of this state is not present at this moment. The First World War took place between 1914 and 1918. But the whole war was not present at 4 P.M. on June 15, 1916.

We have already seen that one of the differences between events and states is that the former have a structured developmental path, while the latter do not. One way to expand on this point is to note that if we divide up an event into shorter temporal segments, we do not typically find that each segment is occupied by an event of the same kind as the original. Suppose that Fraser eats an ice cream. We can divide this event up into segments: Fraser holds the ice cream in his hand, Fraser raises it to his mouth, Fraser licks the ice cream, and so on. These smaller events are not themselves events of eating an ice cream. By contrast, if we divide up a state into temporal segments, what we typically find are merely shorter instances of the very same kind of state. If France is in a state of being a member of the EEC between January 1994 and January 1995, then France is in a state of being a member of the EEC between January and February 1994, between February and March 1994, between March 1 and March 2, 1994, and so on.

This differentiating feature of events versus states appears similar to the mass/individual distinction.[22] Masses, like water or grass, are composed of smaller masses of the same kind. The mass consisting of all the water in the world divides into smaller masses, like the Red Sea and Lake Michigan. These smaller masses may be further divided, arbitrarily, into still smaller ones, until one gets to the basic constituents, the atoms of hydrogen and oxygen, which are not themselves small masses of water. Exactly parallel remarks apply to grass. Individual objects lack this feature: they are usually not composed of parts of the same kind as the original whole. Fraser is a human being, but his arm is not a human being.

Individual objects differ from masses also in that the former can be counted but the latter cannot. We can count the people in the room, but we can't count the waters in Great Britain or the grasses in Kew Gardens. It is true that we sometimes use the count terms *waters* and *grasses*, but these refer either to types of water and grass or to amounts of water and grass that have already been implicitly divided into individual objects by some method: one might order two glasses of water or (clumsily) two bundles of grass by saying *Two waters, please*, or *Two grasses, please*, respectively.

States appear to be like masses, and events like individuals. Thus we can count arrivals or departures, these being events, but we can't count knowledges or latenesses, these being states. States can also be divided up into bounded units in much the way that masses can be divided up into objects. Water can be divided into glasses, seas, and so on. Analogously, happiness can be divided up into particular states of individuals' being happy. If Fraser is happy between 8 P.M. and 11 P.M. on Wednesday evening, then there is a particular instance of happiness, a particular chunk of the larger state that is happiness in general. Recall the lines from the song "Auld Lang Syne": "We'll drink a cup of kindness yet, for Auld Lang Syne." Plausibly, the metaphor makes sense precisely because we can think of states like kindness as being masses—the sort of thing that one could drink cupfuls of (metaphorically). If Fraser is in a state of being kind, then Fraser is, as it were, the cup that holds a dose of kindness.

On our analysis, stative verbs, adjectives, adverbs, and so on, introduce quantification over states. Thus the RHS of (117) includes the clause "for some e, happiness(e)." We could think of this along the lines of quantification with mass terms: *some water* or *some grass*. Thus the RHS of (117) says that there is some of happiness of which Fraser is the Experiencer. Alternatively, we can think of these quantifications as more explicitly introducing the idea of boundedness, along the lines of "there is a particular instance of the state of happiness."

If we think of states in this way, as four-dimensional analogues of masses, then they need not be considered to be abstract entities, in the sense of existing outside space and time. Physical states, such the state of being at 100 degrees Centigrade, are components of the physical world. They have their own (scattered) temporal location and involve their own physical objects and substances. Like physical particulars, states do not exist uninstantiated: if nothing in the entire history of the universe ever attains a temperature of 9 billion degrees Centigrade, then the state of being at this temperature does not actually exist. But if there are such things as abstract objects, then states involving them will be abstract as well. The number 2 is permanently in a state of being between the numbers 1 and 3. If numbers are abstract objects in some "Platonic heaven," then the state of lying between 1 and 3 in the number series is itself a tract of Plato's heaven.

We have not provided anything approaching a complete account of events and states. We have not given any general account of the essential features of events and states (if there are any), nor of how to tell when there is one state or event, or two. This would be a huge project, far beyond the scope of this book. Furthermore, it's known to involve some very thorny problems. Suppose, for example, that the state of having a certain level of thermal conductivity is coextensive with the state of having a certain level of electrical conductivity (as is in fact the case). That is, they involve the very same substances over the same periods. Does this mean that the states are identical? If not, do we have to commit oursleves to additional entities and say that one state is characterized by the substances' possession of one property and the other by their possession of another?

Analogous problems arise for events. It does not seem that we can individuate events purely in terms of the objects undergoing them and their temporal locations. For example, if Fraser laughs while dancing all the while, there would appear two events (laughing and dancing) involving the same individual at the same time. How might they be distinguished? Donald Davidson has suggested that events are individuated by their causes and effects: two events are identical if and only if they have the same causes and effects. But this view suffers from the problem that there might be events that have no causes or effects.[23]

A further question is whether events need involve individuals or substances at all. If there is a change in the intensity of a gravitational or electrical field at a certain location, does there have to be something that undergoes the change? It's not obvious that there is anything playing the Theme role in this case. Perhaps the intensity change simply occurs at the location. The location is not the Theme, it's just where the event takes place.[24]

We will leave the intricacies of the individuation of events and states to professional ontologists. As usual, their work will either accord with the commitments of our semantic theory, leaving its results intact, or else it will clash with our theory, forcing us to reconsider its assumptions. At present, we see no clear implications either way.[25]

12.5   Times

We introduced events originally as a means of relating adverbs to the VPs they modify. Our reasoning was of a very general kind. We had a node whose two daughters we wanted to connect together semantically. We introduced a new object to mediate this connection. The two nodes were joined through a shared individual of which they were both predicated:

(118)

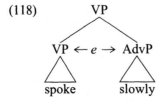

In this section we reapply this reasoning to motivate yet another new object in semantic theory. We do this with a construction that has already come under scrutiny a number of times: secondary predication.

12.5.1 Secondary Predicates Again

Secondary-predicate constructions like *Chris arrives happy* were given as an example of the reasoning sketched above. We proposed that the main and adjunct predicates are united together by being copredicated of a common individual:

(119)

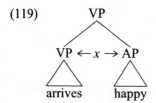

On a standard analysis of adjectives, the truth conditions of *Chris arrives happy* come out as in (120); on our event analysis, they come out as in (121). In either, the shared element in the predications is the individual Chris:

(120) $\exists e[\text{arrival}(e)$ & Theme(Chris, e) & Cul(e) & happy(Chris)]

(121) $\exists e[\text{arrival}(e)$ & Theme(Chris, e) & Cul(e)] &
        $\exists e'[\text{happiness}(e')$ & Experiencer(Chris, e') & Hold(e')]

   On reflection, it is not altogether clear that the shared subject in (120) and (121) is really enough to capture the connection between *arrives* and *happy* in *Chris arrives happy*. The truth conditions in (120) require an event of arriving, and they require Chris to be happy, but no further relationship between the two is mandated. Likewise, (121) requires a event of arriving in which Chris is Theme and a state of happiness with Chris as Experiencer, but that is all. In particular, (121) fails to express something all English speakers know about the sentence in question, which is that Chris's happiness must obtain at the point where his arrival occurs. It is not enough that there be an event and a state. The state must also hold at the point where the event culminates. Neither (120) nor (121) captures this.

   These remarks suggest that our analysis of the connection between the VP and the AP is actually missing something important. Beyond sharing the common individual Chris, we also seem to need some way of linking the culminating of an event and the holding of a state. We have already seen that "Cul" and "Hold" cannot be predicated of the same *e*, on pain of incoherence (recall (88) and its problems). One natural idea, then, is to invoke some as yet undiscovered parameter, ?, that will serve to bring the two predications together —some new individual that will connect "Cul" and "Hold":

(122)

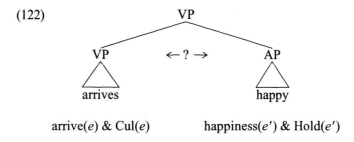

arrive(*e*) & Cul(*e*)   happiness(*e'*) & Hold(*e'*)

12.5.2 Relativizing "Cul" and "Hold" to Times

We introduced "Cul" and "Hold" originally as simple one-place predicates of events. As such, we could have just called them "Event" and "State," since in this form all they really do is to distinguish the two kinds of circumstance. Interestingly, Parsons (1990) gives a more articulated structure for "Cul" and "Hold," one that not only better justifies their titles but also suggests a potential answer to our question about connecting secondary predicates.

Parsons analyzes "Cul" and "Hold" as binary relations holding between events and a new kind of entity: times (τ).

(123) Cul(e, τ)

(124) Hold(e, τ)

Times are viewed in the familiar way, as points that occur in a sequence ordered by a temporal-precedence relation ($\rightarrow$). This relation gives them a direction from past to future. At each point, various things do or do not hold. And one of these points corresponds to the present (now):

(125) Past $\rightarrow$ Future
      .   .   .   .   .   .   now   .   .   .   .   .   .

The understanding of Cul(e, τ) is that the event *e* culminates at time τ. So in the event of house building described by *Jefferson built Monticello*, τ corresponds to the point at which Monticello is finally completed (figure 12.3). The understanding of Hold(e, τ) is that state *e* holds at time τ. So in the state

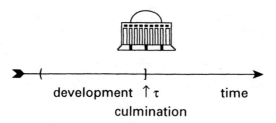

Figure 12.3   For the event described by *Jefferson built Monticello*, τ in Cul(e, τ) designates the time at which Monticello is finally completed.

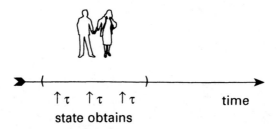

Figure 12.4   For the state described by *Juliet loved Romeo*, τ in Hold(e, τ) designates any of the times when Juliet loves Romeo.

of affection described by *Juliet loved Romeo*, τ is any of the points at which Juliet's loving Romeo obtains (figure 12.4).

The introduction of time points and the relativization of "Cul" and "Hold" to times allows us to express the desired connection in *Chris arrives happy*. We need a T sentence for this example equivalent to (126):

(126) $\exists\tau\exists e$[arriving(e) & Theme(Chris, e) & Cul(e, τ) &
$\quad \exists e'$[happiness(e') & Experiencer(Chris, e') & Hold(e', τ)]]

Then *Chris arrives happy* is true iff there is some time τ such that an event of Chris's arrival culminates at τ and a state of Chris's happiness holds at τ.

The revisions needed to prove (126) are straightforward and fairly mechanical. We must alter our lexical rules and compositional axioms so that times are introduced and passed in appropriate ways. Representative sample axioms include those in (127) to (131):

(127) a. Val($\langle x, e, \tau \rangle$, *walks*, σ) iff walking(e) and Agent(x, e) and Cul(e, τ)
      b. Val($\langle x, e, \tau \rangle$, *ponders*, σ) iff pondering(e) and Experiencer(x, e) and Hold(e, τ)

c. Val($\langle x, e, \tau \rangle$, *arrives*, σ) iff arriving(e) and Theme(x, e) and Cul(e, τ)

d. Val($\langle x, y, e, \tau \rangle$, *kisses*, σ) iff kissing(e) and Agent(x, e) and Patient(y, e) and Cul(e, τ)

e. Val($\langle x, y, e, \tau \rangle$, *admires*, σ) iff admiring(e) and Experiencer(x, e) and Patient(y, e) and Hold(e, τ)

f. Val($\langle x, y, z, e, \tau \rangle$, *gives*, σ) iff giving(e) and Agent(x, e) and Theme(y, e) and Goal(z, e) and Cul(e, t)

g. Val($\langle x, e, \tau \rangle$, *happy*, σ) iff e is a state of being happy and Experiencer(x, e) and Hold(e, τ)

h. Val($\langle x, y, e, \tau \rangle$, *in*, σ) iff Loc(y, e) and $\theta(x, e)$ and Hold(e, τ)

(128) Val(t, [$_s$ NP VP], σ) iff for some x, for some τ, for some e,
Val(x, NP, σ) and Val($\langle x, e, \tau \rangle$, VP, σ)

(129) a. Val($\langle x, e, \tau \rangle$, [$_{VP}$ V], σ) iff Val($\langle x, e, \tau \rangle$, V, σ)

b. Val($\langle x, e, \tau \rangle$, [$_{VP}$ V NP], σ) iff for some y,
Val($\langle x, y, e, \tau \rangle$, V, σ) and Val(y, NP, σ)

c. Val($\langle x, e, \tau \rangle$, [$_{VP}$ V NP$_1$ NP$_2$], σ) iff for some y, z,
Val($\langle x, y, z, e, \tau \rangle$, V, σ) and Val(z, NP$_1$, σ) and Val(y, NP$_2$, σ)

(130) Val($\langle x, e, \tau \rangle$, [$_{AP}$ A], σ) iff Val($\langle x, e, \tau \rangle$, A, σ)

(131) Val($\langle x, e, \tau \rangle$, [$_{PP}$ P NP], σ) iff for some y, Val($\langle x, y, e, \tau \rangle$, P, σ) and Val(y, NP, σ)

The rule for secondary predication must also be ammended so that it binds together the main and adjunct predicate through a shared time point τ:

(132) Val($\langle x, e, \tau \rangle$, [$_{VP}$ VP XP], σ) iff Val($\langle x, e, \tau \rangle$, VP, σ) and for some e',
Val($\langle x, e', \tau \rangle$, XP, σ), where X is A or P

As the reader may verify, these changes will permit us to prove truth conditions equivalent to (126) for *Chris arrives happy*.[26]

12.5.3 Introducing Simple Tenses

As with events, the effects of introducing time points are felt in many other parts of the grammar. We will discuss one such case here, an aspect of sentence semantics that has been conspicuously (and sometimes explicitly) suppressed in our results to this point.[27]

In even the simplest English sentences, verbs are obligatorily marked for what is called **tense**. As illustrated by the examples in (133), there is inflection on the verb to signal past tense (*-ed*) and present tense (*-s*), and marking for the future (what is sometimes called future tense) is accomplished through the modal auxiliary *will*:

(133) a. Jill protest*ed*.
       b. Jill protest*s*.
       c. Jill *will* protest.
       d. *Jill protest.

The difference in inflection corresponds to an important difference in truth conditions. For (133a) to be true, Jill must have protested at some time prior to the moment when the sentence is spoken; for (133b) to be true, on one reading, Jill must protest at the moment it's spoken;[28] and for (133c) to be true, Jill must protest at some time after it's spoken. Tense thus brings in an important element of deixis or indexicality. Tenses force sentences to be evaluated relative to the moment of utterance.

Up till now tense has been ignored as a complicating detail. However taking our earlier work on indexicals together with the introduction of time points, we can accommodate tense phenomena in a straighforward way. Recall that we have already introduced the notion of the **moment of speech** in discussing what we called the fixed "utterance roles" of a sentence. We identified four such roles for any sentence—utterer, addressee, place of utterance, and time of utterance—and we correlated their values with definite positions in any sequence:

(134) a. $\Sigma(u, \sigma)$ only if $\sigma(a)$ = the utterer of u
       b. $\Sigma(u, \sigma)$ only if $\sigma(b)$ = the addressee of u
       c. $\Sigma(u, \sigma)$ only if $\sigma(c)$ = the place of u
       d. $\Sigma(u, \sigma)$ only if $\sigma(d)$ = the time of u

With this apparatus, we could give simple axioms for indexical items like *now*, which always picks out the time of utterance:[29]

(135) Val(x, *now*, σ) iff $x = \sigma(d)$

A similar approach is possible with tenses, which also depend on the moment of utterance. Suppose we recast our basic syntax for S to include a node

(Tns) that contributes tense information:[30]

(136)

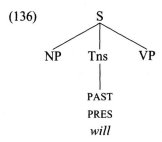

Then we can revise our S rule so that the time coordinate of the sentence is passed to Tns:

(137) Val(t, [$_s$ NP Tns VP], σ) iff for some x, for some τ, for some e,
Val(x, NP, σ) and Val(τ, Tns, σ) and Val($\langle x, e, \tau \rangle$, VP, σ)

Correlatively, we give rules for individual tenses that express relations of τ to the moment of utterance $\sigma(d)$:

(138) a. Val(τ, PAST, σ) iff τ is before $\sigma(d)$
b. Val(τ, PRES, σ) iff $\tau = \sigma(d)$
c. Val(τ, *will*, σ) iff $\sigma(d)$ is before τ

A Sample Derivation

We illustrate these proposals with our example *Chris arrived happy*, which has the syntax in (139):

(139)

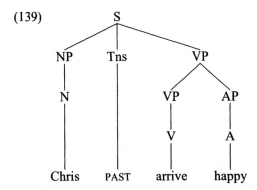

Axiom (137) gives the basic expansion of S:

(140) Val(t, [$_S$ [$_{NP}$ [$_N$ Chris]] [$_{Tns}$ PAST] [$_{VP}$ [$_{VP}$ [$_V$ arrive]] [$_{AP}$ [$_A$ happy]]]]], σ) iff
       for some x, for some τ, for some e,
       Val(x, [$_{NP}$ [$_N$ Chris]], σ) and Val(τ, [$_{Tns}$ PAST], σ) and
       Val($\langle x, e, \tau \rangle$, [$_{VP}$ [$_{VP}$ [$_V$ arrive]] [$_{AP}$ [$_A$ happy]]], σ)

By familiar reasoning with proper NPs, we derive (141):

(141) Val(x, [$_{NP}$ [$_N$ Chris]], σ) iff x = Chris

Analogous reasoning with Tns yields (142):

(142) Val(τ, [$_{Tns}$ PAST], σ) iff τ is before $\sigma(d)$

The more complex VP with adjunct unpacks as in (143):

(143) a. Val($\langle x, e, \tau \rangle$, [$_{VP}$ [$_{VP}$ [$_V$ arrive]] [$_{AP}$ [$_A$ happy]]], σ) iff
          Val($\langle x, e, \tau \rangle$, [$_{VP}$ [$_V$ arrive]], σ) and
          for some e', Val($\langle x, e', \tau \rangle$, [$_{AP}$ [$_A$ happy]], σ)
       b. Val($\langle x, e, \tau \rangle$, [$_{VP}$ [$_V$ arrive]], σ) iff e is an event of arriving and
          Theme(x, e) and Cul(e, τ)
       c. Val($\langle x, e', \tau \rangle$, [$_{AP}$ [$_A$ happy]], σ) iff e' is a state of being happy and
          Experiencer(x, e') and Hold(e', τ)
       d. Val($\langle x, e, \tau \rangle$, [$_{VP}$ [$_{VP}$ [$_V$ arrive]] [$_{AP}$ [$_A$ happy]]], σ) iff
          e is an event of arriving and Theme(x, e) and Cul(e, τ) and
          for some e', e' is a state of being happy and
          Experiencer(x, e') and Hold(e', τ)

Taking these results together we then derive (144):

(144) Val(t, [$_S$ [$_{NP}$ [$_N$ Chris]] [$_{Tns}$ PAST] [$_{VP}$ [$_{VP}$ [$_V$ arrive]] [$_{AP}$ [$_A$ happy]]]]], σ) iff
       for some τ, for some e, τ is before $\sigma(d)$ and
       e is an event of arriving and Theme(Chris, e) and Cul(e, τ) and
       for some e', e' is a state of being happy and
       Theme(Chris, e') and Hold(e', τ)

For *Chris arrived happy* to be true, (144) requires that there be a past time τ at which an event of arriving by Chris culimnated and at which Chris was in a state of happiness. These are the correct truth conditions.

Theory and Exercises

The Theory EC (Event Calculus)

Lexical Axioms

(1) a. Val(x, *Phil*, σ) iff x = Phil
    b. Val(x, *Jill*, σ) iff x = Jill
    c. Val(x, *Chris*, σ) iff x = Chris
    d. Val(x, *Kate*, σ) iff x = Kate

(2) a. Val($\langle x, e \rangle$, *walks*, σ) iff x walks in e
    b. Val($\langle x, e \rangle$, *ponders*, σ) iff x ponders in e
    c. Val($\langle x, e \rangle$, *arrives*, σ) iff x arrives in e
    d. Val($\langle x, y, e \rangle$, *kisses*, σ) iff x kisses y in e
    e. Val($\langle x, y, e \rangle$, *admires*, σ) iff x admires y in e
    f. Val($\langle x, y, z, e \rangle$, *gives*, σ) iff x gives y to z in e

(3) a. Val(x, *quickly*, σ) iff x is quick
    b. Val(x, *locally*, σ) iff x is local
    c. Val(x, *recently*, σ) iff x is recent
    d. Val(x, *late*, σ) iff x is a late

Phrasal Axioms

(4) a. Val(t, [$_s$ S$_1$ *and* S$_2$], σ) iff both Val(t, S$_1$, σ) and Val(t, S$_2$, σ)
    b. Val(t, [$_s$ S$_1$ *or* S$_2$], σ) iff either Val(t, S$_1$) or Val(t, S$_2$, σ)
    c. Val(t, [$_s$ *It is not the case that* S], σ) iff it is not the case that Val(t, S, σ)

(5) a. Val(t, [$_s$ NP VP], σ) iff for some x, for some e, Val(x, NP, σ) and Val($\langle x, e \rangle$, VP, σ)
    b. Val($\langle x, e \rangle$, [$_{VP}$ V NP], σ) iff for some y, Val($\langle x, y, e \rangle$, V, σ) and Val(y, NP, σ)
    c. Val($\langle x, e \rangle$, [$_{VP}$ V NP$_1$ NP$_2$], σ) iff for some y, z, Val($\langle x, y, z, e \rangle$, V, σ) and Val(z, NP$_1$, σ) and Val(y, NP$_2$, σ)
    d. Val(x, [$_X$ Y], σ) iff Val(x, Y, σ) (where X, Y are any nodes)

(6) Val($\langle x, e \rangle$, [$_{\text{VP}}$ VP AP], σ) iff Val($\langle x, e \rangle$, VP, σ) and Val(x, AP, σ)

(7) Val($\langle x, e \rangle$, [$_{\text{VP}}$ VP XP], σ) iff Val($\langle x, e \rangle$, VP, σ) and Val(e, XP, σ)
    (where X is A, Adv)

Production Rules

(UI)   Universal instantiation

For any x, $F(x)$

$\overline{F(\alpha)}$

(SE)   Substitution of equivalents

$F(\alpha)$

α iff β

$\overline{F(\beta)}$

(SI)   Substitution of identicals

ϕ iff for some x, $F(x)$ and $x = \alpha$

$\overline{\phi \text{ iff } F(\alpha)}$

The Theory ECΘ (Event Calculus + Thematic Roles)

Lexical Axioms

(1) a.   Val(x, *Phil*, σ) iff $x = $ Phil
    b.   Val(x, *Jill*, σ) iff $x = $ Jill
    c.   Val(x, *Chris*, σ) iff $x = $ Chris
    d.   Val(x, *Kate*, σ) iff $x = $ Kate
    e.   Val(x, *Fido*, σ) iff $x = $ Fido

(2) a.   Val($\langle x, e \rangle$, *walks*, σ) iff e is a walking and Agent(x, e) and Cul(e)
    b.   Val($\langle x, e \rangle$, *ponders*, σ) iff e is a pondering and
         Experiencer(x, e) and Hold(e)
    c.   Val($\langle x, e \rangle$, *arrives*, σ) iff e is an arriving and Theme(x, e) and Cul(e)
    d.   Val($\langle x, y, e \rangle$, *kisses*, σ) iff e is a kissing and Agent(x, e) and
         Patient(y, e) and Cul(e)
    e.   Val($\langle x, y, e \rangle$, *admires*, σ) iff e is an admiring and
         Experiencer(x, e) and Patient(y, e) and Hold(e)

f. Val($\langle x, y, z, e \rangle$, *gives*, σ) iff e is a giving and Agent(x, e) and
   Theme(y, e) and Goal(z, e) and Cul(e)

(3) a. Val($\langle x, e \rangle$, *quickly*, σ) iff e is a quickness and $\theta(x, e)$ and Hold(e)
    b. Val($\langle x, e \rangle$, *locally*, σ) iff e is a localness and $\theta(x, e)$ and Hold(e)
    c. Val($\langle x, e \rangle$, *recently*, σ) iff e is a recentness and $\theta(x, e)$ and Hold(e)

(4) a. Val($\langle x, e \rangle$, *late*, σ) iff e is a lateness and $\theta(x, e)$ and Hold(e)
    b. Val($\langle x, e \rangle$, *happy*, σ) iff e is a happiness and Experiencer(x, e) and
       Hold(e)

(5) a. Val($\langle x, y, e \rangle$, *in*, σ) iff Loc(y, e) and $\theta(x, e)$ and Hold(e)
    b. Val($\langle x, y, e \rangle$, *on*, σ) iff on(y, e) and $\theta(x, e)$ and Hold(e)

Phrasal Axioms

(6) a. Val(τ, [$_S$ S$_1$ *and* S$_2$], σ) iff both Val(t, S$_1$, σ) and Val(t, S$_2$, σ)
     b. Val(t, [$_S$ S$_1$ *or* S$_2$], σ) iff either Val(t, S$_1$) or Val(t, S$_2$, σ)
     c. Val(t, [$_S$ *It is not the case that* S], σ) iff it is not the case that
        Val(t, S, σ)

(7) a. Val(t, [$_S$ NP VP], σ) iff for some x, for some e, Val(x, NP, σ) and
        Val($\langle x, e \rangle$, VP, σ)
     b. Val($\langle x, e \rangle$, [$_{VP}$ V NP], σ) iff for some y, Val($\langle x, y, e \rangle$, V, σ) and
        Val(y, NP, σ)
     c. Val($\langle x, e \rangle$, [$_{VP}$ V NP$_1$ NP$_2$], σ) iff for some y, z,
        Val($\langle x, y, z, e \rangle$, V, σ) and Val(z, NP$_1$, σ) and Val(y, NP$_2$, σ)
     d. Val(x, [$_X$ Y], σ) iff Val(x, Y, σ)
        (where X, Y are any nodes)

(8) Val($\langle x, e \rangle$, [$_{PP}$ P NP], σ) iff for some y, Val($\langle x, y, e \rangle$, P, σ) and
     Val(y, NP, σ)

(9) Val($\langle x, e \rangle$, [$_{VP}$ VP XP], σ) iff Val($\langle x, e \rangle$, VP, σ) and for some e',
     Val($\langle x, e' \rangle$, XP, σ) (where X is A or P)

(10) Val($\langle x, e \rangle$, [$_{VP}$ VP XP], σ) iff Val($\langle x, e \rangle$, VP, σ) and for some e',
     Val($\langle e, e' \rangle$, XP, σ) (where X is A, Adv, or P)

Production Rules

(UI) Universal instantiation

$$\frac{\text{For any } x, F(x)}{F(\alpha)}$$

(SE) Substitution of equivalents

$$\frac{\begin{array}{c} F(\alpha) \\ \alpha \text{ iff } \beta \end{array}}{F(\beta)}$$

(SJ) Substitution of identicals

$$\frac{\phi \text{ iff for some } x, F(x) \text{ and } x = \alpha}{\phi \text{ iff } F(\alpha)}$$

Exercises

1. The following examples are within the scope of both EC and ECΘ.

   (1) Chris walks quickly.

   (2) Jill kisses Phil recently.

   (3) Kate gives Chris Fido locally.

   - For each of (1) through (3), derive a T sentence in EC. Be explicit, showing all steps.
   - For each of (1) through (3), derive a T sentence in ECΘ. Again, be explicit and show all steps.
   - Extend EC and ECΘ to include the following sentence:

   (4) Rolf admires Kate fervently.

2. For copular sentences involving adjectives and PPs, we adopted a rule that analyzes *be* as a pleonastic verb. In chapter 4, exercise 4.A we considered an alternative analysis in which *be* was contentful, and expressed the identity relation (1):

   (1) Val($\langle x, y \rangle$, be, σ) iff $x = y$

Try to extend the identity analysis of *be* to EC and ECΘ so that appropriate T sentences are derived for (2a, b):

(2) a. Kumiko is happy.
    b. Rolf is in Paris.

What difficulties do you encounter in this attempt?

3. Davidson (1967b) argues that causation is a binary relation holding between events. On this view, the semantic analysis of a causative construction like (1a) involves two events, a causing event and a caused event, (1b):

(1) a. Kumiko made Chris leave.
    b. ∃*e*[Agent(Kumiko, *e*) & Cul(e) &
        ∃*e*′[leaving(*e*′) & Agent(Chris, *e*′) & Cul(*e*′) & Cause(*e*, *e*′)]]

Consider the pair in (2):

(2) a. Fido walked.
    b. Jill walked Fido.

■ Give informal logical representations like (1b) that express the truth conditions of these two sentences.

■ Give lexical axioms for intransitive and transitive *walk* that will allow you to derive the truth conditions you gave above.

4. English contains many triples like those in (1) and (2), consisting of an adjective, an intransitive change-of-state verb, and a causative verb.

(1) a. This is broken.
    b. This broke.
    c. Chris broke this.

(2) a. The door is open.
    b. The door opened.
    c. Kate opened the door.

■ Find additional examples of such triples.

■ Using informal logical representations of the kind we have employed in this chapter, express the truth conditions of (1a–c) and (2a–c) so that the semantic relationships among them are made clear. (Feel free to change the examples in order to eliminate irrelevant details; for example, you may want to consider variants of (1a–c) involving Max, a robot, in order to avoid complications with demonstratives.)

- Construct lexical rules along the lines of chapter 4, exercise 19, that relate the adjective, intransitive verb, and causative verb.

5. Perception-verb constructions in English consist of a verb like *see* or *hear* followed by a clauselike structure:

(1) a. Chris sees [Kate leave]
    b. Kumiko hears [Rolf protest]

Vlach (1983) and Higginbotham (1983c) have proposed that perception verbs express relations between individuals and events. On this proposal, what Chris sees in (1a) is an event of Kate leaving, and what Kumiko hears in (1b) is an event of Rolf protesting:

(2) a. $\exists e$[seeing(e) & Experiencer(Chris, e) & Hold(e) &
        $\exists e'$[leaving(e') & Agent(Kate, e') & Cul(e') & Percept(e', e)]]
    b. $\exists e$[hearing(e) & Experiencer(Kumiko, e) & Hold(e) &
        $\exists e'$[protesting(e') & Agent(Rolf, e') & Cul(e') & Percept(e', e)]]

Give axioms and rules that execute this idea in ECΘ. For concreteness, assume that perception-verb constructions to have the syntax in (3), where SC is a "small clause":

(3)

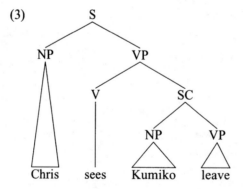

Give a derivation for *Chris sees Kate leave*, illustrating how your extension works in detail.

6. In the text we suggest grounds for viewing nominals as predicates of events or states. The nouns in (1a–c), for example, might be analyzed as true of individual-event pairs:

   (1) a. No dancers were present.
       b. This gift is for Sally.
       c. An admirer walked in.
       d. The recipient was Bill.

   Consider the idea that while the semantics for (1a–d) does involve events, reference to such objects is confined to the internal semantics of the lexical items themselves, as in (2):

   (2) a. Val(x, *dancer*, σ) iff for some e, dancing(e) and Agent(x, e)
       b. Val(x, *gift*, σ) iff for some e, giving(e) and Theme(x, e)
       c. Val(x, *admirer*, σ) iff for some e, admiring(e) and Experiencer(x, e)
       d. Val(x, *recipient*, σ) iff for some e, receiving(e) and Goal(x, e)

   What drawbacks does such an analysis have? Consider phrases like *beautiful dancer* and *fervent admirer*.

7. The need for events and states in the analysis of nouns may seem obvious, given that there are NPs that either describe events directly or are true of certain canonical participants in events. For example, the gerundive nouns in (1a–d) appear to be true of events/states of destroying, giving, admiration, and receiving, respectively:

   (1) a. The destruction of Dresden was horrifying.
       b. Giving money to charity is encouraged.
       c. Phil's admiration of Kate didn't surprise Chris.
       d. The receipt of these goods has been noted.

   Are these data conclusive? Do they argue for axioms like those in (2), parallel to what was proposed in the text?

   (2) a. Val($\langle x, e \rangle$, *destruction*, σ) iff ...
       b. Val($\langle x, e \rangle$ *giving*, σ) iff ...

8. Consider the example in (1a) and its **cleft** counterpart in (1b). Examples (1a, b) have the same truth conditions, but the second conveys the additional contrastive claim that John, and not some other person, was kissed by Mary. It also carries the assumption that Mary kissed someone. To put

things another way, (1b) divides the sentence information into a **focus**, a contrasted subject of assertion, and a **presupposition**, a property asserted of the subject and assumed to be instantiated, (1c):

(1) a. Mary kissed John.
    b. It was *John* Mary kissed.
    c. John = focus
       For some x, Mary kissed x = presupposition

Chomsky (1976) suggests that the partition of focus and presupposition is explicitly represented in syntax. The core of his idea is that focus constructions (which includes clefts) involve an operator-variable structure, (3a), and express a quantification, (3b):

(2) a. It was [John]$_i$ [$_S$ Mary kissed t_i]
    b. [$\exists x : x$ = John] [Mary kissed x]
    c. John = restriction = focus
       For some x, Mary kissed x = scope = presupposition

This analysis yields correct truth conditions and also allows a simple mapping from syntax to focus and presupposition. The clefted phrase representing the quantifier restriction corresponds to the focus. And the phrase (S) containing the trace and representing the quantifier scope corresponds to the presupposition, (3c).

In English, clefted elements are typically argument phrases. However, in a number of languages, predicates too may be clefted. In (4) are some examples of such **predicate clefts** from Haitian Creole:

(3) a. Se   kouri Jan kouri.
      It is run   John run
      'It is run that John did (not, e.g., walk).'
    b. Se anbrase Mari anbrase Jan.
      It is kiss   Mary kiss   John
      'It is kiss that Mary did to John (not, e.g., slap).'
    c. Se anbrase li te di Mari t' ap anbrase Jan.
      It is kiss   he Tns say Mary Tns Asp kiss   John
      'It is kiss that he said Mary did to John (not, e.g., slap).'

As these sentences show, Haitian predicate clefts consist of an initial element *se* corresponding to English *it is*, followed by a clefted predicate (α), followed by a clause (β) containing another instance of the predicate (5):

(4) Se[α] [$_β$ ... α ...]

Extend Chomsky's analysis of clefts to predicate clefts in Haitian Creole. Make sure that the truth conditions and the focal/presuppositional information is correctly captured. You needn't give detailed compositional rules. A general scheme analogous to (2) for each of (4a–c) is sufficient.

9. Consider the following contrast noted by Kratzer (1989):[31]

    (1) a.   Whenever Mary speaks French, she speaks it well.
       b. #Whenever Mary knows French, she knows it well.

The second is decidedly odd. Evidently, the (universal) quantification introduced by *whenever* causes a problem with *know* that it is not present with *speak*.

    Using the parallel of event/count predicates versus state/mass predicates noted in the text, propose an explanation for the contrast in (1). Consider the following additional data:

    (2) a.   Every liquid is precious.
       b. #Every water is precious.

Now consider the further contrast in (3), also due to Kratzer (1989). Both of these examples are fine. In particular, the substitution of an indefinite term *a Moroccan* for the proper noun *Mary* improves (2a) dramatically.

    (3) a. Whenever a Moroccan speaks French, she speaks it well.
       b. Whenever a Moroccan knows French, she knows it well.

Again using the parallel of event/count predicates versus state/mass predicates noted in the text, propose an explanation for the contrast in (3). Consider the following additional data:

    (4) a. Every liquid is precious.
       b. Every cup of water is precious.

    Finally consider the contrast in (5).

    (5) a.   Whenever Mary is happy, she is very happy.
       b. #Whenever Mary is tall, she is very tall.

Can the event/state distinction be invoked to explain the difference in acceptability here?

10. In section 12.4.3 we suggested that adjunct modifiers of nominals might be analyzed as event modifiers, in parallel to the semantics for verbs. The idea was to analyze (1a) as in (1b):

(1) a. a [$_{N'}$ letter to Chris from Kumiko]
   b. Val($\langle x, e \rangle$, [$_{N'}$ letter to Chris from Kumiko], σ) iff e is a state of being a letter and $\theta(x, e)$ and Goal(Chris, e) and Source(Kumiko, e) and Agent(Kumiko, e) and Hold(e)

Consider (2a). Is this rendered correctly as in (2b), parallel to the semantics for verbs? (Ignore the simplication we make in treating *the table* as a referring term.)

(2) a. [$_{N'}$ letter to Chris from Kumiko on the table]
   b. Val($\langle x, e \rangle$, [$_{N'}$ letter to Chris from Kumiko on the table], σ) iff e is a state of being a letter and $\theta(x, e)$ and Goal(Chris, e) and Source(Kumiko, e) and Agent(Kumiko, e) and Loc(the table, e) and Hold(e)

Consider (3a). Is this rendered correctly as in (3b), parallel to the semantics for verbs?

(3) a. [$_{N'}$ letter to Chris from Kumiko last Thursday]
   b. Val($\langle x, e \rangle$, [$_{N'}$ letter to Chris from Kumiko last Thursday], σ) iff e is a state of being a letter and Theme(x, e) and Goal(Chris, e) and Source(Kumiko, e) and Agent(Kumiko, e) and during(last Thursday, e) and Hold(e)

11. Using the sample axioms and rules in section 12.5 as a guide, construct a full theory ET (Events + Tense) that relativizies ECΘ to times and manipulates these entities correctly. Include simple tenses in ET, and show that the resulting theory assigns appropriate truth conditions to (1a–d):

(1) a. Phil gave Kate Fido.
   b. Chris will arrive happy.
   c. Jill protests.

Extend ET to include simple temporal adverbs like *now*, *yesterday*, and *tomorrow*. What truth conditions do your rules yield for (2a, b)?

(2) a. Chris will arrive happy tomorrow.
   b. Jill protests now.

Extend ET to include quantified temporal adverbs like *always* and *sometimes*. What truth conditions do your rules yield for (3a, b)?

(3) a. Chris will arrive happy sometime.
    b. Jill always protests.

12. The analysis of temporal information in the text appeals to time points τ. An alternative explored in the semantics literature on tense is to appeal to time intervals i. For example, we might take states to hold at an interval Hold(e, i), and we might take events to culminate over an interval Cul(e, i) (where the culimination occurs at the last point of i).

The analysis of secondary predication given in section 12.5.2 has the following result in cases where the main predicate is eventive:

■ The time at which the secondary predicate holds coincides with the time at which the eventive verb culminates.

This result was developed for the **achievement** verb *arrive*. Achievements are typically understood as events with little or no development portion.

Consider now the following additional cases of secondary predication, where the main verb is an **accomplishment** verb, a verb with a nontrivial development portion:

(1) a. Chris ran the race injured.
    b. Jill walked home tired.
    c. Kate painted the picture blindfolded.

Does the analysis in terms of time points given in section 12.5.2 extend to these cases? If not, can you suggest modifications to accommodate them using the interval analysis? Assuming that accomplishments and achievements differ in the way indicated, discuss why they show the pattern they do with secondary predicates.

Consider further cases of secondary predication, where the main predicate is stative and neither develops or culminates:

(2) a. John is happy drunk.
    b. Phil stood in the doorway motionless.

Does the analysis given in section 12.5.2 extend to these cases? If not, can you suggest modifications to accommodate them?[32]

13. In chapter 4 we introduced some thought experiments on predication by Gareth Evans. These argued that for an expression to be a genuine predicate, its application conditions have to display sensitivity to the identity conditions of individual objects. For example, for *Warm*! to function as a predicate, its application conditions have to involve entire objects (such as rabbits or huts) being warm. We further observed that predicates are associated with conditions of application to objects: "Each predicate is associated with a condition that an object may meet or fail to meet. If the object meets the condition, the predicate applies to the object. If not, it doesn't" (section 4.2.1).

However, on the view presented in this chapter, predicates like *warm* and *runs* apply not to objects, like huts or rabbits, but rather to states and events.

- Does the event/state analysis of predicates impugn the argument that strong empirical evidence for predication is only available when the speakers' use of the expressions displays sensitivity to the identity conditions of objects? If so, why?

- Is it correct to say that on the event/state analysis, predicates are associated with application conditions on objects? If so, what form would the conditions take? If not, how should the functioning of predicates be explained?

13   Meaning and Knowledge

Cognitivist semantics raises conceptual and methodological questions that have been debated by linguists, psychologists, and philosophers throughout the century. In this chapter we will examine two important issues, both the subject of much current controversy. The first concerns the relationship between an individual's semantic knowledge and features of the individual's physical and social environment. The second is how semantic knowledge, and linguistic knowledge generally, might fit within the wider domain of cognitive science.

13.1   Semantics and Linguistic Individualism

We have pursued semantics from the standpoint of individual psychology, according to which it is not societies or communities that know semantic rules but individuals. Much semantic knowledge is, of course, common among many different individuals. Semantic universals are common across all humans. And different speakers of the same language or dialect share many more specific semantic rules. Nevertheless, there is a lot of room for individual variation. Differences in vocabulary alone will distinguish individuals: no two people know the meanings of exactly the same set of lexical items. And, as we saw in chapter 5, there are other ways in which semantic theories need to be tailor-made for specific individuals. Recall our example of Lori, who had distinct dossiers associated with *Cary Grant* and *Archie Leach*, and the example of Peter who had only one dossier associated with the two names. We argued that our theory of Lori would contain (1a, b), whereas our theory of Peter would contain (1a, c):

(1) a. Val(*x*, *Cary Grant*) iff *x* = Cary Grant
     b. Val(*x*, *Archie Leach*) iff *x* = Archie Leach
     c. Val(*x*, *Archie Leach*) iff *x* = Cary Grant

The fundamental notion of language for the purposes of cognitivist semantic theory is the notion of a personal idiolect: each of us has his or her own idiolect, which is different from everybody else's. But even with this focus on the personal idiolect, issues remain about the extent to which semantics should be construed as an entirely individualistic theory. There are cases suggesting that what individuals mean by their words is itself a partly social matter. It is but a short step from there to conclude that an individual's meanings are not entirely fixed by their own internal states but rather depend partly on external things.

For example, consider cases where we are unable to say what our own words mean and would defer to experts to fix their reference. Many people are unable to tell the difference between chipmunks and ground squirrels. They lack the conceptual means for distinguishing the meanings of the words *chipmunk* and *ground squirrel*. Nonetheless, such people can use the terms appropriately. If they say *I don't know what a chipmunk looks like*, they make a true claim about chipmunks and say nothing about ground squirrels. So their use of *chipmunk* still refers to chipmunks, despite the meager content of their internalized rule.[1] Presumably, this is because they use *chipmunk* with the intention of referring to what persons more expert in relevant ways would consider it proper to call a chipmunk. They defer to experts (zoologists, lexicographers, or whomever) to fix the reference of their own words.[2]

There are also cases in which we would take ourselves to be wrong about what our words mean. Suppose that Maggie believes that, strictly speaking, the culinary term *mousse* applies only to dishes made with eggs. So a dish made of whipped cream and chocolate, no matter how mousselike, does not fall under the term *mousse*, according to Maggie's internal lexicon. Maggie is presented with a dish of the eggless mousse and the recipe comes under discussion. Maggie says,

(2) Oh, no eggs? So it isn't really a mousse then.

But her host, aided with the *Larousse Gastronomique*, demonstrates Maggie's error. Maggie would probably conclude that she had made a mistake: *Oh, I thought a mousse had to have eggs. I guess I was wrong.* And so on. If Maggie's utterance in (2) was false, the word *mousse* in that utterance must have been true of the eggless dish. And if this is right, then the extension of *mousse* in the utterance is not the one specified by Maggie's internalized rule but rather the one agreed on by experts in culinary vocabulary. Here again it looks as though the extensions of our words are fixed not only by our personalized semantic rules but also by the views of others whom we consider to be authoritative.[3]

This last example shows how we can distinguish two notions of what a person means by an expression. The first notion is the socially determined one. We call this **S-meaning**. For Maggie, even before her confrontation with the culinary dictionary, the S-meaning of *mousse* allowed it to apply to eggless dishes. The second notion is the individualistic one. We'll call it **I-meaning**. The I-meaning of a word for an individual is just whatever the individual's internalized theory specifies. Thus the I-meaning of Maggie's term *mousse*, prior to the confrontation, was one that did not allow it to apply to eggless dishes.

There is some appeal to the view that, pretheoretically, we think of meaning as S-meaning. Like Maggie, we regard our own opinions about what our words mean as fallible and subject to correction by others. And a number of linguists and philosophers have held that we should focus on S-meaning as one basic notion of the semantics of an individual's language.[4] But it does not follow from this that S-meanings are the object of study of cognitive semantics, and indeed, we believe that I-meanings should fill this role.[5] The chief reason is that I-meanings are better suited to explain the relevant data: the various semantic judgments that we have discussed throughout. Language users make judgments about what sentences mean, about implication and synonymy relations among sentences, and so on. These judgments are based on the individual's own conception of his or her language, rather than on other people's expertise. This remains true even if we regard some of our linguistic judgments as corrigible by others. For example, most speakers regard (3a) as acceptable but (3b) as somewhat bizarre:

(3) a. John wiped the table clean.
    b. *John wiped the table dirty.

Sentence (3a) is true if John wiped the table with the result that it became clean. Why, then, does sentence (3b) not express the thought that John wiped the table with the result that it became dirty? What explains these judgments?

Adapting a (tentative) suggestion from Higginbotham (1989), we might propose that the lexical entry for *wipe* is along the lines of (4):

(4) $Val(\langle x, y\rangle, wipe, \sigma)$ iff x removes material from the surface of y by lightly rubbing y with something

If speakers had this clause included in their lexical entry, then it would not be surprising if they found (3a) acceptable and (3b) odd.[6] But now suppose that we find a deviant speaker, a child perhaps, who believes that wiping is merely a matter of lightly rubbing. This speaker will presumably not have the same judgments about (3a) and (3b) as we do. He or she might well regard them both as rather odd. Suppose that when we consider the S-meaning of *wipe* for the atypical speaker, we decide that it is the usual one, the one expressed by (4). We use (4) to specify the S-meaning of *wipe* in this speaker's idiolect. It is obvious that we now cannot use S-meaning as part of the explanation of the speaker's judgments. Rather, we have to consider the I-meaning, for it is this that is relevant to the judgments we are trying to explain. The point is, of course, quite general: one's semantic judgments are based on one's internalized semantic theory, not on one's S-meanings.

Some might object here that we are confusing the meaning of a word with the speaker's (possibly mistaken) conception of that meaning. Thus atypical speakers conceive of a word as having a certain meaning, whereas in fact its (S-)meaning is somewhat different. The speaker's judgments can be explained by their conceptions of (S-)meaning, without the need to posit any actual (I-)meaning beyond that of the S-idiolect. I-meanings do no work, the objection concludes.

This objection misses the point, however. The I-meaning is what *gives* the content of the speaker's conception: it is the semantic rule that the speaker has for the word. To say that I-meaning is the object of semantic theory is to say that the cognitive state that explains the sort of data that we are interested in is a representation of a particular set of rules, which set specifies I-meanings. A person's S-meanings are given by a different set of rules, one that doesn't give the contents of the cognitive state in question. Hence the objection is correct in observing that for our purposes, we needn't go beyond a person's conception of the language, but it is wrong to suppose that we can do this without invoking I-meanings.

It is, of course, quite possible to question both the notions of I-meaning and S-meaning. Speakers have I-meanings only if they have internalized semantic theories. So if the basic methodological assumptions of our semantic theory are false, then I-meanings are forfeit. Assuming that semantics of our sort is correct, it makes sense to talk of S-meanings only to the extent that an internalized semantic theory together with our tendencies to defer to experts (and the other factors playing a part in our judgments about what determines the semantic properties of words[7]) generate a coherent and reasonably determinate set of rules for each speaker.[8]

One might wonder how we are to make sense of communication if we are confined to I-meanings. Actually, this is not very difficult. The internalized semantic theories of different people can overlap to any degree: they can be identical, containing exactly the same rules, or they can have not a single rule in common. Where two people's internalized theories overlap, their I-meanings will be shared. An account of communication based on I-meanings deals nicely with cases in which I-meaning and S-meaning diverge. Suppose that both Donna and Laura think that *presently* means 'at present' even though it S-means 'before long'. Donna asks *When is the mailman due?* and Laura says *Presently.* Donna understands this to mean that the mailman is due at the very time of their conversation. And this, of course, is exactly the thought that Laura is trying to get across. S-meanings are of no help here. The same point applies when the speakers' I-meanings differ but they share their S-meaning. Suppose that Donna's internalized rule for *presently* is the refined one stated in the *Oxford English Dictionary*, while Laura takes it to mean 'at present'. Suppose again that the S-meaning is the same for both of them. In spite of the convergence of S-meaning, Donna will not understand what Laura is trying to communicate. There is no meeting of minds here. This failure of communication is, of course, explained by the diverging I-meanings, not the coinciding S-meanings.

13.2 Semantics and Psychoindividualism

We have been arguing for a form of "linguistic individualism" in semantic theory according to which the semantic features of a person's language are whatever his or her internalized semantic theory states them to be. On this view, the semantic theory a person knows doesn't depend on anything outside of his or her mind, such as the opinions of experts or the nature of the surrounding physical environment. Linguistic individualism is in accord with a broader, more general form of individualism, which we may call **psychological**

individualism, or **psychoindividualism** for short. According to psychoindividualism, a subject's possession of a psychological state is entirely determined by the person's internal, physical states. If psychoindividualism is true, it follows that two neurologically identical subjects must be in the same psychological states. A difference in the environment could make a difference to a subject's psychology only if it made some causal difference to the subject's internal, physical states. And presumably the only relevant physical states would be neurological ones.

A number of interesting and widely discussed arguments have been advanced in the philosophical literature that appear to tell against a psychoindividualist conception of semantics. In this section we examine two of these arguments and try to evaluate their force.[9] The first concerns general terms, like the common noun *water*; the second concerns proper nouns and indexicals.

13.2.1 General Terms: Earth and Twin Earth

The central arguments against psychoindividualism in semantics derive from a well-known thought experiment introduced by Putnam (1975). Suppose that in a distant galaxy there is a planet that very closely resembles our own. Its atmosphere and distribution of geographic features are the same as Earth's. And it contains a counterpart for each of us who is similar to us down to the finest synaptic connection. This planet is in fact nearly a molecule-for-molecule replica of Earth, almost an identical twin; hence we can call it "Twin Earth." The only difference between Earth and Twin Earth is that where the former has water, the latter has a substance that, though superficially similar to water, is not H_2O. Rather it has some different chemical composition that we can call "XYZ." XYZ is indistinguishable from H_2O under any normal circumstances. The two can only be told apart in sophisticated chemical laboratories.

Now let's turn the clock back to 1750, a time before either we or the inhabitants of Twin Earth possessed the chemical sophistication to distinguish water from twin water. In 1750 terrestrial English speakers used the word *water* to refer to water. And Twin Earth speakers of Twin English used the word (or word form) *water* to refer to twin water. Consider the following simple question:

(5) Was the lexical entry for *water* in the minds of speakers of Earth English identical to that for *water* in the minds of speakers of Twin Earth?

Notice that if the answer to this question is "no," then a psychoindividualist view of semantic knowledge cannot be upheld. By assumption, Earth and Twin Earth speakers are identical in all local, physical respects.[10] Hence if the psychological states involved in knowing the meaning of *water* are different, then those states cannot be entirely determined by strictly local, internal features of the individuals that possess them.

Many people have held that a "no" answer must indeed be given to (5). More precisely, they have argued that the word form *water* in the mouths of Earth speakers in 1750 had a different extension than it did in the mouths of Twin Earth speakers, and that this entails a difference in lexical entries. The step from premise to conclusion here is a simple one. Suppose we adopt the reasonable view that the extension of a term is determined by the speaker's lexical entry for that term. Then if the extensions are different for different speakers, the lexical entries must be different as well. As we said, this would entail that semantics cannot be psychoindividualist, since, in the case at hand, the speakers in question are physically identical. Accordingly, this argument against psychological individualism in semantics turns strongly on whether the word *water* in 1750 referred to different things for Earth versus Twin Earth speakers.

Putnam has argued that the reference of *water* would have been different for Earth versus Twin Earth speakers. He bases his conclusion on a particular view of how the reference of "natural-kind terms" like *water* gets fixed. Roughly put, his proposal is that a natural-kind term applies to anything that is appropriately similar to a typical or paradigmatic sample of the stuff, where the notion of being appropriately similar means having the same underlying constitution, as determined by scientific inquiry. Thus *water* will apply to anything that is appropriately similar to paradigmatic samples of the stuff. And things will be appropriately similar to a sample of water if they have the same underlying constitution, as determined by chemical investigation.

It's easy to see how this view might lead to the conclusion that *water* on Earth and Twin Earth must refer to different things. In 1750, as now, paradigmatic samples of water on Earth had the chemical composition H_2O. So then, as now, *water* must have referred to H_2O for Earth English speakers. By contrast, in 1750 the paradigmatic samples of water on Twin Earth had the chemical composition XYZ. So then, as now, *water* must have referred to XYZ for Twin Earth English speakers. Note that these results hold even though the Earth inhabitants of 1750 didn't know the true composition of water, and even though, if confronted with XYZ, they would have called it *water*. On Putnam's view, these people would simply have been making a mistake. Just as not everything that looks and feels like gold is gold, not everything that looked and felt like water was water. XYZ would have been a sort of "fool's water" for them. Similarly for H_2O on Twin Earth. Encountering it, the inhabitants of that world might well have referred to it using their term *water*. But they would simply have been wrong in this, since *water*, for them, referred to XYZ, not H_2O. So the argument goes.

Putnam's picture fits well with certain common intuitions. Suppose, for example, that we had discovered the chemical composition of water in the following way. We were investigating the properties of some samples of what we called *water*, and we found that all but of one these samples was largely composed of H_2O. The one oddball sample isn't H_2O, it's XYZ, let us say. Almost certainly, our reaction would go like this: "Ah ha, water is H_2O, but some liquids that we previously thought were water are in fact not so." That is, we would take our previous use of the word *water* to refer to XYZ to have been an error. This means that we do not regard our current, postdiscovery restriction of the word *water* to H_2O to involve a revision of the extension of the old word. The extension of the old word was limited to H_2O as well. These intuitions accord smoothly with Putnam's model: the old term *water* applied to typical samples and whatever else was appropriately similar. Since one sample failed to be typical and failed to be appropriately similar to the examples that actually were typical, it was treated as never having fallen within the extension of *water* in the first place.

More Thought Experiments

The thought experiments described above yield intuitions that support Putnam's model, and hence appear to argue against a psychoindividualist view of semantic knowledge. As it turns out, however, there are further thought experiments and corresponding intuitions that appear to argue for the opposite view. Here is one borrowed from Wilson (1982). Imagine that there exists on a South Sea island a tribe of Druids. It so happens that the only flying things known to the Druids are birds. They call birds *birds*. Now consider the following two alternative scenarios. In the first, an airplane circles the island in full view of the Druids. They say "Lo, a great silver bird flieth in the sky." Thereafter, they call planes *birds*, and they call birds *feathered birds*. In the second scenario, an airplane crashes in the jungle, out of sight of the Druids. When they later discover it, the Druids say "Lo, a great silver house hath appeared in the jungle." Later, when the plane is repaired and takes off, they call it a *flying house*, reserving the word *bird* for birds.

Intuitively, the Druids' usage, and everything else about them and their environment, seems compatible with either of two scenarios described. And as Wilson emphasizes, it is plausible to suppose that in neither scenario would the Druid's feel that they were changing the extension of the original term *bird*. They would not feel as though they were revising their usage. Nor would they feel as though their old usage had proved inadequate to their new descriptive needs, and hence in need of arbitrary refinement or enlargement. In the first scenario, they feel as though their word *bird* always included such things as planes in its extension. In the second scenario, they feel as though their old word *bird* would never have included such things as planes in its extension.

It is not hard to find real examples of this same phenomenon, in which a new discovery leads to a term being used with one extension, while a slightly different historical quirk would have naturally lead to its being used with a different extension. Here is one that Wilson provides: The term *Grant's zebra* was originally applied to a particular subspecies of zebras native to Kenya. A morphologically distinct subspecies of the same species found in Rhodesia was called *Chapman's zebra*. It turned out that the two subspecies interbred near the Zambezi River. The term *Grant's zebra* still extends only over the Kenyan subspecies and not the whole species. But suppose that Chapman's zebras had not been given a name and were first studied by zoologists near the Zambezi, in company with zebras of the Kenyan subspecies. It would have seemed quite natural for the zoologists to say "Ah, there are two subspecies of Grant's zebra." In such a case the term would have ended up extending over the entire species. But at no point would the users of the term felt that they were changing its extension.

It is likewise easy enough to envisage an alternative scenario for Putnam's original Twin Earth case. Suppose that aliens provide a taxi service between Earth and Twin Earth at a time prior to the discovery of the periodic table on either planet. Earth speakers thus encounter large amounts of XYZ, which they naturally call *water*. Later, when chemistry develops, all agree that there are at least two types of water: H_2O and XYZ. At no point do Earth speakers feel that their word *water* was subject to a change of extension.

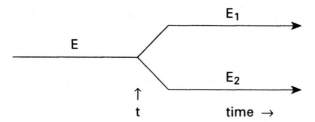

Figure 13.1   The general structure of alternative-scenario experiments. An expression α applies to a definite range of local objects R up to time t. This range R gives rise to a vague notion of the extension of α, call it E. Then as a result of some experience at time t, there is a branching of futures: in one scenario, α applies to a wider extension E_1, and in another scenario, α applies to a smaller extension E_2. Since E_1 and E_2 differ, E can be identical with only one of E_1 and E_2 at most.

The general structure of alternative-scenario experiments is thus the following. There is an expression α that definitely applies to a certain range of items R within the speakers' local environment, up to a certain time t. (For example, water in 1750 definitely applies to H_2O). Call the extension of α, up to t, E, leaving open the question of what might be included in E other than merely the items in R. At a subsequent time, on one branch, the extension of α is wider than just R (*water* extends over both H_2O and XYZ after the introduction of the taxi service). Call the wider extension E_1. At a subsequent time on the other branch, the extension of α definitely excludes some items in E_1. (After the discovery of the periodic table, *water* definitely doesn't extend over XYZ). Call this smaller extension E_2 (figure 13.1). E_1 and E_2 are different, so the original E cannot be identical with both.

In such cases, we have three options: (1) identify E with E_1, (2) identify E with E_2, (3) identify E with neither. Opting for (1) would amount to holding that the extension of water in 1750 included both XYZ and H_2O. When the chemical constitution of Earth water was discovered, the extension altered, shrinking to include only H_2O. Opting for (2) would amount to staying with Putnam's original account. We would then have to hold that in the taxi-service scenario, the extension of *water* altered, widening to include both XYZ and H_2O. It is not so obvious what would be involved in opting for (3), but Wilson offers a suggestion. On his view, the identity of E is indeterminate between E_1 and E_2. Thus it would have been neither definitely right nor definitely wrong to call XYZ water in 1750. Rather, the term has a sort of optional parameter that has not yet been adjusted. Only at the branching point does the parameter get set. In one scenario, it is set to E_1; on the other scanario to E_2.

13.2.2 Accommodating Psychoindividualism

It would be possible to discuss the virtues and vices of each option at length. For present purposes, however, we will simply note that only the third is compatible with psychoindividualism,[11] and we will enter a few considerations arguing that this option is acceptable in its own right.

One point to note is that the third option accords well with our focus on the I-meaning conception of semantics, motivated by linguistic individualism.[12] Recall our thought experiment on the discovery of the constitution of water. Option (3) requires the extension of our term *water* to change when we discover that water is H_2O. On the I-meaning conception, this is accommodated naturally by a lexical revision. Prior to our discovery, our internal lexicon specifies the extension of the term *water* with some clause roughly of the form (6), in which M is some concept in our mental language:

(6) Val(x, *water*, σ) iff x is M

After the discovery, our internal lexicon comes to include the clause (7):[13]

(7) Val(x, *water*, σ) iff x is H_2O

On the I-meaning view, positing this sort of revision would be independently motivated by the changes in our linguistic judgments. For, of course, the judgments we make about the extension of the word *water* change dramatically with our discovery.

Some philosophers find this view counterintuitive, sharing Putnam's intuition that the extension of *water* didn't change when its constitution was discovered (recall our sense that the old word *water* never truly applied to XYZ, no matter what we might have thought before the discovery). Yet, as we have noted, there is an almost equally strong incompatible intuition that there is no change of extension for *water* in the alternative scenario in which *water* ends up applying to both XYZ and H_2O. And it is not clear whether Putnam's intuition is a reliable guide to the truth. Although speakers surely have some authority regarding the current extension of their terms, they have no particular authority with regard to Putnamian thought experiments, which either concern what terms would mean in counterfactual circumstances or what terms did mean when these were used by other people with different linguistic dispositions a long time ago. Speakers are in no privileged position with respect to the semantics of terms in these situations.

A second worry is that there is no principled way of giving the alleged extension of the old word *water* (i.e., of the old concept M from which, on the I-meaning conception, the word inherits its extension). The extension is to include both XYZ and H_2O. But what else? And how is one supposed to tell? These are certainly good questions. And admittedly we lack a well-worked-out theory to answer them. In fact, we lack quite a lot in this general domain: we lack a philosophical theory of what determines the extension a mental concept, we lack a detailed empirical theory of the general nature of lexical entries, and we lack a detailed methodology that would enable us to tell, in a given case, what should and what should not be counted as in the extension of a mental concept. But these failures of omniscience do not jeopardize the overall position. Nobody (to our knowledge) is in a better position with respect to the missing theories.[14] And the currently emerging empirical accounts of lexical knowledge, and the methodology in lexical semantics that will eventually give us much firmer empirical answers to our questions, seem to be fully compatible with psychological individualism, or even to entail it.[15]

Furthermore, we are not in fact completely in the dark as to how one might discover the extension of *water* in the mouth of a 1750 English speaker. True, we don't have such speakers to hand, and so can't actually do the required research. But the ways we could go about it are surely clear enough in principle. We could ask speakers to classify various aqueous samples on the basis of various types of information: what they look like, what they are made of, and so on. We could ask speakers what they took to be the necessary properties of water, what they regard as typical of water but not necessary, and so on. In this way we could surely find out a great deal about the extension of the term. As we said, we don't have a developed theory of lexical entries, so don't know whether this extension-determining information would be best represented as a feature list, as a preference-ranked cluster, in a paradigm/foil format, or in some other way.[16] Our present claim is simply that it is not too hard to see, in rough intuitive terms, how we could work out the term's extension. Given this, there seems to be no particular reason to suppose that a successful psychoindividualistic theory of lexical entries will not be forthcoming in the future.

13.2.3 Singular Terms

Related but different anti-individualist arguments are applied in the cases of proper nouns and variable-reference terms. For terms of both of these kinds, there is a prima facie violation of psychoindividualism in the very semantic theories we have put forward.

Proper Nouns

Consider the following twin example, which relates to PC+.[17] Suppose that we have two Twins, A and B, who are neurologically indistinguishable. Suppose further that A and B are each acquainted with one of two identical twins (with a lowercase t). To make matters more confusing, both of these latter twins are called *Paul*. We can call them "$Paul_1$" and "$Paul_2$." Suppose that everything that A believes about the twin he knows ($Paul_1$), B believes about the twin he knows ($Paul_2$), and vice versa. In PC+ we would have to distinguish the cognitive states of A and B. We would have to deploy axiom (8) for A and axiom (9) for B:

(8) $Val(x, Paul)$ iff $x = Paul_1$

(9) $Val(x, Paul)$ iff $x = Paul_2$

Axiom (8) is appropriate for A because his term *Paul* refers to the particular individual $Paul_1$. Likewise, (9) is the right axiom for B because his term *Paul* refers to the other twin, $Paul_2$. But (8) and (9) are very different claims, attributing different T theories to A and B. This is so in spite of the fact that the only difference between A and B lies outside their heads. Internally, everything is the same for them. So we are forced to write different semantic theories for internally indistinguishable subjects.

If semantic theories are theories of tacit knowledge and we are forced to apply different theories to A and B, then it looks as though we have violated psychoindividualism. For it seems that we are forced to attribute different states of knowledge to the neurally indistinguishable Twins.

There is, however, a way to counter this prima facie argument that PC+ is anti-individualistic. Recall that psychoindividualism is the doctrine that neurally indistinguishable subjects must have the same psychological states. Moreover, it is possible to argue that while there is an obvious sense in which A and B know different things, the Twins' psychological states are nevertheless the same. For the psychoindividualist can argue that states that involve knowing things about particular individuals, for example, knowing that the term *Paul* refers to the particular individual $Paul_1$, can be factored into two distinct components. One component is a purely internal, psychological state of the knower. The second component is purely external and nonpsychological, and this is the individual who is the object of the knowledge. Thus the psychoindividualist would argue that *A* and *B* are in identical psychological states, though these states are about, are directed toward, different individuals.[18]

Another way of putting the point is as follows. The psychoindividualist can hold that in attributing the knowledge that the term *Paul* refers to $Paul_1$, the semantic theorist is indeed picking out a psychological state but is doing so in part via a contingent, relational property of that state: the property of being about the object $Paul_1$. This property is contingent in that the psychological state in question could exist without standing in that relation to that object. A person could be in this very psychological state even if $Paul_1$ didn't exist and the state was about $Paul_2$ or about no existing individual at all. On this view, picking out psychological states in terms of the objects they are about would be somewhat like picking out Jones's height by pointing to someone else, say, Paul, and saying "Jones is as tall as Paul." Obviously, Jones's height is entirely independent of the existence of Paul. But one can still usefully refer to Paul as part of a way of specifying Jones's height.

This move of factoring states of knowledge into two components—the intrinsic psychological state and the external objects that the state happens to be about—needs to be backed up with an account of the alleged internal, psychological state. But in fact we have already provided the beginnings of an account with our story about concepts and dossiers. Recall we proposed that PC+ needs to be supported by a theory of individual concepts. Our understanding a name, on this theory, consists in our having a concept of the individual that the name refers to. And this concept is deployed in our internalized axiom for the name. Thus when we write (8) in our theory of *A*, our metalinguistic term "$Paul_1$" stands in for *A*'s concept of $Paul_1$. We suggested that concepts could be explained in terms of dossiers of information.

It is natural, on this concept and dossier view, to hold that if two individuals have indistinguishable dossiers, then they have the same concept. But now consider *A* and *B* and their concepts of $Paul_1$ and $Paul_2$. And remember that everything *A* knows or believes about $Paul_1$, *B* knows or believes about $Paul_2$. This means that their dossiers might reasonably be regarded as indistinguishable. And so their concepts are the same. They have identical concepts, but concepts of different individuals. So a psychoindividualist would argue.

In summary, if psychoindividualism is true and a psychoindividualistic theory of individual concepts can be provided, then this can fit happily with PC+. PC+ can be regarded as attributing the very same psychological states to A and B. But PC+, in addition to attributing the psychological states, also mentions the individuals that are the objects of these states: it relates A's state to $Paul_1$ and B's state to $Paul_2$. It therefore says different things about the neural Twins but does not thereby attribute different psychological states and does not violate psychoindividualism.

Variable-Reference Terms

When we come to terms of variable reference, the discussion follows a similar pattern. Again, there is a prima facie violation of psychoindividualism in the semantics for these terms, VRTs. We can set up another twin case to illustrate. Suppose that A and B are each looking in the mirror. Each says *I need a haircut*. And suppose further that the neural states of the twins are identical as they speak. Given a VRT treatment, these utterances would have different truth conditions. A's utterance is true just in case A needs a haircut, and B's is true if and only if B needs a haircut.

Once again, there is a reply. Intuitively, there is a clear sense in which the psychological states underlying the twins' utterances are the same. They have the same understanding of the words they are using (they have the same rule for *I* in their internalized lexicons, and so on). And each is expressing the same belief, the belief that he needs a haircut. But intuitively there is also a crucial difference: A says and believes that A needs a haircut, while B does not.

The psychoindividualist will argue, again, that only what is common to the twins counts as genuinely psychological. The difference merely concerns the objects that these states are about. VRT does nothing to undermine the psychoindividualist position. It entails that the twins' utterances have different truth conditions. But, if psychoindividualism is true, this could be dealt with by a two-factor theory of a kind similar to the one we suggested for proper nouns. We could distinguish a purely psychological way of conceiving of the truth conditions from the various external objects that figure in the truth conditions. The former is internal to the subject; the latter external but not psychological.

Once again, it is up to the psychoindividualist to provide a theory of the common psychological states. And VRT already provides some of the materials for this. Recall that VRT provides a theory of the context-independent semantic features of word and sentence types. These are given by the sequence-relative valuation clauses together with Σ theory. Following Kaplan, we called these features of an expression its "character." The character of I, for example, is given by the sequence-relative valuation clause "Val(x, I, σ) iff $x = \sigma(a)$" together with the Σ-theoretic clause stipulating that an utterance selects only those sequences of which the first member is the speaker.

The truth conditions of an utterance are determined by its character, together with the context of the utterance. In the case of utterances with I, the relevant feature of the context is the speaker. This determines which particular object figures in the truth conditions of the utterance: if A is the speaker, then the utterance selects only those sequences with A in their first position, and A becomes relevant to its truth conditions.

When we consider the psychological role of an utterance—the way it is understood, the belief it expresses, and so on—we find that its character appears to play a role and its truth conditions do not. If A and B are sincere in their utterances, then we will make the same predictions about their behavior: we would expect each to try to get a haircut. Thus utterances with the same character support the same psychological predictions, even though they have different truth conditions. By contrast, if A says *I need a haircut* and B, addressing A, says *You need a haircut*, we would predict that A will try to get a haircut. But we would make no such prediction about B. Here the utterances have the same truth conditions, but they have different characters and support different psychological predictions.[19]

This suggests that the following version of a two-factor theory is open to the psychoindividualist. Part of what each twin understands by his utterance of *I need a haircut* is given by his grasp of its character. And this will be the same for the two twins. The truth conditions of the utterances are determined by their character plus features of context. Thus we can regard the character as being part of the way in which the speaker conceives of the truth conditions of the utterance. And we can regard the contextual contribution to the truth conditions as purely external to the speaker's mind. It is composed just of the various objects, and so on, that the speaker's conceptions are conceptions of.

Thus VRT is not only compatible with psychoindividualism but even offers it some support. For it provides an account of character, which gives part of the internal, psychological state that is the speaker's understanding of an utterance.

Other Factors

We say that character provides only part of what is understood by an utterance, because there are typically additional factors inolved. Recall that to compute the truth conditions of an utterance with a term of variable reference, an interpreter always needs to know the various objects relevant in the context. For example, if *A* hears an utterance of *She knows Kate*, where *she* is used to refer to Jill, *A* will need to know that this is the case. Remember the inference (31) from chapter 6, which began with the two premisses repeated here as (10a, b), and concluded with (10c):

(10) a. *u* is an utterance of *She₁ knows Kate*.
     b. Phil uses *she₁* in *u* to refer to Jill.
     c. *u* is true iff Jill knows Kate.

To run through this piece of reasoning and reach the conclusion (10c), *A* will need to have some conception of Jill. And *A* will need to use it to formulate the RHS of (10c). This conception, of course, will not be provided by the character of the expression *she*. It will not even be in the language faculty. It might be a dossier. Or, if *A* doesn't have a dossier for Jill but is looking at her, it might be some kind of visually based conception.

So we can distinguish two different components involved in a subject's understanding of an utterance containing a demonstrative or indexical. The first component is the character. This provides the purely linguistic element of what the subject understands. On the other hand, there is the extralinguistic conception of the objects of reference: dossiers, perception-based concepts, and so on. The psychoindividualist will, of course, have to provide a two-factor account of this second component, distinguishing the purely internal, psychological factor and the purely external object. Evidently, the psychoindividualist project here is independent of VRT and the rest of semantic theory, since it is concerned with concepts outside the language faculty.

We conclude that, in spite of the arguments to the contrary, semantic theory is indeed compatible with psychoindividualism. The extent to which this matters depends, of course, on the extent to which one is concerned with psychoindividualism in general.

Having discussed the individuation of semantic knowledge and its relations to the environment, we turn now to further issues about the nature of semantic knowledge and its relations to the brain.

13.3   Tacit Knowledge

Semantic theory, as part of linguistics, deploys the notion of tacit knowledge as a fundamental part of its explanatory apparatus. The notion of tacit knowledge is in some ways a new one. Around the turn of the century Sigmund Freud was the first to make serious, scientific use of the concept of unconscious knowledge, a notion that is kindred to, or perhaps the very same as, the concept of tacit knowledge used in linguistics and neighboring areas of psychology.[20] This Freudian concept has been the subject of intense debate ever since its inception: some have rejected it as incoherent or empirically misguided; others have defended it or tried to define it. When Chomsky (1965) invoked the idea of tacit knowledge of linguistic rules, the debates took on a new vivacity. It is instructive to examine some of these debates.

People find the unfamiliar mystifying. And so it happens that new theoretical concepts give rise to puzzlement, demands for clarification, and disbelief. This is exactly Quine's reaction. Quine (1970a) offers us the following the distinction between two kinds of relation that may hold between a person's behavior and a set of rules: the person's behavior may merely "fit" the rules, in the sense that the rules correctly describe what the person does. Fitting does not require the person to know or stand in any other cognitive relation to the rules. Thus all of our behavior automatically fits the rules (i.e., laws) of biology and physics. The other relation is that of "guidance." A person is guided by a rule only if they know the rule and can actually state it. Suppose that a given set of syntactic rules generates all and only the grammatical sentences of a given language. The behavior of any speaker who is prone to utter and recognize as well formed all and only the sentences that the rules generate fits the rules. However, the rules only guide the speaker's behavior if he or she can explicitly state them.

Obviously, the cognitivist model accords with neither of these options, as Quine observes: "But now it seems that Chomsky and his followers recognize an intermediate condition, between mere fitting and full guidance in my flat-footed sense of the word. They regard English speech as in some sense rule-guided ..., however unprepared we be to state the rules" (1970a, 442).

The novel intermediate condition recognized by Chomsky and his followers worries Quine, as it does many others. "Implicit guidance," Quine remarks, "is an idea sufficiently moot to demand some explicit methodology" (1970a, 444).

Quine goes on to press the question of how one can decide which particular set of rules a given individual is following. He points out that for any given language, that is, any set of well-formed linguistic structures with specific meanings, there will be many different rule systems that generate it. These rules will "fit" the behavior of any speaker of the language. So the problem is, how can one find a satisfactory empirical motivation for the claim that the speaker is implicitly guided by one of these rule systems, rather than any of the others? Quine and others have been particularly skeptical about semantics. Even if syntactic theory could be given solid empirical underpinnings, the idea of tacit knowledge of reference and other semantic notions has given rise to particular concern.[21]

In this book we have tried hard to be explicit about our methodology. We have tried to show how one can tell which rules are in the semantic module. Throughout we have offered evidence of a variety of kinds and have shown how the evidence bears on the theory. For example, we argued in chapter 3 that the astonishing ability of human beings to quickly learn language strongly suggests that there are strict global constraints on the relation between syntactic and semantic structure and on the general form of semantic rules. The essence of the argument was simply that humans could learn languages relatively quickly if they innately assumed (a) that rules of semantic interpretation apply to some level of syntactic structure (we chose LF in particular) and (b) that semantic rules are strongly compositional. If either of (a) or (b) failed to apply, then the choices left open to the child learning language would be vastly increased, and language acquisition would necessarily be a slow process. If this is right, then there is good empirical motivation for supposing that the semantic rules that speakers tacitly know apply to LF and are strongly compositional. On this basic assumption we were able to motivate further particular claims about the set of rules tacitly known. For example, we argued for a particular treatment of the truth-functional connectives *and* and *or* in chapter 3, and we argued against the Tarskian treatment of quantification in chapter 8.

To be sure, any of these arguments may be questioned, and perhaps ultimately they will be found defective. But the methodology is clear enough: an ordinary instance of inference to the best explanation. In this particular case the explananda are some key aspects of the remarkable phenomenon of human semantic competence. It is true that the idea of tacit knowledge of rules is somewhat novel and that it differs in obvious ways from the commonsense idea of rule following captured by Quine's term "guidance." But science is forever stretching and reshaping commonsense concepts in its endeavour to deepen our understanding of the world. Nobel Prize–winning physicist Richard Feynman expresses this point when he explains, "People often complain of the unwarranted extension of the ideas of particles and paths etc. into the atomic realm." The complaint arises from the fact that the commonsense notions of particle and path do not naturally apply to the rather strange entities of microphysics. But Feynmann responds to the complaint: "Not so at all; there is nothing unwarranted about the extension. We must, and we should, and we always do, extend as far as we can beyond what we already know, beyond those ideas that we have already obtained.... It is the only way to make progress" (1965, 164). The point applies to semantic theory as well: there is nothing unwarranted about the extension of the commonsense idea of rule guidance to help explain semantic competence.

If what we have been saying is right, then tacit knowledge of rules has good scientific credentials. However, the concept is indeed a novel one, and it would be good to be able to say more about it. Linguistics elaborates on the contents, acquisition, and (to an extent) use of tacit knowledge of linguistic rules. But it does not itself attempt to define or present a theory of the notion of tacit knowledge. The position is a standard one in science. Each science has its fundamental notions, notions that are used to give explanations but are not themselves explained. Thermodynamics, for example, takes for granted such concepts as pressure, temperature, and volume; articulates the relations among them ($P = V/T$); and uses them to explain such things as why objects expand when heated. Thermodynamics itself does not offer a theory of these primitive elements. Rather, this is a matter for statistical mechanics, which tells us, for example, that temperature (in a gas) is mean molecular kinetic energy. It is indeed inevitable that any given science will have its unexplained primitives, since explaining one thing always requires taking other things for granted.

In our view, it is not yet clear whether there is currently available a true background theory of tacit knowledge, a theory that stands to linguistics and neighboring areas in cognitive psychology as statistical mechanics stands to thermodynamics. But we do believe that there is a very good contender: cognitive science, with its computational theory of cognitive processes. If the basic explanatory apparatus of cognitive science is correct, then it provides a general theory of tacit knowledge of exactly the kind that would underpin cognitive linguistics. Since this is so, we believe it is worth spending a little space explaining the basic assumptions of cognitive science and their relations to the notion of tacit knowledge.

Before we proceed, we should make our position clear. We do not believe that semantics, or linguistics more generally, stands in any particular need of justification or ratification by some further background theory. Just as the laws of thermodynamics can be confirmed independently of statistical mechanics, so linguistic theories can be confirmed independently of a further theory of tacit knowledge. We do believe that the notion of tacit knowledge, an assumed primitive in linguistics, can in principle be further explained, just as the notion of heat is further explained by statistical mechanics. And obviously such further explanation would be desirable. Moreover (and equally obviously), statistical mechanics does in fact provide deep support for thermodynamics, and a good theory of tacit knowledge would indeed provide deep support for linguistics. Finally, we are tentatively inclined to accept the basic assumptions of cognitive science: they are attractive and plausible and provide an elegant and satisfying account of tacit knowledge. But if cognitive science is eventually superceded by some other theory of tacit knowledge, this will not necessarily impugn linguistics.

13.3.1 A Computational Framework

Modern cognitive science is built on the hypothesis that mental capacities are computational capacities, that the mind is like a computer in fundamental respects. A computer is a machine that computes functions. It instantiates a program, a set of rules or procedures, that determines a specific output for each input from some domain. If a cognitive capacity is computational, then it must be possible to characterize the capacity as a function. Vision, for example, can be characterized as a function from a pair of two-dimensional patterns of light intensity values (retinal images) to the shapes, locations, and orientations of objects in three-dimensional space—the world as it is visually perceived.

A computer performs its computations by processing representations. A representation is the physical form of a symbol or a set of symbols of some language. The computer receives representations of the inputs or arguments of the function, and it reacts by constructing representations of the outputs or values for those arguments. For example, if you type the following sequence of symbols into a pocket calculator: $\langle$"1", "+", "1", "="$\rangle$, the calculator will produce the symbol "2". A computer or calculator can thus be seen as instantiating two functions: a syntactic function from symbols to symbols and a semantic function from what the input symbols represent to what the output symbols represent.

There are three levels of description appropriate to computers, and a complete account of how a computer runs requires all three.[22] The first level (level 1) is the semantic level. At this level we say which function the machine computes and how it computes this function. The specification of the function must be complete: it must be possible to deduce from it the value for each potential argument. The explanation of how the function is computed will usually include a description of the information that the machine draws upon and a "blackbox" breakdown of how it uses this information. The breakdown shows how the task of calculating the value is divided up into subtasks. For example, for a machine that calculates the function $x^2 - 1$, the specification will say whether the machine first calculates x^2 and then subtracts 1 from the result or whether it first calculates the value of $x + 1 = y$ then calculates the value of $x - 1 = z$ and then multiplies y and z.

The information used by the machine will be either explicitly represented or implicitly present. Explicitly represented information is encoded in representations that enter into the computations. It is, as it were, written down inside the machine. Consider, for example, a chess-playing computer that stores a representation of the information that a pawn is worth one point. When faced with the option of exchanging a pawn for another piece, it accesses this representation, which then plays a role in its decision about whether to make the exchange. This is a case of explicit representation. By contrast, consider the machine that computes $x^2 - 1$ in the second way described above. This machine makes use of the information that $x^2 - 1 = (x + 1)(x - 1)$, but this information is nowhere directly encoded within it.[23] Rather, the information is built into the way the system is designed: the machine is wired up so as to make use of the information. This is a case of information that is implicitly present, or, as it is sometimes put, "implicit in the functional architecture."

The second level of description (level 2) is syntactic. The machine operates on the symbols of a formal language. It receives representations as inputs, yields representations as outputs, and usually produces a large number of intermediate representations along the way. Consider again the machine that calculates $x^2 - 1$ in the second way, for instance. It operates on symbols that represent numbers. There are many different languages in which this could be done: Arabic numerals in base ten or base two, Roman numerals, or Chinese numerals. Suppose it does its work with Arabic numerals in base ten. If you type in "11," it will have a processor that produces "12" (i.e., $x + 1$), another that produces "10" (i.e., $x - 1$), and a third that receives these as inputs and yields "120" (i.e., $y \times z$). If the machine operated in base two, then given "11" (representing the number three, not eleven) the first processor will produce not "12" but rather "100." (We leave it as an exercise for the reader to complete the example).

At the syntactic level, we explain how the machine operates in purely formal terms. Nothing at all is said about what any of the symbols mean. The symbols are specified purely in terms of their formal or syntactic properties. Whether they represent numbers or chess moves or the flight paths of aircraft is a matter of indifference. And we are told how the machine works in terms of rules for operating on the symbols as formally defined, in terms of syntactic algorithms. The symbols are like the pieces in a game, and the algorithms are like the rules for moving pieces around and adding new ones. A derivation system in the propositional calculus is like a game for adding representations to a list. You begin with a list of representations. The rules tell you what representation you may write down at the bottom of the list you already have. If you have a representation "p", and a representation "$p \rightarrow q$", then you may write down another token of "q", no matter what "p" and "q" happen to be.

What connects the semantic and syntactic levels, and the functions they instantiate, is a third function, an interpretation function. This last systematically assigns meanings to the formal objects. These three types of functions must be related so that the machine's calculations with the formal system according to the syntactic algorithms achieves the desired result, given the interpretation of the symbols. The symbols in the propositional-calculus derivation game can be interpreted so that it becomes a method for making valid inferences. If you assign the normal meanings to the connective symbols "$\rightarrow$", "$\&$", "$\vee$", and so on, and you make sure that in each derivation the propositional letters "p", "q", etc., receive the same interpretation throughout, then you have a truth-preserving logical system: if the sentences at the top of the list are all true, then every subsequent sentence that you write down by means of the syntactic derivation rules will be true as well.

The third level of description (level 3) is physical. A computer is a physical machine, and its symbols must have some physical realization in the machine. For example, they might be realized by small voltages in silicon chips. A voltage of 0.4 might correspond to the numeral "0", and a voltage of 0.7 to the numeral "1". When the machine performs a computation, the distribution of voltages across the chips will change, and this change will constitute the production of a new set of symbols. Alternatively, the symbols might be physically realized by collections of chalk dust on a blackboard: the machine might consist of a human being, a rule book, a piece of chalk, and the blackboard. The human places marks on the board according to what kinds of marks are already there and what rules are given in the book.

To say that the mind is a computer, or a collection of computers, is to say that it has the semantic, syntactic, and physical properties that relate in the way described above. The symbols will be realized somehow in the brain (perhaps by patterns of synaptic firings), and they will represent the subject matter of our various cognitive capacities. A complete theory of cognitive capacities would encompass all three levels. It would specify the computed functions, the information deployed by the system, a breakdown of the blackbox, the language or languages in which the subject matter is represented, the syntactic algorithms, and the neural realization of the symbols and symbol-processing mechanisms.

There is a serious question as to what confers genuinely intentional (i.e., meaningful) states on a cognitive system. It is reasonable to suppose that the symbols in a pocket calculator only have meaning thanks to us, that they don't have any original or intrinsic intentionality of their own.[24] The states of our brains, however, really do have intentional properties original to them: they mean what they mean, not what someone decides to say they mean. If this is right, then we would ultimately like some account of this difference: why are we genuine intentional systems while pocket calculators are not? A variety of reactions to this question have been offered in the literature, none of which appears wholly satisfactory (as most would admit).[25] The important claim of cognitive science, however, is that brains manipulate representations with genuine semantic properties. It need not in itself be committed to any particular theory of how these properties arise.[26]

13.3.2   Tacit-Rule Following and Computation

The intermediate Chomskyan notion of rule-guidedness and tacit linguistic knowledge can be understood within this general framework. If the computational approach is correct, then linguistics can be seen as one component of cognitive science. Various processors are involved in linguistic tasks. For example, there are presumably one or more processors concerned with interpreting perceived signals (the visual, auditory, and tactile forms of language). These interpretive processors compute a function from the perceived signals to a range of phonological, syntactic, and semantic properties that the signals have. To compute this function, the processors would need access to linguistic rules. This information would be explicitly represented or implicitly present in the processors. Linguistic competence is probably manifested in the computation of other kinds of functions as well. Perhaps speech involves the computation of a function from the thoughts one wishes to express to the physical signals that express them. And language acquisition itself perhaps involves computing a function from perceived speech sounds and their contexts of utterance to facts about language.

If all this is right, then rule-guidedness, tacit knowledge of rules, can be understood in computational terms: to have tacit knowledge of a linguistic rule is to have this rule explicitly or implicitly present in one of your linguistic processors. Attributions of particular systems of linguistic rules would be seen, within this framework, as claims at level 1, claims about what information the linguistic processors use to do such things as determine the structure and meaning of pieces of language.[27] Most of current linguistics is concerned with linguistic rules and would therefore be part of a level 1 theory of language understanding. A complete theory of linguistic competence would offer explanations at the other two levels as well: it would uncover the representational systems used by the processors, and it would explain how the representational systems are physically realized in the brain.

Some linguists and computer scientists are working at level 2: they are attempting to discover the nature of the syntactic algorithms involved in language processing. This is computational linguistics. But it is very important to realize that most of linguistics—most of what is called "generative syntax," "phonology," "morphology," and "semantics"—is not aimed at level 2. It is easy to become confused about this because linguists often do try to present their theories in formal notations appropriate to computation. We ourselves have presented more or less formal theories and derivations throughout this book. The point of this is to demonstrate that the rules we propose are adequate to compute a function from LFs to their interpretations. To do so, it is necessary to formalize the rules in some notation and show that the desired assignments of features can be derived from them. However, we do not intend that the notation of the linguistic theory resemble the representations in our minds, nor that the syntactic algorithms appropriate to the linguistic notation resemble those exploited by the language user. It is the rules represented, not the representations of the rules, that is important. It is what is encoded in the mind, not how it is encoded, that is at issue.

Consider, for example, our production rules such as (SE) and (UI). Strictly speaking, these apply to the syntactic forms of sentences in the metalanguage. Thus (UI) tells us that if we have any sentence of the syntactic form schematically depicted by "For any S, $F(S)$," then we may write down a sentence of the syntactic form schematically depicted by "$F(\alpha)$" (where α stands in for a metalinguistic name of a particular object-language sentence):

(UI) $\underline{\text{For any S, } F(S)}$
         $F(\alpha)$

Our metalanguage is a slightly formalized version of English. The rule (UI) and the other production rules are thus designed to apply to this particular language with its specific syntactic properties. Obviously, such production rules won't apply directly to representations coded in some representational system inside the object-language speaker's brain, with its specific syntactic properties. Rather, the idea is that there are production rules inside the speaker's head that are *semantically equivalent* to those formulated in our metalanguage. Speakers have some representations in their brains that express universal quantifications about object-language sentences and are semantically equivalent to metalanguage sentences of the form "For any S, $F(S)$." And the computational mechanisms inside the speakers' heads infer from these representations other representations expressing claims about particular object-language sentences, these latter representations being semantically equivalent to metalanguage sentences of the form "$F(\alpha)$."

If cognitive science is correct, then we have the desired theory of tacit knowledge of rules. We also have the potential for further confirmation of specific linguistic theories. Such confirmation would be provided by computational theories of the cognitive processors responsible for the deployment of linguistic knowledge. If we knew exactly how these processors work, the syntax of their explicit representations, their overall functional architecture, and their physical composition, we would have the kind of deep confirmation for linguistics that statistical mechanics provides for thermodynamics. If cognitive science is on the right track, then eventually we will have this knowledge.

13.3.3   Against Eliminative Materialism

There is a further important point to be made in favor of cognitive linguistics, with its deployment of tacit-rule following. The point is simply that it is currently the only theory that even begins to offer an account of human linguistic wherewithal. Not only can we stretch and reshape our commonsense idea of rule guidance in our cognitive theory. We must do so. For there is no other theoretical apparatus available with which to address the data. Recall the Feynman (1965) quote above: "We must ... extend as far as we can ... beyond those ideas that we have already obtained.... It is the only way to make progress."

There are those (e.g., Quine [1975] and Churchland [1981]) who hold that we should try to explain all apparently psychological facts in purely neurological terms and avoid any cognitivist notions like tacit knowledge or mental representation. This view is called "eliminative materialism."

This confidence in the possibility of a neurological approach to language is misplaced. To be sure, it is clear that the brain does in fact have a lot to do with linguistic ability, although at present, neurology has very little to say in this domain. Something is known about the areas of the brain that specialize in language. And deficit data point to some interesting connections between the ability to use specific kinds of linguistic structures and the integrity of specific neural structures. Beyond this, neurology is largely silent. Nothing is known about what changes in the brain accompany language acquisition or about the difference between the brain of a Chinese speaker and that of a Turkish speaker. There is nothing that even looks like a nascent neurological theory of language.

It is easy to be misled into thinking that even if there are no neurological explanations of linguistic data at present, such explanations must be possible in principle. One might conclude this on the grounds that the brain is the causal source of all speech, and it is features of speech that we need to explain. But it is important to see that the issue is over which properties of the brain are needed to explain language use and understanding. Brains have all kinds of different properties belonging to the subject matters of many different sciences. The brain has, inter alia, quantum-mechanical properties, thermodynamic properties, evolutionary-biological properties, molecular-biological properties, and neurological properties of many different kinds. And if cognitivism is right, it also has psychological properties, which are essential to the explanation of linguistic competence and which are the subject matter of cognitive linguistics. Eliminativists deny this and hold that only nonpsychological properties of the brain will prove relevant to linguistic competence. But there is no guarantee whatever that nonpsychological properties can do all the work by themselves. We would not expect quantum mechanics or thermodynamics to shed much light on language. What more reason is there to expect that one or another branch of neurology will have adequate resources for the job?

Neurology must eventually, of course, enter into a complete account of linguistic competence. A speaker's brain somehow or other endows the speaker with the ability to understand sentences. But there is no reason to think that the brain's capacity to do this does not involve complex psychological properties. To suppose that we have unconscious knowledge of a semantic theory is to suppose that the brain does its work by containing a representation of this theory and mechanisms that draw upon this representation to yield interpretations of heard utterances. The role of neurology would then be to explain what it is about the brain that constitutes the representations and their deployment.

Noncognitive theories have shown as yet no sign of being able to account for linguistic competence. Nor is there any a priori reason to expect them to do much better in the future. By contrast, cognitive linguistics has a great deal to say about language. The point is not that cognitive theories glow with some irresistible light of plausibility. It is that cognitive linguistics can address a rich array of data that, at least at present, is totally beyond the reach of any alternative theory. It offers the only candidate accounts of the actual details of human languages. It provides, in effect, the only genuine theory of language currently in existence.

It might be objected that this comparison of cognitive linguistics to the alternatives begs the question against the eliminativist. For a consistent eliminativist will reject not only cognitive explanations of linguistic phenomena but also the alleged data to which these are addressed. For these data are themselves described in cognitive jargon: this or that sentence is (un)grammatical or has a certain meaning or is ambiguous, etc. But the status of such alleged facts is itself at issue in the debate. Consequently, the data that cognitive linguistics can allegedly explain does not provide neutral ground on which to judge the competing theories. So goes the objection.

But the objection misses the point. Even eliminativists agree that there are some things to be explained about language. And cognitive linguistics addresses those explananda at a level of depth and detail far beyond any other theory being offered. For example, even the most extreme eliminativist will admit that a remarkable change occurs during the course of language acquisition. Any theory of language must bring this change within its scope. At present, cognitivist linguistics can do this. It can at least produce the outline of a theory of universal grammar with many details fleshed out, and it can provide some fragments of theories about how particular natural languages are generated from universal grammar and its interaction with experience. To be sure, when the linguist explains language acquisition, he or she deploys technical, theory-laden descriptions of the data. But this is a general feature of scientific theories and no peculiarity of linguistics. The linguist's technical descriptions of the data might or might not be adequately motivated, and there might be lengthy arguments on such issues. But the possibility (or actuality) of such arguments does not reduce the extent of the explanatory lead that cognitive linguistics currently has. It has something to say in an area where its competitors are silent.

Of course, being the only theory on the table is not the same as being correct. But it does mean that as long as there exists no principled reason for thinking that the project is doomed to failure, it is worthy of pursuit. Ultimately, a theory must be judged by its successes. If it grows, if disputes get solved, if new predictions are made and verified, and if the theory fits in with other research into the mind/brain, then the theory will be vindicated. If not, it won't. But the only way to make progress is to pursue the theory.

Notes

Chapter 1

1. By "facts" we mean facts or apparent facts. In this section and the next we will sometimes omit the word "apparent" before "facts" and "data" for the sake of brevity.

2. Thematic relations like these are discussed by Gruber (1976), and subsequently in greater detail and depth by Jackendoff (1972, 1976, 1983).

3. In this and the next section we are indebted to Barwise and Perry (1983) and to Lepore (1983).

4. For example, Galileo held that the tides arose from the motion of the Earth, more precisely, from its dual motion about its own axis and about the sun. For a brief history of views on the tides, see Darwin 1898.

5. Here and below we use the terms "knowledge of language" and "knowledge of meaning" to refer to *what* speakers know about their language or about meaning, and not to the mental state they are in when they have this knowledge. For a very useful discussion of this distinction, and of the various confusions that may result when it is ignored, see George 1989.

6. Katz (1972), Partee (1982).

7. Dowty (1979); Dowty, Wall, and Peters (1981); Bach (1989).

8. Katz (1981), Soames (1985). Katz and Soames allow for a research program of "psycholinguistics," which appears to be restricted to the study of the processes underlying knowledge of language, rather than of the content of the knowledge that those processes underlie. For discussion of Soames, see George 1989; for discussion of Katz, see Higginbotham 1983a, 1991b.

9. This discussion is not to object to any of the other disciplines called "semantics," which may be perfectly respectable areas of research in their own right. It is merely

to distinguish our project from others. In chapter 13 we discuss in detail the relationship between the abstract properties of languages and what speakers know.

10. The form of cognitivism that we describe here was developed by Noam Chomsky. Most of the ideas and arguments we present in this section are adaptations of Chomsky's. The application of Chomsky's methodology to semantics in particular has been pursued in a series of articles by Higginbotham, whose ideas we follow in a number of respects (see in particular Higginbotham 1985, 1987, 1991a, 1991b).

11. We explain tree diagrams in detail in chapters 2 and 3.

12. The term "semantic value" was introduced by Dummett (1978) as a technical rendition of Frege's "Bedeutung" (Frege 1893). Frege was the first to develop recursive semantic theories for fragments of languages. His main interest was in providing semantics not for natural languages (a program about which he would have been skeptical) but for constructed formal languages. Nevertheless, his ideas still lead the field in some areas, technical and conceptual.

13. These two sorts of rules are not all that is required for linguistic competence. There are also, for example, phonological rules (for recognizing acoustic forms as elements of language) and morphological rules (for forming complex words from roots and affixes).

14. The acquisition of word meaning has been widely discussed in the psycholinguistics literature. For general discussion, see Clark 1973 and Carey 1978, 1982, 1984, 1985. Keil (1989) discusses children's acquisition of natural kind versus artifact terms. Macnamara (1982) discusses children's acquisition of names. For recent discussion of the acquisition of verbs in relation to syntactic structure, see Landau and Gleitmann 1985, Gleitmann 1990, Naigles 1990, Pinker 1989, and Gropen et al. 1991.

15. The original form of this example is due to Quine (1960, chap. 2).

16. This example and its implications are drawn directly from Gleitman 1990. The reader is referred there for fuller discussion of this and many other interesting examples of environmental underdetermination of predicate meanings.

17. This discussion is drawn from Carey 1984.

18. For an interesting spectrum of views on the so-called **innateness hypothesis** regarding natural language, see the contributions by Chomsky, Piaget, Fodor, and Putnam in Piatelli-Palmerini 1980. These articles are also collected in Beakley and Ludlow 1992.

19. For presentation and discussion of the serial view, see Frazier 1987, 1989. For arguments that parsing is parallel, see MacDonald, Just, and Carpenter 1992. See also the following for arguments that real-world knowledge about events can

affect phrase-structure parsing: Carlson and Tannenhaus 1988, Pearlmutter and MacDonald 1992, Stowe 1989, Tarban and McClelland 1988.

20. For a theory of cognitive processes that make up the gap between context-independent sentence meaning and the interpretation of utterances in particular contexts, see Recanati 1993.

21. This example is from Grice 1975.

22. It is an interesting question to what extent the three kinds of inference are interdependent. It may be, for example, that pragmatic knowledge is sometimes involved in determining the literal meaning of an utterance; for instance, it might help to decide which of two meanings of an ambiguous sentence should be assigned to an utterance. See Sperber and Wilson 1986 for discussion.

23. Invoking modularity in this context carries two main commitments. First, there is commitment to a definite and self-contained set of psychological states that work together to provide the basis for some psychological competence, such as the one that grounds our understanding of the physical world (the physics module), or the mental states of other human beings (the psychology module) This requirement is not trivial: not all cognitive competence will be explainable in this way. There is probably no shopping module or spying module, since these abilities can and must draw on a vast and heterogeneous array of potentially relevant pieces of knowledge.

    Second, there is a commitment to information filtering: some of the information within one module may be unavailable to other modules, or to consciousness. We have already seen this filtering in the fact that information inside our language module is largely tacit and unconscious. Another illustration is provided by visual illusions, such as the familiar Müller-Lyer figures:

(i)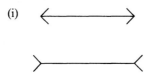

    In this illusion the lower line appears longer than the upper one even though the two are really the same length. Interestingly, the illusion persists even after we convince ourselves that the lines are congruent. This shows that the visual system (the visual module) does not have access to information in the subject's conscious mind. The system continues to construct a representation that presents the lines as being of different lengths despite the countervailing information. As we will see in later chapters, the informational encapsulation of the semantic module plays an important explanatory role.

    The notion of modularity invoked here is different from that in Fodor 1983, from which the Müller-Lyer example is drawn. In fact, there are several different notions of modularity currently used by psychologists. The visual system, for example, is not merely a module in our sense but is also a physical system that receives patterns of light as inputs and constructs representations of the visual world as outputs. Our concept of modularity is probably the least controversial and derives from the work of Freud and Chomsky. See Segal (forthcoming) for discussion of the different kinds of modularity.

24. For a good discussion of the distinction between modular and nonmodular areas of cognition with specific reference to visual perception, see Marr 1977.

25. As far as we understand, Chomsky appears to favor this second possibility. See also Davidson 1986 for a related view.

Chapter 2

1. See, in particular, Davidson 1965, 1967c, 1968, 1970. Our view of the place of T theories in semantics departs significantly from Davidson's in a number of important respects. The formal notion of a T theory originates with Alfred Tarski (1944, 1956).

2. We use the term "relation" loosely. We do not intend to imply that the "*p*" on the right hand side of a T sentence names a state of affairs or proposition or anything that could be considered one relatum of a two-place relation.

3. Since we shall frequently be discussing T sentences and their various parts, it will be useful to introduce some abbreviatory terminology. We will use "LHS" to refer to what appears on the left hand side of the "if and only if" (i.e., "*S* is true") and "RHS" to refer to what appears on the right (what stands in the position occupied by "*p*" in (T)). We will also use "The *S* on the left" to refer to the object-language sentence named on the left. Also, we use italics to display words in the object language, the language under discussion, and we use quotation marks to mention words in the metalanguage, the language being used. In both cases we have language denoting language.

4. The rules in (1) and (2) are formally referred to as **context-free phrase-structure rules**. For more on phrase-structure rules, see chapter 3, section 3.3.2.

5. See chapter 3 for a detailed discussion of phrase markers.

6. More properly, for any phrase markers S, S_1, S_2 whose root node is S. See chapter 3 for more on phrase markers.

7. The qualification "almost" is needed here for at least two reasons. First, some sentences of the form (T*) will be paradoxical rather than true, for example, (ii):

(i) (i) is false.

(ii) *(i) is false* is true iff (i) is false.

Second, object-language sentences with indexicals or demonstratives may falsify (T*) if those words refer to different things in their occurrences on the right- and the left-hand side of the "iff." For example, (iii) can be false if we take the two occurrences of "this sentence" to refer to different sentences:

(iii) *This sentence is on the left-hand side of a biconditional* is true iff this sentence is on the left-hand side of a biconditional.

8. For a different view of the informativeness of homophonic T theorems, see Higginbotham 1989.

9. This is one version of a problem that John Foster (1976) raised for Davidson's original version of the claim that a T theory could serve as a semantic theory.

10. We might also notate this with syntactic turnstiles "$\vdash$" to indicate provability:

(SE) Substitution of equivalents

$$\frac{\vdash F(\alpha) \\ \vdash \alpha \text{ iff } \beta}{\vdash F(\beta)}$$

(SE$'$) Substitution of equivalents, version 2

For any formula β such that α iff β,

$$\frac{\vdash F(\alpha)}{\vdash F(\beta)}$$

11. For logic texts especially directed toward toward linguistics students, see Partee 1978 and Partee, ter Meulen, and Wall 1990.

12. Since $[p \ \& \ q]$ is equivalent to $\neg[\neg p \lor \neg q]$.

13. Truth thus plays very different roles in logic and semantics, despite its central status in both. As Jason Stanley has observed to us, this point entails that it would be misleading to describe a semantic theory as a "logic," or its deductive procedures as "logical inference rules." Such a description would imply the goal of deducing true statements generally, which is not what we are concerned with in semantics. It is likely that a semantic theory will share two important features of standard logical systems: it will be be truth-preserving, and it will be a formal deductive system, in the sense that, for any set of sentences $\{S\}$ and any sentence k of the metatheory, it should be decidable whether k is a consequence of $\{S\}$.

14. Some theorists have addressed the problem of overgeneration by giving the T theory a full set of deductive rules, while permitting only a limited number to appear in the proofs of T theorems (see Davies 1981a). This approach is unsuitable for our purposes, since it is not clear what it would mean for the semantic module to contain deductive rules that are never put to any use.

15. Since we know little about the nature of the processes that deploy the T theorems, we are unable to specify in detail what is involved in their treating the theorems as interpretive. One simple possibility is that the T theorems are fed into a processor that makes the brute inference in (i):

(i) S is true iff p.

S means that p.

The other processors involved in speech, understanding, etc., would receive the outputs of this processor. There are clearly more complex possibilities, however, and we will not speculate on the empirical question of which one is ultimately correct.

16. Notice that part of what's involved in this shift of focus is a move away from the pretheoretical notion of public or communal languages, such as English or French. Public languages do not feature in (29). The concern in (29) is only with what is internalized in the minds of individuals. For ease of exposition, we will continue to talk of, e.g., "English." But this talk is based on the (probably false) assumption that there is a definable, reasonably homogeneous group of individuals collected under the rubric "English speakers." We discuss this point further in chapter 13.

17. The relation between meaning and truth in semantics is analogous, in the respects just discussed, to the relation between acceptability and grammaticality in syntax. Consider the sentences in (i), for instance.

(i) a. *Phil ponders* is an acceptable sentence of English.
    b. *Phil ponders or Chris agrees* is an acceptable sentence of English.

These statements record speaker judgments; they constitute part of the pretheoretical domain of syntax. By contrast, the sentences in (ii) record theoretical results: things that follow as a consequence of an explicit syntactic theory for English.

(ii) a. *Phil ponders* is a grammatical sentence of English.
     b. *Phil ponders or Chris agrees* is a grammatical sentence of English.

Here too the theoretical term ("grammatical") that replaces the intuitive term ("acceptable") describes the data at some remove from what can be directly observed. And here too we find discrepancies between the pretheoretical and theoretical descriptions analogous to those seen in (30) to (32). Consider the sentences in (iii), examples of center embedding with relative clauses.

(iii) a. The woman the girl the man knew knew went home.
      b. The rat the cat the dog worried chased ate the cheese.

Although there are good reasons for wanting principles of grammar to count the examples in (iii) as well formed from a syntactic point of view, native speakers of English are almost unanimous in rejecting of such strings. Judgments of acceptability and deliverances of grammaticality thus part company. Once again, this divergence between grammaticality and acceptability is not a problem for syntactic theory but rather is to be expected, given the gap between competence and performance. And indeed, plausible proposals have been made about the factors responsible for this divergence. Chomsky (1957) suggests that the unacceptability of examples like (iii) results from processing limitations on the ability to apply an operation while the results of that same operation are still being mentally held in store. If this idea is correct, then although the sentences are in fact fully grammatical, they are judged unacceptable because of processing effects.

18. It is important to observe that if we take this general view of ambiguity, then although strings of words may be ambiguous in a language, structural descriptions, i.e., phrase markers, will not be. A structural description will contain sufficient information for a unique T sentence to be proved for it. Thus if T sentences are proved from phrase markers, as in PC, semantic ambiguity will disappear because the structures from which T sentences are proved will themselves be unambiguous.

Notice further that some strings can be assigned two structures though they receive the same or very similar interpretations. For example, (i) can be parsed as either (ii) or (iii), but (ii) and (iii) are logically equivalent:

(i)   The doggy got wet, and the house fell down, and the cow jumped over the moon.

(ii)   [[The doggy got wet and the house fell down] and the cow jumped over the moon]

(iii) [The doggy got wet and [the house fell down and the cow jumped over the moon]]

In view of this it is useful to describe (i) as "structurally ambiguous," and to summarize by saying that whereas all semantically ambiguous expressions are structurally ambiguous in our view, the converse is not true.

19. In fact, its being provable in the T theory that α is true iff it is not the case that β is true is only a *sufficient* condition for α and β to be contradictory. It is not a necessary condition. This does not affect the present point.

20. We discuss commonsense psychology further in chapter 11.

21. The discussion in this section is substantially indebted to Lepore 1983 and Lepore and Loewer 1981, 1983.

22. The Rosetta Stone, discovered at Rashid by Napoleon's defending troops, bore on its face the same text inscribed in three different languages: Egyptian hieroglyphic, heiratic, and demotic Greek. As such it was, in effect, a series of $T^{\dagger}$-like statements correlating sentences of one language with sentences of the other two. The French linguist Jean-François Champollion was able to decipher the previously unknown hieroglyphic writing system precisely because he had disquotational knowledge of one of the three languages, demotic Greek. Without this, the Rosetta stone would

have remained a translation manual between unknown tongues and a frustrating curiosity.

23. The example is from Lycan 1984.

24. (R) is the so-called "Ramsey schema" (Ramsey 1927). T theories employing this schema are discussed by Belnap and Grover (1973), Kripke (1976), Harman (1974), Wright (1981), and Evans (1981). Note that one has to be careful with the way that the quotes are understood in (R). (R) is not to be taken as asserting, "For every sentence *S*, the nineteenth letter of the English alphabet is true if and only if," etc. This is obviously nonsense. Rather, the expression contained within the quotes in (R) must be taken as a simple placeholder for which expressions of a suitable type, here sentences, can be substituted (so-called "substitutional quantification"). Our discussion in this section is indebted to Lepore and Loewer 1983.

25. An example like this, and the points drawn from it, are found in Evans 1981.

26. We appeal to the category clause (Cl) in place of sentence (S) in order to block recursive application of the combination rules, and so confine ourselves to the 24 sentences.

27. See Evans 1981. This paper was written in response to Wright 1981 and inaugurated an interesting series of critical rejoinders and replies to these two papers. For further discussion, see Wright 1981; Davies 1981b, 1987; Peacocke 1986.

28. Davies (1981b) actually produces one such model.

Chapter 3

1. Semantic structure, understood in this way, is also sometimes referred to as "logical form" (see Davidson 1967a, Evans 1976, Platts 1979, and Wiggins 1980a). Since we do not wish to confuse this notion of structure with that implied by the project of logic, we will stick to the more descriptively unambiguous term "semantic structure."

2. This traditional understanding of the term "syntax" contrasts with other broader understandings found in the literature. For example, in some of his writings, Chomsky equates syntax with the study of symbolic systems generally. Under this view, traditional syntax, semantics as pursued here, and phonology as standardly pursued, all qualify as syntax. The issue is purely terminological, and we will stick here to the narrower extension of the term, where syntax is concerned with purely formal principles governing well-formedness, distribution of phrases, possible forms of expression, etc.

3. In more modern times, under the influence of Chomsky, syntactic theory has been reconstrued as the theory of speaker knowledge of natural-language forms. Such knowledge is assumed to include various principles determining how expressions

are structured from their elementary parts (their words and morphemes), how that structure is derived (how it is projected and the transformations it may undergo), what level of acceptability those structures are predicted to have in the judgments of speakers, and so on.

4. For traditional approaches to the study of English syntax, see Burton-Roberts 1986, Huddleston 1982, Quirk et al. 1985. For discussion of syntactic theory within the general Chomskian approach to natural language see Chomsky 1975, 1981, 1986a; Chomsky and Lasnik 1993; Haegeman 1990; Radford 1988.

5. See Russell 1905. For an opposing view, see Etchemendy 1983, 1990.

6. Or rather, a syntactician will be interested in the interpretation insofar as it bears on the form. Thus we saw earlier that ambiguity of meaning in natural language is plausibly analyzed as arising from ambiguity in form. Under this assumption, a syntactician will be be concerned with ambiguity insofar as this always implies a corresponding ambiguity of form.

7. These structures may be generated by the following phrase-structure rules:

    (i) a. S → *Phil ponders*
         b. S → *Jill knows Kate*
         c. S → *Chris agrees*
         d. Conj → *and*
         e. Conj → *or*
         f. Neg → *it is not the case that*

    (ii) a. S → S ConjP
         b. ConjP → Conj S
         c. S → Neg S

8. Structures like (6a) for natural-language conjunctions were originally proposed by Ross (1967) and have been defended more recently by Hale (1992) and Collins (1988).

9. These structures embody so-called "Polish notation" for the connectives.

10. Recall the two theories discussed in section 2.4 of chapter 2.

11. This shows that the properties in question do not necessarily restrict the class of T theorems that can be derived. Rather, they restrict the ways in which we derive them.

12. We will shortly see that it would be more correct to render "Val(t, S)" as "t is *a* semantic value of S," since, in general, expressions can have more than one thing as their values. We thus use the definite description as a temporary expository convenience.

13. For references see n. 4.

14. For a useful presentation of the technical details relating to phrase markers, see Wall 1972. Also helpful is Partee, ter Meulen, and Wall 1990.

15. To adapt from Wall 1972, a phrase marker is a mathematical configuration (N, Q, D, P, L), where

   - N is a finite set (the set of nodes),
   - Q is a finite set (the set of labels),
   - D is a weak partial order in $N \times N$ (the dominance relation),
   - P is a strict partial order in $N \times N$ (the precedence relation),
   - L is a function from N to Q (the labeling function)

   such that the following conditions hold:

   $(\exists x \in N)(\forall y \in N)(x, y) \in D$ (the single root condition)

   $(\forall x, y \in N)(((x, y) \in P \vee (y, x) \in P) \leftrightarrow ((x, y) \notin D \wedge (y, x) \notin D))$
   (the exclusivity condition)

   $(\forall w, x, y, z \in N)(((w, x) \in P \wedge (w, y) \in D \wedge (x, z) \in D) \rightarrow (y, z) \in P)$
   (the nontangling condition)

16. Other verbs assign different thematic roles and different numbers of them; for example, *fall* assigns one role (theme), *annoy* assigns two roles (theme and experiencer), *put* assigns three roles, like *give*, but assigns location in place of goal, and so on. We discuss thematic roles further in chapter 12.

17. There are many subtleties in the application of these principles, of course. Verbs that determine a certain number of thematic roles will allow some arguments to be absent when their content is understood as fixed. Thus although *eat* assigns two thematic roles (agent and patient), it nonetheless permits the bearer of the second role to be formally absent:

   (i) a. John ate an apple.
       b. John ate.

   In this case the object is understood as a meal or some form of food item. Similarly, although *give* assigns three thematic roles, it allows the theme to be absent in certain cases where it understood as referring to money:

   (ii) a. John gave money to charity.
        b. John gave to charity.

   For a fuller discussion of these issues, see Chomsky and Lasnik 1993, Haegeman 1990, van Riemsdijk and Williams 1986.

18. The examples are due to Mark Aronoff and S. N. Sridhar.

19. This is an approximation of the constraints on case assignment assumed in current versions of the principles and parameters theory. For further discussion, see Chomsky and Lasnik 1993, Haegeman 1990, and van Riemsdijk and Williams 1986.

20. In fact, the situation is somewhat more subtle than this. In multiple *wh-* questions, like (i) and (ii), one of the *wh-* words moves between D-structure and S-structure (*who* and *what*, respectively) and the remaining *wh-* word moves between S-structure and logical form (*whom*):

   (i) John wonders who saw whom.
   (ii) Mary asked what John gave to whom.

Chapter 4

1. This point has an interesting consequence in PC+ for cases where a given name such as *Phil* can be used to refer equally to a number of individuals, for instance, Phil Brannigan, Phil Rizutto, or Phil Donahue. In PC+ we are compelled to analyze this as a case of ambiguity, that is, of syntactically distinct proper NPs that happen to be pronounced the same. One way of distinguishing the items is with subscripts, as discussed earlier for *bank₁* and *bank₂*:

   (i) a. Val(x, *Phil$_1$*) iff x = Phil Brannigan
       b. Val(x, *Phil$_2$*) iff x = Phil Rizutto
       c. Val(x, *Phil$_3$*) iff x = Phil Donahue

   With the lexical items distinguished in this way, the requirement of applying to one individual returns. Each proper noun is associated with a condition of singular application.

2. The object dependence of proper nouns is in fact a difficult and complex matter. We will return to it in chapter 5.

3. Gupta (1980) proposes that the distinction be captured by setting the values of common nouns as individual concepts rather than as simple individuals. Individual concepts are, in essence, functions from possible worlds to individuals. We do not develop the apparatus of possible worlds here and so will not attempt to discuss this proposal.

4. These results require us to assume that delineations show a certain kind of consistency. In particular, if there is some delineation for a predicate that Phil meets and that Chris doesn't, there can be no delineation for the predicate that Chris meets and that Phil doesn't. Van Bentham (1983) has referred to this as a "stability principle."

5. The relevant equivalence is the following: for all objects α and predicates F, $\{\alpha\} \subseteq \{y : F(y)\}$ iff $F(\alpha)$.

6. We have relabeled the variables in the lexical axiom for *knows* from $\langle x, y \rangle$ to $\langle r, s \rangle$ in order to avoid any possible confusion with the y and z that already appear in the derivation.

7. The relevant equivalence is the following: for all pairs of objects $\langle \alpha, \beta \rangle$ and relations R, $\langle \alpha, \beta \rangle \in \{\langle x, y \rangle : R(x, y)\}$ iff $R(\alpha, \beta)$.

8. For useful discussion of properties and individuals, see the collection by Loux (1970), and the introductions by Staniland (1972) and Armstrong (1989).

9. Recall our earlier claim that the semantics of predicates is given by a condition of application to objects. We can think of PC^{prop} as an attempt to formalize this idea in a simple and direct way: predicative conditions are reconstrued as Platonic universals, and verbs are held to refer to them.

10. Phrases like "the property of agreeing" and "the relation of knowing" are definite descriptions, whose controversial semantic status we discuss in detail in chapter 9. We are understanding them here as naming a particular property or relation.

11. See Bradley 1930, chap. 3, and Russell 1903, pp. 99–100, for discussion.

12. *Fairly* well understood. See Lewis 1991 for a discussion of some of the conceptual problems.

13. Research continues actively in both areas, however. See, for example, Bealer 1982, 1983, 1989; Chierchia and Turner 1988; Jubien 1989.

14. Evidence like (70) and (71) is sometimes dismissed on the grounds that we can have NPs that appear to refer to a great number of things that don't exist, for example, (i):

    (i) a. The local witch has cursed my cow.
        b. The largest prime number is greater than 101.

    Observe, however, that such examples are simply false, whereas if Chris is happy or if Jill knows Kate, then the examples in (70) and (71) are simply true. More generally, sentences purporting to refer properties and relations are typically judged to be true in just the same circumstances in which their simple predicative counterparts are. There is thus a relation between simple predications and reference to properties and relations that has no parallel with examples like those in (i).

15. Chierchia (1984) provides examples similar to (74b) involving infinitives (i); the general point is the same, however.

    (i) John wants everything Mary wants.
        Mary wants to swim.
        _____
        John wants to swim.

We might also note that there are also paradigms similar to (74b) and (i) that appear to support a PC^{prop}-style theory more directly, for example, (ii):

(ii) John does everything Mary does.
　　 Mary swims.
　　 ————————————
　　 John swims.

We believe that for examples like (i) and (ii) there are alternative analyses in terms of quantification over events instead of quantification over properties. Hence the force of (i) and (ii) is much less than might appear. We introduce the basic elements of event theory in chapter 12.

16. For general discussion, see Caramazza 1988, Shallice 1988, and Ellis and Young 1988. These and the references in the next note are drawn from Carmazza and Hillis 1991.

17. See Warrington 1975; Warrington and Shallice 1984; Warrington and McCarthy 1983, 1987; McCarthy and Warrington 1988, 1990; Basso, Capitani, and Laiacona 1988, Goodglass and Budin 1988; Sartori and Job 1988; Silveri and Gainotti 1988; and Hart, Berndt, and Caramazza 1985.

18. As in PC^{set} generally, (78a, b) will only derive interpretive, *homophonic* T theorems in the presence of additional equivalences from set theory. In this case we need the following:

(i) a. For all x, $x \in X \cap Y$ iff $x \in X$ and $x \in Y$.
　　b. For all x, $x \in X \cup Y$ iff $x \in X$ or $x \in Y$.

19. In fact it is possible technically to analyze t and f as sets, and so bring sentence conjunction under (78). Suppose that we identify f as the empty set $\varnothing$, and we identify t as the universal set $\Im$. Under this idea, we prove statements of the form "Val($\Im$, [$_S$ . . .]) iff . . ." and read them as "[$_S$ . . .] is true if and only iff . . . ." As the reader can show, this view allows (78a, b) to apply correctly to sentence conjunctions and disjunctions. Nonetheless, the assumption that the truth values are sets seems, at the very least, a strange one to be driven to.

20. Again, such an analysis is not impossible to give. If the domain of individuals—including properties, relations, and truth values—is given the structure of a Boolean lattice, it is possible to talk about operations on individuals that are similar to conjunction and disjunction. Furthermore, by defining the truth values as the zero and unity elements of this lattice, the analysis can be generalized to sentence conjunction and disjunction. Again we are compelled to introduce significant metaphysical assumptions about the nature of some objects.

21. For details, see Williams 1983, Stowell 1981, and Kayne 1984.

22. Articulated axioms have played an important part in semantic theories claiming that the class of possible word meanings in English (or any other language) can be

derived from a small set of primitive or "atomic" concepts (see Katz 1972). Such **decompositional** analyses represent one approach to the challenging question of how children manage to learn word meanings so quickly and on the basis of so little evidence. The proposal is that some small set of meanings are unlearned (i.e., innate) and that all other meanings are built up from them by regular semantic operations. A famous example of such decomposition is the verb *kill*, whose meaning was once claimed to be built out of the primitive concepts CAUSE, COME-TO-BE, NOT, and ALIVE. Using axioms like ours, this might be expressed roughly as follows:

(i) Val($\langle x, y \rangle$, *kill*) if x CAUSE [COME-TO-BE [NOT [ALIVE (y)]]]

There are many interesting questions that arise for such an approach, not the least of which is the status of elements like CAUSE, COME-TO-BE, NOT, and ALIVE. The small capitals are intended to show that these are not simply the normal English words "cause," "become," "not," and "alive" but instead elements in a formal theory of concepts. To understand what truth conditions are expressed by a T-sentence like (ii), it is thus necessary to be given some independent account of the semantics of CAUSE, COME-TO-BE, NOT, and ALIVE.

(ii) Val(t, *Kate kills Chris*) iff Kate CAUSE [COME-TO-BE [NOT [ALIVE (Chris)]]]

Lacking this, (ii) is no more intelligible than (iii), where the relevant expressions are replaced by arbitrary typographic signs.

(iii) Val(t, *Kate kills Chris*) iff Kate @ [# [\$ [% (Chris)]]]

At this point there seems to be little agreement among decomposition theorists as to exactly which concepts are the primitive ones.

Chapter 5

1. Throughout this chapter we will accept the intuition that coextensive proper nouns can differ in significance, and we will accept the intuition that empty proper nouns can be meaningful. These decisions are not uncontroversial. Some philosophers follow Mill (1843) in holding that the significance of a name is exhausted by its bearer, and thus appear to disagree with us on both counts. See, e.g., Salmon 1986. However, these philosophers do not regard semantics as a theory of speaker knowledge; hence it is not clear that there is any direct conflict between us. Other philosophers agree with us about coextensive proper nouns but agree with Mill that empty ones are meaningless (see, e.g., Evans 1982 and McDowell 1977). These philosophers are concerned with speaker knowledge, and so are in direct conflict with us. In our view, however, they have no adequate account of the apparent psychological significance of empty proper nouns. See Segal 1989c for further discussion.

2. Another, more technical worry is raised by (8a, b). Axiom (1) identifies the value of *Jill* as the real, existing person Jill. As such, it seems to commit us to the exis-

tence of such a person. If so, then employing (8a, b) would seem to commit us to something false, namely the real existence of Vulcan and Paul R. Zwier.

Standard logical systems forbid the logical equivalent of empty proper nouns precisely because their inclusion would lead to invalid inferences under well-accepted rules of inference. For example, consider the rule of existential generalization (EG) and the already familiar rule of universal instantiation (UI):

(EG) Existential generalization

$$\frac{F(\alpha)}{\text{For some } x, \, F(x)}$$

(UI) Universal instantiation

$$\frac{\text{For all } x, \, F(x)}{F(\alpha)}$$

(EG) allows one to infer a general existential sentence from a singular sentence involving a proper noun. For instance, we would normally take (i.a) to entail (i.b), a result that follows by (EG).

(i) a. Phil ponders.
    b. Something ponders.

But, importantly, if a logic is allowed to contain empty terms, then the two rules, together with standard logical tautologies, will conspire to yield invalid inferences. The argument in (ii) was given by Burge (1974b):

(ii) a. For all x, $x = x$ (tautology)
    b. Vulcan $=$ Vulcan (by (ii.a), (UI))
    c. For some x, $x = $ Vulcan (by (ii.b), (EG))

The premise (ii.a) is surely true. However, the conclusion, (ii.c), is false. From a true premise we thus draw a false conclusion.

Equally, within a T theory containing axioms for empty proper nouns like (8a, b) we can derive invalid results by the rule (EG). From (iii.a) we can conclude the illegitimate (iii.b), which asserts that there is an object that *Vulcan* has as its semantic value:

(iii) a. Val(x, *Vulcan*) iff $x = $ Vulcan
    b. For some y, Val(x, *Vulcan*) iff $x = y$ (by (iii.a), (EG))

In general, a logic for empty singular terms is called a **free logic** and contains modifications of standard logical systems designed to block inferences like that in (ii). Our own metatheory, the axioms of PC+ plus the production rules, is not a logical system. As we explained in chapter 3, semantic theories of the kind we develop in this book are not designed for the study of truth, validity, consistency, and so on. Rather, they are systems that ascribe semantic properties to various elements of the object language and generate statements about their semantic properties. Nonetheless, our T theory does resemble a free logic insofar as it blocks the unwanted inferences through its extremely restricted deductive means. Of the apparatus noted above, PC+ contains only (UI). It contains no tautologies as separate axioms, nor does it contain (EG). Consequently, the inference in (ii) is blocked both by the absence of the initial premise, necessary in the first step, and by the unavailability of (EG), necessary in the last. Likewise, the move from (iiia) to (iiib) is blocked by the unavailability of (EG).

As far as we are aware, PC+ is sufficiently limited to disallow any of the undesirable inferences that free logics are designed to block. Hence PC+-style axioms for empty proper nouns do *not* commit us to the existence of nonexistent things. Adding (8a, b) to PC+ does not entail the existence of Vulcan or Paul R. Zwier.

3. The descriptive-name analysis of proper nouns was first put forward by Russell in his seminal 1905 paper "On Denoting." The form in which we have adopted it here departs from Russell's own formulation to some extent.

4. A prime number is a number divisible only by itself and 1. An even number is a number that is divisible by 2. Only 2 meets both these conditions, hence it is the only even prime.

5. This response is sometimes questioned on grounds of circularity. But the circularity does not seem to be vicious. After all, bearing a name like *Isaac Newton*, *Michael Faraday*, *James Maxwell*, etc., is fundamentally a nonsemantic matter. Surnames are acquired by standing in a particular genealogical relation to someone of the ascendant generation (usually a parent). Given names are acquired at a baptismal of some kind or on a birth certificate, and are typically given by someone of the ascendant generation. When we know of someone that they were called *a*, this knowledge does not presuppose what we are trying to state in the axioms for *a*.

6. See Searle 1958 for a version of this view.

7. There are many parallels in the analysis of how words are related to things and the analysis of how thoughts are related to things. In particular, there are interesting parallels between the descriptive-name analysis of proper nouns and the **mental-image analysis of thoughts**. On the descriptive-name analysis, a proper noun stands for a thing in virtue of being associated with a condition that describes the thing. On the mental-image analysis, a thought stands for a thing in virtue of being associated with an image that resembles the thing. Thus my thought of snow is supposed to be (associated with) a mental image of snow. Interestingly, a number of Kripke's arguments against the descriptive theory of proper nouns closely parallel classical arguments against mental images and the resemblance theory of thought.

8. Some philosophers like to draw a distinction between "conceptual" and "subconceptual" cognition. Conceptual cognition is conscious, while subconceptual cognition is unconscious. These philosophers and psychologists might object to our talk of the semantic module, a subconceptual system, deploying concepts. We

doubt that any such distinction is necessary in linguistics or psychology. But in any event, it is not one that matters to the particular use of concepts that we wish to make.

9. The notion of a dossier we employ here is similar to that in Evans 1973, Perry 1980, and Recanati 1993. Also related is the idea of a **file** from discourse-representation theory (see Kamp 1981; Heim 1982, 1983).

10. In talking about dossiers, we are not talking about something that determines what object a name refers to. We are not claiming that a name refers to an object when and only when all the information in the associated dossier is true of the object. Typically, some of what's in the dossier will be misinformation about the bearer of the name. For reasons we will spell out later, this means that we cannot take the information in the dossier to be responsible for fixing the referent of the name.

11. It would be a mistake to insist that the full theory has to provide the resources to tell in every single case whether a given person has a concept underlying his or her use of a name. There might well be a residue of genuinely borderline cases. This is normal for science and is no embarrassment. We will return to the general nature of concepts and speaker knowledge in chapter 13.

12. See Evans 1973 for substantial contributions.

Chapter 6

1. Actually this is not quite true. The truth of *Arnold is big* will depend on when the sentence is uttered. What this shows is that sentence tense also incorporates an element of variable reference. We will ignore tense for the present and return to it in chapter 12.

2. Similarly for the other singular pronouns *her* and *him*, and for the demonstrative *this*. There is a technical point to notice here. On the LHS of the axioms in (12) the subscript i is standing in for a numerical index on an expression. Thus by he_i we mean the pronoun *he* indexed by any numeral i. On the RHS i talks not about numerical indices (part of the object language) but numbers: "$\sigma(i)$" means the ith object in sequence σ, where i is a number. In view of this, it would be more correct technically to replace (12a) with something like the following: "If n is a number and i is a numeral that names n, Val(x, he_i, σ) iff $x = \sigma(n)$ for all $n \geq 1$."

3. Strictly speaking, this claim demands a proof by induction on sentences. The proof is simple and directly analogous to that found in standard logic texts for the independence of truth values from sequence values for closed sentences of first-order logic.

4. The use of conditional T sentences in interpreting demonstratives was first proposed by Weinstein (1974) and Burge (1974a). See also Taylor 1980 and Lycan 1984 for useful discussion.

5. Once again, deriving these results will involve appeal to inference rules that are not strictly part of the semantics module.

6. Sequences can thus be defined as functions from the positive integers to entities.

7. Sequences thus become functions from the union of the first r letters of the alphabet and the positive integers to entities.

Chapter 7

1. As discussed in chapter 3, the inaudible character of LF representations in the principles and parameters theory is a result of the general organization of the grammar, as given in (i):

   (i)   D-structure
                     $\downarrow$
       PF $\leftarrow$ S-structure $\rightarrow$ LF

   D-structures, which are a pure representation of grammatical relations, give rise to S-structures by means of the rule move α. S-structures are then mapped both to PF (phonetic form) and to LF (logical form). Because only the S-structure is mapped to PF, and not the D-structure or LF, the latter two levels of representation are inaudible.

2. We have altered the category labels in (8b) from those actually given in Kiss 1986. For Kiss, only the highest node in (8b) is labeled S; all of the other instances of S are labeled VP. This revision does not affect the point at issue here, which is that representations involving adjoined quantifiers seem to be available in Hungarian.

3. This is essentially the "substitutional" analysis of quantification. For discussion, see Kripke 1976.

4. For analyses along these lines, see Evans 1977 and Davies 1981a.

5. This point is made in Davies 1981a and Ludlow 1982.

6. See Baldwin 1975, Evans 1977, Davies 1981a for discussion.

7. Axiom (15) is essentially identical to the proposals for the logical form for quantification made by Keenan (1971) and Evans (1977).

8. Partee (1973, n. 3) credits Tarski with the observation that substitutional approaches to quantification (like those discussed here) are noncompositional. The point is also made by Janssen (1986).

9. The semantic analysis of quantification developed in this section is based on Baldwin 1975. See also Chierchia and McConnell-Ginet 1990 for remarks in a similar spirit.

10. In the sequences pictured in table 7.1 and elsewhere in the chapter, we suppress the initial, alphabetically ordered positions associated with fixed utterance roles. Since these are not involved in quantification or sequence variation, the simplification is harmless.

11. The proof is by induction on sentence complexity. For a useful discussion of induction and proofs by induction, see Bergman, Moor, and Nelson 1980.

12. The tripartite division of quantification is introduced in Lewis 1975 and heavily stressed in so-called discourse representation theory (Heim 1982).

13. See, for example, May 1985.

14. Notions of structural prominence have been widely discussed in the linguistics literature, beginning with Klima 1964. The notion of c-command is standardly attributed to Reinhart (1976), although the version adopted here is not Reinhart's own.

15. See, for example, Hornstein 1984; May 1985; Aoun and Li 1989, 1993 for versions of the Scope Principle.

16. See, for example, Lasnik and Saito 1984 for a discussion of this analysis of topicalization.

17. For further discussion and justification of this general analysis of relatives, see Chomsky 1977, Haegeman 1990, Radford 1988, and van Riemsdijk and Williams 1986.

Chapter 8

1. Rescher (1962) and Wiggins (1980a) discuss the need for a relational analysis of determiners in the semantic treatment of natural-language quantifiers like *most* (which resist a first-order analysis). See also subsequent work by Barwise and Cooper (1981), Higginbotham and May (1981), and Keenan and Stavi (1986). Frege himself never pursued the relational analysis formally. Since the technical resources would have been obvious to him, his not having done so is conspicuous. Presumably, Frege thought of the relational terminology as no more than helpful intuitive shorthand. Frege's official account is always both first-level (that is, in terms of objects rather than concepts) and unary (that is, a quantifier always combines with a single complex predicate expression, rather than a pair of predicate expressions).

2. Within generalized quantification theory, the notion of a quantifier is very broadly defined. Essentially, anything corresponding to a predicate of sets counts as a quantifier:

Informal definition α is a generalized quantifier $=_{df}$ α is a predicate of sets.

The idea is that a quantifier is a "predicate of predicates" taking things like VPs as arguments.

3. "$|X|$" is understood in the usual way as denoting the cardinality of the set X, that is, the number of members in X. For a useful discussion of elementary notions from set theory, see Allwood, Anderssen, and Dahl 1977.

4. Since the relations and operations of set theory (subset, superset, intersection, union, difference, etc.) are all defined in terms of individuals and the membership relation, (30a, b), and since set-membership statements of the form "$\alpha \in \{x : \Phi(x)\}$" are all equivalent to simple predications involving individuals, (30c, d), it follows that all T sentences involving set-theoretic relations in GQ will be eliminable in favor of simple predications involving individuals.

5. Note that in (23), the membership condition of the set $\{\sigma'(i) : \text{Val}(t, S_1, \sigma')\}$ involves implicit universal quantification over the objects $\sigma'(i)$, and not over sequences per se.

6. Movement is string-vacuous if it does not change the surface order of elements in a sentence.

7. We are indebted here to discussion with Peter Ludlow.

8. The invalidity of (46b) is straightforward. To see the invalidity of (47b), consider a situation in which many strangers pass by, the vast majority of whom are non-curious. Suppose that John readily talks to these reticent strangers but will not speak to the curious ones. In this situation John often talks to strangers but does not often talk to curious strangers; indeed, he never does.

9. The result that *the* turns out strong in the Barwise and Cooper's (1981) analysis follows from the rather different semantic rule they assign to the determiner. Whereas GQ contains (i) (and so classifies *the* as weak), Barwise and Cooper's proposal is equivalent to (ii):

(i) $\text{Val}(\langle X, Y \rangle, \textit{the}, \sigma)$ iff $|Y - X| = 0$ and $|Y| = 1$

(ii) $\text{Val}(\langle X, Y \rangle, \textit{the}, \sigma)$ iff $|Y - X| = 0$, where $|Y| = 1$

The significance of the "where" clause may be understood as follows: the binary set-relation *the* is taken to be defined only over pairs $\langle X, Y \rangle$ whose second member has a cardinality of 1. For other pairs whose second member is not of cardinality 1, the relation is neither true nor false but rather *undefined* (which may be regarded as a third truth value). Given this, sentences with *the* will yield a determinate truth value only when the set corresponding to N' is nonempty and has cardinality of 1. Accordingly, when they have a defined truth value, sentences of form (iii) will always come out true, and *the* will be classified as strong.

(iii) a. The N' is an N'.
     b. The N's are N's.

10. Keenan's operations are the standard Boolean set operations of union, intersection, and complement.

11. Examples exhibiting no surface predicate (Pred) such as *There is no beer* or *There are few possibilities* (62a–b) may be assumed to contain an implicit predicate equivalent to the prepositional phrase *in existence*.

12. In fact, the result is not fully general but only holds for a particular class of determiners, "conservative" determiners. However, all the determiners we have so far considered are conservative. The result follows from an axiom for interpreting existential constructions together with a particular feature of conservative determiners. For details, see Barwise and Cooper 1981.

13. Of course, the sentence on the LHS of (65a) is ill formed. The idea is that if one were to ignore the ill-formedness and apply the semantic rules to the structure, these rules would generate truth conditions equivalent to those of *Every man is a man*.

14. The notions of definiteness and indefiniteness as defined by the partitive construction and as defined by the *have* and *there be* constructions clearly differ in important respects. For example, NPs containing *most* count as definite in the *have* and *there be* paradigms (see (48g) and (49g)) but as indefinite in the partitive paradigm (see (67g)).

15. More precisely, the weak-crossover constraint forbids a moved operator from simultaneously binding its trace (t_i) and a pronoun (*pronoun$_i$*) that fails to c-command the trace.

16. It is important distinguish reading (87b) from the very different reading in (*i*):

    (i) Only for $x =$ Jill, Jill's mother loves x.

    The latter does not involve variable binding of the pronoun by the quantifier and is not excluded by the weak-crossover constraint.

17. This observation originates with Lindström (1966) and has been developed by a number of subsequent authors, including Higginbotham and May (1981) and Sher (1991). We are particularly indebted to Sher in this section.

18. The quantifier in (98b) corresponds to the boldfaced portion in a sentence like ***There are fewer*** men ***than objects that*** *fly*.

19. This observation is due to Zwarts (1983).

Chapter 9

1. In the predicate calculus, (3b) is rendered as in (i):

    (i) $(\exists x)\ (Fx\ \&\ (\forall y)(Fy \to x = y)\ \&\ Gy)$

2. The GQ axiom for definite descriptions is essentially the same as those proposed in Barwise and Cooper 1981 and Higginbotham and May 1981. See also Evans 1982, chap. 2; Davies 1981a, chap. 7; May 1985; Neale 1990a.

3. Examples like (15a–c) raise problems for an alternative theory of the definite/ indefinite contrast, according to which definites are appropriate for referring to individuals that are *familiar* in the discourse context, whereas indefinites are appropriate for referring to individuals that are *new* or *unfamiliar* (the so-called "familiarity theory of definiteness"). The compatibility of superlatives with definites versus indefinites seems to have nothing to do with the relative familiarity of the denoted individual. The issue appears to be uniqueness, as predicted by Russell's account.

4. The structures in (19) reflect the Stowell and Couquaux analysis of predicative *be* constructions in which *be* underlyingly takes a clauselike complement whose subject raises to becomes the subject of the upper clause. On this analysis, *John is tired* is projected initially as (i):

(i) *e* be [John tired]]

The subject of the embedded clause then raises at surface form to the subject position (*e*) of the matrix clause:

(ii) [John be[*t* tired]]

In (19) this raising involves movement over the modal element *might*, and hence an alteration of scopal relations. See Stowell 1978 and Couquaux 1982 for further details.

5. This point is emphasized in Kaplan 1972.

6. A number of authors have proposed that nominal phrases have a different internal structure, and indeed even a different category, when they occur as arguments versus predicates. For example, de Hoop (1992) proposes that nominals are DPs ("determiner phrases") when they occur as arguments but NPs when they occur as predicates. See also Mandelbaum 1994.

7. See Sainsbury 1979, Davies 1981a, and Neale 1990a for arguments along these lines.

8. Examples (56a, b) are particularly revealing, since they have demonstrative phrases within the existential *be* and *have* constructions in positions typically reserved for indefinites.

9. This example is discussed in Wilson 1978.

10. See Evans 1973, 1982, for discussion of these matters.

11. Use of a demonstrative to refer to different individuals typically involves different indices (e.g., *that*$_{14}$ *man* versus *that*$_{31}$ *man*). Hence it follows that homophonous proper NPs referring to different individuals will be distinguished syntactically on the Burgean account (e.g., THAT$_{14}$ *Kate* versus THAT$_{31}$ *Kate*), as in PC+. Nonetheless, unlike the case of PC+, this structural ambiguity does not correspond to a genuine semantic ambiguity. Demonstratives are not ambiguous in virtue of referring to various objects; rather, they have a fixed meaning that allows their reference to vary with sequences of evaluation. Accordingly, even when THAT$_{14}$ *Kate* and THAT$_{31}$ *Kate* refer to different individuals, this difference does not amount to two different meanings for the NP in question. We are not dealing with ambiguity here but with familiar variable reference.

Chapter 10

1. The general threefold classification of anaphora derives from the work of Evans (1977, 1980) and Higginbotham (1983b). The term "argument anaphora" is adopted directly from Higginbotham 1983b.

2. As we saw in chapter 9, exercise 2, axioms for predicate descriptions can also be applied to definite NPs in argument positions.

3. This suggestion parallels one made by Lycan (1984).

4. Lasnik (1976) suggests this view.

5. Theories similar to that of Evans (1977, 1980) are put forward by Jackendoff (1972), Barwise and Perry (1983), and especially Higginbotham (1983b, 1985). These authors adopt a primitive notion of antecedence in the form of a "table of coreference" (Jackendoff), "antecedence features" (Barwise and Perry), or a linking relation (Higginbotham). We will not attempt to discuss these related proposals here but will confine ourselves to Evans's account. To our knowledge, his account represents the most semantically detailed and explicit version of this general family of proposals.

6. The formal notion of antecedence may be defined via chaining as follows:

   Definition α is the antecedent of β iff there is a chain with head at α and tail at β.

7. This result can illustrated informally by considering a conjunction like *No man smiled, and he sat down* under the chained representation in (i):

(i)

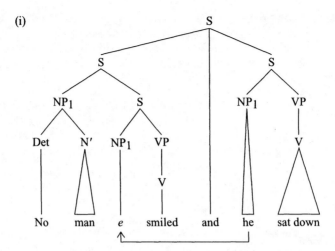

Note that in this structure *no man* fails to c-command *he*, although its trace is in a chain with the latter. In PredC, (the equivalent of) this representation receives the T sentence in (ii):

(ii) Val(t, *No man$_1$ t$_1$ smiled, and he$_1$ sat down*, σ) iff for no σ′ ≈$_1$ σ such that σ′(1) is a man, σ′(1) smiled and σ(1) sat down.

Here "σ(1) sat down" is outside the scope of the quantification over sequences in the first conjunct. Similar results hold for GQ.

8. In Evans 1977, 1980, the chain relation appears to operate wholly internally to sentences. That is, the chaining rule is a rule of sentence grammar. The related "linking theory" of Higginbotham 1983b appears to lift this restriction. Hence Higginbotham's theory is more similar to the sequence view than Evans's own analysis. The restriction must be lifted in view of Higginbotham's analysis of examples like (i.a), which forbid a "circular reading" in which *his wife* is the antecedent of *her* while, simultaneously, *her husband* is the antecedent of *his*. Higginbotham rules this out by proscribing anaphoric linking of the kind indicated in (i.b):

(i) a. His wife loves her husband.

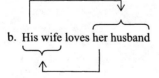

    b. His wife loves her husband

As it turns out, however, circular reference similar to that in (i.a) is also excluded across discourse:

(ii) His wife came in. Her husband was angry.

Hence if Higginbotham's account is to extend to this case as well, linking must plainly be allowed to cross sentence boundaries.

9. It should be noted that this statement does not fully reflect Evans 1977, 1980, in that Evans urges a Fregean approach to the quantifier-trace relation, which is technically different from the Tarskian approach, involving sequences, adopted here. However, this difference does not affect the present point, which is that the syntax and semantics of the two relations is quite different for Evans. It is also worth noting that other Evansesque theories depart from Evans on this point. Thus Higginbotham (1983b) uses a linking relation that is notationally quite similar to Evans. However, this relation is used to represent both the relation between a quantified expression and its trace and that between an anaphoric expression and its antecedent. Hence the separation of the two relations is less decisive than in Evans 1977, 1980.

10. See Fiengo and May 1993.

11. This view is disputed in recent work by Fiengo and May (1993). However, we will assume here that the Lasnik and Reinhart claim is fundamentally correct.

12. Our explication here roughly follows the proposals in Heim 1982 with various differences of detail that are irrelevant for our purposes. It is worth noting that the structures given here (and in Heim 1982) raise a number of important syntactic questions. Thus in (94) it may be fairly asked how the quantified frequency adverb, which appears in the matrix S* in surface form, always obtains its wide scope at LF without leaving a trace in S*. To our knowledge, no serious discussion of the derivation of such LFs has been given within the literature on the NQI theory.

13. As mentioned in note 12, it is not entirely trivial to license such LFs within modern syntactic theory. Determiners like *no* are lexical categories, and current principles within the extended standard theory prohibit such elements from being directly adjoined to a phrasal category such as S.

14. This representation is somewhat simplified. On the normal reading of (106a), the second-person *you* is understood generically and hence as as ranging over various individuals. On a more adequate representation, the pronoun would presumably also be bound by the quantifier "∀."

15. For a more fully worked out version of the unselective theory employing LFs similar to those given here, see Heim 1982. For related recent work on the binding of indefinites, see also Heim 1990 and the papers in Reuland and ter Meulen 1987.

16. The earliest explicit discussion of the proportion problem that we are aware of is Richards 1984.

17. See Parsons 1978 for an approach along these lines.

18. See Cooper 1979 for an approach along these lines.

19. This rule is also equivalent to the principle (P5$_a$) in Neale 1990a, p. 182. See below.

20. Some problems with this general proposal are discussed in Neale 1990a and Heim 1990.

21. For a useful discussion of the uniqueness problem and many of the connecting empirical issues, see Kadmon 1987.

22. The idea of numberless pronouns is briefly discussed in Davies 1981a and developed in considerable detail in Neale 1990a.

23. This idea is discussed in Berman 1987, Heim 1990, and Ludlow 1994a. See Ludlow 1994a in particular for answers to problems for event quantification raised by Heim (1990).

24. The exact nature of the relation R is taken to vary according to context.

Chapter 11

1. The semantic intricacies of clausal complements were first noted by Frege (1893).

2. For the present we abstract away from questions regarding the exact category of complement clauses (S versus IP versus CP) and additional elements of structure that might be present beyond the S node (complementizers, etc.). (Here "IP" stands for "inflectional phrase," and "CP" stands for "complement phrase.") This abstraction appears harmless to the central points discussed in this chapter.

3. The situation here is similar to one encountered with PC′ in chapter 3. Recall that to proceed beyond (i) to (ii), we required a special production rules for disjunction, namely the one in (iii):

    (i)   Val(t, [$_S$ [$_{S_1}$ Phil ponders] [ConjP [Conj or] [$_S$ Chris agrees]]]) iff for some z, z', Val(z, [$_S$ Phil ponders]) and $z = t$ or $z' = t$ and Val(z', [$_S$ Chris agrees])

    (ii) Val(t, [$_S$ [$_S$ Phil ponders] [ConjP [Conj or] [$_S$ Chris agrees]]]) iff Val(t, [$_S$ Phil ponders]) or Val(t, [$_S$ Chris agrees])

    (iii) (DJ) Disjunction

    $$\frac{\phi \text{ iff for some } x, y, \text{ Val}(x, S_1) \text{ and Val}(y, S_2), \text{ and } x = t \text{ or } y = t}{\phi \text{ iff either Val}(t, S_1) \text{ or Val}(t, S_2)}$$

4. The proof of this claim is left as an exercise for the reader.

5. Davidson himself does not hold a quotational theory. On his view, the object of the report is not a sentence but an utterance, which is an event of uttering. See Segal 1989a and Burge 1986b for discussion.

6. This point is made by Partee (1979).

7. See Hintikka 1962, 1969, and Montague 1974 for representative work on clausal-complement semantics within the possible-worlds approach.

8. This theory has been reconstructed in modern times in the situation semantics of Barwise and Perry (1983), and in work by Salmon (1986), Soames (1987), and Richard (1990).

9. This example is drawn from Larson and Ludlow 1993.

10. Various attempts have been made to address this problem for propositional theories. See, for example, Cresswell 1985 and Salmon 1986.

11. The idea of semantically divorcing embedded and unembedded contexts is not unprecedented. In fact, Frege, whose theory of sense we encountered in chapter 5, made just this kind of proposal. Frege (1893) suggests that phrases take their ordinary semantic values in unembedded contexts but refer to their senses in embedded contexts. By adding properties and relations for clausal complements, we would be doing something similar.

12. ILF theories originate with Harman (1972) and have been developed by Higginbotham (1986b), Segal (1989a), and Larson and Ludlow (1993).

13. In fact, although the question of the relation of concept possession to language is not strictly a semantic one, we do address it in chapter 13.

14. To simplify the syntax of this example, we omit the modal from the ILF.

15. Our deployment of the idea that sentences express attitudes is a variant of Davidson's use of "samesaying" mentioned in section 11.2.1. We prefer our expression, since it is not clear whether a sentence can samesay with a belief or desire.

16. See exercise 6 for a potential problem with this proposal.

17. The relevance of phonological information is also correctly predicted by quotational theories.

    Larson and Ludlow (1993) take phonological information to be a part of the lexical information present in a phrase marker, and hence part of their ILFs. The claim is debatable, however, and the issue is subtle one. Much depends on the notion of a lexical item that is relevant to phrase markers, and it is at least arguable that phrase markers do not contain phonological information. Furthermore, under the general model of syntactic organization sketched in chapter 3, it is certainly the true that *some* aspects of phonological interpretation are not represented at LF, since grammatical derivations branch into separate PF (phonological form) and LF (logical form) representations:

(i)   D-structure
                  ↓
      PF ← S-structure   → LF

Any phonological properties imposed in the derivation after the branch to PF will be invisible to LF, and hence absent from ILFs under the Larson and Ludlow (1993) algorithm.

18. There is extensive work in developmental psychology that supports this view. See, e.g., Baron-Cohen 1994, Gopnik and Wellman 1992, Leslie 1994, Segal 1996, Perner 1991, Wellman 1990.

19. See Larson and Ludlow 1993 for a proposal.

20. See Larson and Ludlow 1993 for a proposal.

21. See Segal 1989a for discussion.

Chapter 12

1. Standard evidence for the VP-adjoined position of VP adverbs is that they can either be deleted or stranded by VP ellipsis, (i.a, b), and that they can be carried forward with the verb phrase in VP fronting, (ii):

    (i) a. Chris arrived recently/late, and Jill did [$_{VP}$ *e*] too.
         b. Chris arrived recently/late, and Jill did [$_{VP}$ [$_{VP}$ *e*] late/early].

    (ii) Chris said he would arrive late, and [$_{VP}$ arrive late] he did.

2. In evaluating the examples in (11a–c), care must be taken not to read the doubled phrases as parentheticals ("Chris, the student") or as modifiers ("baby Alice"). The latter have a very different semantics than arguments.

3. Actually, this isn't quite sufficient. Chris's arrival and being late are contemporaneous—something not expressed by the simple conjunction. See section 12.5.1.

4. Barry Schein points out to us that there is a third reading of this example in which *late*, on its "later than expected" reading, is predicated of Chris's arrival. Accordingly, the "late in the day" versus "later than expected" dichotomy does not quite correlate with adverbial versus copredicational interpretation. The presence of this additional reading is irrelevant to the point we are pursuing here, and we will ignore it henceforth.

5. See Davidson 1967a.

6. This analysis has been extensively developed in Parsons 1980, 1985, 1989, and especially 1990. We are heavily indebted to Parsons 1990 in the discussion that follows.

7. Thematic relations like these were first discussed by Gruber (1976), and subsequently in greater detail and depth by Jackendoff (1972, 1976, 1983).

8. This is not to say such parallelisms *cannot* be expressed in a theory without thematic roles. One approach would be through meaning postulates, along the lines of Dowty 1979.

9. The claim of a change in agency in (60) is supported by other linguistic data. Consider the behavior of adverbs like *voluntarily* or *willingly*, which preferentially associate with an agent phrase. In (i.a), Ernie is the one understood as having acted voluntarily. By contrast, in (i.b) *voluntarily* is understood as associated with Kermit, not Ernie:

    (i) a. Ernie bought the block from Kermit voluntarily.
        b. Kermit sold the block to Ernie voluntarily.

10. The view that "psych verbs" like *please, frighten,* and *annoy* involve a subject that is an underlying object was proposed by Postal (1971) and has been defended more recently by Belletti and Rizzi (1988). The position remains a controversial one, however.

11. Correlations between thematic roles and grammatical roles have been proposed to explain a wide variety of phenomena. See, for example, the analysis of Tagalog lexical processes in Carrier-Duncan 1985, English double objects in Larson 1988, nominalizations and experiencer constructions in Grimshaw 1990. Also useful in this context is the general discussion in Rosen 1984.

12. See also Chierchia 1984 and Dowty 1989 for similar ideas. URTR might appear to encounter problems with examples like (i), where Kate and Jill are understood as jointly lifting the piano; such examples seem to involve multiple Agents for the same event:

    (i) Kate and Jill lifted a piano.

    There are at least two different plausible approaches to such examples that avoid any violation to URTR.

    On the analysis of Link (1983) the subject of (i) refers to a plural individual represented formally as the lattice-theoretic join of the individual Kate and the individual Jill. It is this plural individual that is the Agent of piano lifting, not either of its constituent individuals.

    On the analysis of Schein (1993), the event of piano lifting is the mereological sum of events in which Kate was the unique Agent and Jill was the event individual. One way to paraphrase this informally is to say that Jill did something and Kate did something, and those events, taken together, constituted a lifting of the piano.

    For present purposes, the important point is that on neither Link's nor Schein's analysis of (i) is there a violation of URTR.

13. URTR also forbids us from combining events in any simple fashion. For example, it is intuitively plausible to think of a large complex event, for example, a battle,

as composed of many subevents: skirmishes, individual encounters, etc. If x is an Agent in a subevent, it might seem natural to regard x as an Agent in the larger event of which it is a part. URTR forbids this, however. Since events can have at most a single Agent, agency cannot be inherited upward from subevents to superevents.

14. In evaluating this evidence, one must be careful to control for shifts in verb meanings. For example, *know* has both the stative meaning of possessing information or understanding (about something) and the nonstative meaning of coming to possess information or understanding (about something). It is the latter, nonstative meaning that appears in famous examples like (i):

(i) Know thyself!

15. There may be sources of oddness in these examples beyond the eventive/stative distinction. For example, it seems that in addition to requiring an eventive verb, *deliberately* and *carefully* must also have an animate subject. Thus (i) is odd, as indicated by the " # ", even though it involves the eventive *travel*.

(i) #The train deliberately/carefully traveled to Paris.

16. As characterized here, the distinction between eventives and statives resembles the familiar distinction between telic and atelic predicates. The two are not coextensive, however, and should not be confused. As Barry Schein notes to us, the telic/atelic distinction is revealed by the contrast between "in an NP" (telic) and "for an NP" (atelic):

(i) a. *Mary was running in ten minutes.
    b. Mary was running for ten minutes.

The eventive/stative distinction is revealed by the contrast between taking the progressive (eventive) and rejecting it (stative):

(ii) a. Mary was running.
     b. *Mary was knowing the answer.

Our exposition here follows Parsons (1990), who uses Cul and Hold to distinguish eventives and statives. This has the interesting consequence that atelic eventive verbs like *run* are properly analyzed as referring to culminating processes. See Parsons 1990 for justification of this result, and for further discussion of process verbs.

17. These truth conditions evidently ignore the contribution of the past and present tenses. We take up the issue of tense in section 12.5.

18. We also need to accommodate the temporal connection that holds between Chris's arrival and his happiness. We discuss this point in section 12.5.1.

19. See, for example, Siegel 1976a, 1976b; Platts 1979; Higginbotham 1985, among others.

20. The capitalized arguments "*Person*" and "*Dancer*" may be thought of as denoting the attributes of being a person and being a dancer. Thus (97b) is read as "Olga is beautiful with respect to the attribute of being a person," and similarly for (97c).

21. Larson (1983) proposes an analysis of restrictive modification that argues for relativizing noun semantics to events or situations. See also Higginbotham 1985 for a similar proposal.

22. See Allen 1966, Verkuyl 1971, Dowty 1972, Taylor 1977, and Mourelatos 1981, among others, for the idea that the states and events are analogous to masses and particulars, respectively.

23. Quantum fluctuations are a possible example.

24. For more on this topic, see Kim 1976 and Brand 1976.

25. The ontological commitments of semantic theories that include events are further explored by Parsons (1990) and Schein (1993, chaps. 5, 6).

26. For further data on secondary predication that suggest revisions of the simple analysis offered here, see exercise 12.

27. For extensive discussion of how time and tense might be incorporated into a T theory, and various conceptual issues that such attempts raise, see Ludlow 1994b.

28. Although the present tense is used for referring to the present time in English, its usage is notoriously more complicated than this. Reference to the present time occurs primarily in two (somewhat limited) contexts: reports of ongoing action, as in (i), and use with so-called performative verbs, as in (ii):

    (i) He *stops*. He *picks up* the instrument. Now he *looks* around. He *continues* walking.

    (ii) a. I *promise* to deliver three dozen roses.
        b. I hereby *sentence* you to twenty years hard labor.

    Other uses of the present tense not reducible to simple reference to the present time include standard habitual uses, as in (iii), and reports of propensities or qualities, as in (iv):

    (iii) a. Chris reads comic books.
         b. Jill jogs ten miles a day.

    (iv) a. Kate likes chocolate.
        b. Kumiko is vivacious.

29. This analysis of *now* is developed extensively by Kamp (1971).

30. For the motivation of this general syntax for tense and inflectional elements, see Radford 1988 and Haegeman 1990. More recent syntactic analyses have proposed

that tense heads its own syntactic projection (TP). See Pollock 1989 and Chomsky 1991a for developments of this proposal.

31. This exercise and its intended solution were based on ideas by Barry Schein (p.c.).

32. We are grateful to Barry Schein for discussion motivating this exercise.

Chapter 13

1. There are some subtleties concerning exactly how the example is to be taken and what it might show. We might, for example, suppose that the person's internal lexical entries for *chipmunk* and *ground squirrel* are exactly the same, each merely saying, e.g., that the word refers to some kind of small, ground-living rodent. So construed, the example would show that internalized lexical entries don't determine extension. Alternatively, we might suppose that the lexical entries are something like this:

(i)   Val(x, *chipmunk*, σ) iff x is a chipmunk

(ii) Val(x, *ground-squirrel*, σ) iff x is a ground squirrel

In this case the entries are different, so it wouldn't follow that entries don't determine extension. Someone might use the example construed in this way to argue that the identity of the concepts used in the formulation of one's internal lexical entry is partly determined by social factors. In both cases the message is that social factors enter into the identity of a subject's language. But how they enter in is different in the two cases. We are here concerned primarily with the issue raised on the first construal: the extent to which a person's semantics is determined by their internalized rules.

2. The predicament of someone who doesn't know chipmunks from ground squirrels is different from that of someone who has acquired a word that lacks a complete interpretation. If we are mischievously told that a waldegrave is some kind of rodent, rather like a chipmunk or ground squirrel, we might add an entry for this word to our lexicon. However, if we now say *I don't know what a waldegrave looks like*, we are not making a true claim about waldegraves. There is an important difference between the two cases: one can use *chipmunk* to make claims about a particular kind of rodent, but the same is not true of *waldegrave*. The difference obviously doesn't have anything to do with our lexical entries for the words or, more generally, with our beliefs about the language. The contrast between the two sorts of cases is emphasized by Higginbotham: "The learner and the mature speaker will in general have only partial knowledge of their own idiolects, for that will explain the difference between a partly interpreted idiom and a fully interpreted idiom whose interpretation is unavailable" (1989, 159).

3. Kripke (1972) was the first to claim that the rules we take to fix the reference of our terms sometimes fail to specify that reference correctly. Tyler Burge has de-

veloped this line of thought in a series of articles. See, for example, Burge 1979, 1982, 1986a, 1989.

4. Burge's elaboration of this view (in his articles cited in note 3) has been influential. It is defended also in George 1990 and Higginbotham 1989.

5. George (1990) agrees, though he believes that some sense can be made of the notion of S-meaning, and that this notion is required to account for the possibility of linguistic error. Burge and Higginbotham appear to hold that both I-meanings and S-meanings are suitable objects of linguistic study. Burge would further argue that there is no individuating a person's I-meanings independently of his or her S-meanings. This last because the identity of the concepts used in formulating beliefs about language is itself partly determined by the subject's S-meanings: the nature of Maggie's concept of a mousse must itself be understood as partly socially determined.

6. Note also that one can wipe dry but not wipe wet. On the other hand, (4) may not be right, since some people find acceptable the locution "wipe on," as in "wipe on some ointment." For more on resultative constructions, see Carrier and Randall 1992.

7. For example, it seems likely that our judgments about whether a word applies to some newly encountered object involve the use of stored perceptual representations. See Burge 1989, p. 182, and the references cited therein.

8. If they do not, then the claim that there are normative facts about a speaker's meanings that go beyond his or her internalized semantic theory threatens to degenerate into the view that humans tend act as if they believe that there are such facts. The latter is certainly true, but its truth does not guarantee that belief in such normative elements is justified. Chomsky has emphasized this in various places; see, for example, his response to George (1990) in Chomsky 1991b, p. 32. For our purposes, it is not important to resolve the issue. What is important is that the notion of meaning that emerges from cognitivist semantics is I-meaning, rather than S-meaning.

9. We will not be arguing for psychoindividualism here. Moreover, neither our general methodology nor our particular semantic theory in any way depends on the doctrine. The point of this section is simply that if one is independently convinced that psychoindividualism is true and that semantics is part of psychology, no problems of principle arise. For arguments in favor of psychoindividualism, see Fodor 1980; 1987, chap. 2; 1991.

10. We are ignoring here the inconvenient fact that our brains are mostly made of water. This problematic feature of the example is irrelevant to its point.

11. Option (1) is incompatible with psychoindividualism for the reasons given above. Option (2) is incompatible with psychoindividualism for parallel reasons. Rather

than a term's possessing an extension that is determinate with respect to every possible item, it possesses an extension with some items definitely in, some definitely out, and an array of items that are neither in nor out until further notice. But this distribution depends partly on the natives' actual local environment. Thus for 1750 Earth speakers, H_2O is definitely in, and XYZ is neither in nor out. For Twin Earth speakers, the situation is reversed.

12. It is not surprising that psychological and linguistic individualism fit smoothly together, especially since the examples designed to challenge them are the same.

13. The detailed semantics for mass terms is difficult. See, for example, Burge 1972 for discussion. But such technical problems are irrelevant to the present issue.

14. There do exist nonpsychoindividualistic philosophical theories of content, for example, causal and teleofunctional theories, such as those of Dretske (1988), Millikan (1984), and Papineau (1993). But these also encounter familiar objections that (to our knowledge) have never been adequately addressed (for some of these, see Cummins 1989). One obvious problem is that if the extension of a concept is determined by causal interactions with items in its extension, it's hard to see how we have concepts of Santa Claus, phlogiston, virtual lines, triangles, the number 2, aleph null, black magic, to name a few. Various attempts have made to deal with this sort of problem. But these have not tended to convince skeptics.

15. See, for example, Patterson 1991 for a discussion of individualism and conceptual development.

16. Our task in building a theory of how the meanings of individual words generate the meanings of complex expressions such as sentences need not wait on the detailed development of lexical semantics, though evidently we would expect the latter to have some ramifications for us. We have pursued the course of not assuming any structure in lexical entries that does not affect the structure of embedding expressions. This policy has its limitations when it comes to building a theory for a subject whose internalized lexicon contains a term that is not exactly translated by any term of ours. The scientist of 1750 would be a case in point. In such a case we would adopt the policy of introducing a term of art as our translation of his term. Thus we would say something like "*Water* in the scientist's mouth applies to x just in case x is twater (where twater applies not only to H_2O but to any sufficiently waterlike substance)." Segal (1989b and particularly 1991) argues in detail that an exactly parallel policy is pursued by computational theorists of vision articulating the concepts deployed by the visual system. For an opposed view, see Burge 1986a and Davies 1991.

17. The attentive reader will have noted that we haven't actually endorsed PC+ as the correct theory of proper nouns. But we do hold that it is one of the two leading contenders. If proper nouns are really complex demonstratives, as was suggested in chapter 9, section 9.4, then the discussion here applies to them.

18. See Burge 1977, 1982, and Segal 1989c for defense and further elaboration of this view.

19. These points are argued by Perry (1977) and Kaplan (1990).

20. See Freud 1955, Freud and Breuer 1955. Original publication dates are included in the citations to these works.

21. Thus Quine's famous chapter 2 of *Word and Object* (1960), as well as other articles such as Quine 1970b, argue specifically against semantic theory.

22. Our account of computers in terms of three levels is based on David Marr's discussion in Marr 1982, but differs from his account in some details.

23. The example is Higginbotham's (1986a).

24. The term "original intentionality" is due to Haugeland (1980).

25. For a fair survey of views, see the various responses published with Searle 1980, as well as Searle's own influential article and Cummins 1989.

26. For an excellent account of the general methods of cognitive science and some cautionary remarks, see the two articles by Haugeland in Haugeland 1981. Note that Haugeland is committed to a particular view of what warrants the attribution of genuinely intentional states to a computational system that goes beyond anything we have committed ourselves to here. Also recommended are Cummins 1989 and Marr 1982.

27. Peacocke (1986) makes a similar claim.

References

Allen, R. (1966). *The Verb System of Present-Day American English.* The Hague: Mouton.

Allwood, J., Anderssen, L.-G., and Dahl, Ö. (1977). *Logic in Linguistics.* Cambridge: Cambridge University Press.

Aoun, J., and Li, A. (1989). "Scope and Constituency." *Linguistic Inquiry* 20:141–172.

Aoun, J., and Li, A. (1993). *Syntax of Scope.* Cambridge: MIT Press.

Armstrong, D. (1989). *Universals: An Opinionated Introduction.* Boulder: Westview Press.

Bach, E. (1989). *Informal Lectures in Formal Semantics.* Albany, N.Y.: SUNY Press.

Baldwin, T. (1975). "Quantification, Modality, and Indirect Speech." In S. Blackburn (ed.), *Meaning, Reference, and Necessity* (pp. 56–108). Cambridge: Cambridge University Press.

Baron-Cohen, S. (1994). "How to Build a Baby That Can Read Minds." *Cahiers de Psychologie Cognitive* 13:513–552.

Barwise, J., and Cooper, R. (1981). "Generalized Quantifiers and Natural Language." *Linguistics and Philosophy* 4:159–219.

Barwise, J., and Perry, J. (1983). *Situations and Attitudes.* Cambridge: MIT Press.

Basso, A., Capitani, E., and Laiacona, M. (1988). "Progressive Language Impairment without Dementia: A Case Study with Isolated Category Specific Semantic Defect." *Journal of Neurology, Neurosurgery, and Psychiatry* 51:1201–1207.

Beakley, B., and Ludlow, P. (eds.) (1992). *Philosophy of Mind.* Cambridge: MIT Press.

Bealer, G. (1982). *Quality and Concept.* Oxford: Clarendon Press.

Bealer, G. (1983). "Completeness in the Theory of Properties, Relations, and Propositions." *Journal of Symbolic Logic* 48:415–426.

Bealer, G. (1989). "Fine-Grained Type-Free Intensionality." In G. Chierchia, B. Partee, and R. Turner (eds.), *Properties, Types, and Meaning*, vol. 1, *Foundational Issues* (pp. 177–230). Dordrecht: Kluwer.

Belletti, A., and Rizzi, L. (1988). "Psych-Verbs and Θ-Theory." *Natural Language and Linguistic Theory* 6:291–352.

Belnap, N., and Grover, D. (1973). "Quantifying In and Out of Quotes." In H. Leblanc (ed.), *Truth, Syntax, and Modality* (pp. 17–47). Amsterdam: North-Holland.

Bergman, M., Moor, J., and Nelson, J. (1980). *The Logic Book*. New York: Random House.

Berman, S. (1987). "Situation-Based Semantics for Adverbs of Quantification." In J. Blevins and A. Vainikka (eds.), *Studies in Semantics*. University of Massachusetts Occasional Papers in Linguistics, no. 12 (pp. 45–68). Amherst, Mass.: Graduate Linguistic Student Association.

Bradley, F. H. (1930). *Appearance and Reality*. Oxford: Clarendon Press.

Brand, M. (1976). "Particulars, Events, and Actions." In M. Brand and D. Walton (eds.), *Action Theory* (pp. 133–157). Dordrecht: D. Reidel Publishing Co.

Bresnan, J. (1982). *The Mental Representation of Grammatical Relations*. Cambridge: MIT Press.

Burdick, H. (1982). "A Logical Form for the Propositional Attitudes." *Synthese* 52:185–230.

Burge, T. (1972). "Truth and Mass Terms." *Journal of Philosophy* 69:263–282.

Burge, T. (1973). "Reference and Proper Names." *Journal of Philosophy* 70:425–439.

Burge, T. (1974a). "Demonstrative Constructions, Reference, and Truth." *Journal of Philosophy* 71:205–223.

Burge, T. (1974b). "Truth and Singular Terms." *Noûs* 8:309–325.

Burge, T. (1977). "Belief *De Re*." *Journal of Philosophy* 74:338–362.

Burge, T. (1978). "Belief and Synonymy." *Journal of Philosophy* 75:119–138.

Burge, T. (1979). "Individualism and the Mental." In P. French, T. Uehling, Jr., and H. Wettstein (eds.), *Studies in Metaphysics*, Midwest Studies in Philosophy, no. 4 (pp. 73–121). Minneapolis: University of Minnesota Press.

Burge, T. (1982). "Other Bodies." In A. Woodfield (ed.), *Thought and Object* (pp. 97–121). Oxford: Clarendon Press.

Burge, T. (1986a). "Individualism and Psychology." *Philosophical Review* 95:3–43.

Burge, T. (1986b). "On Davidson's 'Saying That'." In E. LePore (ed.), *Truth and Interpretation: Perspectives on the Philosophy of Donald Davidson* (pp. 190–208). Oxford: Basil Blackwell.

Burge, T. (1989). "Wherein Is Language Social?" In A. George (ed.), *Reflections on Chomsky* (pp. 175–192). Oxford: Basil Blackwell.

Burton-Roberts, N. (1986). *Analyzing Sentences.* London: Longmans.

Caramazza, A. (1988). "Some Aspects of Language Processing Revealed through the Analysis of Acquired Aphasia: The Lexical System." *Annual Review of Neuroscience* 11:395–421.

Caramazza, A., and Hillis, A. (1991). "Lexical Organization of Nouns and Verbs in the Brain." *Nature* 349:788–790.

Carey, S. (1978). "The Child as Word Learner." In M. Halle, J. Bresnan, and G. Miller (eds.), *Linguistic Theory and Psychological Reality* (pp. 264–293). Cambridge: MIT Press.

Carey, S. (1982). "Semantic Development: The State of the Art." In E. Wanner and L. Gleitman (eds.), *Language Acquisition: The State of the Art* (pp. 347–389). New York: Cambridge University Press.

Carey, S. (1984). "Constraints on Semantic Development." In J. Mehler and R. Fox (eds.), *Neonate Cognition: Beyond the Blooming, Buzzing Confusion* (pp. 381–398). Hillsdale, N.J.: Lawrence Erlbaum.

Carey, S. (1985). *Conceptual Change in Childhood.* Cambridge: MIT Press.

Carlson, G. (1982). "Thematic Roles and Their Role in Semantic Interpretation." *Linguistics* 22:259–279.

Carlson, G., and Tannenhaus, M. (1988). "Thematic Roles and Language Comprehension." In W. Wilkins (ed.), *Thematic Relations*, Syntax and Semantics, no. 21 (pp. 263–288). New York: Academic Press.

Carnap, R. (1937). *The Logical Syntax of Language.* New York: Harcourt and Brace.

Carrier, J., and Randall, J. (1992). "The Argument Structure and Syntactic Structure of Resultatives." *Linguistic Inquiry* 23:173–234.

Carrier-Duncan, J. (1985). "Linking of Thematic Roles in Derivational Word Formation." *Linguistic Inquiry* 16:1–34.

Cartwright, R. (1987). *Philosophical Essays.* Cambridge: MIT Press.

Chierchia, G. (1984). "Topics in the Syntax and Semantics of Infinitives and Gerunds." Ph.D. dissertation, University of Massachusetts, Amherst.

Chierchia, G., and McConnell-Ginet, S. (1990). *Meaning and Grammar*. Cambridge: MIT Press.

Chierchia, G., Partee, B., and Turner, R. (eds.) (1989). *Properties, Types, and Meaning*. Vol. 1, *Foundational Issues*. Vol. 2, *Semantic Issues*. Dordrecht: Kluwer.

Chierchia, G., and Turner, R. (1988). "Semantics and Property Theory." *Linguistics and Philosophy* 11:261–302.

Chomsky, N. (1957). *Syntactic Structures*. The Hague: Mouton.

Chomsky, N. (1965). *Aspects of the Theory of Syntax*. Cambridge: MIT Press.

Chomsky, N. (1975). *Reflections on Language*. New York: Pantheon.

Chomsky, N. (1976). "Conditions on Rules of Grammar." *Linguistic Analysis* 2:303–351.

Chomsky, N. (1977). "On Wh-Movement." In P. Culicover, T. Wasow, and A. Akmajian (eds.), *Formal Syntax* (pp. 71–132). New York: Academic Press.

Chomsky, N. (1981). *Lectures on Government and Binding*. Dordrecht: Foris.

Chomsky, N. (1986a). *Knowledge of Language: Its Nature, Origin, and Use*. New York: Praeger.

Chomsky, N. (1986b). *Barriers*. Cambridge: MIT Press.

Chomsky, N. (1991a). "Some Notes on Economy of Derivation and Representation." In R. Freidin (ed.), *Principles and Parameters in Comparative Grammar* (pp. 417–454). Cambridge: MIT Press.

Chomsky, N. (1991b). "Linguistics and Cognitive Science: Problems and Mysteries." In A. Kasher (ed.), *The Chomskyan Turn* (pp. 26–53). Oxford: Basil Blackwell.

Chomsky, N., and Lasnik, H. (1993). "The Theory of Principles and Parameters." In J. Jacobs, A. von Stechow, W. Sternefeld, and T. Vennemann (eds.), *Syntax: An International Handbook of Contemporary Research* (pp. 505–569). Berlin: Walter de Gruyter.

Churchland, P. (1981). "Eliminative Materialism and Propositional Attitudes." *Journal of Philosophy* 78:67–90.

Clark, E. (1973). "What's in a Word? On the Child's Acquisition of Language in His First Language." In T. Moore (ed.), *Cognitive Development and the Development of Language* (pp. 65–110). New York: Academic Press.

Collins, C. (1988). "Conjunction Adverbs." Unpublished ms., MIT, Cambridge.

Cooper, R. (1979). "The Interpretation of Pronouns." In F. Heny and H. Schnelle (eds.), *Selections from the Third Gröningen Roundtable*, Syntax and Semantics, no. 10 (pp. 61–92). New York: Academic Press.

Couquaux, D. (1982). "French Predication and Linguistic Theory." In R. May and J. Koster (eds.), *Levels of Syntactic Representation* (pp. 33–64). Dordrecht: Foris.

Cresswell, M. (1985). *Structured Meanings: The Semantics of Propositional Attitudes*. Cambridge: MIT Press.

Cummins, R. (1989). *Meaning and Mental Representation*. Cambridge: MIT Press.

Dahl, Ö. (1972). "On So-Called 'Sloppy Identity'." In *Gothenburg Papers in Theoretical Linguistics II*. Göteborg: University of Göteborg.

Darwin, G. (1898). *The Tides and Kindred Phenomena in the Solar System*. Boston: Houghton, Mifflin and Co.

Davidson, D. (1965). "Theories of Meaning and Learnable Languages." In Y. Bar-Hillel (ed.), *Logic, Methodology, and Philosophy of Science* (pp. 383–394). Amsterdam: North-Holland.

Davidson, D. (1967a). "The Logical Form of Action Sentences." In N. Rescher (ed.), *The Logic of Decision and Action* (pp. 81–120). Pittsburgh: University of Pittsburgh Press.

Davidson, D. (1967b). "Causal Relations." *Journal of Philosophy* 64:691–703.

Davidson, D. (1967c). "Truth and Meaning." *Synthese* 17:304–323.

Davidson, D. (1968). "On Saying That." *Synthese* 19:158–174.

Davidson, D. (1970). "Semantics for Natural Languages." In *Linguaggi nella Società e nella Technica*. Milano: Edizioni di Comunità. Reprinted in Davidson 1984.

Davidson, D. (1984). *Inquiries into Truth and Interpretation*. Oxford: Clarendon Press.

Davidson, D. (1986). "A Nice Derangement of Epitaphs." In E. Lepore (ed.), *Truth and Interpretation* (pp. 433–446). Oxford: Basil Blackwell.

Davies, M. (1981a). *Meaning, Quantification, Necessity*. London: Routledge and Kegan Paul.

Davies, M. (1981b). "Meaning, Structure, and Understanding." *Synthese* 48:135–161.

Davies, M. (1987). "Tacit Knowledge and Semantic Theory: Can a Five Per Cent Difference Matter?" *Mind* 96:441–462.

Davies, M. (1991). "Individualism and Perceptual Content." *Mind* 100:461–484.

De Hoop, H. (1992). "Case Configuration and Noun Phrase Interpretation." Doctoraat in de Letteren dissertation, Rijksuniversiteit Groningen.

Donnellan, K. (1966). "Reference and Definite Descriptions." *Philosophical Review* 75:281–304.

Donnellan, K. (1968). "Putting Humpty Dumpty Back Together Again." *Philosophical Review* 77:203–215.

Donnellan, K. (1978). "Speaker Reference, Descriptions, and Anaphora." In P. Cole (ed.), *Pragmatics*, Syntax and Semantics, no. 9 (pp. 47–68). New York: Academic Press.

Dowty, D. (1972). "Studies in the Logic of Verb Aspect and Time Reference in English." Ph.D. dissertation, University of Texas at Austin.

Dowty, D. (1979). *Word Meaning and Montague Grammar*. Dordrecht: D. Reidel Publishing Co.

Dowty, D. (1989). "On the Semantic Content of the Notion of 'Thematic Role'." In G. Chierchia, B. Partee, and R. Turner (eds.), *Properties, Types, and Meaning*, vol. 2, *Semantic Issues* (pp. 69–129). Dordrecht: Kluwer.

Dowty, D. (1991). "Thematic Proto-roles and Argument Selection." *Language* 67:547–619.

Dowty, D., Wall, R., and Peters, S. (1981). *An Introduction to Montague Semantics*. Dordrecht: D. Reidel Publishing Co.

Dretske, F. (1988). *Explaining Behavior: Reasons in a World of Causes*. Cambridge: MIT Press.

Dummett, M. (1978). "Frege's Distinction between Sense and Reference." In M. Dummett (ed.), *Truth and Other Enigmas* (pp. 116–144). London: Duckworth.

Ellis, A., and Young, A. (1988). *Human Cognitive Neuropsychology*. Hillsdale: Lawrence Erlbaum Associates.

Etchemendy, J. (1983). "The Doctrine of Logic as Form." *Linguistics and Philosophy* 6:319–334.

Etchemendy, J. (1990). *The Concept of Logical Consequence*. Cambridge: Harvard University Press.

Evans, G. (1973). "The Causal Theory of Names." *Aristotelian Society*, suppl. vol. 47: 187–208.

Evans, G. (1975). "Identity and Predication." *Journal of Philosophy* 72:343–363.

Evans, G. (1976). "Semantic Structure and Logical Form." In G. Evans and J. McDowell (eds.), *Truth and Meaning*: *Essays in Semantics* (pp. 199–222). Oxford: Oxford University Press.

Evans, G. (1977). "Pronouns, Quantifiers, and Relative Clauses (I)." *Canadian Journal of Philosophy* 7:467–536.

Evans, G. (1980). "Pronouns." *Linguistic Inquiry* 11:337–362.

Evans, G. (1981). "Semantic Theory and Tacit Knowledge." In S. Holzman and C. Leich (eds.), *Wittgenstein: To Follow a Rule* (pp. 118–137). London: Routledge and Kegan Paul.

Evans, G. (1982). *The Varieties of Reference.* Oxford: Clarendon Press.

Evans, G. (1985). *Collected Papers.* Oxford: Clarendon Press.

Fauconnier, G. (1979). "Implication Reversal in a Natural Language." In F. Guenthner and S. J. Schmidt (eds.), *Formal Semantics and Pragmatics for Natural Language* (pp. 289–302). Dordrecht: D. Reidel Publishing Co.

Feynman, R. (1965). *The Character of Physical Law.* Harmondsworth, England: Penguin Books.

Field, H. (1980). *Science without Numbers.* Princeton: Princeton University Press.

Fiengo, R., and Higginbotham, J. (1980). "Opacity in NP." *Linguistic Analysis* 7:395–421.

Fiengo, R., and May, R. (1993). *Indices and Identity.* Cambridge: MIT Press.

Fillmore, C. (1971). *Santa Cruz Lectures on Deixis.* Bloomington: Indiana University Linguistics Club.

Fodor, J. (1980). "Methodological Solipsism Considered as a Research Strategy in Cognitive Psychology." *Behavioral and Brain Sciences* 3:63–73.

Fodor, J. (1983). *The Modularity of Mind.* Cambridge: MIT Press.

Fodor, J. (1987). *Psychosemantics.* Cambridge: MIT Press.

Fodor, J. (1991). "A Modal Argument for Narrow Content." *Journal of Philosophy* 88:5–26.

Foster, J. (1976). "Meaning and Truth Theory." In G. Evans and J. McDowell (eds.), *Truth and Meaning: Essays in Semantics* (pp. 1–32). Oxford: Oxford University Press.

Frazier, L. (1987). "Sentence Processing: A Tutorial Review." In M. Coltheart (ed.), *The Psychology of Reading*, Attention and Performance, no. 12 (pp. 559–586). Hillsdale, N.J.: Lawrence Erlbaum.

Frazier, L. (1989). "Against Lexical Generation of Syntax." In W. Marslen-Wilson (ed.), *Lexical Representation and Process* (pp. 503–528). Cambridge: MIT Press.

Frege, G. (1893). "Über Sinn und Bedeutung." *Zeitschrift für Philosophie und Philosophische Kritik* 100:25–50. Translated as Frege 1952.

Frege, G. (1952). "On Sense and Reference." In P. Geach and M. Black (eds.), *Translations from the Philosophical Writings of Gottlob Frege* (pp. 56–78). Oxford: Basil Blackwell.

Frege, G. (1953). *The Foundations of Arithmetic*. Trans. J. L. Austin. New York: Philosophical Library. Originally published in 1884.

Frege, G. (1956). "The Thought: A Logical Inquiry." Trans. A. M. Quinton and M. Quinton. *Mind* 65:289–311. Originally published in 1918.

Frege, G. (1967). "The Thought: A Logical Inquiry." Trans. A. M. Quinton and M. Quinton. In P. Strawson (ed.) *Philosophical Logic* (pp. 17–38). Oxford: Oxford University Press. Originally published in 1918.

Freud, S. (1955). *The Interpretation of Dreams*. Trans. J. Strachey. London: Hogarth Press. Originally published in 1900.

Freud, S., and Breuer, J. (1955). *Studies in Hysteria*. Trans. J. Strachey. London: Hogarth Press. Originally published in 1895.

Geach, P. (1962). *Reference and Generality*. Ithaca: Cornell University Press.

George, A. (1989). "How Not to Become Confused about Linguistics." In A. George (ed.), *Reflections on Chomsky* (pp. 90–110). Oxford: Basil Blackwell.

George, A. (1990). "Whose Language Is It Anyway?" *Philosophical Quarterly* 40:275–298.

Gleitman, L. (1990). "The Structural Sources of Verb Meanings." *Language Acquisition* 1:3–55.

Goodglass, H., and Budin, C. (1988). "Category and Modality Specific Dissociations in Word Comprehension and Concurrent Phonological Dyslexia." *Neuropsychologia* 26:67–78.

Gopnik, A., and Wellman, H. (1992). "Why the Child's Theory of Mind Really Is a Theory." *Mind and Language* 7:145–172.

Grice, P. (1975). "Logic and Conversation." In P. Cole and J. Morgan (eds.), *Speech Acts*, Syntax and Semantics, no. 3 (pp. 41–58). New York: Academic Press.

Grice, P. (1990). *Studies in the Way of Words*. Cambridge: Harvard University Press.

Grimshaw, J. (1990). *Argument Structure*. Cambridge: MIT Press.

Gropen, J., Pinker, S., Hollander, M., and Goldberg, R. (1991). "Syntax and Semantics in the Acquisition of Locative Verbs." *Journal of Child Language* 18:115–151.

Gruber, J. (1976). *Lexical Structures in Syntax and Semantics*. Amsterdam: North-Holland.

Gupta, A. (1980). *The Logic of Common Nouns*. New Haven: Yale University Press.

Haegeman, L. (1990). *Introduction to Government and Binding Theory*. New York: Basil Blackwell.

Hale, K. (1992). "Subject Obviation, Switch Reference, and Control." In R. Larson, S. Iatridou, U. Lahiri, and J. Higginbotham (eds.), *Control and Grammar* (pp. 51–77). Dordrecht: Kluwer.

Harman, G. (1972). "Logical Form." *Foundations of Language* 9:38–65.

Harman, G. (1974). "Meaning and Semantics." In M. Munitz and P. Unger (eds.), *Semantics and Philosophy* (pp. 1–16). New York: New York University Press.

Hart, J., Berndt, R., and Caramazza, A. (1985). "Category-Specific Naming Deficit Following Cerebral Infarction." *Nature* 316:439–440.

Haugeland, J. (1980). "Programs, Causal Powers, and Intentionality." *Behavioral and Brain Sciences* 3:432–433.

Haugeland, J. (1981). *Mind Design*. Cambridge: MIT Press.

Heim, I. (1982). "The Semantics of Definite and Indefinite Noun Phrases." Ph.D. dissertation, University of Massachusetts, Amherst.

Heim, I. (1983). "File Change Semantics and the Familiarity Theory of Definiteness." In R. Baüerle, C. Schwarze, and A. von Stechow (eds.), *Meaning, Use, and Interpretation of Language* (pp. 164–198). Berlin: Walter de Gruyter.

Heim, I. (1990). "E-Type Pronouns and Donkey Anaphora." *Linguistics and Philosophy* 13:137–177.

Higginbotham, J. (1979). "Pronouns and Bound Variables." *Linguistic Inquiry* 11:679–708.

Higginbotham, J. (1983a). "Is Grammar Psychological?" In L. Cauman, I. Levi, C. Parsons, and R. Schwartz (eds.), *How Many Questions? Essays in Honor of Sydney Morgenbesser* (pp. 170–179). Indianapolis: Hackett Publishing Co.

Higginbotham, J. (1983b). "Logical Form, Binding, and Nominals." *Linguistic Inquiry* 14:679–708.

Higginbotham, J. (1983c). "The Logic of Perceptual Reports: An Extensional Alternative to Situation Semantics." *Journal of Philosophy* 80:100–127.

Higginbotham, J. (1985). "On Semantics." *Linguistic Inquiry* 16:547–593.

Higginbotham, J. (1986a). "Discussion: Peacocke on Explanation in Psychology." *Mind and Language* 1:358–361.

Higginbotham, J. (1986b). "Linguistic Theory and Davidson's Program in Semantics." In E. LePore (ed.), *Truth and Interpretation: Perspectives on the Philosophy of Donald Davidson* (pp. 29–48). Oxford: Basil Blackwell.

Higginbotham, J. (1987). "The Autonomy of Syntax and Semantics." In J. Garfield (ed.), *Modularity in Knowledge Representation and Natural-Language Understanding* (pp. 119–131). Cambridge: MIT Press.

Higginbotham, J. (1988). "Contexts, Models, and Meaning: A Note on the Data of Semantics." In R. Kempson (ed.) *Mental Representations: The Interface between Language and Reality* (pp. 29–48). Cambridge: Cambridge University Press.

Higginbotham, J. (1989). "Knowledge of Reference." In A. George (ed.), *Reflections on Chomsky* (pp. 153–174). Oxford: Basil Blackwell.

Higginbotham, J. (1991a). "Belief and Logical Form." *Mind and Language* 4:344–369.

Higginbotham, J. (1991b). "Truth and Understanding." *Iyyun* (Tel Aviv) 40:271–288.

Higginbotham, J., and May, R. (1981). "Questions, Quantifiers, and Crossing." *Linguistic Review* 1:41–80.

Hintikka, J. (1957). "Quantifiers in Deontic Logic." *Commentationes Humanarum Literarum* (Societas Scientarum Fennica) 23:2–23.

Hintikka, J. (1962). *Knowledge and Belief.* Ithaca: Cornell University Press.

Hintikka, J. (1969). "Semantics for Propositional Attitudes." In J. Davis, D. Hockney, and W. Wilson (eds.), *Philosophical Logic* (pp. 21–45). Dordrecht: D. Reidel Publishing Co.

Hornstein, N. (1984). *Logic as Grammar.* Cambridge: MIT Press.

Huddleston, G. (1982). *Introduction to the Grammar of English.* Cambridge: Cambridge University Press.

Jackendoff, R. (1972). *Semantic Interpretation in Generative Grammar.* Cambridge: MIT Press.

Jackendoff, R. (1976). "Toward an Explanatory Semantic Representation." *Linguistic Inquiry* 7:89–150.

Jackendoff, R. (1983). *Semantics and Cognition.* Cambridge: MIT Press.

Janssen, T. (1986). *Foundations and Applications of Montague Grammar.* Part 1, *Philosophy, Framework, Computer Science.* Amsterdam: Center for Mathematics and Computer Science.

Jubien, M. (1989). "On Properties and Property Theory." In G. Chierchia, B. Partee, and R. Turner (eds.), *Properties, Types, and Meaning*, vol. 1, *Foundational Issues* (pp. 159–175). Dordrecht: Kluwer.

Kadmon, N. (1987). "On Unique and Non-unique Reference and Asymmetric Quantification." Ph.D. dissertation, University of Massachusetts, Amherst.

Kamp, H. (1971). "Formal Properties of 'Now'." *Theoria* 37:227–273.

Kamp, H. (1981). "A Theory of Truth and Semantic Representation." In J. Groenendijk, T. Janssen, and M. Stockhof (eds.), *Truth, Interpretation, and Information* (pp. 1–41). Dordecht: Foris.

Kanger, S. (1957). *Provability in Modal Logic*. Stockholm: Almquist and Wiksill.

Kaplan, D. (1972). "What Is Russell's Theory of Descriptions?" In D. F. Pears (ed.), *Bertrand Russell: A Collection of Critical Essays* (pp. 227–244). Garden City, N.Y.: Doubleday.

Kaplan, D. (1990). "Thoughts on Demonstratives." In P. Yourgrau (ed.), *Demonstratives* (pp. 34–50). Oxford: Oxford University Press.

Katz, J. (1972). *Semantic Theory*. New York: Harper & Row.

Katz, J. (1981). *Language and Other Abstract Objects*. Totowa, N.J.: Rowman and Littlefield.

Kayne, R. (1984). *Connectedness and Binary Branching*. Dordrecht: Foris.

Keenan, E. (1971). "Quantifier Structures in English." *Foundations of Language* 7:255–284.

Keenan, E. (1987). "A Semantic Definition of Indefinite NP." In E. Reuland and A. ter Meulen (eds.), *The Representation of (In)definiteness* (pp. 286–317). Cambridge: MIT Press.

Keenan, E., and Stavi, Y. (1986). "A Semantic Characterization of Natural Language Determiners." *Linguistics and Philosophy* 9:253–326.

Keil, F. (1989). *Concepts, Kinds, and Cognitive Development*. Cambridge: MIT Press.

Kim, J. (1976). "Events as Property Exemplifications." In M. Brand and D. Walton (eds.), *Action Theory* (pp. 159–177). Dordrecht: D. Reidel Publishing Co.

Kiss, K. (1986). "The Order and Scope of Operators in the Hungarian Sentence." In W. Abraham and S. de May (eds.), *Topic, Focus, and Configurationality* (pp. 181–214). Amsterdam: John Benjamin Publishing Co.

Kiss, K. (1991). "Logical Structure in Syntactic Structure: The Case of Hungarian." In J. Huang and R. May (eds.), *Logical Structure and Linguistic Structure: A Cross-Linguistic Perspective* (pp. 111–147). Dordrecht: Kluwer.

Klein, E. (1980). "A Semantics for Positive and Comparative Adjectives." *Linguistics and Philosophy* 4:1–45.

Klein, E. (1991). "Comparatives." In A. von Stechow and D. Wunderlich (eds.), *Semantics: An International Handbook of Contemporary Research* (pp. 673–691). Berlin: Walter de Gruyter.

Klima, E. (1964). "Negation in English." In J. Fodor and J. Katz (eds.), *The Structure of Language* (pp. 246–323). Engelwood Cliffs, N.J.: Prentice Hall.

Kratzer, A. (1989). "Stage-Level and Individual-Level Predicates." In E. Bach, A. Kratzer, and B. Partee (eds.), *Papers on Quantification*. Amherst: Dept. of Linguistics, University of Massachusetts.

Kripke, S. (1963). "Semantical Considerations on Modal Logic." *Acta Philosophica Fennica* 16:83–94.

Kripke, S. (1972). "Naming and Necessity." In D. Davidson and G. Harman (eds.), *Semantics of Natural Language* (pp. 253–355). Dordrecht: D. Reidel Publishing Co.

Kripke, S. (1976). "Is There a Problem about Substitutional Quantification?" In G. Evans and J. McDowell (eds.), *Truth and Meaning*: *Essays in Semantics* (pp. 325–419). Oxford: Oxford University Press.

Kripke, S. (1977). "Speaker Reference and Semantic Reference." In P. French, T. Uehling, Jr., and H. Wettstein (eds.), *Contemporary Perspectives in the Philosophy of Language* (pp. 6–27). Minneapolis: University of Minnesota Press.

Kripke, S. (1979). "A Puzzle about Belief." In A. Margalit (ed.), *Meaning and Use*: *Papers Presented at the Second Jerusalem Philosophical Encounter* (pp. 239–283). Dordrecht: D. Reidel Publishing Co.

Ladusaw, W. (1979). "Polarity Sensitivity as Inherent Scope Relations." Ph.D. dissertation, University of Texas, Austin.

Lakoff, G. (1970). *Irregularity in Syntax*. New York: Holt, Rinehart and Winston.

Landau, B., and Gleitman, L. (1985). *Language and Experience*: *Evidence from the Blind Child*. Cambridge: Harvard University Press.

Larson, R. (1983). "Restrictive Modification: Relative Clauses and Adverbs." Ph.D. dissertation, University of Wisconsin, Madison.

Larson, R. (1988). "On the Double-Object Construction." *Linguistic Inquiry* 19:335–391.

Larson, R., and Ludlow, P. (1993). "Interpreted Logical Forms." *Synthese* 95:305–355.

Lasnik, H. (1976). "Remarks on Coreference." *Linguistic Analysis* 2:1–22.

Lasnik, H., and Saito, M. (1984). "On the Nature of Proper Government." *Linguistic Inquiry* 14:235–289.

Leech, G. (1974). *Semantics*. Harmondsworth, England: Penguin Books.

Lepore, E. (1983). "What Model-Theoretic Semantics Cannot Do." *Synthese* 54:167–187.

Lepore, E., and Loewer, B. (1981). "Translational Semantics." *Synthese* 48:121–133.

Lepore, E., and Loewer, B. (1983). "Three Trivial Truth Theories." *Canadian Journal of Philosophy* 13:433–447.

Lepore, E., and Loewer, B. (1989). "You Can Say *That* Again." In P. French, T. Uehling, Jr., and H. Wettstein (eds.), *Contemporary Perspectives in the Philosophy of Language II*, Midwest Studies in Philosophy, no. 14 (pp. 338–356). Notre Dame: University of Notre Dame Press.

Leslie, A. (1994). "Pretending and Believing: Issues in the Theory of ToMM." *Cognition* 50:211–238.

Lewis, D. (1968). "Counterpart Theory and Quantified Modal Logic." *Journal of Philosophy* 65:113–126.

Lewis, D. (1970). "General Semantics." In D. Davidson and G. Harman (eds.), *Semantics of Natural Language* (pp. 169–218). Dordrecht: D. Reidel Publishing Co.

Lewis, D. (1975). "Adverbs of Quantification." In E. Keenan (ed.), *Formal Semantics of Natural Language* (pp. 3–15). Cambridge: Cambridge University Press.

Lewis, D. (1991). *Parts of Classes*. Oxford: Basil Blackwell.

Lindström, P. (1966). "First-Order Predicate Logic with Generalized Quantifiers." *Theoria* 32:186–195.

Link, G. (1983). "The Logical Analysis of Plurals and Mass Terms: A Lattice-Theoretical Approach." In R. Bäuerle, C. Schwarze, and A. von Stechow (eds.), *Meaning, Use, and Interpretation of Language* (pp. 302–323). Berlin: Walter de Gruyter.

Loux, M. (ed.). (1970). *Universals and Particulars: Readings in Ontology*. Garden City, N.Y.: Anchor Books.

Ludlow, P. (1982). "Substitutional Quantification and the Problem of Expression Types." *Logique et Analyse* 25:413–424.

Ludlow, P. (1985a). "Substitutional Quantification and Semantic Theory." MIT Working Papers in Linguistics, no. 6. Cambridge: Dept. of Linguistics and Philosophy, MIT.

Ludlow, P. (1985b). "The Syntax and Semantics of Referential Attitude Reports." Ph.D. dissertation, Columbia University.

Ludlow, P. (1994a). "Conditionals, Events, and Unbound Pronouns." *Lingua e Stile* (Bologna, Italy) 29:165–183.

Ludlow, P. (1994b). "The Semantics of Tense and the Metaphysics of Time." Unpublished ms., SUNY, Stony Brook.

Ludlow, P., and Neale, S. (1991). "Indefinite Descriptions: In Defense of Russell." *Linguistics and Philosophy* 14:171–202.

Lycan, W. (1984). *Logical Form in Natural Language*. Cambridge: MIT Press.

MacDonald, M., Just, M., and Carpenter, P. (1992). "Working Memory Constraints on the Processing of Syntactic Ambiguity." *Cognitive Psychology* 24:56–98.

Macnamara, J. (1982). *Names for Things: A Study of Human Learning*. Cambridge: MIT Press.

Mandelbaum, D. (1994). "Syntactic Conditions on Saturation." Ph.D. dissertation, City University of New York.

Marr, D. (1977). "Artificial Intelligence: A Personal Perspective." *Artificial Intelligence* 9:37–48.

Marr, D. (1982). *Vision*. New York: W. H. Freeman.

May, R. (1977). "The Grammar of Quantification." Ph.D. dissertation, MIT, Cambridge.

May, R. (1985). *Logical Form*. Cambridge: MIT Press.

McCarthy, R., and Warrington, E. (1988). "Evidence for Modality-Specific Meaning Systems in the Brain." *Nature* 334:428–430.

McCarthy, R., and Warrington, E. (1990). "The Dissolution of Semantics." *Nature* 343:599.

McCawley, J. (1981a). *Everything That Linguists Always Wanted to Know about Logic* but Were Afraid to Ask*. Chicago: Chicago University Press.

McCawley, J. (1981b). "The Syntax and Semantics of English Relative Clauses." *Lingua* 53:99–149.

McDowell, J. (1977). "On the Sense and Reference of a Proper Name." *Mind* 86:159–185.

McKenna, P., and Warrington, E. (1978). "Category Specific Naming Preservation: A Single Case Study." *Journal of Neurology, Neurosurgery & Psychiatry* 41:571–574.

Mill, J. S. (1843). *A System of Logic*. New York: Harper Brothers.

Millican, P. (1990). "Contents, Thoughts, and Definite Descriptions." *Aristotelian Society*, suppl. vol. 64: 167–203.

Millikan, R. (1984). *Language, Thought, and Other Biological Categories*. Cambridge: MIT Press.

Montague, R. (1972). "The Proper Treatment of Quantification in Ordinary English." In J. Hintikka, J. Moravcsik, and P. Suppes (eds.), *Approaches to Natural Language* (pp. 221–242). Dordrecht: D. Reidel Publishing Co.

Montague, R. (1974). *Formal Philosophy*. New Haven: Yale University Press.

Mourelatos, A. (1981). "Events, Processes, and States." In P. Tedeschi and A. Zaenen (eds.), *Tense and Aspect*, Syntax and Semantics, no. 14 (pp. 191–212). New York: Academic Press.

Naigles, L. (1990). "Children Use Syntax to Learn Verb Meanings." *Journal of Child Language* 17:357–374.

Neale, S. (1990a). *Descriptions*. Cambridge: MIT Press.

Neale, S. (1990b). "Descriptive Pronouns and Donkey Anaphora." *Journal of Philosophy* 87:113–150.

Papineau, D. (1993). *Philosophical Naturalism*. Oxford: Blackwell.

Parsons, T. (1978). "Pronouns as Paraphrases." Unpublished ms., University of Massachusetts, Amherst.

Parsons, T. (1980). "Modifiers and Quantifiers in Natural Language." *Canadian Journal of Philosophy*, supp. vol. 6: 29–60.

Parsons, T. (1985). "Underlying Events in the Logical Analysis of English." In E. Lepore and B. McLaughlin (eds.), *Actions and Events: Perspectives on the Philosophy of Donald Davidson* (pp. 235–267). Oxford: Basil Blackwell.

Parsons, T. (1989). "The Progressive in English: Events, States, and Processes." *Linguistics and Philosophy* 12:213–241.

Parsons, T. (1990). *Events in the Semantics of English: A Study in Subatomic Semantics*. Cambridge: MIT Press.

Partee, B. (1973). "Some Transformational Extensions of Montague Grammar." *Journal of Philosophical Logic* 2:509–534.

Partee, B. (ed.) (1976). *Montague Grammar*. New York: Academic Press.

Partee, B. (1978). *Fundamentals of Mathematics for Linguists*. Dordrecht: D. Reidel Publishing Co.

Partee, B. (1979). "Semantics—Mathematics or Psychology?" In R. Baüerle, U. Egli, and A. von Stechow (eds.), *Semantics from Different Points of View* (pp. 1–14). Berlin: Springer-Verlag.

Partee, B. (1982). "Belief Sentences and the Limits of Semantics." In S. Peters and E. Saarinen (eds.), *Processes, Beliefs, and Questions* (pp. 87–106). Dordrecht: D. Reidel Publishing Co.

Partee, B., ter Meulen, A., and Wall, R. (1990). *Mathematical Methods in Linguistics*. Dordecht: Kluwer.

Patterson, S. (1991). "Individualism and Semantic Development." *Philosophy of Science* 58:15–35.

Peacocke, C. (1975). "Proper Names, Reference, and Rigid Designation." In S. Blackburn (ed.), *Meaning, Reference, and Necessity* (pp. 109–132). Cambridge: Cambridge University Press.

Peacocke, C. (1986). "Explanation in Computational Psychology: Language, Perception, and Level 1.5." *Mind and Language* 1:101–123.

Pearlmutter, N., and MacDonald, M. (1992). "Plausibility and Syntactic Ambiguity Resolution." In *Proceedings of the Fourteenth Annual Conference of the Cognitive Science Society*. Hillsdale, N.J.: Lawrence Erlbaum.

Perner, J. (1991). *Understanding the Representational Mind*. Cambridge: MIT Press.

Perry, J. (1977). "Frege on Demonstratives." *Philosophical Review* 86:474–479.

Perry, J. (1980). "A Problem about Continued Belief." *Pacific Philosophical Quarterly* 5:533–542.

Perry, J. (1986). "Circumstantial Attitudes and Benevolent Cognition." In J. Butterfield (ed.), *Language, Mind, and Logic* (pp. 123–134). Cambridge: Cambridge University Press.

Piatelli-Palmarini, M. (ed.). (1980). *Language and Learning: The Debate between Jean Piaget and Noam Chomsky*. London: Routledge & Kegan Paul.

Pinker, S. (1989). *Learnability and Cognition: The Acquisition of Argument Structure*. Cambridge: Harvard University Press.

Platts, M. (1979). *Ways of Meaning*. London: Routledge and Kegan Paul.

Pollock, J.-Y. (1989). "Verb Movement, Universal Grammar, and the Structure of IP." *Linguistic Inquiry* 20:365–424.

Postal, P. (1971). *Cross-Over Phenomena*. New York: Holt, Rinehart & Winston.

Putnam, H. (1975). "The Meaning of 'Meaning'." In K. Gunderson (ed.), *Language, Mind, and Knowledge* (pp. 131–193). Minneapolis: University of Minnesota Press.

Quine, W. V. O. (1960). *Word and Object*. Cambridge: MIT Press.

Quine, W. V. O. (1970a). "Methodological Reflections on Current Linguistic Theory." *Synthese* 21:368–398.

Quine, W. V. O. (1970b). "On the Reasons for the Indeterminacy of Translation." *Journal of Philosophy* 67:178–183.

Quine, W. V. O. (1975). "Mind and Verbal Dispositions." In S. Guttenplan (ed.), *Mind and Language: Wolfson College Lectures* (pp. 83–95). Oxford: Clarendon Press.

Quirk, R., Greenbaum, S., Leech, G., and Svartik, J. (1985). *A Comprehensive Grammar of the English Language*. London: Longman.

Radford, A. (1988). *Transformational Grammar*. Cambridge: Cambridge University Press.

Ramsey, F. (1927). "Facts and Propositions." *Aristotelian Society*, suppl. vol. 7: 153–170.

Recanati, F. (1993). *Direct Reference: From Language to Thought*. Oxford: Basil Blackwell.

Reinhart, T. (1976). "The Syntactic Domain of Anaphora." Ph.D. dissertation, MIT, Cambridge.

Reinhart, T. (1983). *Anaphora and Semantic Interpretation*. Chicago: University of Chicago Press.

Reinhart, T. (1987). "Specifier and Operator Binding." In E. Reuland and A. ter Meulen (eds.), *The Representation of (In)definiteness* (pp. 130–167). Cambridge: MIT Press.

Rescher, N. (1962). "Plurality Quantification." *Journal of Symbolic Logic* 27:373–374.

Reuland, E., and ter Meulen, A. (eds.) (1987). *The Representation of (In)definiteness*. Cambridge: MIT Press.

Richard, M. (1990). *Propositional Attitudes*. Cambridge: Cambridge University Press.

Richards, B. (1984). "On Interpreting Pronouns." *Linguistics and Philosophy* 7:287–324.

Rosen, C. (1984). "The Interface between Semantic Roles and Initial Grammatical Relations." In D. Perlmutter and C. Rosen (eds.), *Studies in Relational Grammar 2* (pp. 38–77). Chicago: University of Chicago Press.

Ross, J. (1967). "Constraints on Variables in Syntax." Ph.D. dissertation, MIT, Cambridge.

Ross, J. (1981). *Infinite Syntax*. New York: Ablex.

Russell, B. (1903). *Principles of Mathematics*. New York: W. W. Norton & Co.

Russell, B. (1905). "On Denoting." *Mind* 14:479–493.

Russell, B. (1919). *Introduction to Mathematical Philosophy*. London: G. Allen & Unwin.

Sainsbury, R. M. (1979). *Russell*. London: Routledge & Kegan Paul.

Salmon, N. (1986). *Frege's Puzzle*. Cambridge: MIT Press.

Sartori, G., and Job, R. (1988). "The Oyster with Four Legs: A Neuropsychological Study of Visual and Semantic Information." *Cognitive Neuropsychology*, special issue: *The Cognitive Neuropsychology of Visual and Semantic Processing of Concepts* 5:105–132.

Scheffler, I. (1954). "An Inscriptional Approach to Indirect Quotation." *Analysis* 10: 83–90.

Schein, B. (1993). *Plurals and Events*. Cambridge: MIT Press.

Searle, J. (1958). "Proper Names." *Mind* 67:166–173.

Searle, J. (1980). "Minds, Brains, and Programs." *Behavioral and Brain Sciences* 3:417–424.

Segal, G. (1989a). "A Preference for Sense and Reference." *Journal of Philosophy* 86: 73–89.

Segal, G. (1989b). "Seeing What Is Not There." *Philosophical Review* 98:73–89.

Segal, G. (1989c). "The Return of the Individual." *Mind* 98:39–57.

Segal, G. (1991). "Defence of a Reasonable Individualism." *Mind* 100:485–494.

Segal, G. (1996). "The Modularity of Theory of Mind." In P. Carruthers and P. Smith (eds.), *Theories of Theories of Mind*. Cambridge: Cambridge University Press.

Semenza, C., and Zettin, M. (1989). "Evidence from Aphasia for the Role of Proper Names as Pure Referring Expressions." *Nature* 342:678–679.

Shallice, T. (1988). *From Neuropsychology to Mental Structure*. Cambridge: Cambridge University Press.

Sher, G. (1991). *The Bounds of Logic: A Generalized Viewpoint*. Cambridge: MIT Press.

Siegel, M. (1976a). "Capturing the Adjective." Ph.D. dissertation, University of Massachusetts, Amherst.

Siegel, M. (1976b). "Capturing the Russian Adjective." In B. Partee (ed.), *Montague Grammar* (pp. 293–309). New York: Academic Press.

Silveri, M., and Gainotti, G. (1988). "Interaction between Vision and Language in Category-Specific Impairment." *Cognitive Neuropsychology* 5:677–709.

Soames, S. (1985). "Semantics and Psychology." In J. Katz (ed.), *The Philosophy of Linguistics* (pp. 204–226). Oxford: Oxford University Press.

Soames, S. (1987). "Direct Reference, Propositional Attitudes, and Semantic Content." *Philosophical Topics* 15:47–87.

Sperber, D., and Wilson, D. (1986). *Relevance: Communication and Cognition*. Oxford: Basil Blackwell.

Staniland, H. (1972). *Universals.* Garden City, N.Y.: Anchor Books.

Stowe, L. (1989). "Thematic Structures and Sentence Comprehension." In G. Carlson and M. Tannenhaus (eds.), *Linguistic Structure in Language Processing* (pp. 319–357). Dordrecht: Kluwer.

Stowell, T. (1978). "What Was There Before There Was *There?*" *Proceedings of the Chicago Linguistics Society* (pp. 458–471). Chicago: Chicago University Press.

Stowell, T. (1981). "Origins of Phrase Structure." Ph.D. dissertation, MIT, Cambridge.

Strawson, P. (1950). "On Referring." *Mind* 59:320–344.

Taraban, R., and McClelland, J. (1988). "Constituent Attachment and Thematic Role Assignment in Sentence Processing: Influence of Content-Based Expectations." *Journal of Memory and Language* 27:597–632.

Tarski, A. (1944). "The Semantic Conception of Truth." *Philosophy and Phenomenological Research* 4:341–375.

Tarski, A. (1956). "The Concept of Truth in Formalized Languages." In A. Tarski *Logic, Semantics, Metamathematics* (pp. 152–278). Oxford: Oxford University Press.

Taylor, B. (1977). "Tense and Continuity." *Linguistics and Philosophy* 1:199–220.

Taylor, B. (1980). "Truth-Theory for Indexical Languages." In M. Platts (ed.), *Reference, Truth, and Reality* (pp. 182–198). London: Routledge & Kegan Paul.

Van Bentham, J. (1983). *The Logic of Time.* Dordrecht: Kluwer.

Van Riemsdijk, H., and Williams, E. (1986). *Introduction to the Theory of Grammar.* Cambridge: MIT Press.

Verkuyl, H. (1971). *On the Compositional Nature of the Aspects.* Dordrecht: D. Reidel Publishing Co.

Vlach, F. (1983). "On Situation Semantics for Perception." *Synthese* 54:129–152.

Wall, R. (1972). *Introduction to Mathematical Linguistics.* Englewood Cliffs, N.J.: Prentice Hall.

Warrington, E. (1975). The Selective Impairment of Semantic Memory. *Quarterly Journal of Experimental Psychology* 27:635–657.

Warrington, E. (1981). "Neuropsychological Studies of Verbal Semantic Systems." *Philosophical Transactions of the Royal Society of London* 295 (1077, series B): 411–423.

Warrington, E., and McCarthy, R. (1983). "Category Specific Access Dysphasia." *Brain* 106:859–878.

Warrington, E., and McCarthy, R. (1987). "Categories of Knowledge: Further Fractionations and an Attempted Integration." *Brain* 110:1273–1296.

Warrington, E., and Shallice, T. (1984). "Category Specific Semantic Impairments." *Brain* 107:829–853.

Weinstein, S. (1974). "Truth and Demonstratives." *Noûs* 8:179–184.

Wellman, H. (1990). *The Child's Theory of Mind.* Cambridge: MIT Press.

Wettstein, H. (1981). "Demonstrative Reference and Definite Descriptions." *Philosophical Studies* 40:241–257.

Wiggins, D. (1980a). "'Most' and 'All': Some Comments on a Familiar Programme and on the Logical Form of Quantified Sentences." In M. Platts (ed.), *Reference, Truth, and Reality* (pp. 318–346). London: Routledge & Kegan Paul.

Wiggins, D. (1980b). "What Would Be a Substantial Theory of Truth?" In Z. van Straaten (ed.), *Philosophical Subjects: Essays Presented to P. F. Strawson* (pp. 189–221). Oxford: Clarendon Press.

Williams, E. (1983). "Against Small Clauses." *Linguistic Inquiry* 14:287–308.

Wilson, G. (1978). "On Definite and Indefinite Descriptions." *Philosophical Review* 87:48–76.

Wilson, M. (1982). "Predicate Meets Property." *Philosophical Review* 91:549–589.

Wright, C. (1981). "Rule-Following, Objectivity, and Theory of Meaning." In S. Holzman and C. Leich (eds.), *Wittgenstein: To Follow a Rule* (pp. 99–117). London: Routledge and Kegan Paul.

Wright, C. (1983). *Frege's Conception of Numbers as Objects.* Aberdeen: Aberdeen University Press.

Wright, C. (1986). "Theories of Meaning and Speakers' Knowledge." In S. G. Shanker (ed.), *Philosophy in Britain Today* (pp. 267–307). Albany, N.Y.: SUNY Press.

Zwarts, F. (1983). "Determiners: A Relational Perspective." In A. ter Meulen (ed.), *Studies in Model-Theoretic Semantics* (pp. 37–62). Dordrecht: Foris.

Author Index

Subject Index